Unequal Relations

An Introduction to Race, Ethnic, and Aboriginal Dynamics in Canada

Third Edition

D1621708

Augie Fleras
University of Waterloo

and

Jean Leonard Elliott
Dalhousie University

Prentice Hall Allyn and Bacon Canada
Scarborough, Ontario

To "Miss Hahn"
Thank you

Canadian Cataloguing in Publication Data

Fleras, Augie, 1947–
  Unequal relations : an introduction to race, ethnic and aboriginal dynamics in Canada

3rd ed.
Authors in reverse order on 1st ed.
Includes index.
ISBN 0-13-020560-5

1. Canada—Race relations. 2. Canada—Ethnic relations.
3. Multiculturalism—Canada. I. Elliott, Jean Leonard, 1941–   II. Title.

FC104.E44 2000   305.8'00971   C99-930412-7
F1035.A1E44 2000

© 1999, 1996, 1992 Prentice-Hall Canada Inc., Scarborough, Ontario
Pearson Education

Prentice-Hall, Inc., Upper Saddle River, New Jersey
Prentice-Hall International (UK) Limited, London
Prentice-Hall of Australia, Pty. Limited, Sydney
Prentice-Hall Hispanoamericana, S.A., Mexico City
Prentice-Hall of India Private Limited, New Delhi
Prentice-Hall of Japan, Inc., Tokyo
Simon & Schuster Southeast Asia Private Limited, Singapore
Editora Prentice-Hall do Brasil, Ltda., Rio de Janeiro

ISBN 0-13-020560-5

Vice President, Editorial Director: Laura Pearson
Acquisitions Editor: Nicole Lukach
Marketing Manager: Kathleen McGill
Developmental Editor: Lisa Phillips
Production Editor: Cathy Zerbst
Copy Editor: Betty R. Robinson
Production Coordinator: Peggy Brown
Art Director: Mary Opper
Cover Design: Sarah Battersby
Page Layout: Jansom (Janette Thompson)

2 3 4 5   04 03 02 01 00

Printed and bound in Canada.

Visit the Prentice Hall Canada Web site! Send us your comments, browse our catalogues, and more at **www.phcanada.com**. Or reach us through e-mail at **phabinfo_pubcanada@prenhall.com**.

CONTENTS

Chapter 4: Ethnicity: Conflicts and Challenges   103

Chapter 5: Social Inequality: Race, Ethnicity, Class, and Gender   134

PART 2: Diversity in Canada: Peoples, Nations, and Minorities   161

Chapter 6:   Aboriginal Peoples   164

Chapter 7: The Quebec Question   214

Chapter 8: Immigration and Multicultural Minorities   247

PART 3: Multiculturalism and Society Building   287

Chapter 9: Multiculturalism in Canada: "Engaging Diversity"   291

Chapter 10: Putting Multiculturalism to Work   323

Chapter 11: Reconstitutionalizing Canada 365

CASE STUDIES AND INSIGHT BOXES

Chapter 1

Chapter 2

Chapter 3

Chapter 4

Chapter 5

Chapter 6

Chapter 7

Chapter 8

Chapter 9

Chapter 10

Chapter 11

Preface

Few domains in Canada are littered with as much conceptual debris as the fields of race, aboriginal, and ethnic relations. Terms are used "fast and loose," without much concern for precision and accuracy. Concepts such as "multiculturalism," "citizenship," "racism," "equality," "nationalism," and "self-determination" can be stretched to mean everything yet nothing, depending on the context. Gaps in our substantive understanding of "who gets what and why" have also perplexed and provoked. Canadians are living in an astonishing yet bewildering era—both the best of times and the worst of times (Isajiw 1997). To one side, Canada is becoming increasingly open and tolerant. To the other, racial politics and ethnic conflicts continue to threaten to distort and to dismember. Consider only the anomalies that confront Canadians: Race matters at a time when many think it shouldn't. Racism has proven much more tenacious than many would have anticipated in light of energies expended to purge and destroy. Ethnicity is not always about cuddly attachments for display in festivals and food courts. Its potency in advancing ingroup interests at the expense of "others" may impart a chilling twist to the seemingly deceptive euphemism "ethnic cleansing." The application of a three-nations discourse to Canada is equally provocative. The politics of "distinct society" or "nations within" evoke the possibilities of a Canada so recontoured that it may eventually exist on paper only. Fact and fiction mix uneasily in discourses pertaining to aboriginal rights, ethnic nationalism, native title, bilingualism, sovereignty association, and national unity. Debates over immigration and the "refugee question" have proven no less contentious, judging by the degree of media hype and outpouring of public outrage over who should get in, how many, and where from. Tempers flare when politically inspired social experiments such as "multiculturalism" and "employment equity" are drawn into conversation, involving interactants who prefer to "talk past each other." Even the conventions associated with citizenship and belonging are being eroded by the forces of the global market economy and ethnic nationalism. The fact that few Canadians can agree on terms of the debate is worrying in its own right. That even fewer Canadians can concur on a working "constitutionalism" ("first principles") for "belonging together with our differences" can only complicate the society-building challenge in the new millennium.

The third edition of *Unequal Relations* is designed to overcome these lacunae in our knowledge. Part analysis, part consciousness raising, and part antiracist in objective and style, this introductory text comes at a time when the boundaries of "being Canadian" are being pushed to the limit by deep diversities and radical ethnicities. The book begins with the assumption that race, ethnic, and aboriginal interactions are relations of inequality. It continues by emphasizing how these largely inequitable group relationships are constructed, sustained, challenged, and modified by way of official policy and institutional practices. It concludes by focusing on the politics of race, ethnic, and aboriginal relations as they contribute to or detract from the challenge of Canadian society building. The objective in each case is to probe beneath the superficial and discordant in the hopes of uncovering recurrent patterns that animate intergroup relations. Several themes provide a unifying coherence to the text. First, Canada's race, aboriginal, and ethnic relations are essentially intergroup dynamics, and that makes it doubly important to understand how these often unequal relationships are patterned in light of government policies and minority assertiveness. Second, an equally important theme addresses the principles of a political economy perspective: The interplay of institutions and relations that constitute the domain of race, ethnicity, and aboriginality is situated within a context of power. The sorting through of these differentials in power acknowledges the complex web of political and economic relations that generate inequities as well as opportunities (Saggers and Gray 1998). Third, Canadian society is portrayed as a contested site involving competition among race, ethnic, and aboriginal groups as each struggles to define priorities and impose agendas. Ethnic minorities are not simply passive objects acted upon by Canadian society or subject to analysis as objects of study. Minority women and men are active subjects and partners in redefining Canada by shaping political decisions and public policy (Troper and Weinfeld 1999). The repositioning of race, ethnic, and aboriginal relations within the discursive framework of Canada as a site of society-building provides a coherent theme throughout.

Canada's diversity is complex and multidimensional: This multidimensionality reflects patterns in common with other countries. A European-style linguistic dualism, which Canada has in common with Belgium, intersects with an aboriginal/settler/immigrant pattern that Canada shares with the United States, New Zealand, and Australia (Laczlo 1997). Each of these axes of diversity has its own dynamics, yet each is unmistakably interlinked through the interaction of many parts of a whole in ways both mutually reinforcing yet contradictory (Maaka and Fleras 1998). The paradox that subsumes Canada is anchored in its diversity: Differences embody a potential for tension and conflict; they also have the potential to secure the foundations of a distinct society that is increasingly accepting of diversity as a moral good within a common political framework (LaSalva 1996). A vibrant Canadian society that can engage diversity without capitulating to chaos or dismemberment is perhaps the most formidable of the many challenges that await the millennium (Kymlicka 1998). The challenge of living together with our differences in a society both pluralistic and tolerant as well as inclusive and committed makes it especially important to isolate, dissect, and eliminate those social dynamics that erect walls rather than build bridges.

In terms of content and organization, the third edition of *Unequal Relations* may well subscribe to the adage of "continuity in change." There is much that has been retained, including the basic chapter outline, content in terms of concepts and applications to Canadian society, and the theme of race, ethnic, and aboriginal relations as socially constructed and unequal. A certain logic underpins the rationale behind the sequence of topics: Concepts appear before application; theory before practice; abstractions before the concrete. Each section builds upon the other without necessarily precluding the possibility of alternative arrangements for enterprising readers. Highlights appear at the end of each chapter as do key terms and questions for discussion and review.

The first part (Chapters 1 to 5) provides a general conceptual framework for the study of race, ethnicity, and aboriginality. Special emphasis is devoted to the constructs and perspectives employed by sociologists for sorting out intergroup relations. Topics for discussion include models of race, aboriginal, and ethnic relations; race, racism, and antiracist strategies; the ethnicity experience from identity to nationalisms; and inequality and diversity. The second part (Chapters 6 to 8) applies many of these concepts to the emergent realities of an evolving Canadian society. State policies and the politics of government–minority interaction are organized around the division of Canadian ethnicity into "three major diversities": aboriginal peoples, Charter groups (French- and English-speaking colonizers), and multicultural minorities. Each of these "diversities" is shown to occupy a unique constitutional status in Canadian society, both analytically distinct and mutually interconnected, with corresponding differences in outlooks, demands, problems, and solutions. The third part (Chapters 9 to 11) looks at the complex and challenging world of multicultural relations in Canada. An examination of recent developments in official multiculturalism precedes an analysis of multicultural initiatives for engaging diversity at institutional levels, including the media, policing, and education. The book closes with a discussion of the paradoxes that confront society building as Canada grapples with the uncertainties and challenges of forging a new "constitutionalism" for the new millennium.

The third edition is not without changes, as might be expected in a domain where the mix of social patterns and conventional wisdom is rarely constant and often contested. The most noticeable change is in the streamlining of the text. Portions of the text that seem less relevant at present than in the immediate past, including employment equity and gender versus sex, have been discarded or substantially reduced. Many Case Studies have been deleted, or condensed in the hopes of sharpening their focus. New Case Studies have been added as well, on topics such as stolen aboriginal children, multiculturalism in the United States, and identity politics. Content has been revised and updated. The concept of racism has been rethought and modified accordingly, as have the concepts ethnicity, ethnic nationalism, racialization, and official multiculturalism. The reader may also notice a heavier reliance on examples and references from New Zealand and Australia. A stand-alone gender chapter has been jettisoned. The rationale behind this decision was carefully considered: Inclusion of a separate chapter may have had the effect of reinforcing gender stereotypes by "otherizing" the realities of racial, immigrant, and aboriginal women. But by redistributing select aspects of this chapter throughout the book, a gender dimension is imparted instead across a raft of ethnicity issues. Finally, changes to terminology continue to be incorporated, or deleted. Introduction of terms such as "engaging diversity," "subdominant groups," "institutional inclusiveness," and "indigeneity" are not intended to confuse or impress. Rather, they reflect shifts in how people think and talk about diversity at the end of the millennium. Taken together, we hope the cumulative impact of these additions and deletions will craft a new edition both topical and timely without being cumbersome or unwieldy.

Any book of an introductory nature is written with the undergraduate and community college student in mind. Issues are selected for their topicality and relevance to the intended reader. Language is employed that challenges the reader, without losing sight of basic rules for communication. Emphasis is not on correct answers, but on asking the right questions for discussion and debate. Objectives for this book are varied as well, but are generally geared toward personal growth through (a) understanding, (b) explanation, (c) sensitization, (d) criticism, (e) empowerment, and (f) action:

1. To acquaint the reader with an informed understanding of the subject matter encompassed by a sociology of race, aboriginal, and ethnic relations. The text seeks to clarify and rethink perennial debates in this field; it also hopes to avoid sloppy reasoning, mindless clichés, the penchant for simplifying issues, and common sense assumptions at odds with reality.

2. To inform readers by explaining how the patterns and underlying logic that animate race, ethnic, and aboriginal relations are socially constructed and contested rather than

"natural" and "fixed." The challenge rests in going beyond pat explanations and official orthodoxy, but to deconstruct common sense statements by way of multiple perspectives and flexible (sometimes contradictory) interpretations.

3. To sensitize readers to the problems and challenges associated with working through differences in a changing and diverse society. Most of us will come into contact with those who are ethnically and racially different at some point in our daily interaction. Each of us may be a minority in some contexts. Learning to "walk the talk" by walking a mile in someone else's shoes may sound hackneyed and clichéd. Still, the goal of empathizing with minority experiences remains a worthwhile objective for living together with our differences.

4. To promote a critical perspective by confronting the myths and misconceptions about diversity issues. The "debunking" of illusions and half-truths is critical: As "pattern seekers," sociologists are interested in studying human social life to expose the unseen or unspoken by probing beneath the surface of mindless slogans and self-serving platitudes. The sociological maxim that "things are not what they seem to be" ("appearances are deceiving") allows us to "read between the lines" of what is said or done.

5. To initiate a process of personal empowerment. Coping with diversity is no longer an option or luxury that any of us can blithely ignore. Race, ethnicity, and aboriginality are not abstract notions for analysis, but sharply contest the reality at the core of being Canadian or the future of Canada (James 1995). Just as media literacy has grown in stature to equip individuals with intellectual self-defence skills, so too is diversity literacy a prerequisite for personal careers or collective survival.

6. To encourage the reader on a path toward personal actions of antiracism and community. Personal awareness is great; even better is active involvement for meaningful change. The objective of antiracism activity is not wholesale global change—that would be asking too much of anyone—but improvement in one corner of the world (as the bumper sticker says, "think globally, act locally"). Admittedly, the struggle to eradicate racism and injustice even at local levels will be a protracted process, given the tenacity of the problem. But unless racism and discrimination are confronted and challenged through direct action and active resistance, each of us is destined to be part of the problem rather than part of the solution.

It stands to reason that disciplines differ in their approach to the study of race, ethnic, and aboriginal relations. *Unequal Relations* is organized around a macro-sociological perspective, with its focus on the politics and processes of intergroup dynamics against an evolving backdrop of power and domination. A macro-sociological perspective conceptualizes intergroup relations as a patterned yet unequal interaction within broader political and economic contexts. Social relations that exist between and among groups are rooted in intergroup dynamics that incorporate both a social dimension and structural variables at odds with full and equal participation in society (see also Frideres 1998). Conflicts between and within diverse groups do not combust from individual ignorance or irrational fears. Confrontations flare from the processes and paradoxes intrinsic to human social life (see Jaret 1995). At the centre of this macro-analysis is power. As noted by others, power is to society as energy is to physics: without it, nothing happens. Power is situated at the centre of any analysis (Dei 1996), with particular attention on how historically constituted relations of domination and subdomination are embedded in the institutional structures of society. For example, references to prejudice and racism are analyzed as relationships of power within unequal contexts rather than psychological predispositions. The socially constructed nature of ethnic relations makes it amenable to sociological analysis by way of institutional arrangements, intergroup dynamics, policies and practices, and society-building processes.

There are several things the book is not. The book eschews a description of minority groups and Canadian ethnic lifestyles. It does not provide a literary platform for minority "voices" or "stories" by minority authors. Such a perspective may be useful for intercultural understanding (see James and Shadd 1994). With several notable exceptions, our preference rests with the theme of group interaction within unequal contexts. Micromodels of individual behaviour that focus on attitudes or beliefs are not dismissed outright. They simply are postponed as secondary in importance to a focus on institutions, social conditions, and structural level as explanatory variables. Admittedly, we are not interested in everything about race, ethnicity, and aboriginality. Of salience are those social dimensions of diversity that have a bearing on a changing and diverse society. Race and ethnicity affect Canadian society insofar as their influence is a defining feature of Canada, not only in organizing our lives, but also in shaping efforts to integrate diversity with national interests pertaining to unity and identity (Troper and Weinfeld 1999). Nor do we pretend to have all the answers. To think otherwise is both arrogant and controlling; such an attitude also assumes the existence of a discoverable objective reality that unlocks its "truth" to the privileged observer. What we do promise, however, is a galaxy of questions that summon diverse responses to the politics of difference at a time when the challenge of living together with our differences is more pressing than ever. We also want to avoid sermonizing by sanctimoniously talking down to the reader. To enlighten but not abdicate our responsibility to ask tough questions or take unpopular stands is a defining characteristic of *Unequal Relations*. Care is also exercised to avoid regurgitating both blatant government propaganda and ethnic posturing, without dismissing the rationale that may lie behind these positions.

To be sure, not everyone will agree with our analysis or assessment. That much is to be expected: Debates over race, ethnicity, and aboriginality invariably arouse passions by challenging people's sense of identity, self-esteem, core values, sense of place, legitimacy of society, and taken-for-granted privileges (Mulgan 1989). References to race, ethnicity, and aboriginality are not simply descriptive categories about the world out there. Differences do not exist in a social vacuum. More to the point, diversity is relational, insofar as it is inseparable from intersecting patterns of hierarchy which have the intent or effect of denying others on the basis of perceived differences (Fleras and Spoonley 1999). The challenges that confront the sorting through of diversity are daunting: Misconceptions are deeply entrenched and buried under layers of unconscious conditioning and repeated reinforcement. Common sense notions remain resistant to debunking even under optimal conditions. But institutional and cultural practices must be deconstructed if we are to expose hidden assumptions and structural barriers to genuine equality. By tackling issues that foster or inhibit the challenge of living together with our differences, this third edition of *Unequal Relations* hopes to contribute to a Canada both distinctive and compassionate yet unmistakably enriched because of its diversity.

In Memoriam

Jean Leonard Elliott (1941–1995)

It is with lingering sadness that I must remind readers of the death of my coauthor and friend, Jean Leonard Elliott. Jean was one of those rarest of individuals who enjoyed life to the limit, even when confronted with the spectre of death. In her role as a teacher and researcher, she was always the consummate professional. She not only advanced the fields of race, ethnic, and aboriginal relations at a time when many ignored these issues. Her varied writings across a spectrum of topics insisted on a feminist dimension, not because of political correctness, but because of a passionate dislike for inequality and inhumanity of any kind. That Jean lived to see a Canada at the cutting edge of societies for challenging racism and sexism—in principle if not always in practice—is a credit to her tenacity and vision. Even the passage of time has not diminished the untimeliness of her death. If anything, the intervening period has brightened the lustre of working together on projects that arguably remain collaborative in spirit if not in process. It seems only fitting in light of our mutual interests to echo the words of the New Zealand Maori when bidding farewell: Haere ra e hoa—Goodbye good friend. May this third edition of *Unequal Relations* stand as a testimony to Jean's legacy as a keen and courageous individual whose commitment to social justice has proven a beacon to many.

Credits

Case study on Immigrant Women. Printed with the permission of Maria Adasme.
Material used at the beginning of Chapter 9. Printed with the permission of Marita Williams.

Acknowledgments

It's often said that writing is an intensely solitary yet remarkably collaborative enterprise. Perhaps it is the very "aloneness" of the endeavour that enhances the rewards of working with others in thinking things through. With that in mind, I would like to thank my former colleagues in the Sociology department at the University of Canterbury in Christchurch, NZ for their support in rethinking aspects of this text. Two individuals deserve extra praise: Rosemary du Plessis is one of the finest colleagues I have had the pleasure of working with, while Louise Humpage is certainly the most talented student I have ever supervised. I would also like to acknowledge the input and advice of Paul Spoonley of Massey University at the Albany campus at Auckland. And I will always treasure the intellectual stimulation and good "mateship" of Roger Maaka of the Maori department at Canterbury. However, special gratitude must go to Jocelyn and our boys, "J-P" and the "Duke" who proved that physical distances are irrelevant when love and respect are involved. May this edition stand as a testimony to my admiration and love for them.

Thank you also to Prentice Hall's Nicole Lukach, acquisitions editor; Lisa Phillips, developmental editor; Betty R. Robinson, copy editor; and Cathy Zerbst, production editor.

RETHINKING RACE, ETHNIC, AND ABORIGINAL RELATIONS

It has been said that Canada is a solution in search of a problem. Regardless of how interpreted, there is an element of truth to this cryptic comment. Canada continues to be globally regarded as one of the world's best places to live—a society so blessed with physical and human resources that it literally has to "invent" problems that others might ignore. Canadians have much to be grateful for in light of their democratic and open traditions, despite interminable internal bickering that may say more about being pampered than having problems. But being Canadian at the turn of the millennium remains a perplexing and provocative experience. Canadians continue to wrestle over a host of diversity issues that seem frustratingly beyond our comprehension or grasp. The intractability of these dilemmas may be summarized by way of select vignettes, each of which depicts a dimension of race, ethnicity, and aboriginality in Canada.

1. A 1995 amendment to Canada's criminal code requires that judges, when sentencing, give weight to an offender's "Indianness" by paying particular attention to the circumstances of aboriginal offenders. Is this concession a racist attempt to assuage white guilt by bending to the paternalistic pressure of political correctness in suggesting that aboriginal people have a diminished capacity to take responsibility for their actions? Or is the taking of *aboriginal ethnicity* into account a much-needed corrective to the "one-size-fits-all" notion that "everyone is equal before the law"? It should also be noted that prospective jurors may be questioned about their racist views to root out those whose largely unconscious prejudices could prejudge the results.

2. Thirty-five years ago, John Porter, the eminent Canadian sociologist, published *The Vertical Mosaic*. According to Porter, Canada's much-touted mosaic was distorted by differentials in power and income between those of British (and French) ancestry and "other ethnics." The fact that visible minority women and men continue to earn less than the white "malestream" suggests that Canada's mosaic remains vertically challenged. Do we attribute these differentials in income to race or ethnicity or to market forces? Can gaps be diminished by ignoring race or ethnicity as variables, or are solutions based on removal of discriminatory barriers by way of employment equity initiatives?

3. White men can't jump or run? How do we account for the overwhelmingly disproportionate numbers of black males in professional sports such as basketball or football, and baseball albeit to a lesser extent, but virtually nonexistent in professional hockey? Is this pattern explained by reference to race, ethnicity, or social class? Is stereotyping a problem inasmuch as it involves a belief that all individuals will act the same because they are assigned certain traits as minorities? Will whites ever appreciate that much of what they take for granted on a daily basis outside the sports field is not available to others, with the result that people of colour may expend a lot of energy and resources just trying to skirt obstacles that others don't see or experience?

4. The Nisga'a settlement in British Columbia offers a relatively high degree of self-determining self-government for aboriginal peoples. But nonaboriginals who find themselves under Nisga'a governance will not have access to representation. Nor will they have the right to vote or stand for political office. Is this a form of reverse racism or a violation of fundamental human rights? Or is a certain degree of exclusion necessary to put aboriginal *self*-government into practice?

5. Canada's urban regions are becoming increasingly diverse: 42 percent of Toronto's population is foreign-born; the figure for Vancouver is 35 percent, 24 percent for Hamilton, and 22 percent for Kitchener. Yet, levels of interpersonal harmony and intergroup cooperation in Canada are second to none. Is there something about "managing" race or ethnicity in Canada that is likely to defuse rather than detonate race relations? Conversely, why do people continue to call Canada a "racist society"?

6. If there is one word to self-describe Canadians, the most common attribute would be that of "tolerance." Yet Canadians continue to adamantly oppose immigration from Third World countries, bristle at the prospect of moving over and making institutional space for people of colour, and reject initiatives that will have a meaningful and positive impact on levelling the playing field. What is it about such relatively minor adjustments that bring out the worst in a society that espouses the principles of multiculturalism? Why can't we just all get along?

7. White supremacist groups continue to proliferate at grassroots levels by tapping into a groundswell of discontent over social changes. What combination of personal and institutional reforms is required to eliminate this blatant form of racism? Can more subtle expressions of racism be addressed without violating majority rights or core Canadian values?

8. Certain minorities as a group perform well in Canada when assessed by socioeconomic factors; others do not. Still others are perceived as a menace to society because of so-called antisocial tendencies. In what way has crime become "racialized" in Canadian society? How do we account for the criminalization of races? Are racial minorities prone to com-

mit more crime? Are race-based statistics likely to yield answers to this perennial paradox; that is, *it is not differences that matter in terms of who gets what, but how differences are racialized as a basis for unequal treatment.*

9. Canadians seem to be increasingly proud of their ethnic backgrounds, judging by their willingness to use hyphenated Canadianisms or take umbrage with real or imagined insults to their ethnic background. To what extent is ethnicity a progressive or regressive force in terms of Canadian society building? Is it possible to create a Canada that is safe for ethnicity as well as safe from ethnicity?

Responses to these questions about race, ethnicity, racism, and aboriginality underpin the content of Part 1 of *Unequal Relations*. The first part provides a conceptual framework for rethinking race, ethnic, and aboriginal relations in Canada at a time of diversity, change, and uncertainty. Various concepts, definitions, theories, and perspectives are introduced for dealing with the often nuanced and always evolving meanings of race, ethnicity, racism, aboriginality, nationalism, and inequality. This part also demonstrates how race, ethnicity, and aboriginality are properly interpreted as socially constructed relations of inequality, with particular attention to how these unequal relations have been created and maintained as well as challenged and transformed. Finally, Part 1 employs a social problematic perspective in sorting through conceptual issues. The dynamics of race, ethnicity, and aboriginality have been defined by the majority as a social problem, in the process raising the following questions: What is the problem? Who says so and why? How is this problem defined? What solutions have been proposed? What can be done to improve the tenor of race, ethnic, and aboriginal relations?

Chapter 1 begins by exploring the concept of relationships as they apply to race, ethnicity, and aboriginality. We concur with the view that social reality is relational and that relations are prior in the same way that ecology approaches reality as a field of interdependent relations rather than separable entities (see Jackson 1998). Emphasis is aimed at how these constructed and unequal relations are (a) patterned and predictable, (b) evolving and unique to specific historical circumstances, and (c) amenable to study from a variety of different sociological perspectives. Chapter 2 addresses the politics of race in contemporary society. The concept of race may not have biological validity, the chapter concedes, but it continues to be socially significant in shaping the outcomes—both positive and negative—of minority women and men. The origins of the race concept are examined, followed by the utilization of race concepts in the context of European colonialism and historical expressions of racism. Chapter 3 is concerned with the many and bewildering faces of racism in Canada. The chapter demonstrates how racism is vulnerable to shifts in meaning as the social context changes, and it is this fluidity that complicates the problem of isolating and challenging racism. Racism is examined in terms of definitions, properties, diverse types, relationship to prejudice and discrimination, impact, and implications. Antiracist initiatives are also discussed and shown to vary in magnitude from the personal and behavioural to the institutional and structural.

The fourth chapter is devoted to a discussion of ethnicity. The chapter addresses the challenges of the ethnicity experience by references to its expression as (a) community, (b) identity, and (c) social movement. Topics for discussion include the origins and persistence of ethnicity; the surge of ethnicity especially in terms of competition, identity, and nationalist movements; and the implications of ethnicity against the backdrop of Canadian multiculturalism and society building. Finally, Chapter 5 looks at social inequality as it impacts on ethnic minorities. Canada may be perceived as an open and egalitarian society; nevertheless, hierarchies of subdomination continue to mar the lives and life chances of minority women and men. Of particular significance is the interplay of race, ethnicity, gender, and social class in generating intersecting patterns of inequality that are interlocking and mutually reinforcing yet often contradictory in terms of outcomes and process.

UNEQUAL RELATIONS: Patterns, Policies, and Perspectives

1

CASE STUDY 1-1	The Good, the Bad, and the In Between

Canada is widely renown for its many qualities; two, however, appear foremost. First, people around the world marvel at Canada's ability to withstand the pressures of absorption as the fifty-first state of the world's most powerful melting pot society. How, they ask, can Canadians keep the American juggernaut at bay yet pursue a relatively independent course of action at home and abroad? Former prime minister Pierre Elliott Trudeau captured a whiff of that enigma when he startled a Washington audience in 1969: "Living next to you is in some ways like sleeping with an elephant; no matter how friendly and even-tempered is the beast, one is affected by every twitch and grunt. Even a friendly nuzzle can sometimes lead to frightening consequences." That Canadians have managed to keep an anti-melting pot distance without forsaking multicultural commitments

or cooperative Can–Am connections is a testimony to the resilience and adaptiveness of the people.

A second fascination reflects Canada's ability to weave a remarkably united and distinct society from the strands of diversity. How, indeed, has Canada managed to escape the ghettoization and racial violence that periodically engulf the United States, from Los Angeles and Miami to Jasper, Texas? How do Canadians manage to keep a lid on ethnic tensions that have fractured other societies in warring factions? How and why have Canadian cities such as Toronto and Vancouver evolved into the most cosmopolitan and diverse of any in the world without experiencing paralyzing strife? To be sure, the potential for rending Canada asunder is ever present. Nowhere is this more evident than in the paradox of cobbling together a three-nation state of aboriginal peoples and French and English colonizers within an overarching framework of multiculturalism. But while other countries are groping for solutions to "accommodate" diversity, Canada is embarking on a promising if unprecedented quest for balancing the often conflicting demands of diversity in ways that are seemingly workable yet fair. How does this assessment stand up to scrutiny?

The Good

Canada is a diverse and complex society composed of racially and ethnically different groups. Compared with other nation-states that routinely tolerate human rights abuses, Canada possesses an enviable reputation as a tolerant and compassionate country. The "management" of Canada's race, aboriginal, and ethnic relations is widely admired in global circles. People applaud our capacity to forge unity from the fragments of diversity, without forsaking a commitment to prosperity or capitulating to chaos. Many are equally impressed by our collective threshold of toleration for seemingly endless debates over language, culture, and identity. Evidence of this high standing can be gleaned from a list of global firsts in the diversity sweepstakes: Canada's Citizenship Act of 1947 was the first in the world to disregard any distinction between immigrants and native-born. The Immigration Act of 1967 was one of the first to abolish all quotas or preferences on the basis of race or ethnicity. Canada was the first country to receive the United Nations-sponsored Nansen Medal in 1986 for its humanitarian response to the global refugee problem; in 1982 Canada became the first country to constitutionally enshrine aboriginal and treaty rights; and Canada remains the first and only country to constitutionally endorse multiculturalism as a basis for engaging diversity. This hefty reputation is further secured by Canada's consistent high placement in quality-of-life surveys—including its ranking for five consecutive years (1994–1998) as the world's best place to live when measured by a human development index related to wealth, education, and longevity.

The Bad

Some of these accolades in society building are deserved; others, unfortunately, are not. From afar, Canada looks idyllic; up close the picture blurs. Dig deeper and one can unearth a country that has had little to boast about in the mistreatment of minority women and men (Walker 1998). A partial list of shameful episodes would include: xenophobic attitudes and racist political responses to Chinese and East Indian immigrants from the mid-nineteenth century onward (Baureiss 1985); the internment and dispossession of Japanese-Canadians during World War II (Berger 1991); the **segregation** of African-Canadians from mainstream institutions until the 1950s (Walker 1985; Henry 1994); and the pervasive anti-Semitism of the 1920s and 1930s, which culminated in the rejection of Jewish emigrés from Nazi Germany (Abella and Troper 1991). Much to our growing dismay, discrimination and racism are not relics from a bygone era but persist in ways that are difficult to isolate or control. Anti-Semitism continues to persist, with incidents ranging from Holocaust denial to defilement of Jewish properties, synagogues, and cemeteries. The current proliferation of white supremacist groups is no less disconcerting than in the past, given their access to the Internet, even if social climate is much less receptive than once was the case (Barrett 1987). People of colour continue to experience all manner of discrimination at personal and institutional levels (James 1995; Henry et al. 1995). The chronic crisis that pervades police–minority youth relations is but one example of how the system isn't working for people of colour (Cryderman et al. 1998). Mounting evidence of a public backlash over the diversity agenda may point to professed levels of tolerance that are long on principle but short in commitment or practice.

Of particular threat to Canada's national fabric are the ongoing debates between the two "Charter groups" (French- and English-speaking settler groups). Relations between Quebec and Ottawa have hovered between the poles of the sullen indifference ("two solitudes") and open hostility ("two scorpions in a bottle"). This growing estrangement between the French and English may be symbolized by seemingly inexhaustible language controversies. The conflict may also be interpreted as a power struggle over jurisdiction and control within the framework of a federalist system. Issues of language and jurisdiction threaten to polarize the country like never before, as the Québécois struggle for sovereignty in their own right while sharing in the sovereignty of Canada at large. By contrast, English-speaking Canadians are becoming increasingly perturbed over what they see as unrealistic and impertinent demands by a seemingly pampered minority. The escalating clamour of intolerance and prejudice diminishes the potential for voices of moderation to prevail.

A parallel situation applies to Canada's aboriginal peoples (Long and Dickason 1996; Asch 1997). Decades of colonialist subjugation and demeaning clientelism have diminished Canada's lustre as a pacesetter in aboriginal affairs. Annual reports of Canada's Human Rights Commission routinely castigate the government's treatment of aboriginal peoples as the country's most egregious human rights violation. But aboriginal peoples are challenging the status quo by engaging central authorities in a power struggle over who controls what and why (Fleras and Elliott 1992). The quest for self-determination through the implemen-

tation of inherent aboriginal rights and self-governing structures is central to this quest for renewal and reform (Royal Commission 1996). Yet the path toward a workable agenda has proven to be elusive, despite lofty rhetoric to the contrary (Fleras 1996). Political responses are struggling with the unconventional nature of aboriginal demands. Time and again government policies embody false assumptions and dubious tactics, many of which may inadvertently inflame or depress (Ponting 1997). To Canada's discredit and profound embarrassment, aboriginal leaders have turned to world courts and international forums in hopes of hastening the healing process. Even the prospect of violence to achieve aboriginal goals can no longer be discarded, with images of Oka still seared in our collective memory.

The In Between

This admittedly selective overview paints a murky picture of Canadian race, aboriginal, and ethnic relations. Which interpretation is right or wrong? Different answers are possible because no one can agree on the criteria for assessment, with the result that any reference to the "good" or "bad" or the "ugly" may say more about the evaluator and her agenda than about the evaluated or assessed. That kind of equivocation also suggests the possibility of yet another spin; that is, the notion of Canada as lying somewhere in between the extremes of progress or regress. Canada is neither a model of virtue when it comes to engaging diversity nor the "mother" of all evils; it probably falls somewhere in between. Initiatives for "managing" race, ethnicity, and aboriginality are enlightened at times, callously expedient at others, and contradictory at still other times as Canadians stumble around in balancing "national interests" with the rights of minority women and men (also Kymlicka 1998). Compared to a utopia, for example, Canada falls short of the mark.

Yet Canada's record stands as a paragon of virtue in relation with minority rights records in other parts of the world. Even the smallest incidents that would barely rate a mention in many global circles tend to be magnified because of Canada's exacting standards. An appreciation for history also reveals an "in between" quality: In contrast with our lofty expectations for the future, the current situation leaves something to be desired. But in comparison with our past, there is evidence of substantial progress in crafting a more in clusive society—at least at the level of policy and promises if not necessarily in outcomes. Canada today is substantially different from the one that once endorsed the fallacy of assimilation, white supremacy, open discrimination, and institutional segregation. Proof of this shift reflects a growing commitment to proactively engage diversity by acknowledging (a) recognition of aboriginal peoples' inherent rights to self-government, (b) inception of official bilingualism and minority language rights, (c) the implementation of multiculturalism from the federal to the municipal levels, (d) commitment to removal of discriminatory barriers in public life, and (e) introduction of diversity measures within institutional frameworks.

Collectively, of course, much needs to be done. We still have a long way to go in acknowledging the needs and aspirations of racial, ethnic, and aboriginal minorities, let alone in implementing meaningful social reform. Relations between the Canadian state and minority groups tend to hover uneasily between the poles of grudging acceptance and qualified accommodation, with the spectre of public backlash looming in the background. Many are genuinely perplexed because of their failure to grasp the rationale behind government initiatives and minority resistance. Others are frustrated by demands for entitlement that ostensibly conflict with Canada's foundational principles and national interests (Boldt 1993). Assumptions that once defined who got what and why are no longer applicable; promoted instead are appeals that encompass a completely different set of first principles. The margins are now competing with the centre for control over power, resources, and status—not by direct confrontation but by hugging the high moral ground of "victimhood" and "identity politics." With Canada's social moorings increasingly cast adrift and listing dangerously, a rethinking of race, ethnic, and aboriginal relations is timely and necessary. Our aim in this chapter is precisely that, in part by cutting through the conceptual clutter that distorts the dynamics of race, ethnicity, and aboriginality.

INTRODUCTION: INTERETHNIC DYNAMICS—OUTCOMES AND PROCESSES

Any field of study is characterized by a distinctive subject matter. It is also distinguished from related fields by a set of assumptions, an inventory of key concepts, a range of perspectives, methods of data collection, and a body of findings/conclusions. These criteria provide a coherent and organizational framework for sorting out what is relevant for study.

The topic of race, aboriginal, and ethnic relations is no different. Sociologists have long attended to the study of race, ethnicity, and aboriginality, often from a macro-sociological vantage point with its unifying themes of group dynamics and social context. Power is central to a macro-analysis, as many have observed, since nothing happens without it. Certain groups dominate not because of superiority, but because they possess power to control; similarly, subdominant groups are not subordinate or inferior but generally lack access to power except, of course, the veto power to disrupt social definitions and public order. In the final analysis, the concept of race, ethnic, and aboriginal relations points to a specialized form of patterned interaction involving groups who cooperate or compete, depending on the circumstances. These interactional patterns may be relatively equitable when social participants possess equivalent access to power, resources, and decision making. They become unequal, however, if power differentials pervade or intrude—as usually is the case with indigenous peoples or historically disadvantaged minority women and men. The fact that these unequal relations neither originate in a social vacuum nor unfold outside of a wider political and economic context is central in understanding the often confrontational nature of dominant–subdominant interaction.

The contemporary world is comprised of societies that are generally multiethnic or multinational in composition. Of the 200 or so countries recognized by the United Nations, all but a dozen contain a variety of ethnic groups within their boundaries. One of these groups tends to dominate insofar as social institutions are reconstituted around their language and culture; conversely, subdominant groups exist whose members are constrained in the competition for power or privilege. Several patterns of relationships are possible, singly or in combination with others when groups come into prolonged contact (Feagin and Feagin 1993; See and Wilson 1988). First, a dominant group incorporates or annexes a foreign territory by force or "rights of (European) discovery." The British conquest of the French on the Plains of Abraham in 1759 provides an example that even today continues to rankle and provoke. Second, colonization and frontier expansion result in the acquisition of land or resources through peaceful avenues. Territories may be acquired by purchase or treaties such as between Canada's aboriginal peoples and the federal government. Forced migration is a third possibility. A subdominant group is forcibly brought into the country for essentially exploitative purposes. The importation of Africans as slave labour into the United States— and into Canada but on a more limited basis—is a classic example. Finally, we have voluntary migration from overseas. Immigration entails the premeditated and regulated movement of immigrant populations into the host society. These scenarios are not mutually exclusive, of course, but may coexist or overlap as the situation evolves.

Sustained contact involving racial, ethnic, or indigenous peoples invariably leads to a patterned set of responses and relations. Discrepancies in the distribution of power transform this contact situation into a relationship of domination and/or exploitation. The resulting interaction not only crystallizes into an asymmetrical social structure; it also gives rise to a limited number of predictable but unequal outcomes. The range of outcomes can span the spectrum from genocide or subjugation on the one hand to that of accommodation and assimilation on the other, with multitextured layers of separation and pluralism on yet another. The exact response will vary with the nature of the contact situation in terms of duration, timing, balance of power, and magnitude and intensity. For example, early British settlers praised the New Zealand Maori as an evolutionarily sophisticated people—at least once Crown hegemony was firmly established over the land and its peoples. Such labelling made sense in the nineteenth century: Maori were sedentary horticulturalists upon contact with Europeans, readily took to Christianity and education, and proved formidable foes in the struggle for control of New Zealand (Belich 1996). By contrast, the First Australians were contemptuously vilified by early settlers as worthless and beyond the pale of civilization. They were perceived as a physically unattractive species with minimal potential for process. Their crude technology and seemingly random migratory patterns, coupled with an inability to grasp the fundamentals of civilization and Christianity, only confirmed the worst suspicions. Official responses to the status of indigenous peoples in Australia or New Zealand may reflect implicit government guidelines; alternatively, these responses may be codified into an explicit and formal government policy for the management of race, aboriginal, or ethnic relations. In other words, when two unequal groups interact over a period of time, one (or more) of the following scenarios will materialize either as process or outcome: genocide, assimilation, segregation, integration, and cultural pluralism. These models of race, ethnic, and aboriginal relations are not strictly separate from each other. Nor are they internally consistent, despite an internal logic involving a constellation of ideas, policies, and practices that cohere around a core theme and provide the basis for interaction. Nevertheless, their central features are recurrent and amenable to sociological analysis.

Genocide/Ethnocide

An ethnically powerful group may embark on a course of action that seeks to eliminate a weaker ethnic group. **Genocide** (or **ethnocide**) lends itself to different definitions, but most include the notion of deliberate and systematic mass killings of a despised group who dwell in a territory occupied and controlled by the killers (McGarry and O'Leary 1994). The fury and chaos often associated with these vendettas camouflage a hidden logic. This mass liquidation process is not an isolated event by poorly disciplined militia. Nor is it an unintentional and unfortunate byproduct of contact or civil war, much less a spontaneous expression of dormant tribal hatred or uncontrolled primeval rage. Genocide represents a national political decision to achieve political goals or consolidate elite advantage. A calculated and premeditated set of actions is invoked to remove competitors or silence opponents by means of an orchestrated campaign of terror involving a network of institutions, operating procedures, and ideological assumptions that sanction the dehumanization and destruction of the "other" (Hitchcock 1997). Genocide does not necessarily reflect the result of natural differences but the manipulation of these differences by cynical elites who will stop at nothing to retain power, achieve advantage, secure political support, conceal economic difficulties, and distract from internal squabbles (Ignatieff 1995). This raises the question of whether genocide is about politics or passion. To what extent are the conflicts in Rwanda (and elsewhere) the result of pent-up tribal hatred, or is tribalism a convenient covert label to justify power struggles by greedy factions?

CASE STUDY 1-2	Genocide in Rwanda: Power Politics or Tribalism?

Rwanda is a small African country with a population of about 8 million, most of whom are subsistence farmers with an average personal income of about $350 per year (Canada's per capita income is about $22,000 per year). Not only is Rwanda one of the poorest countries in the world; it is also one of the most densely populated at 304 people per square kilometre. Two tribes predominate: the Hutu comprise about 85 percent of the population, with the remainder mostly Tutsi. The fact that the numerically smaller Tutsi have historically dominated Rwanda's politics and economy creates a climate conducive to interethnic strife.

Two decades of relative political tranquillity came to an end in 1990 when Rwanda was plunged into civil turmoil. The country was "invaded" by the Rwandan Patriotic Front, a force of about 10,000 guerillas/refugees predominantly from the outnumbered but politically powerful Tutsi. Prior to Rwandan independence from Belgium in 1962, the quality of Tutsi–Hutu relations had fluctuated over time and from place to place. Colonial politics had exerted an adverse role in fostering a hierarchical racial structure at odds with the largely accommodative relations of the past. First the Germans, then the Belgians bestowed a most favoured status on the Tutsi, largely because of their attractive physical appearance. In return, the Tutsi chiefs were expected to do the "dirty" work in administering a colonialist system of divide-and-indirect-rule. This stratified ethnic classification was secured by way of compulsory identity cards.

Superimposing the rule of the cattle-owning haves (Tutsis) over the horticultural have-nots (Hutus) inevitably set off a chain of events that culminated in open resentment and popular uprising. A Hutu-driven rebellion ended Tutsi domination shortly after Belgium's departure, with thousands fleeing to safety in neighbouring countries. A military coup in 1973 resulted in further bloodshed, with the slaughter of upwards of 300,000 Tutsis followed by yet another massive exodus of Tutsis into neighbouring countries. The Hutu president may have proposed a transitional government based on Tutsi–Hutu power sharing, but continued to pursue a policy of open and institutionalized discrimination through ethnic and regional quotas. But the possibility of compromise collapsed when a suspicious air accident in 1993 killed both the Rwandan and Burundi presidents—an action that was seen by some as a deliberate effort by a clique of extremist Hutus to destabilize the country by sabotaging any challenge to the status quo.

A terrifying orgy of killing followed, instigated in large by Hutu military hard-liners loyal to the president. Hundreds and thousands of unarmed Tutsi civilians *and* Hutu moderates were slaughtered on a scale perhaps unparalleled in recent human history. Few will ever forget the horrific images of machete-wielding youths who hacked at unarmed women and children with a fury that leaped beyond human comprehension or sanity. The Tutsi-led rebel forces eventually proved victorious and installed an interim government by mid-1994, but not before nearly a million Rwandans had been butchered or maimed. These totals were subsequently swollen further still through vigilante violence in Rwandan refugee camps, coupled with reports of planned reprisals by the Rwandan Patriotic Front. The United Nations has officially declared the killings in Rwanda an act of genocide—an orchestrated and methodical slaughter of the "other" rather than a random outburst by undisciplined soldiers.

The carnage in Rwanda poses a challenge to the way we think about the ethnic experience. Can this barbarism be attributed to yet another unfortunate outbreak of some inherent and primordial tribalism that occasionally flares to the surface? Or is ethnicity simply another dimension of a killing machine because of its capacity to incite, demean, or destroy? Responses vary: Many have noted that much of the ethnic hatred is politically driven, with power and economics rather than ethnicity the root cause. Extremists in any conflict are known to use any method available to forestall progressive reforms. Even slaughtering members from one's own ethnic group may be invoked as a tactic for demonizing the "other."

Such a vendetta puts a new and sinister spin on the concept of tribal politics. Ethnocide is about power and politics, in other words, and recourse to ethnicity may or may not deter those who will stop at nothing to procure their blood-drenched goals.

In the United Nations-based genocide convention of 1948, five classes of action have been defined as genocide: (a) members of a group are slaughtered with the intent of bringing about their disappearance as a people; (b) conditions are created that foster the dispersal of the group by destroying the essential foundations of group life; (c) intense psychological abuse or physical discomfort is inflicted, culminating in the dissolution of the group; (d) children are transferred from one group to another, thus bringing about the demise of the culture; and (e) births are prevented through involuntary sterilization, birth control, or abortion. The process of genocide can encompass varying strategies: from those that explicitly seek to exterminate "troublesome minorities" to those that inadvertently erase the cultural basis of minority societies. Annihilation of such magnitude may be attained directly at times through military means. Indirect means may entail the spread of disease or loss of livelihood or resocialization. Group survival is also jeopardized through the introduction of foreign practices such as education and organized religion. Even destruction of the ecosystem by the state or multinational entities may constitute a case of developmental genocide, not in the sense of development to deliberately destroy a people, but in having the effect of doing so because of environmental deterioration (Hitchcock 1997). In the case of ethnocide, the health of a group is eroded through elimination of cultural beliefs and values that provide meaning, identity, security, and community. Customs, values, and identities that threaten dominant rule come under prolonged attack, in the process pushing remnants of the population to the edge from which recovery is difficult.

Examples of indigenous peoples who have (nearly) vanished are not difficult to unearth. Australia's aboriginal populations were deliberately stalked and killed by European settlers in an effort to assert colonial control over what they saw as "pestiferous vermin." Likewise, aboriginal peoples such as the Beothuk in Newfoundland literally became extinct as a result of contact with early European colonialists. The twentieth-century killing fields are no less disturbing: Ukrainians have suffered massive losses in famines engineered by Stalinist purges. Armenians were victimized by genocidal practices under the Turkish regime during World War I. Millions of Jews and other despised minorities were liquidated under the Nazi banner. The blatant mistreatment of indigenous populations by settlers and miners in the Amazonian rainforest has proven destructive (Chagnon 1998). The Iraqi regime has also been accused of genocide and mass extinction (including the use of poison gas) in its efforts to squash the insurrectionist Kurdish populations in the north. Equally genocidal are the "ethnic cleansing" campaigns by Serbs against Muslim populations in Bosnia and Albanians in Kosovo, as were the murderous rampages in Rwanda.

In short, the resurgence of genocide in recent years is as disarming as it is disturbing: disarming because many thought we had put that part of history behind us with the demise of Nazi Germany; disturbing because we may need to rethink the human species as fundamentally flawed in the Hobbesian sense of "nasty, brutish, and short." Should we be asking ourselves if, in fact, the rules of law and reason are contrary to the human grain of violence and fanaticism, and secured only by an unremitting struggle to suppress basic human nature (Ignatieff 1994)?

Assimilation

Assimilation has been referred to as a one-way process of absorption—either deliberate or unconscious. Both formal and informal in structure or function, assimilation involves a process whereby the dominant sector imposes its culture, authority, values, and institutions on the subdominant sector (Gordon 1964). Members of a minority group in turn lose their distinctiveness because of exposure to the forces of conformity. Historically, the concept itself was taken from biology and reflected a scientific belief that social life could be better understood by drawing upon simplified analogies with the natural world (Jaret 1995). In reality, assimilation is a complex and multidimensional process that unscrolls at a varying pace, involves different intensities of absorption, ranges in scope from cultural to institutional, and entails varying magnitudes of conformity (Zhou 1997).

An unflagging commitment to assimilation evolved as the tacit framework for justifying government actions in settler colonies. Assimilation was inseparable from colonialism inasmuch as both entailed a consolidation of imposed power through indoctrination into mainstream norms and values (White 1997). Through assimilation, the dominant element sought to (a) undermine the cultural basis of subdominant society, (b) transform minority members into patriotic and productive citizens, (c) absorb dominant norms as normal and acceptable, and (d) facilitate their entry and transition into the mainstream. Dominant values, beliefs, and social patterns are defined as inevitable or desirable under assimilation; conversely, subdominant sectors are implied to be inferior or irrelevant. Assimilationist policies are rarely intended to transform the subdominant sector in its entirety. The complete absorption of everybody is neither attainable nor always desirable. Few majorities possess either the resources or the political will to enforce total conformity and wholesale conversion. Subsumed instead under assimilation are the virtues of **dominant-conformity** (or **anglo-conformity** in areas under British control). Subdominant group members need only express outward compliance with dominant values and practices. Select elements of their cultural lifestyle are tolerated as long as they (a) are restricted to the private or personal realm, (b) involve only the "cultural" (aesthetic) realm, (c) conform to majority commercial, political, or ideological interests, and (d) do not violate basic moral principles or the law.

As policy or practice, assimilation may be advanced in a variety of ways. Assimilation may occur naturally as immigrant and indigenous women and men are increasingly and inexorably drawn into the mainstream (Alba and Nee 1997). Assimilation may be encouraged informally. Unobtrusive or informal means such as media and education are employed at times to weaken prevailing cultural practices. Explicit or formal government policy and practices may also be activated to foster absorption. Formal initiatives may be directed only at the deserving few, often "half-castes" who unlike "full bloods" are seen as having the potential to progress. Those singled out for assimilationist treatment are often portrayed as "children" in need of guidance, discipline, and control under the ever-vigilant eye of a judicious parent. Assimilation in this case is largely involuntarily through placement and repeated exposure to dominant values and institutions as revealed by the next Case Study on "stolen children" in Australia.

CASE STUDY 1–3	Assimilation By Theft: "People of the Bleaching"

> I would not hesitate for one moment to separate any half-caste from its Aboriginal mother, no matter how frantic her momentary grief might be at the time. They soon forget their offspring.
>
> James Isdell, Chief Protector of Aborigines Western Australia, 1905 (cited in Hedge 1997:B-4)

The distinction between genocide and assimilation is often indistinct if the consequences of the initiatives rather than their intent is taken into account. A policy based on the disappearance of Aboriginal peoples because of dispossession by an allegedly superior culture could be called cultural genocide (Tomlinson 1998). Another policy based on the idea of snatching indigenous children from their families by force, stealth, or deceit, but done in the name of "assimilation" and under Australian law, is equally genocidal in its effect. In the same way that white Australia stole Aboriginal land for minerals or pastures and took Aboriginal women for sex and Aboriginal men for cheap labour, so too did it attempt to complete the process of dispossession by taking Aboriginal children from their families and communities (Human Rights Commission Report on Stolen Children, 1997. Canberra ACT).

Nearly 70,000 Aboriginal children were forcibly taken from their parents between the 1880s and 1960s and placed in government or church missions or with non-Aboriginal families. The objective was to break the Aboriginal spirit by putting children in a Christian environment and away from "pagan" influences. No region was spared, according to the 1997 Human Rights Commission Report on Stolen Children, and nearly one in six Aboriginal children were taken away and put up for adoption, many of whom grew up confused or hostile, prone to destitution or violence, or condemned to an early death (Steketee 1997). Problems related to family breakdowns, drug and alcohol abuse, violence, and mental health are attributed to the trauma of being taken from parents and put in environments where sexual and physical abuse proved rife. The children lost the only thing that little children have: innocence. In the moving words of one mother, "I'm a rotten mother. I don't know how to cuddle my baby. The only time I have ever been cuddled was when I was raped" (reported to Sir Ronald Wilson, President of Australia's Human Rights Commission, cited in Perry 1997:C-1).

The Australian government refuses to make a formal apology or offer compensation for the thousands whose stolen childhood is indeed a national shame. This refusal stands in contrast to Canada where the federal government has "apologized" for also removing children from parents and communities in the name of assimilation.

Possibly an "enlightened" social policy for its times, especially when compared with the alternatives such as segregation or genocide, assimilation gradually lost its prescription as an organizing and guiding principle. The social and political climate that once dismissed group differences as a liability to be overcome through assimilation has given way to positive definitions of diversity as liberating and empowering (Harris 1995). Yet appearances can be deceiving. Although stripped of its explicit normative or ideological pretensions (Alba and Nee 1997), assimilation as a process continues to play a prominent role in shaping subdominant experiences. Assimilation can be seen as a dimension of all government actions. The logical consequences of even seemingly progressive initiatives to assist ethnic minorities may have the effect of drawing them deeper into the "system." In other words, assimilation as a state-imposed policy for eradicating differences may be openly repudiated. However, it remains a key social process that occurs spontaneously if inadvertently in the course of interaction involving subdominant engagement with mainstream institutions and the adoption of dominant cultural values.

Segregation and Separation

The patterns associated with segregation go beyond a physical separation of unequal groups. The dominant group defines itself as superior because of technological, military, social, or moral properties. "Others" are dismissed as inferior or superfluous to the society-building process. Interaction between the segregated sectors is kept to a minimum except in situations of obvious benefit to the controlling sector. This would suggest that segregation is not just a geographical distribution; it is also about a social relationship involving patterns of power and domination (Jaret 1995). In cases of *de jure* segregation, the government deliberately keeps the races apart, thus stigmatizing and handicapping the vulnerable through confinement to inferior facilities; a *de facto* segregation results in the government tacitly condoning forced separation by not actively intervening to dismantle the social cleavages that were intentionally established in the past (Kennedy 1996). Various reasons may account for this enforced separation, for example, ethnocentrism and supremacist ideologies, group preference, socioeconomic differences, fear and hatred of others, resource competition, and discrimination.

One type of segregationist system is known as **plural society** (Furnivall 1948; Smith 1965). Plural societies (not to be confused with cultural pluralism) are segmented into relatively autonomous dominant and subdominant groups. Each sector possesses a distinct and parallel set of institutions except at political or economic levels where a limited degree of interaction must occur. Contact between the two realms is kept to an absolute minimum. Both the dominant and subordinate groups live apart as sharply divided and culturally distinct groups. Interaction is conducted primarily in the marketplace ("selective incorporation") where the dominant group exercises monopolistic control over the economy and distribution of wealth. Compliance and citizenship are not secured by value consensus or social norms; coercion appears as the preferred means (van den Berghe 1970). In the absence of any morally legitimate basis to govern, the dominant group must rely on (the threat of) physical force to compel obedience and order. In short, this system of segmentation and limited incorporation is bound by a combination of racist ideologies, political and economic self-interest, military might, and the long arm of the law. Few cases of segregation have been as highly profiled as that of **apartheid** in South Africa. The implementation of a comprehensive set of segregationist laws and practices virtually compartmentalized blacks from whites into separate groups at social, economic, and political levels. The next Case Study reveals the magnitude and scope of segregation, its impact on South African society, and the challenges of disestablishing the legacy of apartheid.

CASE STUDY 1–4	Apartheid in South Africa: Dismantling a Legacy

Of the many improbabilities within South African race relations, none is as notorious as the political, economic, and social gap between the 4.5 million whites and the 27 million blacks. This gap can be attributed in large part to the effects of a system of institutionalized separation known as apartheid. Apartheid, only recently ended, imposed the organizing framework around which black and white relationships were defined and ranked. Historically, apartheid was formally instituted as law in 1948 by the Afrikaner-based Nationalist Party. Its creation merely codified what had existed informally at political, social, economic, and political levels—the escalating separation of South Africa into the "haves" and the "have-nots." Emphasis was focused on managing the presence of a large black population without undermining white power and privilege.

Two paradoxes sought refuge in the rationale for apartheid. On the one hand, whites wanted to maintain the integrity and unity of their cultural lifestyles, without relinquishing political control and economic domination to the black majority. On the other, they were surrounded by blacks who could not be expelled for a variety of demographic and economic reasons. While whites wanted to incorporate blacks as menial labourers into a resource-based economy, they rejected the idea of including them as equals at the social and political realm. This ambivalent desire to economically incorporate the blacks within a framework of political and cultural separation stimulated the appearance of apartheid. Apartheid envisioned a complex and cooperative social system in which white South Africa would be surrounded by a relatively independent set of satellite black nations or homelands (bantustans). The

bantustan model was allegedly inspired by the system of reserves established in Canada and the United States. Each black belonged to one of these states, such as Transkei; this, in effect, denied individual access to the benefits and privileges of South African citizenship. These homelands provided white South Africa with the labour it required without having to pay the political costs.

To implement the principles of apartheid, a series of laws was passed to separate the races at the political, economic, social, and cultural levels. The Population Registration Act was passed in 1950 to regulate the influx of migrant labourers. Provisions of the act imposed compulsory registration according to race and ethnic group. The Group Areas Act then outlined where blacks could or could not live, although inevitably some breakdown occurred. This was especially evident with the proliferation of black suburbs in Sharpeville and Soweto. These black townships were not intended as permanent residences; the bantustans existed for that. But in light of the need for an accessible labour force, the authorities ignored these violations. Finally, a series of discriminatory practices was instituted to deny black access to normal amenities. These included white-only beaches, the prohibition of mixed marriages or even mixed sexual relationships, and "pass laws" dictating where people could go or live. Many of these were either modified or camouflaged in response to national and international pressure.

The dawning of a new era in South Africa has yielded much promise and potential. The release of black leader Nelson Mandela from prison in 1990, together with the conferral of universal enfranchisement and multiparty elections in 1994, dismantled the infrastructure of apartheid and replaced it with democratic rule and a non-segregationist system of race relations. An interim national unity government under Nelson Mandela and dominated by the ANC (African National Congress) was charged with equalizing access to jobs, schools, health, and housing (Cook 1995). Progress to date has been impressive: since 1994, millions have moved into government-built homes, enjoyed running water and access to electricity, and benefited from accessible and affordable primary care (Schuler 1999).

Nevertheless, the legacy of apartheid continues to distort the society-building process (Pilger 1998). Blacks may control the politics, but whites remain in charge of the economy while the ANC has failed to deliver on promises to create a million new jobs and a targeted economic growth of 6 percent (Schuler 1999). Race-related violence is still rife in rural regions; 80 percent of crime is committed by blacks in black townships, resulting in a 25 percent increase in the money spent on policing and prisons. Unofficial segregation persists as an everyday reality in the cities, where rich whites and poor blacks remain separate and unequal. Wealth continues to be concentrated in the white population, while 70 percent of blacks are below the poverty line (Pilger 1998). Black workers earn about one-eighth of the monthly income of whites; black infants are six times more likely to die than whites; and illiteracy rates are 1 percent

among whites and 46 percent among blacks (*Newsweek*, 9 May 1994). With 5 percent of the population owning 90 percent of the wealth, the battleground has shifted from the politics of race to an apartheid by class (Handelman 1998). The entrenchment of economic inequality suggests that the new South Africa may be little more than a façade behind which apartheid continues by another name (Pilger 1998).

A painful reality is beginning to sink in: It will take more than ballot-box democracy to discard dependency and impoverishment after three centuries of colonialist domination (Watson 1995). The challenge of cobbling together a society of 11 languages and 43 million people with crippling disparities in health, education, and income would be difficult enough under ideal circumstances (Handelman 1998). The prospect of society building against the backdrop of police-state oppression and the racial hostility bequeathed by apartheid makes it much more daunting (Berkely 1996/97). Nelson Mandela deserves the last word in sorting through this conundrum: "We need to understand in a deep and comprehensive way that the country we have inherited is essentially structured in a manner which denies us the possibility to achieve the goal of creating a new people-centred society. Any notion that the revolution ended with the elections of 1994 is both false and dangerous" (cited in Handelman 1998).

Segregation can be imposed as noted above. It can also be generated from "below" by groups who prefer **voluntary separation** from society. Voluntary separation is not the same as segregation or apartheid, despite similarities in appearance and structure. The concept of different rules, structures, or laws for different people in the same society is not segregatory when based on consensual choice or preferred course of action. For example, the Hutterites of Western Canada and other communal religious sects have voluntarily divorced themselves from the outside world through expressions of religion, language, communal lifestyle, dress, and social interaction. Only contacts at the marketplace level are maintained. Elsewhere a separatist relationship can arise from secessionist movements. The emergence of a new global order has opened opportunity for separation from sovereignties once artificially frozen in time because of colonialism or strategic interests (McGarry and O'Leary 1994). The integration of societies in global economies has paradoxically (or perhaps logically) bolstered demands for local self-determination. Emboldened by these postmodernist ideologies, racial, ethnic, or aboriginal minorities are currently seeking new arrangements within existing state systems. Prime examples consist of threats by Quebec and the First Nations to separate from Canada if demands for "peoplehood" status are rebuffed (Nelson and Fleras 1998).

Integration

A fourth outcome reflects a commitment to the principles of **integration.** The shift toward integration in Canada and elsewhere represented a mid-twentieth-century reaction against segregationalist policies or practices. Generally speaking, the concept of integration stands in opposition to segregation. Segregation is defined by forced separation among people who live apart from each other, socially and geographically. Integration, by contrast, refers to a process whereby individuals intermingle with each other at all institutional levels (Jaret 1995). A distinction between desegregation and integration is also useful. Desegregation entails a removal of physical or social barriers to achieve formal equality; integration involves the proactive process of unifying disparate parts into a cooperative and functioning whole. One is about equality before the law; the other concerns the attainment of substantive equality.

Two variations underlie the integration theme. Integration represents a two-way process by which the dominant and subdominant sectors are brought together in a single comprehensive lifestyle, without either losing its sense of distinctiveness. Each is expected to contribute to the construction of the new reality, yet retain a distinguishable presence within the new configuration. Related to this is the variant in which the dominant and the subdominant groups are encouraged to fuse (merge) together like paints in a bucket. The result of this "blending" process is a new cultural entity comprising constituent elements of this admixture. This fusion ("synthesis") of the "modern" with the "traditional" into a relatively homogeneous entity is metaphorically captured by the concept of the **melting pot,** an image that is often invoked to describe the ideal underlying American race and ethnic relations. It also strikes at the core of national identity with its belief that all immigrants can be transformed into new Americans—a new cultural alloy forged in the crucible of democracy, freedom, and civic responsibility (Booth 1998). Yet references to melting "potism" strike a dissonant note when referring to black–white relations in the United States.

CASE STUDY 1–5	From Segregation to Integration/From Civil Rights to Black Is Beautiful

All "men" may be created equal according to the American constitution. But some are born more equal than others, and neither the Declaration of Independence nor the Civil War did much to improve the legal and socioeconomic status of African-Americans. Blacks and whites were unequal and separated by law and custom prior to the Civil

Rights movements of the 1950s and 1960s. Both *de jure* and *de facto* segregation was enforced in restaurants, in public transport, and in major social institutions such as hospitals, churches, and schools. The labour force was racially stratified. Interracial marriages were prohibited in many states. The colour bar led to inferior levels of development among blacks; this in turn became a self-fulfilling prophecy by intensifying discrimination against a segregated population.

The Civil Rights movements established a commitment to integration by dismantling many of the egregious dimensions of segregation. Desegregation sought to undo segregation by eliminating legal and social prohibitions, while integration sought to improve interracial interaction and the participation of African-Americans in all walks of human life (Kennedy 1996). Integration guaranteed all Americans formal equality before the law and expressly prohibited discrimination on the basis of race or creed. A deceptively simple assumption underpinned the promise of integration: Whites will discriminate in favour of themselves if there is a separation of races. The genius of integration is that whites cannot discriminate in favour of themselves without favourably assisting blacks in the process (for example, the best way of guaranteeing black children a good education is to link their fate with white children through integrated schools, even if forced busing is mandated) (Kennedy 1996).

The commitment to integration may have promised much. Passage of the Civil Rights Act in 1964 improved the position of blacks in society, at least in theory if not in practice. But many African-Americans continued to be plagued by the aftermath of segregation. The Civil Rights movement may have envisaged a more integrated society but failed to usher in prosperity for most blacks, many of whom continue to be confined to economic and residential ghettoes (Jaret 1995). Not surprisingly, the Civil Rights movement gave way to the Black Pride movement and to Black Power militants. The shift from Negro to Black as a term of self-description symbolized this rejection of the Civil Rights integrationist ideals. Rather than middle class blacks striving to assimilate into white mainstream, Black Pride represented an identity-building movement that sought to promote the Black Is Beautiful image by politicizing the concept of indigenous ghetto culture as the basis of black unity and separation from whites (Spencer 1994). A demand for affirmative action replaced a commitment to formal equality, since it was no longer sufficient to remove only legal barriers to black advancement but also social barriers by assuring blacks a predetermined share of privileges and rewards (equality of results).

This belief that blacks and whites cannot live together amicably has shattered Martin Luther King's dream of United States as an integrated country of goodwill and equality. Even the NAACP, founded in 1908 by WEB DuBois to combat discrimination through integration and whose greatest triumph in 1954 was the Supreme Court decision to outlaw separate but equal public school facilities, appears to be abandoning the principle of integration in the face of mounting black nationalism for separating the races as a basis for living together with differences (Maxwell 1997).

Many are unsure of how to assess integration: Some associate integration with the positive goals of equality and participation; others conjure up images of unwanted conformity. Some integrationists are inspired by an ethos of human solidarity by endorsing arrangements that encourage universalism; others are inclined to believe that a diverse society requires the protection and promotion of diverse perspectives. In theory, a commitment to integration differs from that of assimilation. Assimilation endorses a one-way process of absorption and surrender of identity into the mainstream. Integration upholds a two-way system of synthesis that ultimately yields a unique cultural fusion. Assimilation is primarily a cultural concept; integration a social concept that rejects any notion of divorcing people from the common life of wider society (Parekh 1997). In practice, however, the outcomes of either may be indistinguishable. In both cases, the subdominant group is absorbed into the basic framework as defined by the dominant sector. For example, although immigrants into the United States are expected to melt into the American pot, this cauldron remains irrefutably white, male, English-speaking, and middle class in orientation. Any restructuring of American society is recast along the lines and priorities of the prevailing institutional framework, which remains essentially intact, while the subdominant sector merely adds a "dash of spice" to an otherwise monocultural stew.

Cultural Pluralism

Government policies that once diminished the value or relevance of diversity are now giving way to alternative arrangements for engaging diversity in a meaningful way. Acceptance of diversity within a national framework is called **cultural pluralism**. Cultural pluralism is more than a description about the presence of racial or ethnic minorities in society. It also constitutes a prescriptive statement that endorses diversity as a key component of an egalitarian society. Ingredients of a cultural pluralism consist of a commitment to secular tolerance, cosmopolitan worldliness, civic nationalism, and rational scientism (Ryan 1997). Neither blatant forms of social inequality nor human rights abuses are consistent with a culturally pluralistic society. The state may have little choice except to intervene to address minority needs by reaffirming individual rights, rectifying past injustices, reducing social inequities through removal of discriminatory barriers, providing positive actions through affirmative (employment equity) action programs, and ensuring protection of traditional language and culture (Helly 1993).

Cultural pluralism can be expressed in diverse ways, including multiculturalism, biculturalism, multinationalism, and cultural autonomy (Fleras 1998). The last section of the book will address the different "isms." Different dimensions of cultural pluralism can also be discerned: Liberal cultural pluralism rests on the principle of nondiscrimination; that is, the government provides no formal recognition to racial or ethnic minorities in pursuit of a colourblind society. A corporate cultural pluralism confers formal recognition on racial and ethnic minorities by acknowledging differences as a basis for entitlement and society building (Gordon 1964). Canada may be perceived as a cultural pluralism in both senses. It promotes the legitimacy of ethnic diversity by creating cultural space for minorities; at the same time it establishes culturally neutral spaces within institutions where all Canadians can interact without fear of ethnic entanglements. Canada's pluralistic commitments are enshrined in the concept of multiculturalism. Multiculturalism has been the official government policy of cultural pluralism since 1971, having undergone several shifts in emphasis and importance, without ever losing its commitment to institutional accommodation. The United States has also experienced a multicultural turn in recent years (Glazer 1997), with a critical, even insurgent, style of multiculturalism that differs sharply from Canada's official consensus multiculturalism (Goldberg 1994).

The religious-ethnocultural group, the Hutterites, provides one of the more vexing examples of cultural pluralism in Canada. Espousing a separatist view of cultural pluralism has resulted in ongoing struggles by Hutterites to protect their identity and distinctiveness in the face of modernizing pressures. In doing so, Canadian multiculturalism has been put to the test by an ethnic group that simultaneously endorses yet repudiates the principles of multiculturalism.

CASE STUDY 1–6   **Cultural Separatism in a Multicultural Society**

The Hutterites can be described as an intensely religious ethnic group whose distinctiveness springs from an agrarian lifestyle and communal ownership of property (Hostetler and Huntington 1980). Centuries of hostility and exposure to assimilationist pressures have not diminished Hutterite resolve to survive as an economically viable, biologically self-reproducing, and culturally distinct people (van den Berghe and Peter 1988). Much of their success can be attributed to the construction of social boundaries against the outside world as a way of securing their separation.

Restricted largely to Canada's west where about 200 colonies thrive, Hutterites are one of three Anabaptist groups (the others being the Amish and the Mennonites) who believe in the separation of state and church—in the process denying the legitimacy of secular authority over them. Unlike other Anabaptists, Hutterites reside in communally based communities of about 10 to 12 families. Up to 200 persons live in these classless colonies in the belief that communal living provides them with the buffer to fend off the temptations of a secular world. Contrasting their simplicity in social and cultural domains is a willingness to utilize modern productive technology to secure an economic base for all to share equally. Their willingness to take advantage of economic opportunities, but unwillingness to integrate into the wider community, has created resentment, at times bordering on open hostility and resulting in

persecution or death. This hostility has had the effect of drawing Hutterites closer together ("siege mentality") by strengthening their resolve to remain apart spiritually, culturally, and socially.

Hutterites have relied on various strategies—both deliberate and unintended—to ensure a degree of cultural separation. Geographic and social isolation are key components: Access to the outside is restricted and carefully monitored by colony leaders (Kallen 1995). Large tracts of land are purchased at some distance from the general population; communities are then constructed in the centre of the tract to minimize contact. Separateness is maintained through structural endogamy ("marriage within the group") and high reproductive rates. Considerable energy is expended on socializing their children into hard-working and God-fearing followers of the colony. An oral history rich with vignettes of persecution and martyrdom has also reinforced perceptions of the outside as evil, corrupt, godless, and untrustworthy. Strong leadership within the commune has kept the faithful in the fold (Boldt 1985). The austerity of communal life provides religious leaders with the latitude to apply diffuse sanctions to ensure compliance with spiritual and social norms. The temptation for youths to stray from the path is defused through a moderate degree of pragmatic accommodation in making concessions to the outside world. This flexibility and moderate receptivity to change suggests Hutterite willingness to "bend rather than break"—provided these concessions do not interfere with the running of the colony or contravene scriptural doctrines (van den Berghe and Peters 1988; Kallen 1995).

In sum, the Hutterites have displayed remarkable success in sustaining a viable lifestyle in the face of insurmountable odds. Part of their success can be attributed to the construction of well-defined boundaries which regulate but with some discretion. Their lifestyle is based on self-sufficiency and in-dependence, with each colony exhibiting a degree of institutional completeness at political, social, economic, and educational levels, in addition to religiously legitimated mechanism for social control (Kallen 1995). A cradle-to-grave-and-beyond security not only diminishes any decision to leave, but also ensures loyalty and commitment beyond the here and now. Such a set of other-worldly commitments makes it doubly difficult to bring Hutterites into the multicultural fold.

To Sum Up   Recurrent responses and patterned outcomes are established when competitively different groups come into sustained contact. The working through of differences in unequal contexts results in a network of patterned relations, many of which become formalized into explicit government policy that denies differences (assimilation), rejects minorities (segregation), demonizes out-groups (genocide), espouses formal equality (integration), and engages diversity (cultural pluralism). To be sure, political strategies for regulating minorities are often mixed and aimed at different target groups rather than being discreet or exhaustive (McGarry and O'Leary 1994). As well, some degree of coexistence and duplication is inevitable, since social reality cannot possibly be carved into mutual discreet and exclusive categories. Table 1.1 highlights some of the key features by way of comparison of ideal types.

TABLE 1.1	Patterns of Ethnic Interaction			
	Definition	**Objectives**	**Means**	**Outcomes**
Genocide/ Ethnocide	Mass annihilation	To eliminate or destroy	Direct (violent) or indirect ("peaceful")	Ethnic or racial purity
Assimilation	Absorption, anglo-conformity	Compliance	Undermine + transform + incorporate	A civilized world
Segregation	Forced separation	Colour bar + discriminatory codes	Threat of force	Separate but unequal
Integration	Incorporate + fuse	Formal equality	Civil rights + education	Melting pot
Cultural pluralism	Engage diversity as different yet equal	Cultural diversity Social equality National interests	Removal of discriminatory (both social and cultural) barriers	Multiculturalism Biculturalism Multinationalism Cultural autonomy (Separatism)

EXPLAINING RELATIONS: SOCIOLOGICAL PERSPECTIVES

Sociology as a discipline is often defined as the scientific study of human society (Macionis and Gerber 1999). Society in turn may be conceptualized as a complex, contested, and evolving system of relations ranging in scope from the interpersonal to the international with intergroup dynamics a focal point in shaping societal outcomes. Several conceptual frameworks furnish a unique perspective on society and how it works. Sociological perspectives of **functionalism, social conflict,** and **symbolic interactionism** provide distinctive yet complementary ways of looking at the social dimensions of race, ethnic, and aboriginal relations. Perspectives vary in terms of the questions asked, the foundational premises, rules of proof, and supporting data. Each perspective highlights certain features of society with respect to intergroup dynamics while excluding other aspects as less important. A functionalist perspective tends to accent stability in intergroup relations and the orderly integration and assimilation of racial, ethnic, and aboriginal groups into a dominant culture. Opposed to functionalism are conflict perspectives that focus on inequalities of power and resources, often in association with the economic institutions of capitalism, the role of government in perpetuating inequality, and resistance of subdominant groups to exploitation or oppression (Satzewich 1998). Still others dwell on race, ethnic, and aboriginal relations as socially constructed and contested interaction within the broader framework of society—itself a human accomplishment. Differences in emphasis notwithstanding, each of these perspectives shares one thing in common: a search for the determinants of human behaviour outside of an individual frame of reference. This commitment to the "bigger picture" distinguishes sociology from other disciplines. Taken together, these multiple perspectives emphasize the relevance of the social and the structural in shaping the relationship of society to race, aboriginal, and ethnic sectors.

Functionalist Models

Each sociological perspective contains foundational premises about the nature of society and human interaction (Burrell and Morgan 1979). For functionalists, society is viewed as a complex whole comprised of interrelated parts that collectively contribute to maintenance and survival. Functionalist perspectives argue that these interrelated parts must be integrated for the system to operate efficiently. Under optimal conditions, all elements of a society are smoothly intermeshed to enhance order and stability. But stresses associated with rapid social change may unravel these relationships to a point of temporary disarray. Countervailing measures are activated to remove potentially disruptive situations and to restore a sense of equilibrium and order within society. In other words, dysfunctions such as conflict and contradiction are viewed as potentially disruptive to an otherwise harmonious society. Corrective measures are thus required to reestablish consensus, stability, and social harmony.

A functionalist perspective on race, aboriginal, and ethnic relations approaches diversity as a potential threat to society. For example, the arrival of immigrants to Canada has proven beneficial to the economic and cultural well-being of society. Immigrants often provide a valuable source of labour to fulfill the needs of an expanding economy. They enliven Canadian society through the richness of their cultural heritages. Yet their entry into Canada is perceived as creating problems ("dysfunctions") because of costs or disruptions. Many new Canadians may have to rely on government assistance for survival because of their marginal status in society. Immigrants frequently are targeted as victims of prejudice and discrimination. Their cultural heritage may be inconsistent with the prevailing value system in Canada, further contributing to problems of incorporation and adjustment. In brief, while their contribution to Canadian prosperity is rarely disputed, certain immigrant groups may be dismissed as dysfunctional to an otherwise stable and integrated society. To thwart any potential conflicts, measures are introduced for damage control and conflict management. A variety of institutional arrangements are put in place to facilitate the entry of new Canadians, not necessarily out of compassion, but because failure to maximize human capital has the potential to lower productivity while sowing the seeds of disarray (Jaret 1995). Assimilationist agencies such as education and mass media complement mechanisms such as multiculturalism to foster consensus and shared values.

Functionalist perspectives have proven useful in drawing attention to government responses to race, ethnic, and aboriginal relations. Government policies such as multiculturalism may be interpreted in the sociological sense of restoring equilibrium and order to situations that may prove problematic (see next Case Study). A functionalist perspective also raises questions about the status and benefits of diversity to society; for example, Is diversity worthwhile from a society-building perspective? How much diversity can be incorporated without undermining the integrity and character of a "functioning" society? What is the absorptive capacity of a society before it becomes "dysfunctional"? Will racial, aboriginal, or ethnic diversity persist in the face of pressures for modernization and assimilation? How can we achieve cooperation and consensus in a system of competitive free enterprise (Troper and Weinfeld 1999)? In answering these questions, functionalist perspectives focus on the mechanisms employed by society to cope with potential disruptions and "troublesome" constituents. It remains to be seen whether functionalist thought is capable of addressing issues pertaining to conflict and change at intergroup levels.

Conflict Models

A conflict perspective on society differs sharply from a functionalist view of society. Whereas functionalists espouse a normative theory of society by emphasizing consensus over rules and values, conflict perspectives assert that social norms reflect the interests of the ruling classes. Conflict is generated by the imposition of ruling class interests against the will or knowledge of the population at large (Green 1994). In contrast with functionalist approaches (with an emphasis on system equilibrium, normative consensus, and institutional integration), a conflict perspective portrays society as a complex system of unequal yet competing groups in perpetual competition over scarce and valued resources, including power, wealth, prestige, and sovereignty (Coser 1956). For **conflict theorists,** then, society represents a contested site where both dominant and subdominant groups struggle to subvert or support the status quo. Dominant groups will rely on peaceful or violent methods to preserve privilege and power. Different strategies of resistance may be employed by subdominant sectors, ranging from outright confrontation to passive resistance.

For conflict theorists, the normal state of society resonates with conflict and change rather than consensus or stability. Society is held together by force or the threat of coercion because of unequal competition for scarce resources and rewards. A conflict perspective is not intended to portray society in a perpetual state of conflict and confrontation. Of interest to conflict theorists are the techniques that are employed to maintain and legitimate a fundamentally unequal order without resorting to heavy-handed tactics. At times, the dominant group is powerful enough to defuse the potential for overt conflict. At other times, group hostilities are open, but may subside during periods of relative calm or consensus. A temporary truce may materialize when opposing groups find it mutually advantageous to lay aside their differences in pursuit of common or specific interests. Consider how official multiculturalism in Canada may constitute an elite consensus for controlling minorities; alternatively, it may be reconstituted as a progressive tool for challenging the status quo (Pearson 1996). This "double-edgedness" suggests that conflict and cooperation involve different aspects of a single process including accommodation with conflict, stability with change, and cooperation with confrontation.

With its focus on inequality and power, conflict models have proven adept in explaining ambiguities in race, ethnic, and indigenous relations. Two variants prevail: According to "moderate" conflict theorists (Dahrendorf 1959), conflict is normal and natural, since all societies are sites of contestation involving competitive struggles by opposing groups to define, control, evade, or collaborate. Relations between race and ethnic groups are sorted out along poles of domination and subdomination. Groups that are politically or economically dominant will take steps to advance and legitimize their own interests—by coercive means if necessary. Control over key institutions is sought through coalition building or strategies of divide and conquer (Jaret 1995). An **internal colonialism** model provides a different reading on conflict perspectives. This approach argues that not all inequities are created the same. Indigenous peoples such as the First Nations in Canada or even the Québécois are not just another ethnic minority. Rather they are a people whose experience of oppression compares with that of indigenes from overseas colonialism (Hechter 1975). Both groups of indigenous peoples are pushed to the periphery by undermining access to land, culture, and identity. A cultural division of labour evolves in which the indigenes occupy the most menial or exploitative occupations. Indirect rule and control are facilitated by the co-optation of indigenous elites or through establishment of a bureaucracy such as the Department of Indian Affairs. The net result is a colonialist relationship that is every bit as oppressive or exploitative as "salt-water" colonies. The concept of internal colonialism will be revisited in the chapter on aboriginal peoples.

Another variant of conflict theory incorporates Marxist approaches. In contrast with internal colonialism, which endorses ethnic differences and class stratification as analytically separate but mutually linked, Marxist conflict theory positions class at the heart of all exploitation and conflict (Feagin and Feagin 1993). Marxists argue that the fundamental contradiction in any complex society is the existence of two social classes: the working and the ruling class. The working class can only survive by selling its labour to the ruling class; the ruling class in turn owns the means of production and will do anything to facilitate the flow of profits by shaving the costs of labour. One tactic is to destabilize the workers by fomenting internal divisions based on lines of race or ethnicity. The working classes prefer to present a united front—at least in theory—by minimizing the salience of race and ethnicity as secondary to class interests. In both cases, racial, aboriginal, and ethnic minorities are portrayed as pawns with little legitimacy beyond their usefulness to the class struggle. But a neo-Marxist variation of conflict theory, known as critical political economy, seeks to transcend the reductionism of class-based determinism (Clement 1998). A political economy perspective seeks to explain the complex and often contradictory relationship between politics and the economy as they effect and are effected by social patterns and cultural life (Saggers and Gray 1998). To be sure, the processes associated with the production, distribution, and consumption of goods are critical to any understanding of social life. But these relations are shaped *only in the first instance* by economic forces. Ideas and ideals are important as well, and that makes it doubly important to understand the ideological and social patterns that inform how society is created and transformed. In short, human action is seen as having considerable latitude of movement by virtue of its active agency, but always within the limits of the structures that constrain and control.

Interactionist Models

Both functionalist and conflict perspectives see society as a taken-for-granted point of departure. Society is portrayed as durable and real, existing above and beyond the individual, yet exerting vast leverage over people's behaviour. By contrast, interactionist perspectives begin with the notion of society as an active and ongoing human accomplishment. Instead of something "out there" and determinative, society is perceived as socially constructed through group interaction. According to this outlook, we do not live in a predetermined world of mechanistic outcomes. Rather, reality is constructed by applying provisional meanings to a variety of situations. Once a situation has been defined and redefined, jointly linked lines of action are developed through negotiation, compromise, and adjustment. The interplay and combination of these joint linkages at a given point in time and place create what we call society. For interactionists, too, society is envisaged as a contested site in which opposing racial, ethnic, and aboriginal groups interact to socially construct realities that foster unity or division. In contrast with Marxist conflict theory, which reduces society to sites of power and inequality, an interactionist approach incorporates a process-oriented and non-deterministic view of intergroup dynamics as continually emerging through the processes of formation, negotiation, accommodation, and definition. Not surprisingly, interactional patterns are best approached in a frame of constant flux, dynamic tension, mutual adjustment, negotiated compromise, and ongoing movement.

A similar line of reasoning applies to race, ethnic, and aboriginal relations. Race, ethnicity, and aboriginality are treated as resources by social actors in defining situations and acting out on the basis of these definitions. Ethnically specific identities are activated as a basis for collective action, especially when there is a competitive advantage to group affiliation in contexts of change or breakdowns in the "racialized" division of labour. Patterned interaction is thus generated and sustained by opposing elements who compete for definitional control of the situation in an effort to attract constituencies and promote interests. Minority groups, as Louis Wirth recognized long ago, may seek one of four broad goals: pluralism, assimilation, separatism, or militarism. Conversely, the majority casts for ways to eliminate, isolate, absorb, tolerate, or incorporate. From a minority point of view, the question revolves around the benefits of working either within the system or outside by way of parallel institutions. From a majority perspective the question is no less perplexing: Should minorities be allowed into the mainstream, or is it better to exclude them from full and equal involvement? These interactional styles and outcomes are not mutually exclusively, but intersect to create interesting group dynamics.

A **collective definition** approach by Herbert Blumer and Troy Duster (1980) provides a window of understanding into the interactional components of dominant–subdominant relations. A collective definition approach emphasizes the process by which intra- and inter-group relations are formulated and reformulated because of opposing tendencies (**dualisms**) that coexist within all groups. Both the dominant and subdominant groups may be internally divided into competing factions known as dualisms. To one side are the dualisms associated with inclusion versus exclusion as opposing tendencies; to the other side are the dualisms of assimilation versus separation as optional choices. Consider the possibilities: One of the dualisms within the subdominant sector may prefer assimilation ("inclusion") into the dominant sector, especially when conditions are ripe for integration. The other dualism in the subdominant sector, however, may reject the legitimacy of the dominant sector, preferring instead to separate ("exclusion") through the creation of parallel institutions as ends in themselves or tactical strategy. The dominant sector is also characterized by dualisms. It too is confronted by the option of exclusion or inclusion in defusing challenges to its privilege. On the one hand are those dominant factions who wish to preserve the status quo by way of exclusionary actions. Elements within this sector may resort to tactics of closure by restricting access to resources and power. On the other hand, there are those who are not threatened by such demands. They are willing to be inclusionary toward subordinate claims and demands, especially if something can be levered by such assimilationist postures. These dual tensions within the dominant sector give rise to an inner dynamic that may elicit mixed messages to subdominant sectors.

The collective definition process is animated by the intersection of these interlocking forces: assimilation/separation versus inclusion/exclusion. The pull and push of these dualisms impart an element of instability in intergroup dynamics, since any one of these dualisms may gain ascendency or decline in response to local, national, or international developments. These dual responses—inclusion or exclusion/assimilation or segregation—are neither mutually exclusive nor fixed in perpetuity, but vary over time. Certain conditions may bring about convergence of dualisms; other conditions may activate exclusionary tactics in mobilizing people for competition with the "other." The interplay of these dualistic oppositions (inclusion–exclusion) helps to explain the diverse range of subdominant responses and dominant reactions. The politics of dualism also provide insight into the unpredictable and often contradictory relations associated with race, ethnic, and aboriginal relations, as the next Case Study on the politics of multiculturalism demonstrates.

CASE STUDY 1–7	Putting Multiculturalism Into Perspective

Sociological perspectives of social phenomena can assist in seeing the familiar in unfamiliar ways. Perspectives such as functionalism, conflict theory, and interactionism not only provide distinctly different ways of looking at social reality; each of these perspectives also casts light on aspects of social reality that the others prefer to gloss over or dismiss. The existence of official multiculturalism in Canada is a case in point.

Everyone agrees that Canada is a multicultural society. Its population is extremely diverse, Canadians generally subscribe to core values of openness and tolerance, and elites are known to rely on multiculturalism to advance personal or national interests (Troper and Weinfeld 1999). Canada is also multicultural in the sense that since 1971 it has had a federal policy of official multiculturalism. Furthermore, multiculturalism was entrenched in the Constitution Act of 1982 and given statutory status with passage of the world's first and still only Multiculturalism Act in 1988. The content of multiculturalism has shifted over time: From an initial period of "celebrating differences" to ensure acceptance of new Canadians, multiculturalism in the 1980s focused on institutional accommodation and removal of discriminatory barriers. In recent years, multiculturalism has shifted to embrace a more inclusive Canada by expanding the participatory principles of citizenship (Fleras 1998).

Canadians have had a love–hate relationship with multiculturalism, despite its pervasiveness, and this ambiguity corresponds to some extent with sociological perspectives on the role and status of multiculturalism. A functionalist perspective on multiculturalism acknowledges its role in creating a distinct, coherent, and prosperous Canada. Multiculturalism is perceived as a device whose function is to defuse ethnic hostilities by making both the majority and minority more comfortable with each other in the public realm. By removing both attitudinal and discriminatory barriers in determining who gets what, multiculturalism resembles a conflict resolution device that fosters a cohesive social climate. A radical conflict perspective disagrees with this positive spin on multiculturalism. According to conflict theorists, multiculturalism is a calculated device by the ruling elites to defuse, distract, and diminish ethnic conflict, thus preserving the prevailing distribution of power and privilege by keeping minorities in their place. Multiculturalism is most effective in terms of fostering a false consciousness: It either camouflages the real source of exploitation in society by suggesting cultural solutions to structural problems, or, alternatively, recourse to multiculturalism creates the illusion of radical change by reinforcing its image as "assimilation in slow motion." Differences between conflict and functionalist perspectives, nonetheless, both acknowledge that multiculturalism makes a contribution of kind to something: for functionalists the stability and order of society, for conflict theorists the power and privilege of vested interests.

Interactionists differ in focus from functionalists or conflict theorists. Rather than assessing multiculturalism on a scale of good to bad, interactionists tend to interpret multiculturalism as a socially constructed human accomplishment. People create multiculturalism and multicultural realities by defining situations in terms of multiculturalism and then acting out on the basis of these definitions by jointly linking these patterns of interaction. Multiculturalism itself becomes a battleground of conflicting visions as opposing interests with varying amounts of resources compete with each other in struggling to impose their definition of the situation at the expense of others. For parts of the dominant sector, multiculturalism is endorsed as a basis for living together with our differences or for cooling out troublesome constituents. Another part of this sector may reject multiculturalism as a recipe for disaster in reinforcing ethnic cleavages and conflicts. Conversely, the subdominant sector may support multiculturalism as a window of opportunity in levelling the playing pitch, or repudiate it as a sneaky device for co-opting minorities into the mainstream. The dualisms in group interaction are readily apparent. Furthermore, multiculturalism is situated within the framework of Canada as a socially constructed reality. That is, Canada is a contested site in which multiculturalism competes with other forms of nationalism such as that of the Québécois or aboriginal peoples. Advocates of multiculturalism are simply one of many players whose competitive struggles contribute to the ongoing dynamic of Canadian realities.

Each of these perspectives provides a valuable insight into different ways of looking at multiculturalism. Multiculturalism is seen by some as good in bolstering the collective sentiments upon which order and stability are conveyed; by others as bad in fostering the illusion of progressive change without really challenging the system; and by still others as critical to an understanding of human reality as social, relational, and constructed. None of the perspectives is inherently superior to the other. Taken together, however, they do provide a complex and multidimensional view of multiculturalism that each, alone, cannot possibly attain. In the final analysis, preference for one perspective over another is not a case of right or wrong. It may reflect one of several sociological perspectives of Canada and the role of multiculturalism in advancing a vision of Canadian society at the millennium.

CHAPTER HIGHLIGHTS

- This chapter provides an overview of race, aboriginal, and ethnic relations as socially constructed and patterned interaction involving diverse groups within contexts of inequality and change.

- Sociologists are not interested in everything about race, ethnic, and aboriginal relations. Their interest is in the social dimensions of group dynamics, with particular emphasis on their relationship to society.

- Canada's record in the field of race, ethnic, and aboriginal relations can be interpreted as good, bad, ugly, or as something in between. A sense of perspective is required in making such an assessment. Much also depends on the criteria employed.

- Sociologists are interested in intergroup relations and may regard the competition and conflict associated with group dynamics as a necessary and normal component of interaction rather than a pathological result of individual prejudices or irrational fears.

- A rephrasing of race, aboriginal, and ethnic relations as dominant–subdominant (majority–minority) interaction draws attention to the importance of power in shaping intergroup dynamics. Race and ethnic relations are treated as relationships of inequality between groups, and sociologists are interested in how these inequities are constructed, supported, challenged, and transformed by way of government practices and minority resistance.

- Patterned interaction is likely to occur when racially and culturally different groups come into prolonged contact and compete over scarce resources. These relations between competitively different groups may crystallize around processes and outcomes related to genocide, integration, assimilation, segregation, and pluralism.

- Genocide represents an orchestrated campaign to eliminate a devalued minority; assimilation consists of a framework for absorbing minorities into the mainstream without necessarily sharing power or cultural space; with its focus on fusion and melting, integration represents a more sophisticated form of assimilation as well as a reaction to segregation; segregation usually implies the rejection and forced separation of minorities from the mainstream; and cultural pluralism acknowledges the legitimacy of diversity as an integral component of society.

- Various perspectives for the study of racial and ethnic relations are explored, with particular emphasis on functionalism, conflict, and interactionism. These perspectives provide distinct ways of looking at diversity, since each has different assumptions and asks different questions about the status, role, and nature of race, ethnic, and aboriginal relations. Inasmuch as group relations are constructed, patterned, and unequal, each of the models provides certain insights into a sociological understanding of diversity in Canada.

- With its focus on societal needs and the importance of consensus and shared values as a basis for stability and survival, functionalist models emphasize the devices for controlling (correcting or eliminating) diversity; conflict models envision society as a site of competition for scarce resources between groups; and interactionist models emphasize the socially constructed and contested nature of group interaction.

- The contested notion of multiculturalism as a means for engaging with diversity makes it amenable to sociological analysis.

KEY TERMS

anglo-conformity (dominant conformity)
apartheid
assimilation
collective definition
conflict theory
cultural pluralism
cultural separation
dualism
functionalism
genocide (ethnocide)
integration
internal colonialism
melting pot
plural society
pluralism
segregation
social conflict
subdominant
symbolic interactionism
voluntary separation

REVIEW QUESTIONS

1. What is meant by a sociology of race, aboriginal, and ethnic relations? Include the notion of patterned interaction in your answer.

2. Briefly compare and contrast the policies and principles of genocide, assimilation, integration, segregation, and cultural pluralism as strategies for managing race, aboriginal, and ethnic relations.

3. Why is it useful to rephrase race and ethnic relations as relationships of inequality?

4. Compare and contrast the major sociological perspectives on society in terms of how they approach the study of racial, ethnic, and aboriginal realities.

5. How does a collective definition perspective contribute toward an understanding of race, ethnic, and aboriginal relations?

6. Select any issue or incident involving racial, ethnic, or aboriginal groups. Analyze the issue or incident from one or all three sociological perspectives on society.

7. How would you assess Canada's record in the treatment of racial, ethnic, and aboriginal peoples? Justify your answer by using specific criteria for your assessment.

THE POLITICS OF 'RACE'

2

INSIGHT 2-1 | **'Racing' Whiteness**

Most Canadians are willing to admit that certain minorities are disadvantaged because of skin colour. Many are also willing to concede that social and economic disadvantages may not result from individual failure. Inequities flow instead from restricted opportunity structures because of discrimination by '**race.**'[1] Disadvantages associated with the colour of one's skin are widely acknowledged, as Henry and Tator (1993) remind us: "In a white dominated society, the colour of your skin is the single most important factor in determining life chances, as well as your dignity, identity, and self-esteem." But few Canadians are prepared to concede how whiteness as a relationship of power may privilege some while disprivileging others. Even fewer are inclined to acknowledge "whiteness" as a category of race—in much the same way that most ref-

erences to gender seem to exclude men from the category. Whites will see "others" as racialized subjects[2] but view themselves as colourless, according to a *Socialist Review* article entitled "White Reconstruction." Yet whites are 'raced' just as men are gendered.

Think for a moment about the privileges associated with whiteness, many of which are taken for granted and largely unearned by accident of birth (McIntosh 1988). Being white means you can purchase a home in any part of town and expect cordial treatment rather than community grumblings about a plummeting in real estate values. Being white saves you the embarrassment of going into a shopping mall with fears of being followed, frisked, monitored, or fingerprinted. Being white means you can comment on a variety of topics without having someone question your objectivity or second-guess your motives. Being white enables you to express anger or indignation without being labelled as aggressive or emotionally unstable. Being white means you never have to say you're sorry or make excuses for the antisocial antics of other whites. Being white provides a peace of mind in that your actions are judged not as a betrayal of or a credit to your race, but in terms of individual idiosyncracies. Or as an Australian Aboriginal woman once put it, "If a whitefella does something wrong, he's wrong; if a blackfella does something wrong, we're all wrong" (cited in Morris and Cowlishaw 1997). Finally, being white ensures one the satisfaction of socializing at night, without being pulled over by the police or patted down.

In short, being white is a privilege that is stamped into your skin. Whiteness is a kind of "passport" that opens doors and unlocks opportunities just as identity cards in South Africa once defined who got what. The privileges associated with whiteness are neither openly articulated nor logically deserved, but assumed and universalized as the norm and beyond definition, scrutiny, or criticism. Yet being white is a meaningful part of how people construct their social identities and organize their activities, even if done unconsciously. As a normative referent, whites are privileged by their skin colour yet unable or unwilling to recognize the cultural and institutional conventions that normalize white invisibility as natural or neutral. Whiteness is the "natural" way of being human; conversely, those with nonwhite skin colour are defined as the "other" and demonized accordingly (Stamm 1993). As Judith Levine (1994:22) puts it:

> Whiteness purports to be nothing and everything. It is the race that need not speak its name. Yet it defines itself as no less than whatever it chooses to exclude. To grow up white is to be the ground zero from which everything else differs....

This tacitly accepted but unmarked category of normalcy not only makes it difficult to accept others. Such ethnocentrism (a belief in the normalcy and superiority of one's ways) also establishes the baseline by which others are judged and compared (Frankenberg 1997). In other words, whiteness as race shapes people's lives by signalling the production and reproduction of (a) dominance rather than subdomination, (b) normativity rather than marginality, and (c) privilege rather than disadvantage. The pervasiveness and stability of whiteness—as location of privilege, as culturally normative space, and as standpoint—are secured and reproduced at the expense of others (Frankenburg 1993). Not surprisingly, whereas whites tend to see themselves as colourless, image-conscious minorities are known to capitalize on skin whiteners in countries where whiteness is associated with beauty, wealth, and status (Easton 1998).

Blackness, by contrast, represents the antithesis of whiteness in terms of privilege or entitlement—a highly visible stigma (or marked category) by which others are denied, excluded, or exploited. Unlike whites who rarely experience whiteness or see themselves as white—they just are—people of colour have little choice except to experience blackness or "Asianness" on a daily basis. No aspect of existence, no moment of the day, no contact, no relationship, no response is exempt from the stigma of blackness, given the nature of the society in which blacks live. M Nourbese Philip (1996: 21) writes to this effect:

> Like blackness, whiteness is highly visible (to Blacks and all those upon whom it impacts negatively) while being simultaneously visible. Invisible, because in a society steeped in racism and ethnocentric ideology, white and whiteness become equated with normalcy, while its effects—primarily negative (for white people as well)—remain visible for all those who care to look.

Whiteness is a relational term; it cannot be understood outside of the context of its relationship to subordinated others (Frankenberg 1997; Kaufman 1998). To be sure, celebrating whiteness is not inherently racist. Rather, the racism associated with whiteness reflects a stubborn refusal to appreciate the largely unearned privileges and advantages of being white by birth. It also reflects the tendency to interpret the world from a white point of view as natural and normal, and assume that others will do so, while ignoring other viewpoints as irrelevant or inferior. Of course, not everyone equates whiteness with an unmarked vehicle of privilege. Whiteness is emerging as an explicit category of self-definition in response to the political and cultural challenges of other racialized groups. White supremacist groups have cleverly victimized the concept of whiteness as an endangered or persecuted race, under threat and challenge by minorities because of quotas or "reverse discrimination"—in much the same way that men's movements have depicted males as victims of uncompromising feminism and reverse discrimination. But challenges to the supremacy of "whiteness" have hardly resulted in any significant shift in power or privilege, which continue to persist along increasingly contested lines. Herein, then, lies the genius of white privilege: Whiteness is everything because it is perceived by whites as nothing. As bell hooks puts it: Most whites are captives of their culture...and they don't know they are captive (hooks 1994). Insofar as all knowledge is particular and situational, moreover, everybody is ethnically and racially located (see Hall 1996). Thus, to exclude whiteness as an unmarked category that stands outside history or convention is to redouble its hegemony by naturalizing it (Bell 1996). Such a naturalization makes it doubly important to decolonize the definition of normalcy by racializing the normalcy of whiteness. For in the final analysis, social equality is attainable only by fostering an awareness of whiteness as a 'race' that confers privileges at the expense of other 'races.'

---

1. Inverted commas, or 'scare' quotes, are often used for bracketing the term 'race' to signal the fundamental ambiguities of a socially constructed concept as well as to dissociate the authors from its popular but erroneous use as a scientifically valid and biologically fixed category.

2. **Racialization:** The idea that race relations do not exist (since there is no such thing as race) but focuses on why certain relations between groups become defined by reference to race. Racialization refers to patterns of interaction that reflect perceptions of biological differences to account for differences and similarities. It also entails the idea that certain ideas or activities become linked with race (racialized). Minorities may also be racialized in that they are invested with negative biologically determined attributes that are seen as creating problems, posing a threat to society, and providing unwanted competition for scarce resources (Ongley 1996).

INTRODUCTION: "WHAT'S THE MATTER WITH RACE?"

'Race,' aboriginal, and ethnic relations are inextricably linked with patterns of domination and control. The previous chapter argued that dominant–subdominant relations cannot be considered apart from group dynamics. These relationships neither exist nor flourish outside a framework of interaction. Nor do they make sense outside the general context in which group interaction takes its cue and direction. Foremost to our analysis is the notion of group relations as patterned but unequal. These patterns of inequality are not random, but tend to cluster around the poles of culture, language, or religious affiliation. No less important a variable in accounting for inequality is that of 'race.'

Few will dispute the significance of race in shaping intergroup dynamics. Race is widely regarded as a key variable in shaping patterns of entitlement and engagement both in the past and at present for people of colour and for whites (Walker 1997). The creation of race categories not only facilitated European colonialization; the resulting typologies also conferred a pseudoscientific legitimacy on sometimes questionable schemes that classified humans into mutually exclusive categories on largely arbitrary grounds. Many of the social policies enacted in recent years have been justified as necessary in addressing the needs, concerns, and aspirations of racial minorities. The concept of race continues to attract attention as a preferred means of (a) explaining group differences, (b) rationalizing unequal treatment, (c) condoning a lack of concerted action, (d) simplifying reality, and (e) securing scapegoats. Admittedly, race is not a "thing" out there—a tangible object that can be isolated and measured as a fixed biological entity. Rather, race is a "process" in which certain groups or activities are defined in race-based terms. This racialization of relationships or activities entails a complex process of interaction in unequal contexts where power is negotiated rather than boxed into discreet categories and isolated from everyday routines and organizational behaviour (Holdaway 1996). In reflecting, reinforcing, and advancing relationships of power, race is not simply about a natural or self-evident category. Race is a historically grounded social construction, both dynamic and shifting as well as contradictory and ambiguous (Morris and Cowlishaw 1997).

Reference to race as an explanatory principle is widely deplored. Critics argue that race is essentially a social construct rather than a biological reality, with next to no scientific value (Miles 1982; 1993). Race has little do with genetics or biology, but everything to do with social construction and politics. Race relations are essentially class relations perpetuated by ideological aspects of capitalism in subordinating particular populations. They can also be seen as predominantly group relations that happen to have a racial dimension. The use of the term itself is seen as racist in its own right. Not only are comfort and aid conferred on forces hostile to minorities; a view of the world is promulgated where social significance is correlated with physical variation. The concept of race is seen as reifying an ideology that has been scientifically discredited, namely, the idea that distinct and fixed groups of people exist whose constellation of racial and cultural attributes can be ranked hierarchically in ascending and descending lines of superiority and inferiority (Holdaway 1996). To the extent that the race concept has no empirical reality, except in its perception as real, it is more accurate to speak of relationships that are "racialized" rather than race relations *per se* (Bonilla-Silva 1996). Inasmuch as there is no such thing as a 'race' that stands in a relationship to another 'race,' the race concept is constitutive of people's perceptions of racial differences as a basis for engagement or entitlement. In other words, the proper study of race is not in the looking at minority attributes or actions; it is focused on explaining why some relationships or activities (but not others) have been linked to race and devalued accordingly (that is, "racialized") in constructing a racially based social order (Ongley 1996; Holdaway 1997).

That race once "mattered" in the historical past is beyond dispute. The classifying of humans into race types furnished a simple yet satisfying account of human diversity during the era of European exploration and expansion, the consolidation of capitalism both in the past and at present, the colonization of new worlds, and the emergence of race consciousness in light of biological discoveries and intellectual trends (Walker 1997; Essed 1991). The fact that race continues to "matter" for precisely the same reasons as in the past—even though we should know better—should be cause for concern. **Race matters** not because groups of people are racially inferior or perceived as such by the dimwitted or politically inastute. Race matters because people perceive others to be different and rely on these perceptions to justify unequal treatment or condone indifference. Race matters because its presence provides privilege and power for some, privation for others. And as long as racism and racialized inequality exist, moreover, race will continue to matter (Morris and Cowlishaw 1997). Race also matters because people continue to rely on socially perceived differences as a source of explanation or rationalization. The so-called race card is routinely invoked to expose the centrality of racism of those decisions that adversely affect minority women and men (Holdaway 1997). For example, the recourse to race in "Black Rage" defence strategies is predicated on the principle that the social context for certain races has contributed to a state of mind that may induce criminal behaviour (Harris 1997). In short, race matters not because of interest in systems of classification, but as a conceptual tool to understand how (a) how differences are used to justify unequal treatment, (b) how power differentials are exercised in a context of domination and inequality, and (c) the process by which society devalues groups or activities (Dei 1996).

The politics of race is seen as one of the more explosive yet divisive forces in shaping the dynamics of contemporary societies. Often unconscious in use or outcome, race remains a potent element in everyday life and encounters, with unlimited potential for conflict and misunderstanding (Holdaway 1996). The concept of race is problematic inasmuch as its meaning is socially constructed and politically contested (Winant 1998). Race consciousness is increasing rather than decreasing as many once predicted. Reactions to race vary, however, and responses are invariably fraught with perils and pitfalls. Those who talk about race tend to reinforce racial hierarchies; refusing to talk about race on grounds of colourblindness also has the effect of perpetuating the status quo. Thinking about race must steer a balance between its dismissal as an "illusion" versus its reinforcement as fixed and objective (Winant 1998). Those who endorse race as a biologically accurate description of humanity find themselves linked with nineteenth-century racist and discriminatory discourses. Those who dismiss race as a fiction may compromise a people's identity by trampling on social history or cultural aspirations. Even if race is a fiction, after all, it is a powerful fiction that provides an important source of meaning and security during times of diversity, change, or uncertainty. For some, race constitutes a primordial fact of life that provides a rational basis for group culture, solidarity, and inclusion. For others, race is used as a social construction that has the intent or effect of excluding others on the basis of artificially constructed boundaries and typologies that spuriously conjoin biology with behaviour. Still others prefer to reconfigure the idea of race by relying on culture rather than biology to essentialize differences between groups. In doing so, culture and ethnicity are racialized through claims of behavioural superiority every bit as powerful as those of biological determinism. And still yet others see race as a source of entitlement rather than an object of scorn or dismissal. Racially based distinctions that formerly stigmatized individuals as inferior or irrelevant are routinely invoked as a criterion for promotion or admission as is the case with racially based employment equity/affirmative action programs.

Most Canadians appear ambivalent about the salience of race in society. This ambivalence explains the controversy over a decision in the 1996 Census data to include a question on racial (visible minority) origins by asking respondents to specify if they were white or black, but also (!) Chinese, South Asian, Arab/West Asian, Filipino, South East Asian,

Latin American, Japanese, or Korean—in effect, confusing colour with nationality and regional variation (see Fellegi 1996).[1] Ambivalence is expressed in other ways: On the one hand are those who criticize treatment of aboriginal peoples on the basis of race for purposes of entitlement; on the other are those who argue that race created the problem; thus race must be part of the solution (see Gibson 1998). The source of such ambiguity is not difficult to discern: The race concept carries a negative connotation at odds with the dynamics of an achievement-oriented, upwardly mobile society. The underlying message of race rankles the cultural sensibilities of many Canadians, insofar as it endorses a belief about a person being an accident of birth, something beyond control, and that alone should determine job, status, and privilege. A focus on race also contradicts the tenets of liberal pluralism; that is, what we have in common is more important than what differentiates us; the content of our character is more important than the colour of our skin; and what we do and accomplish are more important than who we are or what we inherit. Still, it is premature to discount the politics of race in contemporary affairs. No matter how many times it is discredited or dismissed, race continues to bounce back as an ineradicable marker of social differences. How, then, do we account for its popularity and tenacity?

CASE STUDY 2-1	Institutional Inclusiveness: Engaging Diversity or Flirting With Disaster?

One size fits all or levelling the playing pitch? Should there be one set of rules for all Canadians, or should laws be customized to reflect the diverse realities of aboriginal peoples? Should individuals take full responsibility for their actions, or must historical and social circumstances be incorporated in any assessment of wrongdoing? Is it racist and paternalistic to imply that a racial or ethnic background merits special consideration in sentencing? Or does such an enlightened concession acknowledge the importance of the social and the cultural as mitigating factors in a multicultural society?

This debate over diversity as a basis for entitlement has assumed a new twist with a recent and controversial ruling involving an aboriginal woman and the criminal justice system. Issues pertaining to race, aboriginality, differential treatment, political correctness, free will, and cultural defence have been brought into play because of this court case, with interesting repercussions for the ongoing multiculturalization of Canadian society.

First the facts: A Métis woman, Deanna Emard, 28, received a conditional sentence of two years less a day in the British Columbia Supreme Court for stabbing her common law partner, Wilfrid Shorson, 39, in January 1997. She was sentenced to perform 240 hours of community service and to refrain from consuming alcohol. Defence counsel, Peter Wilson, argued that Ms Emard should receive a lighter sentence for the stabbing death (there was no record of domestic abuse in the relationship) because of her "Indianness." In saying that past injustices contributed to the crime, her lawyer argued, she suffered from the systemic problems that plague Canada's First Peoples, including substance abuse, racism, and poverty. The presiding judge agreed: Although her aboriginal background did not absolve her of blame for committing the crime—after all, the jury did find her guilty of manslaughter—the woman had endured an unhappy life through "no fault of her own." The sentence also reflected sentencing guidelines introduced in 1995 to the Criminal Code (S718.2(e)): "All available sanctions other than imprisonment, that are reasonable in the circumstances, should be considered for all offenders, with particular attention to the circumstances of aboriginal offenders." Judges are now required to consider the social, cultural, and historical backgrounds of offenders, particularly the circumstances of aboriginal offenders as a group, to justify a sentence other than imprisonment, as long as the sentencing arrangement does not pose a risk to the public.

Second, the reaction: Reaction to this controversial ruling appeared negative. Some contemptuously dismissed the conditional "discharge" as a "Get Out of Jail Free" card for aboriginal offenders. Others, such as columnist Lisa Birnie, dismissed the ruling as a clumsy, irresponsible, and racist attempt (in suggesting that aboriginal people and children and the mentally ill have a diminished human capacity) to assuage white guilt and defuse political pressure. In expressing concern over the effects of the amendment on the constitutional principle of fairness and equality before the law, Mike Scott, Native Affairs critic for the Reform Party, has said: "You can't right historical wrongs by creating new injustices. When you move away from the principle that we're all entitled to the same treatment in the eyes of the law, you're going down a slippery slope." For still others, such leniency posed a risk in encouraging aboriginal people to commit a similar crime. The victim's family also accused the system of bending to political correctness because the accused was Métis, a woman, and intoxicated. The victim's sister was quoted as saying: "Alcohol is not an excuse, and neither is being a native. There should be justice for everyone—not one system for Indian and Métis people and one for white people."

Third, the interpretation: This incident raises a number of key issues about the changing relationship of Canada to its citizens, but particularly its First Citizens. While the ruling may single out certain races or categories of peoples for differential treatment, all Canadians now have the multicultural right to have their social and cultural circumstances incorporated into the sentencing process. The ruling does not undermine the concept of one law for all and that everyone is equal before the law, at least no more so than the Young Offenders Act absolves youth of guilt or responsibility. In the case of Ms Emard, it was not her guilt that was being disputed; only the appropriate level of punishment. In this sense, the judgment is consistent with other forms of cultural defence such as "Black Rage" strategy, which acknowledges the importance of social context and historical factors in shaping states of mind that may culminate in criminal actions. In other words, individuals may be responsible for their actions; nevertheless, even the most offensive of actions do not occur in a social void, but reflect options and choices that are constrained by extenuating circumstances.

Nor can this ruling be framed as a race issue. The intent is not to define a group of people on the basis of fixed biological features and to hierarchically rank these race categories in a way that denies or excludes. The ruling is not concerned with excusing the criminal acts of aboriginal people or getting them out of jail because of their aboriginality. Central to the debate is the indigeneity of aboriginal peoples, that is, aboriginal peoples have indigenous rights related to culture, land, and political voice that have yet to be extinguished. These rights not only articulate a special relationship with the Crown and the Canadian state. Indigenous rights also provide a rationale for differential treatment when employed to enhance, bolster, improve, or advance. Finally, the broader context needs to be considered. Initiatives to keep aboriginal peoples out of jail may have nothing to do with aboriginal rights, but everything to do with diminishing the number of aboriginal people in overcrowded jails. In a 1996 report, aboriginal peoples were 11 times more likely than nonaboriginal peoples to be in provincial jails and 5 times that of others to be in federal penitentiaries. Prisons for many aboriginal inmates are little more than barbed wire universities that confer revolving-door degrees in criminality. At a time when community-based alternatives to traditional imprisonment are gaining in popularity, the decision to suspend jailing aboriginal offenders suggests that sentences other than imprisonment may better meet the needs of the community or offender than incarceration. This focus on reestablishing aboriginal connections to their community and culture may also concede that the criminal justice system is not working and that aboriginal communities may be better positioned to take over the rehabilitative role of the prison system.

In a multicultural society such as Canada, everyone has the right to equality before the law. Each person also has the right to be culturally different without being penalized. Neither of these "rights" is more "right" than the other. The paradox lies in the "rightness" of both and the fundamentally irreconcilable nature of this conflict between two mutually opposed but equally valid rights. Herein is the challenge for the twenty-first century. How much diversity can be tolerated in a multicultural society? Too little acceptance makes a mockery of multiculturalism; too much diversity precludes any possibility of living together with our differences. Canadians, it seems, will need to accept a certain level of ambiguity and compromise if we hope to constructively engage diversity in the new millennium.

SOURCES: Cori Howard, "Racial Background Key Part of Argument at Sentencing Hearing." *The Globe and Mail.* 11 January 1999; Lisa Birnie, "An Ill-Advised Native Rider." *The Globe and Mail.* 15 January 1999; Editorial, "Crime, Time, and Race." *The Globe and Mail.* 16 January 1999; Jonathan Rudin, "Aboriginal Offenders and the Criminal Code." *The Globe and Mail.* 9 February 1999.

The past twenty years have witnessed a resurgence of interest in the politics of race (Cose 1997). Debates over race strike at the core of some of the most enigmatic of problems in contemporary society: Can people live together with their differences yet acknowledge their commonality in the civic space of community? The prognosis is mixed at best, bleak at worst. Contradictions abound in sorting through this enigma: Race may reflect an accident of birth yet profoundly shape a person or group's lives and life chances; race may be skin deep but provides a basis for judging the worth of an individual or group; race should never justify discrimination against minority women and men, yet it is increasingly assigned a role in defining identity, rewards, and relationships (Fernandez 1997). Race may be socially constructed: *Social constructions are not intended to imply that race is a fiction with no material effects, but to convey how racialized ways of thinking and acting vary from time to place* (Jackson 1998). It is within this context of race as (a) problem and solution, (b) a source of empowerment yet disprivilege, and (c) fact yet fiction that answers must be found, and this chapter attempts to do so by exploring the politics of race in contemporary Canada. The chapter examines the race concept in terms of its (a) meaning and content, (b) genesis and rationale, (c) impact and implications, and (d) validity and value. Attention is aimed at what is meant by the concepts of race and race types/typologies; why these ideas originated in the first place; why they persist into the present; how they justify entitlement and rules of engagement; and what are their consequences for society. Of particular note is the process by which groups and activities become racialized and the extent to which the process of racialization contributes to construction, maintenance, and transformation of unequal relations.

RACE MATTERS

The relevance of race to human affairs is hotly contested. Many would argue that race is worthless as a biological or explanatory concept, with no bearing whatsoever in the sorting-out process. Others disagree: They believe the social world can be partitioned into a fixed and limited number of race types, each with a distinctive assemblage of cognitive and behavioural characteristics. Still others acknowledge the partial validity of both positions. Races do not exist in the conventional, concrete sense; nevertheless, perceptions of race are real. That is, people talk about race *as if* it had objective reality, regardless of its ontological status, proving once again the sociological aphorism that phenomena do not have to be real to be real in their consequences. To the extent that race matters, the end result is a racialization of relationships between and among groups that reflect and reinforce inequities in Canadian and American society.

America the Bad?

That race matters in the United States is taken as self-explanatory. Critics point to a country historically riddled with a legacy of slavery and segregation as well as lynchings and the Ku Klux Klan. American racism was animated by a belief in the innate differences between people as a basis for justifying unequal treatment. Even today the race subtext is unmistakable in public discourses about crime, poverty, and urban decay. Social problems are framed as black or white issues, and everything from welfare to income is refracted through the prism of skin colour (Mitchell 1998). Statistical evidence confirms the notion that race matters when it comes to distinguishing "haves" from "have-nots." The status for many African-Americans continues to deteriorate in the aftermath of the Civil Rights revolution. The real median household income for blacks has declined, while an increasing number of black households and children hover below the federal poverty line. Race can also count in a different way as revealed in the Case Study on the racialization of sport.

CASE STUDY 2-2	Racialization of Sport

Many have invoked the race concept to explain differences and similarities. Race-based explanations possess a certain appeal: They are simple and direct, conform with the canons of common sense, reinforce many of our stereotypes and prejudices, and pander to the lowest common denominator. Yet the popularity of racial explanations does not necessarily equate with accuracy. Explanations by race tend to ignore the social and historical dimensions of individual or group behaviour. The broader social context and cultural values that give shape to patterns of human interaction are also underplayed. The controversial link between race and sport is a case at hand.

Hurdling the Colour Bar

As recently as the late 1940s, blacks did not participate in professional North American team sports. The colour bar kept white from black until 1947 when Jackie Robinson joined the Brooklyn Dodgers, after a minor league stint with the Montreal Royals to gauge the reaction of the crowds. Professional football and basketball blunted black entry until the late 1940s. The last major league sport, ice hockey, was not integrated until Willy O'Ree signed with the Boston Bruins in 1958. To be sure, blacks were tolerated in the minor leagues; as well, blacks played in segregated "Negro" leagues. But owners and players steadfastly refused to integrate teams for fear of alienating sponsors and audiences. By the late 1990s, however, a different picture had appeared: African-Americans dominated three of the nation's most popular spectator sports and had transformed how these sports are played. Blacks comprised two-thirds of the gridiron personnel in the National Football League, over three-quarters of hoopsters in the National Basketball Association, and about one-sixth of the major league ball players. In the 1996 Summer Olympics, only one of 13 gold medals in the track and field went to a white male (for shot put). These figures are striking: The proportion of African-Americans in the United States (about 13 or 14 percent of the population) is disproportionate to their numbers in certain sports. With the growing perception of white male inability to run fast or jump high, white male athletes have become "second class citizens" of the most popular American sports (Sapsted 1998). How do we account for the racialization of North American professional team sports?

Biology or Society

A popular explanation is derived from the "theory" of black anatomical advantages. Black athletes perform well because of natural (biological) factors including bone structure, stamina, strength, coordination, and size. Anatomical differences include (a) leg and calf structures more suitable for jumping, (b) faster twitch muscles (muscle fibres that rapidly burn cell glycogen) for sprinting, (c) more sweat glands (more body surface) for dissipating excess body heat, and (d) darker eye colours for excelling at reactive sports (Jaret 1995). Poor performance in other sports is related to so-called biologically imposed limitations, for example, less buoyancy for swimming sports. While superficially appealing, the notion that blacks rather than whites are biologically better endowed cannot account for variations across sports. For example, blacks may excel in certain sports, but not others such as tennis and swimming. Nor can biological explanations explain the absence of blacks from professional team sports until after World War II—unless one reverts to some wildly implausible genetic displacement in an impossibly short time span.

That leaves social factors to account for these discrepancies. Biological differences *per se* do not make a difference; rather, it is public perceptions and social constructions of these differences that make the difference. To be sure, biological factors are not invalid; after all, biology intersects with culture and society in ways that have yet to be determined. Nevertheless, social factors are more compelling as systems of explanation. First, professional sports are one of the few opportunity structures open for African-Americans (Edwards 1971). Not only do blacks focus on sports to escape the poverty of the inner city, but they also gravitate to sports as an avenue for success beyond the business or professional fields.

Success itself creates role models that provide additional incentive for youth. Second, American sports is a big business that extols winning at all costs. This postwar commitment put a premium on attracting the best athletes—regardless of colour or race. Black athletes were able to overcome discrimination by pursuing those sports whose performance levels could be evaluated objectively by way of statistics. Thus highly quantifiable performances among black athletes (such as pass catching yardage or batting average) proved pivotal in dismantling barriers or suspicion. Third, entry occurred in team-oriented sports where black excellence could be diffused among white teammates and rationalized as integral to team success. Fourth, blacks did not excel in all sports. They tended toward those sports that were relatively inexpensive and accessible.

A Double Racialization

Yet black success in sport is "skin deep." Blacks may do well in team numbers, but they are not randomly distributed across the playing field. Black players tend to cluster around certain positions in a phenomenon known as stacking. In the NFL, for example, blacks predominate in positions such as running back or wide receiver on offence, and cornerback and safety at defence (*USA Today*, 17 December 1991: C-6). Whites in turn prevail at quarterback and kicking on offence; they monopolize the positions of tackle, guard, and centre on defence. Black quarterbacks remain a rarity; few black college-level quarterbacks ever make it to the NFL in that position (usually they are converted to defensive backs), with the first being James Harris of the Los Angeles Rams in 1975. Similarly, stacking occurs in baseball where pitchers and catchers are overwhelmingly white, with blacks predominantly in the outfield. That pattern is not entirely accidental: It reflects a view that whites should monopolize the thinking positions, whereas blacks should gravitate to those that can capitalize on their *natural* talents. The subtext is clear: Whites succeed as athletes through perseverance, brain power, and strategic reasoning; black athletes are successful because of raw genetic prowess rooted in speed and power (see Brunt 1994). Not surprisingly, racial tensions have mounted in the professional leagues, especially in basketball, where blacks who are selected for aggressiveness and transformed into instant millionaires invariably come into conflict with authority—from coaches to managers to owners—most of whom remain white.

In short, the racialization of sport is multidimensional. Blacks are overrepresented in certain sports and positions, underrepresented in others, excluded from the spatial centre of team formations, and denied leadership positions both on and off the field (Smith and Leonard II 1997). Of the 411 major league baseball managers since 1900, according to *Baseball Weekly*, March 10, 1999, 402 have been white. Consider Canadian football: blacks may comprise about 70 percent of the playing personnel, but only one black coach, Willy Wood of the Toronto Argonauts, has made the grade, and even he was fired in 1981 and never rehired. The combination of success and failure among African-Americans is primarily related to social rather than biological factors. Race matters when it comes to sports not because one race has more natural talent than another, but because of a dearth of opportunity structures for blacks outside of sport. Even here success is deceptive: Only a minuscule percentage of black athletes ever fulfill "hoop dreams" or achieve "gridiron success," much to the disappointment and frustration of many aspiring youth. An overemphasis on sport in the community, together with ads that extol sport as a prime avenue of success, may encourage black youth into bad choices about unrealistic expectations.

For African-Americans, then, race does matter, albeit when filtered through the prism of culture and society. The primacy of race defines who you are, what you get, where you live, how you make a living, and when and how you die. Public debates about welfare mothers, inner-city violence, urban decay, and hard drugs are essentially code terms for "blackness." Race remains a significant factor even for middle class blacks; many continue to be rebuked for acting too white or too black. Conversely, race matters for whites, since their whiteness is the norm that confers the privilege of being everything, yet nothing, depending on the circumstances.

Canada the Good?

Canadians and Americans are perceived as poles apart when it comes to managing minority relations. Compared to the United States, the refrain "race doesn't matter here" is widely endorsed in Canada (James 1994:47). We exult in the myth that Canadians have a deep aversion to judging others by the colour of their skin. Canada is widely renown for emphasizing achievement and merit rather than skin colour as the basis for recognition, reward, and relationships. Discussions about race tend to be muted, often employing proxies such as visible minorities or ethnicity for fear of inflaming public passions (Mitchell 1998). A quick reality check suggests otherwise.

Historically, Canada's immigration policy rested on racial factors (Whitaker 1991). A constellation of mechanisms—from head taxes to continuous passage requirements to bureaucratic regulations—combined to protect Canada's perception of itself as a "white man's society." Questions asked of native-born racial minorities such as "So, what island are you from?" attest to the lingering legacy of race in defining Canadian-ness. Statements such as "You're different...," "I'm not a racist but...," and "Some of my best friends..." resonate with racial overtones that say more about dormant prejudices than progressive thinking (James and Shadd 1994). Minorities continue to bear the brunt of negative treatment, from local snubs to half-hearted service delivery. People of colour continue to be employed as cheap and disposable labour in often dangerous and arduous tasks. Participation and decision making are influenced by prevailing stereotypes and racial prejudices, while social rewards are allocated on the basis of racial affiliation. Even the racialization of public discourse and the emergence of race-conscious state policies to ameliorate disadvantage have elicited criticism for being tokenistic or divisive. The following Case Study reveals how race continues to infiltrate Canadian society without much fanfare but with deadly results.

CASE STUDY 2-3	Reality Bites: Tabulating Race and Crime

Racial and ethnic minorities have historically been accused of excessive criminal behaviour. From the nineteenth-century Irish and Chinese to the Italians and Jews in the twentieth, certain groups were vilified as inherently depraved and in need of constant supervision and control. Recent incidents in major Canadian urban centres have again singled out minorities for special attention. Of particular note are renewed demands for keeping track of crime rates by racial origins. High-profile crimes involving suspects of colour will invariably elicit additional calls to collect race-based crime statistics.

The debate focuses on whether having access to this information will reinforce bigotry and exclusion or foster tolerance and ease discrimination (Mitchell 1998). Those who support the collection of race statistics argue that problem areas need to be identified for appropriate solutions. Crime statistics by race would produce a profile of suspected criminals, the kind of crime they engaged in, the contexts behind this criminal behaviour, proposed solutions, and the prevention of future occurrences. Supporters of racially based crime statistics are not necessarily racist; they may or may not believe that certain races are predisposed to certain types of crime. Rather, they may be anxious to see if patterns can be discerned and solutions applied (see Appleby 1998).

Those against the collection of racial crime statistics argue that such data are impossible to collect or are subject to abuse and manipulation. Statistics reflect incidents of crime reported to or by the police rather than criminal offending in society. Statistical information may say more about those collecting the data than anything accurate about minority offending. Publication of such data may reinforce stereotypes unless placed into a broader context. In an era of quantification, moreover, statistical data confer an air of authenticity and objectivity that may be unwarranted from the available evidence.

In short, the collection of race-based statistics is problematic. Totals are skewed because only a small percentage of arrested suspects are eventually charged, and fewer still are convicted. Many crimes are never reported to the police, ranging from domestic crime to white collar crime; even fewer make it to police occurrence sheets. The process of racial identification for the report sheets is a mug's game in its own right: Who decides what category a suspect fits into—the victim, the suspect, the police officer? For example, the category of black can include recent immigrants from Jamaica or refugees from Somalia, or indigenous Canadian blacks—many of whom have been settled in Canada for generations. How will the data be collected? For what purpose? Are the police sufficiently trained and impartial to impose a label? How reliable are victims' perceptions for purposes of identification? Or consider the impact of disseminating these data. However inadvertently, the circulation of this information may (a) reinforce stereotypes and legitimate a racist mindset; (b) promote ulterior motives and hidden agendas; (c) distract attention from the real source of the problem; and (d) strengthen policy-monitoring powers.

In between the critics and supporters are those who do not openly deny the relevance of such data but want safeguards to prevent abuse. In collecting *any* type of information it is important to know who is gathering the data, how this information will be collected, who wants to know and why, and how the data are to be utilized. Do the police want this information to justify bigger budgets or to secure more freedom of movement within minority communities? Do politicians hope to look tough on crime with collection of such data? Will the availability of statistics spur an effort to weed out the criminal element within minority communities? What should be included in the count? Will the inclusion of white collar crime and other types of underreported crime provide a more balanced picture of what "really" happens? Until answers are forthcoming, we would be advised to move cautiously.

There is yet another reason for exercising caution in this area. No matter how accurate the survey or sound the interpretations, a causal relation between race and crime can never be proven. Crime cuts across all groups of people; its detection, however, may be racially motivated. The causes of crime are social and universal, not racial or restricted to certain races. Moreover, only a small proportion of individuals within any community is likely to engage in criminal behaviour. These distinctions make it doubly important to acknowledge the social dimensions of crime-related behaviour, including poverty, unemployment, hopelessness, police harassment, racism, dysfunctional families, disregard for the law, and absence of a work ethic (White 1997). Structural barriers that inhibit minority life chances may magnify encounters with the criminal justice system. Poverty enhances the possibility of crime; crime in turn may intensify poverty by discouraging business initiatives, thus inflating minority unemployment (Loury 1997). Both cultural values and social patterns may lead to behaviour in public that is likely to attract police attention. The prevalence of stereotypes and prejudice may also bolster the like-lihood of apprehension by race (Cryderman et al. 1998).

In short, there is no sociological basis for correlating race with crime. Race cannot account for crime but only public perceptions about "who's committing what." In a culture where blackness is synonymous with evil and threat, it is too easy for the police and the public to assume that African-Canadians are more prone to violence than other groups or more likely to commit crimes (Flynn 1998). Statistics, in turn, can only measure levels of enforcement against targeted minorities. If police create a racial profile that blacks need to be monitored more closely, they will find what they are looking for. Police will then look at the results and say they were justified in conducting more intense surveillance or selective searches (James 1998). Race matters, to be sure—but not because some races carry an antisocial gene. Rather, race matters because people act as if it did by assigning moral force to spurious statistics.

These and related incidents remind us that—like it or not—race does matter. Many Canadians appear to have an aversion to the race concept and everything that it stands for; yet they inadvertently employ it to explain or justify. Race looms even larger outside of Canada: Tribal violence in Rwanda and military repression in Bosnia are conducted and justified on the grounds of race and ethnicity. The globalization of race makes it more important than ever to scrutinize a term that has the potential to destroy lives and life-chances.

THE HUMAN 'RACE': UNITY IN DIVERSITY

It is obvious that race has an existence beyond the biological or scientific. Contemporary science approaches race as a loose description of relatively isolated breeding populations whose members have more physical traits in common with each other than with members of other 'races.' Its widespread use in the vernacular and the everyday is at odds with its marginal status in the sciences. Indiscriminate references to terms such as the "human race" and the "Irish race" compound the difficulty.

Human beings belong to a single biological species (*Homo sapiens*) within a larger grouping or genus (*Homo*). The term "species" is used in the genetic sense of a breeding population whose members possess the capacity to naturally reproduce fertile offspring. Within the human species there are numerous populations that exhibit genetically diverse frequencies. These gene frequencies are manifest in readily observable characteristics including skin colour (*phenotypes*) in addition to less discernible attributes such as blood types (*genotypes*). Biologically speaking, then, the concept of race refers to this distribution of genes based on clusters of phenotypes or genotypes between populations. When applied to humans, it can be defined as a subpopulation of the species in which certain hereditary features appear more frequently in some population pools than others because of relative reproductive isolation (Jaret 1995).

On the surface, it might appear as if human diversity is too broad to qualify as a single species. But appearances in this case are deceiving. Judging by our capacity to propagate with each other, we all qualify as members of the human race (or, more accurately, human species). Several reasons can account for the singularity of the human species:

1. **Speciation** (the process by which new species are generated) can only occur under conditions of relative isolation. With the possible exception of extremely remote areas such as Australia and interior New Guinea, human populations have remained in direct or indirect contact with each other. The creation of a generalized gene pool is a reflection of various social exchange processes associated with migration, trade, or intermarriage between groups.

2. Speciation requires an extensive time period for genetically isolated populations to evolve. Although our ancestors arguably have been around for millions of years, this span of time may be insufficient for even the most isolated populations to speciate.

3. Speciation is likely to occur when organisms adapt to the environment by evolving the "appropriate" biophysical characteristics. But humankind has relied on social and cultural characteristics as an adaptive response to evolutionary pressures. This reliance on culture and society as a primary coping mechanism has created a generalized rather than a specie-leaning gene pool.

We can conclude that human beings constitute a single intrabreeding species with phenotypic and genotypic variation at the subspecies (racial) level. Humans resemble other floral and faunal species in terms of population clusters with varying gene frequencies and distributions. Anatomical differences exist, of course, and span the spectrum from phenotypical features such as skin colour and ear wax (moist or crumbly) to genotypical attributes such as blood chemistry (A, B, O, AB), metabolic rates, and physiological functions such as susceptibilities to disease (Jaret 1995). Most differences reflect adaptations to environmental niches in accordance with modern biological principles of mutation and natural selection. These differences presumably contributed to our collective survival.

No one should be surprised by the scholarly interest in the study of human variation. Physical anthropologists and biologists have explored the limits of diversity in hopes of unravelling human secrets. What is unusual is the obsession by some to study human variation at the subspecies level (race). Plant and animal species also display a random distribution of gene frequencies in response to evolutionary forces. Yet the concept of race is rarely applied to discourses about plant and animal populations. People rarely make references to tulip "races" or a "race" of dogs, or rank each according to superiority. By contrast, there has been no dearth of initiatives to (a) classify people into race categories, (b) attribute certain physical, social, psychological, and moral properties to these categories, and (c) evaluate and rank these categories in ascending/descending order. The following section addresses the paradox of why a biological concept of limited worth has altered the course of human history.

Defining Race

Definitions of race have proven to be elusive (Biddiss 1979). We agree with Ellis Cose (1997:1) when he refers to race "...as a strange and flexible concept, with an endless capacity to confound." The term itself appeared in the English language as far back as the fifteenth century as a device to interpret and classify varied forms of human life as well as to account for intergroup differences and similarities (Banton 1987). Such longevity notwithstanding, it is difficult to think of an English concept with greater ambiguity and emotional baggage than the concept of race (Martin and Franklin 1973). The term has also been applied indiscriminately to a jumble of sociopolitical units, including culture (Anglo-Saxons), religion (Jews), nationality (Irish, Chinese), language (French-Canadians), polity (Irish), geography (Mediterranean, European) (Stepan 1982), and even gender (women as a race as reported in the *New Zealand Herald*, 25 July 1898). This lack of consensus is not surprising, given the politics and perils of extracting social significance from a concept of limited biological utility.

Notwithstanding its elusive and enigmatic character, race can be defined as the classification of people into categories on the basis of preconceived attributes. Under race, each group is defined as different by virtue of predetermined properties that are seen as fixed and permanent because of real or alleged characteristics (van den Berghe 1970). This focus on the socially constructed and contested only partly explains the fascination or repulsion generated by race. Its inclusion into systems of classification and evaluation provides insight into the emotional politics associated with race.

Categorizing Race: Types and Typologies

Early approaches to human variation drew inspiration from the race concept. This preoccupation reflected a nineteenth-century quest for unitary schemes that explained the totality of human experience (Goldberg 1993). Just as early anthropologists devised unilinear evolutionary schemes to explain the coexistence of civilization with barbarism and savagery, so too did social theorists resort to race as an all-encompassing interpretive framework for understanding human differences and similarities (Biddiss 1979). The race concept classified human groups into a finite number of permaneant **race types,** each with a fixed and distinctive assemblage of physical and behavioural characteristics (Banton 1987). Individuals and groups were subsequently slotted into social rankings, or **racial typologies,** that reflected a predetermined hierarchy of superiority and inferiority (Feagin 1984).

A variety of classificatory schemes (or typologies) were hatched from the eighteenth century onward. The Swedish naturalist Carl von Linné (or Linnaeus) posited four races in 1735; since then, the number of races has expanded to as many as 30 by Carleton Coon and even 150 by Quatrefages (Rensberger 1994; Jaret 1995). Typologists became preoccupied with measurement and quantification as proof of fundamental differences. Human skulls were endlessly measured for size while the contours of people's crania were correlated with mental capacities (phrenology) (Stepan 1982). The proliferation of racial typologies reflected a broad failure to agree on an appropriate typology. The most common and widely known system of classification endorsed a threefold division of humanity into Caucasoid (white), Negroid (black), and Mongoloid (Asian or Oriental). Each of these categories was distinguished from the others by virtue of common physical features such as skin colour, hair form (fuzzy, wavy, or straight), eyelid shape, and so on. Each had also evolved (or had been divinely bestowed) its own unique and fixed bundles of characteristics. Only physical intermingling with other "stocks" could undermine the permanency of these types (Biddiss 1979).

Many social scientists are opposed to the race concept. They have rejected the validity of race as germane to the understanding of human diversity. Racial types and typologies have been discredited as pseudoscience and dangerous politics, without any redeeming explanatory value or empirical merit. Aversion to the term "race" itself arose from global revulsion over the murder of 6 million Jews and other undesirables in the name of Nazi racial purity. The common arguments against race thinking are numerous, but include the following:

1. Discrete and distinct categories of racially pure people do not exist. The intermingling effect of migration with intermarriage has made it impossible to draw a line around human populations, with certain characteristics on one side, but not on the other (Martin and Franklin 1973). Explicit boundaries between so-called racial groups are nonexistent (unlike political boundaries, which are fixed at some point in time). Instead, populations with variable characteristics merge into one another, thus forming gradients (or clines). This makes any division between races a somewhat arbitrary exercise that reflects the whims of the investigator rather than anything intrinsic to reality itself. For example, picture ourselves moving from the north of Europe to the Mediterranean and across to Africa. Where do we draw the line between white and black populations? Any proposed demarcation is open to dispute as light-skinned northwestern Europeans merge into relatively darker Mediterranean populations and into progressively black-skinned populations in Africa. The picture is further complicated by the inclusion of millions of Indo-Pakistanis who are defined as Caucasoid for racial purposes. Ultimately such a division is essentially a subjective decision on the part of the investigator. It becomes pointless, in other words, to devote countless studies to the notions of "racial superiority" and "pure races" when the nature of the units under study is inconsistent with reality (Banton 1987).

2. Related to this is the arbitrary manner of selecting traits for inclusion and evaluation. The pigmentation of skin is the most widely used. Nevertheless, outside of convenience, one can justifiably ask, Why skin colour? Why exclude eye colour or earwax type? Better yet, how about the weight of internal organs as a criterion for categorization? Admittedly, skin colour is the most immediately obvious feature. But it distorts the purpose of science to construct an elaborate system of classification around convenience. It is equally fanciful to impute certain social attributes or psychological properties on the strength of superficial properties.

3. Even the integrity of racial typologies is open to question because of high rates of internal variation. Just as physical differences exist among persons whom we categorize as Caucasoid ("Nordic, Alpine, Mediterranean, and Indo-Pakistani"), so too is there equally significant diversity within the Asian and black categories. Differences *within* groups that are defined as races are often as broad as differences between groups. Such internal diversity would appear to invalidate the credibility of any classificatory system that strives for universality and consistency. The options are lose–lose: Either an unwieldily large number of distinct categories are created to account for this diversity, or a restricted number of classifications overlook the rich diversity within the human species.

Yet no system of classification—large or small—can possibly include those that invariably fall in between the cracks.

In addition to conceptual problems, there are practical and moral reasons for rejecting the validity of the race concept. Social scientists do not reject the reality of biogenetic differences between individuals or even groups (populations). Individual differences exist: What do *not* exist are defined populations with fixed inventories of common characteristics. Specific traits can be classified, but not particular groups of people, since all populations are bundles of different combinations of traits (Rensberger 1994). Nor do social scientists deny the validity of studying these differences in an objective and scholarly fashion. What is repugnant are studies of race that isolate differences and rank diversity along an ascending/descending order. Equally reprehensible are doctrines that uphold the proposed superiority of one type over another on the basis of biological justification. Many also object to the linking of select physical characteristics with certain behavioural, moral, or cognitive properties, thereby establishing an unwarranted relationship between culture and biology. The political fallout of such a linkage, it is argued, undermines the legitimacy of the race concept for public debate. Nowhere is this more evident than in the decade-long controversy over the right of Philippe Rushton of the University of Western Ontario to promote race-based evolutionary typologies.

INSIGHT 2–2   Debunking the Rushton Race Myth

Biological theories of race and evolution have come and gone, and in all probability will continue to flourish into the foreseeable future. From the nineteenth-century doctrines of social Darwinism to the pseudoscientific racism of Herrnstein and Murray of the 1990s, efforts to link race with intelligence on an evolutionary hierarchy have proven tempting. A professor of psychology from the University of Western Ontario, Philippe Rushton, has also entered the fray by unleashing a storm of controversy over issues pertaining to genetically based determinants of human behaviour. The question of academic freedom has also moved to the forefront, as have debates over the roles and responsibilities of contemporary postsecondary education.

In his most provocative works, including the recent text, *Race, Evolution, and Behavior: A Life History Perspective* (*NY Transaction,* 1994), Rushton posits a theory of evolution to account for racial differences across a broad and hierarchical spectrum of physical, social,

mental, and moral domains. Rushton argues that separate races, namely, Oriental, Caucasoid, and Negroid, evolved a distinctive package of physical, social, and mental characteristics because of different reproductive strategies in diverse environments. Very simply, high reproductive strategies (many offspring, low nurturing) evolved in tropical climates; low reproductive strategies (few offspring, intense nurturing) in temperate climates. A racial pecking order can be observed, according to Professor Rushton, because of this evolutionary adaptation. Orientals (Rushton's terminology) are superior to Caucasoids on a range of sociobiological factors, who in turn are superior to Negroids (also Rushton) on the grounds of measurements involving skull size, intelligence, strength of sex drive and genital size, industriousness, sociability, and rule-following. Orientals as a group have proven more intelligent, more family focused, more law abiding, but less sexually promiscuous than Negroids. Caucasoids happily occupy the terrain in between—neither too hot nor too cold. The table below summarizes this theory.

How valid is Rushton's thesis? Of course, human differences exist at individual and group levels. But good reasons exist to reject a racial interpretation of human differences and achievement. Very simply, the concept of human race has long been discredited as scientifically valid or biologically meaningful. No empirical evidence supports the existence of fixed categories of humans with unique assemblages of homogeneous and fixed properties. The credibility of Rushton's work has also plummeted because of funding links with a **eugenics**-based (improvement through genetic engineering) movement in the United States. His conclusions are seen as an expression of classic racism, that is, behaviour is linked with genes; this linkage is fixed; differences are ranked along a hierarchy; and an ideology of racial superiority is implied. Likewise, his database has been denounced as outdated, simplistic, highly selective, and calculated to achieve a singular slant in the nature–nurture debate.

Many colleagues of Rushton have supported his right to speak on contentious issues, keeping in mind that freedom of speech is not an absolute right, but entails a degree of social responsibility. The University of Western Ontario also has defended his right to teach despite numerous protests. Others disagree; a preoccupation with race and racial differences is perceived as a ruse for containment of minorities through the "politics of science" (Snyderman 1994:79). Still others are dismayed by the publicity and exposure Rushton has received, all of which has had the unfortunate effect of conferring both a public platform and a degree of legitimacy to his assertions. As to why this type of thinking finds a receptive audience, the answers are less clear. Perhaps such simplistic bioreductionisms possess an intrinsic appeal at times of social complexity and rapid change.

Rushton's Evolutionary Typology

	Negroid	Caucasoid	Oriental
Evolutionary branching from hominid line	200,000 years ago	110,000 years ago	40,000 years ago
Brain size	1,330 cm^3	1,408 cm^3	1,448 cm^3
IQ score	85	100	107
Sexual activity	Intense	Moderate	Weak
Temperament	Aggressive/Excitable	Moderate	Calm/Cautious
Marital stability	Brittle	Moderate	Strong
Social organization law abiding crime rates	Low High	Moderate Moderate	High Low

Race types and racial typologies continue to attract interest despite unease within the scientific community. Not only do these concepts exercise a tenacious hold on our thinking; they also exert a powerful influence in shaping the lives and life chances of racial or indigenous minorities. Such a scenario is perplexing, since neither race nor race types have any empirical validity. Both represent social constructs (ideologies) that reflect human interests rather than anything inherent or self-evident within reality itself (Miles 1982). The race concept also fails as an explanatory concept. A social construct with no basis in reality cannot empirically account for human variations and societal inequality (Miles and Phizacklea 1984). Race relations are not biological relations; in the final analysis, they constitute relations of inequality that have been racialized between groups in order to deny or exclude (Miles 1993). As a social construct, race matters at three levels: (a) as a tool for dominance that has been institutionalized in many cases; (b) as a historical experience that has shaped the lives of designated minorities; and (c) as a distinguishing marker for oppressed groups that is increasingly transformed into a mark of pride, identity, or resistance (Lerner 1997).

Race continues to matter, even when fraught with political overtones and pernicious associations. This confirms the sociological notion that perception *is* reality when it comes to impact. Thus socially defined phenomena do not have to be real to be real in their consequences. Merely defining a situation can make it "realistic." Argued in a parallel fashion, the race concept does not have to be real to exert an impact upon society. The renowned scholar Michael Banton (1967:4) has claimed as much:

> Beliefs about the nature of race—whether true or false—still have considerable social significance, and, when a category is labelled in the popular mind by racial terminology rather than religious or class criteria, certain predictable consequences ensue. The social significance of the racial label...forms part of the study of intergroup relations.

Evidence from around the world has revealed all too clearly the suffering and chaos generated by human fantasies and illusions. To what factors and forces can we attribute the origins, growth, and popularity of the race concept?

THE ROOTS OF RACE: HISTORICAL AND SOCIAL PERSPECTIVES

> There is in the world a hierarchy of races.... [Some] will direct and rule the others, and the lower work of the world will tend in the long run to be done by the lower breeds of men. This much we of the ruling colour will no doubt accept as obvious.
>
> Murrary 1900; cited in Banton 1987:vii

The race concept has enjoyed a long period of grace in the West. The concept itself was a product of a global paradigm that originated with European expansion and conquest. Expansion of Europe in regions with racially diverse populations created a global system in which 'races' were assigned particular economic functions because of their physical appearance, local resources, power to resist, geographical location, and cultural proximity to Europe (Walker 1997). The popularity of the race concept was consistent with Enlightenment philosophies that extolled the virtues of human progress and individual perfectibility. Several questions should immediately come to mind. Why did the race concept originate in the first place? How do we explain this compulsion to pigeonhole human diversity into racial types that are fixed, permanent, and unequal? Why do pockets of openly racist thinking continue to linger on in the public domain? Why are they resistant to reform? Answers to these questions point to a constellation of social forces that have bolstered its legitimacy as an explanatory tool.

On the Origins of Race—European Exploration

A scientific approach toward the concepts of race and types originated in response to a variety of complex factors (Stepan 1982). These included the expansion of the slave trade after the fifteenth century, abolition movements at the end of the eighteenth century, the appearance of human and biological sciences (with their focus on comparative anatomy) around the turn of the nineteenth century, and the "estrangement" of Europeans from non-Europeans in the wake of international competition.

Particular interest in race relations was sharpened during the era of European exploration. European imaginations were intrigued by sustained contact with highly diverse populations whose appearance and culture stimulated an outpouring of amusement, fascination, and repulsion. Exposure to diversity encouraged a system of explanation that would impose a framework of coherence and order. The concept of race types (typologies) proved a "common sense" approach to explaining and sorting out civilizational differences that could not be explained by climate or history. This concept was also invoked to explain why non-Western populations lacked the political acumen and techno-military prowess of imperialistic-minded Europeans. Far from being the product of irrationality or hate, race emerged as a product of the Enlightenment with its rational and scientific commitment to classify, understand, and control the diversity of the world's plants, animals, and peoples according to one grand scheme (Goldberg 1993).

To be sure, race as a social category existed prior to European exploration and expansion. Embryonic forms of race thinking existed among the Chinese and Arabs in the late Middle Ages (Goldberg 1993). Europeans had long relied on other criteria for demonizing those beyond the pale of Christianity. For instance, the Middle Ages world was divided into Christian and non-Christian sectors. Non-Christians were viewed as wild and untamed pagans ("the devil's own handiwork") who had crawled out from beneath the flat world to test Christian patience. Heathens were dispatched to the lower rungs of the creation ladder (a "chain of being")—a stable and static hierarchy that relegated lesser beings to one end and superior races to the other. Primitives and savages were fortunate to have occupied the realms in between. The magnitude and impact of the Christian/non-Christian dichotomy should not be underestimated. The intensity and cruelty of the violence espoused by the Crusades, the Inquisition, and the Protestant Reformation—all in the name of God—will verify that. Still, these earlier schemes were no match for the ruthless destruction unleashed by the race concept. After all, it was one thing to disparage non-Westerners as worthless and unsalvageable for proselytizing purposes. It was quite another to construct elaborate classificatory schemes that invoked pseudoscientific explanations to legitimize worldwide exploitation and domination. When sanctioned by human and biological sciences, these classifications made group differences appear more comprehensive, more entrenched, and more scientifically valid (Stocking Jr 1968; Stepan 1982). When harnessed to military prowess and technological advances, the effects proved fatal to many.

In other words, Europeans did not invent the concept of race and its ramifications. Ancient peoples possessed an intense aversion to those who were different—on the grounds of superstition or ignorance rather than on comprehensive theories rooted in systematic observation and pseudoscientific classification (Jaret 1995). Nor was Europe awash with racists who relished every opportunity to disparage and/or exploit distant peoples. To paraphrase Michael Biddiss (1979), many at this time were genuinely perplexed about the nature and significance of human diversity, but answers were limited. But Europeans were among the first to popularize the race concept as a scientifically grounded formula for explaining away human diversity in an expansionist era. Europeans not only racialized the "other" as unassimilable or as a threat; they also racialized themselves by defining Europeans as a group held together by the inevitable superiority of white to nonwhite. For that reason, Europeans must be held responsible for unleashing chaos and destruction of a magnitude previously unknown.

Putting Race to Work: Imperialism and Colonialism

It has been suggested that Europeans manipulated the concept of race as one way of domesticating global diversity. The proliferation of **racial doctrines** or dogmas stemmed from such a racial mindset. Racial doctrines originated to facilitate and condone the negative treatment of non-Western populations who were racially and culturally different from Europeans. Under the sway of these dogmas, many overseas populations found themselves susceptible to powerful external interests even after attaining nominal political independence.

The nineteenth century is often regarded as the age of **imperialism.** It represented a period of time when various European nations (as well as including Russia and the United States) assumed an inalienable right to conquer, colonize, and exploit overseas territories. A need for foreign markets, investment opportunities, cheap labour, and inexpensive resources reflected the requirements of an expanding capitalist system. It also embraced the stirrings of a religious fervour with its resigned commitment to proselytize the world in the name of Christian duty ("the white man's burden"). In addition, imperialist expansion reflected an obsession among Europeans to accumulate foreign territories for nationalistic or military reasons. This fanaticism for colonial empires may also have been perpetuated for no other reason than "one-upmanship" in an ever-spiralling game of tit for tat, which no side could realistically hope to win except at the expense of others.

A predatory approach toward global relations uncovered a set of existential dilemmas. First and foremost, how could so-called civilized and Christian nations rationalize and justify the blatant exploitation of others? Second, how could self-serving interests be sustained without contradicting the image of Europeans as a sophisticated and enlightened people with a moral duty to civilize and convert? Answers to these uncomfortable questions invited an ideology that condoned the mistreatment of others as natural or normal—even necessary. The contradiction between Christian ideals and exploitative practices was mediated by the racist conviction that indigenous peoples existed at lower levels of civilization and would benefit from servitude and close supervision (Lerner 1997). This ideology not only explained and legitimated the sorting of populations along racial lines; it also set the tone for asserting absolute European supremacy on pseudoscientific grounds. As Martin and Franklin (1973:71) write:

> [The] advent [of race] seemed to be due in large measure to the need for a rationalization of the exploitation of certain groups.... This proposition was also advanced to justify the imperialism and colonialism that flourished.... Racism became a convenient ideological defense for social practices which patently and flagrantly violated basic social and institutional principles.

Racial doctrines arose to "soften" the impact of imperialist encounters throughout Central and South America, the Caribbean, Africa, Australia, and New Zealand. By dismissing overseas peoples as inferior or subhuman, Europeans could exploit and oppress indigenous populations without remorse, guilt, or responsibility. Equal treatment was denied merely because of perceived deficiencies in the mental or moral makeup of primitives. Once racial differences were ingrained as fixed and immutable, moreover, Europeans were absolved of any compelling need for improving the plight of the less fortunate. With consciences salved, they were free to do whatever was expedient to expand or safeguard white privilege. Racial doctrines, in turn, continued to justify systems of exploitation and control.

DOCTRINES OF RACIAL SUPREMACY

Doctrines of racial superiority began to appear once racial types were assigned a fixed moral value. Only a minimal cognitive shift was required to move from racial types to their placement on rank orderings of superiority and inferiority (Biddiss 1979). These hierarchies were intrinsically racist in that they employed the authority of science to confirm the superiority of some groups over others on the basis of arbitrarily defined criteria (Stepan 1982). Their impact was devastating: Racial supremacist doctrines endorsed the dehumanization of minorities as objects for exploitation. In justifying inequality between races, the doctrines also embodied a set of practices and relationships that denied or excluded the "other." The most notorious of these doctrines were social Darwinism, eugenics, and scientific racism.

Social Darwinism

Social Darwinism evolved into a widely acceptable doctrine of racial superiority during the final quarter of the nineteenth century. The doctrine itself borrowed a number of Darwin's biological propositions, then reworked them to further the aims of overseas exploitation. Foremost were the notions of a "struggle for survival" on a global scale and "survival of the fittest" by way of natural selection. Social Darwinism portrayed the social world as a gladiatorial arena where populations were locked in mortal combat over scarce and valuable resources. Those who were better adapted to compete in this ongoing struggle prospered; those with less adaptive attributes were vanquished.

The nations of Europe and the United States defined themselves as evolutionarily advanced. Superior breeding had propelled Western Europe to the top of the unilinear evolutionary schemes that were in vogue at the time. The concept of unilinear evolution had proposed that populations evolved through predetermined and universal stages of savagery–barbarism–civilization. While some with the proper biological stock had progressed to the apex of the evolutionary heap, others, of course, were left behind in the competitive struggle for evolutionary survival. Racial groups were ranked along the evolutionary ladder on the basis of their likeness to standards of European civilization and Christianity. As mentioned earlier, the Maori of New Zealand were prominently ranked because of their military prowess and receptivity to Western customs. First Australians, by way of contrast, were banished to the bottom because of their association with a stone-age culture.

Social Darwinist philosophies played into the hands of western **colonialism.** The subjugation of colonized peoples was condoned on "natural" rather than conventional grounds. In the words of Nancy Stepan (1982:83):

> Evolutionism provided a new emotionally charged, yet ostensibly scientific language with which to express old prejudices.... [T]the "lower races" were now races that had "evolved" least far up the evolutionary ladder, had lost out in the "struggle for survival" and were "unfit" for the competition between tribes. Or they represented the evolutionary "childhood" of the white man.

These doctrines exonerated the colonialists of responsibility in the colonization of African blacks, East Asian populations, Aboriginal peoples, and Polynesian islanders. Racial ideologies not only explained European superiority and justified out-group exploitation; these ideologies endorsed the virtues and inevitability of capitalism and imperialism as integral to human progress and social enlightenment.

Eugenics

Racist doctrines assumed even more sinister proportions at the turn of the twentieth century. A variety of social movements arose in the United States, Britain, Russia, and Japan, with objectives often benign in intent but deadly in consequence. *Eugenics* proposed the idea that the social, mental, and behavioural qualities of the human 'race' could be improved by selective manipulation of its hereditary essence (Kevles 1995). Fortified by the discovery of hereditary laws, the eugenics movement collectively advocated the improvement of human stock by purging the species of undesirables through selective breeding procedures. Eugenics operated on the assumption that the genetically unfit were a threat to society. Defectives such as racial minorities, the congenitally deformed, and the "retarded" would be sterilized as one way of curbing the further "bastardization" of the human species (Banton 1967). By contrast, racially superior stocks were encouraged to freely propagate to ensure perpetuation of the best "stock" (Stepan 1982).

Eugenecists in the United States were instrumental in restricting immigration from less "fit" countries in Eastern and Southern Europe. They promoted passage of sterilization laws that in 31 states disproportionately targeted lower income groups (Kevles 1995). In Canada, the 1928 Sexual Sterilization Act in Alberta condoned the sterilization of 2,822 women, most of them poor or aboriginal, before being repealed in 1972 (Caulfield and Robertson 1996). By the early 1930s, eugenics as a movement had declined, but not before a final burst of compulsory sterilization under the Nazi genocide machine. Eugenics as a doctrine was increasingly criticized. Prominent American anthropologists such as Franz Boas, Ruth Benedict, and Margaret Mead were instrumental in demolishing the validity of biological reductionist arguments. Eschewing racial explanations, they proposed instead the relevance of social and cultural forces as explanatory variables. Cultural explanations of human differences and similarities gained popularity in revulsion to Nazi atrocities. Nevertheless, the idea of eugenicism has persisted into the present, albeit in diverse and somewhat more disguised forms and without the backing of an openly receptive social climate.

Scientific Racism in the United States

Doctrines of racial superiority were not applied exclusively to African, Asian, or South American countries. They also blossomed in North America where racial ideologies arose and evolved in response to the need for cheap and disposable labour, unrestricted access to land and mineral resources, and preservation of white privilege and power. Initially these dogmas were directed at indigenous peoples. Later they included successive waves of incoming immigrant groups. Powerful interests were thus able to exercise control and exploitation under these doctrines that diminished minorities to subhuman status.

Racial dogmas became especially marked in the United States. The existence of an indigenous native population, a more mobile black population, and the ongoing influx of European immigrants created a pressing need to scientifically sort out and impartially arrange this diversity. The search for an appropriate doctrine culminated with the discovery of so-called intelligence tests. The most popular of these was the **intelligence quotient (IQ) test,** which even today continues to fascinate or repel.

CASE STUDY 2–4	**IQ Testing for Race and Intelligence**

American whites have long harboured racist sentiments toward African-Americans. This racism was manifest in a variety of ways during the pre-Civil War era: in the exclusion of blacks from the freedom and equality provisions within the American constitution to the often brutal treatment of slaves on plantations. After emancipation, racism continued to flourish both in the North and the South. In the North this racism became increasingly focused in urban areas where blacks competed with white immigrants over jobs and housing. Blacks were resented for moving into neighbourhoods; they were also disliked even more for engaging in strike-breaking activities at the expense of the European immigrants (van den Berghe 1967). Given such antiblack sentiments, American whites were clearly receptive to any scientific proof for putting blacks back into place.

The growing popularity of ideologies based on **scientific racism** equipped racists with the proof they required. Scientific racism was built on the premise that racial capacities between populations could be measured and evaluated by statistical means. The introduction of the IQ test proved a godsend in supporting this alleged relation between **race and intelligence.** The IQ test itself, called the Stanford–Binet test, was designed at Stanford University by French psychologist Alfred Binet for the discovery of deficiencies in the cognitive skills of French pupils. It was never really intended to measure the amount of intelligence a person possessed. Binet himself believed intelligence could not be correlated with precise mathematical certainty. Nevertheless, American interests co-opted the test and applied it indiscriminately during the latter stages of World War I as a means of sorting raw recruits into two categories: officer rank or cannon fodder. Since blacks for a variety of reasons were more likely to perform poorly on these tests, the IQ test quickly established itself as an instrument for proving racial inferiority.

Repeated testings revealed that blacks on the average scored about 15 percentage points less than whites on the IQ test. This gap was taken as proof that blacks were intellectually inferior "stock" because of hereditary factors. With few exceptions, many believed this biogenetic gap could never be bridged, even with environmental improvements and enrichment programs. That being the case, the implications were obvious. Blacks were destined for menial occupations. They did not require a sophisticated education system, since there was little hope for substantial improvement even with increased exposure or expenditure. The IQ test legitimized this popular conception of black inferiority. It invoked a set of statistics whose "halo effect" proved what many had secretly harboured. But in their hurry to promote white intellectual supremacy at the expense of blacks, the advocates of the IQ test took some unwarranted liberties with the results. For example, while blacks scored consistently lower than whites as a group, the range of variation between black and white scores was comparable. The highest and the lowest scores within each category were approximately the same. Also relevant but widely ignored were variations in group averages. While blacks on the average scored about 15 percent lower than whites, 15 percent of the blacks scored higher than the average score for whites, suggesting by inference that some blacks were intellectually superior to whites. According to Joseph Flynn of the University of Otago in New Zealand, a 24 percent increase in IQ scores since 1948 confirmed the importance of social conditions in shaping outcomes.

The most recent reincarnation of these race-intelligence debates stems from the publication of *The Bell Curve: Intelligence and Class Structure in American Life* (The Free Press, 1994). The authors, Charles Murray and Richard J. Herrnstein, argue that intelligence (as measured by IQ) is inherited. Low levels of intelligence, in turn, are responsible for social problems such as poverty, lawlessness, and dysfunctional families. If this trend is allowed to continue, they warn, the eclipse of the United States as a superpower is assured. Key points in their argument are as follows:

- Intelligence is real and differs among humans.

- Intelligence can be measured by standardized testing such as IQ tests. Properly administered, IQ tests are not biased against racial minorities.

- Intelligence is largely inherited (between 40 and 80 percent); this makes it resistant to reform.

- Intelligence has a predictive value; that is, it correlates with positive (success) and negative (welfare or crime) achievement. Those with intelligence succeed; those without, fail. Those in between, with IQ scores between 76 and 124, are less predictable.

- Intelligence varies with ethnic and racial groups; some races or classes have high levels; others don't; whites, for example, are smarter than blacks and these differences are largely innate.

- Social problems are related to low IQs. The proliferation of intellectually impoverished ethnic and racial groups (by migration or natural birth) will diminish a country's ability to produce, compete, or prosper.

- Innate differences in intelligence should serve as a basis for social policy; why throw good money at bad when compensatory or affirmative-type programs are a losing proposition that no government can afford?

In other words, inequality and class (who is rich and who is poor) are not randomly distributed but dependent on inherited measures of intelligence. Those at the top of their cognitive class are successful; those near the bottom are destined to be dysfunctional. Social problems will proliferate unless something is done to purge the country of the intellectually impoverished underclass.

Many social scientists would strongly disagree with this social Darwinian outlook (Alland Jr 1996). Low IQ scores do not create social problems; rather, social conditions such as class structure and racial discrimination are likely to create lower IQ scores. Social inequality cannot be directly reduced to differences in cognitive ability; differences in cognition may reflect responses to social inequality. To be sure, (a) intelligence may be partly inherited and measureable; (b) heredity and environment may interact in diverse ways to create intelligence; (c) environments can strongly influence a person's intelligence regardless of heredity; and (d) genetic and environmental factors are impossible to separate (Sternberg and Grigorenko 1997). Nevertheless, the assertion that biological pools rather than social conditions shape behaviour has altered how we think about social inequality. Two reasons may account for the tenacity of racial explanations. First, if intelligence is biologically innate and largely impervious to environmental modification, then white America cannot be held responsible for the plight of minority groups. The results of these tests can be used to justify negative treatment of minorities, ranging from segregated facilities to inferior programs. They can also be employed to forestall progressive change. Second, IQ tests are an effective device for explaining away differences through their logical presentation of "facts" and simple causal explanations (Mirza 1998). They possess an aura of scientific validity that is substantiated by the "magic" of quantification and measurement. Yet the use of half-truths in conjunction with reams of graphs and statistics can foster stereotypes or hatred (Callahan 1995). Such accreditation can also create the impression that race is a respectable intellectual position when grounded in "science," with a legitimate place in the national debate on race (Naureckas 1995). Even more disturbing is its potential to foster an undemocratic political agenda and mean-fisted public policy.

To Sum Up The significance of race in shaping intergroup dynamics cannot be underestimated. Public policy in the past served as a source of discrimination by race, as well as enforcing racial discrimination by others (Walker 1997). Yet many are baffled by how such a discredited Victorian-era concept has exerted a profound influence over the course of human history. The race concept originated and evolved in an attempt to explain patterns of inequality, to legitimize conquest and condone exploitation, and to account for human differences and similarities as parsimoniously as possible (see Goldberg 1993). The race concept remains pivotal in the public eye as a means of (a) explaining group differences, (b) justifying unequal treatment, and (c) condoning a lack of action. Race continues to matter in influencing people's lives and life chances, even if dismissed by many as poor science and bad politics. Racial assumptions reinforce how we see the world, think about it, and relate to others—in many cases reflecting an unconscious part of everyday life and common sense views of the world. In short, race matters even if it shouldn't. But because people act as if it does, the issue of race must be confronted squarely if we are to appreciate its role in generating inequities in a society where people should neither be rewarded nor penalized without justifiable cause (Cose 1997).

ENDNOTES

1. Also known as visible minorities. According to Statistics Canada, visible minorities are non-Caucasian in race or nonwhite in colour. The world is divided into areas of nonvisible minorities (Europe, North America, and Australia/New Zealand) and visible minorities outside of these regions. Yet anomalies exist: Turks are visible minorities; Greeks and Bulgarians are not. Arabs are, Jews are not. Those who declare multiple origins are automatically included as visible minorities if someone in their ancestry complied with the definition of visible minority. Not surprisingly, there is widespread hostility to being racially categorized as visible minorities, in effect further confounding the defining process (Gardner 1996).

CHAPTER HIGHLIGHTS

- This chapter has explored the politics of race by looking at the origins of racial types and typologies, the role of racial doctrines as instruments of colonialist expansion, and its status in the comprehension and construction of human reality.

- Race: although there is no genetic basis or scientific validity for it, race continues to polarize people and rouse deep-seated emotions.

- In a racialized society, race continues to matter as a fundamental principle of social organization and group identity.

- Race continues to matter in terms of entitlement or engagement within contemporary society. Race remains a powerful social force that is instrumental in shaping inter-group dynamics since groups are likely to exploit, control, or dominate on the basis of what they "see" in others.

- Race matters when it comes to minority participation in sports. African-Americans excel in certain sports not because of physiological properties (although genetic differences may play a role), but because of social factors and opportunity structures.

- Race and crime do not necessarily correlate, notwithstanding public perception and political clamour to the contrary. Race cannot explain crime (crime transcends racial groupings); race-based crime statistics do not measure crime but rates of minority apprehension by law enforcement.

- The race concept is described in terms of its (a) definition and characteristics, (b) logic and underlying rationale, (c) origins and development during the era of imperialism, and (d) impact and implications for group dynamics.

- The race concept is primarily a social construct, without any biological basis or scientific validity, even if its consequences are real. Race may be a social construction, nevertheless, it is not a social fiction without material consequences. In that sense, race is political because it is associated with debates over who gets what.

- Recourse to the race concept reflected a growing reliance on "scientific" techniques to (a) categorize people into racial groups on the basis of skin colour, (b) provide an explanation for internal diversity among humans, (c) explain the relative achievements of certain groups, and (d) predict the fate of the human species.

- Racism in the United States was conveyed by the vehicle of scientific racism and its expression in intelligence (IQ) testing. The fact that such thinking remains today indicates that race matters as a system of explanation, exploitation, engagement, and entitlement.

- The controversy over IQ and race ultimately hinges on whether the tests measure innate intelligence or socially constructed measures of intelligence.

- The race concept originated and evolved in response to the needs of an expanding Western economy. As an ideology with powerful public appeal, it was employed to rationalize and condone exploitation of colonized groups.

- Doctrines of racial domination, including social Darwinism, scientific racism, and eugenics, were also invoked to establish the desirability and inevitability of white privilege.

- Racial differences exist but races do not, at least not in the sense of distinct and fixed categories of individuals, with a unique assemblage of characteristics that evolved over time.

- People are similar in essence but vary in certain surface differences, mostly in terms of single traits rather than as bundles of characteristics. This suggests that traits can be categorized, not groups of people with their different combinations of traits.

- In theory, the concept of race is not the problem *per se*. The problem lies in arbitrarily dividing the world into fixed categories of people, linking physical differences with social and moral properties, arranging these compendiums of characteristics in ascending/descending order, and establishing ideologies of superiority to explain, justify, exploit, and control.

- Race has long been endorsed as a way of condoning inequality and domination while maintaining a veneer of morality and piety throughout. It has also been employed to explain human differences and similarities under a pseudoscientific mantle.

- The concept of race is not real. The consequences of believing in race are real insofar as actions consistent with this belief have real consequences.

- Race matters not because it is real, but because people respond as if it were real. Race matters not because people are inherently different or unequal, but because perceived differences may be manipulated as a basis for sorting out privilege and power. Race matters not because of biological differences, but because an exclusive preoccupation with genes detracts from the socially constructed character of dominant–subdominant relations.

KEY TERMS

colonialism/imperialism
eugenics
IQ test
race
race and intelligence
race matters
race types
racial doctrines
racial typologies
racialization
scientific racism in the United States
social Darwinism
speciation

REVIEW QUESTIONS

1. How valid is the race concept from a scientific point of view?

2. Race has little to do with genes or biological reality, but everything to do with social constructions and social control; in other words, race is *not* biologically grounded but socially constructed. Explain this assertion.

3. Sociologists have an expression that suggests that phenomena do not have to be real to be real in their consequences. Apply this sociological insight to a discussion of race and racial typologies in terms of their impact on targeted groups.

4. Why did racial doctrines emerge in nineteenth-century Europe, and why did they persist into the twentieth century?

5. What do we mean by the statement that there is no such thing as race relations but only relationships that have been "racialized"?

6. Race matters in that a belief in innate differences between groups of people can serve as a basis of entitlement and engagement. Write a brief essay (about 250 words) on how "race matters" in Canada.

7. Indicate whether there is any validity to the collection of crime statistics by race.

8. Framing the "other" by way of race typologies may say more about "us" than about "them." Explain.

9. It is said that the only way of combating race is by emphasizing what we have in common rather than what divides us racially. Do you agree or disagree with this statement? Why?

10. Demonstrate how race has emerged as a fundamental principle of social organization and racial identity in a racialized society.

C h a p t e r

THE FACES
OF RACISM

**CASE
STUDY 3–1** | **The Unacceptable Face of Canada: "Yellow
Peril" or White Xenophobia?**

Early Chinese immigration provides an embarrassing face of Canada that many Canadians would prefer to forget (Baureiss 1985; Li 1988). From the time of their first arrival in Canada as virtually indentured labour for the construction of the transcontinental railway, Chinese immigrants were subjected to legislation that sought to economically destroy the community, restrict political activity, and inhibit healthy social growth (Vasil and Yoon 1996). A split labour market quickly appeared: Chinese labourers were employed for $1 a day (only 80 cents if they did not buy provisions from the company store), compared to $2 a day for Canadian workers or $3.50 for American labourers (Faces 1996). They were seen as cheap and exploitable work horses for the most hazardous sections of the railway, but expendable once the task was completed (Lee 1997). Upon completion of the railway, many returned to their homelands to buy farms. Others were stranded in Canada because of insufficient funds and sought unskilled employment in laundries and gardens. The Chinese were increasingly exposed to caricature and abusive treatment by the general public and politicians. In the same year the railroad was completed, the BC government passed the 1884 Chinese Regulation Act, arguing that Chinese "were not disposed to be governed by our laws; are useless in instances of emergency; and desecrate graveyards." They were frequently subjected to racial invectives by organized labour who demonized them as strike-breaking "scabs."

Others perceived them as a kind of "yellow peril" that would undermine the purity and integrity of this British outpost. The exploitation of the Chinese as a political football or as electoral scapegoats played into the hands of white supremacist racists. Federal plans to import an additional 5,000 Chinese for the construction of the Grand Trunk Railway elicited an editorial response to this effect from the September 1906 issue of *Saturday Night:*

> We don't want Chinamen in Canada. This is a white man's country and white men will keep it so. The slant-eyed Asiatic with his yellow skin, his unmanly humility, his cheap wants, would destroy the whole equilibrium of industry.... We cannot assimilate them. They are an honest, industrious, but hopelessly inferior race (cited in Fraser 1989:12).

With no political voice or representation, the Chinese were unable to adequately defend themselves. This is not to say that all passively accepted these social injustices; protests, strikes, and lawsuits were often employed in reaction to negative government legislation and discriminatory practices (see Ip 1998). But Chinese efforts to withdraw into their own communities for protection resulted in further hostility and suspicion. Under public pressure, the successive government imposed a **head tax** on each incoming immigrant, culminating with a fee of $500 in the early twentieth century—a sum that was equivalent to the price of a new home in Vancouver. The federal government curtailed Chinese immigration in 1923 in response to public demands to stem the "yellow peril." With passage of the act, the Chinese became the only people to be prohibited from immigrating to Canada entirely because of race. This exclusionary injunction also forced the separation of Chinese men from their wives and partners, in effect curbing population growth (Stasiulis 1997). This racist ban was not lifted until 1947 with repeal of the Chinese Immigration Act and passage of Canada's first Citizenship Act.

Chinese-Canadian relations with society have improved in recent years. Successive generations of Chinese have moved from relative social isolation to active involvement in staking a rightful claim to status as Canadian citizens. But prejudicial and racist attacks continue to linger. Chinese-Canadians have been accused of stirring up a host of social problems, from monopolizing spaces in medical schools to driving up real estate prices in Vancouver. These attacks are less direct than in the past; nevertheless, the undercurrent of thinly veiled hostility is no less disconcerting, suggesting that racism in racialized societies never disappears. Rather it tends to reappear in a variety of different disguises.

INTRODUCTION: FACING UP TO RACISM

From afar, Canada strikes many as a paragon of racial tranquillity. Racism may loom as the single most explosive and divisive force in many societies, including the United States, but surely not in Canada, where racism is publicly scorned and officially repudiated. In contrast with the United States, where race continues to divide or deter, racism in Canada is thought to be relatively muted, isolated to fringe circles, and confined to historical dustbins. Laws are in place that not only prohibit racism and discrimination, but also severely punish those who flaunt Canada's multicultural ideals. Brazen racists such as white supremacists are routinely charged and convicted for disseminating hate propaganda. Race riots are virtually unheard of, while blatant forms of racial discrimination have been driven underground. To their credit, Canadians have learned to "walk their talk": The demographic revolution that has transformed once stodgy cities such as Vancouver and Toronto into vibrant, racially tolerant cosmopolitan centres is but one of many positive indicators (Grayson 1996). The fact that the United Nations has ranked Canada as the country of choice for five consecutive years must surely say something about its peoples and their commitments.

Up close the picture blurs. We could be smug about our enlightened status if racism were a mere blip on Canada's social and historical landscape. This, sadly, is far from the truth. Minority women and men have experienced varied degrees of intolerance and discrimination depending on racial and national origins. Racism in Canada was and continues to be chronic and historically embedded in its culture and institutions, rather than an affliction among individual malcontents, with little or no sign of diminishing (see Satzewich 1998). Even that quintessential of American racist institutions, slavery, existed in Canada as conveyed by this advertisement:

> *TO BE SOLD, A BLACK WOMAN, named Peggy, aged about forty years; and a Black boy her son, named JUPITER, aged about fifteen years, both of them the property of the subscriber. The woman is a tolerable Cook and washer woman and perfectly understands making Soap and Candles. The Boy is tall and strong of his age, and has been employed in Country Business, but brought up principally as a House Servant—They are each of them Servants for life. The Price for the Wowan [sic] is one hundred and fifty Dollars—for the Boy two hundred Dollars, payable in three years with Interest from the day of Sale and to be properly secured by Bond &c.—But one fourth less will be taken in ready Money. PETER RUSSELL. York, Feb. 10th 1806* (adapted from Bristow et al. 1993).

Nowhere was racism more evident than in the business of making a living. Racism furnished the ideological life support for capitalism at large and Canadian society building in general, as the previous Case Study on Chinese-Canadians demonstrated (Bolaria and Li 1988; Satzewich 1991; McKague 1991; McKenna 1994). Canadian society was constructed around the racialization of minorities, and racism proved an integral part in rationalizing the exploitation of certain labour segments. Hate and fear compelled authorities to intern thousands of ethnic minorities, including Ukrainians during World War I and Italians during World War II, at great personal costs to themselves and to their families. A more spiteful internment was inflicted on Japanese-Canadians in British Columbia. Most were rounded up like Jews in Nazi Germany, their property confiscated and civil rights suspended through placement in labour internment camps, which were viewed as a prelude to deportation (Samuel 1997). Restrictions were not lifted until 1949.

The present may be equally racist—at least in consequence if not always in intent. Critics charge that racism is alive and well in Canada; only its worst effects are camouflaged by a Teflon veneer of tolerance and politeness (Henry et al. 1995; Satzewich 1998). Racism may be less blatant than in the United States, but people of colour continue to be politely discriminated against in housing, employment, and access to social services. Cabs don't stop for them; clerks follow them around in stores; elderly women tightly clutch their purses in their presence; if they walk, they get pulled over for loitering or jaywalking ; and if they drive, police suspicions are aroused (Galt 1998). Certain institutions such as the police and the mainstream media are routinely condemned as being as discriminatory and insensitive as their oft-criticized counterparts in the United States. Even Canada's much-lauded initiatives to accommodate diversity through government initiatives are denounced as racism in defence of the status quo (Thobani 1995). Nor can Canadians take much solace in basking over Canada's relatively peaceful "race" relations record. Incidents of racial conflict may confirm the presence of racism; their absence, however, does not disprove the pervasiveness of racist hostility toward out-groups (Brown and Brown 1995). That Canada has managed to escape the debilitating race riots of its southern neighbour is commendable in its own right. Yet such a fortuitous state of affairs may be attributed to exceptional good fortune and a powerful myth-making machine rather than to enlightened policies.

Which picture is more accurate? Is Canada as racist as critics say; or is Canada essentially an open and tolerant society, with only isolated and random incidents of racism? Can Canada be described as a society where individuals are rewarded on the basis of merit, where no group is singled out for negative treatment, and where racial attributes are irrelevant in determining a person's status? Or is this perception at odds with reality? Perhaps the answer to the question of Canada as racist lies somewhere in between the poles of naive optimism and cynical pessimism. Canada contains an awkward and baffling blend of hard-core racists and resolute antiracists, with the vast majority of individuals wavering somewhere in between these extremes. It makes no more sense to exaggerate the notion of Canada as irrevocably racist, with countless hate groups resorting to violence to achieve supremacist goals, than it is to underestimate the tenacity of racism in privileging some, disprivileging others. This ambiguity is expressed in diverse ways: Canada's best-documented race riot in 1933 at Christie Pits in Toronto involving a scuffle between Jews and non-Jews may have claimed a dozen injuries but no fatalities; many immigrants have experienced discrimination and racism, but rarely death or imprisonment; mainstream cultural ethnocentrism, but not ethnic cleansing (Thompson and Weinfeld 1995; Levitt 1997). Even expressions of racism appear selective in targeting victims: People of East Asian origins may be perceived as model minorities, whereas Indo-Pakistanis and African-Canadians score lower on the social acceptance scale (Berry and Kalin 1993). Regional variations are no less noticeable: According to a 1997 survey by the Department of Immigration, Toronto has the highest levels of intolerance scores for any city, despite receiving the highest number of immigrants; conversely, Vancouver, with the second highest number of immigrants, has the lowest score. Racism may "rule," in other words, but its face is shifting in response to a changing and diverse society (McFarlane 1995).

This chapter will explore the many faces of racism in Canada from a variety of different vantage points. It will examine racism in terms of its nature as a concept for analysis as well as a reality for many Canadians. Different dimensions of racism are analyzed and assessed in casting about for a definition, including **racism** as (a) race, (b) culture, and (c) power. The magnitude and scope of racism will be assessed by dissecting its constituent elements, including prejudice (from ethnocentrism to stereotyping) and discrimination (including harassment). The different dimensions of racism are also compared: Those involving the personal, conscious, and deliberate are contrasted with the impersonal and systemic. Racism is also expressed at different levels, from the interpersonal (including red-necked and polite) to the institutional (including the systematic and systemic) to the societal (including everyday and cultural). The understanding of racism in its many guises provides a platform for exploring the concept of antiracism. Antiracist strategies are classified into personal or institutional, then examined with respect to differences in objectives, means, and outcomes. Also included is a discussion on why racism continues to persist, despite the fact that "we should know better."

Certain questions are inevitable in a field as highly charged as racism. These questions impart a conceptual framework for analyzing racism in Canada. They also reveal the degree of complexity in sorting out its magnitude and scope.

1. Are incidents of racism and racial conflict increasing across Canada? Or are Canadians more aware of racism and human rights, with a growing willingness to report violations to proper authorities?

2. Is racism of recent vintage in Canada? Or is racism deeply embedded in Canadian history and institutional structures?

3. To what extent is racism a case of individual ignorance or fear? Are we better off analyzing racism as a structural feature of Canadian society in which access to power and privilege is systematically controlled? Is racism the result of racists with intense dislike toward others, or does it stem from the largely inadvertent consequences of institutional arrangements, ideologies, and practices that hinder or hurt (McCormack 1998)?

4. How valid is the charge that Canada is a racist society? What exactly constitutes a racist society? How many incidents are required before reaching this threshold? Is it preferable to define a racist society as one that officially condones racism or lacks formal mechanisms for controlling—either before or after the fact? Or is the notion of a racist society more systemic and difficult to quantify?

5. In what way is racism a "thing" out there? Is racism better seen as an attribute that is applied after the fact, depending on the context or consequence? Or should racism be interpreted as a system of social relations, with a complex array of practices and discourses that are historically defined, embedded in patterns of power, and woven into the ideological fabric of society (Stamm 1993)?

6. Is it possible for persons to be colourblind yet stand accused of racism? For some, colour consciousness in terms of colour-coded policies or civic culture may be regarded as progressive and nonracist. For others, the idea that race differences should shape identities or define entitlements is racist, since skin colour is equated with determinism (Sleeper 1997).

7. How valid are all references to racism? Is any treatment of people on the basis of race an expression of racism, or does such labelling depend on the context? People may advocate or oppose practices for many reasons, some of which may be openly racist, but others may reflect certain political differences about minority–majority relations or philosophical outlooks on society (Satzewich 1998).

8. Is there a danger of overusing racism? Is any criticism directed at people of colour a form of racism by definition? Or is this assertion itself a kind of racism since it implies that minority actions are beyond reproach or immune to criticism?When is racism an all-purpose putdown for silencing opponents or closing debates? Can constant repetition diminish or trivialize the meaning, specificity, and impact of racism for those who routinely suffer from its presence?

9. In what ways is racism a social problem? Who says so and why (D'Souza 1995)? Is racism "miscast" as an irrational reaction rather than a "rational" response by those who benefit from the suffering of others (see Bonilla-Silva 1996)?

10. Do all minorities experience racism of the same kind and magnitude? In what ways does racism inform institutional structures or inextricably fit in with the values of a

democratic society such as equality? Conversely, does it exist as a situational but unfortunate blip on the social horizon (Henry et al. 1995; Satzewich 1998)?

Responses to these questions are important for two reasons: The manner in which we confront these issues says a lot about our approach to race, aboriginal, and ethnic relations. In contrast with the past, when Canadians were generally reluctant to admit that racism contributed to the marginalization of minorities, the ease with which racism is now invoked to describe a host of ideas, actions, and institutional practices can be seen a positive development (Satzewich 1998). Yet the ubiquity of racism as a sociological concept and political slogan has a downside. Not only has reference to racism silenced individuals and closed off public debate, Satzewich argues, its value as a consciousness-raising exercise has been undermined because of imprecise meaning, insufficient supporting evidence, and random application. These responses also furnish a framework for analyzing the complex, multifaceted, and changing faces of racism in Canada.

DEFINING RACISM: "PASTING JELL-O TO THE WALL"

Racism: liberal racism; aversive racism; "friendly" racism; racism without race; experiential racism; democratic racism; reverse racism, enlightened racism; cultural racism. Judging by the proliferation of terms, racism has undergone a number of shifts in emphasis and changes to content (Solomos and Back 1996). The rhetorics of racism have also varied over time and place; accordingly, a widely accepted definition of racism has eluded our grasp. We know that something called racism exists, but are stumped in trying to figure out what it means. Conceptual uncertainty over racism is a surprising admission in light of its profile and pervasiveness. As many definitions exist as specialists in this area. Certain actions are unmistakably racist; others are defined as such because of context or consequence. Some define racism as a predisposition to "biologize" the intellectual, moral, and social characteristics of a person or group. Dinesh D'Souza (1995), for example, talks of racism as an opinion that acknowledges cultural differences and attributes them to biology. Others prefer to define racism as any act of denial or exclusion against any identifiable group perceived as inferior. Something can be defined as racist if it produces or reproduces a racially unequal social structure by essentializing racial identities or naturalizing perceived differences (Winant 1998). Boundaries are drawn by racializing culturally different groups and signifying them as different and unequal ("**racism without race**") (Malek 1996). Racism is defined by others still as any organized ideology that unjustly diminishes others and justifies this discrimination by reference to race. It provides a biologically based ideology of intellectual or moral superiority, involving a so-called hierarchy of superior and inferior races. Still others see racism as the exercise of power by some groups over others in ways that perpetuate the status quo. Moreover, as we shall see, racism is known to intersect with and be constitutive of other forms of exploitation related to class, gender, ethnicity, or sexual preference—in ways both mutually intensifying yet often contradictory. Such a variety of dimensions and perspectives produces a profusion of contradictory statements about racism, whose combined impact may generate more heat than light in sorting out which are appropriate.

The faces of racism are bewilderingly elastic. Racism is like a moving target: It is difficult to pin down and control. And it can span the spectrum from the openly defamatory to systemic patterns that confer institutional advantage to some, not to others, to the subtle and discreet so that only victims are aware of it (Solomos and Back 1996). Certain types of racist behaviour are unplanned and unpremeditated, but expressed in isolated acts at irregular intervals because of individual impulse or insensitivity. Other expressions of racism are not spontaneous or sporadic; they are systemic and manifest instead through discriminatory patterns that are inextricably linked with society at large. Expressions of racism can be willful, intentional, or conscious; alternatively, they can be involuntary, inadvertent, or unconscious. Racism can be expressed by individuals or entrenched within institutional systems. Some see racism as something individuals do or don't do, while others define it as structural arrangements that exclude and deny. Still others characterize racism as a property attributed to actions by those powerful enough to do so, rather than an attribute inherent in reality. Others still define racism in terms of how victims experience it. As a result, racism means whatever people want it mean. Such subjectivity can only play havoc with consensus.

Part of the problem in securing a definition stems from reality itself. Racism is so expansive, with such an array of meanings from context to context, that it no longer has a meaning in the conventional sense of a single, commonly understood definition (Editorial, *The Globe and Mail*, 12 May 1992). Definitional difficulties are compounded by an indiscriminate use of the term itself. Racism is as an omnibus concept with a remarkable capacity to bend, elude, twist, conceal, and shape, depending on context and consequences. Negative comments involving racially different persons are assumed to be racist; nevertheless, the remarks may more accurately reflect ignorance, bad manners, greed, fear, or laziness on the part of the speaker (Wieseltier 1989). Repeated references to racism as the precipitating cause of behaviour may gloss over the complexity of attitudes in shaping actions (Palmer 1996). Blaming racism for everything when race is irrelevant may be racist in its own right. Doing so may draw attention to racial rather than social causes of minority problems, in effect contributing to perceptions of minorities as victims or villains. Or it can draw attention to the fact that racism is a lot more than name-calling on the playground, as Margaret Cannon (1995) observes, but a world view that entraps both victim and perpetrator. Racism is also vulnerable to manipulation by various interests along the political spectrum. Used as a smoke screen, it can divert attention from the issues at hand; likewise, it may silence others or close debate because of the cringe factor associated with racism. Constant and repetitive use of the term runs the risk of turning it into a harmless cliché, thus trivializing its consequences for victims at large. In short, there is no timeless or absolute standard for defining racism (Winant 1998): Social structures change and discourses undergo constant rearticulation, and it this dynamism that complicates the study of racism.

Dimensions of Racism

Generally speaking, reference to racism is multidimensional (Winant 1998). The multidimensionality of racism appears to sort itself out into three interwoven strands: racism as race, as culture, and as power. Racism is expressed in terms of who people are (race or biology), what they do (culture), and where they stand in the broader scheme of things (power). These distinctions are analytically useful for conceptual purposes but are mutually interrelated in reality, as revealed in the Insight Box on **anti-Semitism** at the end of this section.

Racism As Race

One dimension of racism is derived from the root, "race," with its attendant notion that biology is destiny. Strictly speaking, the concept of race is concerned with differences; racism, by contrast, transforms these differences into an ideology to justify the dominance of one group over another (Jakubowicz et al. 1994). Definitions of *racism as race* entail a belief in innate differences as a basis for justifying unequal treatment within a racialized social context. Racism alludes to an ideological belief that people can be divided into "races" and assessed or treated accordingly. The human world is partitioned into a set of fixed and discrete categories of population. Each of these racial categories contains a distinctive and inherited assemblage of social and biological characteristics that can be arranged in ascending/descending orders of importance. Unequal treatment of others is then justified on the grounds of innate differences between races that are natural and fixed. Racial doctrines not only define certain types of behaviour (such as intelligence) as biogenetically programmed; a moral value of inferiority or superiority is also assigned to human differences. Certain races are judged as inherently unequal because of social or mental deficiencies and subsequently denied rights and opportunities (Jaret 1995). As one prominent scholar in this field has noted in correlating racism with biological determinism:

> [R]acism is an ideology which considers a group's unchangeable physical characteristics to be linked in a direct causal way to psychological or intellectual characteristics, and which on this basis distinguishes between superior and inferior racial groups (van den Berghe 1967).

Racism as biology (or classical racism) is the process of attaching intellectual and moral qualities to biology. It consists of a relatively cohesive set of beliefs ("ideology") and practices that label, classify, evaluate, and rank members of a group along a hierarchy by virtue of their inclusion in a predefined category. Individuals are thought to internalize a set of ideas about the inferiority of others. This intense dislike of others because of what they are leads to racially discriminatory actions (see Bonilla-Silva 1996). In recent years, the focus of racism has shifted: A preoccupation with pigment-based deficiency is being replaced with assumptions about cultural inferiority.

Racism As Culture

Racism is no longer perceived as a universalist discourse of dominance over inferiorized others as was the case with colonialism. The objective then was to destroy the "other," to exploit them on the grounds of their biological inferiority, or to subordinate and assimilate them to the colonizer's concept of progress (Solomos and Back 1996). The new racism is rooted in a dislike toward the "other" not only because of who they are ("biology") but also because of what they do ("culture"). Minorities are denied or excluded by racializing cultural differences as a basis for denial or dislike. Instead of assertions over the differing endowments of different races, this discourse on *"racism without race"* has shifted accordingly. From its reference to inequality, racism incorporates debates over inclusion and exclusion as well as belonging and acceptance within a cultural framework.

This newer racism is rooted in a coded language that links social cohesion with national identity by way of culture (Henry et al. 1995). Under cultural racism, ethnic minorities are no longer dismissed as racially inferior. Dominant sectors are not defined as racially superior but culturally unique and different. Racism as culture is predicated on the principle that the cultural "other" poses a danger or threat to the mainstream. Cultural differences are racialized or vilified to marginalize a group as inferior or irrelevant. Conversely, these differences are subject to intense assimilationist pressure to preserve a preferred way of living (Modood and Berthoud 1997). Culturally different migrants are defined as the source of a society's social problems, Wieviorka (1998) writes, with dominant groups drawing on racial definitions that combine biology with culture to diminish the "other" on the grounds they are too aggressive, too self-confident, too demanding, too successful, or not successful enough. Contemporary racist discourses are aimed at isolating or segregating the "other" when differences are deemed as beyond integration. In more extreme cases, those who do not belong to the cultural ideal are expelled or eliminated.

Racism As Power

Another dimension focuses on the notion of *racism as power*. This broader definition goes beyond racism as a set of ideas or individual actions. It approaches racism as virtually any type of exploitation or exclusion inherent in dominant–subdominant relations that allows the dominant group to institutionalize its privilege and power at all levels of society (Bonilla-Silva 1996). The concept of **hegemony** is critical to this view of racism as power. Hegemony itself refers to a process of control or domination by way of consent rather than coercion. Dominant patterns of power and privilege are secured by manipulating people's attitudes without their awareness that they are being controlled, in effect contributing to their own control. For example, Marxists see racism as the hegemonic means by which the ruling classes justify the exploitation of a divided working class (Bolaria and Li 1988). Racism is perceived as a rationalization (such as slavery or apartheid) that "hegemonizes" the social, political, and economic relations within a racialized social system (Bonilla-Silva 1996). Others do not see racism as an ideological project, but an instrument of policy that is designed to exploit domestic workers, migrants, and refugees, thus preserving white privilege while divesting the state of social costs (Sivanandan 1997). Racism as power also entails the capacity to establish agendas regarding what is normal, necessary, desirable, or acceptable, thus reinforcing the superiority of one group over another. Intent and motive may be less important than the context or the consequences of an action on those without the resources to deflect or defuse them.

At its most fundamental, then, racism is about power, not pigmentation (Khayatt 1994). *Racism refers to the power held by one group or individuals that results in dominance and control over another on the basis of appearance, intelligence, or moral worth* (University of Guelph 1994). Racism is not about differences *per se*. It is about how these differences are racialized by those in power to mediate social hierarchies that deny or exclude because of race. In contrast with the perception of race as prejudicial ideas, racism as power is focused on the primacy of structures, ideologies, and practices in defence of a racialized social order that allocates resources and rewards by race (Bonilla-Silva 1996). To be sure, power is not reduced to the level of static resource, with white people holding all the power in some kind of zero-sum game, but rather as a component in social relations that is subject to competition, negotiation, and compromise (Holdaway 1996). Minorities are not powerless; they may tap into pockets of power to resist, remove, redefine, or renew (but see next Question Box). Still, full-blown racism is embedded in institutionalized power relations that reflect the capacity of some groups to formulate ideologies that legitimize and reproduce relationships of inequality (Guibernau 1996). This power is (a) expressed at the level of dominant–subdominant interaction, (b) embedded within the institutional framework of society, (c) buttressed by a coherent system of ideas and ideals, and (d) perpetuated by vested interests. In short, minority group lives and life chances are circumscribed by those with the balance of power or resources to ensure compliance. This raises an interesting and often controversial point of contention: Can minorities be racist?

Question Box
Is Racism a Two-Way Street?

The correlation between racism and the power of dominant groups raises a vexing question. Can minority group members display racism against the majority sector? Can ethnic minorities be racist toward other ethnic minorities? Is it a case of reverse racism when nonaboriginal writers are openly discouraged from filming or writing fiction about aboriginal themes? Is it racist for aboriginal peoples to accuse whites of genocide in undermining the political, social, and cultural grounds of aboriginal society? Is it racist for black militants to openly display hatred toward whites as an inferior race for return to Europe? Are black leaders who make defamatory remarks about Jews acting in a racist manner (D'Souza 1996)? Answers to these questions may never be settled to everyone's satisfaction, but their very asking provides a sharper understanding of racism.

Consider the cry of reverse racism when the Writers' Union of Canada sponsored a conference in Vancouver in the spring of 1994 that barred white Canadians from some activities. Funded primarily through public monies, Writing Thru "Race"—A Conference for First Nations Writers and Writers of Colour sought a venue for minorities to explore the experiences of racism in a world where, national myths notwithstanding, race matters. The conference justified its decision to exclude whites from one session on the grounds of improving dialogue among the historically oppressed, in the same way women's consciousness-raising movements frequently excluded men. Critics saw this as little more than reverse discrimination on the grounds of race. They resented the notion that people could be singled out and denied access or participation on the basis of race or group affiliation rather than as unique individuals (*Alberta Report*, 25 April 1994).

Was this a case of racism? Much depends on how one defines racism—as race or power? A reading of racism as biology—recourse to innate differences ("race") as criteria for differently treating others—would imply, yes, it was. Majority members would appear to have been denied and excluded primarily because of their race (skin colour). A more comprehensive view of racism as power suggests a different conclusion. Accusations of reverse racism must go beyond superficial appearances. There is a world of difference in using race to create equality (employment equity) versus its use to limit opportunity (discrimination), even if the rhetoric sounds the same. Emphasis must be instead on the context of the actions and their social consequences. The essence of racism resides not in treating others differently because they are different, but in different treatment in contexts of power that limit opportunity or privileges in a colour-conscious climate (Blauner 1972).

In short, racism is about the politics of difference within the context of power. Statements made by a minority group—

however distasteful or bigoted—may not qualify as racist in the conventional sense of outcomes. They are largely preferences or prejudices without the capacity for harm, since minorities lack the institutional power to put bigotry into practice in a way that "stings." bell hooks (1995:154–155) reinforces the notion that racism is not about prejudice but about power when she writes, "Why is it so difficult for many white folks to understand that racism is oppressive not because white folks have prejudicial feelings about blacks...but because it is a system that promotes domination and subjugation. The prejudicial feelings some blacks may express about whites are in no way linked to a system of domination that affords us any power to coercively control the lives and well-being of white folks." To be sure, minorities are not entirely powerless; after all, there is recourse to alternative sources of power brokering such as boycotts, civil disobedience, and moral suasion. Power does not reflect the rigid dualisms of a zero-sum game in which whites hold all the power in all contexts (Holdaway

1996). It is shifting, uneven, and context dependent. Power is not a static resource but aspects of a social relationship in which symbolic and material rewards are negotiated and mobilized in interaction.

Despite a more fluid and dynamic perspective, the equation prejudice + power = racism should not be casually jettisoned. The power that minority individuals wield in certain contexts rarely has the potential to deny or exclude. Minorities neither possess the resources to topple the dominant sector nor have the critical mass to harass, exclude, exploit, persecute, dominate, or undermine its collective self-respect. Conditions of relative powerlessness reduce minority hostility to the level of empty rhetoric or a protective shell in defence of minority interests. In other words, reverse racism may be a contradiction in terms, since those without access to institutionalized power or resources cannot racialize the other in a way that demeans, controls, or exploits. Racism is not a two-way street; more accurately, it resembles an expressway with controlled access points for those privileged enough to hog the centre lane.

Working Definition   We prefer a definition of racism that encompasses all three perspectives. Racism is defined as *those ideas and ideals ("ideology") that assert the superiority of one social group over another, together with the institutional power to put these beliefs into practice in a way that has the intent or effect of denying or excluding by virtue of membership in a devalued category.* This definition is similar to one proposed by Howard Winant: Any action can be defined as racist if it creates or reproduces a racially unequal social system, based on essentialized racial categories that naturalize racial identities and significations as unchanging, impervious to social context, and uniform across a defined category (Winant 1998). Racism is ultimately based on patterns of power involving relations of dominance, control, and exploitation (Schermerhorn 1956). Those in positions of power are able to invoke a doctrine of racial supremacy to ensure a measure of *social control* over those deemed inferior in the competitive struggle for scarce resources. We will explore further the idea of racism as social control, but first a look at the constituents of racism.

CONSTITUENTS OF RACISM

Racism does not exist as a monolithic reality. Nor is it a kind of thing out there that everyone can agree on. Racism ultimately touches on a variety of social processes, from the immediate and everyday to the remote and systemic. Each of the components that comprise racism contributes to its totality as an ideology and practice. The building blocks of racism consist of **prejudice** (including ethnocentrism and stereotypes) and **discrimination** (including **harassment**).

Prejudice

The concept of *prejudice* refers to negative, often unconscious, and preconceived notions about others. Prejudice arises because of our tendency to prejudge persons or situations for imposing definition and order on the world around us. Prejudicial thinking is normal and necessary; it is fundamental to the way that individuals process information with respect to in-group–out-group relations (Thomas 1998). It consists of *pre + judgments* that are irrational and unfounded on the basis of existing or compelling evidence. It also entails a set of generalized attitudes and beliefs that encourage the perception of others in a way that runs counter to objective facts (Holdaway 1996). Unlike ignorance, prejudice is characterized by an inflexible refusal to modify beliefs when presented with contrary evidence.

Many regard prejudice as a psychological phenomenon with a corresponding set of rigid or authoritarian personality traits (Adorno et al. 1950; Allport 1954). Others link these pre + judgments with a visceral and deep-seated fear of those whose appearances, values, or practices threaten a cherished and comfortable status quo. Still others equate prejudice with (a) feelings of superiority, (b) a perception of subordinate groups as inferior, (c) belief in the propriety of white privilege and power, and (d) reluctance to share scarce resources (Essed 1991). In that prejudice may involve a projection of "us" on "them," such beliefs may say more about the "us" and the need to protect this ego from the "them" (Curtis 1997). Finally, prejudices do not materialize out of nowhere; nor are they the byproduct of unhealthy personal development. The nature and content of prejudice are socially constructed and historically embedded in contexts both unequal and evolving.

National surveys confirm what many probably suspect (Henry and Tator 1985): Most Canadians are inclined to negatively prejudge others because of ignorance or visceral dislike. The nature of this prejudice may be changing (Pincus and Ehrlich 1994): The strongly held sense of biological inferiority and the hateful stereotypes have given way to rejection and denial on the basis of cultural differences and unacceptable lifestyles. This cultural prejudice is reflected in and reinforced by **stereotyping,** unwarranted generalizations about others; it also is expressed by **ethnocentrism,** with its belief in the self-proclaimed superiority of one culture over others. It is quite possible that many references to racism are synonymous with stereotyping or ethnocentrism. Nevertheless, the social consequences of such cultural rejection may be racist and controlling, given their potential to perpetuate a racialized social pecking order.

Ethnocentrism

Ethnocentrism can be defined as a belief in the superiority of one's own culture compared with others. It involves the all too common tendency to interpret the world from the perspective of one culture rather than another, and to assume that others will do so as well. It also represents an uncompromising loyalty to and belief in one's own cultural values and practices as natural, normal, and necessary. Other values and practices are implicitly dismissed as inferior or irrelevant. There is nothing intrinsically wrong with endorsing a cultural lifestyle as self-evident and preferable. Difficulties arise when these standards are used as a frame of reference for negatively evaluating others as backward, immoral, or irrational in contexts where power differences prevail. Further problems appear when these ethnocentric judgments are manipulated to condone the mistreatment of others. In other words, ethnocentrism is a two-edged social phenomenon: Favouritism toward one's group may forge the bonds of cohesion and morale; it can also foster intergroup tension and hostility.

Stereotyping

Ethnocentrism often leads to a proliferation of stereotypes about out-group members. *Stereotypes* are essentially generalizations about others, both unwarranted and unfounded on the basis of available evidence. Stereotyping reinforces a universal tendency to reduce a complex phenomenon to simple (or simplistic) explanations that are generalized to a whole category without acknowledging individual differences. It also reflects a belief that all individuals within a certain category will act in a similar way because they are assigned certain attributes on the basis of this membership (Essed 1991). Like ethnocentrism, stereotypes in themselves are harmless. Problems arise when these preconceived mental images give way to discriminatory practices. The dispossession of aboriginal peoples from their lands was facilitated by circulation of negative images of aboriginal peoples as savages, cannibals, and brutes (McKenna 1994). A pervasive antiorientalism in British Columbia fostered hatred against Asian populations, thereby simplifying the task of expelling 22,000 Japanese-Canadians from the West Coast in 1942. And hostility toward Arab/Muslim-Canadians continues to fester in light of demeaning, even belligerent, stereotypes that portray Arab-Canadians as (a) a Third World visible minority, (b) colonized peoples without democratic traditions, and (c) proterrorist religious fanatics that are resolutely anti-Western (Siddiqui 1998; Said 1997).

All negative stereotypes are hurtful; nevertheless, not all negative portrayals have an equivalent degree of impact (Stamm 1993). Context and consequence are crucial variables in shaping different outcomes. For example, members of a dominant group need not be unduly concerned with negative stereotyping about themselves; after all, as a group, they have control over a wide range of representations that flatter or empower. Even a constant barrage of negative images can be absorbed without harm or damage. Stereotypes might make white men uncomfortable, yet many possess the resources to resist or neutralize them. Power and privilege provide a protective layer. For minorities, however, stereotyping is a problem. Each negative image or unflattering representation reinforces their peripheral position within an unequal society.

Mainstream media are a major source of stereotyping. Stereotypes abound in advertising, news casting, TV programming, and filmmaking, in part because of prejudicial attitudes and discriminatory practices. Minorities are portrayed in unidimensional terms such as in comics, as athletes, victims, vixens, and as violent. These images, in turn, can be employed to justify daily violence or structural oppression through the negative effects of a "chilly climate" (Ford 1994). Ethnic jokes are a problem too. Ethnic jokes often portray minorities in a demeaning way, not out of intentional malice, but because such humour by definition is simplistic and prone to exaggeration. The consequences, while unintended, are damaging in unequal contexts. In short, stereotypes are not an error in perception, at least no more so than prejudice is a case of mistaken identity. More accurately, stereotyping is yet another expression of *social control* in preserving the prevailing distribution of power and resources (Stamm 1993).

Discrimination

Prejudice refers to attitudes and beliefs; by contrast, *discrimination* consists of the process by which these prejudgments are put into practice. The term "discrimination" can be employed in different ways. Nonevaluative meanings indicate a capacity to distinguish (for example, a colourblind person may not "discriminate" between blue and green). Evaluative meanings of discrimination can be used positively ("a discriminating palate") or negatively ("a differential treatment"), depending on whether the distinction is appropriate or legitimate. Section 15 of the Canadian Charter of Rights and Freedoms may prohibit discrimination on the basis of race, ethnicity, or origins, yet concedes the necessity for "discriminatory" measures such as employment equity to assist historically disadvantaged minorities to compete on a level playing field. D'Souza (1995) refers to discrimination that is positive when taking evasive action or making a sound judgment on the basis of statistical patterns of behaviour, even if these group generalizations are unfair and reflect badly on targeted group members. Other uses of nondiscriminatory distinctions can be applied to private clubs and in insurance companies, which take into account age and gender in determining levels of benefits or payouts (Schnauer 1997). In brief, some forms of discrimination are inevitable and acceptable—even essential—to the functioning of a complex and democratic society (MacQueen 1994).

Discrimination within the context of unequal relations entails a process of denial and exclusion. It involves the differential treatment of minority groups because of irrelevant characteristics such as skin colour and language preference rather than ability or merit. Individuals are lumped together as members of a devalued group rather than valued as individuals with skills and talents. Intrinsic to all types of discrimination are the realities of *power:* Those with access to institutional power possess the capacity to put prejudice into practice in a way that denies, excludes, or controls. This discrimination may be open and blatant; it may also be covert, thus prompting companies to see whether there is anything in their hiring or promotional procedures that may unintentionally result in the exclusion of otherwise qualified applicants. In some cases, indirect discrimination happens when the outcomes of rules or procedures that apply equally to everybody have the unintended effect of undermining some group's access to benefits or opportunities. Combining these dimensions produces a workable definition: *Discrimination can be defined as any act, whether deliberate or not, that has the intent or the effect of adversely affecting ("denying" or "excluding") others on grounds other than merit or ability.*

What, then, is the relationship of prejudice to discrimination? Although discrimination is often paired as the behavioural counterpart of prejudice, such a distinction or relationship is not as clear-cut as appearances may suggest. Discrimination can exist without prejudice; conversely, prejudice may flourish without its expression in discrimination. Prejudice and discrimination are analytically distinct concepts that can vary independently under certain conditions; that is, an individual can be prejudiced, yet may not act in a discriminatory manner for a variety of reasons (see LaPiere 1934).

Question Box
Prejudice Versus Discrimination?

Do prejudicial attitudes lead to discriminatory behaviour? Social scientists have long pondered the nature of the link between prejudicial attitudes and discriminatory behaviour. One of the earliest studies in this area was conducted by Richard LaPiere and a Chinese couple who travelled throughout the United States during the early 1930s. The pervasive anti-Oriental (Asian) prejudice at the time led LaPiere to assume that his companions would be refused service in most hotels and restaurants they frequented. On the contrary, only one establishment of over 200 refused service to LaPiere and his friends. Several months later LaPiere sent a letter to all the venues they had visited earlier. In the letter he asked if they would accept members of the Chinese race as guests in their establishment. An overwhelming number of establishments (92 percent) that earlier had accepted Chinese guests replied in the negative.

This study was held as proof that there was a poor correlation between attitudes (as manifest in verbal responses) and overt behaviour. People may be prejudiced, but will not necessarily act out these prejudices for a variety of self-serving reasons. But a certain amount of caution is necessary before jumping to conclusions from LaPiere's experiment. For example, no one could determine if the same individuals who provided services responded to the requests for reservations. Did the presence of a white person defuse a potentially discriminatory situation, whereas the letter only mentioned the needs of a Chinese couple? For these and related reasons, we must conclude that a correlation between prejudicial attitudes and discriminatory behaviour is tenuous at best. It is governed instead by a variety of situational cues and opportunity structures. We must also recognize that the equation of racism with prejudice + discrimination is subject to diverse conditions.

In short, prejudice may be divorced from discrimination. Fear, threats, sanctions, company policy, or good sense may encourage individuals to compartmentalize their prejudice from everyday action. By way of contrast, discrimination can prevail in many domains where willful malice is absent. Those who persist in applying similar rules in unequal contexts may have the effect of inadvertently but systemically perpetuating discrimination and inequality. What is critical in defining discrimination is the *context* in which the actions occur and the *consequences* of these actions in unequal situations. This is especially true in situations involving institutional or organizational settings. Here, negative treatment toward out-groups is deeply embedded within formal structures and rules, often beyond the consciousness or personalities of those who occupy organizational offices. Thus institutions can operate on racist principles even if the individuals themselves are free of prejudice. This notion of systemic bias will be explored shortly.

Harassment

Harassment is commonly appraised as a type of discrimination. Racial harassment consists of persistent and unwelcome actions of a racially oriented nature by those who ought reasonably to know that such attention is unwanted (University of Western Ontario 1993). In the words of Monique Shebbeare (McGill 1994:6), harassment involves:

> [t]he abusive, unfair, or demeaning treatment of a person or group of persons that has the effect or purpose of unreasonably interfering with a person's or group's status or performance or creating a hostile or intimidating working or educational environment....

As is the case with discrimination, harassment constitutes an abuse of power that need not be explicitly directed at a specific target. Seemingly minor and isolated incidents may amount to harassment when viewed over time or in context. The creation of a chilly climate or "poisoned environment" because of harassment can also have an adverse effect on work, study, involvement, or well-being (Waterloo 1994). Others disagree: A distinction is posited between harassment and causing offence. Harassment should be restricted to speech or behaviour that targets a particular individual or group in a way that inhibits that person (those persons) from full and equal participation within the institutions. Merely offending someone because of random ethnic jokes or thoughtless racist remarks should not be considered harassment (Stockholder 1997). In both cases, harassment is ultimately defined from the perspective of the victim who determines what the acceptable boundaries are and what distinguishes offence from harassment, consensual conduct from an abuse of power.

To Sum Up   Racism has been defined by some as a combination of prejudice with power and discrimination. To some extent the equation racism = prejudice + discrimination + power has some merit. Racism consists of a complex interplay of ideas and actions, involving an admixture of prejudice (stereotyping and ethnocentrism) and discrimination (harassment). It also encompasses an ideology with a patterned set of responses. These responses combine to explain, justify, rationalize, and legitimize the unequal treatment of minorities through political exclusion, economic exploitation, or social segregation. The key element in this equation is power. When combined with power, the interplay of prejudice and discrimination creates fertile grounds for racism to thrive. The many faces of racism are illustrated in the next Insight Box.

INSIGHT 3–1   **Rethinking the Faces of Anti-Semitism in Canada**

Racism has many faces. These different faces may be analytically separated for analysis but often coexist over time or at a given point in time. This Insight Box on anti-Semitism in Canada exposes the changing face of racism in response to historical and social circumstances.

As one might expect of a country peopled by numerous European immigrants, Canada has historically endorsed racist attitudes toward the Jews. This anti-Semitism has assumed many faces, ranging from violence and outright discrimination in the past to more indirect expressions at present which are no less powerful in their impact. How does anti-Semitism express itself in a society that collectively takes pride in its tolerant and nondiscriminatory ideals?

Open Season

Intolerance and bigotry toward Jews were openly tolerated in the prewar era (Abella 1989). This estrangement between Jews and non-Jews was displayed in numerous ways. One of Canada's best-documented race riots exploded in Toronto in August 1933, when the Swastika Club confronted a group of Jews at a baseball game in Christie Pits field, with a dozen injuries in the fracas. Refusal by Canadian authorities in 1939 to accept 900 German-Jewish refugees who arrived by boat after rejection in Latin American and American ports of call reflected the depth of hostility. These refugees had no choice but to return to Nazi Germany, where many were subsequently forced into concentration camps (Abella and Troper 1991). In other areas Jews were routinely excluded from employment in banks, insurance companies, and department stores. Jewish professors, judges, doctors, engineers, and architects found it nearly impossible to get work. Universities imposed limits on the number of Jewish students who could enroll (Abella 1989). Signs were erected barring Jews (and dogs) from access to Toronto's Lake Ontario beaches, while the Metropolitan Toronto Police posted window signs discouraging Jews and Catholics from applying.

Softening the Stance

Anti-Semitism persists in contemporary contexts. Modern anti-Semitism is more varied than in the past. In some cases, anti-Semitic feelings are invoked through racist slurs, vandalism, or acts of harassment. Incidents involving the defacing of Jewish synagogues with Nazi graffiti in Toronto and Vancouver have shown a marked increase in recent years as documented by the B'nai Brith League. The destruction of property is thought to be the work of red-necked racists, some of whom are steeped in white supremacist ideologies. The fact that 212 cases of anti-Semitism were reported by B'nai Brith in 1997 serves as a reminder that Jews are not entirely acceptable in some sectors of Canadian society.

Blatant expressions of anti-Semitism are no longer tolerated in Canada, although prejudicial attitudes appear deeply embedded in Canadian society. Nearly 50 percent of all Canadians once harboured anti-Semitic prejudice prior to World War II; this figure has dwindled to about 10 percent at present. Discrimination that denied Jews access to housing, employment, education, and club membership is currently illegal under the Canadian Charter of Rights and Freedoms and various human rights codes. But anti-Semitism has not disappeared: What we have instead of open bigotry are increasingly "polite" forms of racism involving the circulation of dogmas and propaganda that perpetuate demeaning images of Jews. Contemporary expressions of anti-Semitism dwell on attempts to deny the Holocaust (Farber 1997). Holocaust-denial theories camouflage anti-Semitism by rejecting the historical fact of Nazi concentration camps in which millions of Jews were incarcerated and slaughtered. Two of the major proponents of this theory, Ernst Zundel, a Toronto publisher, and James Keegstra, an Alberta teacher, have been charged with acts against the Criminal Code for willfully distributing hate propaganda. Allegations continue to circulate about Zionist conspiracies to assert worldwide domination in the fields of business and government. To avoid detection and criticism, anti-Semites are increasingly turning to the Internet as a basis of operation, including the 600 sites in the United States, up from only one in 1991, according to the American-based Simon Weisenthal Centre. Online anti-Semitism allows these fringe groups to situate themselves within the mainstream by appealing to disenchanted youth.

Toward a New Reality

Anti-Semitism represents one of the oldest forms of bigotry and discrimination in recorded human history. Its persistence and pervasiveness have been difficult to account for, especially since anti-Semites have scrambled about for different ways to hate Jews (Farber 1997). Generally speaking, the subtle and more sophisticated forms of anti-Semitism are more common, although explicit provocation and malicious destruction remain in effect. According to Irving Abella, Chair of the Board of Governors of the Canadian Jewish Congress, the old anti-Semitism was social and discriminatory (racism as biology); the new anti-Semitism rests on the belief that Jews have too much power and influence in proportion to their numbers (racism as culture). Affixing the modifier "polite" is not intended to trivialize the impact of racism on the Jewish population. On the contrary, these polite and more sophisticated expressions of racism are just as devastating as the old red-necked variety. After all, both the Holocaust-denial and Jewish-conspiracy theories deny to Jews their collective memory about suffering in the past.They also libel Jews by repeating lies about their collective ambitions in society.

TYPES OF RACISM

Racism is not a uniform concept that reflects a singular experience or common reality. On the contrary, different modes of racism can be discerned which embody variations in intent, levels of awareness, magnitude and scope, styles of expression, depth of intensity, and consequences. These variations have led to the proliferation of diverse types of racism, including (a) *interpersonal* (including red-necked and polite), (b) *institutional* (including systematic and systemic) and (c) *societal* (including everyday and cultural). Comparing and contrasting these admittedly ideal types will reveal the complex and multidimensional nature of racism as theory and practice. The existence of different racisms should also point the way for diverse solutions if we are serious about purging racism from our midst.

TABLE 3.1	Types of Racism	
Interpersonal	**Institutional**	**Societal**
Red-necked	Systematic	Everyday
Polite	Systemic	Cultural

Interpersonal Racism

Interpersonal racism entails a pattern of interaction that occurs primarily between individuals. It reflects a degree of dislike that is directed at another because of who they are or what they stand for. Two types of interpersonal racism can be discerned: red-necked and polite.

Red-Necked Racism

Red-necked racism is the kind of racism that most of us think of when asked to comment on the topic. It refers to the kind of old-fashioned racism that prevailed in the past and continues to exist in the present among a handful of the reactionary or defiant. Intrinsic to red-necked racism is the explicit, highly personalized character of its expression. Whether through physical or verbal abuse, red-necked racism consists of highly personal attacks on others who are perceived as culturally or biologically inferior. These personalized attacks often consist of derogatory slurs and minority name calling. Red-necked racists are rarely intimidated by labels of racism. Unlike many Canadians who cringe at the prospect of being labelled racist, many take considerable pride in—even boast about—such a label.

Even a cursory glance over Canada's past will reveal the tenacity of red-necked racism (Walker 1997). This may come as a shock to many readers. References to the United States as a hotbed of red-necked racism comes as no surprise to most (King 1994). A country with historical claims to slavery and convulsive urban riots is easy to isolate as a bastion of racism. But surely not in Canada, with its espousal of multiculturalism and human rights? Certain myths are deeply entrenched in our collective memories, especially those that extol Canada's progressive outlooks. Foremost is the absence of American-style race riots, the lack of racist symbols, the omission of prolonged slavery, and the entrenchment of multicultural philosophies within Canadian society. How accurate are these perceptions? Are Canadians really superior to Americans when it comes to the treatment of racial minorities? Close scrutiny suggests no. Our treatment of racial, aboriginal, and ethnic minorities since Confederation has left much to be desired. The Chinese, Japanese, Indo-Pakistanis, First Nations, Jews, and blacks have been and continue to be the object of intense racism. Laws and practices were invoked that segregated people of colour, especially blacks, from full and equal participation in Canadian societies until the 1950s and 1960s (Walker 1997). Racist groups such as the Ku Klux Klan have also relied on red-necked violence to cultivate an environment of fear and hatred against minorities throughout the United States and Canada (Barrett 1987).

Stark reminders of red-necked racism in Canada are readily available. Racial violence in recent years has been perpetuated by white supremacist groups ranging from the White Aryan Nation and Western Guard movements to neo-Nazi skinheads in urban areas (Kinsella 1994; Barkun 1994). Perhaps only 1,500 hard-core supremacists operate in Canada, but these extremists have the potential to destabilize a society where prejudice is pervasive (McKenna 1994; Howard 1998). The beating death of a sixty-five-year-old Sikh temple employee in Surrey, BC, in mid-1998 by four skinheads prompted calls to label Vancouver as Canada's racism capital (Wood 1998). These groups are committed to an ideology of racial supremacy in which the white "race" is seen as superior to other races on the basis of physical and cultural characteristics. They are also prepared to transform society along white supremacist lines by seeking out converts to their racist cause (Li 1995). The popularity and potential of white supremacist groups are difficult to gauge. Many supremacists may see themselves as white Christians, fusing race and religion in a single nationalist crusade against the forces of "evil" (Jaret 1995). Hate groups sustain their credibility and legitimacy by capitalizing on a poor economy and social instability. Disaffected youth are an obvious target because of perceived government indifference to their plight in a changing and diverse world. Demographic imbalances resulting from immigration are likely to ignite supremacist ire, as is the perception that certain minorities have hijacked government and business for self-serving purposes. White hate groups have infiltrated the social fabric of Canadian society in different ways, but primarily through telephone hotlines, the Internet, and disinformation campaigns by hate mongers recruited by the movement (see Kinsella 1994). The combination of music, pamphlets, and the Internet concocts a poisonous but appealing mishmash of neo-Nazi philosophies, KKK folklore, pseudo-Nordic mythology, and antigovernment slogans (Wood 1998). To be sure, the courts in Canada have defined these diatribes as "hate propaganda" and a violation of Canada's criminal code. Technicalities, however, have often overturned such verdicts.

Polite Racism

Few people at present will tolerate the open expression of racism. At one time, institutionalized racism was socially and politically acceptable: There was no need for pretence—everything was up-front and openly visible (Griffin 1996). But the risk of social or legal consequences, not to mention the potential for physical retaliation, serves as an inhibitor nowadays. The passage of constitutional guarantees such as the Canadian Charter of Rights and Freedoms and human rights codes has eroded the legitimacy of red-necked racism from public discourse. But while blatant forms of racism have dissipated to some extent, less candid expressions of bigotry and stereotyping remain in force. Instead of disappearing in the face of social reprisals and legal sanctions as might have been expected, racism is increasingly couched in a way that allows people to talk around or disguise their criticism of others by using somewhat more muted (polite) tones.

Polite racism, then, can be seen as a contrived attempt to disguise a dislike of others through behaviour that outwardly is nonprejudicial in appearance. It often manifests itself in the use of coded or euphemistic language ("those people") to mask inner feelings and attitudes (Blauner 1994). In contrast with the open bigotry of the past, racist attitudes are increasingly ambivalent or contradictory and often coded in a way that invokes racism by those looking for a racist message but also rendered deniable and difficult to prove as racist (Wetherell and Potter 1993). This politeness is especially evident when people of colour are ignored or turned down for jobs, promotions, or accommodation (Henry and Ginzberg 1993). For example, an employer may claim a job is filled rather than admit "no blacks need apply" when approached by an undesirable applicant. Or consider how a general principle may be invoked to deny the legitimacy of a specific instance as when refugees are criticized for "jumping the queue." Polite racism may appear more sophisticated than its red-necked equivalent; nevertheless, the effect on victims is similar: It serves to sustain prevailing relationships of control, exclusion, or exploitation.

Canadian racism is often depicted as polite and subdued. Racism in Canada is rarely perpetuated by raving lunatics who engage in beatings, lynchings, or graffiti. Rather, racism among Canadians is unobtrusive, often implicit and couched in political correctness or higher ideals ("everyone should be equal before the law"). Derogatory references about minorities continue to be expressed, but they are usually restricted to remarks in private or to friends. An increasingly educated population has fastened on to the principle of polite racism. With higher education, individuals become more adept at compartmentalizing and concealing racist attitudes, lest they blurt out statements at odds with career plans or a sophisticated self-image (Fleras 1996). This subtlety makes it difficult to confront, let along eradicate, the expression of polite racism.

Institutional Racism

Much of the discussion to this point has dwelt on racism as an individual attribute. Other types of racism go beyond the interpersonal in terms of scope, style, and impact. Racism at the institutional level represents such a shift in expression. *Institutional racism* refers to the process by which organizational practices and procedures are used either deliberately or inadvertently to discriminate against "others." By institutional racism, we are not simply referring to individual acts of racism within the confines of an institution or workplace. Rather, we are referring to the rules, procedures, rewards, and practices that have the intent (systematic) or effect (systemic) of excluding or denying some because of who they are, how they live, and what they do.

Systematic Racism

Systematic racism involve rules and procedures that directly and deliberately prevent minorities from full and equal involvement within society. This institutionalized racism appears when discriminatory practices are legally sanctioned by the state and formalized within its institutional framework, thus reflecting the values and practices of the dominant sector. It consists of norms and corresponding activities that are embedded within the design (structure and function) of the organization to preclude minority entry or participation.

Systematic institutional racism flourished in societies that endorsed racial segregation. The regime of apartheid in South Africa was a classic example, as was pre-Civil Rights United States. Nor was Canada exempt from the tarnish of institutionally racist practices (Reitz and Breton 1994). Institutional racism was once a chronic and inescapable component of Canadian society (Walker 1997). Minorities were routinely barred from even partial participation in mainstream institutions. Predictably, they were subjected to verbal and physical harassment without much chance of recourse or retribution. This racism ranged from the slavery of blacks in Nova Scotia in the pre-Confederation era (Walker 1985) to the disenfranchisement of Japanese-Canadians in British Columbia until 1949 (Sunahara 1981) and the differential admissions policy for Jewish students in Montreal at McGill University during the 1940s. African-Canadians were routinely excluded from entry into theatres and restaurants until these odious distinctions were rescinded in the 1950s (Walker 1989).

Evidence now suggests that minorities are unlikely to be directly victimized by blatant institutional racism. Openly racist platforms find little public acceptance or political support in Canada (Adam 1992). This injunction applies across the board, from institutions to interpersonal relations. Institutions can no longer openly discriminate against minorities, lest they attract negative publicity or incite consumer resistance. Nevertheless, institutional racism continues to exist. It can incorporate various discriminatory actions, from red-necked to polite, all of which are tacitly endorsed by the corporate culture. It can take the form of harassment from supervisors or co-workers—often defended as unintentional or harmless— by way of ethnic jokes, racial graffiti, and racist cartoons, with excuses such as "just a joke," "where's your sense of humour," "didn't mean anything by it," or "it's just the way guys talk" (see Henry 1997). Or systematic racism refers to the way in which organizations deliberately manipulate rules or procedures to deny minority access or participation. The revelation that both Denny's Restaurant chain (USA) and Texaco went out of their way to discriminate against African-Americans provides proof that the more things change, the more they stay the same (also Watkins 1997).

Systemic Racism

There is another type of institutional racism that comes across as impersonal and unconscious. Its unobtrusive and implicit character makes it that much more difficult to detect, much less to isolate and combat. *Systemic racism* is the name given to this subtle yet powerful form of discrimination within the institutional framework of society. It is entrenched within the structure (rules, organization), function (norms, goals), and process (procedures) of social institutions. The standards and expectations inherent within these organizations may be universal and ostensibly colourblind. But they have the unintended but real effect of excluding those outside the mainstream. In other words, the normal operations of an institution will lead to racist results and white privilege.

With **systemic racism**, it is not the intent or motive that counts, but rather the *context* and the *consequences*. Policies, rules, priorities, and programs may not be inherently racist or deliberately discriminatory; that is, institutions do not go out of their way to exclude or deprive minorities. However, rules that are evenly applied may have a discriminatory effect in that they exclude certain groups while conferring advantage to others. Minority experiences and needs are ignored under the guise of formal equality. Minority women and men have no choice but to work in organizational settings that are not of their making, thus creating a poor fit between institutional structures and minority realities. In brief, we can define systemic racism as the adverse yet unintended consequences that result from applying seemingly neutral rules to unequal contexts, but with dissimilar effects on identifiable minorities.

Systemic racism is defined by its consequences. It rests on the belief that institutional rules and procedures can be racist in practice, even if the actors are themselves free of prejudicial discrimination. Institutions are systemically racist when they ignore how organizational practices and structures reflect and reinforce white experiences as normal and necessary. These institutional barriers to minority success are unintentional but hidden in institutional reward systems that penalize some individuals because of who they are, not what they can do. Here, systemic racism is rarely identified as such by those who benefit from such arrangements. Embedded within institutional rules and procedures, systemic racism remains (a) beyond our everyday consciousness, (b) undetected and disguised by universal standards and rhetoric to the contrary, (c) taken for granted, and (d) powerful. Minority opportunities are restricted and constrained by the rigid application of rules and refusal to rethink procedures.

A few examples will demonstrate how the implicit bias of a system designed by the mainstream can create unintended yet negative effects on minority women and men. For years, a number of occupations, for example, the police, firefighters, and mass transit drivers, retained minimum weight, height, and educational requirements for job applicants. In retrospect, we can interpret these criteria as systemically discriminatory because they favoured males over females and white applicants over people of colour. Valid reasons may have existed to justify these restrictions; nevertheless, the imposition of these qualifications imposed a set of unfair entry restrictions, regardless of intent or rationale. No deliberate attempt is made to exclude anyone since standards are uniformly applied. But these criteria have the net effect of excluding certain groups who lack these requirements for entry or promotion. Other examples of systemic racism may include an insistence on Canadian-only experience, the devaluation of minority experiences and credentials, unnecessarily high educational standards for entry into certain occupations, and other demanding qualifications that discourage membership into professional bodies.

Systemic racism can be illustrated in other ways. Minorities have long complained about media mistreatment. For the most part minorities are ignored or rendered irrelevant by mainstream presses (Kunz and Fleras 1998). When reported on, they are portrayed as a social problem (a state for which they are ultimately responsible) or as having problems in need of costly solutions. Some minority groups are depicted as volatile, prone to mindless violence, and having minimal regard for human life. While such violence does occur, the absence of balanced coverage results in a single and distorted image of that minority group. In some ways, the misrepresentation stems from the media's preoccupation with readership, audience ratings, and advertising revenues. To satisfy audience and sponsorship needs, mainstream media will usually focus on minorities only in situations of crisis, conflict, or catastrophe involving natural or human disaster. Otherwise, they are ignored as non-newsworthy. The media may not be aware of such discriminatory effects in this area, arguing they are only reporting the news. The net result, however, is an unflattering picture of minorities that distorts reality and people's perception under the guise of information or entertainment (Fleras 1993; 1995).

In short, rules and priorities that may seem neutral on the surface are not even-handed in terms of who gets what. This hidden agenda imposes certain handicaps on those who are inadequately prepared to cope with organizational demands and routines. Well-meaning people may have drawn up the policies, and the policies may have been administered by caring and concerned employees. The architects and employees typically defend their actions as even-handed. They may be well-intentioned individuals adhering to guidelines which they feel are universal, justified, and fiscally responsible. Nevertheless, the logical consequences of these actions are systemically discriminatory because of misconceptions that underpin these initiatives.

Societal Racism

Societal racism constitutes that level of racism that pervades the general functioning of society. It consists of interactional patterns, often without people being consciously aware of how their actions may inadvertently perpetuate a racialized social order. We make a distinction between the everyday and the cultural: Everyday racism consists of unconscious speech habits that have the effect of denying or excluding; cultural racism reflects ambiguities in our value system, whose resolution has the effect of reinforcing a racialized social order.

Everyday Racism

Contemporary racism is no longer expressed in direct aggression but in more culturally acceptable ways that achieve the same effect without attracting negative attention (Sirna 1998). Certain ideas and ideals are widely circulated that explicitly or implicitly assert the superiority of some people at the expense of others. The internalization of these racist ideas and ideals is called *everyday racism*. It entails racist practices that infiltrate everyday life and become part of what is accepted as normal by the dominant group (Essed 1991). The mechanisms of **everyday racism** are well established. Individuals interact with each other in a way that tolerates and reinforces racism, sometimes explicitly, other times in an implicit or oblique manner. As a process and social practice, racism is created and reconstructed through daily actions that are repetitive, systematic, familiar, and routine. Racist discourses are "prestructured" (Essed 1991) in a manner that constrains individual actors and everyday behaviour. This suggests that the structures and ideologies that underpin racism are produced and reproduced through a complex and cumulative interplay of attitudes (prejudice) and practices (discrimination). This combination (a) is diverse in manifestation but unified through constant repetition; (b) permeates daily life to the extent that it is viewed as normal or inevitable; and (c) implies the notion that the potential for racism exists in all of us, rather than reflecting a division of society into racists and nonracists.

The role of language in perpetuating everyday racism is widely recognized (Essed 1991; Wetherell and Potter 1993; Blauner 1994). Nevertheless, many continue to underestimate the potential of language in shaping thought and action. Language is perceived as a kind of postal or courier system, that is, a neutral system of conveyance between sender and receiver for the transmission of messages created independently through a process called thinking. In reality, language is inextricably linked with the social construction of reality. Language is intimately bound up with our experiences of the world and our efforts to convey that experience to others. Ideas and ideals are "trapped inside" language, with a corresponding impact on patterns of thought and behaviour. Language can be employed to control, conceal, evade issues, draw attention, or dictate agendas about what gets said. Words are not neutral; rather, they have the capacity to hinder or harm when carelessly employed. Words also have a political dimension: They convey messages above and beyond what is intended. Inferences can be (and are) drawn about who you are and where you stand in the competition for who gets what and why. Language, in short, represents an ideal vehicle for expressing intolerance by highlighting differences or sanctioning inequality through invisible yet real boundaries (Sirna 1998).

Language may be used to degrade or ridicule minorities by way of obvious bigotry ("niggers"), colour symbolism (black = bad), loaded terms ("Indian massacres"), and seemingly neutral phrases that are infused with hidden anxieties ("waves of immigrants"). The association of "blackness" with negativity illustrates how certain values are embedded in our everyday speech. Daily speech patterns provide an example of racism as everyday and interactive. Words are a powerful way of conveying negative images and associations. For this reason and others, some Canadians of African ancestry prefer to be called "African-Canadians" rather than "blacks." To be sure, the racism implicit in words and metaphors may not be intended or deliberate. Nor will the occasional use of such loaded terms explode into full-blown racism. Moreover, it is inaccurate to say that language determines our reality; more precisely, it provides a cultural frame of reference for defining what is desirable and important. In other words, perils await those who trivialize the impact of language in perpetuating racism through its cumulative and quiet effect.

Cultural Racism

Cultural racism suggests the existence of cultural values that reinforce the interests of the dominant sector at the expense of the subdominant. These values may be specific in terms of openly compromising the right of minority women and men to equal treatment. Alternatively, they may indirectly endorse dominant value orientations by privileging them as necessary and normal while dismissing others as irrelevant or defective, and the prime cause of minority failures. Cultural racism reflects the outcome of conflict between liberal plural values of universality and the demands of minorities to be different (Wetherell and Potter 1993). Consider the primacy of liberal pluralism in Canadian and American society: Foremost is a belief that what we have in common is much more important than differences; that what we do and accomplish are more important than who we are; and the content of our character is more important than the colour of our skin. Compare this universalism with the particularism of ethnic nationalisms with their focus on difference as pivotal in sorting who gets what. A third expression of cultural racism reflects a certain degree of ambiguity implicit in contemporary cultural values. The "subliminality" of this racism denounces the explicitness of old-fashioned racism yet reinforces racial inequality, however inadvertently, through muted criticism of minority actions that are perceived as too much, too fast, too assertive, or too unorthodox. Perpetrators may be oblivious to their participation in perpetuating patterns of inequality. Still, the net effect is the same, that is, minority groups are cast as troublemakers or problem people, whose interests or means are unacceptable in liberal-democratic societies.

This ambivalence in cultural values may be called subliminal racism (alternatively, "democratic racism" [Henry and Tator 1994]; "nonracist racism" [Elliott and Fleras 1991]; or "aversive racism" [Katz et al. 1986]). It tends to locate conflict and contradictions within the psychological complex of a person's emotional and cognitive makeup (Wetherell and Potter 1993). **Subliminal cultural racism** is found among that class of person who abhors openly discriminatory treatment of minorities. Yet these same individuals are incapable of escaping the cultural or cognitive influences that may encourage a dislike of others because of what they do. Even many of those who profess egalitarian attitudes and a commitment to racial equality are unwilling—or incapable—of realizing the contradiction. The subliminality of cultural racism appears to reflect an inescapable dichotomy in our core values. On the one hand, we place a premium on the public good, with its emphasis on collective rights, special treatment, equality of outcomes, and fair play. On the other, there remains a powerful commitment to competitive individualism, with its focus on personal freedom, self-reliance, meritocracy, and competition. This dichotomous orientation enables individuals to maintain two apparently conflicting values: one rooted in the egalitarian virtues of justice and fairness; the other in beliefs that everyone should play by the same rules in an open competition. Yet those very values that promote a democratic right to compete may be revoked if minorities compete too vigorously or successfully (Henry et al. 1995). These aversive feelings are not about outright hostility or hate, but entail discomfort or unease, often leading to patterns of avoidance rather than intentionally destructive behaviour.

How does subliminal cultural racism work? Evidence suggests that Canadians as a whole are receptive toward the principles of multiculturalism and racial equality (Berry and Kalin 1993). Many Canadians express sympathy for the plight of those less fortunate than themselves; for example, immigrants are frequently portrayed as industrious contributors to Canadian well-being. Yet negative and prejudicial attitudes continue to distort our assessment and treatment of the foreign-born. Minorities are acceptable as long as they know their place and act like the mainstream wants them to. Minority demands that fall outside conventional channels are criticized as a threat to national identity or social harmony (Gaertner and Dovidio 1986). People of colour are chided for making too many complaints or demands or for not taking advantage of the opportunities open to them. Government initiatives to protect and promote diversity are acceptable as long as they don't cost money or impose burdens in terms of sharing power or cultural space. Affirmative or preferential action programs for historically disadvantaged minorities are disparaged as unfair to the majority. Minority espousal of genuine cultural differences is criticized for being too different, especially if these interfere with the rights of individuals, violate the law of the land, or undermine core Canadian values or institutions.

How, then, do we explain this ambiguity in cultural values toward minorities in Canada? Cynics would argue that Canadians are hypocrites whose deep-seated racism is camouflaged by platitudinous pieties. Opposition to multiculturalism or immigration by way of coded or euphemistic expressions is perceived as more acceptable than open expressions of intolerance (Palmer 1996). We agree to some extent, but concede subliminal racism to be different from polite racism. What we have instead is a style of out-group hostility that goes undetected by conventional measures (Katz et al. 1986). Subliminal racism is not directly expressed but embodied in "lofty" opposition to progressive minority policies and programs. The opposition is coded in terms that politely skirt the issue and that rationalize criticism of minorities on grounds of mainstream values, national interests, or appeals to a higher sense of fair play, equality, and justice. For example, refugee claimants are not condemned in blunt racist terminology; their landed entry into Canada is criticized on procedural grounds ("jumping the queue"). Or they are belittled for taking unfair advantage of Canada's generosity or ability to shoulder processing costs. Other examples such as the decision by the RCMP to accommodate the mandatory turban worn by religious Sikh males are denounced as un-Canadian, an affront to majority values, illegitimate, excessively demanding, too costly, unacceptably rapid, or outside due process (See and Wilson 1988).

Clearly, then, a degree of cultural ambiguity is apparent. Individuals may endorse inclusiveness as a matter of principle, yet disapprove of policy implications (the "costs") or minority assertiveness (Essed 1991). Values that endorse racial equality are publicly reaffirmed; nevertheless, there is deep-seated resentment at the prospect of moving over and making space for people of colour. However, the cost of doing nothing is not neutrality; to the contrary, it is a tacit acceptance of a racialized status quo. Failure to realize this mainstream inactivity in a racialized society may have the effect of affirming and supporting the very structure of racist domination and oppression that many profess to see eradicated (hooks 1995). It also raises the issue of the pervasiveness of racism in Canadian society.

| **CASE STUDY 3–2** | **Is Canada a Racist Society? It Depends...** |

Is Canada a racist society? Are Canadians racist? To what extent is racism a major problem in Canada? Answers to these questions are much more complex and problematic than many give credit. What exactly constitutes a racist society? What do we mean when Canadians are accused of being racist? On what grounds can we make a judgment one way or the other? Coming to grips with Canada as racist is not simply an intellectual parlour game, even if raising the question may seem unusual at a time when public acceptance of diversity has never been more conducive to opportunity, understanding, protection, and support (Levitt 1997). National debates over multiculturalism and employment equity would appear to be predicated on the premise that Canadian society is fundamentally racist and Canadians are racists in need of government intervention to break the cycle. How accurate are these appraisals?

Racism and Counterracism in Canada

Canada is widely regarded as a socially progressive society whose initiatives for managing race and ethnic relations are second to none. But there is growing concern that things are not what they seem to be and that racism is flourishing in Canada, albeit in ways that are less likely to conform with classic models of racist thought and practices. Recent incidents would appear to uphold this assessment of Canada as a racist society. Counterbalancing this racist image of Canada is another set of images that imply a more positive reading of Canadian society. The following table demonstrates the difficulty in labelling Canada as racist; that is, for every item of racism there is a counter-item to suggest a different spin.

Racism and Counterracism in Canada

Racism in Canada	Counterracism in Canada
Racism in High School	**Antiracism in High Schools**

Racial incidents have marred social relations at the Cole Harbour High School in Nova Scotia since 1989, when a snowball fight erupted into a brawl between black and white students. At the end of 1997, a school dance led to a racial battle that ended with assaults on two police officers and five arrests. Ten days later another fight escalated into a school-clearing brawl that led to hospitalization of four people.

Both primary and secondary schools are the site of antiracist actions designed to deter the potential for racist encounters as well as to introduce internal reforms that create a more inclusive school environment.

Toronto the Bad

Vancouver the Good/Toronto the Bad?

Canada's most multicultural city, Toronto, may be the home of 44 percent of the country's visible minority immigrant population, but it is also the most intolerant, according to a 1997 report commissioned by Canada Immigration.

A study by York University's International Social Research group (Grayson 1996) found that white Toronto was generally racially tolerant toward others, positively recognized the contributions of visible minorities such as Chinese and blacks to Canadian society, and overwhelmingly disapproved of differential treatment toward visible minorities. In the same survey that branded Toronto as the most racially intolerant city in Canada, Vancouver was deemed to be most racially open despite the large number of visible minority immigrants. Perhaps differences can be attributed to variations in the kind and sources of immigrants.

Hate Crimes: Only the Tip of the Iceberg

Hate Crimes: More Than Meets the Eye

Hate crimes are far more common in Canada than people believe, says a new study by a University of Ottawa criminologist. About 61 percent of the almost 1,000 hate crimes recorded by the police during 1993–94 were directed against visible minorities. According to the author, this figure is misleading; estimates are closer to 60,000 in the nine major cities, since only a small percentage—perhaps 10 percent—of hate crimes are ever reported to the police. Fear of reprisals may account for the discrepancy; there is also the perception that complaints won't be taken seriously by the criminal justice system. Interesting to note is that of the 8,000 hate crime incidents reported to the FBI in 1995, 61 percent were also motivated by racial bias.

It's true that some racial incidents are not reported. But accusations of underreporting should not go unchallenged since we live in an era in which people are more likely than in the past to report racially based slights—real or imagined—to proper authorities. Similarly, increased rates of racial incidents may reflect a growing awareness and willingness on the part of victims and authorities to make public what once was glossed over. For example, twenty years ago a high school scrap may have been dismissed as youthful exuberance (given that boys will be boys); in the current climate of zero tolerance, formal charges are likely to be laid, while the incident is widely publicized and framed as a racial incident. It should be noted that the number of anti-Semitic incidents in Canada has dropped from 331 in 1995 to 212 in 1997.

Cyberhate

Internet Antiracism

Authorities are increasingly worried about the use of the Internet as a source of racism against Jews and visible minorities. Unlike conventional sources that can be monitored and controlled, the Internet is largely impervious to controls, thus giving hate mongers an open hand in spreading anti-Semitic diatribes.

Just as the Internet can provide an environment for racism to flourish, so too can it furnish a lively and open forum for antiracist challenges.

Sorting Through the Issues

The items in the table would suggest that racism exists in Canada. By the same token, the counter-items portray Canada as progressive in designing initiatives to challenge and eradicate racism. The coexistence of these opposing streams reinforces the challenges of labelling Canada as a racist society. Consider some of the difficulties in making such a linkage.

First, what is meant by racism when applied to Canadian society? Racism is not a static and fixed entity, but evolving, elusive and situational. Nor is racism restricted to swastikas and burning crosses. Classic expressions of racism are disappearing, including those that equate society with (a) formally prescribed boundaries within and between institutions; (b) opportunity structures defined by inherited racial attributes; (c) codification of prejudice and discrimination into laws that openly discriminate against identifiable minorities; and (d) conscious exclusion of others from full and equal participation in activities that enhance social and material rewards (Holdaway 1996). A racist society is one in which racism is institutionalized insofar as it is (a) supported by cultural values, (b) expressed through widely accepted norms, (c) tacitly approved by the state or government, (d) intrusive in many interpersonal relations, and (e) part of normal functioning of society (Aguirre and Turner 1995). South Africa's apartheid regime may have been racist according to this set of criteria, but surely not Canada, at least not since the 1950s. But racism has become much more subtle in terms of its process and effects, in the process becoming less visible as Canada becomes more racially visible. Racism is the glass ceiling that prevents visible minorities from advancing in the workplace; racism is the difference that race makes within the criminal justice system: from charges and arrests to convictions and sen-

tencing; racism represents a resentment toward Third World immigrants under the guise of national interests; and racism consists of those tacit assumptions that bolster dominant ways of thinking or doing while cavalierly dismissing minority ways. In short, racism in Canadian society has become increasingly covert, embedded in normal operations of institutions, and beyond the direct discourse of racial terminology. Such invisibility not only complicates efforts at detection and eradication; it also detracts from any consensus over the magnitude and scope of racism in Canada.

Second, what exactly do we mean by a racist society (Fleras and Spoonley 1999)? What would a nonracist society look like? What criteria are involved in making either assertion? Who says so, why, and on what grounds? To what extent are statistics and national surveys valid measurements of racism in society? Is a racist society based on a minimum number of racial incidents per year, or should we look more closely at systemic biases that inadvertently perpetuate a racialized social order? Too much of what constitutes the charge of a racist society is based on measuring racially related incidents. But statistical measures have inherent drawbacks. Statistics cannot reveal the ratio of reported to unreported acts. In some cases, reported acts provide only a small proportion of unreported acts; and increases in the number of reported acts may reflect a decrease in the number of unreported incidents (Levitt 1997). For example, according to Levitt, The League of Human Rights for B'nai Brith Canada reports 331 anti-Semitic incidents in 1995, a 12 percent increase over 1994 and the largest number in the fourteen years of documentation. But such an increase may reflect (a) growth in antiracism awareness in school curricula, (b) greater public awareness and concern, (c) expanding media interest and reportage, and (d) more open access to grievance articulation, such as a hate crime hotline with an 800 number and an incident-reporting form that is advertised at the end of the B'nai Brith audit. Only 244 incidents were reported in 1996, a drop of 26 percent from 1995, followed by only 212 incidents in 1997, another drop of about 13 percent from 1996.

Third, what we see or say about racism may depend on where we stand in society. Many whites do not deny the existence of racism but see it as an isolated and vanishing relic by some knuckle-dragging Neanderthals from the past. Racism is perceived as an irrational aberration from the normal functioning of society. Minority women and men, by contrast, tend to see racism as a central and normal aspect of racialized society in which patterns of power and privilege are reproduced in overt and covert ways. The racism that is experienced by minorities is not the "in-your-face" gesture. More likely, expressions are those subtle remarks or the "look" that "otherize" people of colour as different and inferior and out of place in Canadian society. These discrepancies in perception can create problems when whites voice opposition to employment equity or official immigration policy. White opposition may be voiced on the grounds of a general antagonism to state intrusion, a preference for the values of personal freedom and equal opportunity, or concern over the consequences of immigration. This opposition to change or accommodation may not entail racism *per se*, but involve a complex array of attitude in which race or racism is but one dimension (Satzewich 1998). Yet white refusal to endorse equal rights or measures to produce equality of group outcomes may be perceived as racist and consistent with long-standing practices of white supremacy. This perceptual gap between whites and people of colour makes it difficult to arrive at any consensus regarding the magnitude and scope of racism in Canada, given that perceptions of racism may depend on positioning in society.

Fourth, are Canadians racists? Four criteria are employed to define a racist: (a) a belief in the existence of biologically different races; (b) ranking of these races along lines of superiority/inferiority; (c) conferral of fixed and immutable status to this hierarchy; and (d) use as a base for treating others differently because of membership in these groups (D'Souza 1995). Studies in the early to mid-1980s suggested that many Canadians may have subscribed to such negativity ("prejudice") toward minority groups (Henry and Tator 1985). There is no reason to believe the situation has changed dramatically since then, judging by the degree of public hostility directed at immigration, employment equity, and multiculturalism. But a dislike of government policies or minority initiatives is not necessarily racist, even if the unintended consequences of such a position may help to reinforce a racialized social order. In fact, critics may argue that it is supporters of special programs who are racist in treating others differently because of race, and that to be criticized for being critical of such programs is racist in its own right, since it implies that minorities are immune to criticism. Moreover, the very idea of a nonracist population or society may be an impossibility, given the range of publics that exist in society. Racism and intolerance are unavoidable since Canadians are not perfectly consistent or logical in their actions, with reactionary pockets of resistance inevitable during periods of change and diversity. A certain level of racial animosity is inevitable in liberal democratic societies, and its existence is the cost for living in a society that encourages freedom and individualism, in the same way that we must cut a certain amount of slack for a host of deviant activities if democracy is to prevail.

From Either/Or to Both/And

What can we conclude? There is little doubt that racism exists in Canada, both personally and institutionally, as well as openly and covertly, but that it is not the same as saying that Canada is a racist society. The combination of racist incidents with racist individuals is not synonymous with such a label. Just as we must never underestimate the pervasiveness of racism in sectors of society and display constant vigilance to that effect, so, too, is a degree of caution required in exaggerating the notion of Canada as a racist society. A sense of perspective is critical: Most racist incidents are instigated by a relatively small number of protagonists. The actions of a few are hardly representative of society at large and should not be manipulated as a measure by which to judge the inactions of many. Compare racism in Canada with the situation in Europe, where a European Union survey of 16,000 Europeans in 15 countries yielded staggering results: 55 percent of Belgians identified themselves as very or quite racist; 48 percent of the French, and 35 percent of British (Bates 1997). Comparable figures for Canada are much lower, often in the 5 to 15 percentage range. Nor can we blame racism or racial discrimination exclusively for problems that preclude minority equality or participation in society. A host of factors from culture and history to misguided government policy may also contribute to unequal relations (see also D'Souza 1995). In short, the criteria for labelling Canada a racist society are ambiguous and contested, and it is this very ambiguity that complicates the definitional process. Canadians may not be racists in the conventional sense of open and deliberate acts that deny or exclude. But their racism may be embodied in seemingly neutral acts of behaviour that have the effect of perpetuating a racial and Eurocentric social order. At the same time, the unanticipated consequences of institutional rules and practices—largely created by whites to normalize the preservation of power and privilege—may inadvertently have a cumulative effect of disadvantaging minorities. White experiences continue to be defined as the norm to define the acceptable. When combined with the power to put these normative expectations into practice, an arrangement is created that privileges some, disempowers others. In other words, Canada is racist in the same way that Canadian society is sexist and heterosexist: Racism is manifest in the process by which people are racialized as different and ranked in hierarchies that are used to legitimate relations of power and inequality. Racism is also manifest in the tendency to interpret and evaluate reality from a mainstream perspective as normal and necessary while dismissing other inputs as irrelevant.

Putting it into Perspective

Durkheim and Marx once said that the smallest misdemeanour in a society of saints would be sufficient to incur capital punishment (Levitt 1997). In societies where hatred toward others is the norm, even the most egregious form of racial intolerance will go unnoticed or unpunished. In a society such as Canada, where racism and racial intolerance are socially and legally unacceptable, the slightest provocation is cause for public remorse or vigorous rebuke. And it is precisely these high standards that encourage and simplify the process of labelling Canada as a racist society. The concept of a "racist society" needs to be carefully articulated: A racist society is one that systematically oppresses others by denying or excluding them on the basis of race or ethnicity. A racist society is one in which prejudice toward others is formally institutionalized as a basis for entitlement or engagement in society. Racist societies are those that do nothing to prevent the outbreak of racist incidents at individual or institutional levels and do even less to deal with these violations when they occur. By contrast, Canada possesses human rights legislation, criminal codes against racial hatred, and sentencing procedures that more severely punish hate crimes. On these grounds Canada can no longer be regarded as a racist society, as was once the case in our not-too-distant past, even if racism does exist in Canadian society. Nevertheless, Canada may be racist in the tacit assumption that mainstream values and institutions are natural, superior, and inevitable, while minority experiences and alternatives are dismissed as irrelevant or inferior. Perhaps answers to the question of whether Canada is a racist society must avoid the discursive framework of either/or (yes or no). Proposed instead is a position of both/and (yes and no), depending on the circumstances and criteria.

EXPLAINING RACISM

That racism in one form or another exists in Canada is surely beyond debate at this point in our history. With the benefit of some prodding and sharp reminders, we Canadians are increasingly facing up to our checkered past, with its bewildering mixture of tolerance and repression. Racism may be equated with a particular psychological complex of emotions, feelings, and thoughts; it also entails the symbolic, cultural, and institutional expressions of society that are systematically and systemically organized around the suppression of some, the privileging of others (Wetherell and Potter 1993). Some forms of racism are now widely condemned and detested, even by those who are indifferent toward diversity. Other varieties of racism continue to be endemic to Canada, with few signs of releasing their tenacious grip. Canada was founded on racist principles and continues to be racialized in consequence if not intent, despite a tendency toward collective denial and historical amnesia (Philip 1995; Henry et al. 1995). No less worrying is the persistence of racism, despite public policies that guarantee equal rights and full participation. The threat of social condemnation only seems to have propelled racism to go underground or redefine itself. The fact that racism "reigns" in the face of debilitating costs and destructive effects is cause for concern and raises the question of what, if anything, can be done to crush racism.

Racism does not come cheaply. It represents a blot upon Canadian society that has the capacity to squander our potential as a progressive and prosperous country. Racism costs all Canadians: To tolerate racism is to perpetuate inequality and to infringe on fundamental human rights; racism diminishes the number of people who can contribute to Canada; useless energy is expended that otherwise could be funnelled into more productive channels; institutions that cannot capitalize on a diverse workforce because of racism are destined to lose their competitive edge. Racism also adds an additional burden to minority lives (Ford 1994): Minorities live in perpetual fear of physical retaliation; the loss of personal security intensifies isolation and self-defensive behaviours; they endure a restricted set of economic and social opportunities; and many are constantly burdened by negative media messages (Thomas 1998). Exposure to racism may contribute to poor health, both physical and psychological. A few may even lash out from frustration in occasional acts of rage.

The danger of racism does not reside in creating racist attitudes where none existed before. Rather, the threat is threefold: An environment is fostered where existing prejudices are articulated, legitimized, and defended as a basis for white privilege (McKenna 1994); mixed messages are delivered, many of which contradict the ideals of a socially progressive society; the costs of racism are absorbed unevenly across society, with some capitalizing on racism as a basis for preserving privilege or power while others suffer. Awareness of racism as a costly social problem is gradually expanding. Antiracism has emerged as a powerful and direct challenge that promises to go beyond conventional measures to correct racism. However, its potential for social and cultural change invariably raises concerns about the politics of antiracism. The very act of defining something as a problem is no guarantee of a workable solution within the framework of a democratic society; that is, what, if anything, can be done to curb racism without undermining core Canadian values related to free enterprise, liberal values, freedom of speech, and tolerance for diversity? Negotiating a balance between these values is easier said than done. A more appropriate level of response may stem from the question, Why does racism continue to exist when we should know better? How do we explain its persistence in the face of government initiatives to condemn, curb, and control?

The Broader Context

Many would be inclined to dismiss racism as a relic from the past, at odds with the dynamics of a progressive contemporary society. Yet racism continues to flourish despite laws and social sanctions. How do we account for this anomaly? Is it because of societal inertia or public disinterest, with the result that racism drifts along, irrespective of its dysfunctional effects on society? Some attribute the pervasiveness of racism to our biogenetic wiring—from an evolutionary past when a fear of outsiders elicited a survival response in uncertain environments—that continues to operate in the present so that recoiling from what is different seems only natural. This visceral dislike of out-groups may explain the universality of racism.

Some like to think of racism as the byproduct of ignorance or fear of the unknown because of improper socialization. Racism will vanish with improvements in people's knowledge about differences and minorities. Others believe that racism persists because of its self-serving properties. Put bluntly, racism has a way of making the mainstream feel good about itself. Racism not only bolsters individual self-images, whether people are aware of it or not; it also has the effect of enhancing majority privilege by reducing uncertainty and imposing control. Racism, in short, provides simple but effective explanations to justify why people get what they deserve or deserve what they get. This notion of racism as "functional" for whites is captured in these words by Julian Bond, chair of the NAACP (National Association for the Advancement of Colored People), when referring to the tenacity of white supremacist racism (White 1998:25):

> It's still white supremacy. It still means so much to those who practice it. It defines who they are. It makes them feel that they are better than others. It ensures them positions in employment and college admissions they otherwise might not have. It still puts a lid on the dreams of black people....

Still others look to social institutions as the primary culprit responsible for racism. Mainstream institutions are crafted by dominant groups and either deliberately or inadvertently reflect and normalize dominant values, priorities, agendas, and practices as superior, necessary, and inevitable.

Each of these explanations of racism is accurate. But reference to racism as a function of biology or an individual is secondary to most sociological analyses. Racism does not exist solely in the minds of demented individuals; nor is it an error of perception or belief. The roots of racism go beyond the conduct of aberrant individuals even if individuals are the carriers and targets of hatred. The root problems of racism are similar to the root causes of other social problems; only when racism is addressed accordingly is there much likelihood of positive change. Racism persists because of its location within the capitalist structures of society (Bolaria and Li 1988; Satzewich 1991). The economic well-being, standard of living, and cultural history of Canada are constructed around a contrived hatred toward others, both in the formal and informal sense (McKenna 1994). Through its ideological underpinnings, racism has played and continues to play a formidable role in establishing and maintaining patterns of inequality and control. Racist ideologies are employed for securing ready access to a cheap and disposable labour supply; to destabilize minority movements by undermining any potential show of unity or strength; and to justify intrusive devices for regulating the activities of troublesome minorities (Satzewich 1991; McKenna 1994). The interests of capitalism are also served by a degree of inner turmoil—from racial unrest to class fractions—as long as racism does not unduly interfere with wealth extraction or public order. Rather than a departure from the norm, in other words, racism exists because it is supportive of the system designed to augment white power and privilege. Those in positions of power will do anything to preserve privilege in the competition for scarce resources. Sowing the seeds of racism provides this advantage without drawing unnecessary attention to the contradictions and dysfunctions within the system.

Put bluntly, racism is linked with patterns of social control in contexts pervaded by relations of unequal power. Racism in Canada is neither a transient phenomenon nor an anomalous and unpredictable feature. The origins of racism have deep roots in Canadian society; that is, racism is intrinsic to Canada's historical and economic development; it is embedded within the institutional structures of society; it is endemic to core cultural values; and it is integral to Canadian society building. Racism continues to flourish because of its positive functions in support of white, ruling class interests; not unexpectedly, cultural values and institutional structures have evolved on the strength of racially based social cleavages. It is not a case of false consciousness, moreover. Racism has a basis in real material conditions of social life and the concrete problem of different classes by way of ready explanations to ideologically construct a world in change, under stress, and increasingly uncertain (Henry and Tator 1994). That alone should remind us that in defining racism as a social problem it constitutes a majority (white) problem rather than a minority problem. It should also alert us to the possibility that racism and racial hatred are not always perceived as dysfunctional (abnormal or deviant). Its acceptance as "normal" within the context of a commodity-oriented society only complicates the process of solution.

Not surprisingly, responses to the question of why racism persists continue to miss the mark. The reason why we don't have the right answer is because the question is misphrased. Perhaps the question should not be "why does racism exist" but "why should racism *not* exist in light of capitalist pressures for preserving privilege and power?" Rephrasing the question in this way alters our approach to solutions. Antiracist initiatives that focus on racism as a self-evident social problem are doomed to fail. Misreading the problem creates inappropriate solutions, especially when disregarding the social conditions that give rise to negative beliefs and behaviour. Racism, therefore, cannot be understood apart from the social, cultural, economic, and political context in which it is embedded and nourished. Racism is not a departure from society and its ideals, but a true expression of them. Aspects of government policy in Canada that are predicated on the assumption that racism is an irrational feature of an otherwise rational and sound system are doomed to miss the mark. To the extent that institutions are irrevocably tainted by racism, both covert and overt, personal as well as institutional, the challenge to transcend or eliminate racism may prove formidable.

TOWARD AN ANTIRACIST CANADA

Most Canadians are no longer racists in the classic sense of blatantly vilifying the different races. The days are gone of openly denying and excluding others because of who they are are disappearing, and they are unlikely to return in light of numerous checks and balances to prevent such a recurrence in Canadian society. Yet racism continues to exist in unobtrusive ways—deliberately or unconsciously, by way of action or inaction. Racism persists in tolerating practices and arrangements that have the intent or effect of discriminating against others because of what they do, who they are, and how they live. Doing nothing to confront such racial discrimination is no less racist since fence sitting (through inactivity or silence) is not impartiality or neutrality but tacit acceptance of the status quo. By contrast, **antiracism** can be defined as the process that isolates and challenges racism through direct action at personal and institutional levels (see also Dei 1996). Antiracism entails active involvement in changing the values, behaviour, and structures of society that perpetuate or support racism. It is egalitarian in outlook insofar as equality is sought, not in the liberal sense of everyone being similarly equal, but through structural changes that acknowledge the principle of equally different. Two styles of antiracist strategy can be discerned: one is concerned with modifying individual behaviour through education or interaction; the other with removal of discriminatory structural barriers by eliminating its systemic roots, either democratically through political channels and institutional reform, or through revolution by way of a violent seizure and redistribution of power (Bonilla-Silva 1996).

Interpersonal Levels

The distinction between personal and institutional antiracism is important. Taken at its most obvious level, racism is normally envisaged as a personal problem of hatred or ignorance. There is an element of truth to this assertion. Racism is generally expressed through the thoughts and actions of individuals. Prejudice consists of ignorance or a dislike of others because they are different or threatening. Thus strategies for containment or control are proposed that focus on modifying defective attitudes related to prejudice and stereotyping. Three of the more common personal antiracist strategies for improvement are interaction, education, and law and legal sanctions.

Interaction   Learning through interaction represents one of the many antiracist techniques available for individual change. Interaction with others will remove barriers that stem from ignorance or fear. Lack of knowledge is replaced with mutually reinforcing understanding. But contact in its own right is not necessarily beneficial. It is doubtful if the thousands of tourists that escape to the Caribbean each winter have "improved" race relations given that such interactional patterns are restricted primarily to serving white interests. Under these potentially degrading circumstances, the degree of resentment and contempt escalates in the reconstituting of colonialist patterns of servitude and deference.

Reduction of racism through interaction depends on the nature of the interactional setting. For any positive effect, interaction must be conducted between individuals who are relatively equal in status, who collaborate on a common endeavour in a spirit of trust and respect, whose interaction receives some degree of institutional and societal support, who derive mutual benefit from cooperation, and of sufficient frequency and duration to foster a working relationship (Jaret 1995). Interaction between unequals outside of a supportive context simply upholds the status quo by perpetuating stereotypes and confirms the worst prejudices in a negatively charged environment.

Education   It is widely assumed that formal instruction can reduce racism. Racism is viewed as a case of individuals subscribing to an irrational belief; thus the cure lies in educating people to realize that racism is wrong. Once aware of what they are doing and why, people are deemed sufficiently rational to make the appropriate adjustments. This notion of enlightenment through learning has put schools in the vanguard of institutions for dealing with diversity. Education has long been seen as the most popular policy prescription for curing us of racism (Bonilla-Silva 1996).

Two styles prevail in accommodating diversity within schools: multicultural and/or antiracist (Fleras and Elliott 1992). *Multicultural education* refers to a philosophy for "celebrating differences." It consists of activities and curricula that promote an awareness of diversity in terms of its intrinsic value to minorities and/or society at large. The aim of multicultural education is largely attitudinal, namely, to enhance sensitivity by improving awareness about cultural differences. Emphasis is directed at becoming more aware of ourselves as cultural carriers; of the customs that underpin non-Western cultures; and of the role of ethnocentrism and cultural relativism in supporting or denying diversity. It is also aimed at fostering tolerance. In contrast with acceptance and understanding, tolerance is the putting up with something that one does not like to improve interpersonal interaction or social harmony (Vogt 1997). Strategies for this kind of sensitivity awareness are varied, spanning the spectrum from museum approaches to immersion programs, with cross-cultural enrichment in between.

Multiculturally based training sessions have also proliferated in the wake of "awareness enhancement." Training sessions may involve workshops for new and established employees, with content ranging from cultural awareness modules to cross-cultural communication sessions to pointers about prejudice and ethnocentrism. Police forces in the larger metropolitan areas are increasingly involved in multicultural relations training programs for cadets, patrol officers, and management (Fleras and Desroches 1989). Program sessions are generally geared toward the elimination of discrimination in policing, promotion of cultural diversity within the police force, development of sensitivity to culturally diverse constituencies, improvement of cross-cultural communication, and implementation of community-based policing principles. But diversity training programs can be counterproductive in the hands of poorly trained and inadequately motivated instructors. Blame-and-shame programs can backfire because they are openly confrontational or preachy, put people on the defensive, and often foster resentment among participants because of humiliation, embarrassment, guilt, or shame (Jaret 1995). Even in the hands of skilled practitioners, there is no guarantee of positive change in attitude or behaviour, given the difficulty in isolating let alone unlearning something that was internalized unconsciously and perceived as positive rather than irrational or inappropriate.

Antiracist training seeks to overcome limitations of multicultural education, arguing in effect that the cultural solutions of **multicultural education** cannot adequately address structural problems. **Antiracist education** takes a critical view of power relations in society and directs its attention at how the dominant sector exercises power over subdominant groups (Cheyne et al. 1997). Both blatant and systemic forms of bias are analyzed, as well as stereotypes and discriminations within institutional settings. Antiracist education links racism to politics and economics against the backdrop of policies, practices, and social structures. Not only are the historical relations of domination analyzed and assessed at the level of individuals and institutions, thus exposing both minorities and the mainstream to the structural sources of oppression in society; antiracist education is also focused on encouraging individuals to look inside themselves and their culture as sources of racism. Whites are encouraged to examine their own racism and privileged positions on the assumption that white awareness is a central point in understanding personal privilege and taking responsibility for disempowerment of others (McIntosh 1988).

Law and Legal Sanctions Recourse to law is sometimes upheld as an effective personal deterrent. Laws exist in Canada that prohibit the expression of racial discrimination against vulnerable minorities. The scope of these laws is broad: Some legal measures consist of protection for identifiable minorities through restrictions on majority behaviour. For example, the Supreme Court of Canada has ruled repeatedly that prohibition of hate literature is a justifiable and reasonable limitation on freedom of speech. Other measures are aimed at removing discriminatory barriers that deter minority participation within society. The objective is to make it illegal to discriminate by making people aware of the repercussions for breaking the law.

Passage of these and related laws is not intended to alter people's attitudes, at least not in the short run. A democratic society such as ours entitles people to their own private thoughts, however repugnant or antisocial. But this right disappears when private thoughts become discriminatory behaviour; legal sanctions apply at this point. To be sure, laws are limited in their effectiveness for modifying individual thought and behaviour. The legislative advances of the Civil Rights Act in 1964 in the United States neither resolved African-American inequities nor eliminated prejudice or discrimination. Section 319 of Canada's Criminal Code prohibits the promotion of hatred against identifiable minorities: The positive impact of hate crimes prosecution sends a strong message that one cannot vilify those with identifiable characteristics, according to Lincoln Alexander (1998), and that those who persist will be held criminally liable if they willfully promote hatred against an identifiable group. However well intentioned, this hate law may have the outcome of (a) driving racism underground; (b) reinforcing the in-group's belief in the rightness of their actions; and (c) fostering a sense of hero worship or martyrdom in defence of the cause (Kinsella 1994). Nor can laws eliminate disadvantages by dispersing the concentration of wealth or distribution of power. Passage of laws may be designed to minimize majority inconvenience rather than assist minorities. But laws can modify people's behaviour through the imposition of sanctions. On the assumption that most individuals are law abiding because of the threat of punishment or social ostracism, passage of antiracist laws will ensure compliance with the letter of legislation, at least outwardly if not by personal conviction. In time, however, people may realign their beliefs to match behaviour in hopes of reducing the dissonance between thought and action.

Institutional Antiracism

There is room for cautious optimism when discussing the effectiveness of individually tailored antiracist programs. But are these initiatives of sufficient scope to uproot racism? Are the structures of society amenable to reform through personal transformation? Perhaps a word of clarification is needed about the sociological point of view. With the possible exception of sociobiologists (see van den Berghe 1985), most sociologists would argue that individuals are not biologically programmed to act in a racist manner. There are no genes that express themselves in racial discrimination. Nor is there any compelling reason to believe that people are born with a propensity to hate. To be sure, biological and psychological perspectives are not dismissed outright. There may be good reasons for an evolutionary approach that acknowledges a fear of strangers as a survival value. Nevertheless, our preferences are directed at social explanations: People are conditioned to be racist by environments that foster ethnocentrism, out-group antipathy, and racism. Racism is inextricably linked with the process of social control for preserving the status quo in complex societies. This assertion is consistent with a fundamental sociological premise: The social is real, it transcends individual personalities, it is amenable to analysis and reform, and it helps to account for differences and patterns in attitudes and behaviour. Racism may be expressed in and through people (who may be regarded as precipitating causes), but individuals are merely the conduits of racial antipathy. It is the social context that counts.

Racism can only be resolved by attacking it at its source, namely, within the institutional structures that support a capitalist society. Racism is not just about individuals with regressive beliefs or dormant prejudices; it is rooted in institutional structures and provides justifying ideologies and practices in those contexts where the social order is structured around the placement of minorities in racial categories ("racialization") (Bonilla-Silva 1996). Personal solutions such as antiracist training are comparable to applying a bandage to a cancerous growth—compassionate and humane to be sure, but ultimately self-defeating in light of the magnitude of the disease. The symptoms are addressed, not the cause or source. The problem of racism cannot be eliminated except by confronting it within the wider confines of political domination and economic control. This comprehensive approach will entail a different set of assumptions and tactics than those focusing on personal initiatives.

Antiracist measures may include fighting racist hate groups, direct action through protest or civil disobedience, boycotts, litigation, or legislation (Jaret 1995). The promotion of employment equity is one such measure. Employment equity programs are based on the premise that racially discriminatory barriers do not stem from ignorance, fear, or arrogance. These barriers are systemic and entrenched within existing structures: That embeddedness makes them amenable to reform only through institutional rather than personal change. Equity initiatives are directed at hidden rules and unconscious procedures that inadvertently distort the process of recruitment, entry, treatment, promotion, or reward allocation in favour of one group rather than another. These initiatives hope to identify and eliminate offending practices; they also intend to remedy the effects of past discrimination, to remove systemic barriers in pursuit of equal outcomes, and to ensure appropriate representation of identifiable groups at all workplace levels. The ultimate goal is the creation of a workplace environment where differences are embraced as a legitimate and integral component of "business as usual."

In short, antiracism strategies consist of measures and mechanisms for dismantling the structural basis of institutional racism. The removal of discriminatory barriers is central: Selection and recruitment procedures as well as rules for promotion and reward are scrutinized for hidden bias in the interests of accessibility. Values and practices are monitored that historically have propelled the organization, but are irrelevant in a changing and diverse context. Antiracist strategies must focus on dominant beliefs and values within the institution, the organizational system related to rules and practices, and the experiences and behaviours of organizational actors. These systemic biases are most apt to occur at the level of mission statement, culture and subculture, power and decision making, structures (including rules, roles, and relationships), and resources distribution of physical, financial, and human assets. Any institutional enterprise will foster racism intentionally or unintentionally when it perpetuates mission statements that are exclusionary, refuses to share power or decision making, promulgates a monocultural set of values and beliefs as normal and necessary, maintains an inflexible or unresponsive set of structure and operations, and endorses unequal distributions of resources (Chesler and Crowfoot 1989). These multipronged antiracist initiatives sound plausible in theory; their implementation may be another story.

Toward a Comprehensive Solution: Think Politically, Act Personally

It's relatively easy to dismiss racism as a personal problem. It is equally tempting to situate racism within a system of vast and impersonal forces that are largely beyond individual control or responsibility. Neither of these positions is entirely correct. Individuals may not be the root cause of racism, but racism is located within and carried by the person. Systems may generate root causes, but institutions do not exist apart from individuals who interact to create, support, maintain, and transform patterns of racism. It is implicit in our daily encounters through the perpetuation of countless actions, gestures, and speech patterns. Each of us must be held accountable for our actions, no matter how powerful the social context in which we find ourselves. That much is critical: Unless there is an awareness of our contribution to the problem, it becomes difficult to be part of the solution. Put differently, when applied to the realm of racism and proposed solutions, the personal is indeed the political. The political in turn defines the personal; that is, changing the system invariably changes people's attitudes; changing people's attitudes may result in corresponding alterations in people's behaviour and revisions to society.

Racism is a ubiquitous feature of contemporary society, although often beyond our awareness or consciousness. As individuals, we must reflect critically upon our degree of complicity in perpetuating racism. Racism is embedded in our capitalist society by way of social, economic, and political institutions and practices. This societal racism may be deliberately invoked to control, deny, or exclude. It may also flourish inadvertently in privileging Eurocentric norms, values, practices, and institutions as necessary and superior while ignoring minority experiences as inappropriate. To combat the root cause of racism requires a sociological analysis and critique of how and why racism as an ideology is widely perpetuated. Hence strategies to combat racism must obviously take into account the interplay of social forces and intersubjective experiences of individuals. Only a comprehensive approach can deliver the goods with any hope of success. It remains to be seen whether any system driven by private profit and individual aggrandizement can ever hope to solve any of its problems, since the goals of making money may conflict with the promotion of social values related to diversity, inclusion, and equality. In the final analysis, then, the objective of antiracism is not simply to purge racism from our midst, but to create a new society that is based on "living together with our differences" in ways that enhance diversity without sacrificing equality.

CHAPTER HIGHLIGHTS

- Racism exists and has always existed in Canada, although its magnitude and scope as well as depth and intensity have varied over time. The many faces of racism, both past and present, provide a coherent theme for organizing the chapter.

- Racism is not a recent import into Canada. Even a cursory review of Canada's history reveals otherwise. Racism instead is a chronic and embedded feature of Canadian society that shows few signs of diminishing.

- Racism is not just about individual prejudice, but also a structural feature of society in which power and resources are distributed unequally among socially different groups.

- Defining racism can be a problem. Some of the difficulties flow from the fact that racism is not necessarily a "thing" out there, but rather an attribute conferred on a social relationship within a specific context and having certain consequences.

- Definitions of racism fall into "narrow" and "comprehensive" categories. Narrow definitions (racism as 'race') lean toward racism as a belief in a kind of biological determination and racial inferiority. Racism as culture refers to a dislike of others who are perceived as culturally different and a threat to society. More comprehensive definitions (racism as power) tend to focus on racism as the power of one group over that of another to deny or exclude.

- Racism is defined as a relatively coherent set of *beliefs* about the innate inferiority of some racial groups, combined with the *power* to transform these ideas into *practices* that deny or exclude.

- With its focus on group dynamics within contexts of power and domination, racism is best envisaged as a socially constructed system of control imposed by one group over another in the competition for scarce resources.

- Racism represents a relatively coherent system of beliefs ("ideology") and practices that legitimate the expression of racial inequality in society. It also includes a behavioural component which may or may not entail some element of prejudice. Power underpins all forms of racism: Without it, racism is indistinguishable from a host of negative attitudes and practices.

- Prejudice consists of beliefs about a group, an emotional reaction to that group, and a motivation to act on the basis of these beliefs and attitudes. This constellation of thoughts, feelings, and motives is learned, generalizable from one group to another, often indirect and coded, and may not necessarily lead to discriminatory behaviour (Pincus and Ehrlich 1994).

- Prejudice and discrimination continue to exist. But the once strongly held notions of biological inferiority and hateful stereotypes have given way to rejection on the grounds of cultural differences and unacceptable lifestyles.

- Minorities are unlikely to be racist since, as a group, they lack the power to put prejudice into practice in a way that denies, excludes, exploits, and controls. The notion of racism as folded into the institutional structures of dominant society also shifts blame away from minorities.

- There are many faces of racism, varying as they do along different criteria. Faces of racism discussed include (a) interpersonal (red-necked, polite), (b) institutional (systematic, systemic), and (c) societal (everyday and cultural). The different types of racism can be compared and contrasted along diverse dimensions.

- Expressions of racism are embedded in the institutional structures of capitalist society; they are also grounded in the everyday experiences of people. This distinction between micro-racism and macro-racism is analytically useful; however, the interplay between macro and micro levels provides racism with its staying power.

- The different dimensions of racism make it difficult to precisely define the problem, where it is located, why it exists, and how it should be dealt with.

- Antiracism is an emergent field, both in study and practice, that is concerned with the elimination of racism at personal and institutional levels. Antiracism can be defined as the process by which those institutions, values, and practices that perpetuate racism at personal or systemic levels are identified, challenged, and modified through direct action.

- Antiracist strategies vary with how racism is defined, the magnitude and scope of the racism that has been identified, and its impact. In general, antiracism focuses on personal and institutional strategies for reform.

- Antiracist strategies aimed at personal change are channelled into venues as varied as language, laws, interaction, and education.

- The roots of racism are challenged by antiracist measures at institutional and structural levels. Formidable barriers confront those who want to change society by changing the system.

KEY TERMS

antiracism
anti-Semitism
Cultural racism
discrimination
essentialism
ethnocentrism
everyday racism
harassment
head tax
hegemony
institutional racism
multicultural versus antiracist education
polite racism
prejudice
racism
racism as race
racism without race
red-necked racism
stereotyping
subliminal cultural racism
systematic racism
systemic racism

REVIEW QUESTIONS

1. Compare and contrast the different levels of racism that have been discussed in terms of style, level of expression, and degree of intent.

2. Demonstrate the linkages between racism and prejudice (including ethnocentrism and stereotypes) and discrimination (harassment).

3. Compare and contrast the different but interrelated strands of racism.

4. Racism is not just about race; it is also about power. Expand on this idea by defining racism in terms of power and providing an example to support your answer.

5. Discuss whether or not you think Canada is a racist society. Problematize the notion of a 'racist' society and use specific examples to support your answer.

6. Racism has undergone a number of changes in content and scope. Explain.

7. Select several examples of recent incidents involving racial, ethnic, or aboriginal minorities, and indicate if the issue is one of racism. If yes, what kind of racism is involved?

8. How can we explain the persistence of racism? Be sure to emphasize the social dimensions in your answer.

9. Compare and contrast the strategies of antiracism at the personal level versus the institutional level.

10. Should racism be seen as a psychological complex of beliefs, emotions, and values, or should it be interpreted as the cultural and symbolic expression of a society in which certain groups are systematically and systemically denied and excluded? Justify your response.

ETHNICITY: Conflicts and Challenges

| INSIGHT 4–1 | White Ethnicity—A Contradiction in Terms? |

It's been said that many academic arguments could be solved *a priori* if people took care in defining their terms (Tilley 1997). This principle is aptly demonstrated in the often animated debates over the inclusion of the "white mainstream" as an ethnic group (Bell 1996; Beddgood 1997). Are "whites" ethnic? Do whites have ethnicity? To one side are those who argue that mainstream whites do not have ethnicity because most are unaware of their shared identity as a conscious distinction. They just *are*, and labelling them as ethnic is inconsistent with commonly accepted definitions of ethnicity as shared awareness of ancestral differences as a basis for rewards, recognition, and relationships. To the other side are those who argue that everybody, including whites, is ethnically located, since ethnicity is a key variable in shaping what we do and think and how others perceive and respond to us (Hall 1996; Gillespie 1996). Attributing ethnicity to whiteness reinforces the notion that all discourses about reality are from somewhere ("standpoint"), regardless of intent or awareness. In between these poles are those who concede the existence of the mainstream ethnicity but also acknowledge its tendency to conceal itself by attributing ethnicity only to the "other." For example, the English- and French-speaking sectors of Canada have reaffirmed Frenchness and Englishness as a natural cultural identity that exists as a tacitly accepted norm around which "other" ethnicities orbit. Yet these "orbiting" ethnic groups are only too aware of the dominant group's ethnicity in shaping the values and agendas of society (Doane 1997).

Everyone agrees that Canada is ethnically distinct. Aboriginal communities have a distinctive ethnicity even though the First Nations reject labelling as an ethnic minority, but endorse the status of a people or nation. Migrants from countries such as China and Somalia are generally perceived as having a distinctive ethnicity. Most English-speaking Canadians would concur that the Québécois constitute an ethnicity; Quebeckers may dispute this, preferring, instead, to see themselves as a people rather than a French-speaking aggregate who happen to live in Quebec. Similarly, English-speaking Canadians would be reluctant to define themselves as ethnic even if others, including the Québécois, would disagree by pointing to the politicized consciousness of anglophones in the province in preserving their distinctiveness and privilege. So what is going on? Is whiteness an ethnicity or not?

Much will depend on how we define the criteria for ethnicity. Yinger (1994) indicates that three components must prevail: Members of a group see themselves as different; others see them as different; and they participate in shared activities with the intent or effect of affirming their distinctiveness. Implicit in most definitions of ethnicity is the notion of peoplehood with its reference to *shared awareness* of common history and destiny as a basis for membership or entitlements. Applying this ideal of ethnicity as consciousness would appear to exclude the mainstream, which at best possesses pockets of ethnicity among individuals, often at the extreme right and left of the political continuum. This inability of the dominant sector to identify itself ethnically can be attributed to the nature of dominant group status. In contrast with visible minority ethnic groups, mainstream members are rarely reminded of social and cultural differences on a day-to-day basis, are unlikely to have their identity anchored in overtly ethnic institutions and structures, and are much less likely to have experienced prejudice, discrimination, or dis-

advantage due to ethnicity or race (Doane 1997). In that advantages are often less conspicuous than obstacles in shaping people's experiences, ethnicity for the mainstream plays little or no overt role by intruding in daily thought or behaviour. In short, mainstream groups may be defined as having ethnicity, but this ethnicity is best described as hidden or dormant; that is, an ethnicity that lacks the criterion of "consciousness" but has the potential to be activated or to assert itself when challenged by subdominant groups, as was the case of the English in Quebec during the 1970s and 1980s.

Two points seem uppermost in rethinking white ethnicity. First, the notion of ethnicity as a conscious awareness of differences may need to be rethought and replaced with the idea of "potential" awareness as a defining characteristic. Second, refusal to acknowledge white ethnicity is problematic. This denial has the effect of elevating white existence as the universal or the norm. It also has the consequence of diminishing ethnicity by making it synonymous with being a minority, with a corresponding trivializing of status or achievement. Refusing to "ethnicize" the dominant group as an ethnicity privileges the mainstream as the hidden centre—the unmarked standard—of intergroup relations. Minority women and men, in turn, are discredited as having a "handicap" that must be discarded before full acceptance into society. Thus in masking the contested but ethnic nature of societal values and institutions, the status and interests of the dominant sector are normalized. The consequences are contrary to healthy ethnic relations; after all, to ignore white ethnicity is to redouble its hegemony by naturalizing whiteness (Spoonley 1993:57). The challenge, then, is to first render the mainstream visible as an ethnicity and then question its status as the normative standard by which to judge, compare, and criticize.

INTRODUCTION: GLOBAL IMPLOSION/ETHNIC EXPLOSION

Two distinct but seemingly contradictory dynamics are at play as the twentieth century draws to a close. The coexistence of these ostensibly opposing trends has proven difficult to deal with, both conceptually and politically. On the one hand are the homogenizing forces of **globalization** as labour, markets, and capital move across national boundaries, in effect connecting communities in a new time-space compression. Nation-states are inexorably drawn into a single world economy under globalization. The local and the national are conflated into a single world system of industrialized production, routinized procedures, standardized consumption, and homogeneous monoculturalism. The formidable presence of transnational corporations underscores this universalizing trend, involving technological advancements related to communication, information processing, and transportation in bringing people more closely together than ever. No less important in fostering this interdependence is the circulation of modernist values such as rationality, progress, achievement, universalism, individualism, and equality, all of which have had the effect of eroding the distinctiveness that once flourished in many parts of the world. In place of diversity is a growing trend toward a "McDonaldization" of societies into a single global loop where differences are dismissed or commodified (Nelson and Fleras 1998).

There is a second but equally compelling dynamic that is pushing in an opposite direction, away from the general and the uniform, toward the specific and the particular. The centrifugal forces of globalization are challenged by the centripetal forces of ethnicity, with their tendency to propel the surge of nationalism and ethnic identities in directions both familiar and uncharted. The growing awareness of ethnic differences because of minority assertiveness is matched by a concomitant fear and resentment of others because of these differences (see Persons 1998). The two trends are not unrelated: The very globalisms that threaten ethnicities may also bolster ethnic attachments by creating new hybrid identities that oscillate between old and new without fear of contradiction or transparency (Hall 1996; Gillespie 1996). In an era of global population movements, ethnic identities become increasingly delocalized (deterritorialized), and the corresponding diaspora of ethnic members develops new identities while maintaining a connection across the physical divide (Anthias 1998; Cohen 1998). The more similar people become because of globalism and mass consumerism, the greater the urge to be special or claim differences (Behrens 1994; Fukuyama 1994). Pressures for conformity and routinization have prompted like-minded people to rediscover their ethnic roots as a basis for continuity or competition. This discovery has proven hydra-headed. Ethnic experiences can be "regressive" in their capacity to unleash dormant hatreds and settle old scores. The faith of even the most optimistic has been shaken with the demise of superpower restraints on intertribal strife, followed by an unleashing of deeply rooted ethnic conflicts. Ethnicity can be "progressive" in terms of influencing how we think, who we marry, how we interact, what we do, and when we eat. It can also be "political" in the sense of redrawing the ground rules in competition over scarce resources. Few will question the potential of ethnicity to mobilize individuals into the most formidable of action groups. What is more questionable is whether the ethnic experience can be harnessed to the interests of many rather than a few.

Ethnicity has leaped to the forefront of contemporary society building. Where once society was discussed in terms of a universal sense of common humanity, with differences attributed to uneven development or class conflict, there is growing awareness of ethnic pluralism as a bedrock of the human condition (Kromkowski 1995). But however much ethnicity may be central in helping to explain or justify human behaviour, this powerful explanatory principle can be overused in reducing all confrontation to ethnic conflicts. Because of its capacity to empower or dismember, reaction to ethnicity as a social force has been mixed (Yinger 1994). For some, ethnicity is endorsed as a positive contributor to global survival, reflecting a fundamental fact that differences rather than similarities constitute the definitive feature of the human species. Others denounce the cult of ethnicity as an inexcusable reversion to "tribalism" and groupthink that panders to humankind's basest instincts. Ethnicity is criticized for defining people as members of a group rather than as individuals; for judging others by who they are rather than by what they do; for focusing on their differences rather than commonalities. Ethnically based nationalisms are disparaged as a major contributor to international conflicts because of the instability they pose to the cohesion and integrity of sovereign states. Still others are not sure how to respond. How, they ask, can any society that historically has championed the virtues of homogeneity now deal with the particularist demands of ethnicity? Many are resigned to ethnicity as a persistent presence in human affairs, with potential to harm or help, depending on the circumstances. That being the case, the preferred option is to determine how ethnicity can be put to good use, without capitulating to a worst case scenario. Put bluntly, how do we go about making society safe *for* ethnicity as well as safe *from* ethnicity (Schlesinger Jr 1992)?

Canada is no exception to this global trend. Recent years have witnessed a convergence of controversies and challenges that routinely are labelled as "ethnic." The politics of First Nations ethnicity have catapulted to the forefront of Canadian society in terms of decolonizing aboriginal relations with Canada along the lines of the "nations within." Québécois ethnicity continues to provoke English-speaking Canadians, many of whom are perplexed or apoplectic over Quebec's demands for "sovereignty." Quebeckers, in turn, are equally puzzled by the bull-headed arrogance of the Anglais. Multicultural minorities have been no less adamant in demanding "mainstream" Canadians to move over and make ethnocultural space. What is this enigmatic force that threatens to dismantle the conventional in exchange for the unorthodox? Why has ethnicity come to assume such salience in shaping Canada's destiny and that of other societies? How is ethnicity a key variable in helping to shape and explain patterns of human behaviour at individual and group levels? When does ethnicity become a factor in the competition for valued resources? This chapter explores the "ethnic experience" as a formidable dynamic in reshaping Canada's political and cultural landscape. It focuses on some of the complexities associated with the surge and persistence of ethnicity as a major source of divisiveness and inequality in Canada and abroad. The chapter is concerned primarily with understanding (a) what ethnicity is, (b) why it exists, (c) how it is expressed, (d) its relation to inequality, and (e) its impact and implications for Canadian society building. Particular attention is devoted to the processes and outcomes associated with the (a) ethnic surge; (b) ethnic groups and communities; (c) varied types of ethnic identities, including lived-in, symbolic, insurgent, and postmodern; (d) ethnic nationalism as social movements; and (e) depoliticizing ethnicity. We conclude this chapter by discussing ethnicity in terms of its implications for the multicultural reconstruction of an increasingly diverse Canada.

Two themes provide conceptual bookends: One focuses on ethnicity as inequality; the other emphasizes the link between ethnicity and society building. Ethnic relations are primarily unequal relations in that they deny basic human rights and exclude devalued minorities from full participation in society (Aguirre Jr and Turner 1995; Kallen 1995). By the same token, ethnic Canadians have looked to their ethnicity as a source of empowerment in challenging existing inequities. Attention, accordingly, must focus on the role of ethnicity in creating, supporting, contesting, or modifying these relationships of inequality. Ethnicity is also inseparable from questions of Canadian society building. Canada originated in the context of diversity, especially since settlement relied on the skills of ethnic immigrants. Future prosperity, in turn, may well depend on how adroitly Canadians engage with ethnic differences both nationally and abroad. The challenge of ethnicity cannot be underestimated: Ethnicity is no longer a cuddly security blanket or cultural survival from a bygone era but a powerful social dynamic that is capable of renewing and transforming itself in ways that perplex yet illuminate, unite yet divide. As for the contemporary challenge for society to make room for diversity while ensuring common grounds for cooperation (Underhill-Sem and Fitzgerald 1997), the impact and implications of ethnicity to Canada cannot be ignored. The fact that ethnicity *is* the mainstream in many parts of urban Canada sharpens the need to understand what is going and why.

WHAT IS ETHNICITY

The term "ethnicity" continues to baffle and confuse as well as to infuriate and inflame. *Ethnicity* is an imprecise term of contested meanings, as Marie Gillespie (1996) writes, with a tendency to encompass and derive new meanings from its relationship to different political interests or discursive formations such as race and nation. More a process than a thing, **ethnicity** can be manipulated by insiders and outsiders to put down or empower, to include or exclude, to celebrate or debunk, and can be imposed or voluntarily accepted (Adam and Allan 1995). Ethnicity, like racism, has become bewilderingly loose in practice, in the process acquiring the status of cliché while losing analytical vigour. The term itself seems immune to rational analysis: After all, how do we sort through vagaries as disparate as Kosovar ethnocide on the one side, Québécois ethnic nationalism on the other, and the contrived ethnicity of Kitchener-Waterloo's annual Oktoberfest celebrations on still another? Despite these contradictions and slippages, its popularity both in public and scholarly discourse continues to expand. Ethnicity is often contrasted with or mistaken for the term "race." Or it may be used euphemistically instead of race: As a more neutral category for sociological discourse, the term "ethnic" may be wielded as a dodge to circumvent the more ideologically loaded "r" word, given the latter's propensity to smear or to silence. Ethnicity may be conceived as a property of the social structure, namely, a distinct group defined by its culture, such as European "ethnics." Or it may refer to a fluid process that spans the spectrum from identity formation to material exclusion, with resource competition in between (Smaje 1997). Ethnicity may be employed as an adjective (ethnic identity or ethnic cleansing), a noun (ethnicity or professional ethnics), a nominalization (ethnicization), or even a verb (ethnicize). Such elasticity of usage weakens the case for a commonly accepted definition.

There are additional pressures in sorting through ethnicity. Ethnicity may invoke a putdown that entails some degree of derision, contempt, or condescension, in a sense resorting to its original usage to depict "others" as "outsiders" (Greenfield 1994). References to ethnicity may evoke a kind of verbal code that camouflages a majority disdain for something perceived as inferior or irrelevant. It is something that "those other people have" while the mainstream is exempted from ethnic consideration (Jaret 1995:71; also Bissoondath 1994). Conversely, ethnicity can also be employed in the hyphenated sense to publicize one's political commitments. The politicized and oppositional nature of ethnicity cannot be dismissed lightly. To claim an ethnicity is itself a political act, as Myrna Kostash (1988:58) proclaims:

"Anglo" and "ethnic" have become politicized designations in the same way that the desig-
nation "woman" has become politicized and represents a world view critical of and alternative to male-dominated identity....When I call my self an ethnic I am signalling that I situate
myself obliquely in relation to Anglo-American culture....

In short, ethnicity represents an enigmatic concept that can be stretched to mean everything
or nothing. Ethnicity may be a key variable in generating patterned human behaviour and explaining differences and similarities. But reliance on ethnicity can be overstated by reducing all confrontations with minorities to ethnic conflicts. For example, many Bosnian
Muslims disputed their conflict as ethnic, arguing that the Muslim side contained a multiethnic
mix of Catholic Croats and Orthodox Serbs that challenged the creation of a greater Serbia.

A Working Definition   We prefer a definition consistent with our sociological commitment
to ethnicity as group dynamics in unequal contexts. Broadly speaking, ethnicity consists of a
shared awareness of ancestral differences as a basis for engagement or entitlement. It entails
a consciousness about belonging and loyalty to a particular people, homeland, or cultural tradition. Ethnicity, more specifically, implies a principle of organization whereby ancestrally related individuals are entitled to benefits on the basis of perceived commonality, physical
appearance, subjective identification, stereotyping, and exclusion; that is, ethnicity is a statement of affiliation or attachment involving like-minded people in pursuit of a social activity or
goal. Employed in this sense of belonging or "peoplehood," ethnicity is concerned with classifying persons who are related by birth or common symbols into goal-directed action groups.
    A distinction between *ethnicity* and *ethnic groups* is useful. Ethnicity as a principle pro-
vides the basis for political mobilization or social relations. It connotes a very general label
that is appended to categories by those who define themselves as different or are defined by
others as different by virtue of shared commonalities (Jaret 1995). Ethnicity as classification
also consists of those distinctive attributes that typify and distinguish members of one category from another on the basis of beliefs, values, emotions, and practices (Glazer and
Moynihan 1975). **Ethnic groups,** by contrast, refer to communities of people who act on the
basis of perceived physical, social, cultural, and political similarities, and who see themselves as distinct from other communities by way of boundaries that distinguish "us" from
"them" (Modood and Berthoud 1997). In other words, ethnicity is to ethnic groups as class
consciousness is to class: Ethnicity represents a contingent and changeable set of ideas that
may or may not be activated into action (Gillespie 1996).

Components of Ethnicity

At one time, ethnicity was discussed almost exclusively as a set of objective and specific cultural features. Canadian society, for example, was envisioned as a mosaic of relatively
durable and distinct cultural entities. Ethnicity embraced an objective and immutable laundry list of cultural traits that could be employed to identify a person as belonging to "x"
rather than "y." A set of appropriate symbols and artifacts was attached to a particular community of people (Brown 1989). Explicit and unbending boundaries were drawn around
designated ethnic groups once the inventory of values, language, religion, and culture was
identified. Focusing on the objective dimension of ethnicity culminated in a "cookie-cutter"
approach toward the study of ethnicity.
    This emphasis on objective ethnic content has waned in recent years. In its place has
emerged an interest in the subjective experiences and "symbolic" boundaries that define and

encircle. Subjectivists reject the notion of ethnicity as a clearly demarcated cultural category with an easily defined set of morphological features. Emphasis is focused instead on ethnicity as a transactional process, that is, a socially constructed reality involving interethnic relations in contexts of inequality (Barth 1969; Jenkins 1994; also Kallen 1995 for review). Ethnicity reflects a shared "we feeling" within a collectivity ("groupness") whose symbolic components can vary from time to place. The argument for subjectivity is compelling. But just as an itemized approach to ethnicity is inadequate, so too is an over-emphasis on subjective experience. Ethnicity is more than a feeling of apartness. Select tangible markers are required to validate a sense of continuity and commitment. A limited number of objective features are subsequently incorporated in defining a distinction. These distinguishing markers become relevant only when deliberately chosen or challenged by others. A few of these symbolic markers are openly visible, such as clothing and lifestyle. Others are less apparent, including religious beliefs and attitudes across a broad range of symbols from family obligations to sexual mores. Of those characteristics that serve as indices of ethnicity, the most prominent are birthright, homeland, and language.

Birthright Only persons with proven (or perceived) descent from a common source can claim membership to a particular ethnic group with a consequent entitlement to assistance and security. The notion that "blood is thicker than water" serves as a definitive trait.

Homeland Many ethnic groups have a powerful attachment to a territory or homeland that they have left behind or are bent on reclaiming. This attachment is frequently couched in almost spiritual or reverential terms. Instead of viewing land as a commodity for purchase and profit, ethnic homelands are exalted as an embodiment of the past—worth defending to the death if necessary.

Language Language represents a key component of group distinctiveness (Fishman 1989). As the Québécois have shown, language represents more than a routine way of communication for threatened minorities. Language retention is endorsed as a powerful symbol of identity, cohesion, distinctiveness, and boundary maintenance. The issue of language and ethnic minority aspirations will be discussed later in the chapter on French-English relations.

Ethnic groups select certain items as a basis for carving out a distinctive space in society. These criteria provide a rallying point around which to galvanize ethnically alike people into action. The practice of ethnicity calls forth a combination of subjective experiences, objective markers, and cultural codes of conduct. Certain elements are pivotal in defining the notion of in- and out-group perceptions, commonality of origins and characteristics, shared experiences, and a historically derived sense of belonging. But ethnic group fortunes are known to fluctuate over time, in the process emphasizing or displacing the importance of certain cultural markers in response to changing circumstances.

Maintaining a degree of distinctiveness that distinguishes one ethnic group from another can pose a problem. Countries such as Canada, with our highly democratic and relatively egalitarian outlooks, are particularly hard on ethnic retention. Without external pressure or outside hostility, it is too easy to slip into the mainstream unless vigilance is constant (Abella 1995). *Ethnic boundaries* provide such a protective barrier. **Ethnic boundaries** can be defined as socially constructed barriers that provide some degree of separation between ethnic groups. Neither totally impenetrable nor excessively permeable, these boundaries can be likened to "membranes" that simultaneously inhibit and enhance the flow of individuals into and out of the group. Ethnic boundaries are negotiated and adjusted through social interaction that simultaneously unites and divides into binary oppositions of "us" and "them" (Barth 1969; Nagel 1994). These boundaries are maintained for as long as group members consider themselves under threat because of racist legislation, restricted economic opportunity, restrained cultural expression, and social rejection. Anabaptist groups such as the Hutterites (Chapter 1) clearly reveal what happens at social boundaries as neighbouring groups capitalize on a range of symbols and markers to distinguish the "us" from the "others," neither of which can exist without the other, thus reaffirming how ethnicity and identity are socially constructed if unequal relations.

WHY ETHNICITY? THE ETHNIC SURGE

Virtually all societies are composed of racially and culturally diverse groups. The range of variation is almost limitless. Some societies are relatively homogeneous in terms of composition (Japan and Korea); others have a single dominant majority with numerous minorities in different stages of assimilation (United States); still others consist of dominant and subdominant groups that are locked in competition for power (Fiji); and still others, including Canada, Australia, and New Zealand, are white settler colonies with powerful indigenous or aboriginal sectors.

On the surface it might appear hopeless to extract pattern from such a remarkable range of social conditions. However, two patterns prevail: First, a dominant ethnic group exists whose culture, language, values, and social patterns are upheld as normal and desirable. Such groups possess the power and resources to establish institutional arrangements and ideological systems consistent with their interests (Kallen 1995). Second is the unequally common existence of subdominant groups. Occupying the margins of society in terms of power and resources, these groups are marginalized from the mainstream because of racial composition and cultural differences. Many are under constant pressure to conform with prevailing values, norms, and institutions. A situation is thus created where opposing groups enter into competition to define and protect as well as promote collective interests. It is the tension between these competing forces that generates the double-edged dynamics of society building in Canada and elsewhere.

Dominant groups have dealt with ethnocultural minorities in different ways. Most have sought to diminish ethnic differences through their assimilation into the mainstream. The inevitable demise and dissolution of ethnic communities was widely predicted—and anticipated. Both socialism and liberalism attacked particularist attachments as atavistic survivals at odds with rational, universal progress (Connor 1972). Such "primitive" attachments would erode in the face of social and cultural integration or recede under the relentless assault of an all-pervasive modernist belief that people should be treated as individuals rather than as members of a group (Bell-Fialkoff 1993). Minority values and lifestyles were disparaged as immoral or inimical to the realities of contemporary society. Functionalists, for example, predicted the eventual disappearance of ethnocultural minorities. Ascriptive differences such as race would diminish with exposure to contemporary forces of modernization such as urbanism, industrialization, mass education, and mass communication. A Marxist perspective was equally contemptuous of any ethnic attachment. Class relations constituted the fundamental dynamic in society: Everything else, including ethnicity, was derivative or residual (Bell-Fialkoff 1993). To think or to act otherwise, namely, in terms of ethnicity, could only perpetuate false consciousness and postpone the inevitable reconstruction of the socialist system. In short, both functionalist and conflict theorists alike pounced on ethnicity as stumbling blocks to progress.

Predictions for the decline of ethnicity have proven premature to say the least. In conceding that reports of its demise are greatly exaggerated, ethnicity has proven to be persistent in the face of modernization. Perpetuated at times by individuals as genuine culture (enjoyed for its own right) or as an impetus for mobilizing people into goal-directed action (manipulated as a means), this surge of ethnicity has had a profound effect in unsettling contemporary societies. A new reality has evolved instead since the late 1960s that privileges ethnicity as a cutting edge for collectively challenging the status quo (Nagel and Olzak 1982; See and Wilson 1988). People have turned to ethnicity as a means of protecting their immediate interests, especially when state formations are unable or unwilling to regulate intergroup dynamics (Turner 1994). No longer are ethnic attachments defined as anachronistic survivals from the past—quaint and exotic, perhaps, but irrelevant to the demands and rigours of the twenty-first century. To the contrary, this renewal of ethnic pride and identity has evolved into a formidable power, with the double-edged capacity to enhance personal growth or national interests in some instances yet destroy or dispossess in others.

The rejuvenation of ethnicity in Canada and elsewhere has raised many questions. What do we mean by **ethnic surge**? Why has it occurred? How is it manifested? With what impact? What are the immediate or long-term implications? Answers to these questions require us to revisit the ethnic politics associated with minority assertiveness over identity, land, or political voice. How can the visceral appeal of ethnicity as identity or action possibly supersede the cosmopolitan lure of a modern society? Why, indeed, do people prefer to affiliate along ethnic lines rather than political parties or trade unions? Put crudely, why would anyone want to be thought of as a Québécois or Aboriginal or Vietnamese or Lithuanian-Canadian when they have the opportunity to discard their ethnicity and identify as nonhyphenated Canadians? This and subsequent sections will address the reasons why by examining the principles, processes, and outcomes of ethnicity as a social force in modern Canadian society. Three major explanations help to isolate the factors contributing to this surge in ethnicity: (a) the *primordialist thesis*, (b) the *instrumentalist thesis*, and (c) the *constructivist thesis*.

Primordialist Thesis: "Blood Is Thicker Than Water"

The **primordialist thesis** argues that the boom in ethnicity is essentially an extension of powerful and immutable sentiments that are impossible to suppress. Ethnicity represents an ancient and deep-rooted impulse that reflects a tendency to seek out others of your "own kind" (Jaret 1995). This "survival" from a "primitive" past capitalizes on an inherent need for belonging with others who are similar. Evolutionary adaptation and survival of the human species may have depended precisely on ethnic bonding. Such a genetic inheritance makes it only natural to exhibit such spontaneous feelings and emotional attachments with those of common birthright. People appear to have a genuine preference for confiding in and congregating with people of their own cultural background and have endorsed ethnic groupings as fixed and relatively impermeable organic entities anchored in descent, history, language, and culture to secure identity and belonging (Gross 1996).

In short, individuals affiliate with one another because of personal gain; they also do so because of a "primordial" urge to stick together (Rex 1983). These bonds are primordial in the sense that they are perceived as hereditary, unavoidable, undeniable, and superior to other forms of affiliation (Gross 1996). This intrinsic dimension may help to explain the intensity of passions and emotions associated with the ethnic experience. It may also explain the popularity of rabidly ethnic movements, with their rejection of modernist values and endorsement of essentialist ties as a basis for collective harmony and group cooperation (Bell-Fialkoff 1993).

Within the primordialist camp are various biologically slanted theories, the most popular of which is **sociobiology.** According to this perspective, ethnic interest is biogenetically "wired" into the human species as a mechanism for transmitting genes from one generation to the next. Pierre van den Berghe (1981), for example, traces the origins of ethnic sentiment and racial bonding to an extension of kinship group solidarity. Any kinship group with knowledge of its own common ancestry and descent tends to act in a manner that preserves itself by providing mutual aid and cooperation. Involvement with related others ensures the long-term survival of the "species"—albeit at some expense to any specific individual. It follows from this that even ostensibly altruistic actions that assist our kin have the effect of protecting and promoting our evolutionary well-being. The twin-edged tendency of primordial ethnic identity is clearly apparent: The very bond that unites and secures may also divide and destroy, depending on the circumstances.

On balance, the evidence is insufficient to confirm the validity of the sociobiology theory. Sociologists themselves are split on the merits of sociobiology as an explanatory device, in part because of the ambiguous role assigned to social forces in shaping human behaviour. On the one hand, there is something to recommend in sociobiology. By casting ethnic feelings into our genetic and evolutionary past, sociobiology can explain the tenacity and the intensely emotional appeal of ethnicity, especially when compared to alternative explanations for bonding (Brown 1989). On the other, many are disturbed by the political implications of reductionist arguments that link biology and culture. Culture and environment, after all, intervene in any relationship between genes and behaviour. Our capacity for culture and learning is the trigger that releases us from the imprisonment of our genetic code. We may be genetically predisposed to identify with our "own kind" in preserving our own personal survival. But we are also free to choose otherwise, and many have done so by repudiating their ethnic heritage.

Instrumentalist Thesis: "Continuity in a Sea of Change"

The second set of explanations, the **instrumentalist thesis,** approaches ethnicity as a means to an end. Ethnicity persists because it provides a tool for coping with the globalizing demands of contemporary society. Of particular note is the relevance of ethnicity as a source of identity and meaning in an uncertain world of diversity and change. Ethnicity and the search for identity are primarily expressions of a perhaps universal desire for social space and cultural location in contemporary society. This instrumentalist perspective points to ethnicity as a buffer for insulating individuals from the pressures of a remorselessly amoral and competitive world. In a world of "doing," the appeal of "being" may account for the popularity and appeal of ethnicity. A commitment to ethnicity allows an escape from feelings of irrelevance and powerlessness as well as alienation and impersonality by restoring a measure of meaning in an increasingly meaningless world. Appeals to ethnicity foster a sense of relief, continuity, belonging, importance, and security, especially for those at the margins of society without alternative channels for coping with societal stress.

Ethnic involvements, in other words, permit meaningful identity to be crafted at a time of expanding mass society. A "quasi-kinship" community is sustained that not only accounts for the tenacity of ethnic attachments in contexts of unremitting rationality, especially in light of state-planned social orders to ensure a society-wide level of standardization and central control (Scott 1998). It also helps to explain the intense and universal appeal of such affiliation when confronting the relentless pressures for conformity, brought on in part by the spread of liberal pluralism with its emphasis on commonality rather than difference. To be sure, not all ethnic experiences are instrumental in the sense of providing instant relief in an anomic world. Breakdowns in the modern political process and incongruities in liberal pluralism (especially its rejection of corporate ethnic groups as anathema to individualism) have produced a postmodern expression of the ethnic experiences that is contradictory, fluid, and fragmentary (Gross 1996). As we shall see in the next section, even these fractured ethnic experiences may serve as a workable response in a world where old rules rarely apply but the new have yet to be entrenched.

Constructivist Thesis: "Strength in Numbers"

A **constructivist** explanation of the ethnic surge is located within the framework of group dynamics. Ethnicity is seen as a socially constructed response to political and economic opportunities and the attainment of goals consistent with a group's interests. The concept of social construction is not used in the sense of ideological categories that conceal the real principles of social structure ("false consciousness") (Smaje 1997). Rather, the social constructivist position affirms that there is nothing natural or normal about the world we live in despite continued efforts by vested interests to normalize and naturalize the world out there. Social conventions that guide or organize are continually constructed and reconstructed through a process of human interaction. Similarly, ethnicity is not a natural feature of society, but a constructed response to material exclusion and a search for social meanings in a politically effective manner.

A variation of this explanation, the **resource mobilization thesis,** is firmly grounded in a sociology of group competition. Ethnicity is defined as a catalyst for political mobilization and a vehicle for resource competition, especially in contexts where an ethnic division of labour reflects a situation of uneven economic development (Hechter 1975; Gross 1996). Dominant sectors monopolize the wealth and power at the expense of ethnically different subdominant groups, many of whom are locked into a position of inferiority because of their unskilled status. Resentment over this differential treatment may reach a boiling point when expectations rise. The ethnic division of labour, with its prevailing system of stratification, may buckle under pressure from the forces of mass education, mass communication, improved education, and ameliorative government policies. It is precisely at this point that ethnic activism and conflict are likely to escalate (Nagel and Olzak 1982; See and Wilson 1988). Action groups begin to mobilize around ethnic markers to improve their lot in the competitive struggle for scarce and valued items. Ethnic activism is further bolstered by actions of opportunistic elites and leaders who may articulate personal concerns in the language of group interests.

The resource mobilization theory argues that ethnic minorities will take united action to lay claim to rightful entitlement. Collective action is also taken to thwart state intrusion into minority affairs (Adam 1989). Emphasis on collective rather than individual responses is a preferred course of action. Two questions are uppermost: First, why do ethnic groups prefer to act on a collective basis to achieve their goals rather than as individuals or neighbourhood associations? Put simply, a collective basis is superior for coping with the demands of a complex and bureaucratized society. Only large-scale social movements possess the human resources and critical mass to compete effectively at a national level or to influence central policy structures. Second, why are ethnic attachments important in securing the loyalty and commitment of members? What is the tactical advantage of relying on ethnicity as a basis for mobilizing people into groups? Recruitment by ethnic bonds is perceived as more natural and durable than the "artificial" linkages inherent in political or economic organizations. These bonds are cemented by emotional involvement with persons of one's own kind, a kind of quasi-kinship that needs no justification beyond its own existence (Brown 1989). These quasi-kinship ties infuse the movement with the commitment necessary to wage a protracted struggle against seemingly insurmountable odds. Ethnicity thus serves as a useful criterion for political mobilization, since it combines an objective base (culture, language, religion, institutions) with a common symbolism and shared consciousness.

Any lingering notions about ethnicity as a romantic exercise in nostalgia should be dispelled by now. Rather than a regressive or emotional response to the modern challenges of an increasingly contested world, ethnicity constitutes a rationally constructed vehicle to further collective interests and exploit economic and political opportunities (Gross 1996). Nor is ethnicity simply an affective desire to discover "roots" in the hopes of recovering historical continuities. In many ways, the dynamics of ethnicity resemble contemporary interest groups in function and process (Cohen 1969; Glazer and Moynihan 1970). Under the banner of ethnicity, individuals corroborate to maximize social advantage in a rational and calculated manner (Hechter 1975). This strategic resource model also emphasizes the situational and constructed character of ethnic experiences (Nagel 1994). To the extent that such rational preferences are shared and shaped by structural constraints, the emergence of collective ethnic movements is patterned and predictable and subject to sociological analysis.

To Sum Up   Three approaches attempt to explain why ethnicity persists when many thought it wouldn't or shouldn't. Several dimensions of ethnicity may be concurrent. According to Rudolfo Stavenhagen, (a) ethnicity is an inherent primordial affiliation that reflects a deep sociobiological need for a sense of belonging to one's kind; (b) ethnicity represents a framework of social organization for attainment of expressive goals in a changing, diverse, and uncertain world; and (c) ethnicity constitutes a socially constructed response to uneven distributions of power and wealth, prompting people to emphasize their difference when useful, downplay it when seen as a handicap. Evidence suggests that sociologists are eschewing a static and fixed model of ascriptive ethnicity in favour of a more dynamic model that acknowledges instrumentality, constructedness, and adaptation to new political environments (Gross 1996). Paradigms have changed because ethnic groups have evolved from a premodern outlook (with its internal focus on consolidation and institutional self-sufficiency as the goal) to modern (with emphasis on integration within society at large as the goal) to postmodern (where hybrid identities oscillate between the past and present, involving a multiplicity of crossovers and border crossings in a world of fragmentation, multiplicity, plurality, and indeterminancy [Hall 1996]). It is not our intent to suggest one is better than the other. Rather, each provides an insight into aspects of the ethnic experience in any given situation, namely, its powerful hold on people; its popularity in times of change and uncertainty; and its practicality in the competition for scarce resources. There is no reason why primordial explanations that address the historical meaning of ethnicity cannot coexist with instrumentalist arguments that posit relief and satisfaction in addition to constructivist claims for ethnicity as a competitive edge (Smaje 1997).

EXPRESSIONS OF ETHNICITY: COMMUNITY, IDENTITY, SOCIAL MOVEMENT

Ethnicity can be expressed in different ways. At one level, ethnicity is manifested in ethnic groups who live together in relatively self-sufficient communities. At another level, ethnicity manifests itself through different expressions of identity, ranging in scope and intensity from the individual to the group, from the traditional to the insurgent. At a third level, ethnicity is interpreted as a social movement with nationalistic overtones. These social movements challenge mainstream ethnicities and structures and invariably culminate in a clash of wills over whose agendas will prevail.

Ethnicity As Community

Ethnicity refers to a principle of potential group formation and at times remains highly abstract and hardly extends beyond a symbolic role. It classifies persons with shared and felt identification into a category, but this "collective sentiment" may not be activated into an action group. At other times, ethnicity serves as a principle for uniting ancestrally related persons into ongoing social units. Those with a common sense of history and peoplehood are united temporarily to advance individual or collective claims. In still other circumstances ethnicity provides a basis for relatively permanent communities with stable institutional settings of like-minded individuals. Such group formation reflects both self- and other identifications. In some cases, ethnic groups define themselves as unique and alike by virtue of common ancestry and select cultural symbols. In others, such as the case of early Chinese immigrants to Canada, the host society imposes a demeaning ethnic label on migrants who then resort to community bonds for adaptive purposes in an unfriendly environment.

The ethnic community can be conceptualized in different ways. It can be viewed as a cultural enclave with a distinctive set of values, traditions, and habits that have evolved and have been transformed over time. Institutions are established that offer a number of political, economic, and cultural functions for individuals who are related by descent or kinship. Ethnic communities can also be seen as systems of social relations. These consist of interpersonal and kinship relations for emotional and material support; they also entail a framework for collective activities. Parts of urban Canada are composed of a mosaic of ethnic communities, including the widely renown Chinatowns in Vancouver and Toronto as well as relatively self-sufficient Hasidic Jews in Montreal. Ethnic community organizations may assist in the preservation of language and transmission of culture. They also establish a power base for advancing political consciousness and action. These organizations may attract resources and influence if local leaders can command loyalty within the community and deliver this "commodity" as electoral support for government initiatives. Those communities with a relatively high degree of "institutional completeness" (Breton 1964) equip their members with mutual support, networks, services, and a source of identity. Involvement in these institutions is seen as accelerating rates of integration into wider society without loss of cultural integrity. Recent immigrants in particular may find economic and cultural refuge in communities: Such a social oasis may help in facilitating the transition from the society of origin to urban Canada. Similarly, ethnic communities provide a sense of security in a highly impersonal and mechanized society by buffering the old from the new, the individual from society, and the familiar from the strange (Isajiw 1977).

INSIGHT 4–2	Chinatowns: New Communities For Old

Ethnic communities have a number of functions. Not only do they assist in preserving the past, but they can also serve as a link with the future. Chinatown communities in Toronto provide a useful glimpse into the dynamics of ethnicity in contemporary settings. Chinese-Canadians number about 350,000 in Greater Toronto's urban population of about 4 million. At one time, most Chinese-Canadians resided in the enclave located primarily but not exclusively in the Spadina-Dundas region of downtown Toronto (Gorrie 1991). There has been a recent exodus of Chinatown residents to suburbs such as Scarborough and Mississauga. Compared to the older generations, who prefer the accessibility and intimacy of the downtown area, many new immigrants and younger Chinese-Canadians have opted for the spaciousness and amenities associated with suburban living. Life in the downtown ghetto is dismissed as quaint and as anachronistic as the archaic "ponytail" (Gorrie 1991:18). The suburbs provide a comparable range of benefits, but without the costs of congestion or fear of crime. All manner of services and transactions related to government services or private business are available in English or Chinese. Community centres provide a focal point for interaction and exchange. This suggests that, the lure of assimilation notwithstanding, Chinese-Canadians will remain a distinct population, with a unique constellation of lifestyles, patterns of interactions, and outlooks on what it means to be Chinese and Canadian.

But references to ethnic communities as collective entities should not obscure the prevalence of internal diversity. A residential location and cultural bond are not a guarantee of community harmony or group consensus. Each community may embrace members who vary in outlook and commitment. Political cleavages are readily apparent in some cases, with a potential for factional infighting because of differences in age, sex, income, education, and length of residence (Du Plessis and Alice 1998). Ethnic community members convene not only to promote corporate interests, but they also jockey for leadership and status. An image of corporate unity may be fostered primarily for the benefit of impression management. Beneath the constructed façade may lurk internal tensions that threaten community solidarity or consensus on important group issues.

Younger members may be especially estranged by the contradictory demands of an ethnic community. Of particular concern are the ambiguities in balancing a deference to ethnicity with the pressures of peer group conformity. Consider the dilemmas: If ethnicity is emphasized, ethnic youth may endanger social acceptability or economic opportunity; if ethnicity is deemphasized, it may be difficult to establish an appropriate sense of identity without invoking parental wrath or community ostracism. The paradoxes confronting second-generation youth may be of such magnitude as to call into question the legitimacy of parental ethnicity (Du Plessis and Alice 1998). The main barriers include the following:

1. Language. The language barrier and lack of communication are key catalysts in widening the gap between native speakers and non-native speakers.

2. Demands. Parents expect their children to fulfill various obligations, from church to costume, yet participate and succeed in mainstream institutions such as education.

3. Obedience. Young adults are expected to be obedient to elders and defer uncritically to tradition, even if this deferential respect runs counter to the demands of society at large.

4. Success. Parents expect children to succeed at school, but students are afraid of ridicule, ostracism, or being put down by their peers (tall poppy syndrome) if they excel or achieve in ways that are thought of as "uncool."

In brief, a newly shaped ethnic identity must be forged which may emanate from their parents and community, yet a community-based identity must be adjusted and modified to meet the cutthroat demands of a cosmopolitan and changing society (see also Underhill-Sem and Fitzgerald 1997).

Ethnicity As Identity

Many accept the existence of ethnicity as an organizing principle with remarkable staying power. Ethnicity as a principle establishes guidelines for group behaviour. It also provides a sense of identity for individuals who wish to foster a sense of distinctiveness that distinguishes them from others. Identity entails that part of the person that needs to fit into a group to ensure both a reflection of themselves as well as a sense of safety and security. These identities can be broadly defined as personal attachments to a group (or tradition) on the basis of commonly shared ancestry, experiences, and characteristics (Driedger 1989). In certain cases, ethnic identities are imposed by outside sources; in others, they are voluntarily adopted on the basis of the way individuals or groups feel about themselves. Some identities, such as "white ethnicity," are passive insofar as people are not consciously aware of actively defining themselves by these terms unless challenged to do so. Others may be active in that individuals are conscious of them and act accordingly to protect or promote a cherished identity. Still other identities are politicized in that they provide the basis for collective action to achieve goals. In all cases, identities are relational in that meanings are acquired by way of oppositions to the "other" (Hall 1996).

One of the identities open to many Canadians is derived from ethnicity. In a multicultural society such as ours, many individuals regard their ethnic background as a component of "who I am." Ethnicity and ethnic identity can assume different levels of importance from person to person as well as from one region of Canada to the next (Isajiw 1990). Some reject their ethnic background and want to be identified only as Canadians, except perhaps for special occasions; others maintain a dual identity without much difficulty; still others prefer to retain strong nationalistic feelings and can't wait to return "home." The properties associated with ethnicity and ethnic identities are varied, but may (a) embrace both objective and subjective components, (b) be imposed or voluntarily selected, (c) acquire a variety of overlapping ascriptive loyalties, (d) be for genuine ("primordial or essential") or practical (instrumental) purposes, and (e) be situational and intermittent yet sufficiently durable to persist across a variety of domains. Identities can be positive or negative: An emphasis on ethnicity may imperil mobility and opportunity; an underemphasis may hinder self-esteem and identity (Porter 1965). Some researchers suggest a genetically-wired tendency for individuals to associate with members of their own group over others (van den Berghe 1981). Others suggest ethnic identities arise, persist, and change in response to the vagaries of intergroup behaviour (See and Wilson 1988). This debate over ethnicity as essential or provisional points to the possibility of different "styles" of ethnic identity in modern settings, namely, lived-in, situational (symbolic), postmodern, and insurgent.

Lived-in Ethnicity: Full-Time and Functional Identity

Individuals with common cultural values or religious beliefs may strongly identify with a particular ethnic group. This attachment to the norms, values, and institutions of this group constitutes a serious statement about personal affiliation. Anabaptist sects such as the Hutterites, sociologically speaking, are authentic communities governed by rules, values, and sanctions. Here, the principle of ethnicity is expressed in the organization of viable groups that continue to exert a pervasive influence in shaping members' lives. These individuals admit that their identification with the cultural past makes a difference in how they think and behave. Involvement at this level presupposes a canopy of constraints, demands, and responsibilities for members of the group. Individuals are born into these primary groups, and their membership is irrevocably assigned at birth.

We refer to this type of identification and involvement as *lived-in ethnic identity* (Boldt 1985). A **lived-in ethnicity** extols a difference that makes a difference in terms of rewards, relationships, and recognition. The costs entailed ensure that this style of ethnicity is disappearing in Canada. Restricted largely to rural areas and certain urban enclaves, conventional ethnic groups have lost much of their moral authority in shaping human behaviour. Many of these groups can no longer supply a common set of shared values, enforce mutual obligations or responsibilities, supply incentives or sanctions, or secure compliance from members. Others are gradually being replaced by social categories (people who share one or two characteristics in common) and social aggregrates (people who happen to be there) (see Jaret 1995). An "old-fashioned" style of ethnicity no longer appeals to those who are anxious to derive full benefit from a socially mobile and achievement-oriented society. This lack of formality is creating the basis for a more flexible and fluid arrangement.

Situational Ethnicity: Symbolic and Negotiated Identity

Another kind of ethnic identity is common across Canada. This ethnicity is indeterminate and negotiated; it represents a strategic personal resource that allows individuals to improve their life chances within a pluralistic environment. In contrast with the obligatoriness of lived-in identity, the newer ethnicity emphasizes both choice and flexibility and symbolic commitments and situational adjustments.

The "new" ethnicity reflects a process of adaptation by immigrants in their adopted country. Incoming immigrants who become established through work or social involvement may become estranged from the behavioural aspects of their cultural heritage (in terms of language use, friendship circles, and residential patterns). Many are increasingly attracted to a lifestyle associated with consumerism, career enhancement, and materialism. Ethnic attachments become situational, nonbinding, and tentative, with commitments both provisional and superficial, and lacking conformist demands upon members (Roberts and Clifton 1990). Involvement in ethnic organizations declines (except on isolated occasions or in favourable circumstances) to the point of insignificance—if measured by the frequency or intensity of institutional participation. Yet many new Canadians may retain a strong emotional tie or cognitive commitment to their cultural past. In resisting the lure of wholesale assimilation, they reveal an affective attachment to the community as a reference group. Unaccepted, however, are the restrictions and responsibilities of full-time and lived-in ethnicity (Roberts and Clifton 1990).

Social scientists (Gans 1979; Weinfeld 1985) refer to the emergence of this "part-time" ethnicity as **situational (or symbolic) ethnic identity.** A person's degree of participation in ethnic clubs, knowledge of ethnic language, circle of friends, place of residence, and marital patterns are largely irrelevant with situational ethnicity (Isajiw 1977). Involvement and frequency are not important; what is salient is an identification with that ethnicity and the symbols associated with its distinctiveness. Individuals, in other words, do not so much belong to an ethnic group as they voluntarily affiliate with the symbols of that culture as preferences dictate and situations demand. Ethnic minority members do not necessarily share a common culture; more accurately, they possess a sense of identity or affiliation with that culture on the basis of perceived similarities and common symbols. Not everyone, of course, has such a choice of options: Because of the centrality and constraints of visibility this option may be less applicable to people of colour. Even here, however, the prominence of race does not necessarily diminish the importance of other interlocking identities such as gender, with the primacy of one rather than another a function of context (Omi and Winant 1993). In short, ethnicity for most represents a resource that can be manipulated in the search for identity or struggle to gain advantage. It goes without saying that references to ethnicity as situational or manipulated are not intended to trivialize or demean the ethnic experience as inauthentic, but to demonstrate its underlying logic.

The situational nature of contemporary identity provides answers to vexing questions about Canadian ethnicity. Three questions prevail. First, can distinct ethnic identities survive in situations where the traditional past has disappeared to meet the needs of modern society? Second, can individuals continue to identify themselves as "ethnics" long after abandoning all involvement in group activities? According to the logic of situational ethnicity, the answer to both questions is yes. The decline of a particular lifestyle will not necessarily diminish the validity of the ethnic experience. After all, what is critical is the identification with select aspects of that cultural lifestyle—not the degree or intensity of involvement. This style of identity is relatively painless and voluntary as well as abstract and effortless. It is also well suited to the needs of a socially mobile and competitive society.

Third, is a hyphenated Canadian possible? Is it possible to identify and participate as a Canadian, yet retain an affiliation with a certain ethnic heritage such as Lithuanian (or Chinese or aboriginal)? Again, the answer is in the affirmative. Dual identity entitles people to compartmentalize their secondary ("ethnic") identity from their primary ("citizen") identity. The demands of a particular context as well as the nature of the ethnic group will determine which identity is to be activated. Affiliation with select symbols should not be regarded as necessarily incompatible with involvement in mainstream values and lifestyles. Dual identities are not mutually exclusive; rather, they may complement each other in fulfilling diverse personal needs and goals. Nor does identification with select symbolic elements necessarily interfere with the business of making a living, provided identification is restricted to the cognitive rather than the behavioural level. That allows everyone to regard themselves as an "ethnic" while maintaining full and active participation within the institutional framework of Canadian society. Having the best of both worlds also helps to explain the popularity and persistence of situational ethnicities.

Postmodern Ethnic Identities

Most perspectives on ethnicity tend to reflect a "structuralist" or "modernist" approach to intergroup dynamics. Structuralists see structures (namely, those of institutions, groups, roles, tribes) as the primary source of human identity and group relations; hence ethnic identities are thought to be organized around membership in lived-in "structures" such as nations, tribes, subtribes, bands, and communities. Membership within these structures or organizations is regarded as fixed and closed, with the result that there is little movement in or out of these groups (McHugh 1998). Such a structuralist approach may have the benefit of simplicity and certitude; it may even provide a proactive response to ensure cultural survival in the teeth of mainstream encroachment. This essentialism also runs the risk of reifying the fluidity of social life into a host of coordinate points around which a person or group must identify for entitlement, regardless of whether any of this bears any relationship with reality.

Structuralists tend to see structures as determinants of thought and behaviour; poststructuralism (or postmodernism) defines structures as the consequences of largely personal choices and subject to perpetual process. In contrast with the modernist assumptions about a coherent and singular ("essentialist") identity rooted in land or ancestry, identities are perceived as relational and contextual as well as negotiated and contingent, both individually and collectively, resulting in compromise or contradiction by way of self-identification and political action (Castells 1997). Such provisional identifications are neither stable nor coherent, much less fixed in some kind of essentialized past, as Stuart Hall (1996) reminds us, but evolving and subject to continuous play of history, power, and culture—never completed, always in process. The provisionality of **postmodern ethnicity** explores the diverse ways in which identity is constructed and reconstructed without having to conform to conventions, consistencies, or boundaries. Ethnic identity is acknowledged as complex and multitextured, inherently open, constantly negotiated, layered and contradictory, contextual in varying with time and place, and involving a constant series of borders, crossings, and recrossings across varied frontiers. Ethnic identities tend to be crafted and recreated without any degree of certitude and prediction in a changing world of fluidity and flux, thus enhancing the possibility for recombinant ("hybrid") mixtures to emerge (Giroux 1995). Such identities tend to be provisional and contingent in oscillating between tradition and translation and marked by a degree of "in-betweenness" as traditional sources of authority and identity are contested by fragmentation, uncertainty, and plurality (see Gillespie 1996).

The relationship between structures and identity is undergoing a significant shift. Ethnic groups (tribes, communities, etc.) are not fixed and durable entities, but more closely resemble rhizomic webs of interconnected associations as people shift from one to another as the situation demands (Gross 1996). Structures, in turn, are seen as emergent and provisional instead of rigid and determining, in a perpetual process of becoming through meaningful interaction. Nowhere is this more evident than in transmigrational ethnic communities: When ethnic minorities are uprooted because of migration from a homeland, innovative patterns of ethnicity and identity emerge that may be only tangentially connected to those left behind (Cohen 1998; Anthias 1998). The emergence of identity politics as a major force is a consequence of these new ethnicities.

INSIGHT 4–3	Identity Politics: Postmodern Ethnicities in a Postcolonizing World

Human beings are identity-seeking animals, both as individuals and as collectivities.

T.K. Oommen (1997:20)

Debate over identity has emerged as one of the more vexing but controversial topics in contemporary cultural politics. Put baldly, identity is at the heart of all contemporary politics. The drive to have a particular identity acknowledged and respected is a pivotal determinant in influencing the shape of group dynamics (Salée 1995). Few should be surprised by such a turn of events. With the demise of Marxist notions of class conflict as grounds for explaining political involvement to achieve desired goals, people are casting about for new ways to be rewarded and recognized (Gillespie 1996). But the eclipse of Marxist foundationalism has not resulted in a rush to embrace broader national or international identities (Littleton 1996). To be sure, national identities such as being Canadian continue to provide meaning for life, secure a sense of self-respect, and furnish a sense of belonging and security (Nielson 1996/97). However, this identity does not exhaust people's sources of identity; nor is it necessarily the one that people embrace as the most important to their lives. This is especially true with regard to cultural minorities such as indigenous peoples, many of whom are moving to define who they are and what they would like to be. Instead of seeing themselves as citizens of the world or of a nation-state in pursuit of common interests because of shared humanity, indigenous people increasingly prefer to define themselves as members of an ethnicity (or nation) and often are fiercely protective of their choices.

This profusion of these largely nominated identities is hardly surprising. There is little doubt that people are drawing their sense of identity from a much broader range of interests and sources than was once the case, given the loss of stable group membership, meaning in a meaningless world, advances in communication technologies, and control over life and life chances (Gillespie 1996). The postmodern world we live in is a pluralistic world where immigrants mingle with national minorities and indigenous peoples, where cultural boundaries are constantly invented, renegotiated or hybridized, and where new social movements assert the attractiveness of new patterns of belonging based on gender, sexual preferences, indigeneity, and ethnicity. This is especially evident at the level of ethnicity: Its centrality to all forms of cultural identity is widely acknowledged, even if an ethnic attachment does not exhaust all channels of identification but complements or competes with other axes of difference such as gender (Littleton 1996). Ethnicities formerly suppressed or stigmatized are reasserting themselves and defiantly reclaiming their rightful place in a postcolonizing, postassimilationist society. After all, the Civil Rights movement may have secured legal representation and equal institutional access. It did not, however, address the issue of minority cultural representation. This omission has left minorities at a distinct disadvantage, both politically and economically, without the tools to transform public perception of the historical past. The claiming of ethnic identities may be one way of drawing attention to injustices and defining new popular images. But this process may be so charged with emotion and experience, that acts of violence and heroism are routinely invoked in resisting and defending such claims and counterclaims.

The prominence of identity politics in a postmodern world cannot be discounted.

Individualized identities may be too "small" to cope with processes of change, diversity, and uncertainty, while national identities are too "large or remote" to solve the problem of meaning, distinctiveness, and security. Shared ("universal") identities as humans may become secondary to particular identities as members of a definable group. Individuals are seeing themselves as more than rights-bearing organisms or citizens of the state. Preference is aimed at connecting with specific identity-conferring communities from which individuals draw their sense of security and belonging in an otherwise atomized world (Sigurdson 1996). With identity politics, differences become politicized and employed in the political struggle for recognition or resources (Spoonley 1993). In situations where identities provide a base for political action and where individuals routinely think of themselves in terms of "who they are," identity politics involve the decolonizing of minorities "from within" through creation of liberating identities with corresponding values and outlooks. These politicized identities are collectively organized around and constructed through political action in pursuit of identifiable goals such as gay rights and black pride. In short, identity politics are underpinned by three key attributes: (a) the perception of difference as fundamental, (b) its distinctiveness and exclusiveness as the basis for engagement and entitlement, and (c) the expectation that this difference will be recognized and respected (Littleton 1996). A preoccupation with identity as the basis for a politics of difference is played out in different ways, from the exclusionary strategies of separate classrooms to the atrocities of Balkan ethnic cleansing.

Identity politics are often described as the politics of naming oneself in relationship to others. At the core of identity politics is the privileging of difference as fundamental in defining who we are, what we get, and how we relate to others. The politics of difference acknowledge differences rather than commonalities as a basis for entitlement. Differences rather than commonalities are also used to define how people relate to each other and engage society at large. This politicization of difference as differenced puts identity politics at odds with postulates of liberal pluralism, thanks to the latter's denial of group differences as relevant because of universalistic assumptions and abstract individualism (Schneiderman 1996). Liberal pluralism endorses the universal notion that what we have in common is more important than what separates us; that what we accomplish as individuals in an openly competitive environment is more important than who we are as members of a group; that the content of our character is more important than the colour of our skin or national origins; that participating freely in the open space of public life is more significant than locking people into localized and particularistic concerns; and that reason and compromise are more important than raw experience as a basis for knowledge, rewards, or relationships. Not only does identity politics challenge each of these postulates; proposed instead by identity politics is a recognition that the subject is socially constitutive within a context of group differences. Society can only become equitable and inclusive if identity-related differences are taken into account, as are the perspectives of minorities whose distinctiveness provides a legitimacy for defining rewards, recognition, and relationships. Advocates of identity politics may argue that recognition and acceptance of differences are critical to an inclusive citizenship. But it is equally obvious that liberal democracies are poorly positioned for endorsing concrete policy measures to satisfy the demands of identity seekers for inclusion on their terms, especially if these concessions involve parallel institutions, relatively autonomous self-governing structures, and separate power bases (Salée 1995).

How do we account for this commitment to politicize, that is, to create, protect, or preserve, group identities in the face of globalizing assimilation or localized dispersion? The magnitude and pace of contemporary social change may be largely responsible. Certainties once associated with the modern world are vanishing in the face of intense global competition, radicalized individualism, a disintegrating civil society, increasingly porous territorial borders and erosion of the nation-state as the primary source of legitimacy, and cultural upheavals created by the proliferation of information and computer-mediated technologies. The seemingly fixed and clearly defined identities of universal humanity or sovereign statehood are eroding, and this erosion hastens the fragmentation of the postmodern self as relatively free floating and detached from conventional anchors of identity formation. Postmodern identities reflect the predicaments of a postmodern era: Instead of single unified (and centred) individuals, we have become vessels of multiple identities and provisional subjectivities that may have more in common with those around the world than the immediate locale. The dissolution of the familiar and reassuring may result in people losing their sense of social belonging, a rootedness in traditional collectivities such as kinship or community. The confluence of uncertainty and change compels individuals to withdraw into social groups that are familiar and emotionally satisfying (Littleton 1996). As Manuel Castells (1997:66) writes:

> When the world becomes too large to be controlled, social actors aim at shrinking it back to their size and reach. When networks dissolve time and space, people anchor themselves in places, and recall their historic memory.

Identity politics may be the definitive social force of the late twentieth century. But many are critical of this preoccupation with

identity and the celebration of identity-related differences as a basis for engagement or entitlement (see Schneiderman 1996). Critics dislike the kind of identity politics that parcels people into relatively self-contained cultural groups, knowable only to their members with the result that only a black can talk about black experiences while any external criticism is rejected especially if not reflecting "raw" experience (see Eisenstein 1996). This concern over identity as an excuse for standing apart rather than working together is aptly captured by Richard Sigurdson (1996:59), who claims:

> To the extent that individuals identify with their own ethnic or cultural groups, there will be a tendency to withdraw into the confines of that group. The result is a sort of cultural ghettoization, with each group retreating into its own territory and tending to its own parochial interests, without much attention to the cultivation of a larger societal culture.

Others are critical of the abandonment of principle under the relativism of identity politics. The potential for social transformation through collective action is compromised by this preoccupation with the self. As Myrna Kostash (1996) writes, those in positions of power can afford to luxuriate in a decentred subject when they are already at the universal centre of subjective. Those who are powerless, by contrast, need principles to assert claims and challenge the status quo. Yet others are concerned over identity politics as a cultural solution to a structural problem. A focus on identity by way of cultural politics may expand middle class opportunity, yet prove irrelevant to the marginal classes in need of structural solutions to fundamental problems associated with alienation and marginalization (Pearson 1996). Reducing disadvantage to the level of identity loss rarely constitutes a threat to the underlying social relations in a capitalist society, thus reinforcing the marginalization of those already at the edges. Such a depoliticization of grievance may pose only a limited threat to the state which in the past has shown a remarkable resiliency in co-opting the rhetoric of cultural nationalism into the language of politics or reform without necessarily having to make substantial adjustments (Poata-Smith 1996).

Insurgent Ethnic Identity: "Ethnicity That Stings"

Both lived-in and situational ethnic identities appear to be relatively innocuous. With few exceptions, these identities endorse the multicultural axiom of "live and let live" or the slogan about "agreeing to disagree." *Insurgent ethnic identities,* by contrast, are much more assertive about what they believe is right or wrong, are highly politicized in terms of what they want, and more aggressive in their approach to goal attainment. Affiliation with insurgent ethnicity transcends mere identification or celebration. Insurgent ethnicity takes this notion of a shared attachment to a people, tradition, or territory and pushes this consciousness to an extreme, often violent, limit. The sense of belonging, so critical to the concept of ethnicity, is directed inward and outward in casting for new relations with the "other." In place of coexistence is a politicized assertion of peoplehood for establishing a new political order based on self-determination and autonomy. More importantly, an intense dislike of others, especially when religion or language differences are incorporated, provides a defining feature of **insurgent ethnicity.** Such a collectivity is willing to take whatever measures necessary, including the revival of dormant grievances, to achieve their goals of an exclusive, essentialized identity. Expressions of this deep-seated dislike of anyone outside your group can range from the open hatred of white supremacist groups or Louis Farrakhan's Nation of Islam, to the violent actions associated with "final solutions" and "ethnic cleansings."

The playing out of insurgent ethnicities invariably leads to ethnic conflict. Admittedly, ethnic differences do not automatically generate confrontation (Banton 1997). Conflict, however, can make people much more conscious of ethnic differences. The exclusive, often essentialized nature of insurgent ethnic identities is conducive to actions that pit one ethnicity against another in the competition for space or resources. Many of these conflicts have deep colonial roots. Ethnicity as insurgency signals the undoing of centuries of colonial damage by breaking up the artificial and contrived nation-states established by colonial powers. Consider Africa, where boundaries between states were created for political, military, economic, and diplomatic reasons, with little regard for ethnic differences and tribal borders. These expedient states are brittle and prone to fracture by tribal groups who seek a degree of autonomy at the expense of others. Ethnic conflicts inevitably arise from the clash of opposing principles, that is, state territorial integrity versus national self-determination, especially in those countries where there is a lack of "fit" between the political borders of the state (a political organization) and the cultural borders of the nation (a politicized ethnic group). In this sense, the uncoupling of an ethnic nation from state is not abnormal but a logical and necessary response to a nineteenth-century problem. Similar situations exist in Canada where ethnic conflicts involving the three major nations can be attributed to our colonial past.

The notion of insurgent ethnicities may strike many as illogical or irrational, at least when interpreted from the perspective of the nation-state, with its commitment to civic nationalism and secular coexistence. Emotions run high with radical ethnicities, and this affectivity often goes beyond rational analysis or behaviour modification. Not surprisingly, insurgent ethnicities rarely respond to so-called rational solutions: Sanctions as varied as international censure, trade embargoes, and military force do not carry as much moral clout as the ethnic imperative. If anything, the threat of external force is likely to fortify ethnic resolve against meddlesome outsiders. Nor can UN-based initiatives guarantee compliance; by definition, insurgent ethnicities refuse to play by conventional rules. That defiance alone makes insurgent ethnicity a potent force in destabilizing a national or international order. Nowhere is this more evident than in the growth of social movements that advance the expression of an ethnicity that stings.

Ethnicity As a "New" Social Movement

The dismantling of the Berlin Wall in 1989 was widely heralded as a defining moment in global history. Many saw its demise as a triumph of universalism and reason over the irrationalities of ideologues, rampant prejudices, and petty hostilities. But the promise proved short-lived: Predictions of a new global order with its commitment to create culturally homogeneous consumers have not materialized. Nor has the proposed ascendancy of liberal democracy, with its notion of a nation as a community of equal individuals, both secular and tolerant, and united in patriotic attachment to a shared set of political practices and democratic values. What is increasingly evident instead is an intensely parochial era in which the "key narrative of the new world order is the disintegration of nation states into warring factions; the key architects of that order are warlords; and the key language of our age is *ethnic nationalism*" (emphasis added) (Ignatieff 1994). With several exceptions, virtually all conflicts since 1990 have involved confrontations between ethnic groups within existing borders, largely because of the political vacuum created by collapsed states and stagnant economies. Ancient animosities and dormant hatreds have been resurrected by these national cultural minorities with a passion and fury that had rattled an abiding faith in the decency of human nature (Behrens 1994; Kymlicka 1995). This ethnochauvinism has challenged the fundamental tenets of liberal society, in effect giving rise to ethnic-based social movements.

These ethnic insurgencies constitute what are known as "new" social movements. In contrast with traditional social movements that often revolved around issues of labour and class, new social movements rely on ethnic identities to galvanize like-minded individuals into action for a cause. Ethnicity as a social movement entails the idea of peoples engaging in collective action to achieve the political goals of identity, voice, or land. Ethnicity provides a basis for mobilizing individuals into collective action; it also provides the motivation and rationale to achieve ethnically defined goals. This surge of ethnic movements has come about for various reasons. The collapse of superpower colonialism has given rise to social formations that emphasize ethnic loyalties rather than the abstractions of citizenship (Ignatieff 1994). Tribal conflicts, once suppressed by colonialist control and Cold War politics, have found receptive audiences. The UN-based principle of national self-determination continues to provide a normative basis for making ethnic political claims against the state (Bell-Fialkoff 1993). Structures that formerly colonized national ethnic minorities are no longer acceptable. Proposed instead are new arrangements that sharply curtail state jurisdiction while bolstering a people's model of self-determination (see Alfred 1995). Nationalist movements involving ethnic groups are known as **ethnic nationalism.**

Ethnic Nationalism

Ethnic nationalisms are not new social phenomena. They entail an age-old quest for autonomy, unity, and identity, often at the expense of those who fall outside that collectivity (Fawcett 1996; Smith 1996). The origins of ethnic nationalism can be traced to nineteenth-century European Romanticism, with its disavowal of Enlightenment ideals. Romanticists disagreed with Enlightenment ideals of universal human progress by way of reason and science. This nineteenth-century ideal of a sovereign state as the politicized expression of a single people in a particular territory continued to be manipulated to justify all manner of violence and oppression (Graff 1994). Endorsed was the notion of a **nation** as a community of people who were racially uniform and culturally distinct (Jakobsh 1994). Unlike a **state,** which is essentially a political and administrative system, a nation consists of people who believe they are different and deserving of political autonomy on those grounds. Membership is defined on the basis of birthright and descent from a common ancestry. Loyalty to the community or homeland ("nation") precedes any commitment to nation-states or social classes. The territorial rights, distinctive language, and shared ethnicity of this imagined political community must be defended at all costs from hostile outsiders. Recourse to violence may be permissible not only to preserve autonomy or authenticity, but to consolidate the bonds of belonging by defending the homeland against enemies, both internal and external, by whatever means necessary.

Central to these nationalist movements is a guiding ideology involving a collective sense of peoplehood (Smith 1994; Freeden 1998). As an ideology and social movement, nationalism constitutes the political expression of a people who believe they have a common ancestry and shared destiny to govern themselves in a place they associate with their history and its fulfillment (Wiebe 1996/97). Nationalism asserts a belief that the world is divisible into states (a political organization with authority over a territory) or nations (as politicized ethnicity with a people's self-assertion of autonomy over identity and homeland), with rights to self-determination either as self-governing entities ("nation-states or countries") or as subunits within society ("nations"). Each of these entities is unique and distinctive, according to the tenets of nationalism, and their full potential can only be realized by entrenching autonomy. Nationalism as a cultural ideal concedes the possibility that many personal identities may exist, but none so important as identification with the nation or the state as the primary form of belonging and security. All expressions of nationalisms are grounded in this idealization of group exclusiveness and maintenance of internal cohesion and collective loyalty because of perceived external threats or unresolved grievances (Rothchild and Groth 1995).

But not all nationalisms are the same, with a common distinction distinguishing "ethnic" from "civic" nationalism (see Insight 4–4). Claims to ethnic nationalism are based on the principle of self-determination: National minorities strive to become majorities by revamping the existing political arrangement. They see themselves as fundamentally autonomous political communities, both sovereign in their own right and sharing in the sovereignty of society at large if necessary (see also Asch 1997). In doing so they hope to establish jurisdictional control over a defined homeland, in addition to the sovereign status denied to them as a subject people (Graff 1994). People want to become "normal," as the Québécois remind us; they want to be a majority in their own homeland rather than a minority in somebody else's. The path to ethnic nationalism can take different routes. Peaceful channels are pursued in some cases; in others, long-suppressed grievances and a craving for settling scores are more important than scoring points with the United Nations. Nationalism may be most violent when there are small differences between groups, confirming once again that hatred between kin (for example, Cain and Abel) is more ferocious than between enemies (Ignatieff 1995). The violence factor may be intensified when religious differences are at play, creating untold misery on both sides of the dispute. At times, ethnic nationalism represents a revolt against the modern and the universal, with a preference for the traditional and particular. At other times, it is essentially forward looking in crafting innovative political orders for working through differences. Sometimes, expressions of hot-blooded ethnicity are genuine; other times ethnicity represents a convenient front to camouflage or distract, to conceal or evade, or to deter or preserve. What is too often common among most of these movements is a re-luctance to concede a reciprocal right to live and let live (Havel 1994). This difference in out-look reveals the existence of competing nationalisms, as the next Insight Box demonstrates.

INSIGHT 4–4	**Nationalisms in Collision**

Contemporary societies, including Canada, are engaged in a protracted exercise known as society building. At the core of society build-ing is creation of a nationalism that provides a basis for securing consent and loyalty. Yet nationalisms exist that are contrary to soci-ety building. Canadians are witnessing the confluence of two competing nationalisms, or, more accurately, two groups of elites es-pousing nationalistic aims that are at cross-purposes. One nationalism seeks greater autonomy from the state: This move toward "independence" is rarely secessionist in ori-entation except, perhaps, as strategic rhetoric, given the costs and logistics of formally sep-arating. Preferred instead is a working rela-tionship between interdependent peoples as a way of working through differences in a spirit of constructive engagement. The other na-tionalism is geared toward Canada's ongo-ing growth as a distinct but cohesive society. This nationalism seeks to emulate the nine-teenth-century ideal of a sovereign state as the political expression of a single people within a particular territory. The ideological position of a nationalism is adopted with a view toward legitimizing attempts to mould, homogenize, and create a country (or soci-ety) out of various ethnic, indigenous, and immigrant groups (Connor 1972).

All nationalisms vest political sovereignty in the people. But different nationalisms ar-ticulate a different definition of who consti-tutes the people of a territory. Two patterns are discernible, in theory at any rate, based largely on divergent patterns of belonging, namely, *civic* and *ethnic nationalism*. Civic nationalism is concerned with society build-ing by strengthening the organization of the state. It maintains that society should be com-posed of all individuals, regardless of race or ethnicity, as long as they subscribe to the ideals of this constructed community. This nationalism is called civic, Ignatieff observes, because it envisages society as a constructed community of equal rights-bearing citizens organized around the pursuit of an idea. Ethnicity is largely irrelevant in determining belonging or inclusion. Membership in a civic society is open to anyone who agrees to comply with core values; those of liberal pluralism provide an ideological base for civic nationalism (see Smith 1994).

By contrast, ethnic nationalism is aimed at building nationhood by strengthening a "people" (or nation) at the expense of others if necessary. Membership in the nationhood is restricted to those who can demonstrate common roots ("bloodlines or descent") rather than shared attachments to key institutions. Unlike a state, which is comprised of numerous nations, a nation constitutes a moral community in which members feel themselves emotionally involved and responsible to each other, with a passionate attachment to a homeland as the site of pre-existing ethnic entitlements (Mead 1993). This nation is the sole source of political power; group loyalty overrides others.

Everyone belongs to the nation, and the world would be a better place if people's full potential was realized under this community of like-minded individuals. Attainment of an ethnically pure community may entail the removal or "purging" ("cleansing") of those outside the preferred ethnic mould. The table below provides a brief comparison and contrast on the basis of select criteria.

Typologies of Nationalism		
	Civic Nationalism (state building)	**Ethnic or Indigenous Nationalism (nation building)**
Driving force	Statehood/society building	Peoplehood/nation building
Direction	Outward and future oriented (progress)	Inward looking and glorify past
Challenge	Construct an (imaginary) community of equals from diversity	Protect and promote the integrity of a people
Nature of belonging	Citizenship (community of equal individuals)	Bloodlines (being with your own kind)
Source of belonging	Consent (contractual ties to an idea)	Descent (primordial attachments to a place/homeland)
Outcome	Multiculturalism/biculturalism	Binationalism
Basis of social order	Rule of law	Birthright
Rationale	Appeal to reason—an *idea*	Appeal to heart, spirit, and blood —the *tribe*
Status of diversity	Ethnic coexistence/symbolic ethnicity	Insurgent ethnicity/ethnic "cleansing"

The distinction between these nationalisms reflects ideal types that rarely are found in reality. The attributes differ from each other for the sake of argument, but none is intuitively obvious and each is contestable. Civic nationalism is about state building. It is concerned with forging unity from diversity by braiding immigrant, ethnic, and indigenous strands into a coherent and cosmopolitan community of equal individuals with shared loyalty and common attachments. It is based on the state-building premise that individuals of disparate backgrounds can come together under a shared citizenship without relinquishing their distinctiveness as the price of entry. By contrast, ethnic nationalism is about nation building. Its concern is

not unity from diversity but protecting ethnic diversity from state unity. Ethnic nationalism is aimed at preserving the integrity of a moral community of like-minded individuals whose exclusivity to a group and loyalty to a homeland supersede all other attachments. Differences between groups are perceived as real and powerful, largely unchangeable, and provide an exclusive basis for engagement and entitlement. To be sure, the distinction breaks down upon closer scrutiny: Even civic nationalism is ethnic to some extent, since there is no purely neutral concept of the state (Nielson 1996/97). Nevertheless, as ideal types, ethnic nationalism (exclusive, based on descent/bloodlines, affective, and rights rooted in place) differs from civic nationalism (inclusive, based on commitment to shared culture and citizenship, rationalistic, and rights rooted in territory). One is not better than the other, only different in terms of underlying logic and outlook.

Canada's nationalisms are increasingly polarized around the civic–ethnic continuum. National cultural minorities, such as First Nations, do not agree with the vision espoused by successive waves of immigrants who are increasingly defining Canada as a civic community of citizens (Boismenu 1996). The indigenous nationalism of the First Nations and the Québécois is directed at nationhood by seeking innovative patterns of belonging as a distinct people; in contrast are the forces of civic nationalism involving state efforts for forging a diverse society around ideas that we have in common as citizens. These competing discourses, which contest the sovereignty of Canada, are of such magnitude that the Crown is drawn into the most contentious of political relations: the relationship between peoples, each of whom claims inherent authority over internal jurisdiction pertaining to land, identity, and political voice. Is it possible to forge a working relationship that acknowledges Crown sovereignty with recognition of aboriginal peoples as original occupants? Differences are irreconcilable under these circumstances; so too is conflict. This clash between state and nation, between citizenship and peoplehood, is double-edged: The potential to craft an innovative political order is counterbalanced by the potency to dismember Canadian society into warring factions.

To Sum Up A revisiting of ethnicity is now securely established. No longer can we think of ethnicity as some primitive or transient whimsy in a cultural backwater outside the path of rational progress and liberal democracy. Ethnicity, especially when harnessed with a vibrant nationalism, is a powerful political force and potent social movement. Its potential for greatness or depravity is magnified even more when coupled with religious grievances. It remains to be seen whether the new international order can cope with the multiplicity of ethnojingoistic demands. Coexistence will depend on the need to understand and adapt to the ethnicities of others as legitimate and equal (Havel 1994). Differences that are seen as absolute rather than relative diminish the chances for global survival. Endorsement of differences as natural, normal, and beneficial bolsters the probability of living together with our differences.

DE-POLITICIZING ETHNICITY: MAKING SOCIETY SAFE FOR ETHNICITY/SAFE FROM ETHNICITY

The world of the 1990s is a bewildering place (Smith 1996). Gone are the global certainties of the past, including (a) division of the world into competing superpower blocs, (b) Cold War patterns of defence and foreign aid, (c) a global alignment in which everyone knew their place and played by the rules, and (d) games of political chess camouflaged by acts of espionage, political double dealing, and propaganda. The simple verities of a predictable if somewhat tense order have been superseded by a complex and multipolar world in which former ethnical certainties have been replaced by a degree of moral ambivalence and political ambiguity. The sovereignty of the state has been "outflanked" and compromised by the global movement of capital, labour, investment, and information. No comparable political or military power has rushed in to fill the political vacuum created by the disintegration of the

USSR, thus encouraging both intermediate powers and ethnic nationalisms to compete for vacated space. Ethnic forces have rushed into this political void, in effect destroying the balance of power. Not surprisingly the very forces that were supposed to dissolve the potential for group conflicts have actually increased ethnic confrontation. This surge of ethnicity is not some throwback to an earlier era or a passing phenomenon. The ethnic experience is but one of many resurgences since the French Revolution, and as postmodernity "bites" deeper, an intensification of ethnic conflict is widely predicted (Smith 1996).

A new international disorder is gradually taking shape. Even the very concept of a sovereign state is under siege because of shifting global and ethnic trends. Once assumed to be the bedrock of international order as well as a natural focus of group solidarity, the nation-state can no longer automatically command the loyalty of its citizens. Perceived by some as too big for small problems and too small for big problems, the very concept of a sovereign nation-state runs the risk of drifting into irrelevance because of capital mobility and ethnic jockeying (see Aguirre Jr and Turner 1995). The double-edged quality of contemporary dynamics makes the nation-state less capable of preserving its boundaries against forces "from below" or "from above" (Smelser 1993). Negotiating the fine line between the forces of "implosion" and "explosion" could result in a global order altogether different than the current arrangement. Instead of nation-states as we know now, boundary lines will be redrawn to reflect a loose confederation of ethnic communities within the framework of regional or global trading blocks.

Canada as the world's third oldest federal system is not unaffected by these pressures. The dual challenges of ethnicity and globalism have infiltrated every aspect of our social fabric and personal existence. Rules that formerly defined right from wrong are openly challenged or increasingly irrelevant. What once were virtues are now vices and vice versa. Forces of change have shaken those institutions and values that once imposed security and meaning on social life, including the authority of the Church, the State, and elite politics. How can national unity be secured in the face of forces whose potential to divide is legendary? Both ethnicity and globalization may enrich a society by weaving national unity from the strands of diversity; alternatively, either may ignite a chain reaction that could culminate in destruction and decline. That raises the question of whether an ethnically diverse country such as Canada can remain cohesive when ethnic ties are becoming brittle, when the cultural centre appears to be eroding, and when group conflicts are escalating (see also Aguirre Jr and Turner 1995).

Multiculturalism represents one of Canada's response to the challenges and paradox of ethnicity. Canada has chosen to pursue the path of unity through diversity. Its attachment to the "mosaic" as an egalitarian ideal departs from the "melting pot" blueprint of the United States, with its commitment to unity within homogeneity (but see Reitz and Breton 1994; Kallen 1995). But protection and preservation of ethnocultural diversity come with a qualifier: Canada's multiculturalism is planted firmly within the framework of symbolic ethnicity. Under official multiculturalism, all Canadians are encouraged to identify and participate as individuals in the cultural heritage of their choice. Multiculturalism in Canada is not concerned with the enhancement of ethnic communities, let alone the preservation of ethnic nationalities. Few societies could survive the strain of multiple competing groups with clearly demarcated sovereign boundaries, a separate power base, and parallel institutions. Even fewer are equipped for addressing the often unprecedented demands of ethnic nationalists. Ethnicity within the framework of society building can only exist when stripped of its potency to divide or incite, then folded into the prevailing social and cultural system of society.

Herein lies the appeal of situated and symbolic identities within a multicultural society. Promotion of ethnic identity at situational or symbolic levels comes across as relatively harmless, since the political and economic status quo is left intact. In that sense, multiculturalism does not exist to promote ethnicity. Multiculturalism is a tactical strategy for creating a society in which ethnicity is accommodated as integral and legitimate but without undermining the interconnectedness of the core. Put baldly, multiculturalism is concerned with **depoliticizing ethnicity** as part of the society-building exercise. This "consensus-based" multiculturalism represents Canada's response to the conundrum of making society safe for ethnicity as well as safe from ethnicity (Fleras 1998). Whether this level of inclusiveness will be sufficient for those ethnicities that are seeking to make diversity *safe* from society is an issue that will be addressed later.

CHAPTER HIGHLIGHTS

- The centrality of ethnicity in complex, urban societies ranks as one of the more remarkable features at the end of the millennium. Nevertheless, our understanding of ethnicity is subject to ongoing revision and new interpretations in light of uncovered evidence.

- Sociologists tend to see ethnicity as a key variable in shaping what we think and do and how others respond to us. It is also seen as important in helping to explain patterns of similarities and differences in human behaviour at individual and group levels.

- Ethnicity is examined from three perspectives: as group relations in competition for scarce resources, as a key variable in shaping unequal relations, and as an exercise in society building or society bashing.

- The emergence of ethnicity represents a powerful theme in the reconstruction of contemporary societies like Canada. The world is being pushed and pulled by diametrically opposed forces. A multinational-driven globalism is pushing the world together ("homogenizing") in a rational and calculating way. The forces of ethnicity, in turn, are pushing it apart.

- Nation-states appear to be the main casualties in this worldwide tug of war between ethnicity and globalization. It remains to be seen if nation-states are indeed "too big" to handle "small" problems of ethnicity or "too small" to cope with big problems of a market-driven globalism.

- Ethnicity is a powerful force that is capable of arousing both deep and irrational feelings as well as a sense of identity and continuity in times of uncertainty and change. These emotional and cognitive dimensions can be manipulated as a political organizing tool.

- Ethnicity at personal levels involves a search for continuity, community, and commitment in a world of diversity, change, and uncertainty. At the group level, ethnicity refers to a strategic device for improving advantage in a competitive context. At societal levels, ethnicity represents a way of organizing social relations in terms of who gets what.

- Ethnicity can be defined as a shared awareness of differences as a basis for engagement or entitlement. It can also be defined as a principle of organization for mobilizing individuals into action groups on the basis of self-definition and shared characteristics.

- Confusion can sometimes arise from failure to separate ethnicity as a "thing" (the objective components that comprise an ethnic group) from ethnicity as a "process" (including subjective experiences and intergroup relations).

- From a sociological perspective, ethnicity arises primarily (but not exclusively) from intergroup conflict and competition. It represents a dynamic resource that can be

called into action by emphasizing community, continuity, and identity during periods of stress and change. Individuals and groups rely on ethnicity to define an appropriate self-image, to articulate demands, and to express dissatisfaction.

- The surge in ethnicity can be explained in primordialist, instrumentalist, and constructivist terms. Inasmuch as ethnicity resembles a practical response to modern
problems, the "instrumentalist" perspective provides an interpretation that complements the "primordial" and "constructivist" hypotheses.

- Ethnicity is manifested in several ways, including that of ethnic communities, ethnic
identities, and social movements.

- Urban Canada continues to be the site of ethnic enclaves that provide a degree of
community and continuity for more traditional members as well as social and institutional support.

- Ethnicity can provide an important component of identification for many Canadians.
Ethnic identities can be expressed at the level of "lived-in," "symbolic," "postmodern,"
and "insurgent."

- Ethnicity is increasingly expressed in terms of social movements. Commonly called
ethnic nationalism, the politicization of ethnicity has grave consequences for the survival of the modern nation-state.

- Civic nationalism differs from ethnic nationalism in several ways. At the core of civic
nationalism is a belief that people should be identified and evaluated on the basis of
their commitment to an *idea*, not on who they are as members of a "tribe."

- Ethnically diverse countries are faced with a challenge with respect to national identity and unity. Initiatives such as Canada's official multiculturalism are best seen as
moves to depoliticize ethnicity as a means of national survival and society building.

KEY TERMS

civic nationalism
constructivist thesis
depoliticizing ethnicity
ethnic boundaries
ethnic groups
ethnic nationalism
ethnic surge
ethnicity
globalization
instrumentalist thesis
insurgent ethnicity
lived-in ethnicity
nation
postmodern ethnicity
primordialist thesis

radical ethnicity
resource mobilization theory
situational (or symbolic) ethnicity
sociobiology
state

REVIEW QUESTIONS

1. Globalism and ethnicity represent two powerful trends at present. Explain the magnitude and scope of these forces in terms of their potential impact on a nation-state such as Canada.

2. Three major approaches—primordialist, instrumentalist and constructivist ("resource mobilization")—have historically been utilized to explain the ethnic surge. Compare and contrast.

3. Compare and contrast ethnic nationalism and civic nationalism in terms of their underlying logic.

4. How is ethnicity expressed? Focus on the notions of community, identity, and social movement.

5. What are the impact and implications for ethnicity in Canada's continuing efforts to make the country safe for ethnicity as well as safe from ethnicity?

6. Explain the logic that links the notion of insurgent ethnicity with the notion of ethnic nationalism.

7. Ethnicity is seen by sociologists as a key variable that accounts for patterns of human behaviour. Explain, with examples.

SOCIAL INEQUALITY: Race, Ethnicity, Class, and Gender

CASE STUDY 5–1	A Vertically Challenged Mosaic: Ethnicity As Inequality in Canada

John Porter's seminal study, *The Vertical Mosaic* (1965), provides a useful introduction to the concept of ethnic inequality. Identified by many sociologists as one of the most important publications in the annals of Canadian sociology (Helmes-Hayes and Curtis 1998), the book explores the nature of the relationship between ethnic origin and social class and power in Canada. For Porter (1965), Canada's tapestry of cultural differences was stratified vertically along ethnic lines, hence the expression "vertical mosaic." That this term is now thoroughly ensconced in Canada's sociological discourse attests to its power as metaphor and explanation.

Porter argued that ethnic groups in Canada were arranged hierarchically. The British and, to a lesser extent, the French played the role of gatekeeper, regulating who would enter the corridors of power. Based on an analysis of census data between 1931 and 1961, he found that the British and the French (Canada's "Charter groups") were in control of privileged positions by an accident of history. The other groups to emigrate to Canada occupied an inferior or "entrance status." According to his "ethnicity blocked mobility" thesis, ethnic immigrants tended to reflect lower socioeconomic attainments because of their lower status upon entry to Canada. Retention of ethnicity also hampered the upward mobility of ethnic minorities, leading to what Porter called an ethnic mobility trap. For immigrant groups, ethnicity and inequality proved a paradox. If they wanted to achieve social mobility and shed their lowly entrance status, it was necessary to reject their cultural background and assimilate into the mainstream. But severing their ties with their ethnic community also increased the risk of discarding an invaluable support system. To the extent that racial and ethnic groups became trapped in self-contained communities, Porter claimed, social mobility would be beyond their grasp.

For Porter, ethnic inequality and ethnic group solidarity were persistent. This persistence was unfortunate, since it violated the principles of liberalism and meritocracy that Porter admired, especially in their purest embodiment in the United States (Brym 1991). Porter was dismissive of ethnic cultures, seeing them as residues of the past—simultaneously dysfunctional and irrelevant in a modern context. Minorities are socialized in a culture that does not adequately prepare them for the demands of a complex and advanced industrial system. This, of course, does not suggest that racial or ethnic minorities are "inferior" in the absolute sense. Rather, their social and cultural background is defined as "deficient" in comparison with mainstream values. Rightly or wrongly, according to Porter, ethnic differences would vanish in the face of modernist pressures and global development. But the path would be uneven at best. Not surprisingly, Porter chided the Canadian government for its misguided efforts to encourage ethnicity by way of multiculturalism. Not only would multiculturalism entrench social inequality by relegating ethnic minorities to perpetual lower class status; the promotion of ethnicity would also postpone the onset of national prosperity.

How accurate was Porter's assessment of Canada as a vertical mosaic? Do his conclusions stand up to the test of time? Since the publication of *The Vertical Mosaic*, there have been many attempts to verify his observations (Helmes-Hayes and Curtis 1998).

Many researchers now disagree with Porter's conclusions (see Brym 1991). Some of the key disagreements are the following:

1. He overstated the differences between Canada and the United States in attitudes toward and treatment of minorities (Palmer 1975; Reitz and Breton 1994).

2. Ethnic stratification is less entrenched than in the past. For example, ethnic differences in occupational status have declined over time for European groups (Breton et al. 1990). However, this flattening process has not necessarily extended to people of colour.

3. Strong ethnic group cohesion does not necessarily curtail mobility rates. Ethnic attachments (including accent and ethnic work enclave) may impede mobility and exert economic costs but are selectively imposed (Reitz and Sklar 1997).

4. Ethnicity is not necessarily a strong predictor of socioeconomic status or mobility (Breton et al. 1990).

5. Ethnic inequality is decreasing, even as inequality in general is expanding, with members of most European ethnic groups experiencing some degree of upward mobility over time (Isajiw et al. 1993).

In short, many have contested Porter's key arguments underpinning his theory of the vertical mosaic. There are growing doubts about the determinacy of ethnicity in shaping Canadian stratification. Many European-based ethnics have been incorporated into Canadian society as social equals, but without having to relinquish affiliation with selective elements of their traditional past. A study by Raymond Breton and his associates (1990) found that "white" ethnic minorities in Toronto, especially the Germans and Ukrainians, had achieved a high level of incorporation into society as measured by economic rewards and sociopolitical acceptance. Ukrainians were also most protective of their ethnocultural background and select aspects of their ethnic identity; conversely, Germans exhibited the least amount of ethnocultural retention. The status of Jews was ambiguous. Although economically successful and politically incorporated, they as a group were more likely to experience discrimination and social rejection. Their commitment to ethnic retention was highest among the eight groups studied by Breton ct al. (1990). Finally, birthplace is critical: For example, ethnic attachments have more significant economic costs for European-born immigrants than for native-born members of European origin groups (Reitz and Sklar 1997).

Not all ethnic minorities are so "lucky." For racial and visible minorities, considerable stratification does still seem to exist. Chinese and West Indians remain poorly in-tegrated into the culture and economic structure of Canada. Not only do they rank near the bottom of scales for employment opportunity and social acceptance, but these groups also score poorly in terms of identity, cultural preferences, residential segregation, social bonds and interaction, and levels of political activity. In short, as Breton et al. (1990) concede, the vertical mosaic concept needs to be rethought. Certain ethnic groups have little or no trouble with mainstream integration, even when they do maintain their ethnocultural identity. The same degree of mobility does not apply to all ethnic minorities, especially those who are racially visible. Perhaps the metaphor of a mosaic is too rigid and static to capture the dynamics of inequality. References to a kaleidoscope, with its constantly changing patterns and nuanced rearrangements, may prove more enlightening.

INTRODUCTION: RETHINKING THE MOSAIC

The twentieth century may well be remembered as the dawn of egalitarianism (Pinkerton 1998). A combination of forces, from class warfare and welfare states to human rights and cultural politics, has eroded nineteenth-century structures of class and hierarchy that once demanded the poor and different to "know their place in society." This egalitarian revolution not only unfettered historically disadvantaged groups from social bondage; it also resulted in a reevaluation of diversity in society. The suppression of differences as inimical to national interests is being replaced by increased acceptance of diversity in countries such as Canada. Canada cherishes its image as an egalitarian and largely middle class society, with supposedly few extremes in poverty or wealth. This portrayal is arguably true in a relative sense, given the magnitude of inequities and racial oppression elsewhere. Canada indeed represents a remarkably open and pluralist society with a powerful commitment to equality before the law, regardless of a person's background or beliefs. Ideally, all parts of the national "mosaic" are envisaged as contributing equally to the whole. These diverse components are also viewed as deserving of a fair share of the entitlements of wealth and power.

Appearances, however, can be deceiving. Canada is more accurately a society of unequal shares with wealth concentrated in the hands of the few; for example, the richest 1 percent hold 25 percent of Canada's wealth (Goar 1995). Economic gaps have broadened in recent years. In 1971, the richest 10 percent of the population earned 21 times the amount of the poorest 10 percent; in 1996, the ratio had increased to 314 times the total (Editorial,

Toronto Star, 24 October 1998). As a result, Canada can be conceptualized as three disjointed "demographics": one growing more prosperous and powerful, another squeezed by stagnant incomes, and another drifting into increased poverty and powerlessness (see also Fischer et al. 1998). Income and opportunity gaps involving dominant and subdominant sectors have created a pattern of ethnic inequalities, as articulated by the eminent Canadian scholar John Porter. Inception of official multiculturalism and employment equity initiatives have not appreciably altered this arrangement, with some measures having had the somewhat perverse effect of perpetuating inequality. Racial, aboriginal, and ethnocultural groups continue to be sorted out unequally against a "mosaic" of raised (dominant) and lowered (subordinate) tiles (Tepper 1988). Pyramids of privilege exist that elevate white, male, middle class, middle-aged, and the able-bodied to the top of the scale, others to the bottom. Those of Northern European origin seem to have more options and opportunities when reflected by their place in the economy (see Jaret 1995). In other words, all the deeply ingrained myths in the country cannot disguise the obvious: Canada remains a stratified society where differences in pigmentation and ethnic background continue to make a difference. It is in the self-interest of all Canadians to challenge this inequality and ensure a more equitable distribution of resources (Nelson and Fleras 1998). Failure to do so could well increase the likelihood of conflict between ethnic groups, with corresponding social and economic costs (Fernandez 1997).

That Canada is stratified by race and ethnicity should come as little surprise (Curtis et al. 1993). Some minorities do well because of or in spite of their ethnicity; others suffer; and still others do not appear adversely affected one way or the other. The theme of this chapter is predicated on the premise that social inequality is not natural or "fated" but socially constructed and amenable to analysis, challenge, and transformation (also Fischer et al. 1998). Inequality is shown to be the result of public policies, social structure, and human behaviour rather than culture, psychology, or human nature. Such a macro-perspective exerts pressure on understanding how these inequities were created, sustained, and challenged. This chapter draws on these themes by exploring the inequitable relationship of minority groups to society at large and argues that inequality in Canada is not randomly distributed but patterned around the poles of race, ethnicity, gender, and social class. These mutually intersecting "variables" not only reflect fundamental inequities in Canadian society; they also have an effect in shaping patterns over who gets what and what needs to be done to improve the situation. Chapter content is organized around responses to such concerns as: (a) the nature of ethnic inequality; (b) how this inequality is manifested; (c) why it exists; and (d) what can be done about it. We begin by looking at the magnitude and scope of ethnic inequality in Canada. This is followed by a brief insight into the ambiguous but revealing socioeconomic status of blacks in the United States. Social inequality is examined next within the framework of ethnic stratification and how the interplay of social class, race, ethnicity, and gender combines to create interlocking patterns of inequality that are durable and seemingly impervious to change. Particular attention is devoted to how each of these inequities is an aspect of social differentiation in its own right, with a distinctive dynamic, rationale, structure, and history. Nevertheless, all are interconnected with each other in ways that create distinct but overlapping hierarchies of subdomination that are mutually reinforcing yet contradictory. The chapter concludes with a look at the reconceptualization of inequality and equality in light of evolving definitions and changing demographies. The principles and practices of employment equity are shown to embody this "structural" shift in redefining dominant–subdominant relations.

ETHNIC STRATIFICATION IN CANADA

Even a cursory inspection of Canada's race relations record is a testimony to inequality (Henry et al. 1995; Breton 1998). In the past, immigrants to Canada were frequently imported as a source of cheap menial labour—either to assist in the process of society building (for example, the Chinese for the construction of the trans-Canada railway) or to provide manual skills in labour-starved industries such as the garment trade (Bolaria and Li 1988). Once in the country, many became convenient targets for abuse and exploitation. Immigrants could be fired with impunity, especially during periods of economic stagnation. Promotions, of course, were entirely out of the question. Political and civil rights were routinely trampled upon without many channels for redress. Racism and discriminatory barriers proved to be common stumbling blocks, as were the imperatives of a capitalist system. Those on the bottom provided a grim reminder to others of the fate that awaited anyone who refused to play by the rules.

The situation has improved somewhat, thanks to the passage of human rights and multicultural legislation. Yet both native-born and foreign-born minorities continue to be shunted into marginal employment ghettos with few possibilities for escape or advancement. A study for the Human Rights Commission indicated that only 4.1 percent of federal public servants in 1995 were visible minorities, compared to 12 percent in the private sector, despite a federally mandated employment equity program since 1986 (Foster 1997). Immigrant labourers from the Caribbean are brought into Canada on a temporary basis for seasonal employment primarily in agricultural fields. Domestic workers ("nannies") from the Philippines are taken advantage of by those middle class families who should know better. Working conditions are reported to be among the worst of any occupation, and many domestic workers are denied fundamental workers' rights by discriminatory laws (Stasiulis and Bakan 1997). African-Canadians are routinely denied equal access to housing and employment (Henry and Ginzberg 1993; Henry 1994). For black youth, relations with the police border on the criminal in certain urban areas (Cryderman et al. 1998). Indo-Pakistani Canadians continue to experience widespread dislike and resentment if national attitudes surveys are to be trusted (Berry and Kalin 1993). These and related expressions of exploitation or dislike confirm what many prefer to ignore or reject: Various ethnic and racial groups are earmarked for the bottom of Canadian society without much hope for escape or redress.

Canada is characterized by layers of inequality among aboriginal, racial, and ethnic groups. This inequality is not distributed evenly or randomly; it is concentrated among certain minority groups who tend to cluster around certain nodes on the socioeconomic continuum. Herein lies the genesis of what popularly is known as **ethnic stratification.** The term "ethnic stratification" can be employed in two ways (See and Wilson 1988). First, it refers to hierarchical systems in which scarce resources are unequally and vertically distributed among diverse minority groups. Second, it consists of highly segmented systems in which minority groups occupy specialized occupational statuses (sometimes referred to as a cultural division of labour). Taken together, stratification can be thought of as a hierarchical structuring of society into "strata," or "layers," by which racial or ethnic minorities are unevenly ranked in descending/ascending order because of differences in wealth, status, or power. Any society predicated on unequal relations, regardless of the criteria employed including race or ethnicity, can be defined as socially stratified (Kallen 1995). These ranked differences are not randomly scattered across the population. Nor are they of a transitory nature, that is, reflecting the "costs" of initial adjustment. Rather these differences are patterned in the sense that they are accorded social significance, and their placement is predictable, enduring, and difficult to dislodge.

Inequality remains a fact of life in Canadian society (Curtis et al. 1993; Matthews and Lian 1999). John Porter convincingly argued that ethnic groups in Canada were arranged hierarchically, with the British and French near the top and other minorities ranked accordingly. Despite initiatives in multiculturalism, employment equity, and human rights legislation, national studies continue to expound what many "intuitively" know: That not all Canadians are created equal when it comes to sorting out the "goodies." Earning differentials among ethnic groups in Canada continue to reveal marked disparities according to 1991 Census data. Pendakur and Pendakur (1995) point to significant earning differences between (a) whites and visible minorities; (b) native-born and foreign-born; (c) women and men; and (d) aboriginal and nonaboriginal populations (see Table 5.1). These differences remain in effect, albeit to a lesser degree, even when controlling for individual characteristics such as age, education level, language knowledge, full-time status, household type, and occupation.

TABLE 5.1	Mean Earnings By Visible Minority Status			
Sex	**Immigrant Status**	**Visible Status**	**Earnings (Mean)**	**Earning (% difference)**
Males	Canadian-born	White	$36,563	—
		Visible	$31,653	−13.4%
		Aboriginal	$28,725	−21.4%
	Foreign-born	White	$38,456	+5.2%
		Visible	$28,285	−22.6%
Females	Canadian-born	White	$23,173	—
		Visible	$23,149	−0.1%
		Aboriginal	$19,887	−14.2%
	Foreign-born	White	$22,498	−2.9%
		Visible	$20,132	−13.1%

Note: Adapted from Pendakur and Pendakur (1995). Based on Census Public Use Microdata, Individual File, 3 percent sample of the Canadian population. Population includes permanent residents age 20 to 64, not in school full-time, living in Montreal, Toronto, Hamilton, Edmonton, Calgary, and Vancouver; does not include persons not reporting an education level, a household type, occupation, or industry, or immigrants arriving after 1989.

Canadian-born visible minority males earn considerably less than Canadian-born white males even when educated and socialized in Canada (Pendakur and Pendakur 1995). Variation exists within the categories themselves: Canadian-born men of Greek, Portuguese, Black, and Chinese background earned between 12 and 16 percent less than males of British origin. Foreign-born visible minorities, in turn, earn substantially less than Canadian-born visible minorities. Regional variations are noticeable: The wage gap for Canadian-born visible minority men in Toronto was 9 percent, 17 percent in Montreal, but only 4 percent in Vancouver (see also Turner 1996). Foreign-born males of colour fare worst, with those in Toronto earning 16 percent less, in Montreal 20 percent less, and Vancouver 13 percent less. Aboriginal peoples confront negative earning differentials of between 15 and 19 percent. Earning differentials between men and women are significant; nevertheless, different earning patterns within each gender are less striking. Compared with men, income differences between Canadian-born white females and visible minority females were minimal. The same applied to foreign-born white females and Canadian-born white and visible minority women. By contrast, aboriginal women earned less than any group of foreign-born and Canadian-born women. Also evident were regional variations: Foreign-born visible minority women earned 20 percent less than white Canadian-born women in Montreal, 6 percent in Toronto, and virtually the same wage in Vancouver. These earning gaps for women and men, the authors of the report conclude (Pendakur and Pendakur 1995), cannot be dismissed because of cultural differences, education quality, or language skills. Rather, these disparities are suggestive of labour market discrimination.

Patterns of ethnic stratification on the basis of income provide insight into the expression of inequality. This emphasis on income may be misleading since the possession of wealth or assets is a more reliable measurement of who gets what (Oliver and Shapiro 1995). Income is what people earn from work or receive from government transfers for purchase of goods or services; wealth is what people own (from stocks and bonds to home ownership) and signifies command over financial resources that a household has inherited or accumulated over a lifetime by which to create opportunities, secure a desired status, or pass status on to children. Command over wealth is more encompassing than income in determining access to life chances. For example, most university students living away from home may be income-poor and fall far short of the federally regulated poverty (low-income cutoff) line. Nonetheless, they are asset-rich because of the marketability of their pending degree. Focusing on wealth rather than income also casts a new light on inequality and ethnic stratification: Minority women and men may possess approximately similar levels of income compared with the mainstream. Yet many are asset-poor, thus foreclosing opportunity structures. For example, middle class American blacks may earn about 70 percent of white middle class incomes, but only own about 15 percent of the wealth held by middle class whites (Oliver and Shapiro 1995). This lack of wealth undermines the creation of a sound economic foundation to provide stability and security.

Patterns of ethnic inequality and stratification prevail as well in the United States. Evidence is clear in confirming vast gaps in the income status of whites and nonwhites. The following Insight Box focuses primarily on African-Americans in the hopes of demonstrating that references to ethnic inequalities are not always what they seem to be.

| INSIGHT 5–1 | **Revisiting the Colour Bar** |

WEB DuBois predicted in 1903 that the problem of the colour bar would prove to be the key issue of the twentieth century. A Swedish observer of American politics, Gunnar Myrdahl (1944) reiterated this point at mid-century, declaring the race problem to be the quintessential paradox in challenging American democracy (see Loury 1998). Nearly one hundred years after DuBois' prediction, the colour bar remains a central fact of American society and continues to partition and provoke both white and black Americans (Johnson 1998). The struggle that secured legal equality for blacks following a century of second class citizenship does not appear to have eroded the substantive inequalities that appear immune to laws or affirmative action programs (Loury 1998). White racism and the racial otherness of blacks may be so deeply embedded in the collective consciousness that it not only resists change but also refuses to accommodate (Loury 1998). To be sure, opinion is divided: Some say race relations have improved; others say no. Some believe affirmative action has fostered racial progress; others disagree (Shipler 1997).

For blacks, the socioeconomic figures are dismaying. Thirty-five years after Civil Rights legislation and affirmative action programs, the paradox of the colour bar continues to be manifest at the levels of crime, drug addiction, family breakdown, imprisonment, welfare dependency, and community decay that are virtually unrivalled in scale and severity to anything found in the rest of the Industrial West (Loury 1998). Take income, for example. According to the Census Bureau numbers issued in October 1997 (reported in *Society,* March/April 1998), Asian-Americans had a median household income in 1996 of $43,276 (US), $37,161 (US) for whites, $24,906 (US) for Hispanics (of any race), and $23,482 (US) for African-Americans. The annual income of African-Americans who are employed in full-time jobs amounts to about 60 percent of that of whites. The black unemployment rate is double that of the whole nation; one-third of all blacks, including one-half of all black children, are poor (live below the poverty line). The situation in Canada is comparable: Blacks earn an average income of $20,617 compared to $24,001 for the general population, while 31.5 percent of blacks compared to 15.7 percent of the general population fall below Statistics Canada's low-income cutoff line. Homicide is the leading cause of death for black males between the ages of fifteen and twenty-four, while the life expectancy of sixty-five years for American black men is comparable with some Third World countries (D'Souza 1995).

Black–white gaps have been variously explained. Those on the liberal side tend to attribute the chasm to a combination of white racism, racial segregation, black poverty, and inadequate funding of black schools. The causes of black poverty are both structural and behavioural, in other words, and solutions must focus on the twin realities of white

racism, black initiative, and structural adjustments in preparing blacks for the new economy (Gates Jr 1998). The most common conservative explanations tend to focus on genetic differences, the **culture of poverty,** and single motherhood (see Jencks and Phillips 1998). The differences in definition are reflected in general remedies: Whereas the conservatives believe that success would follow if blacks only "get their act together," liberals are more inclined to see how deeply rooted political, economic, and legal practices in American history are linked to contemporary impoverishment. Solutions vary accordingly: To one side is the struggle for equal treatment and civil rights against the backdrop of a colourblind society (Sleeper 1997). To the other side is the expression of black nationalism as a response to white domination (Marable 1998). Core elements in the different black nationalisms are varied, but include the following: First is the belief that African-Americans are an oppressed minority trapped inside a white society. Blacks are not Americans who happen to be black but Africans who happen to live in America. Second is the assertion that an oppressed society could survive in a hostile environment only if they constructed their own institutions, supported their own enterprises, established black homelands, and espoused black cultures and values.

But improvements are apparent even if the results are mixed and ambiguous (Shipler 1997). This social transformation in American race relations since 1945 has yielded positive outcomes: Official segregation and a caste system of domination has been eradicated; black demands for equal citizenship rights and equal opportunity are upheld by law and embraced by political institutions; and black participation in economic and political life of the nation has expanded impressively (Loury 1998). In 1940, 60 percent of employed black women worked as domestic servants in contrast with only 2.2 percent at present; today, 60 percent of black women hold white-collar jobs. The number of college and university professors has doubled since 1970, the number of physicians tripled, the number of engineers almost quadrupled, and the number of attorneys has increased nearly sixfold. The shift in public attitudes is no less impressive. In 1958, 44 percent of whites said they would move if a black family moved next door; today the figure is down to 1 percent. As recently as 1964, only 18 percent of whites claimed to have a black friend compared with 86 percent who say they do now (Thernstrom and Thernstrom 1998). According to a 1994 National Conference survey, whites feel most in common with blacks who, paradoxically, feel little in common with whites (conversely, Latinos feel most in common with whites who in turn feel little in common with them) (Hochschild 1998). Other trends are difficult to fathom: In 1971, the average seventeen-year-old African-American could read no better than an eleven-year-old white; by 1988, the gap had closed to 2.5 years, only to have increased to 3.9 years by 1994, with similar patterns for math and writing (Thernstrom and Thernstrom 1998).

Overall improvements notwithstanding, the colour bar remains firmly in place. The Civil Rights movement may have expanded the access agenda for blacks. But an expanded legal representation could not redress the cultural exclusiveness that continues to deny the value of black history and collective landmarks with which to signify their importance to society at large (Marable 1998). Nevertheless, it would be misleading to fixate only on the divide between whites and blacks: An equally distinctive and widening rift can be discerned between underclass blacks and middle class blacks. To one side is the plight of the black underclass, which has been stereotyped and stigmatized because of their purported criminality, sexual excesses, and intellectual deficiencies, to the

point of being objects of public derision and cast into a pariah status (Loury 1998). To the other side of this shifting colour bar is an increasingly affluent middle class black America. Over 40 percent of blacks now consider themselves to be middle class; 42 percent own their own homes (75 percent if only black married couples are included); 33 percent live in suburbs; and black two-parent families earn only 13 percent less than those who are white (Thernstrom and Thernstrom 1998). In short, middle class blacks have never been more prosperous or more secure, argues Henry Louis Gates Jr (1998); yet a large part of the black underclass appears unable to benefit from openings in American society, and this inability to benefit would seem permanent. As a result, there is a greater disparity between the top fifth and the bottom fifth of African-Americans with respect to income, education, victimization by violence, occupational status, and electoral involvement than between the top and bottom fifths of white Americans (Hochschild 1998).

This bending of the colour bar has not appreciably altered the American discourse on race relations. Moreover, the black underclass continues to define the "essence" of black America to much of the public (Thernstrom and Thernstrom 1998). Both public and media preoccupation with ghetto culture, hip-hop, and gangsta, together with the perception that success in the "whitestream" is selling out, has had the effect of glossing over the achievements of those who have hurdled the colour bar. The colour bar may be real, but its reality should not blind to the fact that blacks are no less heterogeneous than whites when it comes to the socioeconomic status. Perhaps that is the real success story of the Civil Rights movement: the right of black Americans to be successes and failures without drawing excessive attention.

EXPLAINING ETHNIC INEQUALITY

Question
How can we explain the fate of a twenty-four-year-old Caribbean-Canadian woman whose parents were manual workers and is bringing up two children on her own in the Jane-Finch corridor of York, and who now has to choose between low-paid work as a hospital domestic or dependency on benefits? Is this set of circumstances the result of gender or race or class or ethnicity?

Possible Answers
Do we explain her fate because of gender, which finds her confronted with responsibilities for child-care without male assistance and a limited range of labour market options? Is it racism that ensures that the only job available is the stereotypical servant role that historically has been assigned to black women? Is it class that compelled her to leave school without marketable qualifications? Is it ethnicity that imposes cultural values and group expectations at odds with mainstream success?

Plausible Answer
All of the above.
(adapted from Gillespie 1996:19)

We have already emphasized that race and ethnic relations are ultimately relationships of inequality. Class relations also constitute a type of unequal relation. Race and social class provide two of the grounds upon which inequality is constructed, organized, and perpetuated. What, precisely, is the nature of this relationship between *race* and *class* in explaining who gets what? Which of these key explanatory variables is logically prior in shaping intergroup dynamics? The debate touches on a number of related points regarding the true source of exploitation in society. Can inequality be explained by reference to "individual responsibility," "a pervasive racism," or "economic structures and restructuring" (Fischer et al. 1998)? Alternatively, is inequality explained by references to genetic inferiority (race), cultural deficit, or cultural discontinuity (Taylor 1998)? Are people unequal because of who they are (race) or because of what they do (class)? Are group conflicts in Canada the result of ethnic tensions or class confrontations? For example, did nineteenth-century Chinese immigrants experience discrimination because of a pervasive anti-Orientalism (race) or cultural anxieties (ethnicity)? Or should the treatment of the Chinese be assessed because of their occupational status (class) as essentially disposable labour for Canadian nation-building purposes? Are both interpretations correct in part?

Both race and class provide the foundation upon which social inequities are constructed and maintained. As we shall see, gender and ethnicity as key explanatory variables are no less important in shaping intergroup relations. The intersection of race and class with gender and ethnicity reflects a growing interest in tracing the interlinkages involving multiple dimensions of inequality (Kallen 1995; Yuval-Davis 1997). Nevertheless, each factor can be isolated and analyzed to appreciate the underlying debate.

Social Class

Many would argue that *social class* logically precedes race (as well as gender and ethnicity) as a source of inequality. **Social class** can be defined as a principle of organization that differentiates groups of individuals because of their unequal involvement in the economy. It consists of those who occupy a similar position in a stratified social order when measured by such criteria as income, education, occupational status, prestige, ownership of property, and socioeconomic power. With class at the core of a capitalist society, race relations are merely an extension of a more comprehensive category of social inequality (Li 1988; Bolaria and Li 1988; Wotherspoon and Satzewich 1993).

The primacy of class is anchored in Marxist analysis of capitalist relations. Capitalism is properly seen as a system for the rational pursuit of profit and capital accumulation by way of privately owned means of production and the production of goods (commodities) for sale in an unlimited and competitive marketplace. The centrality of the profit motive culminates in the establishment of class relations, with the productive property-owning class squaring off with the working class over who gets what. Shared experiences notwithstanding, the working class is neither homogeneous in composition nor uniform in outlook. It is internally divided since all workers by definition are exploited, but some more so than others because of gender or race. For example, white male workers often are better paid than nonwhite workers. Males in general earn more than females of all ethnic groups. In addition to income differentials, males generally have access to more secure types of employment with greater opportunities for promotion and career enhancement. Competition between subclasses serves to reinforce a system of stratification as well as a pattern of domination that is sustained through racist ideology.

The property-owning and working classes are in a constant struggle for control over power and wealth. The ruling class enhances its profit-making capacity by fostering internal divisions along lines of race and ethnicity (Rex 1983). Racial factors serve primarily as a basis for destabilizing class relations (Li 1988). This fragmentation and the corresponding ideology stigmatizes certain groups as undesirable and less marketable. It also provides a constant supply of cheap and unskilled labour. These class fractions can also be manipulated to foster what Marx termed "false consciousness." Instead of directing their hostility at the source of their exploitation and domination (that is, the capitalists), workers misplace their antagonism toward each other. This has the effect of fostering social cleavages within the working class. Nevertheless, class relations remain at the root of this conflict. Racial differences and confrontations are simply aspects of the wider struggle between classes. Minority concerns merely complicate the issue by distorting ("mystifying") the reality of domination and cause of exploitation. Thus conflicts between racial groups are ultimately conflicts within and between classes—whether people are aware of it or not.

Race

Can race as a source of exploitation or denial be subsumed under stratification and class conflict? Race theorists dispute the validity of this reductionist assertion. Issues pertaining to race, racism, and racial discrimination are *not* reducible to class relations. Nor are they a derivative of economic forces. They constitute forces in their own right, with a distinctive set of explanations (see van den Berghe 1981). Race has historically (and geographically) preceded class relations as an organizing principle. Class divisions are merely superimposed over existing racial patterns without diminishing the significance of race as an antecedent force for organization, differentiation, and stratification. As well, attachments created by racial bonds are more durable than the "contrived" bonds generated by class affiliations. Race-based connections are perceived as natural and "authentic" because of their conception from birth or descent. These relationships provide the basis for group affiliation, with its lure of emotional security, interest satisfaction, and accessible appeal for adherents (Brown 1989). Such is not necessarily the case with class. Members of a particular class may possess little in common except a similar relation to the means of production. Class ties are perceived as brittle and are subsequently prone to rupture in the face of concerted pressure.

How valid is this argument when applied to Canada? York University professor Frances Henry (1994) has argued that the differential treatment of Caribbean-Canadians can be attributed primarily (but not exclusively) to racism and racial discrimination, a refusal to appreciate visible minority needs, and failure to accommodate Caribbean cultural values within institutional structures. Class issues are subsumed under the more inclusive category of racial conflict. This reading is consistent with public perception of group conflict in Canada. Reports of group confrontation are "framed" as conflicts between racially or culturally different sectors, whether they be French–English strife, aboriginal–nonaboriginal tension, and police–visible minority hostility. Confrontation between groups is rarely framed within the discourse of class conflicts. Of course, one might argue that this merely represents the victory of the ruling class in distracting us (through dominant ideologies) from the root cause of exploitation and domination ("false mystifications"). Difficulties obviously exist in attempting to prove or disprove this position.

The relationship between race and social class can be analyzed in three ways. First, social class is logically prior to race as a system of exploitation and explanation. Race relations are merely an appendage of this more comprehensive system of domination and control. The second option privileges race as logically prior to class in terms of exploitation and explanation. Social class affiliation is simply superimposed over preexisting racial patterns and antagonisms, yet exist independent of class factors. Third, neither race nor class is logically prior, but they coexist as interdependent forces of a more generalized kind. Race and class are analytically different expressions of oppression that require separate entries. Each represents a relatively autonomous organizing principle of social relations in its own right with independent effects on the hierarchy of social life (Bonilla-Silva 1996). At times, race overlaps with class; at other times, it displaces class as a system of organization or differentiation (Rex 1983). At still other times, neither race nor class determines the final outcome, since additional factors such as gender and ethnicity may intensify patterns of inequality. At still other times, class relations *in the first instance* influence race relations but invariably are mediated and transformed by patterns of domination in ways that intersect and mutually reinforce.

Gender

Both minority women and men experience denial or exclusion because of their race and lower class status. Consider the case of immigrant women and men. Their lives are constrained by Eurocentrism and the centrality of Anglo-Canadian concerns to the exclusion of others (see Carty 1993). Immigrants confront formidable pressures to succeed in their adopted land, even if many are without the language skills or credentials to make an immediate adjustment. Both genders encounter discrimination and racism, since their visibility compounds the difficulty of integration. With respect to class, both men and women of colour are usually ghettoized into menial, sometimes dangerous occupations, with low pay and lower chances for promotion. Even highly accredited persons may be forced to accept demeaning labour if they are without the requisite amount of Canadian experience or credentials. With such pressures, it is not surprising that some individuals give up on the system, preferring instead a street life that may be nasty in outcome, but easier to understand and deal with in the short term.

It is widely acknowledged that minority women and men suffer discrimination and drawbacks because of colour, country of origin, racial background, or ethnic tradition (Satzewich 1998). But minority women (women of colour, immigrant women, and aboriginal women) are doubly disadvantaged as a result of their membership in the historically devalued category of gender. But the literature on gender and ethnicity—at least compared with race and class—is not well established, and this lack of analytic sophistication has created gaps in our knowledge (Du Plessis and Alice 1998). Ethnicity may impose cultural expectations on both minority women and men often at odds with mainstream definitions of success or safety. For women, however, gender is also known to block, inhibit, deter, or distort by way of stereotypes, double standards, glass ceilings, and restricted opportunity structures. Gender contributes to the subdomination, not in the mechanical sense of three cumulative forces, but in a complex interplay of amplification and intensity (Stasiulis 1990). The simultaneity of subdomination by women of colour cannot be underestimated (Hurtado 1996). Those minorities who are low on more than one hierarchy are subject to additional discriminatory forces. Persons who are socially devalued in two or more characteristics are more vulnerable to denial or exclusion. Inclusion in several devalued but interlocking categories of subdomination inflates the "**multiple jeopardies**" that women of colour confront. Thus gender is thought to intersect with race, ethnicity, and class to generate overlapping hierarchies of subdomination in ways that are mutually reinforcing yet contradictory in the struggle for equality (Bottomley et al. 1991). How, then, do women of colour simultaneously inhabit the social space encompassed by race and gender (see also Uebel 1997)?

Unlike men, minority women face sexist barriers that arise from their status as women in a predominantly patriarchal society. Patriarchy is characterized by the institutionally enforced authority of males over females and children that permeates the entire organization of society, from politics to culture, from the private to the public (Castells 1997). But gender is experienced differently by women of different races (Awatere 1984). Each subdominated group in Canada is positioned in a particular and distinctive relationship to white patriarchy, and each expression of subdomination is shaped by this relational position (Hurtado 1996). Women as a group may be united in a common experience of male dominance, but experience this patriarchy differently because of differing situations for different groups of women (Gillespie 1996). The allegiance of white women to white men through familial ties and integration around centres of power means that they cannot be subdominated in the same way as women of colour. As Hurtado (1996) observes in acknowledging how gender subdomination is experienced differently, women of colour are rejected whereas white women are seduced into corridors of power. White women are largely concerned with projecting private sphere issues into the public realm (such as unequal division of household labour, media double standards, daycare at places of employment, and childhood identity formation); women of colour focus on public issues related to employment equity, racism, and healthy children. Even strategies for change differ. In contrast with white women, women of colour are not in a position to divorce themselves from the men of their group since neither can exist without the other in the struggle against oppression (hooks 1994; 1995). Nor are they in a position to compartmentalize their concerns as women from broader struggles for land, identity, or political voice. In the words of Donna Awatere (1984:43–44), when chiding white feminists for ignoring the double colonization of indigenous women:

> For Maori women, all our concerns as women centre around the fact that we and our people have no say in the shaping of our destiny as a people.... The Maori language is a feminist

issue, the land is a feminist issue, separate development is a feminist issue, the venomous hatred of the Maori by the Pakeha is a feminist issue.

Women of colour also confront discrimination because of race and racism, a situation compounded by the marginality of class status. After all, to be poor in a society that privileges wealth is to live with shame. To be poor and different—and a woman—may consign some to the margins of society.

What, then, is the nature of the relationship between gender and other domains of inequality? Can gender as a form of exploitation be reduced to class, race, or ethnicity without overlooking the unique and oppressive experiences of women? We believe the answer is no, and the OJ Simpson verdict demonstrated how black women may be trapped in choosing between these intersecting options. African-American women found themselves having to take sides: white women, with whom they share gender and sexist discrimination, and their menfolk, with whom they embrace race, ethnicity, and social class while uniting against racism, ethnocentrism, and classism. The contrasts are unmistakable: To the extent that white women do not experience race, they are free to focus on sexism. To the degree that black women must confront racism, ethnocentrism, and classism, they cannot privilege gender as the primary site of struggle but regard it as equal to race, class, and ethnicity. The feminism of minority women is not against white women *per se*. Rather, it challenges women of privilege to acknowledge how the inequities and challenges that confront women of colour or aboriginal women often differ from the generalized oppression of visible minority or particularized oppression of all women.

Yet commonalities prevail. Neither minority nor mainstream women are content to be differentiated as objects to be acted upon. There is mounting resentment toward being "factored" in as a "variable" for analysis or assessment (Gillespie 1996). Increasingly, women of all colours are repositioning themselves as multiply-organized subjects whose activities and discourses are socially constructed by women for women in contexts and relationships that are contested and evolving (Larner 1996). Socially stigmatized groups such as women have reclaimed history by taking previously denigrated attributes and transforming them into positive affirmations of self (see Uebel 1997). In the same way that gender is a source of subdomination, so too can it be used to liberate and empower, just as black liberation employs skin colour to overcome disadvantage by conveying the message of black is beautiful.

Ethnicity

Ethnicity is also a key variable in shaping unequal outcomes. Ethnicity-based inequities are generated in two ways. First, ethnic groups may be singled out as inferior or irrelevant and dismissed accordingly. Second, ethnic groups may possess cultural values at odds with those of the dominant stream. Endorsement of these values, such as obligations to kin or obedience to tradition, may prove a barrier in the competition for scarce resources. The ethnicity factor may be experienced differently by the different genders.

Minority women are subtly, yet profoundly, undermined by ethnicity. Women in many ethnic communities are expected to know their place and do as told. Actions by women that do not conform with tradition or male values may be criticized as a betrayal to the cause or the community. Severing connections with the past proved problematic, as this excerpt reveals:

Being a Canadian-born Chinese I tried to follow the ways of Canadians. Yet I found it difficult at times because of respect and obedience to my mother (Mrs L., as quoted in Nipp
[Burnet 1986]).

For the sake of appearances, many women of colour are expected to defer to the authority
of tradition and community. Such passivity and submissiveness may foster the façade of
unity and cohesion; it also inhibits the expression of skills necessary for women to excel in
society at large. Assertiveness or freedom can lead to conflict when it interferes with deference
to tradition-bound males. Minority women remain the "hushed-over" victims of violence. This
violence results from cultural traditions that (a) normalize male abuse of women, (b) naturalize abuse as a male right and a rite of passage for both women and men, and (c) discourage public disclosure because of family honour or community pride. The family may be
widely regarded as a bastion of privacy that shuns or punishes those who refuse to shield un-
pleasant issues from the public (Buckley 1996). This indictment is not to suggest that domestic
violence is more prevalent in minority or immigrant communities. But its effects on women
may exert a different impact because of ethnicity. Patterns of domestic abuse may intersect with the vagaries of loneliness, dependency, homesickness, lack of knowledge of
English or access to services, and the threat of social ostracism, to provide few options for
escape or recourse (Ip 1990; Easteal 1996).

Exposure to double standards is a burden for many women. Tradition may dictate a
double duty for women: As well as outside employment, many are expected to maintain
responsibility for raising children. That type of dual responsibility comes with its own set of
problems: Many immigrant children want to be accepted as quickly as possible into the
mainstream. Their ethnicity is a constant reminder of how different they are from the friends
and routines they are trying to emulate. Parents, by contrast, may be anxious to impose culturally conservative codes of behaviour, including strict sexual propriety, respect for authority, particular dress styles and appearances, and compliance with tradition. Youth are
trapped in a complex balance between the culture of the home and the culture of the peers.
Some enjoy the challenge of picking and choosing the best of both worlds. Others find it a
wearying struggle to reject parental values and authority, while endlessly explaining strange
customs and defending practices to friends. To be a minority youth, in other words, is to find
oneself suspended between two cultures, fully acceptable in neither yet seemingly rejected
by both.

To Sum Up: A World of Jeopardies   Recognizing the multifaceted nature of social inequality helps to account for the dynamic interaction between different forms of subdomination and the different ways in which each is experienced in and through the other (Bottomley
et al. 1991). Race, gender, ethnicity, and class may be treated as analytically distinct dimensions of inequality; nevertheless, their conceptualization as interlocking and mutually reinforcing categories is increasingly central to social analysis (Patterson et al. 1996). Gender,
ethnicity, race, and class may possess different ontological bases and separate discourses, as
Yuval-Davis (1997) concludes, but each is constituted within each other and articulated accordingly in real social contexts. For example, women of colour experience racism differently from visible minority men, and differently among themselves depending on age, class,
ability, sexual preference, and place of residence. Women of colour experience gender differently from white women because of racism and ethnicity.

In short, neither gender nor ethnicity can be subsumed under social class or race. Both
constitute relatively independent if mutually interconnected patterns of discrimination.

Moreover, neither race and ethnicity nor gender and class are defined as fixed identities. Rather than a fixed or essential subject category rooted in bodies or geographical location, they are perceived instead as dynamic modes of cultural practice and relative points of convergence among culturally shifting and historically specific sets of relations (Uebel 1997). That makes it increasingly urgent to focus on the different ways in which each intersects with the others to create interlocking but relatively autonomous hierarchies of inequality in shaping the realities of immigrant, aboriginal, and visible minority women and men.

CONTESTING INEQUITIES

Perspectives on social inequality vary among sociologists. Some regard inequality as a social problem for solution; others believe inequality is necessary and desirable. Both functionalist and conflict theorists differ in analyzing and assessing ethnic inequality when applied to minority women and men. Each also raises the question of whether ethnic inequality is a social problem.

Functionalist Models

The economic division of labour is the starting point for functionalist models. For society to operate smoothly, functionalists argue, positions in the economic structure, such as jobs and careers, must be filled with suitable personnel. Since these jobs differ in skill and importance, people need to be rewarded appropriately for doing tasks of differing complexity. The occupational prestige hierarchy is the result of these differential rewards. We accept as "natural" that physicians are compensated more for their services than plumbers even though, arguably, both are crucial for our well-being (Davis and Moore 1945). Leading sports figures are paid more than common labourers (in the United States the average major league baseball player earns about $1.7 million per year in 1999, while a child-care worker makes less than $14,000). This discrepancy arises not because one is more important to society. Salary and status gaps exist because certain skills are in short supply compared with the demand. Those skills that can generate more wealth for their owners are in even shorter supply, and paid accordingly.

Functionalists acknowledge the existence of minority inequities. They argue that the failure of minorities to penetrate the market may reflect a lack of expertise or credentials. Efforts to boost their "cultural capital" would focus on improving minority education levels to those consistent with competitive labour force needs. Once opportunity is equalized, the modern forces behind a rational meritocracy will ultimately sort out people on the basis of ability. Cultural or racial considerations will be rendered superfluous when employers overcome bias and simply hire the best. A modern technological society—if it hopes to prosper in an intensely competitive and global market economy—has to be "colourblind" in capitalizing on the entire spectrum of brainpower and talent.

In sum, functionalists distinguish between "good" (functional) inequality and bad (dysfunctional) inequality. Inequality is "good" when achieved "fair and square"; it is "bad" if unfairly achieved. Functionalists recognize and decry the existence of racism and discrimination. Yet the pernicious effects of racial discrimination can be diminished by liberal appeals to fairness through objective testing for education and job entry. Functionalists also accept the inevitability of innate differences, not necessarily in a racial way but in cultural capital that individuals bring to the marketplace. Wealth and poverty are equally functional for society—the wealthy, because of what they do; the poor, as an incentive to work hard and play by the rules. In that sense, functionalists argue, inequality is necessary and desirable in a merit-based, openly competitive society. But inequities by virtue of ascribed racial or ethnic differences are not. This makes it doubly important to ensure that steps are taken to purge ascriptive indicators from determining who gets what. A fair and open competition demands nothing less.

Conflict Models

Conflict theorists share with functionalists the view that a capitalistic society is differentiated by competition. They differ in their assessment of the role played by inequality. For the functionalists, society exists as an ongoing entity inasmuch as a consensus of values secures social cohesion. The inevitability of inequality—a basic tenet of functionalism—is an anathema to the Marxist variants of **conflict theory.** For Marx, inequality is *not* natural or normal; it is "naturalized" or "normalized" only in those societies geared toward the rational pursuit of profit. Private productive property and class relations that pit one class against another are largely responsible for these inequities.

Society, for conflict theorists, is composed of opposed groups who compete for scarce resources. One set of competing pairs has the ruling class on one side, the subdominant class on the other. Conflict theorists argue that ruling class interests are advanced by sowing the seeds of dissension within working class ranks. Fomenting racial prejudice and outgroup hostility helps to perpetuate the status quo, prevents the formation of worker solidarity, improves capital formation, destabilizes countermovements, and militates against the development of class consciousness. This infighting also has the effect of foreclosing the ability of workers to "unite and throw off their chains." Under conflict models, in other words, race-based inequalities are functional for some, dysfunctional for others.

Is inequality a social problem? The sociological response is mixed. For functionalists, inequality (within limits) is inherently good in advancing a complex and productive society. Conflict theorists disagree, arguing that inequality is necessary only in capitalist societies and that it is inherently bad for those who are its primary victims. Neither answer is more correct or insightful; both shed light on diverse aspects of the inequality paradox. In other words, sociological perspectives do make a difference in how to respond to questions about the inevitability and legitimacy of inequality in an ethnically diverse society.

Rethinking Ethnic Inequality

Two sets of explanation have been employed to explain ethnic inequality and stratification. One of these is a functionalist perspective, most closely identified with Porter's "ethnicity blocked mobility" thesis. According to this line of thinking, ethnic affiliation is likely to undermine the status aspirations and achievement goals of those ethnic minorities whose cultures are inappropriate or devalued. The second explanation is more closely related to conflict theories. The inferior status of ethnic minority groups can be properly explained by reference to differential opportunity structures, especially racial prejudice and discrimination (see Reitz and Sklar 1997). This shift toward structures as key explanatory frameworks reflects a repositioning of ethnic inequality. Instead of focusing on the individual or ethnic culture as a source of the problem, the trend is toward structural factors that encompass class, organization, racism, government policies, and systemic barriers (Brym 1991).

Emphasis is on the relational rather than distributional component of diversity with particular attention on how inequities are created, expressed, maintained, challenged, and transformed at the level of collective action or public policy. Focusing on the structures of society
as the problem has compelled a rethinking of federal and provincial policy initiatives, most
notably those dealing with employment equity programs. The reasons behind this change in
thinking are numerous; essentially, however, both changing demographics and shifting cultural politics have been central in rethinking both problem and solutions.

The Ethnicity Paradox: "The Old Vertical Mosaic"

The concept of ethnic inequality and stratification was once most commonly couched within
the context of a 1970s-style democratic liberalism (see Agòcs and Boyd 1993). Democratic
liberalism endorsed the principle that commonalities prevailed over differences, while doing
and accomplishing were deemed to be more important than being or birthright. At the core
of this democratic liberalism was a commitment to individual rights and formal equality as
a basis for national unity and prosperity. Canadian society was envisaged as an open and competitive marketplace in which individuals competed as equals and were rewarded because of
their skills or production. Individual success or failure reflected a person's amount of human
capital; that is, those people with training, skills, and education succeeded; those without did
not. To expand opportunities for all new Canadians without incurring a public backlash,
institutions would be "multiculturalized" by defining them as public spaces, thus ensuring
equal treatment irrespective of ethnicity and without the threat of messy ethnic entanglements
(Breton 1998).

Imperfections, of course, existed within the system. Ignorance and prejudice on the part
of employers hindered a natural sorting-out process and posed a threat to themselves and society. Economic success belonged to those who hired individuals only on the basis of merit.
Discrimination in the workforce would vanish once basically rational employers were shown
the irrationality of prejudice against ethnic minorities. Acceptance of ethnic differences
was critical in bolstering the national interests of social harmony and cohesion. By the same
token, ethnic minorities had to overcome the debilitating aspects of their ethnicity for success in the marketplace. Ethnic differences had to be suppressed (except at personal or private levels) to diminish their potential to divide, exclude, incite, or destroy (Breton 1998).
Alternatively, ethnicity could be promoted as it was after 1971, but only to the extent that
everyone was different in the same kind of way. The role of the government throughout
this adjustment process was essentially passive—to improve access and eliminate discrimination by ensuring a level playing field for all the contestants. The introduction of a multicultural policy in 1971 was viewed as a way of eliminating prejudice in the workplace
through removal of negative mainstream attitudes (Fleras 1994). It also sought to depoliticize ethnicity by eliminating its salience as a basis for entitlement or engagement in society.
In short, ethnicity was perceived as a problem under the old vertical mosaic, and steps were
taken to neutralize its potentially divisive effect.

The Power of Structures: "The New Vertical Mosaic"

By the early 1980s, thinking about inequality underwent a shift in emphasis (Fleras 1993).
Emphasis shifted from a focus on prejudice and ethnicity as problems and solutions to a
growing concern with structures and discriminatory barriers. The primary catalyst for this

cognitive shift was a dramatic increase in immigrants from developing countries, coupled with a growing chorus of complaints over the lack of progress in mainstreaming diversity. In contrast with European ethnic minorities, whose concerns were mainly (but not exclusively) over the preservation of language and culture, new migrants worried about institutional impediments and racism that precluded full and equal participation. The discourse on inequality shifted accordingly, from individual to structure, from ethnicity to race, and from a commitment to equality to that of *equity* with its focus on substantive differences and equal outcomes as part of this transformation.

A new paradigm was proposed to explain institutional resistance to accommodating diversity. According to this perspective, the problem did not rest with individuals or attitudes *per se*. Rather, the source of the problem was seen to be rooted in the institutional *structures* of society. Inequality and barriers to advancement were derived from structural constraints that were largely systemic and reflected a job market constructed by the "malestream" for self-serving purposes. These barriers to success were subtle but numerous. There was a greater awareness that workplace climates fostered unequal treatment of minorities because of harassment, double standards, and tokenism (see Kanter 1977). In applying the metaphor of a competitive footrace with staggered starting blocks, it was obvious that not all contestants were in a position to compete equally in the labour market. The race was rigged because of ascribed characteristics that handicapped certain individuals because of skin colour or lifestyle preference. As barriers, racially ascribed characteristics were just as real and debilitating as those encountered by individuals with disabilities. In both cases, the onus lay on the government to smooth out the playing field through legislation that would ensure at least the appearance of nominal equality.

Responses to the problem of racial inequality underwent a corresponding change of direction. The open marketplace was no longer thought to be an appropriate solution; it was identified instead as contributing to inequality through such entrenched barriers as segmented labour fields, racial division of labour, dual labour markets, and systemic structures of discrimination. Solutions that focused on individual shortcomings to eradicate inequality from the public domain did not capture the gravity of the problem. A "blaming the victim" approach could only apply superficial solutions to fundamental (structural) problems. It was the institutions, not the participants, that were in need of an overhaul for attainment of anything beyond the façade of equality. Attention thus shifted to employment equity as a policy framework for removing structural inequalities. Concurrent with this shift was a rethinking of equality as a basis for engaging diversity on a more equitable basis (see next Case Study).

From Equality to Equity

That most minorities aspire to social and economic equality is surely beyond dispute or debate. Many Canadians would also agree that equality is to be preferred over an inequality that is unfairly achieved. But the concept itself, "equality," is subject to diverse interpretations. Mutually opposed definitions may be endorsed by different groups, by different individuals across the spectrum of society, or by competing factions within the group. The situation is further complicated by the possibility of concurrent versions at a given point in time in response to changing circumstances. This proliferation of definitions has led to confusion and misunderstanding over the issue of entitlement, that is, who gets what and why. This element of uncertainty has also complicated the process of solving problems. Without new solutions to the old problem of inequality, the goal of equality will remain lofty but elusive.

Competing Equalities

The concept of equality is employed in three different ways. First, equality is used as synonymous with sameness. Everyone is treated the same regardless of their background or circumstances. No one is accorded special privileges in a system designed around equal opportunity and universal **merit**. This type of "formal" equality is focused on due process and legal equivalents. Second, equality is used in the sense of numerical, or "proportional," equivalence. Under systems of preferential hiring and promotion, each group is allocated positions according to their numbers in society or the workforce. Third, the concept of equality is aimed at the principle of "equity." References to equality as equity consider the unique circumstances of a person or group as a basis for differential treatment and institutional adjustments. Emphasis is on the attainment of equal outcomes (or conditions) rather than the abstract principle of equality of opportunity. Consider, for example, the "special" treatment that extends to individuals with disabilities. Concessions such as wheelchair ramps, closed-caption TV, and designated parking spots are common enough. But these concessions can hardly be thought of as special or preferential, but rather as removing barriers to ensure an equality of opportunity. Likewise, historically disadvantaged minority women and men also encounter barriers that are every bit as real as physical impediments, and equally in need of removal for levelling the playing field. In other words, those with socially defined disabilities also require different treatment if only to ensure their right to compete with others on an equal basis.

Each of these perspectives on equality differs from the other in terms of objectives and scope. **Formal equality** is concerned with mathematical equivalence and a market-driven means for establishing who gets what. It tends to treat individuals as asexual, deracialized, and classless without a history or context (McIntyre 1993). Any measure that rewards individuals on grounds other than merit or competition is criticized as contrary to the natural sorting-out process. This perspective is at odds with more substantive versions of equality known as equity. Under **substantive equity,** differences are taken into account as salient. A one-size-fits-all mentality can produce unequal results and perpetuate group-based inequities, according to Ontario's Human Rights Commission Annual Reports, especially when everyone is treated the same irrespective of differences or circumstances. This makes it imperative for social policies to take into account inequities derived from gender, race, and class (McIntyre 1993). Such a claim also raises a host of questions about which version of equality should prevail. Is one more important than the other, or is it a case of one serving as a necessary if insufficient precondition for the other?

Equity = Opportunity + Outcome

The distinction between equal opportunity ("competition") and equal outcomes ("conditions") is critical. Equal opportunity focuses on the rights of individuals to be free from discrimination when competing for the good things in life. By contrast, equal outcomes concentrates on the rights of individuals for a fair and equitable share of the goods and services in society. A commitment to equal opportunity openly advocates competition, inequality, and hierarchy as natural and inevitable. An equal outcomes perspective is concerned with controlled distribution and egalitarian conditions for members of a disadvantaged group. Differences are taken into account to ensure substantive equity. This perspective recognizes the need for collective over individual rights when the situation demands it. It also endorses the principle of social intervention for true equality, since equal outcomes are unlikely to arise from competitive market forces.

By themselves, equal opportunity structures are insufficient to overcome the debilitating effects of systemic discrimination and institutional racism. Additional treatment is required over and above that available to the general population, particularly when the application of equal standards to unequal situations merely freezes the status quo. Context and consequences are as important as abstract principles of equal opportunity in righting the wrongs. Taking context into consideration may mean the necessity for differential treatment in some cases to achieve an equality of outcome. Taking consequences into account suggests that intent and awareness are less important than the effects of practices, since the same treatment may have the effect of fostering unequal results. The unintended consequences of even seemingly neutral practices may lead to the unintentional exclusion of qualified personnel, regardless of motive or consciousness. Equity-based equality accepts the idea that superficially neutral rules may exert an adverse impact on certain minority groups and that reasonable accommodation is required to ensure that everyone has an equal opportunity to participate.

An outcome-oriented equity is derived from the principle that treating everyone the same is not equality or justice. But this outcome-based equity is not opposed to equal opportunities in defining equality. On the contrary, a commitment to the principle of equal opportunity constitutes a necessary first step in overcoming entrenched racism and discrimination. But ultimately such a commitment cannot achieve a fair and just equality in an unequal competition, especially in contexts where a segregated division of rewards exists. Only a dual commitment to equitable outcomes and equal opportunities can free up the playing field for open competition.

CASE STUDY 5–2	Employment Equity: Addressing the New (In)Equality

What Is Employment Equity?

Initiatives pertaining to a results-oriented equality derive legitimacy from the concept of **employment equity** (also known as affirmative action in the United States). Equity initiatives are aimed at proactively assisting minorities who have been excluded through no fault of their own from full and equal workplace participation. To its credit, the Canadian government has pioneered such measures through its Employment Equity Act of 1986, even though discrimination in the workplace had been illegal since 1962. The act sought to:

> ...achieve equality in the workplace so that no person shall be denied employment opportunities or benefits for reasons unrelated to ability...by giving effect to the principle that employment equity

means nothing more than treating persons in the same way but also requires special measures and the accommodation of differences.

Instead of passively responding to complaints of discrimination, the act sets out to proactively identify and eliminate systemic discrimination in the workplace and to remedy the effects of past discrimination. Terms of the act apply to all federally regulated employers (with 100 or more employees), public sector companies, and crown corporations. These companies were obligated to publish annual reports on the composition of their workforce, with particular reference to the number and type of work performed by women, visible minorities, people with disabilities ("differently able"), and aboriginal peoples. Minorities were to be hired and promoted in numbers commensurate with their ratio in the general workforce. Also falling under equity provisions are federal contractors with at least 100 employees. Each has to sign a certificate of commitment to comply with equity provisions ("contract compliance") if they wish to bid on government goods or services contracts worth $200,000 or more. All organizations are expected to file an annual report outlining their progress in this area. However, no penalties for noncompliance appear in the act.

Employment Equity: Policy and Philosophy

Employment equity has been defined in different ways, reflecting variations in emphasis on what employment equity looks like and does, and what it should look like and should do. Problems have arisen from failure to distinguish philosophy from policy. Employment equity as a philosophy is concerned with the principle of "institutional accommodation" through the removal of discriminatory barriers. It is based on the belief that all persons, regardless of colour and gender, should be treated equally within the workforce. That is, they should be recruited, hired, promoted, trained, and rewarded like any other person—assuming they are qualified on the basis of job-related skills and that positions are available—without barriers that discriminate against them because of membership in certain devalued groups.

By contrast, employment equity as a policy constitutes a legislated program with a formal set of practices to achieve government goals. As a principle, it points to a set of ideas and ideals; as a policy, it embraces a political solution to a social problem. One is concerned with the goal of justice and fairness; the other is compromised by the expediency that for justice to be done it must be *seen* to be done. Toward that end, employment equity consists of a comprehensive set of strategies designed to:

- ensure equitable representation of designated groups throughout all occupational and income levels at numbers consistent with their percentage in the regional workforce (Jain and Hackett 1989);
- identify and remove employment practices that create discriminatory and systemic barriers against identifiable and devalued groups;
- remedy adverse effects of past discrimination through positive programs for the recruitment, selection, and training of minorities;
- ensure reasonable progress in meeting numerical goals and timetables as proof of a more inclusive workplace (Jain 1988).

Assumptions and Rationale

Employment equity is ultimately concerned with institutions moving over and making space. This is particularly true of traditionally male occupations such as firefighting; for example, of the 1,143 firefighters employed by the City of Toronto in January 1996, 10 were women, 48 were members of visible minority groups, and 8 were aboriginal peoples. Employment equity begins with the premise that equality of opportunity and the hiring of individuals on the basis of merit *eludes* the four targeted minorities (women, persons with disabilities, people of colour, and aboriginal people). After all, if discriminatory employment barriers did not exist, all sectors of the workforce would theoretically be evenly distributed along all occupational and income levels in accordance with their numbers in the population (allowing, of course, for individual and cultural pressures, which may restrict occupational choices) (Regional Municipality of Waterloo 1986). Conditions such as gender, race, and disability, which are unrelated to merit and ability, must be neutralized as a basis for eliminating workplace discrimination. Minorities are not the problem, in other words; institutions are. As a result, it is institutions that must accommodate and change rather than the disadvantaged.

Employment equity is also based on the idea that workplace discrimination is systemic rather than personal. Discrimination may be defined systemically, that is, in the application of ostensibly neutral rules and conditions of employment that adversely affect certain minorities because of their culture or appearance. Systemic discrimination can vary in form and style. Often, it is inherent in universal employment policies and practices that uphold qualifications (such as those based on weight, height, gender, and experience). The rules, when applied evenly, have a dissimilar effect because they are unrelated to successful job performance, do not compensate for the disadvantages of a late start, and fail to incorporate minority needs or experiences. Positive and intrusive measures are required to redress what goodwill and best intentions cannot. Left on their own, organizations will tend to reproduce themselves unless an outside force is applied to break the circularity. Achievement of such long-range goals may require temporary colour-conscious initiatives on the assumption that race problems only respond to racial solutions, structural problems to structural solutions.

Setting the Record Straight

Criticism of employment equity is common enough. Decades of race-based equity programs have not resulted in unity, equality, and fairness, but in discrimination, division, grievance, and political correctness (Loney 1998). Certain minorities have felt exposed and vulnerable because of employment equity in the struggle to balance ambition and success with social responsibility (see also Slambrouck 1999). Confusion about employment equity continues to prevail as well. The three most common misconceptions are

those that link it with **reverse discrimination,** violation of the merit principle, and the imposition of **quotas.** Employment equity is frequently accused of "reverse discrimination." If it is unfair to discriminate against minorities, critics say, it is just as wrong to give preference to minorities and treat whites unfairly. All distinctions based on race, gender, or ethnicity are discriminatory and wrong, writes Sidney Knowles in a letter to the editor of *Society* (November/December 1998), especially when the discrimination is endorsed by the government under the guise of fairness or equity. Others disagree: Reference to context and consequences is important in sorting out this issue, as Cyril Levitt responds to the editor. Racial discrimination, by definition, is aimed at preserving privilege by denying or excluding minorities. Employment equity measures, by contrast, are geared toward greater inclusiveness through removal of discriminatory barriers (see Fish 1993). Equity programs are not intended to discriminate against white, able-bodied males (although the unintended consequence of such actions would appear to disqualify whiteness *and maleness from certain consideration*). Nor are employment equity initiatives designed to confer preferential treatment for designated minorities. To the contrary, the objective is to expand the number of qualified candidates by eliminating the bias that historically has rewarded certain sectors at the expense of disadvantaged groups.

With regard to merit, employment equity is not in business to hire or promote unqualified personnel. If anything, the removal of discriminatory barriers is intended to expand the pool of qualified applicants in the competition for employment. Employment equity also strives to make the competition more equal by opening it up to those formerly excluded from fair and just participation because of membership in a devalued group. Historically, of course, a preference for white males has long been the norm in society, in effect suggesting that merit was never the principal basis for hiring but, rather, an excuse for excluding unwanted minorities. Under employment equity, however, minorities are now considered on the basis of merit and credentials, in contrast with the past when people were hired because they fit the right type or had the right connections. To be sure, the concept of merit may need to undergo a rethinking in a world engulfed by rapid change, increased diversity, and painful uncertainty. Employment and promotions based on credentials are no longer guarantors of success. In fact, merit as a narrow set of abstract qualifications may well inhibit organizational effectiveness by obstructing the talent needed to survive in a competitive global economy.

Finally, employment equity is not about government-mandated quotas and deadlines. American-style quotas consisted of an externally imposed system of fixed percentages to be achieved within a certain time frame. Not surprisingly, unqualified personnel were hired to comply with the law or circumvent penalties. By contrast, employment equity goals are much more flexible; they reflect "reasonable expectations" about hiring and promotion from qualified designated group members when and if available for employment. The emphasis on improving the future rather than remedying the past diminishes the rationale for quotas under employment equity. In the final analysis, employment equity is aimed at creating a workplace culture, both inclusive and equitable, as well as progressive and productive.

CHAPTER HIGHLIGHTS

- The relationship between inequality and ethnic minority groups is a complex and evolving one. Generally speaking, Canada remains stratified by race and ethnicity despite moves to improve and accommodate. What is less well known is why this inequality exists and what, if anything, should be done to bridge the gap.

- Functionalist and conflict perspectives differ in how they approach minority in equality. Functionalists tend to see inequality as necessary and normal in a complex society; conflict theorists prefer to think of inequality as inevitable only in capitalist-type societies.

- The colour bar remains in effect in the United States, where African-Americans continue to bear the brunt of inequality, despite impressive gains by a rapidly emerging middle class.

- Evidence suggests that minorities in Canada are not equal when it comes to income. People of colour and aboriginal people tend to gravitate toward the bottom; whites and European ethnics are at the top.

- Some explanations of inequality assign a priority to race as the source of domination. Others explain ethnic stratification primarily as a result of social class. Still others suggest that race and class originate simultaneously, in the process reflecting relatively independent systems of explanation and prediction.

- Equally relevant as a source of exploitation or explanation are gender and ethnicity. Both race and class as well as gender and ethnicity intersect with each other to create interlocking and mutually intensifying patterns of inequality and stratification.

- The whole notion of racial and ethnic inequality is currently under reconsideration. This is especially evident in terms of causes and cures. The emphasis on ethnocultural differences and individual attitudes as the source of the problem (the ethnicity paradigm) is shifting toward structural factors as they relate to institutional rules, processes, and outcomes (the **equity paradigm**).

- This focus on structures of society as the problem has altered government solutions, with growing emphasis on institutional accommodation through removal of discriminatory barriers.

- Employment equity can be interpreted as a solution to the structural problem of inequality. A distinction needs to be made between employment equity as a principle (which many accept) and its application as a government program (which many reject).

- **The new equality** rejects the notion of equal in the sense of formal equality or mathematical precision. The application of equal ("identical") treatment to unequal situations simply "freezes" (however unintentionally) the status quo. It focuses instead on an equality that incorporates differences and focuses on equal outcomes (conditions) as a basis for entitlements.

KEY TERMS

conflict theory
cultural capital
culture of poverty
employment equity
equity paradigm
ethnic stratification
ethnicity paradox
formal equality
interlocking (or multiple) jeopardies
merit
multiple jeopardies
the new equality
new vertical mosaic
old vertical mosaic
quotas
reverse discrimination
social class
status attainment model
substantive equity

REVIEW QUESTIONS

1. Describe patterns of stratification in Canada by race and ethnicity.

2. Gender intersects with race, class, and ethnicity to create interlocking patterns of inequality that are mutually reinforcing yet analytically separate. Explain, and provide an example.

3. Compare and contrast the approaches of conflict versus functionalist theory as a means for explaining inequality and social stratification.

4. Point out how race and class offer different explanations for the source of group inequality. Which do you think is correct?

5. Our thinking on inequality has evolved in recent years. The equity paradigm (the new vertical mosaic) is replacing the ethnicity paradox (the old vertical mosaic). Explain what has happened and why.

6. The concept of equality can mean different things. Discuss the different meanings of equality as they pertain to race and ethnicity.

7. Stanley Fish has posed an interesting question: Whites once set themselves apart from minorities and claimed privileges while denying them to others. Now, on the basis of race and employment equity, people of colour are claiming special status and reserving for themselves privileges that they deny to others. Is one form of "discrimination" as bad as the other? Why or why not?

8. Cyril Levitt has referred to employment equity as a solution in search of a problem. Discuss what he might have meant by this expression.

P a r t

DIVERSITY IN CANADA: Peoples, Nations, and Minorities

Canada encompasses a formidable array of racial, aboriginal, and ethnic minority groups. Such a profusion of riches poses a problem of who to incorporate in an introductory textbook. Should our sample of minorities include the descendants of the original occupants who populated Canada thousands of years before the earliest European settlement? Logic would dictate the inclusion of aboriginal peoples. How much attention should focus on the British and French components? Again, an adequate level of coverage would appear necessary, given their importance as Charter (foundational) members of Canadian society. Who do we select among other ethnic minority groups in Canada? The rationale for choosing one group over another cannot be taken lightly. Should coverage encompass numerically large ethnicities such as those with Germanic or Ukrainian descent? Or should emphasis be directed at primary targets of Canadian racism, such as Indo-Pakistani Canadians or African-Canadians (see Buckner 1993)? Can the inclusion of certain minorities be justified on the grounds of sympathy or visibility? Is the decision to be based on practical concerns, such as access to research material? The range of possibilities can be discussed indefinitely. Nevertheless, the problem should be self-evident at this point: In the face of a bewildering array of diversity, who do we select for study and how do we justify our choices?

Specialists in this field have explored different ways to impose some semblance of coherence on an otherwise sprawling subject matter. They have tried to organize this diversity into manageable proportions in the hopes of imposing an element of logic in the sorting and selection process. One solution proposes a classification of Canadian ethnicity into a limited number of categories by virtue of shared similarities in history, status, and structure

(Elliott 1983). The social relations that arise between groups are rooted in patterned inter-group dynamics incorporating both situational factors and structural variables and are amenable to analysis and assessment (Frideres 1998). Our text follows this proposal. Canada is partitioned into three major ethnic "forces" on the basis of (a) legal status in society, (b) major problems, (c) proposed solutions, and (d) anticipated goals. According to this classi-ficatory scheme, most Canadians can be classified into one of the following ethnic cate-gories: (a) **aboriginal peoples;** (b) Charter group members, and (c) multicultural minorities, such as immigrants, refugees, landed residents, European ethnics, and native-born people of colour. Each of these three major ethnicities is associated with a set of distinctive and shared properties, and each is known to confront a host of unique problems in defining its place in society. All three are also likely to espouse strategies commensurate with their interests, concerns, and priorities. The table below compares the three major ethnicities on the basis of the aforementioned criteria.

Three Major Ethnicities in Canada: A Comparison and Contrast				
	Legal Status	**Basic Problem**	**Proposed Solutions**	**Anticipated Outcome**
Aboriginal peoples	Original occupants	Internal colonialism	Decolonize by self-determination	Nations within
Charter members Québécois	Founding Nations	Blocked nationalism	Sovereignty association	Distinct society
Multicultural minorities				
Visible	Citizenship	Discrimination	Inclusion	Equity
Nonvisible	Citizenship	Culture loss	Celebrate diversity	Mosaic

This table clearly demonstrates how Canada's three major ethnicities differ in terms of (a) who they are, (b) what they want, (c) how they propose to attain goals, and (d) what barri-ers preclude goal attainment. Very briefly, the status of aboriginal peoples as Canada's orig-inal occupants is inseparable from the politics of aboriginality. In contrast with the human rights of ethnic minorities, aboriginal peoples possess political rights that stem from injus-tices perpetuated by the colonization project, including rights to self-determine both mem-bership in and intergovernmental relationships with the Canadian state (Bell 1997). The aboriginal agenda is driven by a commitment to decolonize their relationship from within through incorporation of aboriginal models of self-governing, self-determination over land, identity, and political voice. Aboriginal leaders are pursuing a national political agenda that focuses on wresting jurisdiction away from federal/provincial authorities, while reaffirming their status as fundamentally autonomous political communities, each of which is sover-eign in its own right yet sharing in the sovereignty of Canada at large (Royal Commission on Aboriginal Peoples 1996; Asch 1997; Ponting 1997). Ottawa–Quebec relations are con-structed around the constitutional status of founding members. French–English (or, more ac-curately, French- and English-speaking) conflicts are sharply animated by failure to craft an innovative political order that concedes "peoplehood" to Quebeckers. To justify demands and actions, both aboriginal peoples and the Québécois draw on the notion of nationhood, with its connotation of a psychological bond of peoplehood, an aversion to being ruled by others, common history and customs, and a qualified form of self-determination within the context of Canadian federalism (Bell 1997). Finally, multicultural minorities confront a different set of pressures than aboriginal peoples or Charter members in staking out their place in society. Minority women and men are entitled only to individual equality rights of citizenship rather than any collective agenda-setting status in making claims against the state. Their concerns are directed at the institutional inclusion of diversity and equality through removal of discriminatory barriers rather than jurisdictional debates over self-determination as is the case with indigenous peoples. A distinction in the different priorities of visible and nonvisible minorities is duly noted, but is not systematically pursued in light of space limitations.

We believe this system of classification provides a convenient organizing principle for what to study and how. Exceptions abound in this kind of typology, to be sure, including anomalous status minorities such as Hutterites and francophones outside of Quebec. The very nature of "ideal types" is prone to simplification or reductionism; after all, as the sociologist Max Weber once noted, the goal of any typological exercise is not to replicate reality in its exactitude, but to render it intelligible for description or analysis, even if some degree of exaggeration is necessary. The classification of minorities into major ethnic groups solves several problems in one swoop. Recurrent themes and predictable patterns in group behaviour can be emphasized without lapsing into a welter of detail. Specifics are sacrificed along the way; nevertheless, much can be gained from examining the logic rather than the details behind the politics of diversity in Canada. This "big picture" approach also reinforces a macro-sociological view of society as a dynamic of competitively different groups in the ongoing struggle for scarce resources within unequal and changing contexts.

Part 2 is organized around this macro-level of analysis. In Chapter 6, recent developments in the field of aboriginal peoples–government relations are explored in light of the government's recent decision to acknowledge original occupants as "peoples" with an "inherent right to self-government." Much of the chapter concentrates on the following issues: (a) the dispossession of aboriginal peoples because of colonization; (b) government policy response to solving the so-called "Indian problem"; and (c) aboriginal proposals for atonement and renewal through constructive engagement. Chapter 7 analyzes the politics of English–French (Charter members) relations within the framework of an increasingly contested Canadian federalism. A closer look at the language issue will demonstrate its ability not only to advance Québécois ethnicity, but also to address the jurisdictional wrangles at the core of French–English misunderstanding. Chapter 8 looks at a variety of concerns that confront multicultural minorities as they cope with the challenges of survival and attainment of success in Canada. Primary attention is centred on various issues pertaining to immigration, including a review of immigration policies, immigration patterns in the past and present, debates over the pros and cons of immigration, and an assessment of the costs and benefits with respect to Canadian society building. Part 3, on multiculturalism and institutional inclusiveness, will deal more specifically with official attempts to engage diversity in ways that are workable, necessary, and fair.

ABORIGINAL
PEOPLES

CASE STUDY 6–1	**Nunavut: Decolonizing the North**

The principle of aboriginality as a new paradigm for redefining aboriginal peoples–government relations has gained both constitutional and legislative strength in Canada's Arctic. The old paradigm of treaties, reserves, and outdated colonialism was never practical for the circumpolar peoples, given geographical and demographic considerations (Quassar 1998). The evolving paradigm is squarely rooted in the principle of aboriginal self-determination over their cultural and social affairs. It is also grounded in the notion that control over material resources and economic self-sufficiency are key in giving practical effect to self-governing initiatives. But the gap between the ideal and reality may prove especially daunting in the implementation, and this Case Study will highlight some of the difficulties in putting an Inuit government into practice in Canada's North.

The Nunavut Nation

The Inuit of the Canadian Arctic have undergone considerable change in response to political and social pressures. Once isolated and without a common awareness for collective action, the Inuit have taken steps since the early 1970s to redefine themselves in relationship with each other and with the Canadian state. In the Eastern Arctic, Inuit aspirations were couched within the framework of Nunavut, the Inuktitut word for "our land" and also the name of a group of Inuit living in the Eastern Arctic. To date, the concept of Nunavut remains unrecognized in the constitution; nevertheless, the process of defining it and its ratification in 1993 allow us some glimpse into the magnitude of the task that awaits implementation of Nunavut government on 1 April 1999.

The Eastern Arctic Inuit themselves number about 20,000, scattered across a tract of land the size of Argentina. Unlike status Indians in the South, the Inuit were the undisputed landlords of the North, having never entered into treaty arrangements with federal or provincial governments. Legally, however, the Inuit possessed the same status as aboriginal peoples elsewhere in Canada because of a 1939 Supreme Court ruling. Until the 1970s the Inuit did not share a common sense of peoplehood. Political, geographic, dialectical, and jurisdictional problems militated against promotion of a shared and united front under the aboriginal banner. This inability to foster a pan-Inuit identity and aboriginality undermined efforts to exert pressure on central authorities to negotiate territorial self-determination.

The Vision of Nunavut

The vision and struggle for Nunavut gathered momentum during the early 1970s. This redefining process was derived from aboriginal movements in Canada and the United States as well as throughout the world. In 1976, the Inuit Tapirisat submitted its first proposal for the establishment of Nunavut. The plan sought to establish a single Inuit homeland across the Arctic, covering nearly 2,000,000 km^2 of land and adjacent offshore areas, modelled largely on the Cree land claim settlement negotiated with the Quebec government as part of the James Bay agreement. Eight years later, in 1984, the agreement still unsigned, another group, the Inuialiut Inuit, signed a second land claim settlement in the Western Arctic, including $152 million in cash, 91,770 km^2 of land, and various guarantees, consultation rights, and developmental funds (DIAND

[**Department of Indian Affairs and Northern Development**], *Information*, October 1996). Having settled their grievances, the Inuvialiut Inuit were free to align themselves with either the more limited proposals of the Denendeh in the Western Arctic or the broad vision of the Nunavut of the Eastern Arctic. For various political, geographical, and cultural reasons, the Inuvialiut cast their lot with the Denendeh.

What exactly does the Nunavut vision consist of? Nunavut conjures up the same emotional appeal that "mon pays" does for the Québécois. The sustaining vision of Nunavut is a society with full control over its culture and language, its resources, and its environment. Proposals for Inuit public government, in which all residents have voting rights regardless of racial or cultural background, rather than **aboriginal self-government,** reflect the unique demographics of the North, with its high density of indigenous peoples compared to nonindigenes (numbering about 5,000). Equally important is the settlement of Nunavut land claims for securing rights to wildlife and mineral harvesting. The need for such an overarching plan was evident; the social and economic needs of the Inuit were desperate in some cases and forecast to worsen if current trends continued. Forces that were undermining efforts at culture and language preservation were increasingly difficult to control without redefining the government structures of the territorial system. In addition, a diversified economic base was required to meet the material needs of a growing population.

A Vision Realized

The vision of Nunavut came to fruition in May 1993 when the Nunavut Act and Nunavut Land Claims Agreement were signed by federal, territorial, and the Tungavik Federation, making it the largest comprehensive land claim settlement to date in Canada (DIAND, May 1997). Under the terms of the agreement, the

Inuit will receive ownership of 350,000 km² of land, including access to 36,000 km² of mineral rights. The agreement provides financial compensation of $1.14 billion to be paid out over 14 years. A $13 million Training Trust Fund will be established to ensure the Inuit have the skills to implement the terms of the settlement. A key benefit will be a new type of land–sea resource management structure, with Inuit comprising half of the representatives in these decision-making bodies. The final agreement also made provisions for the establishment of a Nunavut Territory and a "public" government, which will cover about one-fifth of Canada's land mass and came into effect 1 April 1999. The Nunavut Assembly will not resemble aboriginal self-government in the "sovereign" sense, but will operate as part of Canada's Parliamentary system, with the Inuit in effective control by virtue of the fact they comprise 85 percent of the population.

To be sure, formidable problems threaten to derail the implementation process, including a continued dependency on federal funding to underwrite the costs of putting the vision into practice. With a population base of around 25,000, including 3,500 in the capital, Iqaluit, Nunavut simply does not have the critical mass of tax base to be self-sufficient and will continue to rely on Ottawa for 98 percent of its funding (Henton 1998). The combination of soaring costs of living and deeply anchored social problems will also hinder progress and elicit criticism (Smith 1995; Anderssen 1998). Still, the fact that the Inuit have already begun to implement wildlife-harvesting rights and participate in environmental exercises suggests that the vision of Nunavut is rapidly becoming a practical reality in a country that itself is still in the process of society building (Légaré 1997; Amagoalik 1998).

INTRODUCTION: THE FIRST PEOPLES

What a difference a few decades can make. As recently as 1969, Canada's aboriginal peoples were poised on the brink of legal extinction, thanks to the assimilationist intent of the government's White Paper bill, under then Indian Affairs Minister Jean Chrétien. Aboriginal concerns tended to dwell on basic survival strategies, and many seemed resigned to powerful outside forces beyond control. In reaction to the White Paper, however, aboriginal protest mobilized against what many perceived as a thinly veiled pretext for cultural genocide. By 1978, a sense of revolt was palpable over government indecision to address aboriginal issues, a move that nearly toppled Trudeau's efforts at repatriating the constitution during the early 1980s. The constitutional entrenchment of aboriginal and **treaty rights** in 1982 clearly confirmed that aboriginal peoples had arrived. By 1992, aboriginal leaders were engaging with First Ministers in Charlottetown in hope of hammering out a workable post-Oka relationship with the government. Principles became practice when the Liberal government leader, Jean Chrétien, acknowledged the "inherent right" of Canada's aboriginal "peoples" to self-government. Another conference of provincial premiers in 1997 in Calgary further assured aboriginal leaders of their participation in all constitutional matters involving aboriginal peoples. The shift in the balance of power is cryptically captured by this fractured howler:

> Before we [aboriginal peoples] had to play a sort of poker. But the civil servants dealt us our cards face up, kept theirs close to the chest and asked us how much we wanted to bet. But we Natives don't have to play poker any more because we've learned how to play *bridge* (emphasis added) (Gene Rheaume, commenting on the Mohawk blockade of the Mercier Bridge in Montreal during the Oka Crisis, quoted by Viola Robinson in National Proceedings 1993:38).

The distance travelled by aboriginal peoples in such a relatively short time period—from irrelevancy to robust political actors on the Canadian state—underscores one major theme of this chapter. The distance that is yet to be traversed before aboriginal peoples assume their rightful place in society is yet another theme. Canadians have been slow in recognizing the central reality that must be addressed if productive relationships are to be reconstructed: aboriginal peoples have historical rights. These rights focus on aboriginal peoples as fundamentally autonomous and self-determining political communities with rights to self-determination over land, identity, and political voice (Royal Commission on Aboriginal Affairs 1996; Asch 1997; Maaka and Fleras 1998).

It is not coincidental that we begin Part 2 with an analysis of aboriginal peoples (also called First Peoples or First Nations, indigenous peoples, Native Indians, or Indians, as the context suggests). The term "aboriginal" itself refers to the original or indigenous occupants of this country. This status as original occupants provides aboriginal peoples with the moral and legal authority to press claims against the Canadian state on the basis of common law **indigenous rights.** The term "first" can also be used in a less flattering way. Aboriginal peoples are "first" in those social areas that count least (unemployment, undereducation, suicide, and morbidity rates), but last in realms that matter most. Aboriginal peoples are exposed to prejudice and discrimination; nevertheless, the major obstacles are in the colonialist and institutional structures of society that inhibit full and equal participation (Frideres 1998). With the possible exception of French–English relations, they also are "first" in terms of media exposure: Some of this publicity is sympathetic; much reflects a degree of hostility or intolerance in endorsing a popular view of aboriginal peoples as "problem people" who "have problems" or "create problems" that cost or provoke (Switzer 1998). Others dismiss aboriginal issues as a "quagmire" in which public understanding is sacrificed for the "...sinkholes of Orwellian language games, financial sleight of hand, and treacly Noble Savage romanticism" (Mulgrew 1996). The circulation of this misinformation is unfortunate for two reasons. First, a considerable amount of public sympathy and goodwill is squandered because most Canadians are generally unaware of what aboriginal peoples want, why they want it, and how they propose to achieve their goals (Ponting 1997). Second, aboriginal efforts at renewal and healing are often underappreciated or underreported in spite of nationally recognized accomplishments in fields as diverse as art, literature, and academics.

Canada's mistreatment of the aboriginal peoples has been called a national tragedy and a shameful disgrace. A UN Human Rights Committee has ruled the treatment of aboriginal peoples to be in violation of international law and the most "pressing human rights facing Canadians" (cited in Gordon 1999:A–12). Canada may be perennially ranked by the United Nations as the world's best place to live, but aboriginal peoples on reserves are ranked sixty-third on a human development index. The fact that aboriginal peoples live 12 years less and earn about one-quarter of what Canadians do (according to 1991 statistics) puts aboriginal reserves on the same par as medium developed countries, such as Mexico and Thailand (Anderssen 1998). The overtones of neglect, indifference, and expediency represent nothing less than Canada's great moral failure, Richard Gwyn (1998) writes, since only aboriginal peoples possess the status of the dispossessed, the demoralized, and the dysfunctional. But aboriginal peoples have not stood by as passive and defeated victims. Many have taken the initiative in reconstructing their relationship to society, and it is these initiatives rather than "problems" that anchor the content of this chapter. The complex and difficult issues associated with this reconstruction process should never be underestimated. Aboriginal demands are organized around the principle of nationhood rather than social integration, with the result that there is much to be gained in approaching the concept of aboriginal self-determination within the context of the "nations within" (Fleras and Elliott 1992). Colonial arrangements are no longer applicable in this postcolonizing era (Alfred 1995; Salée 1995). Proposed instead as part of the renewal process is the idea of a new political order in which aboriginal peoples comprise a third tier of government, each of which is sovereign in its own right yet sharing in the sovereignty of society at large by way of multiple, interlocking **jurisdictions** (Royal Commission on Aboriginal Affairs 1996; Maaka and Fleras 1997). Insofar as the aspirations of Canada's aboriginal peoples are not altogether dissimilar from indigenous aspirations in Australia and New Zealand, the situation is ripe for a comparison and contrast that may well sharpen our knowledge of aboriginal peoples–state relations in terms of underlying logic, hidden agendas, current dynamics, and future outcomes (Fleras and Maaka, forthcoming).

This chapter is not intended as a history or description of aboriginal traditions or lifestyles. Nor is it intended to present a litany of aboriginal social problems. The chapter is organized around the theme of "aboriginality" in reframing the relationship of aboriginal peoples to society. Placement of aboriginal peoples–state relations within the context of a "contested politics" provides insight into how this relationship of inequality is defined, expressed, maintained, contested, and modified by way of state policy and aboriginal initiatives. The chapter begins with a brief overview of aboriginal peoples with respect to legal and socioeconomic status. This is followed by an examination of policy changes that historically have shaped aboriginal peoples–state relationships. Aboriginal policy is shown to have generated as many problems as it set out to solve, partly because of faulty premises and partly from privileging "national interests" over aboriginal concerns (Boldt 1993). The creation of an appropriate working agenda for aboriginal peoples–government relations is focused on aboriginal proposals as a blueprint for reconstruction. Comparable initiatives by aboriginal peoples elsewhere in the world are also discussed as grounds for contextualizing Canada's experience within a broader perspective.

A word of warning to the reader. Neither of the authors is of aboriginal ancestry, so we cannot speak from an aboriginal perspective (also Ponting 1997; Cockerill and Gibbins 1997). Our analysis cannot capture the experiences, aspirations, and constraints that routinely confront the original occupants of Turtle Island (North America) because of colonialist pressures. All we can do is reflect upon our research experience in Canada and elsewhere as a basis for assessing the contemporary situation. This limitation, of course, need not be fatal since an outsider's point of view can augment an insider's interpretation. Reliance throughout this chapter on the works of aboriginal scholars and colleagues will serve to lessen the potential for distortion.

Second, limitations of space cannot be ignored. It is impossible to compress into a single chapter all there is to know about aboriginal peoples, either in the past or at present. Nor can we conflate the diverse concerns of aboriginal women and men into a coherent statement, especially when differences within groups may be greater than differences between groups. The necessity to be selective leads us to concentrate on a single dimension of aboriginal life, namely, the evolving political relationship of aboriginal peoples with the Canadian state (or government) as reflected and reinforced through the prism of official policy and aboriginal assertiveness. Admittedly, this decision to concentrate on the politics of power will diminish the richness associated with aboriginal existence. However, there are numerous aboriginal works on the market that deal with issues of spirituality, cultural traditions, and oral histories, and readers are encouraged to seek these out. But in going with our strengths and interests, we firmly believe that the political dimension offers the most comprehensive and provocative insight into the challenges of constructively reengaging aboriginal peoples with Canadian society building.

Third, our discussion of aboriginal peoples is confined to general terms. This increases the risk of ignoring the historical and social specifics of different tribes and bands. Aboriginal peoples themselves are legally divided into status, nonstatus, Métis, and Inuit, each with a specific set of problems and solutions. Variation can be found among aboriginal groups in the Atlantic provinces, Central Canada, the Western Plains, Yukon and the Northwest Territories, and the Pacific West. The diversity is conditioned by ecological adaptations to unique physical environments, along with corresponding differences in the symbolic and material cultures. Adjustment problems vary for aboriginal peoples in remote and rural reserves, in contrast with those who reside in towns and cities. Compounding geographical variations are individual differences based on age, gender, education levels, and socioeconomic status. The political aspirations of aboriginal "elites," with their focus on "inherency" and "self-governance," may be at odds with the more pragmatic local concerns for healthy children and indoor plumbing. In short, there are numerous traps in discussing aboriginal peoples as if they were a relatively homogeneous entity with a shared sense of where to go and how. Common sense will dictate they are as heterogeneous as nonaboriginal Canadians in political outlook and cultural aspirations. To say this is not to diminish the value of broad brush strokes. It is simply to warn readers of the perils in sorting through debates in a field of burgeoning complexity.

CONTEMPORARY STATUS

Aboriginal peoples comprise an extremely diverse constituency, with numerous tribes of varying size, access to resources, development levels, and social health. According to the 1996 Census, nearly 800,000 people reported they were aboriginal, of which 554,000 were "North American Indian," 210,000 Métis, and 41,000 Inuit (Canadian Press, 14 January 1998). It is interesting to note that in the 1991 Census, aboriginal peoples comprised about 3.7 percent of Canada's population, with 1,002,675 reporting aboriginal ancestry, up 41 percent since 1986 because of natural increases and different means of enumeration. Differences between the 1991 and 1996 figures may depend on how "Native American Indian" is defined. Social and cultural differences among aboriginal tribes remain as real as they did prior to European contact (Frideres 1998). Aboriginal communities vary in terms of development and socioeconomic status; differences also exist between rural and urban aboriginals as well as between aboriginal women and men. Even the term "aboriginal peoples" is misleading, since this constitutional status can be further subdivided into the categories of *status Indians, nonstatus Indians, Métis,* and *Inuit.*

Legal Dimensions

Aboriginal peoples with the highest profile in Canada are **status Indians**. With some exceptions, membership to status Indians is defined by (a) admittance to a general registry in Ottawa, (b) affiliation with one of 605 bands, (c) entitlement to residence on band reserve lands, and (d) jurisdiction under the Indian Act (Frideres 1998). The current population of status Indians stands at 553,316, up from 230,902 in 1967. These numbers are expected to increase to about 750,000 by 2005, primarily through reinstatement of individuals who had lost status through marriage or other means. Ontario has the largest population of status Indians, with 121,867 followed by British Columbia with 90,769 (Canadian Press, 14 January 1998). Status Indians reside on one of 2,597 reserves across Canada, ranging in size from a "few" on one Pacific coast reserve to nearly 19,000 at the Six Nations Reserve near Brantford, Ontario. The majority of status Indians (59.2 percent in 1992) live on reserves created by one of 61 treaties signed with the Crown. These numbers can vary because of fluctuations in the pattern of rural–urban migration (Dosman 1972). The interests of status Indians are represented by 633 chiefs who comprise the Assembly of First Nations. These interests are supported by the federal government, which targets over $5 billion per year to this group because of treaty and fiduciary responsibilities. Only a small percentage (about 4 percent) of this amount is directed at aboriginal economic development, primarily in the form of loans for business (Buckley 1992), with the bulk monopolized by administrative costs and social spending.

The second category of aboriginal peoples comprises the **nonstatus Indians.** The exact population is unknown, but estimates fluctuate between 75,000 and 750,000. Unlike status Indians, nonstatus Indians are exempt from provisions of the Indian Act and dictates of the Department of Indian Affairs. Some individuals relinquished their official status in exchange for the right to vote, drink alcohol off the reserve, or (in the case of women) to marry a non-Indian. Others are nonstatus because of having never entered into any formal treaty agreement with the federal government. Nonstatus Indians do not live on reserves (only status Indians are entitled to reserve life and receive band inheritance); they are scattered in small towns and large cities across Canada. This geographical and social isolation is not conducive to preserving language, culture, and identity. Despite this formal estrangement from their roots, many nonstatus Indians continue to identify themselves as aboriginal peoples because of shared affinities. Inclusion of nonstatus Indians as aboriginal peoples by the Canadian Constitution of 1982 has legitimated the identity and concerns of nonstatus Indians. Still, relationships between nonstatus and status Indians have been fraught with tension and disagreement because of competition over limited federal resources. Currently, nonstatus Indians are represented by the Congress of Aboriginal Peoples.

The third class, the **Métis,** constitutes a contested category comprising the offspring (and descendants) of mixed European–aboriginal unions. Numbering in the vicinity of 100,000 to 400,000 persons, the Métis initially were restricted to those descendants of the Red River Settlements in Manitoba who identified with the Métis nation. Many Métis at present dwell in relatively remote communities throughout the Prairie provinces without much land base to secure economic prospects. The Métis may be officially regarded as a distinct aboriginal peoples with constitutional protection and corresponding guarantees. But the lack of judicial recognition on par with status Indians undermines the legal authority of the Métis to negotiate claims over traditional lands, the assumption being that the Constitutional rights of 1982 can only be enjoyed by those who can prove original occupancy, exclusive relationship to the land, and can exercise the rights to **aboriginal title** (Bell 1997; Spiers 1998). The Métis continue to be hampered by difficulties in defining who is Métis and the jurisdictional debate between Ottawa and the provinces over who is responsible for off-reserve natives. In late 1998, the Ontario provincial court ruled that the Métis have as much right to hunt and fish for food as status Indians. The ruling also confirmed the Métis as a culturally distinct aboriginal people (Anderssen 1998). The Alberta government has also recognized Métis self-governing rights along with the right to limited institutional autonomy. The 192,000 Métis across the Prairies are represented by the Métis National Council.

The **Inuit** constitute the final category. The 41,000 Inuit (or 55,700, according to DIAND figures) enjoy a special status and relationship with the federal government despite never having signed any treaty arrangements. Vast changes in Inuit culture in the past decades have not yet substantially altered subsistence and cultural patterns. Inuktitut is widely spoken in Inuit communities across the Northwest Territories and Northern Quebec and Labrador. Many continue to rely on hunting and trapping to secure food, clothing, and shelter (DIAND, *Information,* October 1996). Despite an enviable degree of cultural integrity, deeply rooted social problems are endemic, including soaring rates of teenage pregnancies, substance abuse, suicide rates, accidental deaths, and diabetes (Anderssen 1998). At local levels, the Inuit are governed by municipal councils, with various committees to discharge responsibilities over health and education. Inuit interests at national levels are represented by the Inuit Tapirisat ("an association of various Inuit leaders") of Canada. The Inuit have recently concluded successful negotiations with Ottawa for control over their homeland—Nunavut—in the Eastern Arctic. Since the 1970s, Inuit groups have negotiated several other **comprehensive land claims,** including the James Bay and Northern Quebec Act of 1975—the first of its kind in Canada—as well as the North East Quebec Act of 1978, both of which involved transfers of land and extinguishment of aboriginal rights for cash, land, co-management bodies, and hunting and trapping rights.

Socioeconomic Status

Nearly four hundred years of sustained contact and interaction have left aboriginal peoples–government relations in a state of disarray and despair. The imposition of a colonialistic framework in this country exerted a powerful, negative effect on aboriginal peoples (Bienvenue 1985). In some cases, government policies deliberately undermined the viability of aboriginal communities in the never-ending quest to divest aboriginal peoples of their land, culture, and tribal authority. In other cases, the demise of aboriginal peoples came about through unobtrusive but equally powerful measures pertaining to education and missionization. In still other cases, the often unintended effects of possibly well-intentioned but ultimately misguided programs, for example, residential schools, have had lingering repercussions in marginalizing aboriginal peoples.

No matter how evaluated or assessed, aboriginal peoples as a group remain at the bottom of the socioeconomic heap. Housing is inadequate or overcrowded on many reserves, failing to meet basic standards of amenities and structure, including an absence of sewer or water connections (Frideres 1998). With rates nearly three times the national average, unemployment is a major cause of aboriginal distress in leading directly to poor housing, illness, a sense of powerlessness, cultural disintegration and social decay, and cycles of poverty (Drost et al. 1995). On certain reserves, up to 95 percent of the population subsists on welfare or unemployment benefits. Individual incomes are half of that of all Canadians, while the ratio of social assistance to aboriginal peoples is five times that of the population at large (Purvis 1999). The $2.5 billion the government spends just to offset poverty, including $1 billion on social assistance, is really closer to $7.5 billion if one takes into account lost productivity, income, and potential taxes. The awkward location of many reserves and their limited resources remain key problems, but many residents are reluctant to abandon them for fear of losing reserve entitlements. The situation is equally grim for those who have drifted into cities. Many have few skills, experience high unemployment, live in derelict housing, are exposed to inadequate services, and are cut off from federal funding or reserve benefits. Only a small percentage (about 20 percent) of aboriginal students even finish secondary schooling, let alone go on to postsecondary levels. Still, enrollments in postsecondary education have escalated from about 200 in the 1960s to 14,242 in 1987, and doubled since then to 27,487 in 1997 (Simpson 1998).

Equally worrying is the demographic time bomb that is ticking away in many aboriginal communities. The aboriginal population has been rapidly increasing since the 1960s because of high fertility and dramatic declines in infant mortality (Canadian Press, 14 January 1998). With a birthrate that is 70 percent higher than the general population, the youthfulness of many aboriginal communities is causing concern, given the average age of 25.5 years compared with 35.4 in the nonaboriginal population. The aboriginal cohort aged 15 to 24 is expected to increase by another 26 percent by 2006; the demand for access to education and social services will increase correspondingly. Nearly one-third of aboriginal children under 15 years live with a lone parent, twice the rate in the general population. The implications of this demographic reality are staggering.

Deterioration of aboriginal cultural values has compounded the difficulties of identity and adjustment. Numerous aboriginal languages are currently under threat of disappearing because of pressure from the English (and French) in the schools and media, with only three (Ojibwa, Cree, and Inuktitut) on relatively solid footing (Fleras 1987). The psychological effects derived from a sense of powerlessness, alienation, and irrelevance have been no less detrimental (Shkilnyk 1985). As noted by David Courchene, a former president of the Manitoba Indian Brotherhood:

> One hundred years of submission and servitude, of protectionism and paternalism have created psychological barriers for Indian people that are far more difficult to break down and conquer than the problems of economic and social poverty (Buckley 1992:24).

Aboriginal individuals may transform this powerlessness and impotence into an expression of self-hatred. The internalization of white racism and/or indifference is reflected in violent death rates, which are up to four times the national average. Infant mortality rates are about 60 percent higher than the national average. Alcohol and substance abuse is widely regarded as the foremost problem on most reserves, with alcohol-related deaths accounting for up to 80 percent of the fatalities on some reserves (Buckley 1992). Domestic abuse is so endemic within aboriginal communities, according to some observers (Drost et al. 1995), that few aboriginal children grow into adulthood without first-hand experience of interpersonal violence. Violent deaths and suicides are also disproportional when compared to the general population. With a suicide rate of six times the national average for certain age-specific groups, aboriginal peoples represent one of the most self-destructive groups in the world at present.

Aboriginal involvement with the criminal justice system is deplorable as well. Nearly three-quarters of aboriginal males will have been incarcerated in a correctional centre at some point in their lives by the age of 25. Aboriginal inmates occupy 64 percent of the federal penitentiary population in Western Canada, according to Statistics Canada, but only about 12 percent of the Prairie population (Editorial, *Globe and Mail,* 2 February 1998). Admittedly, some degree of cautiousness must be exercised: Statistics may be misleading since offenders may be convicted for relatively minor offences and serve time for offences that require only a fine. As well, only a small number of individuals may get in trouble with the law, but on a repeated basis (Buckley 1992). Nevertheless, the statistics are damning: The revolving door of incarceration and recidivism has stripped many aboriginal peoples of any positive self-concept, in effect leading to self-fulfilling cycles of despair and decay. Nor can we disregard the sometimes disastrous consequences of often well-intentioned but misguided government policies and programs (Shkilnyk 1985).

Question Box
Who's to Blame?

The Stoney Reserve west of Calgary has attracted the kind of publicity that most aboriginal communities would prefer to avoid. The 3,300 strong reserve is one of the wealthiest in Canada, with annual revenues of around $33 million, including $20 million from the federal government and $13 million from natural gas royalties (Flanagan 1997). That amounts to approximately $10,000 per year, tax-free, for every man, woman, and child (Bercuson and Cooper 1997). But these figures conceal a more unnerving reality. The Stoney Reserve has a deficit of $5 million, its electrical power is being threatened because of unpaid bills amounting to $750,000, almost 90 percent of reserve residents are unemployed, 66 percent are on welfare assistance, and 28 people have died violently since 1995, including 8 suicides. What makes these figures more disturbing still is the location of Stoney Reserve, midway between the boom city of Calgary and the perpetually labour-starved resort town of Banff (Flanagan 1997).

So, what is going on? Who is to blame? Why is it that $6 billion in federal expenditures for aboriginal programs is doing little to heal the ills that plague aboriginal communities (Cheney 1998)? Is it a case of colonial practices by successive government policies that historically have encouraged poor opportunity structures, lack of education, unemployment, welfare dependency, and racism within society (Fontaine 1998)? Band councils continue to be governed by the Indian Act with little control over the political process. There is no incentive to modify current funding arrangements,

since reserve communities have no taxation base, are dependent on the government for expenditures, and devoid of individual private property (Flanagan 1998). Is it because of cultural differences, that is, are aboriginal cultures, with their emphasis on sharing, diametrically at odds with the demands of success in a competitive, individualistic, and globalizing economy (Drost et al. 1995)? Is the blame to rest with federal officials, who on the one hand tolerate loose auditing practices and nonexistent accountability procedures to the community but on the other provide little guidance on spending priorities or conflict of interest rules in communities dominated by power and divided by politics with few checks and balances (Flanagan 1998)? Is it a case of a small number of well-connected leaders and insiders skimming off the wealth at the expense of the vast majority who continue to wallow in welfare (Cheney 1998)? Or have the media imposed a double standard in criticizing aboriginal inequalities: After all, as Phil Fontaine (1998) observes, when whites get rich, it's good for the economy; when some aboriginal peoples get rich, it becomes a national disgrace.

With respect to the Stoney Creek Reserve, no one is taking responsibility (Bercuson and Cooper 1997). The chiefs blame their predecessors; the province says it's a federal problem; federal officials say the problem is under control; and the Department of Indian Affairs is blaming residents for not taking the chiefs to task. Is the problem one of leadership, involving arbitrary exercises of power, nepotism, or a general cronyism (see Gibson 1998)? Should fingers be pointed at the ready accessibility of welfare and social assistance payments for creating a climate of dependency that demoralizes peoples and erodes initiative, especially when "dole" payments are higher than most entry-level jobs (Flanagan 1997)? Is the legacy of welfare colonialism too much of a handicap to overcome in the face of government policy that treated aboriginal peoples as helpless children or dependent wards of the state? Or are the causes deeper, reflecting a general despondency when aboriginal cultures are stigmatized as irrelevant or inferior? Do we look to youth, many of whom are suspended between the past and the future, rejected by their tradition yet unacceptable to the mainstream, while coping with both at once? Whether any of these questions are answerable is open to debate. Without answers, however, the suffering will continue.

Of course, not all aboriginal peoples are destined to fail—even when measured by mainstream standards. Aboriginal peoples are gaining access to substantial sums of money and resources because of successful land claims settlements. Success stories abound, including the recent selection of a formerly poverty-stricken Quebec Cree community (Ouje Bougoumou) as one of the fifty places around the world that best exemplifies the objectives of the United Nations (Platiel 1995). There are currently 10,000 aboriginal businesses, 50 financial institutions, a native trust company, and a native bank, thus confirming the relationship between possessing wealth and exercising power. Nor should success be evaluated on such narrow grounds. There are individuals who possess secure and satisfying prospects and exceptionally enriched lives without rejecting one or both cultures. As a group, however, most live under conditions that evoke images of grinding Third World poverty.

Urban Aboriginals

Reserves were once regarded as tools of colonialism or locales of chronic poverty. Increasingly, however, they are endorsed as enclaves of aboriginal identity, sites of self-sufficiency and self-government, and engines for renewal. That points to a striking ambiguity: The very isolation of these reserves fosters the "essence" of aboriginal being, both physical and psychological. Yet their remoteness creates problems with attracting investment. The fact that they serve as a refuge from and buffer against a hostile outside world also complicates adjustment problems (Buckley 1992). Reserve communities furnish spiritual assistance and social security for aboriginal persons, despite unacceptably high levels of unemployment and dilapidated living conditions. Yet nearly 42 percent of Canada's First Peoples live off the reserve, and that number has increased by 50 percent in the past decade (Purvis 1999). About one-fifth of urban aboriginals live in seven cities: Regina, Winnipeg, Calgary, Edmonton, Saskatoon, Vancouver, and Toronto (Canadian Press, 14 January 1998). Winnipeg has the largest number of aboriginal residents; at 46,000 it might well be called Canada's largest reserve, well above the 19,000 at the Six Nations of the Grand River Reserve near Brantford, Ontario. On the strength of these urban figures, the highest concentrations of aboriginal peoples are in the Prairie provinces, including Manitoba at 12 percent, Saskatchewan at 11 percent, and Alberta at 5 percent. Aboriginal peoples may comprise only 1 percent of Ontario's population, but at 140,000 are the most numerous in absolute terms, with British Columbia next.

Reasons for migration are numerous, but often reflect "push" factors (lack of resources, opportunity, or excitement) and "pull" forces related to employment, education, and lifestyle. Structural (band size, proximity to urban centres), social (poor housing, unemployment), and cultural (socialization) factors are important in making the decision to leave—or return (Frideres 1993). People leave because of misguided reserve policies and fiscal mismanagement in which the well-endowed few grow rich at the expense of the increasingly impoverished masses within a social context of corruption and political repression (Cheney 1998). For some, the move to cities is positive. There are aboriginal lawyers, teachers, nurses, and successful entrepreneurs, many of whom earn high incomes and are actively involved in the community. For others, there are numerous difficulties in coping with the demands of a large urban centre (Frideres 1998). Life off the reserve is beset with missed economic opportunities, abysmal living conditions and homelessness, exposure to substance abuse, discrimination and lack of cultural awareness, and repeated brushes with the law. Consider the province of Saskatchewan: The unemployment rate among urban aboriginals stands at 30 percent, compared with a provincial rate of 5.1 percent. Urban aboriginals comprise 39 percent of the province's welfare caseload but only 15 percent of the population. Cities like Saskatoon and Regina have the highest overall crime rate (including incidents of violent crime) at a time when overall rates are decreasing across Canada (Eisler 1996). Similarly, in Ontario: In Toronto, for example, an estimated 3,750 natives, or about 10 percent of the population, live on the streets, with the result that they account for 15 percent of the homeless but only 2 percent of the population (Philp 1998).

Imbalances in the city and on the reserve have led some aboriginal migrants to accept dual residence (see Dosman 1972): Home in the winter may be the city where welfare and heated accommodation make life bearable; summer sees an exodus back to the reserve for the company of relatives and rural lifestyles (Comeau and Sandin 1990). The federal government, for its part, offers little in the way of services to off-reserve aboriginals, citing jurisdictional problems with the provinces as a stumbling block. Established government institutions are ill equipped (both in terms of resources and needs assessments) to provide adequate, culturally sensitive services to aboriginal clients (Maidman 1981). Many aboriginal-run voluntary agencies have been established to address issues of health care, traditional healing, shelter, and criminal justice. For example, Native Child is both a United Way member agency and the only aboriginal-controlled child welfare agency in Ontario that, with its $4 million budget and 45 staff, offers services to the 40,000 natives in Greater Toronto, including 10,000 children under 14. Programs incorporate a strong cultural dimension and emphasize prevention, and include everything from aboriginal head start incentives to assistance to aboriginal mothers. Nevertheless, the gap between supply and demand continues to escalate.

Aboriginal Women

The plight of aboriginal women is gaining prominence. But both formal studies and personal testimonies indicate that aboriginal women rank among the most severely disadvantaged people in Canada (see Silman 1987 for similar assessment in the United States). Economically, they are worse off than nonaboriginal women and aboriginal men in terms of income levels and employment options, with the result that the feminization of poverty bites deeply, especially for lone parent women in cities (Williams 1997). Social hardships are numerous and include reports of abusive male family members, sexual assaults and rapes, inadequate housing, squalid living conditions, unhealthy child-raising environments, and alcohol and drug abuse. Levels of violence directed against aboriginal women and children are extremely high: As explained by the Native Women's Association of Canada in a 1991 brief (quoted in Razack 1994:910):

> We have a disproportionately high rate of child sexual abuse and incest. We have wife battering, gang rapes, drug and alcohol abuse, and every kind of perversion imaginable has been imported into our lives....

Depression and self-hatred among aboriginal women is vented in high rates of suicide, alcohol dependency, and neglect of children. Nearly 6.4 percent of aboriginal children (status Indian) in 1986 were in protective care compared with only 1 percent of the general population (Comeau and Sandin 1990). To that volatile mixture add the pressure of derogatory stereotypes about aboriginal women to experience a sense of marginality (Witt 1984; also LaRoque 1975; 1990).

Negative images make it difficult to recognize the positive contributions of aboriginal women to community life and social change. Historical and social factors work against adequate recognition. Those who lost status because of marriage to nonaboriginal males have been penalized through deprivation of Indian rights, for example, ostracism from band life and exclusion from housing and jobs. Not even the repeal of the offending passage (Section 12(1)(b) of the 1985 Indian Act) has eased the barriers for some women. Their status and that of their children has been partially reinstated, but resource-strapped bands have refused membership and residence for political and economic reasons. Bill C-31 women were not given the right to pass full status to their children, with the result that status disappears completely by the third generation. That anomaly explains why country-pop diva Shania Twain can claim Indian status (she may have no aboriginal blood but was adopted by her Ojibwa father), whereas the former chief of the Assembly of First Nations, Ovide Mercredi, cannot pass status to his children (Ovide's mother was reinstated as a "Bill C-31er," but because his children are half white they cannot claim full status) (Anderssen 1997). Efforts by aboriginal women to do away with blatant forms of discrimination have met with resistance on the grounds that tampering with the status quo could further jeopardize federal fiduciary ("domino effect") obligations as set out in the Indian Act (Weaver 1993).

To Sum Up   The abysmal circumstances that confront aboriginal peoples are a scathing indictment of the status quo. Aboriginal people tend to score poorly on those indicators that count and rank high on those that don't. But not all Canadians are convinced by the gravity of the situation, and studies suggest that perhaps a small percentage (around one-third) believe aboriginal peoples are worse off than nonaboriginals, while another portion (26 percent) think aboriginal peoples are better off than most Canadians (Nadeau et al. 1998). But the federal government operates on the assumption that poverty exists and has responded by "throwing money at the problem." Announcements of new funding programs by the government are usually prefaced with references to deplorable living conditions in the hopes of garnering public support by tapping into the sense of fairness that many Canadians profess (Platiel 1996). This focus on problems is problematic, however. The impression is created that poverty will disappear with better opportunities, thus ignoring structural problems and the fundamental changes needed to a system that continues to portray aboriginal peoples as a drain on public coffers. Improvements will occur only with changes that provide aboriginal control over institutions, a share of revenue from reserve mineral resources, and aboriginal title to land. The importance of indigenous control over land and resources is nicely captured by Matthew Coon

Come, grand chief of the Grand Council of Crees in Quebec: "But without adequate access to lands, resources, and without the jurisdictions required to benefit meaningfully and sustainably from them...no number of apologies, policies, token programs, or symbolic healing funds are going to remedy this fundamental socio-economic fact" (cited in Barnsley 1999:1). Focusing on problems has the effect of "framing" aboriginal peoples as a problem people who have problems or create problems. Such a focus not only glosses over the fact that the aboriginal plight may arise from repeated Crown violations of treaties (George 1997). It also reflects the persistence of a neocolonialist mentality with its commitment to control and co-opt without appearing to do so. Finally, the underlying logic of a problem approach may have to be rethought: It's not a case of aboriginal peoples as problems. Rather, what is it about Canadian society that makes it so problematic for First Nations people to find their rightful place?

ABORIGINAL POLICY: FROM COLONIZATION TO CONDITIONAL AUTONOMY

> We believe that there is an inherent right to self-government, that the inherent right stems from powers, and if you will, sovereignty, which existed prior to 1763, certainly existed prior to 1867, and certainly existed prior to 1982.
>
> Bob Rae, Premier of Ontario, in his first major speech after being sworn into office, 1990

To what extent has the state by way of government policy contributed to or detracted from aboriginal aspirations for control or consent? Do state initiatives facilitate the achievement of aboriginal claims to self-determination and innovative patterns of belonging? Or do they have the effect of blocking or undermining aboriginal jurisdictions over land, identity, and political voice (Fleras and Spoonley 1999)? The role of state policy and administration in the dispossession of indigenous peoples has been well documented. Little can be gleaned by rehashing the negative consequences of even well-intentioned actions by Indian Affairs officials, often more interested in careerism and empire building than in fostering aboriginal empowerment (Ponting and Gibbins 1980; Ponting 1986; also Shkilnyk 1985). What more can be added to the sorry legacy of official indigenous policy, with its focus on promoting "national interest" rather than protecting aboriginal concerns? But the verdict in assessing state performance may be more accurately described as ambivalent. The state is capable of progressive policies that enhance indigenous rights; it is equally capable of regressive measures that may exclude, deny, or exploit (Spoonley 1993). Policies of disempowerment tend to delimit the actions and options of indigenous peoples; by contrast, enabling policies provide a window of opportunity for empowerment (Hinton et al. 1997). Moves to expand jurisdiction may inadvertently and simultaneously restrict options because of unforeseen circumstances.

A similar assessment can be applied to Canada, where aboriginal relations with the state have long been mediated by legislation and policy yet marred by duplicity and expediency. Aboriginal affairs policy can be seen as evolving through a series of overlapping stages, with their focus never wavering from a fundamental commitment to foster aboriginal self-sufficiency. An initial period of cooperation and accommodation gave way to a largely misguided and paternalistic policy of assimilation, with its underlying racist assumptions of white superiority as a basis for control and coercion. Treatment of aboriginal peoples as captive "wards" was intended to facilitate the eventual absorption of aboriginal peoples into the mainstream, but with little success. A shift from assimilation to integration and "ordinary citizenship" gathered momentum after the late 1940s. Integrationist policies and programs sought to "normalize" relations with aboriginal peoples by terminating their unique relationship with the Crown and placing them on the same footing as ordinary Canadians. Yet federal efforts to integrate by "mainstreaming" aboriginal peoples had the catalytic effect of mobilizing aboriginal peoples in protest against the ill-fated **White Paper** of 1969. Federal policy discourses shifted toward **devolution** from the 1970s onward, in part to acknowledge aboriginal jurisdiction over land, identity, and political voice, in other part to confirm the legitimacy of **aboriginal rights** as a basis for belonging, rewards, and relations, and in still other part to defuse mounting resentment and international disapproval. Recent government and aboriginal initiatives have tended to endorse a **conditional autonomy** model by exploring the implications of aboriginal peoples as "peoples" with an "inherent" right to self-government, albeit within the framework of Canadian society. The emergence of three general themes—renewing the partnership, strengthening aboriginal governance, and supporting strong communities—suggests a continuing commitment to redefine aboriginal people–state relations (see also Frideres [1998] and Ponting [1997] for overview).

Acknowledging Aboriginality: The Royal Proclamation (1763)

> And whereas it is just and reasonable, and essential to our interests, and the security of our Colonies, that the several Nations of Tribes of Indians with whom We are connected, and who live under our protection, should not be molested or disturbed in the Possession of such Parts of Our Dominions and Territories as, not having been ceded to or purchased by Us, are reserved to them or any of them, as their Hunting Grounds.... And whereas great frauds and abuses have been committed in purchasing Lands of the Indians, to the Great Prejudice of Our interests and to the Great Dissatisfaction of the said Indians....We do, with the advice of Our Privy Council, strictly enjoin and require, that no private Person do presume to make any purchase from the said Indians of any Lands reserved to the said Indians, within those parts of our Colonies where, We have thought proper to allow settlements; but that, if at any time any of the said Indians should be inclined to dispose of the said Lands, the same shall be Purchased only for Us, in our Name, at some public Meeting or Assembly of the said Indians....
>
> Royal Proclamation, 1763

Aboriginal policy in the broadest sense began with the Royal Proclamation of 1763. The Proclamation sought to establish the principle if not the practice of Crown sovereignty over the unexplored interior of Turtle Island. But it also acknowledged that aboriginal interest in land was a preexisting right rather than a right delegated by the Crown (Slattery 1997). Those vast tracts of land encircled by the Thirteen Colonies, Rupert's Land, and the Mississippi River were subsequently designated as aboriginal hunting grounds. To ensure orderly settlement and Crown preemptive purchase, "Indian" lands were closed to European trespass. To underwrite the costs of colonizing Canada, the act prohibited individual purchase without express approval of the Crown (Rotman 1996). The vision of a working partnership was clearly articulated: Proclamation not only recognized aboriginal land title under traditional use and ancestral occupancy; it also established the basis for a political relationship anchored in mutual noninterference and friendship.

The Royal Proclamation may be seen as laying down a blueprint for defining aboriginal peoples–state relations. But interpretations vary over the intent, scope, and implications of the Proclamation. Some have argued that the Proclamation acknowledged aboriginal tribes as "nations within" with jurisdictional rights over land and claims to nation-to-nation status

(Clark 1990; Fleras and Elliott 1992). The Supreme Court of Canada has ruled to this effect, arguing that British protectorate status did not extinguish aboriginal rights or aboriginal orders of government, but reinforced their status as distinct political communities with exclusive authority over jurisdiction within their borders (Henderson 1997; see also Nisga'a Case Study later in this chapter). Contemporary aboriginal peoples–state relations tend to be at odds with the principles of the Royal Proclamation as manifest in (a) violation of agreements, (b) suppression of culture, and (c) disregard of legal obligations. Others, however, disagree with that assessment. Under the Proclamation the British Crown asserted its sovereignty over the people and the land, with propriety rights to aboriginal land by virtue of the doctrine of "first discovery" (Boldt 1993). In other words, Crown objectives were purely pragmatic in establishing control over settlers and property interests. They also sought to curb American territorial expansion, establish control over the newly acquired colony of Quebec, and prevent outbreak of costly Indian Wars (Rotman 1996).

"No More Indians": Assimilation As Colonial Policy (1867–1945)

An initial period of cooperation characterized the post-Proclamation relationships. Encounters involving aboriginal peoples, French and British explorers, missionaries, and traders were based on a principle of self-serving coexistence, involving reciprocal trade and practical accommodation in areas such as subsistence and miscegenation. The British were few in number and militarily weak; the benevolence of their aboriginal allies was crucial for survival (Rotman 1996). The forging of military alliances with powerful tribes was no less critical in pursuing imperial interests. From 1755 to 1812, the British Indian Department (forerunner of the Department of Indian Affairs) implemented the key tenet of British policy, namely, to blunt American and French imperial interests by fostering allegiances with aboriginal tribes (Allen 1993). But once the British assumed paramountcy as the major European power in Canada, this symbiotic relationship began to unravel (Purich 1986). Termination of the War of 1812 with the United States eliminated the need for aboriginal allies, thus rendering them expendable and subject to expedient actions. Crown commitments and responsibilities that had been incurred through interaction or treaties were now displaced by covetous interest in land, minerals, and settlement at the expense of aboriginal peoples. The Crown unilaterally asserted sovereignty over people and lands; aboriginal consent was simply assumed or deemed irrelevant (Jhappan 1995). Aboriginal tribes may have had "natural title" to land by virtue of prior occupancy, but their uncivilized status enabled the British to rationalize moral and legal justifications for dispossession in the name of civilization, Christianity, and progress (Allen 1993). The post-1815 era was subsequently dominated by this commitment to pacify aboriginal tribes through conquest-oriented acculturation and displacement into increasingly remote areas.

Colonization refers to a process in which imperial powers established European sovereignty over the various areas of Canada. Generally, it entails the subjugation of a people who happen to live in a territory that is being colonized by Europeans. More specifically, it involves a process of (a) dispossessing indigenous lands, (b) imposing British legal systems and jurisprudence over indigenous systems of law, (c) the amalgamation of existing political structures, and (d) assimilation of indigenous peoples (Bell 1997). The Dominion of Canada operated as the colonizing arm of the British Colonial office. It assumed the rights and responsibilities of the Imperial colonizer with the Constitution Act of 1867 and imposed British rule through occupation, negotiated settlements, and the threat of force

(Bell 1997). The 1867 Constitution Act enshrined state responsibility for aboriginal peoples by conferring federal jurisdiction over aboriginal lands and affairs (Ponting and Gibbins 1980; Kulchyski 1994). Confirmation of federal jurisdiction over aboriginal affairs was abetted by the establishment of the Indian Affairs branch under the Secretary of State (Ponting and Gibbins 1980). Canadian federalism tended to dismiss any thought of aboriginal peoples as political communities, preferring, instead, to see them as wards of the state with limited civil rights but fully entitled to federal custodial care (this trust relationship was subsequently transformed into a fiduciary responsibility) (Jhappan 1995). The theme of assimilation was endorsed for solving the "Indian problem": In the pithy phrasing of Sir John A Macdonald in espousing a "no more Indians" national policy: "The great aim of our civilization has been to do away with the tribal system and assimilate the Indian people in all respects with the inhabitants of the Dominion, as speedily as they are fit for the change" (cited in Miller 1989). Federal responses left much to be desired in light of racist and evolutionary philosophies that disparaged aboriginal peoples as inferior and impediments to progress (Weaver 1984). The concept of guardianship reinforced the stereotype of aboriginal peoples as childlike wards of the state who were deemed too incompetent to look after themselves except under the tutelage of Crown-appointed guardians (Ponting and Gibbins 1980; Ponting 1986). Aboriginal languages, cultures, and identity were suppressed—ruthlessly at times—while band communities were locked into patterns of dependency and despondency with little opportunity for development or dignity. The signing of 11 numbered Treaties and Williams Treaties between 1871 and 1923 established a system of reserves, thereby allowing the Crown to simultaneously open land for settlement while advancing the cause of assimilation.

Legislation served as an important tool in controlling aboriginal peoples and divesting them of their resources (Rotman 1996). The Gradual Enfranchisment Act of 1869 sought to eliminate "Indian" status through enfranchisement and comingling with the "...white race in the ordinary avocations of life" (quoted in Allen 1993:202). Passage of the Indian Act in 1876 may have intended to codify the Canadian government's regulation of aboriginal peoples. But its avowed commitment to protect and civilize also had the effect of controlling rather than empowering or developing aboriginal communities. The imposition of the Indian Act bestowed sweeping state powers to invade and regulate the minutest aspect of reserve life, even to the point of curbing constitutional and citizenship rights (Morse 1985). The Indian Act defined who came under its provisions, what each status Indian was entitled to under the government's fiduciary obligations, who could qualify for disenfranchisement, what could be done with reserve lands and resources, and how local communities were to be ruled. Traditional leadership was stripped of its authority as a legitimate political voice (Dickason 1992). Local governance took the form of elected band councils, many of which were perceived as extensions of central authority, with limited powers at the beck and call of Ottawa (Webber 1994). Even economic opportunities were curtailed. Under the Indian Act, aboriginal people could not possess direct title to land or private property; they were also denied access to revenue from the sale or lease of band property. Punitive restrictions not only foreclosed aboriginal property improvements; they also forestalled the accumulation of economic development capital for investment or growth, especially since aboriginal land held in Crown trust was immune to mortgage, collateral, and legal seizure (McMillan 1988; Eckholm 1994). In that the Indian Act was an essentially repressive instrument of containment and control, its role in usurping aboriginal authority and replacement by federal jurisdiction could not have been more forcefully articulated. To the extent that the Indian Act continues to divide and rule 125 years after its inception, the words of Donna Isaac of Listuguj Quebec (1997) cannot be lightly dismissed:

> The Indian Act system of government imposed on us so long ago has created such divided communities. We are immobilized by internal political strife. Half of the community often gets ahead at the expense of the other half. Hurt leads to contempt, division brews, and co-operation becomes impossible as hatred grows.

The next Case Study provides yet another example of the long-term consequences of assimilation, regardless of the motive behind the move to "kill the Indian inside."

CASE STUDY 6–2	"To Kill the Indian in the Child": Assimilation Through Education

The Canadian government recently apologized to the First Nations for decades of systematic assimilation, theft of their lands, suppression of cultures, and the physical and sexual abuse of aboriginal children. For over a century, thousands of aboriginal children passed through the residential school system, where many were exposed to an inferior education in an atmosphere of neglect, disease, and abuse. The government acknowledged its role in enforcing policies that forcibly removed children from their families and placed them in residential schools often hundreds of kilometres from their community, leaving behind a legacy of emotional scars because of intense homesickness and pain. "To those who suffered the tragedy of residential schools," the Minister of Indian Affairs, Jane Stewart, announced, "we are deeply sorry." As a token of atonement, the government pledged $350 million to fund counselling programs and treatment centres for residential school victims of emotional, sexual, and physical abuse. To be sure, not everyone agreed with this assessment: To demonize all residential schools as symbols of cultural genocide, critics argued, tended to accentuate the negative at the expense of the positive, dismissed the testimony of those who enjoyed the experience, relied heavily on vague and unsubstantiated testimony, stigmatized the schools as scapegoats for aboriginal suffering, and fed into white liberal guilt by cultivating grievances (Donnelly 1998).

Still, the statement of reconciliation caught many off guard because of its unprecedented nature. Central authorities have historically been reluctant to apologize or even acknowledge responsibility for past misdeeds, since admitting liability may encourage lawsuits. But the government may have had little choice but to apologize, despite the risk of being sued, not necessarily to right the wrong or to accept responsibility, but as a plea bargain to limit damages from further revelations regarding the more sordid dimensions of the residential school experiment (Coyne 1998).

Content

Founded and operated by Protestant and Roman Catholic missionaries but funded primarily by the federal government, residential schools (or industrial schools, as they were called initially because of the emphasis on manual skills acquisition) for aboriginal children were built in every province and territory except Prince Edward Island, Nova Scotia, and Newfoundland, with the vast majority concentrated in the Prairie provinces. From 2 residential schools at the time of Confederation, the number of schools expanded to 80 by 1931: 44 Roman Catholic schools, 21 Anglican, 13 United Church, and 2 Presbyterian (Matas 1997). Between 100,000 and 125,000 aboriginal children (about one in six) entered the system before it was closed down in the mid-1980s, although four residential schools continue to operate but under aboriginal jurisdiction (Miller 1996). To be sure, Canada was not the only country to remove children from their parents and resocialize them in schools or foster families. From the 1910s to the 1970s, about 100,000 Australian part aboriginal children were placed in government or church care in the belief that Aborigines would die out, a practice that was deemed tantamount to cultural genocide, according to Australia's Human Rights Commission.

Rationale

From the mid-nineteenth century onward, the Crown engaged in a variety of measures to assert control over the indigenous peoples of Canada (Rotman 1996). The Indian Act of 1876 was ultimately such an instrument of control—a codification of laws and regulations that embraced the notions of European mental and moral superiority to justify the dispossession and subjugation of aboriginal peoples. The Indian Act provided a rationale for misguided, paternalistic, and cruelly implemented initiatives to assimilate aboriginal peoples into white culture. The mandatory placement of aboriginal children in off-reserve residential schools fed into these racist assumptions of white superiority and aboriginal inferiority. With the assistance of the RCMP when necessary, the government insisted on taking aboriginal children away from their parents and putting them in institutions under the control of religious orders. The rationale for the residential school system was captured in an 1889 annual report by the Department of Indian Affairs:

> The boarding-school dissociated the Indian child from the deleterious home influence to which he would otherwise

be subjected. It reclaims him from the uncivilized state in which he has been brought up. It brings him into contact from day to day with all that tends to effect a change in his views and habits (quoted in Roberts 1996:A7).

The guiding philosophy embraced the adage that "how a twig is bent, the tree will grow." Federal officials believed it was necessary to capture the entire child by segregating him or her at school until a thorough course of instruction was acquired. However, the residential school system had a more basic motive than simple education: The removal of children from home and parents was aimed at their forced assimilation into nonaboriginal society through creation of a distinct underclass of labourers, farmers, and farmers' wives (Rotman 1996; Robertson 1998). This program not only entailed the destruction of aboriginal language and culture, but also invoked the supplanting of aboriginal spirituality with Christianity in the hopes of "killing the Indian in the child" for future preparation in a nonaboriginal world (Royal Commission on Aboriginal Affairs 1996).

Reality

This experiment in forced assimilation through indoctrination proved destructive. Many of the schools were poorly built and maintained, living conditions were deplorable, nutrition barely met subsistence levels, and the crowding and sanitary conditions transformed them into incubators of disease. Many children succumbed to tuberculosis and other contagious diseases (Fournier and Grey). A report in 1907 of 15 schools found that 24 percent of the 1,537 children in the survey had died while in the care of the school, prompting the magazine *Saturday Night* to claim: "Even war seldom shows as large a percentage of fatalities as does the education system we have imposed upon our Indian wards" (quoted in Matas 1997). Other reports indicate that disciplinary terror by way of physical or sexual abuse was the norm in some schools according to the Royal Commission on Aboriginal Affairs (1996). As one former residential school student told the Manitoba Aboriginal Justice Inquiry:

> My father, who attended Alberni Indian Residential School for four years in the twenties, was physically tortured by his teachers for speaking Tseshalt: they pushed sewing needles through his tongue, a routine punishment for language offenders.... The needle tortures suffered by my father affected all my family. My Dad's attitude became "why teach my children Indian if they are going to be punished for speaking it?"...I never learned how to speak my own language. I am now, therefore, truly a "dumb Indian" (quoted in Rotman 1996:57).

Punishment also included beatings and whippings with rods and fists, chaining and shackling children, and locking in closets and basements. Reports of abuse appeared in anecdotal form by the 1940s, went public during the 1960s and 1970s, but did not capture the public imagination until Phil Fontaine, the National Chief of the Assembly of First Nations, disclosed his personal experiences in 1990. Admittedly, some aboriginal children profited from the residential school experience. Others suffered horribly: Children grew up hostile or confused, caught between two worlds but accepted in neither. Young impressionable children returned as older, Western educated people; having lost their identity and the ability to converse in their own language, many could neither communicate with older members of the community nor identify with their community ways (Rotman 1996). Adults often turned to prostitution, sexual and incestuous violence, and drunkenness to cope with the emotional scarring from the residential school system.

Implications

This misguided and destructive experiment in social engineering makes disturbing reading when judged by contemporary standards of human rights, government accountability, participatory democracy, and aboriginal self-determination. Admittedly, it is easy to judge and condemn actions in hindsight, especially when implemented by people who may have genuinely believed that one's own culture and assumptions were of universal applicability and value. Negative impacts may stem instead from the logical consequences of well-intentioned programs that are based on faulty assumptions ("progress through development"), an inaccurate reading of the situation ("eliminate poverty by throwing money at the problem"), or cultural misunderstanding ("they want to be like us"). Many may have believed that they were acting as good Christians by improving the lot of First Nations and congratulated government initiatives as enlightened or necessary (Editorial, *Globe and Mail*, 8 January 1998). Nor should the role of aboriginal parents be ignored: According to Miller (1996), aboriginal leaders insisted on a European-style education for their children, while federal authorities acknowledged a fiduciary obligation to oversee such education. Finally, incidents of abuse and violence are likely especially during an era when corporate punishment was routinely accepted as part of the "spare the rod, spoil the child" mentality.

Still, the Royal Commission concluded that the residential school system was an "act of profound cruelty" rooted in racism and indifference and pointed the blame at Canadian society, Christian evangelism, and policies of the churches and government. The apology and proposed reparations may prove a useful starting point in acknowledging the injustices in the past that denied recognition of the moral and political stature of aboriginal people as full and complete citizens and human beings (Editorial, *Globe and Mail*, 8 January 1998). It remains to be seen whether psychologically scarred natives, broken families, and dysfunctional aboriginal communities will respond to the balm of healing and counselling centres and establishment of programs to reverse the genocidal consequences of the residential school experiment.

Integration: Normalizing Indianness (1945–73)

Neither assimilation as policy nor the reserve system as practice brought about the goal of "no more Indians" (Smith 1993). Rather, this ambitious experiment in social engineering proved disruptive in seeking to erode the social and cultural foundations of aboriginal society as the price of admittance to society (Frideres 1993). Failure to bring about the intended results exerted pressure to rethink the aboriginal affairs policy agenda, especially after World War II, when the contradiction of fighting for freedom overseas clashed with a host of domestic human rights violations. An official commitment to assimilation merged with the principles of integration as a blueprint for reform. Strategies to desegregate once isolated aboriginal enclaves through integration into the mainstream proved increasingly attractive for political and economic reasons. Aboriginal services were costly to maintain; their effectiveness was questionable; and they represented an international embarrassment to Canada. A discussion paper to solve the "Indian problem" by doing away with aboriginal peoples as a legal construct was tabled by then Minister of Indian Affairs, Jean Chrétien. The White Paper proposed to terminate the special relation between aboriginal peoples and the Crown, thus eliminating the status of aboriginal peoples as a collective entity (Weaver 1981). Federal responsibility over aboriginal peoples would be transferred over to the provinces. Both the Indian Act and the Department of Indian Affairs were to be dismantled, while aboriginal assets (including lands) would be divided on a per capita basis for "disposal" as individual owners saw fit. Also recommended was the eventual abolition of aboriginal treaty privileges and special status as a precondition for "normalizing" entry into Canadian society.

Political calculation or economic expediency could not entirely account for the tabling of the White Paper. Pierre Elliott Trudeau, the Prime Minister of Canada, worked on the assumption that a "just" society was unattainable without guarantees of formal legal equality for everyone regardless of race or ethnicity. The isolation of aboriginal peoples on reserves and through legislation had contributed to their inequality, decline in social and cultural conditions, and lack of participation in Canadian society. But the government badly misread aboriginal aspirations. What government endorsed as progressive and inevitable was roundly condemned as regressive by aboriginal elites and leaders. The White Paper stood accused of everything from cultural genocide to callous expediency in offloading federal costs and reneging on Crown responsibilities. Aboriginal peoples possessed a special, one-of-a-kind relationship ("**sui generis**") with the Crown in Canada, aboriginal leaders argued, and they could not afford to sever this legally obligatory ("fiduciary") relation for the uncertainties of provincial jurisdiction (Rotman 1996). Aboriginal groups galvanized into protest action, including establishment of the first national body of status Indians, the National Indian Brotherhood, in the hopes of shelving the White Paper in exchange for a new "Indian" agenda (Allen 1993). This collective show of strength chastened central authorities. They were left with little option but to rethink aboriginal demands for control of their destiny and lands without jeopardizing Canada's integrity as a united and prosperous society in the process.

Devolution: "Power to the People" (1973–90)

A general commitment to the principles of devolution eventually replenished the policy vacuum created by the White Paper void. This shift was preceded by a period of impasse—even paralysis—as government response lurched from crisis to crisis with little vision of how to bridge the gap of misunderstanding across a cultural divide. The Calder decision in 1973, with its qualified support for the idea of aboriginal rights and title, proved a starting point for reassessment. Two trends eventuated from this ruling: On the one hand were aboriginal moves to transform the federal policy agenda in a way that enhanced aboriginal autonomy over land, identity, and political voice. This focus on self-determination through self-government became more politicized with the constitutional entrenchment of collective aboriginal rights. On the other were government initiatives to expand aboriginal jurisdictions over domains of relevance to aboriginal peoples. In 1986, the government announced as an interim measure a devolutionary program of community-based, municipal-style self-government in conjunction with Cabinet-approved guidelines for community self-sufficiency, to be pursued on a band-to-band basis and outside any federally imposed blueprint. The Sechelt of British Columbia were among the first bands to take advantage of this federal legislation by establishing municipal-level self-governing structures beyond the scope of the Indian Act (Taylor and Paget 1989; Hawkes and Devine 1991; Price 1991). Currently, 13 First Nations in Ontario, British Columbia, Alberta, and Saskatchewan have negotiated self-government arrangements, with another 350 communities currently engaged in discussions to capture local control over future destiny through tribal structures.

A revised social–political contract involving aboriginal jurisdiction over local affairs both reflected and reinforced developments within the Indian Affairs Department. The Department had moved away from a control-and-deliver mentality that had prevailed as a blueprint since 1876. Reorganization of the federal department into a decentralized service delivery through direct band involvement drew its inspiration from three assumptions: first, the need to establish aboriginal rather than federal control over community affairs; second, a perception that properly resourced communities were better equipped to solve local problems; and, third, a suspicion that centralized structures are ineffective for problem solving when dealing with a geographically disperse and cultural diverse people. The shift toward devolution resulted in the establishment of community-based control over local jurisdictions related to aboriginal administration of departmental programs, local decision making, and mutual accountability. Service delivery on a program-by-program basis was replaced by more flexible funding arrangements to improve management of service delivery, develop long-term expenditure plans, reduce administrative burdens, and emphasize local responsibility for good program management. In time, 82 percent of the department's program expenditure was administered by aboriginal governments. With a broad spectrum of comprehensive funding arrangements at their disposal, in other words, each First Nations government was now expected to assume ownership over program delivery at a pace consistent with community interests and local control.

Funding arrangements are not simply administrative widgets for transferring federal monies to the First Nations. They also constitute the "sharp end of the stick" for (a) carrying out Canada's constitutional and fiduciary responsibilities; (b) aboriginal empowerment through management of band affairs; (c) improving effectiveness in the delivery of services and programs; (d) transferring responsibilities and accountability to local communities; (e) increasing local autonomy and self-government practices; and (f) acknowledging the reality of government-to-government relations (Prince 1994). The transformation was unmistakable: DIAND repositioned itself as a developmental and advisory agency for the transfer of federal funds to community-based self-government structures in the same way that provinces receive federal block funding for programs and services (Fleras 1996).

Aboriginal peoples–government relations have continued to explore the limits of devolution. The 1982 constitutional entrenchment of aboriginal and treaty rights made Canada the first country to embark officially on such an unprecedented path. Enshrinement of aboriginal rights from common law to constitutional principle established grounds for recognition of legal status and preferential treatment. At the same time, however, it also imposed limits on these "existing rights" by restricting them to the survivors of the exercise of federal powers prior to 1982 and incorporating them within a constitutional framework that assumes the legitimacy of Canadian jurisdiction over all people and lands (Bell 1997). The principle of aboriginality was put to the litmus test with several court rulings that confirmed aboriginal rights over procurement of wildlife foods. A series of First Minister Conferences between 1983 and 1987 yielded few concrete results; nevertheless, they did have the effect of sensitizing decision makers to aboriginal grievances and demands for self-government (Brock 1991). But advances were matched by stagnation: Despite impressive gains in establishing jurisdiction over land, identity, and political voice, aboriginality as a principle continued to be undefined and excluded from the national agenda. Nor was there any urgency on the part of the government to restore aboriginal rights in crafting a new political order that acknowledged the principle of aboriginality as a basis for engagement or entitlement. That indifference was abruptly halted by the 78-day Oka Crisis that sharply refocused political attention on aboriginal affairs.

Conditional Autonomy: "Toward Self-Governance" (1990s–)

Recent developments entail rethinking the place of aboriginal peoples within the constitutional framework of Canadian society. Four policy pillars—accelerated land claims settlement, improved socioeconomic status on reserves, reconstruction of aboriginal–government relations, and fulfillment of aboriginal concerns—were introduced immediately after the Oka Crisis in September 1990. By mid-1991, arguably in response to the Oka Crisis and threats of further civil disobedience, Ottawa had officially endorsed a parallel aboriginal constitutional process that culminated in full assurances of their historic right to negotiate on a government-to-government basis, that is, as a distinct tier of government, with corresponding rights to sit with Canada's First Ministers and debate constitutional reform. Terms of the doomed Charlottetown Accord included constitutional entrenchment of aboriginal self-government both inherent in nature and sovereign in sphere, but circumscribed in extent by virtue of the Canadian Constitution and Charter of Rights (no external sovereignty). Even the notion of inherent self-government proved palatable as long as inherency was not used to declare independence or undermine Canadian sovereignty. In short, a threshold in restructuring aboriginal peoples–state relations had been scaled: This baseline would henceforth represent the minimum starting point for future negotiations, and the Liberal government took advantage of this momentum by eventually accepting aboriginal peoples as peoples with an inherent right to self-government as a basis for new partnership (Government of Canada 1994).

Current government policy objectives are aimed at exploring the reality of inherent aboriginal self-government rights. Such a recognition signifies a remarkable departure from even the immediate past when governments were resolutely opposed to any concessions that might encourage international recognition of peoplehood, with its tacit connotation of sovereign self-determination over land, identity, and political voice. Much of the impetus for this push originated with the Conservative government proposals in 1990 to (a) accelerate land claims settlement; (b) improve socioeconomic status on reserves; (c) rebuild aboriginal peoples–government relations; and (d) address aboriginal concerns. The Liberal government continued in this path by expanding its commitment to the principle of inherent aboriginal self-government rights. In the words of the former Minister of Indian Affairs, Ronald Irwin:

> The federal government is committed to building a new partnership with Aboriginal people, a partnership based on mutual respect and trust. Working steadily towards the implementation of *the inherent right of self-government is the cornerstone of that relation* (Government of Canada 1994) (emphasis added).

Jane Stewart, the current Indian Affairs minister, has also endorsed the principle of inherent aboriginal self-government. The minister is equally insistent on "restoring jurisdiction" as a touchstone for sharing power under the current government initiative of "gathering strength" (*Windspeaker,* December 1997). A commitment to renew aboriginal relations with the state by recognizing and strengthening aboriginal governments is also captured in a parallel document, "An Agenda for Action with First Nations" (Frideres 1998). Restrictions still apply: Aboriginal inherent self-government rights are "contingent" rather than sovereign, according to the 1995 Federal Policy Guide on Self-Government; they are also intended to be based on practical, negotiated arrangements rather than Constitution or court decisions. It is worth noting that Canada's representatives to the Third Session at the United Nations Human Rights Working Group (Pritchard 1998) have confirmed this country's commitment to aboriginal self-government over a broad range of jurisdictions as long as this recognition does not impair the territorial integrity or political unity of Canada, is consistent with the Charter of Rights and Freedoms, and does not interfere with the participation of aboriginal peoples in society. The paradoxes of an autonomy that is conditional will be explored later.

TABLE 6.1	Stages and Milestones in Aboriginal Policy
Stages	**Milestones**
Accommodation (to 1820s)	Royal Proclamation (1763)
Assimilation (to 1960s)	Indian Act (1876/1951)
Integration (1940s to 1970s)	White Paper (1969)
Devolution (1970s to 1990s)	Calder Decision (1973)
	Constitution Act (1982)
Conditional autonomy (1990s–)	Oka Crisis (1990)
	Charlottetown Accord (1992)
	Royal Commission on Aboriginal Affairs (1996)
	Delgamuukw Ruling (1997)
	Nisga'a Agreement in Principle (1998)

To Sum Up Historically, Canada's aboriginal policy can be described as a contested and evolving site involving overlapping interests and divided loyalties, against a backdrop of "national interests" (see Boldt 1993). To be sure, the attainment of self-sufficiency has always underpinned the logic behind governments' aboriginal policy. Only the means have changed, with assimilation strategies giving way to the principles of integration and different levels of autonomy. Canada's aboriginal policy can also be depicted as racist and destructive in outcome if not intent. Consider this disclosure by Jane Stewart from the document entitled "Statement of Reconciliation: Learning from the Past" (cited in the *Globe and Mail,* 8 January 1998):

> Sadly, our history with respect to the treatment of Aboriginal people is not something in which we can take pride. Attitudes of racial and cultural superiority led to a suppression of Aboriginal cultures and values. As a country we are burdened by past actions that resulted in weakening the identity of Aboriginal peoples, suppressing their languages and cultures, and outlawing spiritual values. We must recognize the impact of these actions on the once self-sustaining nations that were disaggregated, disrupted, limited or even destroyed by the dispossession of traditional territory, by the relocation of Aboriginal people, and by some provisions of the Indian Act. We must acknowledge that the result of these actions was the erosion of the political, economic, and social systems of Aboriginal people and nations

Overt policies of integration and assimilation have been shelved in favour of recognizing aboriginal rights for purposes of entitlement and engagement. Sections 25 and 35 of the 1982 Constitution Act have opened and expanded areas of jurisdiction that were denied or constrained under the colonialist era. Reform is increasingly structural, collaborative, and cooperative: from welfare to self-government; from dependence to autonomy; and from government assistance to self-determination. Emergence of a commitment to self-determination by way of self-government represents the latest initiative to expand aboriginal control and consent by sharply curtailing state jurisdiction. Aboriginal peoples are increasingly relying on the principles of sovereignty and tribalism as a basis for bringing about a workable arrangement between themselves and existing governments (Frideres 1998). Further changes are anticipated in light of the 1994 agreement to dismantle DIAND in Manitoba by repealing the Indian Act in this province. To date, however, moves to cede departmental jurisdictions to Manitoba's First Nations have not as yet produced any transfer powers (*Kitchener-Waterloo Record,* 2 August 1997). Nevertheless, the principles of conditional autonomy as a basis for restructuring the relationship remain in effect.

TOWARD RENEWAL AND REFORM

Aboriginal leaders reject the label of aboriginal peoples as a social problem (although they acknowledge the many difficulties that confront aboriginal communities). Physical poverty, they contend, is not necessarily responsible for aboriginal marginalization in Canadian society. Powerlessness associated with colonization and denial of aboriginal rights is far more worrying. Stereotypes that portray aboriginal peoples as slaves of customs or hopeless welfare dependents are rejected. So, too, is the notion of aboriginal cultures as relics of the past—little more than impediments to a secure and satisfying coexistence in Canadian society. Retention of aboriginal cultural values not only provides a source of identity and resourcefulness, but also serves as a basis for a community-based renewal or healing.

Aboriginal peoples have struggled to counteract the vicious cycle of exclusion and demeaning clientelism that has historically entrapped them (Salée 1995). Collectively and individually, they have explored ways to survive by asserting control over their lives and by reclaiming a rightful place in society without having to deny their uniqueness. Three themes appear recurrent throughout this process of renewal: retention of **"indigenous-plus"** status; promotion of aboriginal models of self-determination over land, identity, and political voice; and acknowledgment of aboriginal title and treaty rights for securing an economic basis.

Indigenous-Plus: Aboriginal + Citizenship Rights

Aboriginal peoples have refused to be labelled as another ethnic or immigrant minority. They prefer to define themselves as a people whose collective rights to self-determination are guaranteed by virtue of their ancestral occupation, not because of difference, need, or disadvantage. There is little enthusiasm to being integrated as an ethnic component into a Canadian multicultural mosaic, with a corresponding diminishment of their claims. Proposed instead is recognition of their sovereign status as the original occupants of Canada as well as a founding nation, not unlike that of the French in Quebec. Claims to sovereignty are defended either by appeal to natural law or by reference to spiritual grounds (Ahenakew 1985). As the original occupants whose inalienable rights have never been extinguished by treaty or conquest, aboriginal peoples do not seek sovereignty *per se*. Rather, they see themselves as having sovereignty, at least for purposes of entitlement, and only requiring appropriate mechanisms to put this autonomy into practice.

Aboriginal rights are sui generis, that is, they differ from citizenship rights because only aboriginal peoples can possess these rights. Sui generis rights are based in sources of law that reflect the unique status of original occupancy (Borrows and Rotman 1997). These sui generis rights are collective and inherent: inherent in that they are not delegated by government decree, but intrinsic to aboriginal peoples because of first principles; collective in that aboriginal communities can exercise jurisdictions over the individual rights of members of these communities (Denis 1997). Aboriginal rights encompass those rights that ensure survival of aboriginal people as aboriginal people, including the right of ownership and use of land and resources, the right to protect and promote language, culture, and identity, the right to political voice and self-governance, and the right to aboriginal models of self-determination (McKee 1996). Three dimensions are prominent (ATSIC 1994/95): autonomy rights to control lives and life chances, identity rights to preserve distinctiveness, and land rights to ensure economic self-sufficiency.

Underlying this notion of aboriginal rights is the concept of aboriginality. Strictly speaking, the word "aboriginality" is the nominalization of the adjective, aboriginal. The relationship of aboriginality to aboriginal is equivalent to that between ethnicity and ethnic in that both aboriginality and ethnicity refer to the process of a shared awareness of defined differences as a basis for entitlement or engagement. In the case of aboriginality, this difference is based on original occupancy and corresponding rights of indigenous occupants as fundamentally autonomous political communities (Denis 1997). More broadly, the principle of aboriginality expresses a statement about power. Aboriginality asserts a special relation between aboriginal peoples and the state, together with a corresponding set of rights and powers that have never been extinguished but flow from this relationship. Aboriginality, in other words, encapsulates a politicized set of claims and entitlements against the state with respect to the redistribution of power and resources. This claim is manifest in calls for self-government over agendas pertinent to aboriginal realities. Programs and policies that apply to other Canadian minority groups are dismissed as inapplicable—even counterproductive—in light of unique historical–legal status and special aboriginal concerns. As we shall see, a rights-based focus on aboriginal peoples–state relations works best when situated within a context of constructive engagement (Asch and Zlotkin 1997).

What, then, do aboriginal peoples want? The most direct response is, the same things as all Canadian citizens. All aboriginal peoples want to live in a just and equal society wherein (a) their cultural lifestyles and language are protected from assimilationist pressure; (b) select elements of the cultural past can be incorporated within the realities of the present; (c) bureaucratic interference within their lives is kept to a minimum; (d) they are not victimized by racism or by indifference by politicians, bureaucrats, or the general public; (e) there is reliable and culturally appropriate delivery of government services; (f) there is collective access to power and resources; and (g) they retain meaningful involvement in decision making and power sharing. Most of us would agree that these objectives are consistent with the principles of citizenship.

Despite these commonalities, aboriginal peoples have also expressed a desire to be different. Many want to transcend the constraints of formal citizen status and explore novel ways of expanding Canadian citizenship to include aboriginal rights. In conjunction with the concept of "indigenous-plus," they espouse a decided preference for treatment that is cognizant of rights that flow from original occupancy. Recognition of unique status is paramount and is the constant that underpins all aboriginal aspirations. Without differences, after all, aboriginal people are in no position to press home their claims. Equal opportunity or equality before the law is necessary but insufficient, since the promotion of mathematical equality in unequal contexts is tantamount to freezing the status quo. Treating everyone the same merely entrenches the prevailing distribution of power and societal resources. In the belief that equal standards cannot be applied to unequal situations without perpetuating the inequality, aboriginal leaders have reinforced the commitment to unique status and equivalent treatment.

In other words, aboriginal peoples have claimed the right to be different as well as the right to be the same (hence the expression indigenous-plus). Equality of treatment ("formal equality") as befitting all citizens is critical; so too is the demand for additional rights ("equality of outcomes") because of their unique legal status as original occupants. Aboriginal peoples do not see any contradiction in making these demands. As far as they are concerned, these concessions have been paid for with the loss of land, lives, livelihood, and cultural lifestyles. Nor do Canadian politicians and policy makers dispute the validity of aboriginal arguments for the rights to self-determination. Debate continues over the magnitude and scope of these rights with respect to specifics such as costs and jurisdictions.

Self-Determination Through Self-Government

Five centuries after European colonization nearly destroyed the original occupants of Turtle Island, Canada's aboriginal peoples are in the midst of a drive to regain control over their lives and life chances. Central to this reconstruction process is the notion of an aboriginal right to *self-determination*. The concept of self-determination rejects the legitimacy of existing political relations and mainstream institutions as a framework for attainment of aboriginal goals. Proposed instead is the restoration of aboriginal models of self-determination that sharply curtail state jurisdiction while enhancing innovative patterns of belonging to the land (also Alfred 1995). Key elements of this self-determination project include control over the process and power of local governance, the attainment of cultural sovereignty, and a realignment of political relations as expressed by formal self-governing arrangements in key jurisdictional areas related to power, resources, and status (Mercredi and Turpel 1993). Aboriginal leaders have endorsed self-determination as essential to breaking the cycle of deprivation and dependency. A commitment to self-determination is seen as critical in moving from the colonialist mentality of the Indian Act to an aboriginal renaissance as a people whose distinctiveness and independence are predicated on aboriginal control over social, cultural, political, and economic issues of relevance (McKee 1996). Arguments for self-determination are justified on the following grounds: (a) A United Nations statement that aboriginal peoples have the right to control their destiny; (b) international law (to which Canada was a signatory in 1967) stipulates the right for all peoples to self-determination; and (c) the moral claims of aboriginal peoples for control to avert the further loss of traditional social and cultural patterns. Put candidly, aboriginal peoples are seeking to expand control over internal matters in the same way the Québécois are seeking a certain level of autonomy over domestic affairs.

Self-determining models will be varied and are expected to evolve in accordance with community needs and local circumstances. Some will reflect a government model, others an aboriginal model, and still others will combine elements of both. Four self-determining possibilities exist: (a) statehood, maintaining complete independence and no external interference; (b) nationhood, within the framework of society but retaining authority and jurisdiction over internal matters; (c) municipality, retaining control over internal affairs by way of parallel institutions but limited by interaction with comparable mainstream bodies; and (d) institutional, having meaningful decision-making powers through representation and involvement in the general political and institutional order. Table 6.2 summarizes these possibilities, with respect to self-determination at self-governing levels.

TABLE 6.2 Levels of Self-Determination/Self-Government	
Statehood	**Nationhood**
Absolute (*de jure*) sovereignty	*De facto* sovereignty
Internal + external jurisdiction	Self-determining control over multiple but interlinked jurisdictions within framework of shared sovereignty
Complete independence with no external interference	Nations within/province-like
Municipality	**Institutional**
"Nested" sovereignty	Nominal sovereignty
Community-based autonomy	Decision-making power through institutional accommodation
Internal jurisdictions, limited only by interaction with similar bodies and higher political authorities	

Aboriginal Self-Government

Few should be surprised that the politics of aboriginality are channelled into debates over self-government for aboriginal peoples (Fleras 1999). Canada itself is a territoriality-based polity involving an intricate allocation of separate but overlapping jurisdictions, and this division of jurisdictions between Ottawa and the provinces is being played out at the level of aboriginal self-government. According to the Royal Commission on Aboriginal Affairs, Section 35 of the Constitution Act confirms the status of aboriginal peoples as equal partners in Canada. Aboriginal governments should be recognized as one of three distinct orders, each of which is internally sovereign by virtue of inherent (rather than delegated) or constitutional status, yet sharing in the sovereign powers of Canada by way of overlapping and exclusive jurisdictions (Royal Commission on Aboriginal Affairs 1996). This commitment to aboriginal self-government invariably raises questions about feasibility, costs, and options. Questions also arise over the degree to which contemporary initiatives for self-government are consistent with Canada's "national interests".

Aboriginal self-government is already an emerging reality in Canada (Hylton 1994). Passage of the 1984 Cree Naskapi of Quebec Act inaugurated the concept of aboriginal self-government legislation in Canada (Price 1991). Acquisition of self-government in 1986 by the Sechelt of British Columbia's west coast also proved pioneering insofar as it represented specifically designed legislative authority rather than being subject to the operation of the federal Indian Act. Self-government models will continue to vary, with differences being contextual rather than categorical, that is, in accordance with community needs and levels of local development. Many will seek reforms or integration within the existing federal framework, in part because they lack any viable indigenous political alternatives. A few want a fundamental restructuring of their relationship within a truly confederal Canada (Alfred 1995). Patterns of jurisdiction are open to negotiations, ranging from shared arrangements on the one hand to exclusive tribal control over land ownership and membership up to and including autonomous political structures (inherent self-government) and cultural sovereignty on the other, as long as these reflect a community-derived legitimacy and the consent of the people. Core jurisdictions entail those matters of vital political, economic, cultural, and social concern to aboriginal peoples, do not have a major impact on adjacent jurisdictions, and can be exercised without federal or provincial input (Royal Commission on Aboriginal Affairs 1996). Peripheral jurisdictions include those realms that have an impact on adjacent jurisdiction or attract federal/provincial interest. Jurisdictional matters are expected to vary from band to band; nevertheless, they are likely to include (a) control over the delivery of social services such as *policing*, education, and health and welfare ("institutional autonomy"); (b) control over resources and use of land for economic regeneration; (c) control over the means to protect and promote distinct cultural values and language systems; (d) control over band membership and entitlements; and (e) control over federal expenditures according to aboriginal priorities rather than those of the government or bureaucracy. This is not to say that all aboriginal communities possess the jurisdictional capacity to fully engage in self-government, given the associated costs and responsibilities, but many do and are casting for ways to establish arrangements that will divest all vestiges of internal colonialism in exchange for political self-determination.

The range and scope of self-governing jurisdictions has yet to be decided. It is also anticipated that the right to self-government will be vested in aboriginal nations rather than communities, that is, a sizable body of aboriginal peoples with a shared sense of national identity that constitutes a predominant population in a certain territory (Royal Commission on Aboriginal Affairs 1996). Between 60 and 80 aboriginal historically based nations can be discerned from the 1,000 or so aboriginal communities, based on economies of scale and natural ties, thus reviving the nation-way in which aboriginal peoples once were organized. Generally speaking, aboriginal claims for self-governmenthood are consistent with the model of "domestic dependent nations" in the United States. American First Nations do not possess external sovereignty (for example, they cannot raise an army); nevertheless, these "domestic dependent nations" retain considerable control over internal sovereignty, subject to certain restrictions at the federal and state levels. To date, the Canadian government has offered a level of self-government with powers that go beyond a municipality jurisdiction but encompass less than a nation or province. Aboriginal leaders publicly endorse a model somewhere between nationhood/provinces and statehood but appear willing to compromise, depending on particular circumstances.

The concept of *inherency* is critical to the principle of aboriginal self-government (Penner 1983; Little Bear et al. 1984; Royal Commission on Aboriginal Affairs 1996). Inherency suggests that the legitimacy of aboriginal law, authority, and governance goes beyond external sources such as the Crown, parliament, or constitution. *Legitimacy* is derived instead from original occupancy, bequeathed by the Creator, legitimated by the consent of the people, and consistent with treaties, international law, and cultural minority rights (Macklem 1993; Bell 1997). The origins of inherent self-governing rights reside with aboriginal peoples as autonomous political and cultural entities; they also reflect aboriginal possession of their territories and customary political rights prior to European contact. In other words, self-governing rights are inherent and inalienable, implying that aboriginal rights can never be extinguished without explicit consent, a concept vigorously defended by Elijah Harper (Royal Commission on Aboriginal Affairs 1992:19):

> Self-government is not [something] that can be given away by any government, but rather...flows from Creator. Self-government...is taking control and managing our own affairs, being able to determine our own future and destiny.... It has never been up to the governments to give self-government. It has never been theirs to give.

An inherent right to aboriginal self-government is widely endorsed within aboriginal circles. The rationale for support reflects several lines of reasoning, including: (a) all aboriginal peoples have the right to control their destiny by virtue of original occupancy; (b) international law stipulates the right for all peoples to self-determination; and (c) treaty rights affirm rather than deny aboriginal self-government. Nonaboriginal opinion is often less enthused. Concerns are raised over costs, feasibility, effectiveness, degree of legitimacy, and belief that self-government is not the cure to all problems (Editorial, *Globe and Mail,* 1998). Some see aboriginal self-government as a "recipe" for social disaster and disunity; others query the soundness of a system based on race and separate status, and still others express concerns over the implementation or implications (Smith 1995; Gibson 1998). A flourishing aboriginal grievance industry is seen as little more than blackmail to support the lavish lifestyles of affluent and corrupt aboriginal leaders (Cheney 1998; Anderssen 1998). Appeals to aboriginal self-government are criticized as a simplistic solution to a complex problem espoused primarily by aboriginal elites, who are removed from urban realities and out of touch with local needs (Editorial, *The Globe and Mail,* 1998). The dangers of a new aboriginal bureaucracy and increased dependency on federal transfers are also raised (Mulgrew 1996).

Of particular concern is the spectre of separation under self-government. Contrary to popular belief, however, most aboriginal proposals are not interested in making a total break with Canadian society. With few exceptions, aboriginal demands for self-governing sovereignty rarely extend to calls for political independence or territorial autonomy. Proposed instead is a relationship of relative and relational autonomy within a noncoercive context of cooperative coexistence (Scott 1996). This excerpt from the Royal Commission on Aboriginal Affairs (1996:xi) is typical and should allay alarmist fears:

> To say that Aboriginal peoples are nations is not to say that they are nation-states seeking independence from Canada. They are collectivities with a long shared history, a right to govern themselves and, in general, a strong desire to do it in partnership with Canada.

In other words, inherent self-government is not same as secession or absolute sovereignty. What is entailed is a *functional* sovereignty where First Nations are treated *as if* sovereign for purposes of entitlement and engagement. The intent is not to demolish Canada but to dismantle that part of Canada that has precluded them from their rightful place as original occupants and the nominally sovereign cofounders of this country (Borrows and Rotman 1997). Aboriginal peoples are not attempting to erect subversive enclaves within "foreign" territories. Efforts are directed at repatriating their spiritual and cultural homeland, whose sovereignty was never relinquished. By the same token, aboriginal leaders categorically reject the view of themselves as individual Canadian citizens who happen to live on reserves. No less dismissive is the labelling of aboriginal peoples as yet another ethnic or immigrant minority. Aboriginal peoples define themselves as a *de facto* sovereign political community whose collective rights to self-government are guaranteed by virtue of indigeneity (ancestral occupation) rather than because of need, disadvantage, or compensation. Admittedly, attainment of aboriginal status as peoples as a nation will require a reversal of colonialist assumptions that historically have distorted aboriginal realities. It will also have to overcome a hardening of Canadian attitudes toward First Nations, together with a public perception of Canada as essentially sound and beyond the need of a major overhaul (Monti 1997).

Aboriginal Title and Treaty Rights

The process of renewal and reform is anchored in the recognition, definition, and implementation of *aboriginal title and treaty rights.* Enforcement of federal treaty obligations is particularly important in advancing aboriginal interests and aspirations. Treaties were seen as a fundamental component of aboriginal diplomacy with European powers and the medium by which aboriginal peoples and the state continue to regulate their relationship with each other (Rotman 1997). The British in particular insisted on observing legalities: Treaties represented practical nation-to-nation relationships between European colonizers and tribes; they also provided a foundation for the principle of private property, since only land that had been properly acquired ("without encumbrances") could be sold, mortgaged, used as collateral, or employed in a productive manner in a free enterprise economy (Walkom 1998). Treaties continue to be regarded as ongoing and organic agreements that reaffirm the distinctive legal status of aboriginal nations. They also serve as a basis for meaningful political interaction at government–aboriginal levels.

Aboriginal leaders have long upheld treaties as semi-sacred and binding documents. Land and resources were exchanged for treaty rights that guaranteed perpetual access to goods, services, and a reserve homeland. For example, consider the terms of agreement in Canada's treaties with the First Nations of Manitoba and the Northwest Territories:

- Aboriginal tribes would relinquish all their rights and title to the great region from Lake Superior to the foot of the Rocky Mountains.

- Land would be set aside as reserves for homes and agriculture. This land cannot be sold without Indian consent and only then for their benefit.

- Indians would be granted the right to hunt and fish over these Crown lands until sold into private hands.

- An annual payment of $5 for each man, woman, and child ($25 for chief, $15 for councillor). Suitable clothing, medals, and flags to the chiefs.

- To assist in agricultural endeavours, each band will receive implements, herds, and grain.

- Establishment of schools on reserves.

- Prohibition of the sale of alcohol on reserves (see Price 1991).

A conflict of interest was evident from the start. For the most part, European governments saw treaties as legal surrenders of aboriginal land. Treaties would provide legal title to under-occupied land, foster peaceful settlement, avoid costly wars, and deter American annexation or expansion (Price 1991). For aboriginal peoples, the treaties were viewed as mutually rewarding and binding contracts insofar as they entailed a reciprocal exchange of rights and responsibilities. Land and resources would be shared in exchange for Crown assistance to make the transition to the new economy while securing traditional lifestyles and livelihood. As far as aboriginal leaders are concerned, the government remains bound to honour the contractual obligations of these treaties. Access to benefits and services (such as free education and tax exemptions) is not a charitable handout; nor can it be considered a benevolent gesture on the part of an enlightened authority. Treaty entitlements are a legally binding exchange that aboriginal peoples have paid for over and over again with the loss of their lives and life chances.

Two types of treaty rights exist: one is based on specific claims to existing treaty violations, and the other involves comprehensive (modern-day treaties or regional settlements) settlements. A series of treaties were signed between 1763 and 1867 involving the governments of Britain, Eastern Canada, and aboriginal nations. The earliest treaties resembled peace compacts to facilitate trade, secure allies, and preempt European rivals (McKee 1996). Between 1867 and 1923, 11 numbered (1–11) treaties were signed, involving a surrender of aboriginal interest in land to the Crown across much of the Prairies and parts of the Northwest Territories, British Columbia, and Ontario (DIAND 1997). These historical Indian treaties set out the promises, obligations, and benefits of both parties to the agreement. Aboriginal peoples surrendered title to land and received in return reserve lands, agricultural equipment, ammunition, annual payment, and clothing. Their right to hunt and fish on ceded Crown land remained in effect as long as these lands remained unoccupied. The Crown also promised schools on reserves or teachers when requested.

The treaty process was often marred by willful duplicity, leading to specific grievances by aboriginal peoples (Price 1991). Most grievances involve failure to live up to Treaty promises by cutting back on benefits. Miserly payouts proved a problem as well. Another source of grievance entails the unauthorized and uncompensated whittling away of reserve lands because of fraud, expropriation, or government theft (Spiers 1998). So too is the misappropriation of aboriginal monies from government sale of resources or mineral rights held in trust by the Crown. Ambiguities in the misinterpretation of treaties have also come under scrutiny, with the result that the government is expected to give a "fair, large, and liberal interpretation" by providing the benefit of the doubt to aboriginal peoples. Finally, interpretations diverge because of different approaches to the treaties. While the Crown signed treaties to formalize surrender of aboriginal title, aboriginal peoples saw treaties as reaffirming their autonomy and territories by sharing resources in exchange for Crown assistance to pursue their traditional lifestyle while making a transition to the new economy (McKee 1996; DIAND 1997).

By contrast, comprehensive claims consist of modern-day treaty arrangements over disputed ownership of land. Comprehensive claims do not deal with redressing specific claims. Rather, modern-day treaties address the need to establish treaty relationships with those who had never signed a treaty in the past in order to clarify the rights of ownership to land and resources (Purvis 1999). Securing certainty over control of "untreatied" land and resources is imperative: For the Crown, certainty of ownership is a prerequisite for investment and development; for aboriginal peoples, only a solid economic base can secure the basis for social and cultural self-determination. Negotiated settlements provide aboriginal communities with protection for traditional land-based interests related to wildlife harvests, resource management, some subsurface mineral rights, and regulated development. Economic benefits can be derived by renting out lands and resources at rates that are favourable to aboriginal interests. Benefits also can be achieved through local development (in tandem with public or private interests) at a pace that reflects community priorities and developmental levels. In short, any fundamental changes in the status of aboriginal people is more likely when negotiating from a position of economic strength and the political power that sustains it. To date, ten comprehensive claims settlements have been concluded since 1973, including the Nunavut Agreement in the Case Study, while others are in various stages of settlement.

The resolution of land claims settlements in Canada is predicated on the principle of *aboriginal title.* Broadly speaking, aboriginal title specifies aboriginal rights of use over land and resources whose ownership ("title") has not yet been legally extinguished and transferred to the Crown (Gray 1998). According to the *Delgamuukw v British Columbia* ruling in 1997, aboriginal title entails a right to land that was previously occupied by aboriginal peoples; it also involves a right to use land for a variety of activities that are integral to the distinctiveness and survival of aboriginal societies. The principle itself revolves around the question of who owned or occupied the land prior to the unilateral assertion of Crown sovereignty: If aboriginal peoples can prove they had continuous and exclusive occupation of the land prior to sovereignty, they can claim aboriginal title; otherwise, the land reverts to Crown possession (Editorial, *Globe and Mail,* 13 December 1997). Because it has no counterpart in English common property law, aboriginal title is unlike other forms of property ownership, hence "sui generis": Aboriginal title cannot be extinguished or transferred to anyone but the Crown, is sourced in original occupancy, and is collectively held in perpetuity for the benefit of future owners. Under the **Delgamuukw Ruling,** aboriginal people can use the land or resources in almost any way they wish above and beyond traditional customs, except in the destructive sense that may imperil future use (Gray 1997). And until aboriginal title is settled, moreover, not a single tree can be cut by nonaboriginal interests until those who claim to own title are consulted, compensated, or cede it voluntarily, even in cases where infringements on aboriginal title lands are for public purposes or national interests (Matas et al. 1997).

How, then, does aboriginal title apply to Canada? The Calder decision of 1973, which acknowledged the possibility of aboriginal title to unceded (unextinguished) land, was silent on what this entails, thus hindering land claim negotiations. But the Delgamuukw Ruling in 1997 overturned an earlier BC Court decision that dismissed aboriginal title to land as impossible to determine, even if it existed. The ruling concluded a legal campaign by 51

Gitskan and Wet'suwet'en hereditary chiefs whose predecessors struggled since the 1880s to reclaim aboriginal title to their lands. Delgamuukw recognized the validity of aboriginal claims to certain lands they had never ceded in treaties or agreements. Under Delgamuukw, the Court has ruled that aboriginal peoples have a constitutional and exclusive right of use and ownership to land they can prove was occupied by them prior to European arrival, in effect going beyond an earlier conception of aboriginal title that included only the right to traditional hunting, fishing, and food gathering. Delgamuukw advanced the concept of aboriginal title by defining the support base for proving title, thus eliminating one of the impediments to the settlement of comprehensive land claims, even if aboriginal peoples must turn to courts to prove its existence. To assist in proving claims, oral traditions are now as admissible as evidence as written documents in deciding aboriginal title, in effect tipping the burden of proof from the Crown to the claimants. The consequences of Delgamuukw cannot be underestimated: Not only has Delgamuukw forever changed the ground rules that will shape the future direction of aboriginal peoples–state relations; the Supreme Court has also equipped aboriginal peoples with leverage in changing the rules of the game that once fostered dependency and underdevelopment.

CASE STUDY 6–3	Nisga'a: Apartheid or Standing Apart to Work Together?

It has been said that a little knowledge is a dangerous thing. That well-worn adage was given a thorough airing by the wave of reaction to the proposed settlement of British Columbia's first but longest-running land claims test (Gibson 1997). The gist of the arguments falls into a pattern (see Varadarajan 1998): According to critics, an "extraordinary agreement" with the Nisga'a Indians of British Columbia has "raised the spectre of racially separate development across Canada." This precedent-making treaty is perceived as the "first" of its kind in British Columbia and entails the following perceptions: (a) it provides the Nisga'a with more autonomy and self-government than that accorded to Quebec; (b) it empowers the Nisga'a to pass laws on any matter other than defence, currency, and foreign affairs; (c) it ensures exclusive access to ancestral lands and total control over resources; (d) it confers benefits unavailable to other Canadians based solely on culture or skin colour; (e) it is proceeding without public mandate; and (f) it prohibits non-Nisga'a from voting for the region's administration, thus disenfranchising local residents. The agreement's principles are criticized for recontouring the way the province works, since aboriginal rights are seen as taking precedent over Canadian citizenship rights (see Mickleburgh 1998). The more extreme critics persist in pushing all the "right buttons" by demonizing this pact as the evil reincarnate of apartheid, nothing less than the much-hated bantustans of South Africa, and the only jurisdiction in Canada where some Canadians can be taxed without representation or cannot vote because of race. Finally, even aboriginal leaders are upset with what some perceive as a "sell-out deal" that extinguishes aboriginal claims over land. How do these accusations stand up to scrutiny?

First, the background. Early relations between Europeans and aboriginal peoples rested on striking deals through treaties. Such initially was the case in British Columbia: The English governor signed treaties for the purchase of Vancouver Island, but when the Colonial office refused to underwrite the costs of governing the Empire, Victoria found itself without a tax base or treasury to purchase land for white settlers. The governor simply and unilaterally declared the land and minerals to be property of the Crown and ceased to sign any treaties (Mulgrew 1996). Even when British Columbia joined Canada in 1871, the federal government refused to enter into treaties, despite aboriginal bitterness at the legal theft of aboriginal land. In what amounted to a tacit admission of guilt and to compensate in lieu of a treaty, the government allocated $100,000 per year (upped to $300,000 in 1979) to be allocated on a per capita basis. This state of affairs existed until 1973, when the Supreme Court Calder decision rejected Nisga'a land claims but triggered a rethinking of government policy by suggesting the possibility of aboriginal title. Still British Columbia refused to sign treaties or acknowledge aboriginal title until 1991, arguing that aboriginal proprietary rights to land were extinguished by virtue of discovery, declaration of British sovereignty and common law, and the realities of Crown rule.

Second, the facts: Nisga'a have looked to Ottawa for redress since 1885. They petitioned the British Privy Council in 1913 and in 1968 took their case to court. The Calder decision in 1973 ruled against the Nisga'a but indicated that aboriginal title had never been extinguished in British Columbia and that the government had to do something about it (Walkom 1998). It was not until the mid-1990s that a tentative settlement was reached: Actual terms of the agreement (not a treaty) are commonly known. The Nisga'a agreement would provide 5,500 members of bands who live 800 km north of Vancouver a land base of 1,900 km (a fraction of the amount originally proposed), control of forest and fishery resources, $200 million in cash, release from Indian Act provisions, a municipal level of government including con-

trol over policing, education, community services, and taxes, and eventually eliminate on-reserve tax exemptions (Matas 1998). To pay for this culture, Nisga'a will receive forest and timber cutting rights, oil and mineral resources, 26 percent of the salmon fishery plus $21.5 million to purchase boats and equipment, and fishery-conservation trust. It is expected that this transfer in wealth and control will help to alleviate the social conditions in the Nisga'a community, including high levels of unemployment, criminal activity, and crowded homes. In exchanging the extinguishment of aboriginal title for control over destiny, the Nisga'a will have severed the bonds of dependency and created the conditions for self-determination (Molloy 1998).

Third, the reality: The Nisga'a agreement in principle (it has yet to be ratified) is not the first this century. Canada has signed nearly a dozen comprehensive agreements with indigenous tribes since passage of the 1975 James Bay and Northern Quebec Act. To be sure, this proposed settlement is the first in British Columbia since 1859 and the first of 50 outstanding land claims encompassing the entire province. Further, to suggest that the Nisga'a will have more powers of self-determination than Quebec is stretching the truth to the breaking point. Quebec is often treated as a "distinct society" in Canada, with wide-ranging powers from controlling immigration to establishing diplomatic relations with foreign powers. By contrast, Nisga'a self-governing powers are restricted to those of a municipality, including policing, education, taxes, communities services, with a few provincial bits thrown in for good measure. The settlement is worded to protect federal jurisdictions in criminal law and the Charter and provincial authority over aspects of policing and justice. Health, education, and child welfare services must meet provincial standards, although the Nisga'a government will have exclusive jurisdiction in matters related to language and culture in addition to citizenship and property, even when these conflict with federal/provincial laws (Walkom 1998). Under the treaty, in other words, Nisga'a governments will reflect a "concurrent jurisdiction," since both Nisga'a laws as well as federal and provincial jurisdiction will continue to apply to communities, citizens, and lands (Gosnell 1999).

Contrary to popular belief, Nisga'a will not be the only jurisdiction in Canada to restrict voting rights. Admittedly, in most liberal democratic systems, individual rights are acquired by residence, that is, if you live in Toronto, you can vote in Toronto. In contrast, rights in the Nisga'a nation are based on ethnicity with the result that only the Nisga'a can claim rights of citizenship or vote for government. For the first time in Canadian history, Thomas Walkom (1998) concludes, government is being established on a foundation that is fundamentally ethnic. But this assertion is not entirely true: There are in excess of 2,500 reserves across Canada that also restrict voting to membership in one of 603 bands. Besides, what is the point of self-government if "*others*" can vote and undermine the very point of self-rule and aboriginal self-determination?

Fourth, the interpretation: Criticism of Nisga'a reflects "errors" of interpretation that border on fear mongering involving a worst-case scenario. The powers negotiated by the Nisga'a are vastly overstated by critics. Nisga'a self-governing powers may be constitutionally protected—a status that no municipality has—and not subject to override except by federal, provincial, and aboriginal agreement (Walkom 1998). In reality, Nisga'a powers are circumscribed (a super municipality) and considerably less than those implied by federal recognition of Canada's aboriginal tribes as "peoples" with an "inherent right to self-government." Terms of all inherent self-government agreements are set out in a 1995 federal policy document: Inherent self-government is based on contingent rather than sovereign rights, that is,

aboriginal self-governments must operate within the Canadian federal system, be in harmony with other governments, be consistent with the Canadian Charter of Rights and Freedoms, and *enhance the participation of aboriginal peoples in Canadian society* (emphasis added). In other words, Nisga'a self-government is firmly located within the framework of Canadian society where the right to be different cannot violate the laws of the land, the rights of others, or fundamental values of society. The Nisga'a will not become a state within a state, in other words, but remain citizens of Canada and be subjected to its constitutional provisions.

Even more disconcerting is critics' penchant with "racializing" the Nisga'a pact. Nisga'a is not about racially separate development by restricting the rights of other "races." Nor is it about race-based governments in the mould of apartheid; after all, apartheid was forcibly imposed on South African blacks to exclude, deny, and exploit in contrast with self-government arrangements that work on the voluntaristic principle of standing apart in order to work together. Nisga'a is about *indigenous rights* and the right of indigenous peoples to construct aboriginal models of self-government over jurisdictions of land, identity, and political voice. It is about the rights of six generations of Nisga'a who since 1887 have tried to achieve self-government and establish native title to ancestral land that had never been surrendered to European powers.

Fifth, the future: Canada is widely renowned as a country constructed around compromises. The Nisga'a settlement is but another compromise in crafting an innovative political order in which each level of government—federal, provincial, and aboriginal—is sovereign in its own right yet shares in the sovereignty of Canada as a whole by way of multiple and interlocking jurisdictions. A settlement of such magnitude—like that of Maori tribes such as the Tainui and Ngai Tahu in New Zealand—is not intended to be divisive or racial. The objective is to find some common ground for constructive reengagement between founding peoples. The Nisga'a settlement is intended to improve the certainty over who owns what, since investment is deterred by uncertainty of ownership (see *Financial Post* 1998). The point is to establish an element of certainty by balancing and reconciling the preexistence of aboriginal societies with the sovereignty of the Crown in a way that is workable, necessary, and just.

PUTTING PRINCIPLES INTO PRACTICE

It is one thing to promote aboriginal proposals for renewal and reform. It is quite another to put into practice the goals of indigenous-plus, self-determination, and aboriginal title and treaty rights. Aboriginal leaders have relied on various tactics and strategies to get the message across. Political authorities, ever fearful of losing power or control, have responded with a host of delaying or defusing tactics. And the Eurocentrism inherent in Canada's neocolonial structures makes it difficult to escape the hidden agenda that envelops aboriginal reality.

Aboriginal Initiatives

Aboriginal responses to redefining their relationship to society are varied by gender, age, location, legal status, and socioeconomic standing. Principles and philosophies span the spectrum of "radical" to "moderate": To one side are those who believe in political revolution in which aboriginal people become sovereign (Mercredi and Turpel 1993); to the other are the moderates who endorse a conciliatory bit-by-bit approach that cuts deals, enhances local autonomy, improves job opportunities, and fosters dialogue with private sectors (Fontaine 1998; also Gray 1997). Generally speaking, aboriginal leaders prefer to press for change through conventional channels of dialogue, consultation, and persuasion with central policy structures. Tactics include recourse to parliament, the existing court system, public opinion polls, and special interest/lobby groups such as the Assembly of First Nations. Courts are seen as valued venues for exerting pressure on the government to honour their constitutional obligations; they also provide a forum for thrashing out the aboriginal issues pertaining to land, identity, or political voice. Constitutional forums have been employed for redress of historical inequities and promotion of collective interests. A series of First Ministers conferences in the 1980s sought to clarify the specific nature of aboriginal rights, but made little headway except for enhancing issue recognition (Brock 1991). Aboriginal leaders have also relied on international forums and agencies for assistance. They have gone to the United Nations, to Britain, and to the Vatican in the hopes of putting international pressure on the Canadian government for broken promises, miscarriages of justices, and pervasive paternalism. These tactics have attained a measure of success, partly because of Canada's vulnerability to international criticism over aboriginal rights violation.

Alternative strategies have been adopted as well, because of the failure of political and constitutional channels to adequately address local grievances and national concerns. A variety of activist measures have been advocated, ranging from civil disobedience to threats of violence in some cases. Flamboyant and theatrically staged protests involving the mass media are particularly important in tweaking the conscience of a publicity-conscious government. The use of negative publicity to embarrass the government is especially effective because of Canada's publicly articulated commitment to human and individual rights (see Marcus 1995). Acts of civil disobedience have proven successful. National and international attention was captured in the late 1980s when the Lubicon Indians in Northern Alberta erected a blockade in protest of government failure to acknowledge their grievances. More recent tactics have also paid off, including the successful secondary boycott of Daishawa's corporate customers that put a halt to logging in Lubicon until resolution of the land issue. Finally, there have been occasional threats to employ violence if necessary in defence of aboriginal demands. With few exceptions such as Oka, Ipperwash, and Lake Gustaffsen, the threat of violence has not moved beyond rhetoric. How long this will remain the case is open to conjecture, given the urgency of aboriginal grievances and impatience of younger activists.

Aboriginal demands are consistent with their preferred status as a unique nation within a federalist framework. Central to their aspirations is the middle way: to strike a balance between extremes. Aboriginal peoples don't want to separate from Canada in the territorial sense, but they also reject any move toward assimilation with a corresponding diminuation of their unique status. A separate country is not the agenda; proposed, instead, is a consensual partnership in running Canada by way of overlapping circles of governance, with a sharing of jurisdictions in some areas such as health in addition to exclusive jurisdictions in other areas such as education for aboriginal communities and defence for federal authorities (Purvis 1999). A commitment to self-governing status is endorsed as a compromise between the extremes of separatism and absorption. Second, few want to preserve their cultural lifestyle in timelessness for the edification of purists or tourists. Nor is there any desire to impose their vanishing lifestyles on the non-native group. But equally strong is the refusal to abandon their language and culture in exchange for an alien and incompatible set of Eurocentric values and beliefs. Preferred instead is the forging of relevant elements from the past with the realities of the present for advance into the future (Alfred 1995). Aboriginal peoples want to be modern, in other words, but not at the expense of abandoning traditional values. Third, aboriginal peoples are pragmatists who wish to achieve a working balance between the cultural and spiritual values of the past without rejecting the technological benefits of modern society. Fourth, achievement of political and economic power is viewed as critical for rebuilding communities into flourishing centres of meaningful activity. But political and economic successes are unacceptable if attained at the cost of undermining their social obligations, collective and community rights, and cultural/ spiritual values.

Political Reaction

Central authorities for the most part have stumbled in responding to aboriginal demands for indigenizing aboriginal peoples–state relations. The promises of lofty rhetoric notwithstanding, there remains a noticeable lack of political will for implementing much of this rhetoric (Weaver 1993; Macklem 1993). Politics and initiatives continue to be guided by polls, since politicians are known only to go as far as the polls permit (Ponting 1997; Barnsley 1999; Purvis 1999). Political perception of a poorly informed public contributes to this policy-making inertia: A study conducted in 1997 indicated that nearly two-thirds of 3,946 respondents did not think aboriginal peoples were worse off than the rest of Canadians; 26

percent thought they were better off (Nadeau et al. 1998). In another survey conducted by the Assembly of First Nations involving 1,500 adult Canadians, 39 percent believed that aboriginal peoples brought problems on themselves (Barnsley 1999). Government initiatives have come under criticism for capitulating to aboriginal demands while sacrificing national interests through restitutional expenditures and power giveaways (Smith 1995). In other words, Canadians appear to be broadly supportive of aboriginal concerns and sympathetic to aboriginal problems. Nevertheless, public support may be "skin deep" thus making any government fearful of moving too quickly.

Policy officials are understandably wary of dissolving once habitual patterns of domination for uncharted waters of aboriginal nationhood or sovereignty (Levin 1993). A dichotomy is apparent in shaping federal reaction to aboriginal demands. On the one hand, political authorities appear receptive to aboriginal claims—if only to avert a crisis of legitimacy and restore some semblance of political tranquillity. Political awareness is growing that the Crown acted irresponsibly in dealing with aboriginal peoples, in effect reneging on the trust implicit in this relationship, such as in selling reserve land cheaply to vested interests or squandering proceeds from land sales (Lahgi 1997). Also evident is political willingness to negotiate over issues related to self-determination and self-government to compensate for past wrongs, albeit not to the extent of condoning territorial secession and dismemberment of the state. On the other hand, a willingness to acknowledge aboriginality in redefining aboriginal peoples–state relations is counterbalanced by fears of dismantling Canadian society (Levin 1993; Webber 1994). Government officials prefer to endorse aboriginal self-government as a political concession, both contingent ("qualified") and delegated on a band-to-band basis, with accountability to Parliament and the Constitution, rather than as an inherent right derived from common law. At the core of this impasse is failure to appreciate the politics of aboriginality as a politicized ideology for radical change. Aboriginality is political in that choices about who gets what are politicized and out in public for debate. These debates are concerned with rules of engagement and patterns of entitlement with respect to the allocation of powers and resources (Sharp 1997). The discourse is political as well because aboriginal demands constitute grievances against the state. Initiatives that once focused on cultural preservation and formal equality before the law are now channelled into struggles for jurisdictional control of power and wealth (Levin 1993).

Even the tabling of aboriginal demands is inherently political. Political parties became entangled in controversies dealing with aboriginal issues. The state itself is implicated in these controversies when its legitimacy as a territorial sovereignty is directly challenged. This political aspect is embedded not only in the partisan sense of political parties and party agendas; it is also manifest in the broader sense of value judgments about the preferred vision of society. Strategies for the containment of aboriginal peoples have varied in the past, but most called for their placement as subordinates into a settled hierarchy of status and roles, with all sectors sharing a common goal and an agreed-upon set of rules (Sharp 1997). The politicization of aboriginality has overturned the dynamics of the governing process: It draws the state into the most contentious of all relations: the shifting and openly contested relationship between equals in the political arena, with each claiming intrinsic authority and separate jurisdiction over powers, resources, and status. In brief, aboriginality as principle and practice poses an unprecedented challenge to the balancing act in any society constructed around a series of compromises. The prospect of reconciling Canadian society building with the realities of aboriginal nationhood is daunting, given the challenge of fundamentally separate structures with a distinctive power base and parallel institutions.

Central authorities prefer to work with a benign neocolonialist arrangement that compartmentalizes the aboriginal platform into packages of institutional flexibility and delegated responsibility. Inasmuch as the intent is to simply rearrange the furniture without altering the floor plan, the government's aboriginal agenda is more likely to focus on appearances rather than substance.

Aboriginal peoples in Canada and throughout the world have taken the initiative in politicizing their demands for a radical restructuring of society along the lines of the "nations within" (Fleras and Spoonley 1999). Resistance has shifted from a focus on survival and consolidation to challenging the distribution of power within a reconstituted state. Many Canadians understandably are alarmed by the radical nature of aboriginal proposals. Contrary to popular belief, however, aboriginal demands are not radical in the conventional sense. Their demands rarely invoke the overthrow of Western-styled values or institutions; after all, it is hardly in their best interests to destroy the source of their unique relations. Few actively espouse the dismemberment of Canadian society or the imposition of aboriginal cultural values on society. Endorsed instead is a fundamental redistribution of power and resources. If these demands appear threatening to Canadians as a whole or if they seem unrealistic in light of contemporary realities, consider the alternatives. A continuation of ineffectual government interference and paternalistic handouts is not the answer. Nor is throwing more money at the problem or expanding the legion of experts in this field. In other words, the costs of restructuring may be formidable; the costs of doing nothing or carrying on as before will be even more prohibitive.

Institutional Inertia

Few politicians can afford to cavalierly dismiss aboriginality or deny the existence of aboriginal rights. What are debated instead are ideas over defining their limits and how best to concede these rights without destroying the social fabric of society in the process. In the last two decades, there has been a shift in how society, including the legal system, defines aboriginal rights and the relationship of aboriginal peoples to society at large. Nevertheless, the debate over aboriginality remains so steeped in the colonial–Eurocentric constitutionalisms ("first principles") that the prospect for fundamental change is compromised. Contrary to popular and political belief, Canada has not discarded the colonialism of the past, only its most egregious forms (Denis 1997). The legacy of Eurocentric-based colonialism continues to shape how the legal system identifies and interprets aboriginal rights and relations, in effect, reinforcing the view that Canadian law is not neutral or impartial, but a means by which dominant values are imposed and enforced under the guise of neutrality and objectivity (Asch 1997). As a result of this systemic bias, dominant power and privilege are inadvertently bolstered, while aboriginal peoples are labelled as defiant or unreasonable in pressing their demands for rethinking Canada. To the extent that these same systemic structures in defence of dominant discourses can be used to challenge the status quo, court rulings, for example, from Calder to Delgamuukw, are indicative of how law is indeed a two-edged instrument, depending on the context.

How is this neocolonial relationship manifest (Denis 1996; 1997)? Neocolonialism works on the assumption that people appear to be free. But this is an illusion, since hidden agendas continue to frame, control, and constrain. Neocolonialism is predicated on the acceptance of assumptions that define issues and frame responses, however unobtrusively this may appear. Power may be expressed in the guise of impartial standards of fairness.

Consider how aboriginal peoples–Crown relations remain rooted in the assumption that the Crown owns all the land outright. Aboriginal title and rights to land exist only to the extent they impose a burden on underlying Crown title, with the result that any transfer of use or possession from Crown to aboriginal peoples is to be tolerated as a concession to be proven on a case-by-case basis. But who has the right to define aboriginal title as a legal burden on the title of the Crown and its land-related management activities? Should a postcolonizing mindset call into question this assumption of aboriginal title as a "default option," and assert instead that it is Crown claims that impose a burden on aboriginal title, thus necessitating some kind of process by which to substantiate Crown claims to ownership of land (Venne 1998)? But as Sharon Venne (1998) points out, there is no legal proof to establish the legality of the Crown's unilateral assertion over aboriginal jurisdictions. Such neocolonial arrogance, Venne asserts, is nothing more than a "political statement" dressed up in "hocus pocus rules and regulations designed by the colonizers to dispossess indigenous peoples of our land and territories."

Second, Canadians continue to be trapped within a neocolonial constitutionalism that privileges Eurocentric values and institutions while diminishing aboriginal equivalents. A pervasive Eurocentrism has the intent or effect to do the following: (a) dismiss aboriginal rights, values, or traditions as irrelevant or inferior much less as empowering and legitimate; (b) naturalize Eurocentric ways of seeing and doing as natural and normal; and (c) assert the superiority and dominance of conventional patterns and institutional structures. The demeaning of differences under the cloak of Eurocentrism often reinforces the very problems that solutions are trying to solve. Canada's liberal pluralism is infused with such commitment to commonalities (thanks, in part, to the Charter, which, in defining all Canadians as equal, has conveyed the impression that they are all the same) that differences are tolerated only to the extent that they are acceptable to the mainstream. For example, the government's commitment to inherent aboriginal self-government rights is negated by insisting that all self-governing arrangements must be situated within the framework of Canadian society and entirely subjected to the Constitution of Canada (Venne 1998). Claims to land or government are acceptable as long as they do not affect most Canadians, do not cost exorbitant sums, and can be used as leverage against the interests of the Québécois. But for aboriginal peoples to be equal, they must be different (see Denis 1996). Otherwise, there is a risk of being muscled into agreements that secure colonialism, deny indigenous rights as rights, and undermine any serious government commitment to implement inherent self-governing rights, except as some minimal respect for distinctive culture or aboriginal disadvantage (Venne 1998). The words of Noel Lyons (1997) are especially timely in drawing attention to the idea that colonial arrangements that once suppressed aboriginal peoples are no longer acceptable as a basis for reform:

> As long as the process continues to be defined by rules and standards set by the dominant society, no measure of real self-government is possible because the process itself is a denial of the inherent rights of self-government of Aboriginal peoples. In other words, we cannot de-colonize peoples by relying on the rules and standards that were used to colonize them in the first place....

How, then, will aboriginal peoples and the Crown relate to each other in terms of power and jurisdiction? In situations of conflicting interests and wills, when is the will of the Crown to be legally disabled in those areas of exclusive aboriginal jurisdiction, and when is it to have supreme authority? Conversely, when is the will of the aboriginal nation to count exclusively, and when is it to be disabled under joint arrangements and overlapping jurisdictions (personal communication, Richard Dawson, 28 January 1999). That responses to these questions have yet to be formulated points to the tenacity of "colonial constitutionalisms." One way of escaping this colonialist conundrum is through a power-sharing partnership that sharply curtails state jurisdictions in the hopes of establishing innovative patterns of constructive engagement.

FROM CUTTING DEALS TO CONSTRUCTIVE ENGAGEMENT

Aboriginal struggles to sever the bonds of colonialist dependency and underdevelopment appear to be gathering momentum. Several innovative routes have been explored for improving aboriginal peoples–state relations, including constitutional reform, indigenization of policy and administration, comprehensive and specific land claims, constitutional reform, Indian Act amendments, devolution of power, decentralization of service delivery structures, and, of course, self-government arrangements (Prince 1994). The distributive ideals associated with "aboriginality" are varied, as might be expected in light of diverse constituencies and specific histories, but typically involve demands for aboriginal jurisdiction over land, resources, culture, and identity. But the politics of jurisdiction are not without its costs and consequences that inadvertently may be reinforcing the very colonialisms that aboriginal peoples are seeking to escape. Reliance on confrontational models for allocating power and resources are self-defeating if the debate over "who gets what" is without a unifying vision or set of principles. That makes it doubly important to revisit the politics of jurisdictions (Fleras 1996).

Jurisdictions By Jurisprudence

One of the more striking developments in aboriginal peoples–state relations is a growing reliance on restitutional claims making (**"regional agreements"** or "comprehensive land settlements) for sorting out who controls what and why (McHugh 1998). The logic behind a claims-making approach is relatively straightforward: In an effort to right historical wrongs by settling outstanding complaints against the state for breaches to indigenous rights, the government offers a compensation package of cash, land, services, and controlling rights to specific indigenous claimants in exchange for "full and final" settlements of treaty-based grievances. In Canada these regional agreements, from the James Bay–Cree settlement of 1975 to the Nunavut Agreement in 1993, involved extinguishment of aboriginal title in a region in exchange for a package of (a) perpetual aboriginal rights to various categories of land, from absolute freehold title to usufructuary rights to hunt and fish, (b) comanagement and planning in various socioeconomic and environmental issues, (c) hefty compensation payouts for unauthorized use of land to foster aboriginal economic develop and political infrastructures, and (d) various self-management arrangements (Jull and Craig 1997).

References to "regional" and "comprehensive" are central to these agreements (Richardson et al. 1994). Agreements go beyond simple land tenure settlements for aboriginal land claims. They are designed to not only recognize the unique relation of aboriginal peoples to land and sea as a basis for political and legal claims; also included under these comprehensive and regional agreements is a set of legal frameworks and procedures that link aboriginal self-determination with social justice, economic development, and environmental protection over large areas. After all, as Richardson et al. (1994) conclude, the management and protection of environmental rights can only succeed when decision making is organized over a broad area. Moreover, while these agreements do not confer sovereignty in the traditional sense, they do provide a range of political and economic benefits that ensure the following outcomes: (a) a significant degree of self-management and autonomy; (b) a new legal and political relationship between aboriginal communities and representatives of the Crown; (c) a clearer framework regarding who controls or has access to land or resources in a manner that accommodates aboriginal needs and concerns; (d) an improvement of the basis for cultural and spiritual growth; and (e) securing those self-governing and developmental bases that enable more effective involvement in decision making.

Governments have taken to regional agreements as one way of coping with the "**Indian problem**." Regional settlements are endorsed as a case of restorative justice in compensating historically disadvantaged peoples for unwarranted confiscation of land, while securing a resource base to offset corresponding social and cultural dislocations (see Wilson 1995). But critics and supporters disagree on whether regional agreements are a catalyst for crafting a new political order or an administrative quick fix to make the "Indian problem" go away. Supporters point to regional agreements as an innovative, even unprecedented, process by which two peoples negotiate the basis by which they would share territories, public revenues, decision making, and economic development through a mix of pragmatism, recognition, accommodation, and tolerance (Jull and Craig 1997). Critics point to the unintended consequences of agreements that impart a new twist to the Canadianism, "two nations warring in the bosom of a single state" (Fleras and Maaka 1998). A claims-making approach for reconstituting state–aboriginal peoples relations embraces an underlying agenda, the sum total of which has transformed the challenge of working through differences into a zero-sum game of winners and losers. However unintended, the consequences of the claims-making process foster an adversarial mentality: Disputants are drawn into a protracted struggle between opposing interest groups over "mine," "yours," and "ours" that concedes as little as possible. Issues, in turn, become occluded inside a rigid format that complicates the process of securing a compromise without losing face. Levels of rhetoric under a claims-making model are stretched to the breaking point as each party attempts to manoeuver itself for maximum effect. Rhetoric tends to get blown out of proportion to enhance the number of media "hits." The claims-making game compels aboriginal peoples to articulate their aspirations in the language of the protagonist, with the result that indigenous aspirations are distorted to fit a "westocentric" framework.

Difficulties are also further heightened when central authorities and indigenous peoples operate at cross-purposes in the claims-making process (Minogue 1998). Governments prefer a full and final settlement of past injustices if only to eliminate uncertainty from any further governance or development (Graham 1997). Such pragmatism misreads indigenous perceptions of settlements as a precondition for constructing relationships that secure cultural survival, recognition as a people, and sufficient resources to bolster the prospect of self-determination (Coates 1998). For indigenous peoples, the resolution of claims provides not an end in itself, but a means to this end (including acquisition of administrative powers, financial compensation, and control of traditional lands/resources), one stage in an evolving and ongoing relationship between partners over time. Or as Peter Jull and Donna Craig (1997) put it, when arguing for the primacy of relationship rather than results, albeit in a different context, attainment of indigenous autonomy is not so much a farewell but the beginning of a new relationship, and indigenous models of self-determination are not about separation from society but the beginning of full participation in national life.

Reengaging Constructively

A restitutional claims-making policy environment has proven a double-edged success. Claims-making resolutions are undeniably important as part of a broader exercise in relations repair but, on its own and divorced from the bigger picture of rethinking relationships, such a preoccupation is fraught with hidden messages and underlying contradictions (Rotman 1997). Reliance on claims making as aboriginal policy in the absence of clear principles is counterproductive and may accentuate power-conflict models that secure the status quo. Grievances remain grievances no matter how much money is being exchanged, without a corresponding state commitment to restore the relationship in a generous and unquibbling fashion (see Milroy 1997). A preoccupation with contesting claims to the exclusion of engagement has also had the effect of glossing over the central element in any partnered interaction, namely, the managing of a relation in the spirit of cooperative coexistence and relational autonomy (Henare 1995; McHugh 1998).

Pressure is mounting to transcend claims making as an exclusive model for defining state–indigenous peoples relations. Proposed instead is a more flexible approach that emphasizes engagement over entitlement, relationships over rights, interdependence over opposition, cooperation over competition, reconciliation over restitution, and power sharing over power conflict (Fleras and Maaka 1998). Advocated, too, is a policy framework that acknowledges the importance of working together rather than standing apart, even if a degree of "autonomy" may be inescapable in the constructive "partnering" of indigenous relations with the state. Emergence of a *"constructive engagement"* model of interaction to replace the claims-oriented "contestation" mode may provide a respite from the interminable bickering over "who owns what," while brokering a tentative blueprint for working together by standing apart.

At the crux of a **constructive engagement** policy model is endorsement of aboriginality as a basis for reconstructing state–aboriginal peoples relations. This commitment to aboriginality as a framework for renewal and reconciliation entails a fundamental constitutional shift. Foremost is the radical notion that aboriginal peoples are essentially autonomous political communities, each of which is sovereign in its own right yet sharing in the sovereignty of society at large by way of overlapping and interlocking jurisdictions pertaining to land, identity, and political voice. Among the key planks in advancing a postcolonial relationship are the following preconditions for constructive engagement:

1. Aboriginal peoples do not aspire to sovereignty *per se*. Strictly speaking, they already have sovereignty by virtue of original occupancy, never having relinquished this independence by explicit agreement. The fact that aboriginal peoples are sovereign for purposes of entitlement or political engagement would imply only the creation of appropriate structures for its practical expression.

2. Aboriginal peoples are not looking to separate or become independent. Except for a few ideologues, appeals to sovereignty and aboriginal models of self-determination are discourses about relationships of relative yet relational autonomy within the context of nondomination between interconnected peoples (Young 1990; Scott 1996). Relations repair is the key rather than throwing money at the problem.

3. Aboriginal peoples are neither a problem for solution nor a need to be met. They are a people with **inherent rights** to benefits, recognition, relations, and identity. Nor should they be considered a competitor to be jousted but a partner with whom to work through

differences in a spirit of cooperative coexistence. In acknowledging that "let's face it, we are all here to stay," Chief Justice Antonio Lamer has observed, is there any other option except to shift from the trap of competing sovereignties to the primacy of relations between partners (McHugh 1998)?

4. Acknowledging the fundamental autonomy of aboriginal peoples as a political community is critical in crafting a new political order (Chartrand 1996). The rights of aboriginal peoples as original occupants must be accepted as having their own independent sources rather than being shaped for the convenience of the political majority or subject to unilateral override (Asch 1997).

5. Power sharing is pivotal in advancing cooperative engagement and coexistence. All internally divided societies that have attained some degree of stability entail a level of governance that connotes a sharing of power (Linden 1994). Precise arrangements for rearranging power distributions are varied, of course, but predicated on some degree of relative autonomy for operationalizing indigenous models of self-determination over shared but separate jurisdictions.

6. Innovative patterns of belonging are integral to constructive engagement. Indigenous proposals for belonging to society are anchored in primary affiliation with the ethnicity or tribe rather than as individual citizens, thus implying that peoples can belong in different ways to society, without necessarily rejecting citizenship or loyalty to the whole. This would suggest a dual citizenship as a basis for belonging, that is, to society as well as to one's people (Royal Commission on Aboriginal Affairs 1996).

7. Placing constructive engagement at the centre of a relationship entails a fundamental rethink in sorting out the "goodies." As with dispute resolution in general, engaging constructively eschews any game involving winners and losers, but advocates a problem-solving exercise in which both sides have a stake in coming to an agreement (see Campbell 1998). Parties must enter into negotiations not on the basis of jurisprudence but on the grounds of justice, not by cutting deals but by formulating a clear vision, and not by litigation but by listening.

8. Constructive engagement also goes beyond the dualities that polarize and provoke. Dualisms establish a confrontation between two entities: A choice must be made in terms of this opposition, thus disallowing the possibility that each of the opposing terms requires and draws upon supposedly the opposite (Fay 1996). A dialectical mode of thinking is proposed instead in which differences are perceived not as absolute or antagonistic, but as deeply interconnected and existing in a state of creative tension with potential opportunity.

9. Last but certainly not least is the centrality of conciliation in any constructive engagement. A commitment to reconciliation is meant to exorcise the pain and humiliation endured by aboriginal peoples. An expression of regret for the deplorable acts of a colonial past is not meant to humiliate, embarrass, or extract reparations. The atonement is intended to create the basis for healing and restoration of aboriginal pride and dignity.

To Sum Up An adherence to constructive engagement is shown to transcend the legalistic (abstract rights) or restitutional (reparations), however important these concerns in identity building and resource mobilization. Increasing reliance on contractual relations as a basis for sorting out ownership may have elevated litigation to a preferred level in resolving differences (Spoonley 1997). But this reliance on the legalities of rights and reparations tends to emphasize continuities with the past at the expense of social changes and evolving circumstances (Mulgan 1989). By contrast, a constructive engagement constitutionalism goes beyond the idea of restitution as an excuse to cut deals. It is focused on advancing a relationship on an ongoing basis by taking into account shifting social realities in sorting out who controls what in a spirit of give and take. Policy outcomes with respect to jurisdiction cannot be viewed as final or authoritative, any more than they can be preoccupied with "taking" or "finalizing," but must be situated in the context of "sharing" and "extending." Wisdom and justice must precede power, in other words, rather than vice versa (Cassidy 1994).

REMAKING CANADA: "MUDDLING THROUGH"

> Canada is a test case for a grand notion—the notion that dissimilar people can share lands, resources, power, and dreams while respecting and sustaining their differences.
>
> A Word from the Commissioner's Highlights of the Report
> of the Royal Commission on Aboriginal Affairs (1996:ix)

Canada is struggling to recast its relationship with aboriginal peoples in response to massive disparities, mounting resentment, and emergent political realities. The interplay of racism, paternalism, and disempowement has inflicted a scandalous toll in terms of social, health, economic, and cultural costs. Many aboriginal peoples have lost their language and identity as well, and this spiritual loss is compounded by skyrocketing rates of alcoholism, substance abuse, domestic violence, suicide, diabetes, and heart disease (Rotman 1996). The need for structural change is broadly acknowledged by aboriginal and nonaboriginal leaders alike, but disagreements vary on how to hasten this transformation from colonized subjects to self-determining peoples (Fontaine 1998). The distance travelled has been impressive: In the space of just over two decades, aboriginal peoples have recoiled from the brink of dependency and disappearance to resume a pivotal role in the reconstruction of Canadian society. Such a reversal originated and gained legitimacy when the "costs" of excluding aboriginal peoples from the national agenda proved unacceptably high in social, political, and economic terms (Fleras and Krahn 1992). However much the distanced travelled, there is much more to cover in establishing a genuine partnership in the remaking of Canada.

The start of a new millennium may well see Canada on the threshold of an aboriginal paradigm shift. To be sure, the condition of aboriginal peoples continues to represent Canada's great moral failure, of a people both demoralized and dispossessed by a division of wealth in the land that has passed them by (Gwyn 1998). But recognition of aboriginal peoples as peoples with an inherent right to self-government rather than wards of a guardian state holds promise of a new beginning. Governments have accepted the idea that aboriginal peoples (a) are a distinct society, (b) possess a threatened culture and society, (c) depend on government trust responsibilities for survival, (d) desire more control in line with local priorities, and (e) prefer to achieve their goals in partnership with central authorities. Government acknowledgment of aboriginality as a government-to-government relation is a positive sign (Fontaine 1998). So too is the promise to treat aboriginal peoples as equal partners in all relevant constitutional talks (Denton 1997). And the courts have continued to provide an expansive interpretation of aboriginal and treaty rights, from the Calder decision to the recent Delgamuukw Ruling (Rotman 1997).

The rhetoric of revolution may be compelling; it is also premature, despite the collapse of egregious colonialist structures. Aboriginal efforts to redefine their relationship with the people of Canada are fraught with ambiguity and deception in light of competing paradigms and entrenched interests (Fleras and Elliott 1992). The politics of restructuring often conceal hidden agendas and contested realities between the "two solitudes." The government continues to call the shots regarding what is acceptable and desirable, while aboriginal values and aspirations are overwhelmed by the priorities and constraints of the majority "whitestream" (Denis 1996). The fundamental objective of aboriginal affairs policy agendas—to eliminate the aboriginal "problem" through attainment of local self-sufficiency—has scarcely budged with the passage of time (Ponting 1986) and is repeated again in the 1995 Federal Policy Guideline. Only the means have changed, with crude assimilationist strategies conceding ground to more sophisticated channels that not only co-opt aspects of aboriginal discourse for self-serving purposes, but also have the effect, however inadvertent or unintended, of advancing a corporatist agenda.

Aboriginal peoples–state relations in Canada are currently under reassessment at policy and administration levels. A proposed paradigm shift is gathering momentum, partly in response to escalating aboriginal pressure and prolonged public criticism and in other part to deflect a growing crisis in state legitimacy. But the widely heralded realignment of jurisdictions is riddled with inconsistencies and contradictions as competing interests clash over a new aboriginal agenda. To one side, the contestation paradigm, with its roots in the "old rules of the game," appears to be drawing to a close, but not without a struggle (Borrows and Rotman 1997:31). To the other, a new postcolonizing paradigm based on empowerment and autonomy through constructive engagement has not yet taken hold, in spite of its lofty ideals to promote a nation-to-nation relation that endorses aboriginal differences and inherent self-determining rights (Fontaine 1998). Instead of a paradigm shift, in other words, a paradigm "muddle" has evolved instead. Aboriginal peoples–state relations are imbued with an air of ambivalence as colonialist paradigms grind up against postcolonizing realities, as the old ("contestation") collide with the new ("constructive engagement") without displacing the other. Metaphors borrowed from plate tectonics and continental drift suggest diverse viewpoints on collision course, as perspectives slide into each other, past each other, around each other, and over or under each other. Each of the "plates" tends to "talk past the other" by using the same words but speaking a different language. Neither paradigm is strong enough to dislodge its conceptual counterpart, with the result that the renewal process is enlivened by discordant amalgams of progressive and traditional. Such a state of tension and conflict is likely to persist until such time that conventional thinking accepts a unifying "vision" of Canada as a symmetrical partnership of three founding peoples—aboriginal, French, and English—each sovereign in its own right yet sharing in the sovereignty of a postcolonizing Canada.

CHAPTER HIGHLIGHTS

- Canadian race and ethnic relations revolve about the interplay of three major ethnicities. Aboriginal peoples, Charter members, and multicultural minorities are actively involved in the competition for power and scarce resources.
- Each of these ethnicities occupies a distinct relational status in Canadian society, with a correspondingly different set of problems, strategies for solution, and prospects.

- Aboriginal peoples (including status and nonstatus Indians, Métis, and Inuit) constitute one of these forces. The depressed social and economic status of many aboriginal peoples has earned them the title of a "social problem" or as "having problems" in need of solution through government intervention.

- The construction of state–aboriginal peoples relations is conducted through official policy and administration, yet secured at the level of tacit assumptions and reinforced through patterns of entitlements, symbols, and discourses.

- Aboriginal policy has evolved through several stages: reciprocity, assimilation, integration, devolution and conditional autonomy. Consistent with this evolutionary development are perception of aboriginal peoples as "allies," "children," "citizens," "minorities," and "peoples." The notion of aboriginal peoples as autonomous political communities may be gaining support.

- Government policies and programs have largely failed to hasten the decolonization of aboriginal marginal status. Aboriginal peoples subsequently have sought to politicize their relationship with the government through political, constitutional, and judicial channels.

- Foremost in terms of this redefinition have been the (a) promotion of self-determination through self-government within the framework of Canadian federalism; (b) recognition of aboriginal and treaty rights; and (c) acceptance of aboriginality as a cornerstone of Canadian society building. Clearly, then, aboriginal resistance has jumped from a focus on cultural survival and formal equality to a highly politicized demand for radical renewal and power-sharing reform.

- Much of the tension underlying aboriginal peoples–government relations reflects debate over the politics of self-government. Issues pertaining to jurisdiction are particularly important in deciding who controls what, and why, under self-governing arrangements.

- The current crisis in aboriginal–state relations is generated by competing claims over who controls what with respect to self-government, land claims, and treaty rights.

- The restructuring of aboriginal relations with the state is propelled by a mutual commitment to "indigenize" the aboriginal agenda through government recognition of aboriginal peoples as "peoples" with an "inherent right to self-government."

- Initiatives to accommodate aboriginality as a basis for claims making are subject to controversy, primarily because aboriginal aspirations are perceived as a direct challenge to the legitimacy of state control over aboriginal jurisdictions.

- Aboriginal aspirations revolve around a "middle way" by working through conventional channels of reform.

- Political concessions to aboriginal demands for inherent self-governing rights are tolerated only to the extent that they reflect historical disadvantage or cultural difference rather than stem from aboriginal rights or veer outside the framework of Canadian society.

- Recent developments in redefining aboriginal peoples–Crown relations revolve around the issue of aboriginal title. The Delgamuukw Ruling in late 1997 indicated that aboriginal peoples have a constitutional right to land they have occupied and have not as yet extinguished through treaties. The Ruling also declared aboriginal title to land as a legal fact, land as an integral part of aboriginal identity, and constitutional protection of collective title to land.

- Major court decisions from Calder to Delgamuukw have established the legitimacy of aboriginal claims to land and political voice, and prompted the government to negotiate with them.
- Efforts to decolonize the aboriginal agenda are widely anticipated as necessary and overdue; nevertheless, proposals for re-constitutionalizing aboriginal peoples–state relations must contend with political and bureaucratic interests, both of which resist fundamental change for fear of destabilizing the status quo.
- The concept of constructive engagement provides an ideal model for establishing a new constitutionalism between aboriginal peoples and the Crown. Still, it remains to be seen if creation of a more positive relation can overcome neocolonial hurdles to remaking of Canada along the lines of aboriginality.

KEY TERMS

aboriginal peoples
aboriginal rights
aboriginal self-government
aboriginal title
aboriginality
comprehensive land claims
conditional autonomy
constitutionalism
constructive engagement
contested site
Delgamuukw Ruling
Department of Indian Affairs and Northern Development
devolution
"Indian problem"
indigenous (or aboriginal) rights
indigenous-plus
inherent rights to self-government
internal colonialism
Inuit
jurisdictions
Métis
postcolonizing
regional agreements
specific treaty claims
status versus "nonstatus" Indians
sui generis
treaty rights
White Paper

REVIEW QUESTIONS

1. Compare and contrast the three major forces in Canada in terms of their legal status, core problem, proposed solution, and anticipated outcome.

2. Provide a brief description of the social, economic, political, and cultural problems that confront aboriginal communities. Who is responsible for these problems? Justify your answer.

3. Demonstrate how an internal colonialism model can provide insights into the current status of aboriginal peoples.

4. With regard to government policy, briefly trace the stages in the evolution of aboriginal peoples–government relations in Canada from early contact to the present.

5. Outline the current demands of the aboriginal peoples with respect to improving their relational status in Canadian society. How do aboriginal demands compare with the solutions proposed by the federal government?

6. Why do political authorities have such difficulty with aboriginal demands?

7. The concept of aboriginal self-determination through inherent aboriginal self-government is slowly gaining acceptance in Canada. What is meant by this concept? How is it justified? What does it propose to accomplish? How does it differ from government proposals in this area?

8. Discuss how and why aboriginal peoples–government relations can be described as existing in a "muddled" state.

9. In what do the principles of constructive engagement promise to revise the thinking behind aboriginal peoples–state relations?

THE QUEBEC QUESTION

World Languages: Towers of Babel or Bridges to Prosperity?

Canada strikes many as a complicated, even ungovernable society. Its sprawling size and regional distinctions contribute to this image, as does an ongoing struggle to cope with the competing concerns of its diverse ethnicities. The role of nonofficial languages (sometimes called community or **heritage languages,** but will be referred to as **world languages**) has proven particularly challenging in forging unity from diversity (Cummins and Danesi 1990). The preservation of world languages is endorsed by some as a renewable resource of inestimable value to different interests, including (a) minority individuals (in terms of intellectual development and academic success), (b) ethnocultural communities (with respect to survival), and (c) Canada's (inter)national interests (by enhancing international competitiveness in a freewheeling global economy) (Samuel 1997). Others disagree; they see world languages as complicating the natural unscrolling of Canada as a bilingual society (Parel 1992). World languages maintenance is denounced as a costly luxury for a cash-strapped economy, with the potential to sever the social fabric if left unchecked. Government support for world languages has faltered because of these political worries or economic costs, both real and imagined, despite statutory regulations to "preserve and enhance the use of languages other than English or French..." (Multiculturalism Act, July 1988).

That world language rights are arguably part of Canada's multicultural package is reasonable enough, even if federal support can be described as long on principle but short on practice. Failure to secure world language rights under federal multiculturalism may stem from contradictions within the diversity agenda rather than from negligence or conspiracy. Paradoxes that underlie the logic behind Canada's language policies need to be examined in light of broader political developments and the politics of society building.

Canada's Language Policy Context

The status of Canada's world languages can only be understood within the context of the federal government's formal language policy. A two-tier system prevails at present, although a third tier may emerge because of First Nations pressure to avert the alarming decline of Canada's 53 different aboriginal languages (Fleras 1987; Hassan 1995).

Tier 1: Official Languages

The first tier consists of Canada's official languages. French and English stand in a privileged position as the official languages of political and public discourse. By virtue of the 1969 Official Languages Act, both French and English are equal in the institutional sense; that is, French and English represent the languages of official communication in domains under federal jurisdiction. All individuals are entitled to federal services in either French or English where significant public demand exists. Federal employees not only have the option to communicate in their preferred official language in the workplace; they also have the right to equitable employment and promotional opportunities regardless of their language of choice (Annual Report 1992). In keeping with Canada's language duality, official language minorities (French-speaking Canadians outside Quebec; English-speaking Canadians in Quebec) are accorded equal protection under the Charter of Rights and Freedoms and the Official Languages Act. Official minority language gains have been less impressive in reality, although francophone minorities across parts of Canada have managed to secure limited control over provincial services and local education boards.

Tier 2: World Languages

The second tier consists of nonofficial world languages (languages other than French, English, and aboriginal). World languages are a formidable presence in Canada. According to the 1996 Census, 59.8 percent of the population indicated English as their mother tongue (language first learned at home during childhood and still understood), 23.5 percent reported French as the first language, and 16.6 percent identified a language other than French or English. Compare these figures with the 1951 Census, which showed English at 59.1 percent, French at 29.0 percent, and other languages at 11.9 percent. The most frequently reported home languages other than French or English were Chinese (736,000), up 42 percent since 1991, followed by Italian, German, and Spanish. Of the 4.7 million who reported a mother tongue other than English or French, 2.4 million lived in Ontario, or about 22 percent of the province's population. One in four people in the Toronto area speak a foreign language at home, followed by Vancouver at 22 percent and Montreal at 12 percent. Over half of all school children in Toronto and Vancouver possess a nonofficial language background. As might be expected, ethnolanguage use and identification are highest among new Canadians, with sharply declining rates for subsequent generations (Kralt and Pendakur 1991). With immigration totals currently at postwar highs, language diversities are likely to further escalate (Samuel 1997).

Much of the current debate about world languages is centred around the theme of survival. Three strategies for world language survival exist in varying degrees across

Canada (see Cummins and Danesi 1990; Cummins 1994). First, there are the bilingually based world language programs. World languages are employed as languages of instruction through their incorporation into the school curriculum. The Prairie provinces have long supported such bilingual programs for transitional or maintenance purposes: Up to 50 percent of the classroom instruction may be conducted in a world language, mainly German or Ukrainian, but also Yiddish and Mandarin in cities such as Edmonton. The second type of program is conducted within the school system but outside the core curriculum. Instruction may be held after class hours, as part of an extended school day, or outside school hours, such as on weekends. For example, Ontario, under its 1977 Heritage Language Program, is obligated by law to implement school-based heritage language programs in response to requests by community groups who can supply a minimum of 25 pupils (Cummins 1994). But instruction is conducted outside the normal school day, even with enrollment figures at nearly 120,000 students in 60 languages across Canada. The third type consists of heritage language programs under the auspices of ethnocultural communities. Ethnocultural communities have long supported such initiatives; however, government funding has materialized only in the past 15 years (Cummins 1994). These largely private initiatives may utilize school resources even if they are only marginally tied to the educational system.

Balancing the Tiers

Promotion of nonofficial languages poses a perennial challenge to a democracy that endorses diversity, that is, how to expand the scope of world languages, without incurring the debilitating costs of such an accommodation or infringing on primacy of official bilingualism. A comprehensive multiculturalism is almost inconceivable without a languages component, since language and culture are closely intertwined (Dore 1993). The symbolic importance of language for indigenous and ethnic minority groups goes beyond political interests or commercial value (Edwards 1985; Fishman 1989). An ethnolanguage is revered as a satisfying means of communication, especially when alternative outlets of expression are unacceptable. A language heritage serves as a highly visible manifestation of a people's aspirations, self-hood, world view, and aesthetics (Laurin 1978). Language not only symbolizes cultural distinctiveness and identity; it also facilitates ethnic boundary maintenance and intragroup solidarity in contexts both changing and diverse (Bourhis et al. 1979; Fleras 1987; Henderson 1993).

But what binds together may also rend asunder unless appropriate safeguards are secured. It is this potential for divisiveness that complicates the relationship of world languages with Canada's linguistic duality. To one side, access to world languages is endorsed as a basic human right (Yalden 1993). Minorities in Canada are entitled as individuals to employ the language of their choice in personal settings, within their own communities, in creative capacities, and for school instruction on occasion. To openly discriminate against world languages would transgress constitutional guarantees for protection and pose a grave risk to our national self-image and international obligations. Yet formal recognition of world languages would be equally disruptive. Consider only the chaos in communication from a linguistic free-for-all. Even more mind-boggling are the punishing economic costs and crippling administrative burdens incurred by a totally nondiscriminatory policy. World language programs have drawn flak for being "socially divisive," "excessively costly," and "educationally retrograde" (Cummins and Danesi 1990). Others condemn world languages as a recipe for disaster that is likely to (a) balkanize the school system, (b) detract from the school curriculum, (c) shortchange minority children in the outside world, (d) foster linguistic and cultural barriers, and (e) deter newcomers from learning English or French and becoming Canadian. With such an array of criticism, who can be surprised by government caution in this area, especially when national surveys underscore public resentment toward language funding (Angus Reid 1991; Berry and Kalin 1993)?

In short, what sounds good in theory may not work in practice. This is particularly true in Canada, where a multiplicity of languages are contesting for social space. The Canadian state is ensnared in a paradox: It must strike a balance between competing forces by reconciling the human rights principle that all languages are equal, with the realization that some languages are manifestly *unequal* when it comes to social utility or public power. Walking this linguistic tightrope has proven challenging, especially for those who believe that multiculturalism without multilingualism is a contradiction in terms (see Yalden 1993).

Sunset For World Languages?

Canada's world languages policy originated in the context of official multiculturism. But language retention policies did not materialize until the creation of the Cultural Enrichment Program in 1977. This program made provisions for a variety of initiatives, including supplementary school assistance, heritage language teaching aids, and teacher training support—all on a shoestring budget. Passage of the Multiculturalism Act in 1988 further boosted the fortunes of world languages. The act established a Heritage Cultures and Languages Division within the federal Department of Multiculturalism, with its focus on identity, the mainstreaming of ethnic artists, and promotion of language and ethnoculture. It also cleared the path for a proposed Canadian Heritage Language Institution in Edmonton, although this institute continues to languish in some Byzantine administrative limbo, despite conferral of royal assent.

Official multiculturalism is shifting from an endorsement of ethnicity. A commitment to antiracism and institutional accommodation has diminished support for world languages initiatives. Direct financing of world languages instruction has given way to funding *in support of* infrastructures for advancing the teaching and learning of these languages. Attention is focused on the need to "support and promote innovative approaches to the learning of heritage languages…to develop expertise and teaching materials for heritage language classes…to research and promote heritage language" (Annual Review 1993:11). Few are convinced of government efforts to justify this move toward "referral" or "facilitator" as nothing more than a shift in responsibilities rather than outright abandonment. The fact that federal spending for world languages has fallen to about $750,000 for 1993–94 does not bode well for the future. Compare this anomaly in expenditure with the current $1.1 million as a base grant for Basketball Canada or the estimated $550 million for implementing official bilingualism. Such narrow sightedness may yet prove the cliché of "penny wise, pound foolish." Rather than a tower of Babel, world languages may play a key role in bridging those channels that separate Canada from untapped global markets.

INTRODUCTION: "SCORPIONS IN A BOTTLE"

Canada is widely regarded as the world's best place to live if judged by a United Nations Quality of Life Ranking that combines tangible measures related to traditional income, in addition to less quantifiable dimensions, such as political freedom, environmental sustain-ability, and racial and gender equality. Yet for all its resources and resourcefulness, Canada stands in danger of splintering along ethnic fault lines. Canada is not alone in this predica-ment: The forces of ethnicity (as well as language, region, and religion) pose a greater threat to the sovereign integrity of states than the danger of external invasion or erosion of na-tional borders by a freewheeling globalization (Simpson 1993). Traditional cross-border wars in the conventional sense of using force to capture coveted territory have been re-placed by ethnic upheavals from within. Ethnic conflicts do not disappear when countries modernize, as sociologist James McKee reminds us in his book, *Sociology and the Race Problem: The Failure of a Perspective* (1993). No matter how much effort is channelled into getting people to think of their commonalities, old loyalties and identities rarely vanish. This is especially true if the aggrieved minority must submit to the rule of society that is per-ceived as nonresponsive to their collective concerns (Farley 1995). The global drive for na-tional affirmation together with the collective touchstones of identity, including race or ethnicity, may pose the definitive challenge to the stability of the new world order (Smith 1996). But existing states seem curiously incapable of engaging with these nationalisms because of structural constraints or constitutional limitations (Simpson 1996).

This enigma in society building is sharply expressed in Canada, where French–English relations (or, more accurately, French- and English-speaking relations) have coexisted un-easily since 1841, when Upper and Lower Canada combined into an incipient nation-state, a situation aptly described by Lord Durham as the equivalent of "two nations warring in the bosom of a single state." Interaction has vacillated from stretches of sullen isolation ("two solitudes") to periods of convulsive social change (the "Quiet Revolution"), with oc-casional flashes of violence in between ("two scorpions in a bottle"). In between are posi-tions of noninteraction and mutual incomprehension, a stance stunningly captured by Alice Simard, mother of Quebec Premier Lucien Bouchard, when conceding: "I've never met an English-speaking Canadian, but I'm sure they're as nice as any other foreigner" (cited in *Report on Business,* January 1996). The fact that the vast majority of Canadians cannot even communicate with each other, given the monolingualism that pervades most of the country, speaks volumes of the challenges in forging a common ground. Points of conflict are varied and numerous, from interminable language rights battles to provincial–federal squabbling, but tend to coalesce around Quebec sovereign aspirations as a "nation" or "peo-ple" within a vastly revamped federalist framework. The Québécois constitute a powerful po-litical community of people who claim some degree of sovereignty ("autonomy") by virtue of a shared history, a collective vision, a set of grievances, and collective goals and whose distinctiveness as a nationality is derived from common ancestry. In contrast with a deep emo-tional attachment to their homeland of last resort, Quebeckers see English-speaking Canada as a remote, even unfriendly place, with its own set of priorities and preoccupations, few of which concern or apply to Quebec (Gagnon 1996; Conlogue 1997). In reaction, English-speak-ing Canadians perceive Quebec as a province of narrow-minded ideologues whose single-minded jingoism erodes the ideals of a plural and democratic society. The clash of these perspectives has intensified pressure for reshaping the political contours of Canadian soci-ety. Their lack of satisfactory resolution has also propelled Canada perilously close to the brink (see also Burgess 1996; Boismenu 1996; Jenson 1996).

The potential for misunderstanding is complicated by the **politics of language.** Debates over bilingualism have infuriated and divided the country as few other issues. Quebeckers dismiss bilingualism as an act of appeasement bereft of any moral legitimacy; by contrast,

English-Canadians bristle at the inconvenience that bilingualism entails. Francophones throughout Canada have depicted English-speaking Canadians as callously insensitive, not only to Quebec's language aspirations, but also to its legitimate interests as cultural homeland of last resort. French language and culture may not be under threat; nevertheless, perceptions of a threat are a powerful determinant in stimulating Québécois **nationalism** (Schmitt 1997). English-speaking Canadians, in turn, have dismissed the Québécois as rabid nationalists, with little or no respect for liberal values and individual rights. Reintroduction of Quebec's language police has reinforced this perception and elicited howls of derisive contempt over the sometimes absurd zeal of these "tongue troopers" (White 1997). Sensitivities are further inflamed when the English-speaking media pounce on minority issues to portray Quebec as harsh and intolerant (Sniderman et al. 1993), in effect contributing to a siege mentality that boxes Quebeckers into a perpetual defensive. Nor has the cause of bridge building been advanced from insinuations by Morley Safer in CBS's *60 Minutes* (8 February 1998) that the "expulsion" of 250,000 anglophones since the introduction of stringent language laws is little more than a genteel "ethnic cleansing."

In short, both sectors are locked into seemingly unflattering images of the other as racist, rigid, and intolerant. Each regards its counterpart as the "problem": English-Canadians tend to support a Trudeauian vision of Canada with a strong central government, multiculturalism, no special status for Quebec, official bilingualism, individual rights, and equality of provinces. This vision has less currency in Quebec, where the commitment lies in strengthening Quebec, enhancing French language, assimilating immigrants, and seeking special arrangements for Quebec within a renewed federalism (McRoberts 1997). Quebec has made some important gains as part of a restructuring within Canada, yet it continues to chafe under federal containment and anglophone insensitivity. The continued political blackmail of Canada for more money, power, and autonomy is perceived as essential for the long-term survival of Quebec (Thorsell 1998), a perception deeply resented by English-speaking Canadians, as Jan Wong (1998:A29) observes:

> Quebeckers don't really want to separate. They just want to keep getting pregnant so they'll receive a bigger welfare cheque from the rest of Canada.... Quebec is like a madman who keeps taking himself hostage. Every year or so he whips out a gun and shouts, Give me all your money or I'll shoot myself!

Many Canadians outside Quebec appear increasingly opposed to fundamental concessions, preferring a status quo federalism of formally equal provinces (McRoberts 1993). Even the distinctiveness of Quebeckers is denied. As Michael Ignatieff writes in his book, *The Warrior's Honour*, Quebeckers are just North Americans who happen to speak French but inflate minor differences for self-serving purposes (see also Yakabuski 1997). Fewer still have any sympathy for or understanding of Quebec's preoccupation with the humiliation of the Conquest. To the extent that Quebec is denounced for approaching Canada as a treasure trove for plunder rather than a community to nourish, the potential for conflict is ever present.

Failure to foster a *rapprochement* between two of the founding nations strikes at the very core of Canada's survival. But moves to establish a partnered working relationship are proceeding at snail-like pace. The shock of the October 1995 referendum (50.6 percent for federalism, including about 95 percent of the "ethnic" vote; 49.4 percent for sovereignty, including about 60 percent of the francophone vote) does not appear to have activated any urgency to cut deals, with the possible exception of the Liberal Government's Plan A for national unity through job creation and social reform, followed by Plan B for negotiated Constitutional settlement (Honderich 1996). Proposals for a "social union" are the latest in a line of initiatives to forge a workable division of power and jurisdiction between federal authorities and Quebec (as well as the other provinces). Solutions become even more improbable when polls elicit conflicting messages: Quebeckers believe that separation is inevitable, while many sovereigntists prefer a renewed deal within Canada. Up to 85 percent of Quebeckers think Canada is a good place to live, yet 54 percent would vote yes in a referendum (*Globe and Mail,* 24 February 1996). In other words, Quebeckers are attached to Canada but their attachment is conditional (Stewart 1997). Similarly, English-speaking Canadians may be positively predisposed to Quebec but not if any constitutional deals are involved.

This chapter examines the political dimensions of Québécois ethnicity by exploring the logic behind the potentially explosive relationship between the French and the English in Canada. This analysis of the politics of ethnicity is framed within the broader context of Canadian federalism on the one side, the process of Canadian society building on another, and Quebec's nation-building moves on yet another. Emphasis is on the patterned interaction that has evolved as the constitutional partners continue to jockey for control over jurisdictions pertaining to collective rights, sovereignty, peoplehood, and nationhood. Particular attention is paid to *how* language strikes at the heart of Québécois ethnicity, followed by *why* language issues have assumed such a profile in driving the agenda, even if concerns over power, wealth, and jurisdiction provide the catalyst for the language wars. Prospects for arriving at a mutually satisfactory solution remain elusive because of radically different visions of Canada and Quebec's place within the constitutional framework. Nowhere are the prescriptions for redefining French–English relations more hotly contested than in the duelling nationalisms that engulf aboriginal peoples and the Québécois in the struggle to determine who controls what in Quebec. The emergent notion of Canada as a **multinational three-nation state** has further complicated the task of constructing a society around compromises, although, paradoxically, this balancing act may cast illumination on the Quebec question.

A note on terminology. The chapter makes repeated references to anglophones and francophones as well as to Québécois and Ottawa. Chapter contents are focused primarily on the relationship of French-speaking Canadians in Quebec (the Québécois or Quebeckers) to the English-speaking Canadians in the rest of Canada and centred in the nation's capital of Ottawa. Within Quebec itself, there are additional solitudes such as Québécois of "old stock," old anglophones and allophones (such as European ethnics), and new visible minorities, including over 400,000 people of colour in Montreal, many of whom are unhappy with their status or benefits and are as removed from Québécois mainstream as the rest of Canada (Siddiqui 1998). Some attention is paid to the 1.6 million French-speaking persons outside of Quebec, including the 500,000 Franco-Ontarians and 300,000 Acadians in New Brunswick who occupy a different legal status than the Québécois. Francophones outside of Quebec face a different set of challenges as an official language minority. While the concerns of the Québécois revolve about power sharing, jurisdiction, and language survival, non-Quebec francophones are more likely to worry about assimilation without adequate guarantees of French-speaking educational or provincial services (Gray 1994). A reluctance by Quebec to endorse the struggles of francophone communities in other provinces attests to divergences of outlook and aspirations.

The term "English-speaking" also requires some clarification. Rather than an ethnic group, this category refers to a rather broad description of those Canadians who reside primarily outside Quebec and rely on English as the primary language of communication. English-language minorities who live in Quebec are often called anglophones. Those anglophones who meet the criteria as stated in Section 23(1a)–(1b) of the Charter qualify as the "official language minority" and are certified to educate their children in English:

> Citizens of Canada whose first language learned and still understood is that of the English or French linguistic minority population of the province in which they reside...have the right to have their children receive primary and secondary school instruction in that language in that province.

Immigrants and refugees in Canada whose first language is neither French nor English are called allophones. Finally, references to the term "Ottawa–Quebec" (or Quebec–Canada) relations are employed as a convenient shorthand to capture the politics of English–French interaction (or, more accurately, French- and English-speaking relations).

THE LANGUAGE OF ETHNICITY/THE POLITICIZATION OF LANGUAGE

Canadians appear to possess a remarkably high threshold for debate on language issues. Passage of the Official Languages Act in 1969 followed by promotion of multiculturalism as government policy in 1971 have contributed to the controversies. The existence of the **two-tier language policy** (official + nonofficial) is no less contentious: French and English constitute the official and equal languages of public communication. Both world languages and the 53 different aboriginal languages comprise the unofficial sector. It is common knowledge that French- and English-speaking relations are driven by language politics. But Canadian language debates are not only confined to the realm of official languages. Diverse language groups such as the Ukrainians in Western Canada have lobbied hard to entrench nonofficial languages ("heritage languages") across the school system, on the assumption that official multiculturalism is inseparable from linguistic diversity. Aboriginal peoples have also taken steps to avert the decline of indigenous tongues, including the establishment of aboriginal language preschools and related measures (Hall 1986; Fleras 1987).

Language conflicts are not restricted to Canada. Language controversies culminating in violence and bloodshed are surprisingly common throughout the world. Efforts to accommodate minority language groups are evident in European countries, for example, Belgium and Switzerland, as well as in African and the South Pacific countries. Developing nations that are anxious to purge themselves of imperialist stigmas have replaced colonialist English with indigenous languages. The institutionalization of Swahili throughout central Africa is a clear example of linguistic engineering in support of nationalist endeavours. Language chauvinism also plays an important role in furthering nationalist ambitions in powerful nation-states such as France. The French are proud of their language and envision it as a sign of intelligence, cultural sophistication, social acceptance, and career advancement. The French Language Academy is under constant pressure to maintain the purity of French by purging it of contaminations from English "junk" culture. Even that bastion of English speakers—the United States—is not immune to language politics. Lobbying by the group U.S. English has entrenched English as the official language in nearly half of the states in the union. The lobby group has also attempted to constitutionally enshrine English as the sole official language of the country.

What is it about language that gives it such appeal in cases of interethnic strife? Any ethnic group that wants to remain distinct must activate certain symbols to express and preserve its uniqueness. Language fits the bill. It is proven as an agent of social and political change with respect to the competition for scarce political and economic resources. Language conflicts have the capacity to sharpen political objectives by raising levels of awareness over majority–minority relations. Debates about language also have the potential to camouflage and conceal when necessary, thus advancing practical interests behind an altruistic banner.

Language and Ethnic Politics

Efforts to restructure ethnicity are increasingly dependent on the powerful role of language (Taylor and Giles 1979; also Kramarae 1984; Shkilnyk 1986). Ethnic movements are rooted in the need to establish positive social identities, and language is often a distinguishing characteristic of such identity and a vehicle for the assertions of identity-related claims. Such a linkage is to be expected, given the intimate relationship between language, identity, and cthnicity (Kennedy 1983; Edwards 1985). The link between language and identity is a powerful one for mobilizing individuals in pursuit of collective interests (Edwards 1985). It is also important for securing the social cohesion of otherwise disparate populations (Bourhis et al. 1979; Ross 1979). A common language allows minority members to become situated in a web of satisfying relationships and meaningful activities (Rubin 1983). The Supreme Court of Canada has stated as much even when overruling Quebec's controversial **Bill 101.** While criticizing provisions in the **French Language Charter,** the Court has endorsed the relevance of language as highly visible manifestations of a people's aspirations, self-hood, cultural distinctiveness, world view, and aesthetics (also Nadkarni 1983; Sutcliffe 1986):

> Language is so intimately related to the form and content of expression that there cannot be true freedom of expression by means of language if one is prohibited from using the language of one's choice. Language is not merely the means or medium of expression; …[it is] a means by which a people may express its cultural identity.

In other words, minority languages serve as a vessel for sustaining ethnic consciousness and interaction (Harries 1983; Hewitt 1986). Leaders will capitalize on threats to minority language as a way of galvanizing an otherwise inchoate group into protest action. Minority languages can compress group aspirations into definable proportions for political expression. The recasting of political concerns into linguistic issues can transform the often abstract demands of minority sectors (for example, "**distinct society**" or "self-government") into something of substance for manipulating the levers of power (Fleras 1987).

Majority languages are often devalued as viable communication in highly politicized contexts (Watson 1983). Rather than neutral vehicles for conveying impartial information, dominant languages are perceived instead as ideological extensions for majority rule and co-optation. Certain racial or class biases are inherent within majority speech habits. These distortions render them inappropriate for nationalist movements (Bones 1986). Minority use of dominant speech patterns is dismissed as disloyal and counterproductive to the movement (Rubin 1983). Those whose language is secure may not appreciate the emotion and passion evinced by minority language aspirations. Many are oblivious to the symbolic and emotive properties associated with minority language use. Since theirs is a universally accepted lingua franca that is rarely threatened or challenged, English-speaking individuals, like fish in water, tend to be blasé about its value and power. English is treated as little more than a routine and tacitly accepted form of communication. Only under threatening conditions (such as that which confronted the anglophone community in Quebec) is English embraced as a symbol of anglo-identity and distinctiveness. In short, language debates are not about the freedom of personal expression, but about the politics of power in societies undergoing social change.

La Langue Française As Resistance

Nowhere are the politics of language more evident than in Quebec, where the Québécois have relied on language legislation to repel English-speaking threats to their existence. Promotion of French is justified for various reasons (Laurin 1978). Language represents a complex and powerful system of communication: It not only reflects the foundation of their cultural existence ("ground under their feet"), but also serves as a repository of past values and historical beliefs. As well as a symbol of identity and nationhood, the French language provides a buffer against central authority intrusion. Political objectives are clearly established through the manipulation of these symbols of protest. With its capacity to inflame passions and to trigger demonstrations of public support, the French language allows Quebec leaders to retain the upper hand in negotiating with federal authorities.

Language issues have become even more important because of cultural changes. French–English differences are widely assumed as self-evident—from the seemingly insignificant (French-Canadians prefer Pepsi over Coke) to the more substantive (the French and English belong to different nations and draw upon different constitutional traditions). Nevertheless, what is shared between English and French in Canada is equally impressive (Yakabuski 1997). Cultural convergence is reflected in mutual endorsement of democratic and liberal values, a commitment to protect human rights and freedoms, and willingness to address a pluralist agenda in a way that accommodates diversity without undermining the centre. Differences are rapidly vanishing because of consumerism and mass technologies. Only language remains a distinct feature to be nurtured and protected. That alone exerts additional pressure for protective measures.

Even more intriguing is the capture of French to advance concerns pertaining to the Quebec economy. The conflict between Quebec and Ottawa is not about language *per se:* Power and control are central issues. The Parti Québécois had proposed to reclaim the economic centre of decision making by way of state enterprises and regulation of nonfrancophone ownership in the financial/commercial centre. The economic rather than ideological intent of Bill 101 was expressed by Guy Rocher, a University of Montreal sociology professor. According to Rocher, the legislation sought to francicize the workplace, thus enhancing the competitive advantage of French-speaking workers and managers. The objective was to francicize the economic structure so that francophones could work in French and have access to senior positions. In redefining an anglo-dominated workplace, the rules of Quebec's economic game underwent change. Such a competitive handicap resulted in a massive flight of English-dominant companies, for example, Sun Life Insurance. A number of anglophones at middle and upper management levels also fled. The subsequent vacuum created by these departures enabled the French middle class to move in. Control of the economy subsequently moved from being predominantly in English hands to being almost exclusively in those of the French.

In short, language plays a dual role in Quebec's politics. Language issues possess a kind of visceral appeal to the Québécois, as they do for many minority groups, including English speakers. That alone makes language an effective symbol for mobilizing the masses in defence of minority interests. But language as a trump card can be overplayed. Primary contests in Quebec are not necessarily about language or ethnicity; they are equally concerned with power and resources to exercise control over jurisdictions that "rightfully" belong to Quebec. Language grievances may be manipulated as leverage against Ottawa. The symbols of language and ethnicity provide an emotionally charged vehicle for politicizing the more practical concerns of the Québécois in a manner both socially acceptable and easily identifiable. Interestingly, Ottawa too has capitalized on the politics of language to co-opt Québécois aspirations and advance "national" interests.

OFFICIAL BILINGUALISM: A FAILED SOCIAL EXPERIMENT?

Canada can be described as a linguistic duality whose national language policies are simultaneously a source of unity and disunity. Problems in communication and accommodation can be expected in a country of two major languages with three-quarters of the population speaking one language, one-quarter the other. The problem is compounded by a linguistic divide: The vast majority of English-speaking Canadians outside of New Brunswick and north-east Ontario cannot speak French; most francophones in Quebec outside of Montreal cannot speak English. Such a communications gap poses a threat to Canada. A series of responses, including official bilingualism, have evolved to address the national unity crisis.

Bilingualism itself comes in different shapes and sizes. Under **individual bilingualism,** each person is expected to become proficient in two or more languages in the country. **Territorial bilingualism** is another option; it reflects a division of language use along geographical lines. For example, Belgium and Switzerland are divided into regions where one of the official languages predominates (Linden 1994). Finally, there is **institutional bilingualism,** with its focus on mainstreaming bilingualism at organizational levels, including the creation of bilingual workplaces and delivery of services.

All three styles of bilingualism are found in Canada. There is an unofficial territorial bilingualism, namely, the division of Canada into two language heartlands—Quebec and the rest of Canada—with a limited number of bilingual districts adjacent to Quebec, such as Ottawa and New Brunswick. Increasing numbers are attracted to this type of bilingualism in light of demographic realities that show a rapid assimilation of francophones outside of Quebec in conjunction with the abandonment of Montreal by Quebec's anglophones. Individual bilingualism also exists in Canada; nearly 17 percent of the total population in the 1996 Census possessed fluency in both languages, up from 13 percent in 1971, including 38 percent of the residents in Quebec, 33 percent in New Brunswick, and 12 percent in Ontario. Officially, however, Canada endorses an institutional bilingualism. It acknowledges the equal and official status of French and English as languages of communication in federal institutions across the country. How, then, do we assess official bilingualism as an initiative for national unity through minority language protection?

Federal Bilingualism: Institutional-Style

Canada's experiment with federal bilingualism began in the 1960s. Efforts to strengthen French language rights in exchange for social peace culminated in a typical Canadian compromise: the right of federal public servants in 1966 to conduct business in either French or English. Passage of the **Official Languages Act** in 1969 formalized linguistic duality as a fundamental characteristic of Canadian society. Implicit in this unity formula was a vision of Canada that allowed speakers of either language to feel at home in all parts of the country (Goldbloom 1994; Commissioner of Official Languages 1995). The Official Languages Act confirmed the right of Canadians to work in French or English in federal organizations, to receive federal services in either language, and to guarantee official language minority rights across Canada. No less implicit were political goals; that is, passage of the act sought to "cool out" troublesome Québécois dissidents without any fundamental transfer of power or independence for Quebec.

Provisions of the act acknowledged the presence and legitimacy of both French and English as official and equal languages throughout Canada. The courts and Parliament, in addition to the central offices of all federal government institutions, were to be bilingual. The rights of official-language minorities would protect French-speaking Canadians in English Canada and English-speaking Canadians in Quebec. The act stipulated that official language minorities were entitled to federal services in either French or English, in areas where numbers warranted or demand was significant. It also confirmed the right of federal employees to work in the official language of their choice. Equal opportunities for French and English speakers in the public service were guaranteed as well. Bilingualism was expressed in federal documents, signs in national parks, parliamentary proceedings, court cases, and federally chartered passenger vehicles from Air Canada planes to shuttle buses at Point Pelee National Park. Recent efforts to update the Official Languages Act (1988) to conform with the 1982 Charter's equality provisions have reaffirmed Ottawa's commitment to bilingualism by strengthening official language minority control over education and school boards (parents who speak one of the official languages have a right to educate children in the preferred language) where they constitute viable communities.

Bilingualism in Practice

Nearly thirty years of the Official Languages Act has proven inconclusive as a tool for national unity. Both political and public response to national unity is polarized, involving a mixture of support, rejection, expediency, and indifference. Critics tend to exaggerate the magnitude and costs of official bilingualism; supporters prefer to exaggerate its benefits. Levels of support for bilingualism vary with the phrasing of questions on national surveys. A slight majority of Canadians appear to support Canada's language duality, the principle of bilingualism, and the provision of bilingual government services as a blueprint for intergroup relations—at least when issues are couched in terms of responsiveness and accommodation rather than government intervention (Commissioner of Official Languages 1995). Popular too is the extension of French language social services into areas of high francophone concentration. As well, highly motivated parents have enrolled their children in language immersion programs across Canada. In such a climate of acceptance and rejection (or resignation), it is conceivable that myths and half-truths have appeared with the potential to blunt the potential of bilingualism for society building, as the following FYI points out.

FYI | **Bilingualism: Hits and Misses**

1. Corn flakes boxes have been bilingual since 1907. So much for the perception that French is "being crammed down our throat because of current government policy."

2. A person cannot receive English or French services on demand anywhere in Canada. Most bilingual and official language minority services are offered only where numbers warrant or a significant demand exists. In other words, one is not likely to receive bilingual postal services in tiny Tobermory, Ontario, except perhaps using a 1-800 telephone number.

3. Federal service in Quebec is available in English in 98.8 percent of the cases, according to the Commissioner of Official Languages, but only 72 percent of the time for French federal service for francophones in the other provinces (Stewart 1998).

4. Official bilingualism does not mean that everyone has to be fluent in French and English. It means that *no one* except civil servants in certain federal postings needs to be bilingual for information or services.

5. The provision of information and services in two languages applies only to the federal sector in each province including Quebec. Provincial services are exempt from being bilingual because of a constitutional division of jurisdiction.

6. The assimilation of francophones and the decline of French spoken in the home outside of Quebec have declined to the point where the percentage of people speaking French at home now stands at 0.5 percent in British Columbia, 0.6 percent in Saskatchewan, and 0.7 percent in Alberta, despite official minority language guarantees.

7. Why don't we all speak English? Well, nearly 4 million francophones speak no English. If we exclude the island of Montreal, 83 percent of Quebeckers do not speak English. Ninety percent of English-speaking Canadians do not speak French. Such a staggering solitude creates a strong need for bridging devices.

8. Census figures in 1996 indicate that 17 percent of Canadians identify themselves as bilingual. The vast majority of bilingual speakers are inhabitants of Quebec and francophones outside of Quebec, in effect putting the onus of bilingualism squarely on the shoulders of those it was supposed to help (Auger 1997).

9. Official bilingualism and protection of official language minorities do not come without cost. In 1996, federal expenditures amounted to $549 million for bilingual service delivery and federal transfers to provincial education. Critics argue that this figure ignores the cost of public servant training and private industry compliance for labelling.

10. In 1993, according to a report from the Commissioner of Official Languages, 30 percent of federal civil service jobs, or 64,086 jobs, had been designated as bilingual in order to accommodate significant demand for two-language services. About 50 percent of the bilingual placements were in Quebec; by contrast, only 3 percent of the federal civil service jobs in Western Canada were posted as bilingual.

Federal and provincial authorities have wavered in their endorsement of official bilingualism. Generally speaking, the reality of bilingualism is restricted to (a) federal institutions, (b) communities with a high proportion of French-speaking residents such as Eastern and Northern Ontario, (c) the delivery of some essential provincial services, and (d) select school children in larger urban centres. Only the province of New Brunswick is officially bilingual. Even here, hostilities arise between French-speaking Acadians, who want to expand French language services, and the English-speaking majority, who prefer the status quo. The Northwest Territories has also acknowledged French and English as official languages; official status has also been extended to six aboriginal languages for a total of eight official languages. Nunavut will have three official languages—English, French and Inuktitut.

Another six provinces are nominally unilingual. Resistance to official bilingualism is couched in economic terms ("too costly"), political terms ("too divisive"), cultural terms ("too irrelevant"), and social terms ("too undemocratic"). English remains the *de facto* language of communication in the delivery of service, although French language concessions have been introduced for a variety of reasons. Ontario is a good example of a province that has moved toward limited French language services. Its French Language Services Act (Bill 8) in 1986 enshrined the delivery of French language services when warranted by numbers (namely, where the French-speaking population reaches a total of 5,000, or represents 10 percent of the population). Despite this concession, Ontario refuses to constitutionally guarantee bilingual rights across the province. Other provinces, including Nova Scotia and British Columbia, have barely implemented minimal concessions to official minority language education, despite constitutional guarantees to that effect (Goldbloom 1994). Elsewhere, Franco-Manitobans have experienced difficulty in having their constitutionally entrenched rights recognized.

Three provinces are now officially unilingual in opposition to the spirit of the Official Languages Act. Alberta and Saskatchewan have enacted legislation making English the sole provincial language. This decree ensures the primacy of English for business, commerce, administration, and provincial court activities. In fairness, there exists limited but inconsistent access to French language services. It might be noted that ethnically powerful groups such as the Ukrainians have been successful in incorporating their language into the school curriculum in certain regions throughout Western Canada. The third unilingual province is Quebec. Quebec has endorsed official unilingualism since passage of the French Language Charter (Bill 101) in 1977. French is the only language of communication, although Quebec's 667,000 anglophones, almost 9.7 percent of the population, benefit from guaranteed English language services in health and education. By all accounts, Quebec's French-only unilingual initiatives have proven a success. According to Professor John Richards, an economist from Simon Fraser University in a paper to the CD Howe Institute, nearly 100 percent of all Quebeckers who learn French as infants speak it at home as adults. Yet Quebec's unilingual language laws appear to contravene constitutional and statutory guarantees for official language minorities. Section 23 of the Charter stipulates that the official language minority has the right to instruction in their mother tongue, the right to autonomous school facilities, and the right to the management and control of these schools. How does this apparent contravention stand up to scrutiny? The next Case Study will examine the slippery slope of language politics.

CASE STUDY 7-2	French Language Charter: Bête Noire or Sacred Cow?

Many of the language issues that confront Canadians are based on efforts to reconcile conflicting rights as well as competing realities. Continued discussion and disagreement over Bill 101 constitutes one example. Passage of Bill 101 completed the initiatives of Bill 22, which transformed French into the preferred language of the province for work, education, commerce, and service delivery.

Bill 101 went one step further and prohibited the use of English in public. This French Language Charter asserted French to be the sole official language on the grounds that Quebec had as much right to be French as Ontario did to be English. The act was prompted in part by fears over language loss due to declining francophone birth rates in Quebec and allophone preference to send children to English-speaking schools. English would be permitted in certain constitutionally designed areas such as education and health (and federal services would continue to be bilingual). But for all intents and purposes, English was restricted to the personal and private, thus robbing it of its usefulness as a language of public power (Daost-Blais 1983).

Equally controversial was passage of **Bill 178** in 1988. In 1985, Robert Bourassa regained power on a platform to promote the French face of Quebec from within a framework of bilingual federalism. The Liberals pledged to revoke the French commercial signs provisions of Bill 101 and institute bilingual storefront signs. Both Quebec's Superior Court and the Supreme Court of Canada had acknowledged Quebec's right (by way of Bill 101) to take necessary steps in promoting French as the working language of the majority in that province. But banning the use of English on storefronts was ruled by both as unconstitutional and in violation of Canadian human rights. In other words, although the Quebec government could promote the prominence of French on commercial signs, it could not expressly prohibit the use of other languages such as English without infringing on official language minority rights. Bourassa responded by invoking the notwithstanding clause within the Constitution to override both the Canadian and Quebec Charters of Rights and Freedoms for five years. Under Bill 178, French-only signs were permitted outside an establishment; bilingual signs were allowed inside, provided the presence of French prevailed. Few were satisfied by Bourassa's *inside–outside* compromise for reconciling the demands of Quebec nationalists and anglophone federalists. Nationalists scorned any concession to the hated *anglais* as appeasement. Anglophones by contrast resented the primacy of Quebec's collective rights over individual language rights. To be sure, protective measures for the survival of French could be justified, but surely not by tram-

pling on the constitutional rights of official language minorities.

In Defence of Collective Language Rights

How justified were the Québécois in passing a law that violated both the spirit of official bilingualism and the individual equality provisions of the Canadian Charter of Rights and Freedoms? Does suppression of English language rights by the Quebec legislation constitute a justifiable limit on individual rights in a free and democratic society? Responses to these questions seem to begin with "it depends." Right or wrong depends on whose perspective is taken into account. As Victor Goldbloom, Commissioner of Official Languages, notes, Quebec's sense of collective destiny, including fears of being swallowed up by an English-speaking continent, continue to clash with the rest of Canada and its strong attachment to individual rights and freedoms. As a result, even if all Canadians were bilingual, they would still talk past each other by using the same words but speaking a different language (from Campbell 1997). From an anglophone perspective, Bill 101 is a serious infringement on the constitutional rights of individuals and official language minority rights. Anglophones perceive francophones as a bullying majority in the province who prop up their linguistic and cultural insecurities by picking on minority individual rights. No democratic government has the right to prohibit the use of another language in public, even if certain concessions may be possible under limited circumstances. From Quebec's point of view, the promotion of **collective rights** as implicit within Bills 101 and 178 is justified. Proponents have stoutly defended Bill 101 as the minimum necessary to neutralize the impact and assimilative pressures in a continental sea of English. Moreover, because Quebec is not a province *comme les autres,* neither English-speaking authorities nor the Charter of Rights has any right to interfere in determining the fate of North America's only French-speaking jurisdiction (Gagnon 1993).

Several lines of argument are employed in defence of collective language rights. First, the Québécois define anglophones as part of a huge English majority in Canada and the United States scarcely in need of protection, despite their minority status in Quebec. Infringement of anglophone rights to free speech, though regrettable, does not threaten the survival of English as a language. By contrast, the 8 million Québécois see themselves as imperilled by a continental tide of 267 million North Americans with designs (both conscious and by consequence) to remove the French face of Quebec. The precarious status of French in the homeland of last resort demands special measures to promote Quebec's collective rights, even if these should infringe on anglophone individual rights. As far as francophones are concerned, the prohibition of English on Quebec storefront signs constitutes a reasonable restriction for the preservation of its French character. Even anglophones agree that special language policies are permissible. But these constraints must be designed in a way that bolsters French without penalizing English.

Second, with passage of Bill 101, Quebec is only doing what other provinces have historically done, which is to deny the right for francophones outside of Quebec to protect their language. If Quebec is restricting the language rights of anglophones, its actions are no worse than those of other provinces who routinely infringe on minority language rights. Even then, Quebec's anglophones already possess the best constitutional protection of official minority rights in Canada—unlike the French in other parts of Canada, where services depend on provincial political whims or numerical calculations. With nearly 500,000 franco-Ontarians in the province, Ontario refuses to guarantee access to French-speaking schools or the delivery of social services except in designated areas where numerically warranted to justify the expense. By contrast, the anglophone minority in Quebec is guaranteed access to these services by way of law that cannot be revoked by government decree.

Third, those who regard Bill 101 (and Bill 178) as a blatant violation of the Charter's equality provisions have had to rethink the application of abstract individual rights in contexts of inequality. For the Québécois, the protection of its French culture and language is prior to individual rights. Without this collective guarantee there is no context for the expression of individual rights. Evidence indicates that members of dominant groups can afford the luxury of promoting individual rights. That luxury is not necessarily a viable option for minorities where a threatened cultural existence may require collective defence. The promotion of collective over individual rights is thus justified under certain circumstances. Both political elites and High Court officials have defended the collective right of francophones to protect their language because of their status as a cultural enclave in North American society. This override of collective rights is permitted as long as the concession is reasonable, set out in law, and demonstrably justified in a free and democratic society.

The Politics of Compromise

In late 1993, Quebec passed Bill 86 following the expiry of the notwithstanding exemption for Bill 178. Bill 86 watered down some of the controversial provisions of Bill 178 by allowing languages other than French on commercial signs—as long as the French was dominant (Picard 1994; Francis 1996). According to this compromise, French had to be twice as large as English on commercial signs; alternatively, there had to be twice as many French signs. Outstanding charges against merchants who violated the French-only commercial sign law were dropped as a gesture of good faith. The bill also abolished the so-called language police, "Commission de Protection de la Langue Française." These compromises were rooted in pragmatism rather than ideology, according to Quebec's Language Minister, Claude Ryan. The "inside–outside" compromise may not have provoked the public outrage of its predecessors. But clashes are anticipated following reinstatement of the language police in 1997 to placate Quebec's "language hawks" (Ha 1997) for noncompliance with commercial sign laws. An underlying message can be discerned from these language politics: Quebeckers may be a majority that exerts power and control in their province; outside this jurisdiction, however, they are a linguistic minority, and any concession to anglophones must be avoided on the assumption that if you give the anglais an inch, they take a mile (Ha 1997). With the language hawks nipping at their heels, Quebec's political leaders simply cannot afford to look "soft" on the language question.

Putting It in Perspective

Twenty years of what some regard as one of the most pivotal—and controversial—pieces of legislation in Canada continue to evoke strong feelings (Ha 1997). Lauded by some, but reviled by others, passage of the bill on 26 August 1977 remains a lightning rod for English resentment, yet a beacon of pride for French speakers. Benoit Aubin (1997:D-3) captures a sense of the ambivalence when he writes:

> Bill 101 has represented the best and the worst.... It has been called, variously,

the beginning of a new era, a vile instance of state driven discrimination, and the most ambitious piece of social engineering ever attempted in Canada. It has given rise to petty and mean spirited abuse; language cops pouring over business cards or labels on kosher products to see if they contained the prescribed proportion of French words. It has led to ridiculous extremes, as can happen when controversial laws fall into the hands of lawyers.

Debates remain over whether to tighten, to ease, or to scrap Bill 101. All agree that the bill has proven an instrument of cultural affirmation and social change. With the stroke of a pen, businesses had to operate and offer services in French, immigrant children had to go to French schools, and English disappeared on public and commercial signs. Today, francophones are in charge of the province's economy, French is common in the workplace and the language of communications within companies, and French-speaking residents do not earn less than English-speaking counterparts (Fournier 1994; Synnott 1996). In short, Bill 101 has modified the cultural and political landscape of Quebec and Canada in ways that went far beyond what its proponents envisaged. And perhaps the greatest irony of all, by allaying the linguistic and cultural insecurities of many Quebeckers, Bill 101 may have inadvertently saved Canada by cutting the main fuel line of discontent to the separatist engine (Aubin 1997).

Official Bilingualism: Success As Failure

Has thirty years of official bilingualism been a success or failure? Has it contributed to Canadian unity by keeping Quebec in Canada, or will it provide the catalyst for further political turmoil? Are the costs justified in light of the paltry returns, with estimates ranging from $549 million in 1996 to $2 billion annually if hidden costs are factored in? Or should its worth be measured in terms of fostering a new national identity and improved Canadian awareness of French–English relations?

Answers to questions about success or failures will depend on how these terms are defined, by whom, on what basis, and what for. Responses will vary with the criteria employed, including location (British Columbia versus Ontario versus Quebec), age, socioeconomic status, gender, and ethnicity. A broad spectrum of opinion is evident: To one side, Max Yalden, a former Commissioner of Official Languages, has described the Official Languages Act as one of the most innovative and important social revolutions ever brought about peacefully in a democratic society (cited in Campbell 1997). To the other, such as described by Scott Reid in his 1993 book, *Lament for a Nation,* bilingualism is chided for its failure to bring Canadians closer together. In between are the critics who pounce on official bilingualism for not making Canadians more bilingual, in contrast with Quebec's success in advancing French in the province by way of admittedly controversial legislation (Auger 1997). The number crunchers are equally outspoken. Some point to the 63,000 public servants who have taken bilingual courses as a sign of success, in addition to the 31 percent of federal civil service jobs that are declared bilingual. Others applaud the expansion of bilingualism across Canada, but are concerned that the costs may not justify the results. Despite massive annual outlays, the number of bilingual speakers in Canada outside of Quebec has remained relatively constant: 7 percent in 1971 and 10 percent in 1991. The figures in Ontario show an increase from 9.3 percent in 1971 to 11.6 percent in 1996.

How does official bilingualism contribute to or detract from Canadian society building? Kenneth McRoberts (1997) suggests official bilingualism originated in large part to counter the surge of nationalism in Quebec. It arose to restore national unity by offering Quebec the promise of participation and opportunity throughout all of Canada. As a "society-saving" strategy, this national language policy responded to Quebec's discontent and threat of separation by depoliticizing language through its institutionalization at federal levels. Official bilingualism addressed the national unity question, not by making Quebec more distinctive or power sharing, but by making the rest of Canada more like Quebec. In the words of William Thorsell, editor in chief of the *Globe and Mail*, 30 March 1991:

> In essence, Ottawa tried to dilute Quebec nationalism by dispersing it across Canada, most obviously in the form of official bilingualism. The strategy was basically this: Ottawa would deny Quebecers additional powers in their own province in exchange for additional rights in Ottawa and all the other provinces.

The intent was purely political: Official bilingualism sought to advance national unity by the simple expedient of making Quebec francophones feel more at home across Canada. Any wholesale power sharing or promotion of collective rights was not on the table. But this Trudeau-inspired national unity strategy reflected a misreading of Canada (at least according to the elite consensus and its expression in the Royal Commission on Biculturalism and Bilingualism). It also underestimated the scope and intensity of Quebec's ethnic nationalism. Measures such as official bilingualism were predicated on the assumption of denying to francophones their historically distinct national collectivity. In its place, Quebeckers would adopt a reading of Canada that included multiculturalism, individual rights, and the equality of all provinces. But this national unity strategy failed to dampen Quebec's nationalism. If anything, Kenneth McRoberts (1997) notes, it has solidified Quebec's resolve to see itself as a people and a nation. By contrast, official bilingualism (in conjunction with multiculturalism and the Charter of Rights) has had a powerful effect in transforming how English-speaking Canadians think of Canada in terms of national identity.

There is much to commend in this view of official bilingualism as a conflict management device to diffuse Canada's national unity crisis. However effective in keeping Canada together during the 1970s and 1980s, recent events and polls indicate that federal bilingualism is largely irrelevant as a response to Québécois assertiveness. Efforts to integrate Quebec into the national political community by way of language policies rather than power sharing appear to be self-destructing. This would suggest that federal bilingualism is a necessary but insufficient component of a national unity strategy and must be supplemented by arrangements that ensure Québécois mastery of their house.

CLASHING VISIONS: PROVINCE OR PEOPLE?

Language wars have long rattled the foundations of Canadian society The genesis of language conflicts can be gleaned from a brief history of Quebec in its evolution as a French-speaking nation within Canada. From 1841 onward, when Upper (Ontario) and Lower (Quebec) Canada were united, French–English relations have drifted toward disagreement and open hostility (Rioux 1973). The seemingly opposed forces of federalism and nationalism have coexisted uneasily in response to divergent visions of Quebec's place in Canadian society. The forces of modernization and economic growth have exerted equally ambiguous effects (Whitaker 1993). The cumulative impact of these pressures has consolidated Quebec's commitment to construct cultural and political space for themselves within Canadian federalism. It has also raised questions of how two people can live together with their differences in a common civic culture.

Quebec is historically a part of Canada's federalist system. The Constitution Act (formerly known as the BNA Act) of 1867 introduced a federal system as yet another compromise in balancing the demands of those who wanted a single unitary system as bulwark against American might and those who preferred a decentralized arrangement that acknowledged the fundamental duality of two peoples. The political compromise established a centralized system; it also incorporated Quebec's linguistic, legal, and social distinctions into the constitutional fabric, in effect confirming Quebec's special place in Confederation without undue interference from Ottawa, except in cases involving national concerns (Burgess 1996). But federalism as a system of political compromise between Quebec and Ottawa invites diverse interpretations of Canada. Is Canada properly envisaged as a "**contract**" between federal authorities and the provinces? Or is it better seen as a "**compact**" between the French and English? A third vision— Canada as a "three-nation" state—is slowly gaining credibility, but not without resistance, especially when the interests of different nationalisms intersect. The coexistence of these competing "constitutionalisms" generates the dynamic underlying French–English relations. They also help to explain why the two solitudes continue to talk past each other.

Canada As Contract

According to the first interpretation, Canada constitutes a federalist system of ten equal provinces under a central authority in Ottawa. A *contract* exists between the provinces (of which Quebec is one) and the federal government. The provinces (including Quebec) as well as the federal system are sovereign within their own jurisdiction as set out in the Constitution; neither can usurp the authority or powers of the other. The Constitution Act of 1867 specified the limits and scope of provincial versus federal powers. Canadian history can be interpreted as a struggle between provinces and federalist forces over who has control over what jurisdictions, with the balance of power in recent years tilting toward the provinces.

Two variations of the contract thesis exist. First, provinces are equal to each other (including Quebec), but subordinate in status and power *vis-à-vis* central governing structures. Conferral of federal priority is justified because of its responsibility for advancing Canada's national interests both at home (comprehensive social programs) and abroad through diplomatic or military initiatives. Second, federalism is defined as a partnership of relatively autonomous provinces who freely have entered into accord with the federal government. Under the terms of the agreement, Ottawa has assumed those duties and responsibilities that the provinces were unable—or unwilling—to carry out. As a result of this freely agreed-upon division of power, all 11 partners are equal in status, with a corresponding division of jurisdiction as outlined by constitutional decree. Demands for greater decentralization with attendant powers and levels of autonomy are consistent with this perspective. Quebec is perceived as equivalent to the other provinces in legal status; nevertheless, some concessions may be tolerated for Quebec to pursue its language and culture objectives, even if these should compromise fundamental Charter rights (Chodak 1994).

Canada As Compact

A second vision interprets Canada as a *compact* between English-speaking and French-speaking Canadians. This vision is strongly endorsed by the Québécois, who reject definitions of themselves as ethnic minorities or as mainstream Canadians who happen to speak French or live in Quebec. Even the notion of Quebec as a province in the conventional sense is dismissed. Proposed instead is a vision of Quebec as a people or a "distinct society" with inherent rights to nationhood by virtue of popular sovereignty. Charles Taylor captures the essence of this ethos:

> ...Quebec is not a province like the others. As a jurisdiction at the heart of the French zone in convergence, it has responsibilities and challenges unlike those of other provinces.... This is not to say that each and every province is not also different from others in its own way. But only Quebec is different in this way: that it sustains a society converging on French within a continent in which English massively predominates (cited in Chambers 1996).

According to the compact thesis, Canada is not a union of one central authority with ten equal provinces, of which Quebec is but one province. Rather, Canada represents a compact, or "covenant," between the French (Quebec) and the English (Ottawa). This dualism is rooted in constitutional law and long-standing political agreement, from the BNA Act onward. Quebec entered into Confederation with assurances that it would retain its status as a nation and entitlements as a Charter member. To be sure, the notion of Canada as a "covenant" between two founding nations dominated political discourse into the late 1960s. But the concept of Canada as an equal partnership of "two" founding nations was abandoned by Trudeau, who favoured a constitutionalism based on the principles of a centralized Canada, strict equality among provinces, the primacy of individual rights, and a national unity strategy around a multiculturalism within a bilingual framework (McRoberts 1997; Seguin 1998).

A compact perspective endorses a vision of Quebec as a "nation within" the Canadian state whose self-governing powers are equivalent to those of English Ottawa. Quebeckers see themselves as a "people" with a shared language, culture, and homeland rather than another province with equal rights or an ethnic group whose differences are charming but irrelevant. They constitute a "nation" not only deserving of recognition of its differences, but also entitled to those powers for securing their distinctiveness against outside intrusion (McRoberts 1996). But even this concept of nation is changing. Moves to affirm themselves as "maîtres chez nous" and to redress the political and economic imbalances have resulted in shifts to democratize their political, social, and educational institutions during the 1960s. Quebec has repositioned itself from a defensive inward-looking community to an active and open society (Salée and Coleman 1997). Its emergent nationalism is increasingly liberal and open, and couched in universalistic value-neutral terms. Admittedly, Quebec's relationship with "ethnic others" is complicated by the challenges of modernizing without discarding tradition, of becoming more cosmopolitan without dismantling a French-dominated framework for public affairs, and of being open to the other without discrediting its uniqueness (Nelson and Fleras 1998). As a result, developments in Quebec vacillate between democratic impulses for inclusiveness and enlarged citizenship to one side and concerns over losing its distinctiveness, historically determined identity, and political relevance to the other. This ambiguity is fundamental to Quebec's perception of itself, and those who misread this ambivalence run the risk of misunderstanding Québécois nationalism.

But the distinction between civic nationalism (good) and ethnic nationalism (bad) is not so simple (Neilson 1996). Canada's much-touted civic nationalism is a post-1970s emergence and contains ethnic dimensions related to the idea of British nationality and Canada as a White Dominion (McRoberts 1997). Moreover, Quebec's nationalism is much more civic oriented than many give credit. Quebec finds itself in a quandary since its nationalism touches on two dimensions: an ethnic dimension, reflecting the original white French Québécois who comprise 82 percent of the population, and a civic dimension, which is anchored in progressive anti-imperialist notions (Swift 1996). To be sure, Quebec's national identity was inextricably ethnic prior to 1960. Since then, however, the shift toward a more territorial ("civic") nationalism has embraced Quebec as the homeland of a society French in language and culture but inclusive of all Quebeckers, new and old (McRoberts 1997). Most francophones appear committed to the creation of a modern, open, and technologically advanced society, but must struggle with the demands of balancing modernity with distinctiveness as a French-speaking jurisdiction (Whitaker 1996). Their nationalism is rooted in a desire to exist collectively and to have this collective existence recognized at political levels (Balthazar 1993). This distinctiveness is driven by identity politics, not in the abstract sense of association with territory or government jurisdiction, but in terms of a "people" with a particular historical experience, shared sense of collective grievance, a will to survive, and aspiration toward collective historical destiny (Whitaker 1996). To the extent this transition from ethnic to civic is proving more awkward than anticipated, it remains to be seen if Quebec can establish a new kind of identity from a synthesis of ethnic and civic ("territorial") nationalism. Inasmuch as the interplay of intersecting nationalisms will profoundly reconfigure the contours of Canadian society in general, and those of Quebec in particular, the society-building project in each of these jurisdictions is far from completed.

Interpreting French-English relations as a compact casts light on the logic behind Quebec's aspirations, concerns, and political moves. It also points to potential sources of conflict. Quebeckers perceive the English as politically and economically powerful agents for assimilation whose agenda reflects a commitment to a unitary federal state by centralizing its powers at the expense of other provinces. Quebec likes to see itself as a francophone island surrounded by an anglophone sea and in constant danger of being swamped by an assimilationist tide, either through intent or by consequence. Not surprisingly, Quebec's leaders have sought to establish some distance between Ottawa and Quebec. They have looked for ways to transfer power and resources from Ottawa for fulfillment of Quebec's ambitions. Public support has been galvanized to legitimate their nationalist policies as well as to strengthen Quebec's hand in dealing with Ottawa. Québécois leaders have capitalized on the public's inclination to equate language issues with the status of French–English relations. Widespread public support for language support is thus manipulated as leverage for extracting various concessions from the federal government.

Canada As a Three-Nation State

A new and more inclusive vision of Canada is slowly gaining ground. Canada is neither a contract between a centre and the provinces nor an exclusive compact between Ottawa and the French. Rather, Canada is properly seen as a three-nation state, comprising French, English, and aboriginal peoples, each of which is sovereign in its own right yet sharing in the sovereignty of Canada as a whole by virtue of distinct but overlapping jurisdictions pertaining to land, political voice, and identity (Kaplan 1993; Webber 1994; Royal Commission on Aboriginal Affairs 1996). In that Canada contains distinct collectivities that see themselves as territorially grounded "nations" and as culturally specific "peoples," Kenneth McRoberts proffers, Canada may well be described as a "multinational" society (Seguin 1998). Inclusion of aboriginal people as a founding people and a foundational nation may complicate an already complex balancing act involving the two Charter members. But the intersecting of sovereignties encompassed by these competing nationalisms will yield new possibilities and alliances, as indicated below (Whitaker 1997).

INSIGHT 7–1 | **Duelling Nationalisms/Intersecting Sovereignties**

In terms of legitimacy, the aboriginal peoples, the aboriginal nations on this territory, are quite ahead of the francophones in Quebec, the anglophones of Quebec, and all the Europeans and other nationalities on this territory.

Daniel Turp, Legal Advisor,
Bloc Québécois

The Cree people are neither cattle nor property, to be transferred from sovereignty to sovereignty or from master to master. We do not seek to prevent the Québécois from achieving their legitimate goals. But we will not permit them to do so on Cree territory and at the expense of our fundamental rights, including our right to self-determination.

Mathew Coon Come, Chief,
James Bay Cree Nation,
quoted in *This Magazine*, June 1994

If Quebec can separate, so can the Indians.

Kahn-Tineta Horn, quoted in
Windspeaker, 6 November 1994

Ethnic nationalisms threaten the territorial integrity of every society. Central authorities fear the balkanizing effect of ethnic nationalisms, with their capacity to fractionalize the country like pieces of a jigsaw puzzle. From the vantage point of ethnic nationalisms, however, a centralized system that seeks to control by standardizing differences is equally divisive. Quebeckers may be politically divided, but many are unhappy with the current federalist arrangement that collapses them into one of ten relatively equal provinces rather than a founding nation. Federalist and nationalist forces may agree on Quebec as a distinct society, with a unique and distinctive assemblage of cultural and linguistic characteristics; disagreements tend to reflect different means— flexible federalism or secession—for preservation of Quebec as a French-speaking homeland.

Quebec is not alone in pushing for distinct society status. The indigenous occupants of Quebec have also staked a claim for ownership. The seeds of this discontent were planted with the Oka Crisis and energetic opposition to Hydro Quebec's megaprojects. Quebeckers were obligated to discard folkloric images of the first inhabitants as museum pieces for anthropological study and confront, instead, questions about autonomous governments by those claiming to be legitimate owners of the land and resources (Leger 1994). The furor over Quebec's future has escalated further following the election of the Parti Québécois in 1994, with its promise of a future referendum to determine the relational status of the Québécois. At the core of this debate are the politics of recognition (Salée 1995). Peoples are increasingly in the vanguard for acknowledgment and respect of their particular identities, together with inclusion of these differences on their *own* terms rather than those dictated by others. What happens when competing nationalisms come into conflict over who is more sovereign than the other?

Contested Claims

The peoples that comprise the 60,000 strong First Nations in Quebec (including the Cree, Inuit, Mohawk, Huron, and Algonquin) are adamant that Quebec does *not* have a legal claim to their lands. They see themselves as no less sovereign as nations, with as much right to remain in Canada as Quebec has a right to secede. According to indigenous leaders, up to 80 percent of Quebec is under aboriginal control: Certain lands have never been ceded while others have yet to be resolved through treaty or aboriginal rights claims. For that reason alone Quebec's aboriginal

peoples cannot afford to abandon the financial security of remaining in Canada. The 1996 Cree document, Sovereign Injustice, reinforced their refusal to incorporate themselves unwillingly into an independent Quebec, arguing that their fiduciary relationship with the Crown through the federal government cannot be extinguished or unilaterally transferred from Ottawa to Quebec.

The Quebec government disagrees. Quebec's boundaries are inviolate, as far as the Québécois are concerned, and its territoriality is sovereign and beyond negotiation or dismemberment. Quebec's territorial integrity is not on the agenda, even with recent provincial initiatives to establish a structure of self-government that would send aboriginal representatives to Quebec's legislature, provide taxation powers to aboriginal communities, and entail revenue-sharing schemes in new projects as part of a new partnership (Seguin 1998). As far as Quebec's leaders are concerned, aboriginal rights to Quebec's land no longer exist; instead they were extinguished when the Canadian state transferred Ungava to provincial jurisdiction at the turn of the century. The James Bay Agreement in 1975 also signed away aboriginal "interests" (although a federal act in 1977 also said that the Cree and the Inuit would retain the "benefits and rights of all other [Canadian] citizens." A hardening of their position is understandable. On the one hand, Quebec believes its treatment of aboriginal peoples is second to none, given the government's willingness to recognize aboriginal self-government (within the framework of Quebec society), ownership of land and resources, and protection of language and culture (Gourdeau 1993). On the other, Quebec can hardly afford to capitulate to aboriginal peoples (and indirectly Ottawa) for fear of losing "face" in addition to enormous reserves of surface and subsurface resources, both of which are indispensable for any newly independent state in search of economic viability and international acceptability.

This three-ring tag team match is animated by the prevalence of competing nationalisms. Aboriginal peoples constitute a form of ethnic ("indigenous") nationalism with its focus on peoplehood. As peoples, they have the right to self-determination by virtue of the doctrine of popular sovereignty (sovereignty from the people). By contrast, the federal government prefers to define itself as a civic nationalism in seeking to establish a community of rights-bearing, equality-seeking citizens. Federal ministers such as Stephane Dion like to portray Canada's nationalism as democratic, pluralist, rational, universalist, and progressive in contrast with Quebec's ethnic, exclusivist, antidemocratic nationalism (see David Seljak, Letter, *Globe and Mail,* 8 October 1997). According to federalists, Quebec's nationalism cannot respect diversity and fundamental rights because membership is inherently ethnic and reserved for those whose ancestors are of New France vintage ("la pure laine"). The "money" and "ethnics" postreferendum speech by Premier Parizeau, which blamed immigrants for the defeat of sovereigntist forces, simply confirmed what many had suspected: The Québécois are prone to closedness when it comes to diversity (see Editorial, *Globe and Mail,* 1 December 1997). Suspicions have been further inflamed by the manner of the twentieth anniversary celebrations of Bill 101 with advertisements paid by the Quebec government that appeared in Quebec's papers and reprinted by Jeffrey Simpson in his regular *Globe and Mail* column (28 August 1997). Translated: "In Quebec, We work in French/We laugh in French/We think in French/We love in French/We sing in French/We dream in French/We build in French/We grow in French/We play in French/We live in French." Appeals to inclusiveness and pluralism are seen as hypocritical when the political culture is so blatantly jingoistic.

Whose Rights? The Politics of Jurisdiction

What does international law have to say in sorting out the validity of these contested claims? Under international law, colonial peoples (those who live in a defined territory but under a foreign power) have the right to secede. This right to independence and self-determination does not apply to either Quebec or the Cree. Under international law, only "salt water" (overseas) colonies have the right to unilateral secession. Since both international law and the United Nations are constructed around the inviolability of sovereign states, there is no enthusiasm for compromising state interests by extending sovereign rights of secession to internal cultural minorities. The obligation to respect minority rights but not to the extent of secession is clearly outlined in this passage from a United Nations declaration:

> States shall protect the existence and the national or ethnic, cultural, religious, and linguistic identity of minorities within their respective territories and shall encourage conditions for the promotion of that identity.... Persons belonging to national or ethnic, religious, and linguistic minorities...have the right to enjoy their own culture, to profess and practise their own religion and to use their own language, in private and in public, freely and without interference or any form of discrimination.... States shall take measures where required to ensure that persons belonging to minorities [are able] to express their characteristics...except where specific practices are in violation of national law and contrary to international standards.... Nothing in the present Declaration may be construed as permitting any activity contrary to the purposes and principles of the United Nations, including sovereign equality, territorial integrity and political independence of states (United Nations Declaration on the Rights of Persons Belonging to National or Ethnic, Religious and Linguistic Minorities).

In other words, a "people" have the right to self-determination and autonomy. But a people or a nation or a province does not have the rights to secession except under exceptional circumstances, and even then only through negotiation and compromise.

This compromise appears to be consistent with the demands of aboriginal peoples in Quebec. Quebec's aboriginal peoples are adamant that if Canada can be divided, so can Quebec, especially if the original occupants exercise their international right to self-determination to stay in Canada (Grand Council of Crees 1995). Any unilateral secession would abrogate constitutionally protected aboriginal and treaty rights; hence any constitutional amendment on Quebec independence is contingent on aboriginal consent. Moreover, the special trustee relationship with the Crown puts the onus on the federal government to protect aboriginal interests within the framework of Canada. Or, as Claude-Armand Sheppard, counsel for the Cree, put it: just as the federal government has repeatedly indicated it does not want to keep Quebeckers in Canada against their will, so, too, are aboriginal peoples asking that they not be taken out of Canada against their will (cited in Brydon 1998). Agnes Laporte, counsel for Kitigan Zibi Anishnabeg, captured the politics of the situation when declaring that aboriginal peoples are not simply assets and liabilities that Ottawa and Quebec can negotiate away as part of any divorce settlement, but a people with an inherent right to self-determination over where they belong.

Duelling Nationalisms

Both Quebec and the First Nations are recognition seekers. The politics of recognition is steeped in the struggle for control over jurisdictions related to power and resources. Their relationship is complicated by competing efforts to draw the attention of the Canadian state to their respective griev-

ances and identity claims (Salée 1995). But dangers await whatever course of action federal authorities choose. Siding with the Québécois against aboriginal nationalism could spark a First Nations backlash that could make Oka seem a light-hearted rehearsal. That may explain a statement by Ron Irwin, former Indian Affairs Minister, in defending aboriginal rights: "The separatists say that they may have a right to leave, then why don't the aboriginal people who have been here 20 times as long have the same right. It only seems logical to me." Yet playing off one against the other might play into Québécois hands; after all, if the federal government can recognize aboriginal peoples as "peoples" with an inherent right to self-government, why not Quebec?

The Canadian state is precariously perched between these intersecting yet rival nationalisms. It stands to lose because neither of these sovereignties is compatible with national interests. The federalist strategy rests with playing one group off the other in the hopes of neutralizing the combined impact. Ottawa sees the Cree as allies and a negotiating chip in bargaining with Quebec, even if the government has, until recently, repudiated any recognition of aboriginal peoples as "peoples" with inherent rights to self-determination. John McGarry, a political scientist from The University of Western Ontario, writes: "[T]hey will be happy to use the Native position on Quebec as a club with which to beat the separatists, and a convenient tool to minimize the amount of territory they can take from Canada" (*Globe and Mail*, 15 October 1994). Yet Canada may have no choice but to close ranks with Quebec in that neither side is anxious to transfer vast tracts of disputed land over to aboriginal ownership and control.

Nevertheless, there is room for optimism. Perception of Canada as a binational society has proven problematic in the past. The existence of two principle ethnic nations complicated the goals of compromise and accommodation; it also undermined the politics of coalition shifts (Schmitt 1997). The potential for conflict becomes more pronounced and more difficult to mediate when policy issues are perceived as a zero-sum game where one side wins, the other loses. But the addition of another key player enhances the possibility of policy tradeoffs; coalition shifts become increasingly less problematic. If several nations share power, David E Schmitt (1997) writes, it becomes possible to make less glaring compromises or to hide losses to each group behind more complex plans. The playing off of one group against another by central authorities may backfire, but demands of any one group can be deflected or resisted. It can also allow each party to be part of a winning coalition on particular issues. In that sense, the assertiveness of Quebec's First Nations may prove to be the catalyst that complicates Quebec's demands for separation, thus securing the unity of Canada.

SOVEREIGNTY WITHOUT SECESSION

French–English relations remain as fraught with discordance as they did prior to the 1995 referendum. There has been a lot of talk between the two solitudes, but little dialogue, or, more accurately, a "dialogue des sourds" (of the deaf), as both sides continue to talk past each other in a spiral of mounting animosity (McRoberts 1997; Conlogue 1997). The unthinkable—the spectre of Quebec separating from Canada—is now actively contemplated in the aftermath that nearly rendered Canada asunder. Polls conducted since then paint an inconclusive picture: A majority of Quebeckers endorse some form of renewal within the present federalist system. Fewer appear inclined toward any outright separation or status quo. Contradictions abound: A sizable majority want Quebec to be sovereign; an overwhelming majority want Quebec to remain in Canada (Gagnon 1996). Ambiguity is at the core of Québécois aspirations and opinions, and only those leaders who intuitively understand this ambivalence between Quebec nationalism and Canadian federalism can hope to send different signals to different audiences for maximum effect (Simpson 1998). Even that most conservative of constituencies, Quebec's business sector, approves of disassociation from Canada in light of that province's economic strength, abundance of human and natural resources, and the need to stabilize the present political and investment climate.

A healthy skepticism toward polls and statistics is called for. But no one should dismiss their potential in capturing trends on the future of Canadian society. Three scenarios are possible: First, we are presiding over a turbulent period of intensive social change from which Canada will emerge a strengthened and restructured union. Second, we are witnessing the transformation of Canada into a "Swiss cheese" federalism of relatively autonomous political entities without much centre or unity. Third, it will be back to business once all the bluff and the brinkmanship subsides. No one can predict which scenario will prevail, but we can ask, What, then, do the Québécois want, and what is English-speaking Canada willing to concede in addressing these demands? Admittedly, we could just as easily ask what English-speaking Canadians want from Quebec and what the Québécois are doing to accommodate these demands. Unfortunately space limitations are a factor.

What Does Quebec Want? Recognition, Power, and Money

It is unfair to imply that the Québécois have a uniform set of expectations and aspirations. In the past forty years, Quebeckers have lost the apparent certainties and securities of a world defined by rigid Catholic-dominated social orders of religion and class. The shock waves created by the Quiet Revolution have bewildered many Québécois as they cast about for a fixed identity and point of reference. Responses range from those who endorse the status quo or moderate changes to those who advocate a radical restructuring of Quebec's relationship with Canada, up to and including the point of outright secession. For example, consider an Eikos poll between 12 March and 23 March 1998 involving 2,042 respondents, including 496 in Quebec. When asked to choose between complete independence and status quo, 59 percent of the Quebec respondents chose status quo, 31 percent for independence. When offered more choice than these two extremes, 11 percent chose independence, 32 percent sovereignty association, 22 percent decentralized federalism, and 30 percent the status quo (Greenspon 1998). The sense of belonging to the province remains higher than attachment to Canada at 68 percent versus 54 percent, but represents a drop from 87 percent after the referendum and a lower figure than that expressed by Canadians in other provinces. Responses to the "Quebec question" do not always reflect a perfect consistency. Ambiguities often prevail that vary with situational circumstances and reflect a fundamental ambivalence toward Canada. For example, the prospect of cultural security and political determination may be appealing; nevertheless, the economic disadvantages of severing ties with Canada may be an equally powerful disincentive. Isolation is desired, but so too are increased decision-making powers in Ottawa (Siddiqui 1998). In brief, the Québécois want the best of both worlds; or as quipped by Yvon Descamps, a French-Canadian comedian: "They want an independent Quebec inside a united Canada" (cited in the *Globe and Mail,* 18 June 1994).

Terms such as sovereignty and separation continue to generate more heat than light. Meanings are bandied about and vary in context from person to person without much regard for precision. Sovereignty defined as a final authority that brooks no external interference over internal jurisdictions may be less important than arrangements between fundamentally independent political communities that reflect patterns of relative autonomy within a context of relational, nondominating interdependence (see also Scott 1996). The distinction between separation and sovereignty is subtle but valid. Sovereignty is what the Québécois already possess, as far as many are concerned, because of Quebec's Charter group status and evolution as a distinct society. Separation, by contrast, may be advocated by only a small percentage of Québécois under normal circumstances. Thus sovereignty is not merely a softer version of separation; nor is it a sign of confusion in the minds of a confused electorate, but a nuanced reading of the Canadian federal system and Quebec's place in a globalizing and interdependent world (Editorial, *Globe and Mail,* 11 March 1994). Quebeckers may not want to quit Canada, to be sure, but neither do they want to appear weak or vacillating by caving in to English-speaking intransigence.

Broadly speaking, all Quebeckers appear anxious to maintain the French character of their society. Envisaged here is a set of arrangements, both political and economic, to preserve Quebec's distinctiveness as the homeland of last resort in North America. But agreement over goals does not always translate into consensus over means (Fournier 1994). On the one side are the **moderates** who generally prefer accommodation within the framework of Canada. Proposed is a strengthening of Quebec's position within the federalist system, in large part by reinforcing Quebec's presence in Ottawa and in other part by expanding Quebec's access to power and resources. A new constitutional division of powers is also anticipated to ensure that each level of government controls what it does best (Johnson 1995). Moderates may even define themselves as "soft" sovereigntists but disagree with the principle of separation, preferring instead a kind of flexible federalism with sovereign control over internal jurisdictions of relevance. Affiliation with Canada as their country is accepted, but primary identity points to Quebec as their homeland.

Radical perspectives espouse some degree of separation from Canada. Many *independantistes* are tired of being labelled a minority group that English-Canadians stigmatizes as a costly problem people. They prefer a space that Quebecker can call their own, where they are the majority and call the shots. Quebeckers want to be in the big leagues—a state within a state—not just an administrative subunit of Canada (Latouche 1995). Or, as put by Louise Beaudoin of the Parti Québécois, "I want to be a majority in my own country" (Editorial, *Globe and Mail,* 1 March 1995). The high risk of being permanently out-maneuvered (the "tyranny of the majority") is sufficient to justify a radical shakedown of power, and was recognized a generation ago by a Canadian national unity commission:

> Quebec is distinctive and should, within a viable Canada, have the powers necessary to protect and develop its distinctive character. Any political solution short of this would lead to the rupture of Canada (Task Force on National Unity, Pepin-Roberts Report 1977–79).

Many are also weary of those English-speaking Canadians who reject even minimal concessions to confirm Quebec's distinctiveness. English-speaking insensitivity is seen as stemming from a reluctance to discard a conquest mentality. This insensitivity is also attributed to a lack of distinct cultural identity. While Québécois know who they are, English-speaking Canadians are perceived as bereft of common vision or grand design, except in opposition to something else. Such a cultural vacuum inhibits their capacity to accept Quebec for its differences and history. Taken to its logical conclusion, English-Canadians do not even constitute a people in the sociological sense in having a shared experience or common history and culture, in effect relinquishing the right to deny "real peoples" the right to sovereignty (see McRoberts 1998; Seguin 1998). Others argue that the federal system is no longer viable: Quebec cannot possibly associate itself with a system that is incapable of dealing with its own problems (Castonguay 1994). Federalism does not pay; rather, staying in Canada extracts a heavy economic cost because of the perpetual gridlock between Quebec and Canada over costly overruns, needless duplication, and jurisdictional wrangles (Fournier 1994).

Separatists believe Quebec is poised to go it alone: It has a broad industrial base for wealth creation, a healthy government financial structure, a shared sense of culture and community, and autonomous sources of revenue. Only procedural questions remain: Can Quebec secede only with public opinion and international law on its side, or must it abide by constitutional law and provincial consent? Secessionist moves come in different packages, from outright separation to sovereignty association, but most proposals entail some degree of political independence (including control over culture and language), without loss of close economic ties such as free trade and common currency. Admittedly, sovereignty will come with economic and social costs, but ethnicities everywhere have shown a willingness to pay for heroic ideals, and Quebeckers appear ready to embrace such a tradeoff as part of a sacred duty. To be sure, sovereignty will not solve all of Quebec's problems, concedes Jacques Parizeau (1996), but it will create a more normal situation by sharpening the lines of who controls what.

What Is English Canada Willing to Concede?

In August 1998, Canada's longest-running political drama took another turn. Three matters of policy required clarification: (a) Can Quebec legally and unilaterally secede from Canada? (b) Does international law or the right of self-determination condone the right to unilateral secession? (c) Which body of law would take precedence in case of conflict between domestic and international interpretation over Quebec's proposed secession? To the delight of federalists, Canada's Supreme Court ruled unanimously that Quebec does not have the right to unilaterally secede from the rest of Canada. Any decision to declare Quebec's independence must be balanced by the realities of a federal system with its varied interests and various minority groups (Pearlstein 1998). But the ruling was hardly a victory for federal forces. To Québécois delight, the nine judges also made it clear that if Quebec voters were to embrace secession by way of a referendum, the federal and provincial governments would be required by Constitution and international law to negotiate in good faith the complex process of amending the country's basic governing Charter for engineering the division of Canada.

This ruling—yet another example of the compromises that constitute the balancing act called Canada—appears consistent with the federal position B plan. Under the B plan, the federal government concedes the right of Quebeckers to determine their future, provided the sovereignty question is fair and a clear majority agree. However, Quebec does not have the right to secede unilaterally, but must negotiate its way out through a long and laboured process. Stephane Dion, federal minister for intergovernmental affairs, indicated as much in a letter to his Quebec counterpart, Jacques Brassard. Canada, he argued, would accept the right of Quebec to secede but only if Quebec voters clearly indicated a desire to become independent through establishment of clear conditions for secession. In short, Canada may be divisible in theory, but probably not in practice, given the vagueness of the terms of divorce and corresponding hurdles of a constitutional labyrinth.

The politics of partition seem to lead to one conclusion: Canada's political elites appear willing to make major concessions to Quebec by recognizing its special place in Confederation and its unique character as fundamental to Canada (Editorial, *Globe and Mail,* 16 September 1997). As the First Minsters at the Calgary Conference reiterated, there is greater inclination to modify the existing federal system but resistance to any massive transfer of power to Quebec (Editorial, *Globe and Mail,* 18 October 1997). More expansive visions are available: English-speaking academics have proposed a radical restructuring of the Canadian political order along the lines of a sovereignty-association relationship (McRoberts 1997). Under confederalism, most of the functions performed by Ottawa would be transferred to Quebec. A new federal government would be established with authority over the rest of Canada while continuing to control foreign affairs, currency, and defence. With this arrangement, Quebec would not be sovereign in the classic sense, but its jurisdiction would transcend that of a province. This kind of arrangement would acknowledge Canada as a multination society in much the same way as Switzerland and the United Kingdom. Peoples within a multinationality do not need sovereignty state status to flourish; what is required is autonomy over jurisdictions under their control. Thus national unity is not achieved in the conventional sense of single state or unitary citizenship. Proposed instead are new patterns of belonging that entail accommodation and consensus among the diverse collectivities. Such a proposal has met with a cool reception, to the surprise of no one, in part because it is too radical for moderates, but too moderate for committed separatists.

A REGRETTABLE NECESSITY

> What is wanted is a larger bed (more space for each partner) maybe even twin beds. But there is definitely a desire to continue sharing the bedroom. This is a marriage not of passion but of reason and convenience—a fine arrangement based on common history, shared interests, and mutual respect.
>
> Lysiane Gagnon, 27 July 1996

Tension between Canada's French- and English-speaking communities is as old as the country. French-Canadians have complained of second class status ever since the British red-coats defeated the French forces on the Plains of Abraham outside Quebec City in 1759. Paradoxically, pressures for independence appear to be mounting just as Quebec gains increased political power, economic control, and cultural autonomy (Pearlstein 1998). To many Canadians, we are forever hovering on the brink of self-destruction despite our success as a country. To others, Canada is envied as a place that works, a solution in search of a problem, as one Mexican ambassador put it. It constitutes a possible model for countries such as Spain and Russia, who are also struggling to divide power between the centre and cultural regions (Drohan 1997). An element of envy is understandable: Whereas an estimated 100,000 people died in Russia's efforts to crush the Chechnya separatist movement (York 1997), only one person has been killed because of political struggles between Quebec and Ottawa since 1960. In the words of Professor Xavier Arbos, a Catalan and president of the International Council for Canadian Studies: "Canadians have reasons to be proud of a country that is balanced, democratic, a country that cares, where there is less violence...." Canada may not be perfect, he adds, but looks a lot better than most.

The picture at present is transitional. There is room for a guarded optimism, but a foreboding that Canada's map is about to be redrawn. Canada's federal system is remarkably flexible in its capacity to endlessly tinker over the balance of power between Ottawa and Quebec. *De facto* ("informal") arrangements have been worked out that recognize the distinctiveness and relative autonomy of certain provinces. Quebec, for example, has its own pension plan, its own system of private law, levies its own income tax, and exercises a degree of control over immigration that is unprecedented for any federal system (McRoberts 1996). In many ways, Quebec resembles a quasi-state, according to Stephane Dion, a key constitutional adviser for the federal Liberal government, with control over powers for setting provincial priorities and controlling jurisdictions (Stewart 1994). With or without constitutional guarantees, in other words, Quebec is acting as if it were a distinct society by exercising powers of a relatively sovereign nation.

Ad hoc arrangements for conceding to Quebec's demands are not the problem. The stumbling block resides in moves to *legally* recognize Quebec as a people with a distinct society status. As Charles Taylor (1993) notes, English-speaking Canadians may be willing to accept negotiated and pragmatic arrangements. But many balk at the idea of formalizing any arrangements that (a) oppose conventional views of Canada (as a social contract); (b) violate certain values related to formal equality (the principle of equal provinces), and (c) create imbalances within Canada's federal system because of preferential treatment. Even fewer are willing to acknowledge the possibility of Quebec as a fundamentally autonomous political community whose self-determining rights are independently sourced rather than being shaped for the convenience of Ottawa or subject to meddlesome interference (see also Asch 1997). There may be an additional barrier: Formal recognition may give Canadians more political unity than they really want (in the words of Professor John Richards). After all, one way of solving a complex problem is by ignoring it. The words of the Quebec nationalist poet, Gilles Vigneault, seem especially apropos: "Mon pays ce n'est pas un pays, c'est l'hiver"/My country is not a country, it is a winter (cited in Leslie de Freitas 1996:21). Canadians may be defined by the snows of winter, de Freitas writes, but snowflakes melt when examined too closely in the palm of our hands. Too much scrutiny and debate in sorting out who controls what may also melt Canada's fragile bonds in the heat of nationalist passions.

Forging a workable accommodation between Ottawa and Quebec is unlikely without a major reappraisal of Canadian society. Fundamental to this reassessment is whether two communities with such divergent interests can share a common political space (Salée 1996; Salée and Coleman 1997). Flag waving or finger pointing will not solve what many perceive to be a structural problem rather than a simple case of mutual pigheadedness. The Quebec question appears inseparable from the very strengths that served Canada well in the past. Simply put, Canada's federalist system may be inadequate for coping with the demands of contemporary multinational society. Just as the idea of provinces may be antiquated and irrelevant (Diamond 1997), so too is a federal political process designed for a small agricultural unitary state (Gillies 1997). The very thought of relying on a nineteenth-century political framework for solving the twenty-first century problems of a three-nation state may be misguided or counterproductive, especially in the face of freewheeling global forces and inward-looking identity politics. Engin Isan of York University writes of the need to reconsider the Quebec question within the changing and shifting identities of the new world order:

> [P]olitical boundaries no longer represent the social and economic realities facing Canadian provinces today. Loyalties of Canadian citizens and their sense of belonging are divided along other lines than the nineteenth century territorial boundaries represented by the provinces. There are many other territorial identities and regions that are articulated into the different spheres of the global economy, rendering provincial loyalties and identities increasingly not only banal but counter-productive (1996:6).

In other words, the Quebec question is really a Canadian quandary. Federalism as a system for co-opting Quebec may have worked in the past for dampening dormant nationalisms. Whatever its merits for society building or the representation of diverse interests over vast distances, the federal structure of Canada's political system greatly impedes the recognition of the "nations within" and exacerbates the normal tensions of a binational society (Schmitt 1998). With the reemergence of Quebec nationalism and the vibrancy of indigenous nationalisms, its effectiveness in addressing the multinationalisms of a three-nation state is sharply contested (Burgess 1996; Balthazar 1996). Problems will remain until Canadians embrace a vision of Canada as a unique and independent country with its own culture and constitutionalism rather than one based on a British model of a single culture, language, and constitutionalism (Rimmer 1998). The words of Sir John A Macdonald in 1872 are perversely prophetic, albeit not in the way they were originally intended: "Confederation is only yet in the gristle, and it will require five years more before it hardens into bone" (cited in Olive 1996:13). Such ossification may need to be softened up before the diverse solitudes decide that this regrettable necessity called Canada is not such a bad arrangement after all.

CHAPTER HIGHLIGHTS

- Canada represents a multicultural and bilingual society whose French–English duality constitutes a fundamental and powerful characteristic. The French and the English represent two of Canada's founding nations, or Charter members, with the right to formulate Canada's political agenda.

- However basic this duality, it is an uneasy coexistence, since French–English relations originated in conquest, are inflamed by cultural differences and power differentials, and are the centralizing tendencies of the federal system.

- The politics of language reflect and reinforce the tempestuous character of French–English relations. But linguistic efforts to resolve this problem have proven inadequate. Federal bilingualism is viewed as appeasement without power; Québécois language rights come across as infringements on the individual rights of official language minority in Quebec.

- French- and English-speaking interactions are portrayed as relations of inequality in the competition over scarce resources and jurisdictional control. Language politics are central to these power struggles: Language serves as a key ethnic marker that not only reflects Quebec's distinctiveness, but also provides a vehicle for conveying political aspirations while enhancing economic competitiveness.

- Bilingualism has not appealed to the other provinces of Canada (except New Brunswick). Three provinces are now officially unilingual. Nevertheless, all provinces are constitutionally bound to respect official language minority rights, although the magnitude of concessions can vary from one province to another.

- Language debates may prevail in Quebec, but many of the language issues are ultimately about power, access to resources, and control over jurisdiction.

- A central question in this chapter asks, What is really going on in terms of Quebec–Ottawa relations? Answers to this question suggest the necessity to see Canada from a variety of diverse perspectives, including Canada as a contract, a compact, and a three-nation state.

- The second question asks, What do the Québécois want? While answers are varied and reflect a certain ambiguity, consensus points to a need to protect and promote the conditions that will enhance the distinct and sovereign character of Quebec's identity, language, and culture. Ambiguities in response may reflect the diverse means employed to achieve these goals, including those of moderates who are willing to work within the federalist system on one side and those of radicals who want to scrap federalism in exchange for some degree of separation on the other.

- Quebec–Ottawa relations are currently a contested site. Opposing interests are locked in a struggle to define the nature of the relationship of Quebec with Ottawa and decide how best to restructure this relationship in a way that each acknowledges the agendas of the other without necessarily capitulating to their entire package.

- Competing ethnic nationalisms continue to complicate politics in Canada. Quebec's First Nations argue for the right to stay in Canada if they choose, should Quebec decide to secede. As one might expect in light of its mandate and makeup, international law appears to be siding with the Canadian state.

KEY TERMS

Bill 101 (French Language Charter)
Bill 178
collective versus individual rights
compact federalism

contract federalism
distinct society
flexible federalism
individual bilingualism
institutional bilingualism
moderates
multinationalisms
nationalism
The Official Languages Act
politics of language
radical
sovereignty-association
sovereignty versus separation
sovereignty without secession
territorial bilingualism
three-nation state
two-tier language policy
world (or heritage) languages

REVIEW QUESTIONS

1. With reference to the struggles of French-speaking Canadians, indicate why language issues appear to elicit such strong passions in the competition for scarce resources.

2. Indicate the rationale behind Quebec's language legislation in terms of what it is trying to do and why. Do you agree or disagree with these initiatives? Why?

3. Quebec's demand for distinct society status as "nation" and "people" strikes at the core of the debate between ethnic nationalism and civic nationalism. Explain.

4. Compare and contrast the differing visions of Canada and its relationship to Quebec. Which do you think is the most correct reading of Canadian society?

5. Explain Canada's two-tier language policy. Do you think this is the best possible arrangement? Why or why not?

6. If someone were to ask you what you thought Quebec wants, how would you respond?

7. What does English-speaking Canada appear willing to concede to Quebec? Be sure to cover the range of responses to meeting Quebec's demands.

8. Indicate the nature of the sovereignty debate that is going on in Quebec between Quebec nationalists and aboriginal peoples? Whose argument do you support and why?

9. The federal government asked the Supreme Court in 1996 for its opinion on a major question: Can Quebec secede unilaterally from Canada under the Constitution or international law? How did the Supreme Court respond in 1998? How would you respond on the basis of the material in this chapter?

IMMIGRATION AND MULTICULTURAL MINORITIES

8

Voices
Caribbean Women, Canadian Experience

There are many obstacles to achieving equality in Canadian society for Caribbean immigrant women. The two most prominent obstacles are the attitudes of some white Canadians and the attitudes of some members of the Caribbean community, both male and female. Unless the reasons behind these attitudes are understood, improvements and changes will be long in coming.

Most people dislike the social change that immigrants create. These feelings occur because people in general fear that immigrants will not be able to cope successfully with the changes in culture and values of a new society. Some people also fear that immigrants will bring about changes to culture and norms of the society of their adopted country. Fear is common to humankind; different racial groups react similarly. Some whites as well as some blacks tend to oppose equality for black women—the whites because they fear that it threatens their privileged status, the blacks because of insecurities and conflict of interest. These fears and insecurities impact heavily on some Caribbean women.

Between the early 1960s and the mid-1970s there was an influx of immigrants from the Caribbean to Canada. They came in both genders and from all socioeconomic strata. There were nurses, engineers, doctors, dentists, clerical workers, teachers, domestics, and short-term migrant farm workers. Then in 1980, because of the fear of Jamaican Prime Minister Manley's version of socialism, there was a mass exodus of professional and businesspeople from Jamaica to Canada. This scenario best illustrates the "push" and "pull" factors in immigration—the "push" because of the political situation in Jamaica, the "pull" toward a stable lifestyle in Canada.

In no group were the "push" and "pull" factors more strongly felt than in that of Caribbean women. Caribbean women are an ambitious, industrious, and adventurous lot, who are always striving for a better lifestyle for themselves and their children. Their decisions to immigrate were often made with deep anguish; however, they were certain that they had no alternative if they wanted to improve their own and their children's lives. Consequently, many of them immigrated, some to join spouses already settled here, others coming independently, leaving spouses behind. But in most cases they left children behind with relatives, often grandparents.

Once in Canada, these women found themselves in a strange, cold, and often hostile environment. The friendly white faces they saw in the Caribbean were now almost nonexistent. They often encountered hostility, racial stereotyping, bias, discrimination, and prejudice in employment, education, and housing. Sometimes there was even an overt anti-foreigner attitude, which continues to come across today in a vicious backlash in Canada's national politics.

To many of these women Canada presents a contradiction in attitudes: On the one hand, they are welcome to low-paying, low-status jobs no one else wants, but on the other hand, they are accused of taking jobs away from work-ing class Canadian women. They are often bewildered by this attitude, since many of them earn low wages, have poor working conditions, little work stability, and little or no chance for advancement. They perceive themselves as paying an exorbitant price to be members of Canadian society. Since many of them were teachers and clerical workers in their home countries, they feel cheated of the promise of a better lifestyle as they try to eke out a living working at jobs that are below the level of their social strata and educational qualifications.

Many of them have made the transition into Canadian society successfully and are working as teachers, nurses, and office managers. Still, many others are relegated to jobs in service industries, such as domestics, nannies, hospital aides, beauticians, and seamstresses in garment factories. These women realize their predicament as they try to adapt physically to the climate and housing as well as psychologically adapt to a new social environment—different habits, social life, and social structure. They now find themselves in a society where gender, race, and class are deeply embedded in the structure and relationships among people. Their's is a double jeopardy—they are "black women."

Gender and race have made a significant impact on their lives. They are female as well as a racial minority. Like many other females, a large number of them are at the lower end of the income scale. In addition, many of them are single mothers and heads of their households. They are cut off from the support system they had in the Caribbean. Many of them have no friends, and they experience enormous stress and anxiety as they try to integrate into a new and different society on their own. They feel inadequate, homesick, depressed, hopeless, and helpless as they face the new reality. To combat these bad feelings, most of them work relentlessly to amass money so that they can be reunited with the family they left behind. Others work to send remittances "back home" to support the children they left behind, until they are established and able to provide a home for them in Canada. Ironically, some of their first jobs in Canada are looking after other women's children.

Those who are unattached work to buy houses here in Canada or build their retirement homes back in the Caribbean. Notwithstanding the odds, they all stay and brave the cold, hostile physical and sometimes emotional environment—because they have no choice. The economic conditions are better here in Canada than they are in the Caribbean. So they amass physical goods to compensate for and to fulfill emotional needs.

There are many adjustment problems encountered by the Caribbean women and their children when they are reunited after the long separation. On arriving in Canada, the children must learn to adapt to the climate as well as a new and different culture. Sometimes the mothers are unable to assist them because they have not yet adjusted to the new culture either or because there is a cultural difference between mother and child. This difference could be at a generational or gender level, where mother and child are not sharing similar situational experiences, so they have no common ground.

If the children are of school age, they attend school where most likely there are few peers with similar backgrounds with whom they can associate. They have to cope with a new education system which is biased against them and peers who are prejudiced and sometimes hostile. They often find it difficult to understand their teachers and peers when they speak, and

are frequently teased about their Caribbean accents. They desperately try to hide their differences by losing their accents and casting off any affiliation with the Caribbean as they come face to face with an identity crisis and culture shock. However, they cannot hide their physical characteristics.

As the children lose their Caribbean identities and assimilate, mothers and children become more and more estranged. Mothers try desperately and sometimes futilely to keep the culture alive in their children. The harder they try, the more alienated their children become. This results in the mothers feeling disappointed, betrayed, and hated by their children. They perceive that their hard work and sacrifices were made in vain for children who have proven ungrateful. This creates conflict, tension, and stress in the household.

To compound their stress, most Caribbean immigrant women worry about career opportunities for themselves as well as their children. Most working class Caribbean women are upset and humiliated by their own status. They see themselves as being exploited in the labour market and do not want their children to become exploitable labour for the future. The professional women find many barriers and obstacles placed in their way toward upward mobility. There are hardly any black headmistresses in the school system, black members of parliament, or nursing administrators, and only a handful of black women have advanced to lower and middle management in business. The working class women realize that at their socioeconomic level they will not be able to finance postsecondary education for their children. They come to accept that the Canadian dream is "but a dream" for black women.

Caribbean immigrant children arriving in Canada are confronted with many shocking realities. While back in the Caribbean they thought that their mothers were wealthy and lived opulent and easy lives. In one mother's words: "They think money grows on trees here." Upon arrival, they quickly learn that blacks in general are denied acceptance and economic opportunities in their adopted country and that their mothers work long and hard just to make ends meet. Consequently, they too feel cheated. They develop a sense of hopelessness which turns into rebellion against their mothers as well as the Canadian norms. Some of them become delinquents, join youth gangs, and engage in many antisocial activities. The failed dreams and hopes for their children are sources of great distress and anguish for Caribbean women.

Many Caribbean women are happily married and enjoy gratifying and fulfilling relationships with their Caribbean husbands. Nevertheless, a number of Caribbean women have few relationships with men. When they do, it is generally sexual in nature. Many of them are afraid to have relationships with Caribbean men whom they regard as unfaithful, fickle, and exploitative. Some of them feel this way from personal experiences: They have sponsored lovers and fiancés, who have left them as soon as they established themselves in Canada.

It is extremely difficult for professional Caribbean women to find suitable unmarried partners of their peer among Caribbean men. Therefore, many of them are unmarried or have affairs with married men who are their professional peers. Frequently, these women bear children for these men rather than establish relationships with other partners they deem "unsuitable," because they are not as educated, refined, and sophisticated as the women are.

Caribbean women who left spouses back home are eventually joined by them. These reunions are not always happy. They are sometimes the source of great disappointment and unhappiness because of the stress and strain that the adjustments place on the marriage. The Caribbean male has difficulty adjusting to the change in climate, lifestyle, and norms of the Canadian society. In the patriarchal Caribbean society male and female have the traditional sex roles. Thus Caribbean men become confused when faced with the more egalitarian nature of sex roles in Canada. In one man's words: "Women in this country don't know their place, because they have too many rights."

Moreover, many of these men are torn between enforcing their traditional roles and losing their spouses or conforming and losing face before their peers. To their male friends they have to appear to be in control of their households; if not, they run the risk of losing their respect and being teased that "their wives wear the pants in their families." Therefore, to save face, they live by the roles of the "old country." They refuse, or are reluctant, to do household chores, to grocery shop, or participate in child-rearing activities. As a result, enormous stress is placed on the women who have the double responsibilities of full-time jobs in and outside the home.

Some Caribbean men feel out of control and inadequate in Canada, as they encounter racism, prejudice, stereotyping, and discrimination. Their self-esteem becomes very low. More than anything else they want to feel in control and respected. To compensate for their lack of control outside the home, they attempt to exercise control inside the home. Their families become their objects of control. This control extends not only to wives but to children as well. Children growing up in Canada are not always as respectful as they are in the Caribbean, so they sometimes defy their fathers. This is a source of great displeasure to the fathers, who experience feelings of humiliation and disrespect. Hence in a family scenario these men are constantly in situations where these feelings surface.

Some feel so threatened that they batter their wives and children in vain attempts to reassert their authority and masculinity and gain control of the family. These beatings are frequently not reported to the police. According to one source, "Caribbean women do not like to air their dirty laundry in public." This violent behaviour creates animosity, frustration, resentment, and discontent in the family relationship. This behaviour is a double-edged sword: Instead of gaining the respect they so badly crave, it ends up costing these men the love, trust, and respect of their families.

Caribbean men may become so disillusioned they leave their wives and children and go back home. Others experience impotence with their wives because of their inability to cope with their problems at home. Many leave the marriage to pursue extramarital relationships, sometimes with younger women in order to prove their virility. This most often compounds their problems, since they lack the financial resources to support two homes. As a result, they abdicate their responsibilities to their wives and children and relegate them to a life of poverty. Others turn to women of different racial groups as a panacea for what ails them.

One major problem for the Caribbean immigrant woman is that Caribbean women are separated along the lines of length of residency in Canada, education, and socioeconomic strata. They do not perceive themselves as sharing many common goals and interests. The established female immigrant sometimes looks unfavourably on the new arrivals and refers to them as "J J C," or "Jane Just Come," which is a term of disdain and derision. She has assimilated into Canadian society and amassed some personal belongings. Therefore, she sees the new arrival as a constant reminder of her past, one of which she is no longer very proud and would like to forget. She makes no effort to get close to her, to point out pitfalls, explain or interpret the ways of life in the new country to help her to adapt. She keeps her distance, avoids all contact, and behaves outwardly as if she was born in Canada and does not share a common cultural ancestry.

Friendships between the educated and uneducated are virtually nonexistent. The educated woman finds the other ignorant, crude, and unsophisticated, someone with whom she has nothing in common apart from the colour of her skin. Although many professional Caribbean females immigrated to Canada, the majority of them came as domestics and went back to colleges and universities to acquire professional qualifications. Having worked so hard to get where they are, they are not sympathetic and responsive to the needs of women who did not bother to upgrade themselves or to "pull themselves up by the bootstrap." They see the working class women as lazy and unambitious and therefore unworthy of their friendship. The now professional women feel themselves to be "better" than the others are, because they have taken the time to improve themselves.

If some Caribbean men and women would only take the time to get together and relate they would discover common ground. They would realize that they are not each other's enemy, but that they have a common enemy: racism. If they could put aside their negative attitudes about gender and class and present a united front, they could challenge the real enemy and work toward gaining equality for themselves and their children. Then, and only then, will Caribbean women gain their equal and rightful place in the Canadian mosaic.

SOURCE: Marita Williams. Written expressly for *Unequal Relations.*

INTRODUCTION: THE PARADOX OF IMMIGRATION

In this era of increased human uprootedness, interest in the study of immigration and debate over immigrants has expanded accordingly (Ucarer 1997; Castles and Miller 1998). This is notably true of Canada where immigrants have long proven pivotal to the society-building project. On the whole, Canada has become a more vibrant and dynamic society because of immigrants. Immigrants have contributed to Canada's cultural diversity and economic prosperity without destroying its social fabric in the process. Canadians for the most part have embraced immigration with the kind of civility and open-mindedness that is becoming a trademark of Canadian society (Siddiqui 1998). But there is an undercurrent of concern or confusion over the social implications that come with being one of the world's more proactive immigration societies (Avery 1995). Canada remains a "reluctant host" whose ambivalence—even hostility—toward certain foreign-born is palpable beneath a veneer of tolerance. Migration into Canada is increasingly seen as a threat to internal security and scarce resources. Linking immigration with numerous social ills that confront society ensures a frosty reception, especially for immigrants from nonconventional sources. Both immigrants and refugees may possess the rights of citizenship and the multicultural right to be different yet the same; nevertheless, many encounter unacceptable levels of prejudice and discrimination in the process of settling into Canada.

Immigration has emerged as a pivotal dynamic at the end of the millennium (Thompson and Weinfeld 1995). In capitalizing on their determination and drive, family connections, global links, and financial support of community institutions, immigrants are reclaiming abandoned industries, derelict neighbourhoods, and declining services and bringing hope to blighted areas of Canada (see also Millman 1997). But the importance of immigration to society goes beyond the question of demography or economy. Patterns of immigration have irrevocably altered the very concept of Canada by transforming British Canada into a rich, English-speaking mosaic of different cultures and languages (Dyer 1998). Immigrants from the United Kingdom are no longer an identifiable ethnic group with a collective historical memory and a privileged agenda-setting status. In the space of a generation, immigration has revolutionized the social face of urban Canada more quickly than an aging population or high aboriginal birthrates, with potentially profound implications for longstanding French–English relations (see Passaris 1998). Immigrants continue to fuel the spark for rethinking and rebuilding Canada: As a former minister of immigration and citizenship once commented when observing the relationship between society and immigration: "Immigration is fundamentally about nation-building—about deciding who we are as Canadians and who we want to become.... We need a clear and practical vision of the kind of nation we want to build" (Sergio Marchi, Annual Report 1994:iii). The role of immigration in the reenvisioning of Canada is reflected in the kinds of questions that invariably are raised by immigration, including:

- What does it mean to be a Canadian?
- What kind of country is envisaged for the future?
- Where does diversity fit into the future of Canada?
- What is Canada's perception of itself *vis-à-vis* the world at large?
- Which core values must be protected, and which values are open for negotiation?
- How do immigrants contribute to or detract from a progressive and pluralistic Canada?

Answers to these questions require careful deliberation beyond the realm of political slogan or public posturing. There is no single correct way to frame immigration issues, according to Joel Millman (1997:1), since immigration can be interpreted as a "numbers game, a morality play, a legal debate, and a market model." But however successful the multicultural experiment in Canada, Canadians continue to grapple with a host of thorny immigration questions: Why should Canada accept immigrants? Who should be encouraged to come to Canada? How many immigrants (if any at all) should be accepted? From what countries should Canadians accept immigrants? And which skill level of immigrants is preferred? Responses to these questions involve debates over the future of society and the relationship of immigrants to particular visions of what is or should be. Disagreements over the degree of openness or restrictiveness often lead to provocations or partitions, thus necessitating a broader understanding of immigration in terms of policies, patterns, and practices.

It is within the context of concern and comprehension that this chapter explores the social dimensions of immigration by looking at the relationship of immigration to multicultural society building. Our interests are not in the entire spectrum of immigrant issues; nor are we concerned exclusively with costs or benefits at political, economic, or cultural levels. This chapter explores the social dimensions of immigration by examining the emergence of immigrants as an emergent and evolving third "force" in Canada's multicultural society. The linking of immigration with multiculturalism is deliberate; after all, the two are interrelated insofar as immigration provides the rationale for multiculturalism; multiculturalism, in turn, secures a receptive social climate for migrant adaptation. The study of specific multicultural minority groups is not pursued in this chapter. Rather, both foreign-born and native-born multicultural minorities are examined as a general social category whose relational status is distinguished from aboriginal peoples and Charter members at the levels of needs, concerns, entitlements, and aspirations. Particular emphasis is devoted to the largely ambiguous status occupied by immigrants and refugees in Canada's historical past and contemporary present. A review of immigration policy and practices, in addition to a look at the pros and cons of immigration as well as costs and benefits, confirms what many have suspected: The relationship of multicultural minorities with "mainstream society" is pervaded by patterns of inequality. Canadians proclaim an egalitarian society but gaps between "white" and "nonwhite" persist beneath a sheen of multicultural platitudes. Efforts to isolate, challenge, and transform these inequities are fraught with tension and ambiguity as competing sectors struggle for control of the national agenda. The fact that many new Canadians encounter a less than hospitable climate in adjusting to the demands of Canadian society ensures a lengthy struggle before the vision of genuine "multiculturalism" becomes a reality in Canada.

The chapter begins with an overview of Canada's multicultural minorities in terms of demographic composition and geographical distribution. It continues with a closer look at the collective transformation of Canada by means of past and present immigration trends. This is followed by an examination of policies and principles that have governed the movement of immigrants into Canada. Of particular note is the creative tension between continuity and changes at the core of immigration policy and practices. Such ambiguity is especially evident at the level of public and political opposition to "undesirable immigrants" as this category has evolved over time (see also Avery 1995). Yet the need for immigrants to fuel capitalist expansion has never wavered (Bolaria and Li 1988). Also open for discussion are many of the controversies associated with immigration as debates escalate over who will come in, on what grounds, from where, what for, and at what level of acceptance. Proposed changes to Canada's immigration policy provides a useful basis for asking some "tough" questions about the whys, hows, whats, and wheres of immigration. A number of misconceptions and half-truths about immigration and immigrants are dissected and debunked. The problems and the pressures that multicultural minorities confront in securing an adjustment to Canadian society are also discussed.

A chapter on multicultural minorities could not possibly hope to engage all topics about this diversity without stretching its resources to the point of superficiality and gloss. We have decided to focus primarily on foreign-born multicultural minorities from so-called non-conventional countries of origin. Emphasis is centred on immigrants and refugees in terms of their adjustment to Canadian society under a bewildering array of policy circumstances and social pressures. Specific groups are not dealt with *per se*. Our intent is to provide a useful overview of multicultural minorities *as if* they comprised a relatively uniform category *for analytical purposes*. This *ideal-typical* stance runs the risk of oversimplification or essentializing (treating everyone in a category in a fixed, homogenous, and singular fashion). Others might argue that minority voices are being silenced by this reliance on analysis. There is some validity to these charges. Immigrants do exhibit a broad range of internal diversity because of age, gender, culture, socioeconomic status, length of residence, sexual preference, and country of origin. Patterns of adaptation and rates of success differ considerably for the rich versus the poor, for men versus women, and for youth versus adults, each of whom is anxious to establish his or her own identity and social space in Canadian society. Consider also the category of South Asians as exemplified by federal government employment equity projections: This can incorporate individuals from the Indian subcontinent as well as from Pakistan, Bangladesh, and Sri Lanka. The subcontinent in turn is partitioned into Punjab, Bengali, and South India. Major religious affiliations divide into Hindu, Sikh, Muslims, Christians, Buddhists, and Jains. The term "Indian" also refers to those of Indian ancestry by way of Africa, Britain, Trinidad, and Guyana. The content of these experiences is varied, of course, but common ground exists in shaping group interaction at this level, and it is our intent to examine the nature of these shared commonalities.

ETHNIC DIVERSITY IN CANADA: WHO ARE MULTICULTURAL MINORITIES?

Canada embraces a diverse collection of immigrants and refugees from different parts of the world. The first of many movements was inaugurated by East Asian populations across the Bering Strait as far back as 50,000 years ago. These "immigrants" now constitute the indigenous peoples of Canada whose status as original occupants has proven both provocative and perplexing. Both French and English traders/adventurers/explorers comprised the second wave of immigrants. These colonizers eventually displaced the aboriginal populations and unilaterally assumed official status as the foundational (Charter) members of Canada. The third wave consisted of various non-English- and non-French-speaking immigrants who arrived *en masse* during the twentieth century as part of Canada's society-building commitments. In recent years, the rate of immigration has maintained historically high levels, with the majority of immigrants from nonconventional sources.

Canada's demographic composition has turned on its head since inception of the BNA (Constitution) Act of 1867. Only 8 percent of Canada's population was not of British or French ancestry at the time of Confederation (Palmer 1975). Between 1896 and 1914, the balance began to shift when up to 3 million immigrants—many of them from Central and Eastern Europe—arrived to domesticate the West. Immigration increased substantially prior to and just after World War I, reaching a peak of over 400,000 in 1913. Another wave of Eastern European immigrants during the 1920s brought the non-British, non-French proportion up to 18 percent. The post-World War II period resulted in yet another influx of refugees and immigrants from the war-torn European theatre. Sources of immigration since the 1980s have also shifted toward so-called nonconventional countries such as Asia, the Caribbean, and South and Central America. This infusion of visible minority immigrants has rekindled controversy over the direction of Canada's immigration policies and programs. It has also fostered considerable debate regarding the role of foreign-born multicultural minorities in forging the demographic basis of Canadian identity and unity.

Who are multicultural minorities? In general, **multicultural minorities** consist of those Canadians, both native- and foreign-born, who are not of (or who choose not to identify with) British, French, or aboriginal ancestry. Or structurally speaking, they can be defined by who they are not. Both aboriginal peoples and Charter members possess a distinctive sense of who they are and what they want. National agendas have been constitutionally constructed and organized to protect and promote their political and cultural priorities. Canada's multicultural minorities occupy an entirely different status, both historically and legally. Their status in Canada is not derived from "first principles"; it is based instead on their placement as immigrants or descendants of immigrants, with rights to citizenship but no formal rights to defining national agendas except within the context of Canada's multicultural commitments. Certain multicultural minorities have encountered formidable barriers in adapting to a country whose agenda caters to the first and second "forces." This "marginalization" may explain the preoccupation with the multicultural concerns of equality and institutional accommodation in contrast with the more political demands of Canada's founding peoples (Kymlicka 1995). The entrenchment of multiculturalism in Canada has established a collective platform for articulating issues of relevance to this sector. Yet Canada's multicultural minorities are rarely in a position to present a coherent and united front to central policy structures. Social cleavages are prevalent because of geographic dispersal, cultural heterogeneity, political powerlessness, public unease, and general lack of economic clout. It is from the perspective of inequality and power involving both foreign-born immigrants and native-born descendants of immigrants that this chapter derives its impetus and organization.

A note on terminology. There is no one term that adequately encapsulates all Canadians who do not fit the category of aboriginal peoples or Charter members. Expressions such as "immigrants," "ethnic group," "people of colour" and "racial minorities" are used but may be inadequate because, paradoxically, they are too broad or too narrow. Other expressions, such as **visible and nonvisible minorities,** are widely accepted as administrative labels, albeit with limited emotional appeal. The term "visible minority" refers to an official government category of native- and foreign-born, nonwhite, non-Caucasoid individuals, including blacks, Chinese, Japanese, Koreans, Filipinos, Indo-Pakistanis, West Asians and Arabs, Southeast Asians, Latin Americans, and Pacific Islanders. This administrative category does not always square with popular perceptions of what constitutes visibility (Worthy 1996). We have tried to resolve this dilemma in terminology by referring to this sector as *multicultural minorities.* This descriptive category includes those whose legal rights are derived from their status as immigrants or descendants of immigrants rather than as founding peoples. Collectively, they look to official multiculturalism as a source of entitlements and the basis of their relationship to society. Even the concept of multicultural minorities requires some clarification. Multicultural minorities include the foreign-born, namely, **immigrants** and **refugees**, as well as native-born (or descendants of immigrants). This term may refer to both immigrants from Europe and developing countries as well as native-born Canadians who possess some non-British, non-French, nonaboriginal ancestry. By contrast, *immigrants* refers to persons born overseas, with permanent residency in Canada, including successful refugee claimants but not temporary residents, such as foreign students. Immigrants themselves can be classified into four categories, depending on motive for leaving (economic or political) and the extenuating circumstances that prompted the emigration (voluntary or involuntary).

Canada's multicultural diversity is captured by the array of terms that describe and categorize. Expressions such as (a) multicultural minorities (both visible and nonvisible as well as native-born and foreign-born), (b) visible minorities (native-born or foreign-born people of colour), and (c) immigrants (foreign-born visible and nonvisible minorities) are analytically distinct yet mutually overlapping. Of Canada's total population of approximately 30 million in 1996, the following ethnic breakdowns were tabulated:

- Nineteen percent, or 5.3 million, reported "Canadian" as their single ethnic origin. (Most of these respondents were Canadian-born and indicated either French or English as their mother tongue.)
- Seventeen percent, or 4.9 million, reported British Isles-only ancestry.
- Nine percent, or 2.7 million, reported French-only ancestry.
- Ten percent, or 2.9 million, reported a combination of British, French, or Canadian origins.
- Sixteen percent, or 4.6 million, of the population reported having some non-British, non-French, or non-Canadian origins.
- Twenty-eight percent, or 8.1 million, of the population reported having no British, French, or Canadian origins. Of these, 3.7 million were of single European origins, while 1.9 million had single Asian origin.
- Three percent, or 1.1 million people, are of aboriginal ancestry.

It should be noted that 64 percent of the population reported one ethnic origin, while 36 percent reported multiple ethnic origins.

A breakdown of those reporting non-Canadian origin reveals interesting patterns. The most frequently reported ethnic origins were Scottish, with 4.3 million responses; Irish, with 3.8 million; German, with 2.8 million; Italian, with 1.2 million; Ukranian, with 1 million; and Dutch, with 900,000. Of the 3.2 million visible minorities, or 11.2 percent of the population, that currently live in Canada, those of Chinese origins are the most populous visible minority, with a total of 860,000 persons, or 26.9 percent of the visible minority population, followed by South Asian with 671,000, or 21.0 percent, and black with 574,000, or 17.9 percent. Over half of all immigrants since the 1970s are members of visible minorities, as are nearly three-quarters of immigrants who have arrived in the 1990s. British Columbia and Ontario accounted for nearly three-quarters of all visible minorities. The proportion of visible minorities varied from a high of 18 percent of the population in British Columbia and 16 percent in Ontario to less than 1 percent in Newfoundland.

Canada is home to approximately 5 million foreign-born Canadians. The proportion of immigrants relative to the population at large (17 percent) has remained relatively consistent since 1951, despite ebbs and flows in immigration totals. Regional and municipal variations in ethnic composition are noticeable. Ontario has the largest number of persons with non-British, non-French origins, with over 5 million. This is followed by British Columbia and Alberta with just over 2 million each, and Quebec with just over 1 million. The Atlantic provinces have relatively small totals. The distribution of visible minorities continues to be uneven: In the early 1990s, 52.6 percent of all visible minorities lived in Ontario, 20.7 percent in British Columbia, 13.6 percent in Quebec, and only 2.3 percent in Saskatchewan and the Atlantic provinces combined. By 1996, visible minorities comprised 17.9 percent of British Columbia's population, 15.8 percent of Ontario's population, and 10.1 percent of Alberta's population, but only 1.1 percent of the population in New Brunswick and Prince Edward Island and 0.7 percent in Newfoundland. Multicultural minorities continue to reside in large urban regions. Both absolute numbers and relative percentages make Montreal, Toronto, and Vancouver more diverse than provincial or national averages. In 1996, according to Statistics Canada, 85 percent of all immigrants, including 93 percent who arrived between 1991 and 1996, lived in metropolitan areas. Toronto, Vancouver, and Montreal accounted for about three-quarters of all arrivals. These three metropolitan regions are also important centres for visible minorities: The percentage of Toronto's visible minority population by Census Metropolitan Area in 1996 stands at 31.6 percent, Vancouver's at 31.1 percent, and Calgary's at 15.6 percent. Compare this with the total percentages in Trois-Rivières at 0.9 percent and Chicoutimi-Jonquière at 0.4 percent. The vast majority of visible minorities reside in major urban centres for reasons related to opportunity, sociability, and transition. That concentration, in turn, proves irresistible as a magnet for the next wave of immigrants and refugees. Arguably, then, Canada can be best described as an uneven mosaic: Relatively concentrated pockets of urban multicultural diversity are interspersed with vast stretches of ethnically monochromic hinterland. Such a distribution of diversity is likely to foster misunderstanding between the metropolitan areas and the hinterland regions. The following FYI Box provides some valuable statistical data on immigrants and refugees.

FYI	Immigration Facts and Figures

1. There are 5 million immigrants in Canada, or about 17 percent of the total Canadian population. Those from Britain and other European countries comprise 47 percent of this total.
2. In the decade since 1990, an average of 220,000 immigrants have come to

Canada each year. In the 1980s, the average was 126,000; 144,000 in the 1970s, and 137,000 in the 1960s. The highest ever annual intake was 401,000 immigrants in 1913; by contrast, the record low was just under 7,600 immigrants in 1942. Recent highs and lows include 256,000 immigrants in 1993 up from the 84,000 new Canadians in 1985.

3. With a population of about 30 million and an annual intake of 220,000 immigrants per year, Canada's acceptance rate stands at 0.7 as a percentage of the total population. Compare this level of acceptance with Australia at 0.4 as a percentage of the population, the United States with 0.2 percent, and Britain and France with less than 0.1 percent. Germany, Luxemburg, and Switzerland may have the highest acceptance rate, but most immigrants are seen as "guest workers" and are generally disbarred from citizenship.

4. Let's put Canadian immigration into perspective: In 1997, Canada will bring in one legal immigrant for every 143 residents; Australia, with a population of 18.5 million, will accept 73,000 immigrants for a ratio of 1 to 253; New Zealand, with a population of 3.8 million, will accept about 15,000 net immigrants for a ratio of 1 to 233; and the United States, with a population of 280 million, will accept 720,000 immigrants (perhaps as many as 1.2 million if illegal immigrants are included) for a ratio of 1 to 388.

5. In 1966, about three-quarters of all immigrants to Canada arrived from Europe or the United States. By 1981, the proportion was reversed, with about three-quarters of immigrants from Asia, Africa, the Caribbean, and Central America, but only 25 percent from Europe or the United States. By 1996, immigrants from Europe and the United States declined to just over 20 percent. Just under half (48 percent) of all immigrants between 1991 and 1996 were born in Asia, with Hong Kong (10.5 percent), People's Republic of China (8.5 percent), the Philippines (6.9 percent), and India (6.9 percent) leading the way.

6. Of all immigrants, 13 percent were born in the United Kingdom, down from 17 percent in 1991. Seven percent were born in Italy, while 5 percent were born in each of China, Hong Kong, India, and the United States.

7. Over half of all immigrants (55 percent) live in Ontario, with the result that one-quarter of all Ontarians (and British Columbians) are immigrants. Of all recent arrivals, 42 percent settle in Toronto; as a result, 48 percent of Toronto's population is foreign-born, including one in ten since 1991, reflecting 169 different countries and about 100 different languages.

8. Between 90 and 95 percent of all immigrants live in Canada's larger cities, with the majority in Toronto (36 percent), Vancouver (13 percent), and Montreal (12 percent).

9. Approximately 42 percent of new arrivals speak neither French nor English.

10. Of the projected 215,000 immigrants for 1998, around 60 percent of all immigrants will be from the skilled worker and business class, around 30 percent will be from family class, about 10 percent from the refugee class, and a small number from caregiver programs and special categories.

11. In 1971, the percentage of visible minorities in the Toronto Census Metropolitan Area was about 1 percent. The percentage of visible minorities in Toronto at present is approximately 32 percent. Nearly 42 percent of Canada's visible minorities live in Toronto, prompting the United Nations to designate Toronto as the world's most ethnically diverse city.

12. There are about 25 million refugees and another 25 million displaced persons in the world today. Canada accepted 26,000 refugees in 1996, of which 15,500 were

refugee claimants (arrived unannounced), with Sri Lanka heading the list at 2,964 claimants, followed by Chile (2,646), Iran (1,725), and Israel (1,221).

13. Of the 95,500 refugee claimants between 1993 and 1997, 42 percent were accepted, 33 percent rejected, and 25 percent not finalized or ineligible. Canada's acceptance rate of 58 percent in 1996 may be down from the early 1990s, but is considerably higher than the 5 to 15 percent rate for all other countries. More than 5,000 former refugee claimants who are facing deportation cannot be located, Ottawa has conceded (Laghi 1999).

14. In 1980, sponsored refugees ("approved from abroad") outnumbered refugee claimants ("announced at arrival") by 39,992 to 718. By 1992, refugee claimants outnumbered sponsored refugees by 37,152 to 14,726. The ratio is about equal at present.

CANADIAN IMMIGRATION: POLICIES, PRACTICES, AND TRENDS

Canada is one of the few countries in the world that regards itself as an immigration country (Ucarer 1997). The United States and Australia are two notable immigration countries, so too are Brazil and Argentina, several Latin American countries, and most recently New Zealand. Three characteristics distinguish immigration countries from nonimmigration countries: First, policies exist that attempt to regulate the flow of immigrants into the country. Second, programs are put into place to assist in the assimilation and integration of migrants. This absorption not only includes social and material adjustment; immigrants also receive all civil and political rights associated with citizenship in that country. Third, immigration is viewed as a key part of society building. Immigrants are expected to assist in the social, economic, and cultural development by taking up jobs, filling in underpopulated areas, contributing to population growth, and making international linkages. Compare this with nonimmigration countries such as Germany with policies that stabilize inflows, limit long-term stays, discourage permanent residences, label immigrants as guest workers, and withhold citizenship and attendant rights (Ucarer 1997). Those of German parentage are automatically granted citizenship because of kinship ("bloodlines"); by contrast, foreigners and their children are generally excluded from citizenship even if born and raised in the country. Very simply, immigration in nonimmigration societies does not fit into the long-term plans related to national identity or society building.

Canada is frequently praised—or pilloried—as a country of immigrants (Foster 1998). As one of a small handful of immigration countries in the world, immigration has played a pivotal role in Canada's national development and will continue to do so in the foreseeable future. The increasingly unfettered movements of people, ideas, labour, and investment across cultural borders will see to that. With the exception of aboriginal peoples, all Canadians are immigrants or descendants of immigrants. Yet Canadians seem curiously ambivalent about immigration and immigrants, despite a long-standing reliance on immigrant labour as a catalyst for development (Li 1996). Antipathy toward new Canadians borders on the xenophobic at times, with calls for Rights of Landing Fees, DNA testing, and vigorous deportation procedures. At other times, there are calls for vigorous debate over immigration questions regarding "how many," "where from," "what sort," and "why not" (Denley 1998). Despite its importance to Canada, immigration as a sociological phenomenon has not received the kind of analytical attention it deserves. The next section will partially atone for that neglect by exploring patterns in Canada's immigration at the levels of policies and practices, both past and present.

Early Policy and Practices

Canadian immigration policies have evolved noticeably since Confederation (Foster 1998). Policy content and objectives were shaped historically by a combination of ideological considerations, political expediency, international obligations, and economic requirements. Outcomes were decided by an interplay of factors, including racism and ethnocentrism, the agricultural bias of Canada's early immigration policies, the pivotal role of private interests, economic imperatives, tension between business and labour over who to let in, and high levels of out-migration to the United States. The cumulative impact has transformed immigration policy and practice into a kind of contested site in which competing interests have struggled to impose their agenda and definition on who should come, what for, from where, why, and how many.

Initial policies could be described as essentially racist in orientation, assimilationist in objective, nativist ("Canadianist") in content, and exclusionary in outcome. As much energy was expended in keeping out certain "types" as there was in encouraging others to settle (Whitaker 1991). The 1869 Immigration Act and subsequent amendments excluded certain types of undesirables, such as criminals and the diseased, while imposing strict limitations on the Japanese, Chinese, and East Asians (Avery 1995). A "racial pecking order" (Lupul 1988) was established by sorting out potential migrants on the basis of racial affiliation and capacity for assimilation (Walker 1997). Preferred categories of immigrants were drawn from the so-called superior stock of Great Britain or Northwestern Europe. Immigration from "white" countries was encouraged to ensure the British character of the Dominion. This category was virtually exempt from entry restrictions except for certain visa formalities (Abella and Troper 1991). At the bottom of this pecking order were blacks and Asians, both of whom were seen as inherently inferior and ultimately unassimilable. In between these two poles were the nonpreferred classes, consisting of immigrants from Eastern and middle Europe and Russia. While admired for their brawn and industry, Canadians harboured a degree of suspicion toward these "dangerous foreigners," particularly those who dared to challenge the principles of free enterprise (Avery 1995). A special "restricted" permit class was aimed at Jews and Mediterranean populations.

Moves to settle the Prairies saw preferential treatment extended to more assimilable Europeans, once preferred sources dwindled. Canada's first Immigration Minister, Clifford Sifton, made virtue of necessity in 1896 when he encouraged immigrants from Eastern Europe despite a chorus of criticism about introducing foreign or alien "bohunks" into a "white man's country." Clifton resolutely opposed the import of urban factory workers, many of whom were seen as degenerate, subject to economic unrest, or fodder for radical agitators. The agricultural bias of early immigration was eloquently expressed when Clifton mused about "stalwart peasants in a sheepskin coat, born on the soil, whose forefathers had been farmers for ten generations, with a stout wife and a half-dozen children" (quoted in Whitaker 1991:7). But not all immigrants saw themselves as farmers. Over time, migrants shifted from agricultural to nonagricultural jobs involving wage employment in labour-intensive industries such as railroad construction, mining, and construction work (Avery 1995).

Promotion of immigration from across Europe provoked debate over the direction of Canada's national identity (Lehr 1987). Political parties engaged in endless polemics over who was desirable or assimilable. But all agreed that the survival of Canada was dependent on the absorption of alien groups into Anglo-Celtic culture. Until World War I, Canadian immigration policy was split into two streams: private interests, who recruited immigrants for national economic development, and the immigration branch, which recruited agriculturalists for Western Canada (Avery 1995). Once the apparatus for entry was established, the state was content to leave the actual process to market forces and private companies (Whitaker 1991). In 1925, the Liberals transferred the administration of government immigration policy to the CNR and CPR, both of whom had a vested interest in attracting unskilled labour and hardy farmers, regardless of whether they came from nonpreferred classes (Thompson and Weinfeld 1995). The CPR actively recruited immigrants, since profit margins required a mobile population willing to pay going freight rates (Simpson 1994). In its role as agent for the government, the CPR established a Department of Colonization and Immigration for expediting the movement and settlement of new Canadians, in effect confirming the view that immigration was "...simply part of the economics of transportation in a developing country dependent on staple extraction within a wider imperial framework" (Whitaker 1991:5). The government's involvement in immigration was restricted largely to issuing visas and compiling medical checks. Corporate interests declined only with the collapse of small-scale farming in the 1930s.

Widespread racism did not deter the entry of so-called "undersirables." Asian immigrants such as the Chinese and Indians were tolerated only as "fodder" for Canadian capitalist expansion. The Asian tap was turned on when needed, turned off when their usefulness disappeared. Restrictions for entry were imposed, ranging from head taxes to restrictive quotas. Hardships were compounded by exclusion of undesirable immigrants from organized labour movements in Canada. Immigrants from nonconventional sources who entered and survived were expected to quietly toil away in regions and at tasks (for example, railways, mines, lumber camps, domestic work) below the dignity of native-born Canadians. Public and political reaction to immigrants tended to reflect divergent interests: Business and powerful transportation companies exerted pressure on the government and private interests to increase immigration levels on the grounds that a prosperous local economy was dependent on a steady supply of labour; by contrast, organized labour and public sentiment generally favoured a restriction of those who were "repugnant to Canadian identity" or would "lower [the] Canadian standard of living" (Avery 1995). Short-term economic interests came into conflict with long-term national development strategies and goals. The government was sandwiched in between, sometimes taking the high ground, other times capitulating to private or public interests as the circumstances dictated.

Early immigration policies were based on practical considerations that coincided with Canada's economic needs. Immigrants were selected on the basis of their ability to fill slots in the expanding economy. The resulting taps-on and taps-off approach reflected and reinforced a cautious estimate of Canada's absorptive capacity. Western settlement required large numbers, with immigration peaking at 400,870 in 1913; wars and Depression conditions resulted in lower figures, bottoming out in 1942 at 7,576 immigrants. This stop-and-go mentality exposed Canada to criticism that it was merely operating a guest-worker system; that is, foreigners were welcome when the economy boomed, but rejected when recession set in. It took a lot of convincing to get people to come. Even more inducements were required to make them stay. Many new Canadians promptly left for the United States, in effect reinforcing a perception of Canada as little more than a transfer point (Whitaker 1991) between the United States and Europe. Canadian immigration remained expansionist until World War I. Depressed rates of immigration accompanied both the Depression and World War II, but annual rates sky-rocketed in the wake of Canada's postwar boom economy. Even with the demands of labour-starved industries, postwar immigration reflected a preference for Northwestern Europeans, many of whom were selected from displaced persons camps under international supervision. A new Department of Immigration and Citizenship was established in 1950. It introduced im-migration reforms related to reunification of families and a sharp shift toward skilled nona-gricultural workers, but with orders to maintain a strict eye on Canada's absorptive capacity (Whitaker 1991). Strict quotas remained in place for most non-Europeans.

An expansionist immigration policy in the 1950s and 1960s reflected a seemingly in-satiable demand for skilled and unskilled labour for feeding Canada's expanding economy and a "heady optimism that Canada was an evolving major world power" (Avery 1995). Altruism dovetailed with self-interest as guilt over Canada's heartless denial of sanctuary for victims of the Holocaust meshed nicely with greed in fuelling the industrial boom (Thompson and Weinfeld 1995). But a rethinking of who "got in" was prompted by changes in the world economy. By 1962, Canadian immigration laws underwent a major shift when Canada broadened its acceptance of migrants on grounds of human capital rather than national ori-gin. Several reasons accounted for this shift: (a) to satisfy the need for more skilled labour in the newer economy; (b) to offset the decline in European immigrants; and (c) to compensate for the loss of skilled personnel to the United States (Li 1996). Canada became one of the first countries to remove overt racial criteria from its immigration policies (Hawkins 1974). Independent-class immigrants were admitted on the strength of their capacity for productivity and technical/professional qualifications. Their value also lay in offloading the educational and training costs in producing and reproducing a skilled workforce (Li 1996). **Sponsored immigrants** included close relatives of permanent residents, whereas the **nominated class** of more distant relatives was subject to certain restrictions. Clauses were inserted, how-ever, to prevent Asians and African-Canadians from sponsoring distant relatives.

The criteria for entry underwent further reform in 1967. Canada's expanding economy re-quired educated and skilled labour; yet economic recovery in Europe had sharply usurped Canada's favourite taproot. Skilled immigrant labour could only be found in those quarters of the world that historically fell outside of Canadian customs and practice (Foster 1998), so that immigration pipelines opened to nonconventional sources, including countries in Asia and Africa and South and Central America. A **points system** of evaluation was introduced: Independent applicants were numerically assessed according to their possession of requisite language skills, occupational expertise, and disposable resources. Establishing a formally colourblind immigration policy minimized the salience of racial or ethnic criteria for entry. Still, the system was not free of systemic bias because of discriminatory barriers against the acceptance of the poor or culturally different. The points system also confirmed the link be-tween immigration and the employment market, given the priority assigned to the economy's absorptive capacity as a key variable in determining who got in and how many.

Contemporary Developments

Historically, Canadian immigration responded to the realities of a changing labour market. Questions regarding who was admitted and how many have been determined by three fac-tors: the state of the economy, a commitment to admit only British or British-looking peo-ple, and compliance with international obligations and laws. To date, Canada has never had a clearly articulated national consensus about immigration and its relationship to society building (Knowles 1992), with the possible exception of the **1976 Immigration Act** and minor amendments in 1989 and 1993. Policy itself is accused of being driven by well-intentioned "warm fuzzies" to assist others less fortunate, together with an implicit belief that increasing the size of Canada's population will make it bigger and better (Denley 1998).

The Immigration Act of 1976 codified immigration amendments from the 1960s and 1970s. It also attempted to specify the economic, humanitarian, and legal objectives of Canada's immigration commitment, and included the following political, demographic, social, and cultural dimensions:

- family reunification
- protection of legitimate refugees
- enhancement of Canada's prosperity and global competitiveness
- preservation of Canada's integrity

Canada's immigration policy extends to the settlement and integration of new Canadians. Direct assistance is provided by nonprofit organizations who specialize in language training, employment counselling, and translation services. The objective is to ensure immigrants become self-sufficient and contributing members of society. It should be noted that the federal government exercises primary responsibility in this area; nevertheless, it shares jurisdiction with the provinces through consultations over immigration levels and settlement measures. Only Quebec at present possesses unilateral powers of immigration selection.

Current immigration policy reflects a commitment to moderate and controlled intake as grounds for economic growth. It also acknowledges a rethinking in the relationship between immigrants and society with respect to the economy. Prior to the late 1980s, immigration policies tended to respond to shortages or surpluses in the labour market. This taps-on, taps-off approach was gradually replaced with the idea of immigration as an integral component of a sustainable economic growth policy. Immigrants did not just serve the needs of labour, but also provided consumers, investors, and marketers with the demographics to improve Canada's economic performance. Such a shift in thinking may help to explain the relatively high and constant rates of immigration despite recessionary pressures and public disgruntlement. Current immigration flows also embrace a balance of the enlightened with the practical to ensure fairness without loss of control (Knowles 1992). Refusal to drastically reduce refugee and family reunification classes, even in the face of mounting criticism, suggests a firm commitment to humanitarian values. But pragmatism prevails, and the practical aspects of Canada's immigration policy are manifest in different ways. The primary reason Canada wants immigrants is to offset the effects of an aging population, because Canadians are not reproducing fast enough to maintain a steady population growth, and to generate a basis for a sustainable economic growth (Foster 1999). Only those with requisite skills and resources are allowed entry when applying as independents. Those immigrants who are willing to invest in Canada through creation of employable industries are actively courted. The need for cheap, disposable labour also is critical. Current examples include the importation of migrant workers on a cyclical basis from the Caribbean to harvest fruit and vegetables in southern Ontario and the domestic workers scheme to alleviate the crisis in child-care. Canada, of course, is not the only country whose immigration practices reflect political calculation and economic expediency. European countries have demonstrated all too readily their willingness to accept immigrants to feed a labour-starved economic boom, but an equal disdain when the downturn returns.

Policy modifications are anticipated to respond to recent talk of reform (see Foster 1998). Many of the initiatives for reformulation are drawn from a three-person committee under the Immigration Minister, Lucienne Robillard, who published a report in January 1998 entitled "Not Just Numbers: A Canadian Framework for Future Immigration." The report emphasized the need to tighten up the immigration program by imposing more restrictions on entry, focusing on immigrants who can integrate quickly into the workplace and society, and increased user fees for processing and settlement (Thompson 1998). Its major recommendations included (a) imposition of language fluency in French or English for all **business class immigrants,** (b) imposition of a tuition fee/head tax on all members of the family class who lack fluency in one of the two official languages, (c) elimination of the points system for skilled workers and emphasis instead on education, work experience, and income-generating potential, and (d) toughening up of sponsorship rules by way of contracts and rights to garnishee wages. The Minister has wisely introduced nationwide consultation over these issues before tabling legislation in light of lively reaction from ethnic community and immigration lobby groups. Nevertheless, talk of reform reflects an unspoken assumption that immigrants are a burden on Canadian society and this cost must be minimized to ensure ongoing acceptance (see Editorial, *Toronto Star,* 1998).

To Sum Up Certain trends can be discerned in analyzing immigration policies and practices. The following shifts are most noticeable in defining policies and trends:

- from a focus on immigration from short-term labour supply to that of sustainable economic growth;
- from unskilled agricultural/manual workers to skilled professionals for knowledge-based industry;
- from an emphasis on racial and national origins as a basis for selection to that of colourblindness;
- from a reliance on European sources to that of Asia and other nonconventional origins;
- from a purely pragmatic focus to a balancing of practical with the compassionate;
- from a loosely monitored administration to a tightly regulated system.

Despite these shifts in trends, one theme appears to be constant: Immigration remains a response to capitalist demands for skilled or unskilled labour (see Li 1996). The fact that the types of labour needs have varied from one historical context to the next does not invalidate this underlying commitment.

IMMIGRATION PROGRAM: "WHO GETS IN?"

Passage of the 1976 Immigration Act consolidated the range of admissible immigrants. It also articulated the entry conditions for admission into Canada. Three possible avenues of acceptance exist: *family, independent,* and *refugee.*

Family Reunification Class

The *family class* recognizes the need for families to stay together if only to stabilize the process of integration into Canada. Immediate members of the family—a spouse and dependent children under 19—are automatically allowed into Canada provided they are of good health and without a criminal record. Until recently, parents and grandparents were also included; a separate entry stream is currently under consideration. More distant relatives must "top up" with points from the independent class to secure entry into Canada. The vast majority of family class immigrants come from India (at 17,081 in 1993), followed by Hong Kong, the Philippines, China, Vietnam, and Jamaica, according to Citizenship and Immigration Canada (24 October 1994). Currently, the family reunification category accounts for about 30 percent of all immigration to Canada, a figure that has slowly declined in recent years.

Independent Class

The *independent class* includes skilled workers and businesspeople (both entrepreneurs and investors). Skilled workers are assessed under a points system that emphasizes their suitability on the grounds of job-related skills, age, official language knowledge, and education as well as a personal assessment by an immigration officer (see Table 8.1). The number of points required for entry varies: Business class (both investor and entrepreneur) requires only 25; self-employed and skilled workers need 70, although they are automatically entitled to a large bonus because of their talents. Assisted relatives also receive credit as nominated immigrants, but require additional points elsewhere to qualify for the necessary 70 points.

TABLE 8.1 The Immigrant Selection System	
Factor	**Maximum Units**
Education	16
Specific vocational preparation	18
Experience	8
Occupational demand	10
Arranged employment/designated occupation	10
Demographic factor	8
Age	10
Knowledge of official language(s)	15
Personal suitability	10

SOURCE: Immigration Canada, 1994

To enter, skilled workers must pass the usual health and security clearances. It is interesting to note that Canada does not allow an unlimited number of independent class immigrants (Sarick 1997). Annual targets are set for each of Canada's visa points; in 1997, Buffalo's visa post was entitled to process 22,000 independents for all of Canada and 1,000 for Quebec; the office in Delhi, India, was allocated 10,500 spaces for Canada and 320 for Quebec; Sydney, Australia, had 1,000 for Canada and 5 for Quebec; and Lima, Peru, had 125 final dispositions for Canada and 80 for Quebec.

A subcategory of the independent class entails a transfer of funds as the price of entry into Canada. The "business" or "entrepreneurial" program selects immigrants with an ability to establish businesses that will generate employment opportunities for Canadians. Under the investment program, applicants must meet the usual immigration criteria and a demonstrated net worth of $500,000. In exchange for investing $350,000 in a Canadian fund for five years, a business applicant receives landed immigrant status (a permanent resident visa). As of July 1998, this amount increased to $450,000 for those willing to invest their money in Ontario, Quebec, British Columbia, or Alberta. Nearly 20,000 immigrants have taken advantage of this program since its inception in 1986, with a total investment of $4.3 billion in exchange for resident status for themselves and their families (Jimenez 1999). But the program has also been plagued by abuse and mismanagement. Plans are in place to transfer more responsibility to the provinces for the monitoring of investment funds.

Refugee Class

The *refugee category* is the third and perhaps most controversial of immigrant streams into Canada. Refugees are accepted as part of Canada's humanitarian and legal obligations to the world community. Canada has performed admirably by comparison with countries that perfunctorily deny basic human rights or deport refugees as part of a general crackdown. Since World War II, Canada has officially admitted over half a million refugees, with recent annual intakes in the vicinity of 20,000 to 35,000. Canada's apparent generosity and support of international refugee programs has been amply documented, especially with receipt of the Nansen Medal in 1986, the first country ever to be bestowed such an honour by the United Nations.

Two categories of refugees are "recognized," neither of which requires points for entry. One category constitutes sponsored refugees. **Sponsored refugees** are preselected abroad either by government officials or by private agencies, individuals, clubs or church groups, with private sponsors obligated to provide support for up to ten years. Both government and privately sponsored refugees receive landed immigrant status before arriving in Canada and assistance through government programs once they arrive. A second category of refugees consists of **refugee claimants** who arrive unannounced by foot, boat, or plane, often without documentation such as passports, and claim refugee status upon arrival to Canada. Refugee claimants did not become an issue until 1982, when the numbers doubled from 558 to 1,162 and again in 1991 when numbers quadrupled from 8,328 to 29,092. Refugee claimants have outnumbered sponsored refugees in each of the 1990s decade years. In contrast with sponsored refugees, refugee claimants are not entitled to some of the social services that Canadians take for granted. Until recently, moreover, they were also ineligible for work until they had an initial hearing, thus imposing an additional burden on cash-strapped provinces and work-deprived refugees. Such exclusionary practices have raised the profile of refugees as a "social problem," as the next Case Study reveals.

CASE STUDY 8-1	The Refugee Crisis: Whose Crisis?

Debate over refugees has provoked Canadians as few other issues have. This is not surprising, given the magnitude of this global problem. At present, there are up to 25 million refugees worldwide, an increase from 2.5 million during the 1970s. Another 25 million are displaced from their homes but still reside inside their country in makeshift government-sponsored camps with few amenities or prospects for placement. Most refugees have fled war-torn countries; others from regimes who routinely violate human rights as state policy. Establishing a fair and just system to cope with this human crisis would appear a simple enough challenge. Yet the refugee question remains complex and contested with perennial controversies over "who is a refugee," "how do we find out," "is the system working," and "how many can Canada handle" (Bauer 1994).

Much of the debate over refugees to Canada seems to pivot around two axis points (Plaut 1989). One mindset wants a generous acceptance as a litmus test of Canada's humanitarianism; the other associates refugees with social problems (Avery 1995). Many Canadians recognize and accept Canada's humanitarian commitments to those less fortunate. This sector is inclined to see the refugee process as protecting the lives of endangered human beings. The objective of a humane policy is to cast as wide a net as possible for refugees, then dispose of those who don't fit, keeping in mind that refugees from a disordered society are hardly in a position to adhere to bureaucratic regulations (Plaut 1989). An opposing view sees refugee claimants as a potential threat to the integrity of Canada's immigration system. Refugees are perceived as frauds and manipulators anxious to take advantage of Canada's generosity: Loopholes are exploited by these refugees, while the system is subject to abuse by unscrupulous lawyers, gullible refugees, scheming refugee and ethnic organizations, and incompetent **Immigration and Refugee Board** (IRB) members (Bauer 1994). Not surprisingly, the preferred approach is to exclude as many refugees as possible, leaving room only for genuine cases such as those from Kosovo (Francis 1999).

Defining Refugees

Defining a refugee is not as straightforward as it might appear. According to the United Nations Human Rights Convention of 1951 (to which Canada is a signatory) and Canada's Immigration Act of 1976, **conventional refugees** constitute a class of individuals who have left their country and cannot return because of a well-founded fear of persecution for reasons of race, religion, nationality, group membership, or political opinion. These criteria are difficult to "operationalize"; for example, what precisely is the distinction between outright persecution and ordinary discrimination, between individual harassment and generalized violence? In contrast with conventional refugees, nonconventional refugees may be in need of protection from a dangerous situation but only for a short duration (Stoffman 1997). As a result, even those who have fled famine or civil wars, in some cases suffered hardship or death of family members, may not qualify as conventional refugees under Canadian law if they have not been singled out for persecution because of their affiliation to a particular religion, race, nationality, political opinion, or group membership (Bauer 1994). In May 1997, Canada expanded its definition of refugee status to include people who had been displaced within their own countries because of war or terrorism (Waldie 1998). Conversely, Canada's decision to accept refugees from Mexico and China (important trading partners), Israel (diplomatic allies), and Turkey (military allies) has offended diplomatic friends and trading partners, none of which like to be singled out as possible human rights violators (Shallot 1994). For example, the government is accused of selecting sponsored refugees (7,710 in 1997) not on the basis of individual need but on their ability to contribute to the Canadian economy without excess cost to the taxpayer (Knox 1998).

In theory, a political dimension separates conventional refugees from immigrants who migrate primarily for social or economic reasons. Reality, however, is not so accommodating (Thompson 1997). Politics once played an important part: Historically those who fled Communist regimes were happily accepted as refugees, while those escaping from right wing coups loyal to America such as that in Chile in 1973 have received a cool reception, since they lacked "Cold War credentials" (Whitaker 1991:22). Certain groups who do not conform with the letter of the refugee law are accepted, including those who experience refugee-like conditions, such as political oppression or environmental disaster. Moreover, economic factors are increasingly important in determining who gets in: Refugee status may be granted to minorities such as gypsies, who do not face overt state persecution yet fail to receive state protection from open discrimination and denial of services. Refugee status is now being claimed on gender grounds, such as in cases of abusive domestic situations, exposure to mutilation, or forced marriage and sterilization. Canada became the world's first country in 1993 to recognize gender persecution as legitimate grounds for entry. Finally, refugee claimants whose applications have been rejected and appeals exhausted are not being deported because of dangerous or unstable conditions (Thompson 1994).

Sorting Out Refugees

Even those who are highly critical of government restrictions concede that Canada cannot possibly accept all refugees. The sovereignty and prosperity of Canadians depend on securing its boundaries against the random flow of newcomers. Yet sheer numbers appear to be overwhelming the system: Since the 1990s, the total number of claimants is far in excess of what the system was designed to handle, with the result that refugee workers are overworked and claimants encounter lengthy delays. Arrival at Canada's borders activates a set of refugee determination procedures. The logic behind these procedures reflects a 1985 Supreme Court ruling that entitled anyone who so much as set a foot on Canada the rights of due process as guar-

anteed in the Charter of Rights and Freedom. A lengthy process may be required to determine if the claimants in question qualify as bona fide refugees under the 1951 Geneva Convention statutes (Jackson 1991). The old system of refugee determination proved cumbersome, involving a seven-step process that culminated in delays of five years. Bottlenecks ensued, with an 80,000 person backlog by 1988, despite an administrative review to clear unprocessed applications. A new streamlined two-step refugee determination system was put in place on 1 January 1989 to clear up the refugee backlog and fast-track current claims.

The current system consists of a simplified procedure that purports to balance fairness with efficiency. Within 72 hours of entry, a refugee claimant is interviewed and assessed by a senior immigration official. If the claim is upheld as credible, the refugee is then expected to attend a more detailed hearing by the IRB, a quasi-independent tribunal created in 1989 after a scandal involving political and diplomatic interference in the refugee determination process. Claimants are given a month or so to provide basic data in support of their claim (Bauer 1994). They also are entitled to legal aid in preparing a case or filing an appeal. Those claimants who are almost certain of entry are conferred what is called an "expedited hearing" to speed things up and prevent a backlog. If the claimant is not given expedited treatment, another hearing is held in several months with a two-member panel from the IRB in one of its offices across Canada. Endorsement by one of two panel members is required to confer refugee status to the claimant; a unanimous decision in writing is required for a rejection. That entire process may take up to three years if appeals are exhausted. Those who have exhausted all appeal routes are slotted for deportation, but few ever are, partly because of compassionate grounds and administrative bungling.

Is the System Working?

By world standards, Canada's refugee determination process is generous and regarded as one of the world's best by the United Nations Commissioner on Refugees, despite criticism from refugee lawyers and advocacy groups who believe the system is too tough on refugees (Simpson 1997; Mawani 1997). Others think the system is too lax, including William Bauer and Daniel Stoffman, who point out that Canada accepts refugees claimants at six times the international norm and even approves claims from citizens of democratic societies such as Israel, the United Kingdom, and the United States. Of the 95,500 refugees who made claims to the IRB between 1993 and 1997, according to the auditor-general, 42 percent were accepted, 33 percent were rejected, and 25 percent were not finalized or ineligible. In 1997, the IRB finalized 21,803 claims of 30,756 cases: 9,541 were positive, 7,037 were rejected, and 5,225 were withdrawn prior to adjudication. There are currently in excess of 29,000 claims waiting to be heard. Another 8,500 cases of rejected claimants are undergoing a review process to determine if deportation is likely to pose a risk (Thompson 1997). The average processing time for a case before the IRB is about 13 months; the postdetermination process takes about 7 months. Of the 31,200 claims rejected between 1993 and 1997, only 22 percent have confirmed their departure from the country.

These figures can be read in different ways. The worst spin suggests that Canada's refugee determination system is absurdly generous. Numerous loopholes and vulnerabilities are exploited that can cost about $1 billion per year, once legal, welfare, and administrative costs are factored in (Stoffman 1997). That being the case, why not accept all refugee claimants and dispense with the costs involved in deporting the few who fail to meet our standards? An intermediate position is echoed by the auditor-general (see Thompson 1997), who believes the current system is ensnared in a paradox: As it stands, it does not reply quickly enough to those in genuine need of protection, nor does it deter bogus refugees who do not require or deserve Canada's protection. A third interpretation is predicated on the principle that all refugees are deemed to be innocent ("genuine") until proven guilty ("bogus"). However generous and compassionate, such a commitment (Mawani 1997) will invariably generate bottlenecks in a system designed to be efficient as well as generous and fair.

COSTS AND BENEFITS: THE PROS, CONS, AND THE IN BETWEENS

All indicators suggest a continuation of Canada as a favourite destination for those fleeing political oppression, ethnic conflicts, demographic pressure, and economic stagnation. Immigrants and refugees are not only "pushed" from their homeland, but also "pulled" to Canada because of opportunity and freedom. Invariably this raises the question of whether immigration provides a benefit or extracts a cost. Canadians, in turn, have reacted to immigrants and immigration in different ways, ranging from enthusiasm and endorsement on the one hand to resentment on the other, with a combination of indifference, resignation, and indecision in between. A step back from the fray can help to keep things in perspective. Nevertheless, there is still much that is unknown about the impact of immigration. There is even less consensus about the value of immigration (Isbister 1996). Such indecision raises the questions, What kind of country do we value? How do immigrants contribute to or detract from this vision?

Pros

Increased immigration into Canada has been justified or vilified on various grounds. Canada is a land of immigrants whose prosperity and identity are dependent on the perpetual movement of people (Tepper 1988). Studies in other parts of the world, such as Australia, New Zealand, and the United States, confirm the notion that, on balance, immigrants are a net contributor to society— demographically, socially, culturally, and economically (Isbister 1996; Millman 1997; Castles and Miller 1998; Fleras and Spoonley 1999). The same conclusions exist for Canada: These outcomes, however, are not distributed equally, with some provinces, such as British Columbia, receiving a disproportionate slice of benefits because of more affluent immigrants (Matas 1994).

Many tout the economic perks of immigration (Cohen 1997; Corcoran 1999; but see Stoffman 1998). Immigrants will enhance Canada's ability to compete in the global economy, as Gwynne Dyer likes to remind us, because Canada itself is a global society by virtue of its multicultural character, both domestically and globally. Immigrants create more jobs than they take; as consumers they provide markets for Canadian goods, they are more likely to start businesses than other Canadians, are better qualified in terms of education, and pay more in taxes than they receive in social services. Immigrants not only ease labour shortages during phases of capitalist expansion, but also secure employment in jobs that Canadians dislike. Immigrants tend to possess drive and vitality, with boundless energy and optimism, and a willingness to take entrepreneurial risks by capitalizing on international links to improve Canada's competitive position in a global economy. After all, a global economy requires a continuous two-way flow of skilled workers and capital for investment. In general, then, rather than hurting an economy, immigrants are apt to provide a much-needed kick start.

Social benefits can also be discerned. Immigrants are more likely to be married than Canadian-born and less likely to divorce, with rates below those of Canadian-born. Most immigrants do not soak up welfare rolls or commit a disproportionate amount of crime. To the contrary, with the possible exception of one or two groups, they are less likely to end up in the criminal justice system or engage in criminal activity despite irresponsible media sensationalism. The demographics of Canada also work in favour of increased immigration. An aging population pyramid, with declining birthrate totals (1.7 children per family, which is below the replacement rate of 2.1 and growth rate of 2.3), puts the onus on younger immigrants for future support of social programs. Immigrants are also likely to integrate into Canadian society. A long-term study of 1,348 Southeast Asian refugees that began in 1981 indicates that 78 percent are employed, 18 percent are self-employed, two-thirds feel at home in Canada, with no strong desire to return, and 99 percent have taken out Canadian citizenship. On the downside, two-thirds are unhappy with their command of English.

Cons

Canadians as a whole possess ambivalent attitudes toward the presence of immigrants and refugees. Many people are supportive of immigrants and refugees as hard-working and positive contributors to society. But others dislike what they see as threats to Canada's economy and cultural identity. People tend to be comfortable with immigrants who are poor, appear to be grateful for the opportunity, and are willing to start at the bottom as cooks, labourers, and farmhands. They are less sure of how to "cope" with those who are affluent, confident, assertive, and highly qualified; unwilling to put up with slights or slurs as the price of admission or staying; and are willing to shop their talents wherever the global economy will take them (Siddiqui 1999). Immigrants are deeply resented and fiercely resisted as "scroungers" who steal jobs, housing, and education; who undermine moralities and foster crime; and who swamp access to increasingly scarce services (see Cohen 1997). Others deplore immigrants for making unreasonable demands on Canadian society when it should be Canadians who call the shots. Consider this statement by Ted Byfield in an 18 July 1996 issue of the *Financial Post,* when reminding immigrants that (a) Canada possesses a distinctive culture; (b) this culture is superior and should supersede immigrant cultures; (c) immigrants may retain aspects of their culture that are compatible with Canada's and does not drain public monies; (d) immigrants know their place in society and prove themselves by starting at the bottom and working their way up; (e) immigrants are "guests" in this country, and they should fit into Canada rather than the other way around; (f) immigration should be shaped by national needs rather than by immigrant wants or ethnic lobby groups pressure; and (g) Canada should be able to cut back on immigration when it chooses to do so.

These ideas may or may not reflect concerns of many Canadians. Nevertheless, polls confirm that many believe there is too much immigration of the wrong kind at the wrong time. Canadians as a rule may accept the necessity or inevitability of immigrants and refugees, but bristle at legislative loopholes and unscrupulous stakeholders, especially when dysfunctional government policies prevail because of a small number of vocal clients ("clientele capture") with a vested interested in preserving the status quo (Stoffman 1994). Some criticize what they see as excessively generous concessions to immigrants at a time of relentless cutbacks in services and benefits. The government should be looking after "our own," it is argued, rather than throwing money at refugee determination processes and immigrant resettlement programs (Sudol 1998). Others take exception to the integration costs of immigrants (for instance, the costs for language training, which in the 1997–98 fiscal year amounted to $387.1 million at federal, provincial, and local levels [Galt 1998]). Still others are concerned about the "problems" that immigrants bring with them to Canada. These include allegations that immigrants are using their ties abroad to establish illegal international distribution systems for contraband drugs, loan sharking, prostitution, and smuggling of illegal aliens into Canada, while victimizing those already in Canada through extortion rackets (Madely 1994). The growing fear of undermining the WASP-ish character of Canadian society through unrestricted entry is palpable as well. Finally, there is a perception that vested interests are driving the immigration agenda. Michael Valpy (1994) writes of the sectors that stand to gain from immigration:

> They serve ethnic groups who want easy access to the country for their relatives…. They serve capitalism's desire for cheap labour. They serve immigrant lawyers' desire for a steady supply of customers. They serve the intellectual convictions of those who believe virtually everyone outside Canada can qualify as a refugee.

A powerful ethnic voting block may also explain why politicians are fearful of tampering with the status quo, despite a growing chorus of concerns over policy and practice.

The In Betweens

Joel Millman (1997) provides useful insight. He argues that no person, no matter how opposed he or she is to immigration in principle or practice, is without some sympathy for the plight of the world's poorest. Similarly, no person is without some concern over the negative impact of immigration on some sectors of society, regardless of how pro-immigrant that person is. Somewhere between the "yeahs" and the "nays" are those who are unsure of what stand to take. They acknowledge certain costs associated with immigration, and it is these costs that tend to make people ambiguous about aspects of immigration. Some Canadians, such as unskilled workers, may be penalized by immigration; others such as real estate agents and immigration lawyers may prosper; the vast majority of Canadians may be only marginally affected (Stoffman 1998). Business may flourish, but taxpayers may be forced to foot the bill with respect to social costs and escalating pressure on existing services (Smith 1997). The changing ethnic mix is endorsed as enriching the Canadian landscape; yet fears mount over the potential for social friction or diminution of core Canadian values (also Isbister 1996). Costs are inevitable: A country cannot expect to have a policy of immigration-driven sustained economic growth without some social and economic repercussions. With an intake of approximately 220,000 new Canadians each year, many with radically different lifestyles and outlooks, a degree of friction and annoyance is inevitable, given the likelihood of crowding, pressure on existing services, inflated markets, and congested roads. Cultural clashes are inescapable, but most controversies tend to involve modest demands or the accommodation of outwardly superficial symbols, such as the ever-contentious turban issues, rather than any fundamental shift in power or resources. A sense of proportion is badly needed: If Canadians value the cultural and economic benefits associated with immigration, they must be prepared to make adjustments for these differences.

Criticism and dialogue are important. To be sure, opposition to immigration that is articulated solely on the basis of skin colour or national origins is racist. But people should be able to express informed opinion on immigration and criticize policies and practices that are inconsistent with ideals or goals. Concern over immigration because of Canada's absorptive capacities or competition over scarce resources is legitimate, and does not necessarily reflect bigotry or racism. People acknowledge the partial validity of arguments, both for and against. They also acknowledge that answers to questions about immigration are never right or wrong, but both right and wrong, depending on the context. Few solutions to immigration questions are of an either/or variety but rather both/and. Inflated claims on both sides of the debate often conceal whatever truths they contain. As well, people intuitively recognize that constructive answers with operationalizable goals and realistic procedures are subject to never-ending debate. A balance is often required, with national interests on the one side and the needs of those in search of opportunity or freedom on the other. A sample of the questions that might be raised yet which do not admit of ready answers follows:

1. *Does Canada accept too many immigrants?*

   Critics say that Canada is stretching its "absorptive capacity" by accepting too many immigrants and refugees. Immigration into Canada is currently in the 220,000 range. Some argue for an increase in numbers to about 300,000 (reflecting 1 percent of Canada's population); others propose 150,000 as the preferred figure (it brings Canada in line with its postwar average and with worldwide proportions). Which figure is acceptable?

What is "too much," and how can we determine an acceptable figure? When is the absorptive capacity stretched to the limit? What kind of criteria do we employ to justify any proposed levels?

2. *Does Canada take in too many Third World immigrants?*

Since the 1980s, the largest percentage of immigrants to Canada has arrived from non conventional countries. Should Canada seek more European or American immigrants? What is the proper proportion, and how would you justify your answer, keeping in mind that Canada no longer has complete freedom in choosing who it admits, especially since Americans and Europeans have no compelling reason to come? Besides, Canada is in competition with other industrialized countries to attract the best human capital (Report, *Not Just Numbers,* 1998).

3. *Does Canada entice the wrong "class" of immigrants?*

Canada's immigration quotas are divided roughly among the family reunification class, the independent class, and refugees. Some argue that we need more independent immigrants with the social and economic skills to contribute directly to Canada. Does Canada really need highly skilled personnel when such jobs are unavailable in a downsizing economy? Why does Canada set out to attract expertise whose foreign qualifications are not readily accepted or are in direct competition with professional bodies and Canadian-born university grads? Moreover, Canada already skims off the best and the brightest from the developing world, without cautioning them about the obstacles in finding employment consistent with skills, experience, and credentials (Siddiqui 1999; Bragg 1998). Perhaps immigrants are required for the kind of work (from service jobs to manual labour) that many native-born regard with contempt. Others believe that the integrity of the family is uppermost in building a strong Canada, yet concerned that Canada cannot control the quality ("qualifications") of immigrants under family reunification. How do you sort out who is right or wrong? What is the proper mix of categories? On what basis do you justify this answer?

4. *Are immigrants of economic benefit?*

Some say yes, others say no, and still others say maybe or not much. Perhaps the answer lies in acknowledging that certain immigrants provide immediate benefit (especially independent class immigrants), some don't (refugee class), and others do so indirectly or eventually (family class immigrants). Some parts of the economy benefit from immigration ("real estate"), others suffer ("manual labour"), but the average person may be largely unaffected.

5. *Are immigrants not adapting?*

There is an underlying perception that immigrants are making an inadequate effort to become Canadian. They are seen as dogmatically protecting their culture while huddled together in ethnic enclaves. Reality suggests otherwise. Immigrants do not come to Canada to perpetuate a way of life that many are trying to escape. Many (but especially the young) are anxious to integrate as quickly as possible—without necessarily abandoning everything that provides a sense of meaning or continuity. Those who do settle into ethnic communities often leave for the suburbs after an initial adjustment period, leaving behind older members who lack the resources and resourcefulness to cope with the outside.

6. *Do immigrants commit more crime?*

Statistics indicate that, with the exception of several ethnic groups, immigrants commit less crime than native-born Canadians. To be sure, criminal elements are part of the immigration saga; after all, they are lured by the same market opportunities that attract the law-abiding. Nevertheless, these are exceptions to the immigration rule and constitute aberrations even within their own communities (Isbister 1996). Lower rates may be attributable to age (average age of immigrants in 1991 was 29, and youth are much more likely to commit crime), education (immigrants have higher levels of education than native-born, and reported crime is a function of the lesser educated), marital status (immigrants marry and stay married longer than native-born, and those who are married are less likely to commit crime), income (immigrant families generally have a higher income, and criminality rates are higher for lower income brackets), and, finally, tight screening procedures that are unlikely to admit those of a criminal bent. According to John Samuel (1998), the highest rate of crime was found for immigrants born in the United States, followed by Scandinavia and the United Kingdom. Italians have the lowest crime rate among the foreign-born, but score high on certain offences ("gaming") and low in others (property crime).

7. *Does Canada need immigrants?*

Why does Canada accept immigrants and refugees? Canada may want more immigrants because of tradition, openness, obligation, or compassion for the less fortunate. But does Canada *need* more immigrants (Stoffman 1998)? Some say no: The vulnerability of Canada's economy, coupled with the allegedly fragile state of its social and cultural fabric, may dictate against immigration. Others say yes: Immigrants and society building are strongly linked and of proven benefit. Immigrants provide economic benefits, they enrich Canadians through diversity, replenish emigrants lost to the United States, and they foster international reputations and global linkages. And others still want to open the door wide: After all, does Canada have a moral right to keep out those less fortunate because of an accident of birth (Coyne 1998)? On what grounds can we justify securing our privilege while others suffer and perish? The words of Joel Millman (1997:317) seem appropriate in rounding off this section:

Our future is being born today in a village somewhere far away. Our welfare depends on the quality of our welcome when that future arrives.

IMMIGRATION SETTLEMENT: CHALLENGES AND PROSPECTS

The relationship between society and its immigrants is underpinned by two modern assumptions that secure an unspoken moral covenant (Parekh 1997): Society expects immigrants to identify with prevailing societal norms; society, in turn, promises to treat them as equals with the rest of its citizens. This arrangement is widely endorsed because (a) it reinforces the values of a liberal-plural society, (b) it provides a workable balance between the equally legitimate claims of society and immigrants, and (c) it makes provisions for constructing a cohesive society. But difficulties will arise if the need to identify with society tilts toward assimilation into the mainstream, thus robbing immigrant women and men of any sense of self-definition at individual and group levels. Further difficulties are anticipated if all dimensions of equality are not explored. Eliminating glaring inequalities is a good start, as Bhikku Parekh (1997) intones, but until subtle inequities are addressed, society cannot claim full equality for all its minorities.

A similar line of thought can be applied to Canada. Certain immigrant and refugee groups have experienced difficulties in making an adjustment to Canadian society. Problems may arise not only because of personal shortcomings related to culture shock, lack of political power, loss of economic well-being, and personal isolation, but because of discriminatory barriers that preclude entry or acceptance. Compounding these adjustment problems are those Canadians who resent the minorities and lash out at the prospect of moving over and making space. To be sure, many immigrants and refugees appear to be relatively satisfied with the quality of life in Canada, the opportunities and services available to them and their children, and the promise of human freedom and market transparency. They have used their talent and expertise to enrich themselves and Canadian society at large (see Millman 1997). Nevertheless, many will confront a series of problems that have accompanied them into Canada or encounter problems upon entry and settlement. These problems are in some ways similar to, yet also different from, those experienced by native-born multicultural minorities.

Concerns

Generally speaking, the primary concerns of immigrant multicultural minorities are practical and survival related. Foremost is the desire to "put down roots" and to "fit in" to Canadian society, without necessarily severing ties with their cultural tradition. More specifically, their needs can be summarized as follows:

1. The elimination of all forms of discrimination, racism (including stereotyping), and exploitation in the workplace.

2. The expansion of opportunities in the labour and education markets as well as ease of access to services in housing, government institutions, and mass media.

3. Conferral of full citizenship rights, including the right to pursue interests and activities without undue bureaucratic interference or central surveillance.

4. Access to the best Canadian society has to offer without diminishing their children's sense of cultural identity.

5. Immigrants should be capable of expressing themselves in terms of their identity, yet possess the capacity to construct a successful world around them.

6. Formal equality is fine but so is equal respect for their difference and public acceptance of immigrants as a legitimate and valued part of society (Barekh 1997).

Taken together, immigrant multicultural minorities want the best that both worlds have to offer. People want to be treated as individuals and accepted for what they do rather than what they are, yet want others to appreciate them for where they came from and what group they belong to. Immigrant women and men are anxious to participate in the modern without forsaking the traditional. In seeking to merge the old with the new, there is a commitment to belong to the present by retaining an identity with the past. Culture, history, and language are important, but no more so than meaningful involvement in the wider sector. Equality (to be treated the same) and full citizenship rights are important, but so too is recognition of their cultural worth if they choose to identify with their traditions, without enduring taunts of being less Canadian. In other words, abandoning a cultural identity as a condition of acceptance may not be acceptable for many. As pointed out in Chapter 4, identities are integral to peoples' sense of who they are, instill a sense of community and continuity, and provide resources to find their feet in society and feel secure enough to creatively interact with it (Parekh 1997). In this passage, the notion of intercultural mixing—and the subsequent creative tension—is eloquently articulated by a Pakistani-Canadian who concedes a Pakistani origin but a Canadian commitment:

> Alongside this love for Canada, however, there remains in us a bond to Pakistan. The ideal of Pakistan, its Islamic spirit, masala cuisine, Arabesque architecture, draping fashions, fragrant mangoes, love-triangle movies, super-extended families, and respect-laden values.... Emotions still pull, and the senses still gravitate.... The Canadian influence is secular, commercial, experimental and bracing. The Pakistani wave is spiritual, traditional, poetic, and tropical. The combination, like the mixing of the Gulf Stream and the Atlantic Ocean, creates something new and exhilarating. This synergy, this ability to register experience from a CanAsian perspective, is at once a source of great richness and recurrent struggle (Qaadri 1997).

Challenges

Immigrants have long endured racial abuse and discrimination in the fields of employment, education, housing, and government services (Report, *Equality Now,* 1984). Licensed occupations, including medicine and dentistry, continue to impose restrictions and deny accreditation, which results in blocking the entry of immigrants with foreign degrees or credentials outside Canada. New Canadians find themselves segregated in menial and unskilled occupations with little in the way of security or prospects for promotion. Their visible status has had the effect of precluding a smooth transition into Canadian society, while public reaction to their physical appearance and cultural differences can only complicate the settlement process. A Catch-22 is a constant: Without Canadian experience, many cannot get certified even with extensive retraining; without a certificate, they cannot get the experience to secure employment or peer acceptance (Van Rijn 1999). Even those immigrant women and men who have "made it" continue to feel undervalued and underappreciated, looked down upon by the dominant sector, and torn between the cross-cutting pressures of affirming their distinctiveness while accepting the norms and practices of middle class society (see also Shipler 1997). The immigrant experience may prove less gratifying than originally anticipated. Andrei Codrescu (1995:47) writes of the bittersweet experiences of his Romanian mother, but with a message that applies to many:

> Most people come here because they are sick of being poor. They want to eat and they want something to show for their industry. But soon enough it becomes evident to them that these things are not enough. They have eaten and they are full, but they have eaten alone.... This time they are lacking something more elusive than salami and furniture. They are bereft of a social and cultural milieu.... Leaving behind your kin, your friends, your language, your smells, your childhood, is traumatic. It is a kind of death. You're dead for the home folk and they are dead to you.

For refugees, the situation may be grim. Traumatized by emotional and psychological abuses en route to Canada, refugees are expected to adapt to the unique social, cultural, and geographic climate with only minimal outside assistance. No one should trivialize the impact of cultural shock because of exposure to radically different lifestyles, expectations, rapid social change, and inhospitable climate. The transitional stresses that accompany refugee claimants are compounded by their language difficulties, shame at their inability to work, and low self-esteem due to loss of control over destiny. Even after they secure a work permit, refugees still suffer from lack of Canadian experience, are vulnerable to recession or restructuring in the workplace, encounter discrimination at work, and must cope with language barriers.

Immigrant and refugee school children are subject to a host of conflicting demands and pressures. Some may perform poorly because of racial stereotyping, low teacher expectations, curricula and textbooks at odds with minority experiences, and lack of positive role models among school staff. Others experience a sense of social dislocation as they drift apart from the senior generation, younger women chafe over traditional roles and pervasive paternalism, and educated elites become estranged from the community at large. Obedience, deference to authority, and loyalty to family are paramount, but may lead to conflicts as parents and offspring struggle to find a workable balance between the "anything goes" mentality of contemporary society versus the culturally steeped and religious-infused traditions of new immigrant groups (Tomlinson 1998). Additional problems can arise from concern over the gradual loss of cultural identity, especially among those who appear ambivalent toward their adopted country and their country of origin, belonging to both yet fully to neither (Horn 1997). And difficulties mount when, as Hansen's law describes, the second generation of immigrants seeks assimilation with a vengeance while the third wants to rediscover its ancestral roots that have since been forgotten.

Non-English-speaking immigrant women encounter additional problems because of gender and race constraints. Many women of colour find themselves restricted to the lower echelons of the Canadian labour force where they are slotted into low-paying job ghettoes such as manufacturing, service industries, and domestic work. Domestic workers on two-year probationary periods are particularly vulnerable to exploitation and abuse. Women of colour are also victimized by policies and programs that keep them illiterate, isolated, and vulnerable to abuse. For immigrant women, Canada may be a "cage," as Melody Neufeld-Rocheleau and Judith Friesen (1987) write, because of the loneliness stemming from isolation (limited language, lack of training opportunities, child-rearing and school-related problems, racial prejudice, underemployment, lack of "Canadian" experience, and limited services to cater to their unique situations). The Report of the Ontario Joint Task Force on Immigration and Women put it this way:

> A Canadian-born woman may have difficulty reconciling the conflicting demands of home-making, motherhood, and a paying job. The immigrant woman, however, must face these same problems while having to learn a new language, adjust to a different culture, often while living in overcrowded conditions due to the low earning power of both her husband and herself.

In an attempt to organize for change that reflects their distinct needs and experiences, immigrant women have begun to look for support outside conventional feminist groups.

Prospects

How, then, do we assess Canada's record as an immigration country? Few have demonstrated the same degree of generosity, openness, and tolerance that Canada has, especially since the late 1980s. Admittedly, there remains an element of incompetence and racism, but these appear to be situational rather than systemic (Avery 1995). Canada's commitment is reflected in the positioning of immigration within the context of national development and society building. Canada may not be perfect in this regard; perhaps, however, it is less imperfect than other countries in living up to an ideal, as articulated by this 1862 pamphlet to entice prospective German settlers:

Canada is the land of peace, order, and abundance.... The immigrant when he arrives is protected and guided by government officials.... Canada is about the only country in which the...immigrant practically as well as before [the] law is seen as immediately equal to the native born (cited in Avery 1995:239).

There is another dimension. Canadians for the most part have not yet fully confronted the reality and challenges of a racially and cultural diverse society (Whitaker 1991). Reluctance to endorse measures that encourage inclusiveness and accommodation is one sign of this denial. Growing anti-immigrant sentiment is another, even though any backlash will be constrained by (a) human rights codes that restrict the public articulation of racist views, (b) a pervasive liberalism within the political cultures, and (c) a lack of institutional base with both labour unions and churches onboard the immigration express. The likelihood of reverting to an openly racial basis for selection or treatment of immigrants once in Canada would appear remote. Still, immigrants continue to experience barriers that have a discriminatory effect. In a research paper by Shiva Halli and Abdol Mohammad, entitled "Poverty and Intergenerational Mobility of Immigrants in Canadian Cities," the authors indicate that, on the basis of 1991 Census data, certain minority groups, such as Indo-Pakistanis and South Americans, experience levels of poverty that are twice the national average and that the second generation of immigrants may be poorer than their parents, despite not having to face language and cultural obstacles (cited in Roberts 1999). The last Voices Box in this chapter suggests that for some immigrants the experiential gap between the ideal and the real is widening. In this powerful and moving indictment of a Chilean immigrant woman's experience in Canada, Maria Adasme debunks any notion of Canada as an inclusive society.

Voices
"A Layer Too Low For Our Voices to Be Heard"
Why I Do Not Feel Canadian

I arrived to Canada as an independent immigrant in the spring of 1974. I am putting in writing some of my thoughts about my immigration experience in the summer of 1995; twenty-one years have gone by.

The majority of us immigrants migrate in order to escape the socio-political-economic systems prevailing in our homelands, which deprive us of our primary rights to existence. Humans migrate intranationally or internationally in search of better pastures, as do other species in the animal kingdom. Human beings, irrelevant of creed or ethnicity, struggle to reach higher levels of subsistence or existence. This drive for improvement is instinctual and universal; it is part of our essence. Do you know any person who would not aspire to a better type of existence? Consequently, no human should be penalized for this innate aspiration. Humans inhabiting extremely unequal societies do not live; they just exist. They experience a continuous sense of physical and/or emotional and intellectual starvation. They feel suffocated by the society they live in. Their awareness of being impotent to rectify their society's imperfections makes them deal with that reality by abandoning it, when they have the opportunity to do so or are forced to. The settlement countries of the world are the utopian societies that offer such escape. The oppressed members of the oppressed societies of the human race perceive the so-called First World nations: Canada, Australia, New Zealand, etc., as little "pockets of paradise" on earth. One has the perception that in these developed societies the primary human needs—food, shelter, clothing, education—are met and that the more sophisticated needs leading to self-fulfillment or maximum life satisfaction are within reach for anyone who strives enough to attain them. The international media, sponsored by First World nations, implants in the potential immigrant splendorous images: In the "free countries" humans are allowed to develop their own philosophies of life and express them. Members of these societies can even experience the luxury of openly disagreeing with the prevailing system of values, mores, and ideas, and all these privileges are protected by the law of their lands. Prior to migration, would-be migrants have heard, read, seen, or fantasized what it's like living in a society based on the principle of freedom and equality. All these and much more constitute our premigration perceptions.

Once one is granted immigration permission, the basic premise in one's mind—whatever way it might be phrased—is "I will stop existing. I will start experiencing life." I use this expression in a serious way. I am not implying "experiencing life" as in a nonresponsible form or without effort involved. Prior to migration, one has the image that being a total participant in the affairs of this new social world is implied by becoming an immigrant.

In their lands of origin, migrants were in a no-win position; their potentials, desires, and goals were supposed to remain suppressed, dormant within themselves for life. Here, I am excluding the "life-satisfied immigrants" who migrated in search of adventure or more stimulation. In this writing, my thoughts are focused on the average underprivileged men and women of any society on earth, because the privileged minorities and the ones orbiting their circles have their own golden little worlds in the midst of the multitude's despair in any latitude on earth.

Migrants, knowing that their homeland societies promised similar cycles of oppression to their descendants, assumed that by being accepted as a member of a developed settlement nation they would be able to break the cycle of underprivilege.

Once in Canada, I realized that for most immigrants the state of oppression is not left behind. The first encounter with this reality is the realization of being absorbed into the underprivileged strata of the host society, and in most cases becoming a permanent resident of that particular floor in the hierarchically stratified social building. A layer too low for our voices to be heard.

This is how the immigrant's odyssey starts. The immigrant, particularly the one arriving from the traditionally undesirable zones of the earth—Africa, Asia, Latin America—starts sharing the destiny of the minorities of the First World nations such as the aged, the Native, the poor Anglo-Saxon, who is also discriminated against, if not on account of ethnicity, on account of socioeconomical status.

In my land of origin, I learned the meaning of the concept "underprivileged." I had the status and played the role. Minorities individually and collectively lack power. This state of impotency renders them unable to cut off the ropes of dependency which make them geographically, intellectually, socially, and economically stationary. In all these areas of human endeavour, they can only move within certain boundaries and only with the approval of the majority group, which is minority in number, but majority in power and status.

I was denied self-realization in my land of origin, and my adopted country reemphasized the denial. This realization was one of the saddest intercultural shocks that I have experienced. I have gone through a replication of my original social experience. Consequently, in Canada, I did not have to go through a role preparation process to adapt to it.

My society of origin represents an experience of the past that opened my eyes to the social reality present on the planet. My adoptive country—Canada—representing my very present, has reemphasized the inequality of this social reality.

The cross-cultural experience I have gone through has revealed that First World countries and Third World countries are not fundamentally different, but only superficially different. Both possess foundations designed with the aim of creating inequality. Both nations suffer from a similar social malady. One of the major superficial differences is that the First World countries pass on to their underprivileged large quantities of disposable items—cars, appliances, clothing, etc. Their underprivileged play the role of recycling machines for the privileged. This is what gives the apparent images of equality; for instance, from a Third World perspective it is amazing that a cleaning lady drives a car to work, just like the woman she works for does. However, from a Canadian perspective, there is nothing amazing about it. Chances are that the cleaning lady will remain a cleaning lady for the rest of her life while the woman she works for will be presented with opportunities to move up educationally, occupationally, economically, etc.

Once in Canada, I realized that equality was not a fact, but a myth. The socio-political-economical structure of both cultures is designed to give opportunity and life chances to a sector of the members of the population at the expense of the most vulnerable sector of it. In both cultures, self-realization is not a right but a privilege reserved for sectors of the population, which through history and diverse geographical locations have self-proclaimed to be superior to others. This self-proclaimed superiority, whether based on ethnicity, family name, etc., has given them access to the best that the planet and society have to offer in terms of resources, accommodation, relaxation, security, prestige, etc.

The more I make parallels between Canadian society and my original society, the blurrier the demarcation line between the two of them becomes. In both societies, being privileged is equated with morality, decency, and intellectual capacity; on the contrary, poorer members of society are looked upon with suspicion equating poverty with lack of morality, faulty intellectual capacity, or no capacity at all. My personal conclusion based on my cross-cultural experiences is that First World Nations are not fundamentally different from other categories of nations; if I had the power, I would start by eliminating the labelling.

I ask a psychologist or expert in the field: What is the emotional and intellectual effect on an individual of being labelled twice, in his or her society of origin and in the adoptive nation, a "second class citizen"? I doubt that this person—immigrant—can still preserve his or her sense of self-esteem.

In order to solve this social puzzle I find myself in, I ask myself, What are the essential attributes that the privileged sector possesses that give them the authority to think prejudicially and act discriminately toward people who possess a different ethnicity? One factor that seems to play an essential role is their seniority as immigrants to Canada. This stands to reason in the sense that it is a law of nature that the senior precedes the junior. However, this seniority does not make the majority group less ethnic or less immigrant themselves. It only indicates that their period of residency on Canadian soil is lengthier than that of more recent immigrants. If seniority of residence was a valid reason to exercise social control over the rest of the people in a nation, then Anglo- and French-Canadians and all the posterior ethnic groups arriving onto Canadian soil should be under the social control of Native Canadians.

One way of understanding the predicament immigrants find themselves in would be to ask a hard-core, prejudicial Anglo-Canadian to imagine herself being transplanted overnight to an alien culture where she does not know the language, norms of behaviour, religion, food, etc. And being left there to survive on her own in the midst of the unknown, having to take care of herself and her sons and daughters. In a situation like this, would she not appreciate a human heart and helping hand to lead her and the family around?

Usually the response that the undesired immigrant gets from the majority group conveys annoyance, disregard, or indifference. In cases where the ethnic adult has need of an interpreter, another ethnic person, if available, offers his or her help. However, in cases of emergency, in particular, the ethnic woman has to turn to her own children for help. It is not uncommon to see children between the ages of seven and eleven act as interpreters.

The immigrant's son or daughter acts as a middleman between the majority group and the minority group parent.

When the children of immigrants see their parents being disrespected, if not at a conscious level, they themselves lose respect for their parents, who have turned into a source of humiliation for them. In order to escape this embarrassment, if possible, the children start to hide their true identities. In the process, the adult and the young ethnic are victimized. This victimization is one of the first stages in the process of disassociation between the first generation of immigrants and their offspring. This gap is gradually increased as the children of the immigrants are integrated into the Canadian educational system.

Consequently, yes, we immigrants do lose our uniqueness, distinctiveness, and sense of self-identity. My Canadian immigration experience—I am talking about my experience; someone else's might be different—is inconsistent with the "Canadian mosaic" idea found in traditional sociology textbooks and similar material.

I have been socially censored a couple of times for not acting or feeling Canadian, for instance, for not wearing a poppy on Remembrance Day and not participating at the ethnic festival at the local park on Canada Day. To me, participating at the ethnic festival on Canada Day is unrelated to the degree of how much Canadian one feels. I perceive the ethnic festival as an occasion for the majority and minority groups to entertain their palates with ethnic food and drinks and their eyes and ears with a colourful spectacle.

According to my logic, feeling or acting Canadian is an impossibility if one is not allowed to become one. Give me the life opportunities that mainstream

Canadians offer to one another, and after that criticize me if I do not feel or act Canadian. As an experiment in patriotism, think about a majority member of Canadian society, someone in a position of authority and control over other individuals. Mentally strip that person and his family of the privileges that they take for granted. Rob them of their life opportunities and ask yourself if and to what extent their feelings and behaviours would not change in relation to their allegiance to their country. Chances are they would feel less than Canadian because their sense of identity would be in shambles.

Now, occupationally speaking, the occupation that one individual holds is one of the strongest links between him- or herself and society. Immigrants occupy the most powerless jobs in the occupational setting. We are destined to Canadian kitchens, bathrooms, walls, and floors. There is nothing wrong with it if one is allowed to move away from that setting (through educational opportunities, etc.), if one feels the need to do so. But there is something very wrong if one has to remain a janitor, sewing machine operator, etc., for life, if I am experiencing lack of job satisfaction, feeling enslaved to that occupation. The types of occupations reserved for the majority of us place us at the bottom of the occupational ladder. There are almost no opportunities down here, only limitations. Consequently, the occupations that most immigrants perform are a powerful indicator of the lack of life opportunities open to us.

If one takes into account the linkage between the occupational and educational systems, it can be perceived that immigrants are not channelled according to their potential into the different areas of education. Most are streamed into vocational schools, irrelevant of their academic potential. Our sons and daughters are trained to supply the job market with the necessary personnel to do the menial but necessary jobs that the parents of mainstream children would avoid performing as their life occupational careers.

Over a period of twenty-one years of immigration experience, I have witnessed immigrants being subjected to a whole rainbow of inequalities. This experience supports my beliefs and statements and gives me the confidence to speak about our reality as it is. I also wish to emphasize that the source of abuse does not concentrate in the controlling mainstream social group only, but also among some immigrants who occupy positions of authority in immigrant-related organizations. Some of them are also control- and power-thirsty. Once elevated to certain positions of authority, they adapt the perspective of the mainstream Canadian and start to mortify their own. They delude themselves into believing that they are perceived as full-fleshed Canadians by the majority group. The reality is that, in most cases, they are still perceived as ethnics by both factors. In the process of distancing themselves from their roots, they try to identify themselves with the Anglo-Saxon, losing their own sense of identity. This is a case of "self-inflicted" ethnism/racism. It is the case of a man or woman who turns against himself or herself in his or her search to comply, adapt, or conform. I realize that most of us are "tolerated" by the host society, but tolerance is not enough. In order for us to heal our psychological wounds, we need to be "accepted." Acceptance conveys liberty. Tolerance communicates a false sense of freedom. While expressing my thoughts on my Canadian immigration experience, I have not lost perspective that Canada is the only nation on earth having been distinguished by the United Nations' Nansen Medal on account of its humanitarianism toward refugees, and that is the notion that provides the best standard of living on Earth. The persons who are full participants in the nation's economic and social rewards have more than enough reason to feel proud of holding the Canadian citizen status. Lamentably, there is a large sector of the population—minorities—who cannot share in this distinction. Honestly, I wish we could because it must be a great feeling having a clear sense of identity and being proud of it.

The existence of armies of socio-economically unfulfilled individuals in deprived nations is not a phenomenon that would cause surprise. However, a similar phenomenon causes surprise and is not justifiable in the midst of riches. Canada has plenty for all of its residents. There is no room for deprivation in Canadian society.

Knowledge and education on the subject of immigration will decrease the amount of energy wasted on ethnic tensions. This energy can be rechannelled into reaching positive, desirable goals for all of us as a single Canadian society, which inhabits the same soil and struggles for a better type of existence as a whole and for all. Let us give one another the opportunity to coexist like "rational," "humane" human beings.

I arrived in Canada at the prime of my age. My most productive years are gone. If I had the power to reverse my Canadian immigration social experience, I would give myself the employment that I have been denied. I would change the ideologies and patterns of behaviour that teachers and school administrators have toward ethnic members of society. This would ease the feelings of embarrassment and humiliation that I have gone through when dealing with the Canadian educational system. I would give myself valuable information withheld from me with the covert intention of denying me participation in the social and economic rewards of this society. I would erase from my mind all the expressions of annoyance, smirks, demeaning remarks, the "I am sorry, the position is taken," "call again," "come back next week," "next month," "next spring," "get out of my face." Yes, Canada is a prejudicial and discriminatory nation. The fact that the prejudice and discrimination are mostly covert does not make it any less antiethnic.

Even though I am geographically removed from my land of origin, I have not escaped from the political-social-economic system I was born into. I did not leave it behind; it is still very much a part of my life. I have not reached and I have been penalized for aspiring to a better type of existence. The penalty is the "double denial" to experience self-realization imposed by the host community I presently live in.

I abandoned an unequal society to replace it by another. The "pockets of paradise" on earth are not pockets of paradise for all.

I remember at this moment the Canadian citizenship ceremony when I was awarded Canadian citizenship status. The judge stated: "Now you are one of us. You have the same rights and obligations that we have. Now you have all kinds of opportunities available. Now you can even run for political office if you want to...congratulations to all new Canadian citizens."

Probably my status changed in theory after being awarded Canadian citizenship; however, in actual practice self-fulfillment as a human, as an individual, who is unique and irreplaceable will continue being an impossibility for as long as Canada continues—like other societies—being an unequal society.

SOURCE: Maria Adasme. Written expressly for *Unequal Relations*.

CHAPTER HIGHLIGHTS

- Immigrants and refugees as multicultural minorities occupy a relational status in Canada at variance with the legal status of aboriginal and Charter members with respect to history, problems, solutions, entitlements, and outcomes.

- The relationship of multicultural minorities to society can be analyzed in different ways. A focus on immigrants and immigration provides a useful organizational device that acknowledges the unequal relations of multicultural minorities with society.

- The demography of contemporary Canada reveals an increasingly diverse society. According to the 1996 Census data, over 50 percent of all Canadians possessed some non-British, non-French ancestry. People of colour ("visible minorities") now comprise 11.2 percent of the total population.

- Immigration currently stands at about 220,000 per year, with the majority arriving from Asia, Africa, and South and Central America. Most immigrants move to Ontario, followed by British Columbia, Quebec, and Alberta. The Atlantic provinces are not a favourite destination. Large urban centres, mainly Toronto, Vancouver, and Montreal, are primary destination points.

- Several themes can be discerned to describe Canada's immigration policies and practices. Historically, immigration selection was racist and nativist, geared toward agricultural needs, highly contested by business and labour for control of the agenda, conducted on a taps-on/taps-off mentality, and anchored by economic calculation and political expediency with a dash of compassion.

- During the 1960s, Canada's immigration policy shifted toward skills rather than national origins as a basis for selection.

- Canada's 1976 Immigration Act is committed to the principle of family reunification, Canadian economy, protection of refugees, and preservation of Canada's integrity.

- Immigration selection is divided into three categories: Family reunification is based on sponsorship of close and distant relatives; independent class is based on the points system as it applies to skilled workers, business investors, and entrepreneurs; and finally there is the refugee class, both sponsored and claimants.

- Recent changes to the immigration policy have focused on reducing total levels to about 200,000, placing more emphasis on the independent rather than the family class, ensuring fluency in English or French, and securing more responsible sponsorships. The rationale is that Canada no longer needs unskilled immigrants; nor is Canada prepared to accept the escalating costs of immigration settlement and integration.

- The benefits of immigration are numerous: increased overall levels of skills, knowledge, and experience; established international links; cultural diversity and entrepreneurial spirit; and critical mass for economic growth as well as to offset the costs of an aging population. The costs are no less real and often reflect the flip side of benefits.

- Immigrant needs and aspirations have been misportrayed. Few, if any, want to establish ethnic enclaves or to change Canada to suit their images. Most want to put down roots in their adopted country, contribute to its growth, receive benefits that all Canadians are entitled to, and get the best for their children without necessarily losing that which provides a line of continuity with the past.

- Refugees continue to be seen as problematic, particularly for those who are not conventional refugees but refugee claimants. Canada may have a relatively high rate of acceptance of refugee claimants, although others disagree, but the system for determination is overworked and underresourced. The Immigration and Refugee Board must also walk a tightrope between those politicians/publics who think it should do everything to encourage entry or to keep them out.

KEY TERMS

business class immigrants
conventional refugees
family reunification class
immigrants
Immigration Act, 1976
Immigration and Refugee Board
independent class immigrants
multicultural minorities
nominated class
points system
refugee claimants
refugees
sponsored immigrants
sponsored refugees
visible versus nonvisible minorities

REVIEW QUESTIONS

1. Briefly review the trends and premises underlying immigration policies in the past and at present.
2. Discuss the benefits and drawbacks of increased immigration to Canada.
3. Briefly describe the changing nature of Canada's demographic composition.
4. Compare and contrast the aspirations of multicultural minorities in terms of needs and goals.
5. The voices that appear at the beginning and the end of the chapter seem to reflect different experiences of immigration to Canada. Discuss.
6. Point out the issues that are contributing to a "crisis in refugees" in Canada.

MULTICULTURALISM AND SOCIETY BUILDING

The upsurge of racial pride and ethnic affiliation is well documented in Canada (Herberg 1989) and abroad (Spoonley et al. 1996). Central authorities have responded to this unprecedented surge in a variety of ways, ranging from indifference to rejection on the one hand to its acceptance and promotion as a potential society-building asset on the other. Countries such as Australia (Vasta and Castles 1996) and New Zealand (Pearson 1996) have also implemented strategies to address the following dynamics: (a) influx of immigrants; (b) proliferation of identity politics; (c) salience of ethnicity as meaning or mobilization; (d) tenacity of racism; and (e) ascendancy of nationalist movements. But traditional initiatives such as assimilation and segregation are losing their moral authority as a basis for engaging diversity. Race and ethnic relations have been recast instead within the framework of multicultural policies and polyethnic practices as governments and minorities alike struggle to advance the cause of equality, extension of human rights, recognition of culture, and access to scarce resources. Yet the challenge of society building remains as formidable as ever: How to create a society in which different groups can maintain and develop their culture while coexisting and interacting within the framework of a single multiethnic society (Smolicz 1997).

Of those societies at the vanguard for "accommodating" diversity, few can match Canada's pace-setting properties. With the emergence of Toronto and Vancouver as two of the world's most polyethnic cities, Canada has transformed itself into one of the world's most interestingly diverse societies (see also Patience 1998). Canada is widely admired for its commitment to multiculturalism as a catalyst in "managing" race and ethnic relations (Kurthen 1997). Under the banner of multiculturalism, Canada has implemented a bold but largely untried strategy to secure a society, both united and distinct as well as diverse and committed. Drawing on its liberal tradition of tolerance and egalitarianism, Canada affirmed in 1971 the right for people to keep in touch with their roots while sharing in the core values of Canadian society at large. Official multiculturalism has served admirably as a proactive device for defusing intergroup tensions by promulgating the once unthinkable idea that people with different ethnocultural backgrounds can coexist and cooperate. Under multiculturalism, people are accepted as racially or ethnically different yet no less Canadian, with a corresponding set of citizenship rights, duties, and entitlements, regardless of origin, creed, or colour. Its role as a policy blueprint provides Canadians with a map for sorting through issues as varied as cultural retention and social equality to one side and societal integration and national unity to the other. Entrenchment at constitutional and statutory levels has further reinforced the reality of multiculturalism as an idea whose time has come. To be sure, Canadians are not nearly as multicultural as our collective pride would imply (Fleras 1997); in some ways we are less diversity-minded than our melting pot neighbours to the south (Reitz and Breton 1994; Simpson 1998). Still, the promotion of multiculturalism has engineered a reconfiguring of Canadian society in ways that have evoked both international acclaim and envy.

References to multiculturalism have an uncanny knack of meaning different things to different people. For some, multiculturalism is synonymous with Canada's official multicultural policies, and alternative readings are simply unthinkable (Fleras 1998). For others, multiculturalism invokes a subversive challenge to the cultural status quo (Goldberg 1994). For others still, multiculturalism provides an empty category in which many meanings can be absorbed without much fear of contradiction or consistency. Such flexibility can pose problems of consensus or debate; it may also endow multiculturalism with the resiliency to adapt and evolve. Even a cursory overview of cross-national initiatives reveals recurrent themes in the multicultural engagement with diversity, including the following (Hudson 1987):

- to harmonize group relations through intercultural exchanges;
- to eliminate discrimination, both personal and systemic;
- to reduce minority disadvantage at social and economic levels;
- to expand minority opportunities through institutional participation;
- to assist individuals in preserving their cultural identities;
- to (re)educate the public about the virtues of tolerance and cultural diversity;
- to establish a voice for hitherto neglected and historically disadvantaged minorities;
- to challenge the existing balance of cultural power;
- to foster a transformation of the social world in terms of who gets what.

It should be obvious that multiculturalism encompasses a comprehensive process of social change that entails a multitude of interrelated dimensions. Multiculturalism is linked with the society-building goals of cultural identity, social justice, citizenship, national unity, societal integration, and equality (see Goot 1993). Multiculturalism has the potential to provide an alternative way of viewing the world, thinking about society, codifying reality, processing information, and relating to diversity. It also furnishes an official framework for the reconstruction of majority–minority relations that bolster the chances of living together with our differences. Such a revised and more inclusive relationship represents a significant departure from the past when philosophies of assimilation or segregation prevailed—to the detriment of minority survival.

But multiculturalism as an official doctrine remains vulnerable to criticism. Of the trip wires and cultural landmines laid across the Western landscape in recent years, Michael Posner (1997) writes, few have triggered as much vitriol or controversy as official multiculturalism. Those on the left dismiss multiculturalism as a capitalist ideology to divide and distract the working classes; on the right are those who condemn multiculturalism for diluting core values, unity, and identity; and in between are the liberals who believe cultural solutions cannot solve structural problems. Multiculturalism embraces contradictions that strike at the discordancy of contemporary society, while raising a host of troubling questions about working through differences as a basis for belonging. Multicultural discourses reflect an unobtrusive theorization of power and meaning, that is, multiculturalism establishes a framework of symbols, rules, and priorities that constitute a reality for both the powerful and the powerless. Debates over multiculturalism have unmasked a number of political and economic agendas, many of which may compromise minority concerns and aspirations. Ambiguity and conflict are likely to prevail in these contested situations, as both political and minority sectors apply different spins to multiculturalism by improvising self-serving lines of action. The downside of multiculturalism may include a host of consequences, both intended and inadvertent:

- imposing social control;
- cultivating social divisions;
- encouraging ethnic conflict;
- fostering "slow motion" assimilation;
- entrenching inequality;
- fomenting racism;
- dismembering a country.

The charges against multiculturalism are as compelling as arguments in its favour. This simultaneous duality—multiculturalism as progressive as well as regressive—raises a key theme in this section: To what extent does multiculturalism contribute to or detract from society building, and how do we weigh the evidence for one position over another?

This final section deals with the concept of multiculturalism as a society-building strategy for engaging with diversity. Emphasis is on the social dimensions of multiculturalism: The relationship of multiculturalism to society is explored in terms of how multiculturalism contributes to or detracts from social inequality and the way in which this relation is crafted, maintained, challenged, and transformed. Multiculturalism is analyzed from different viewpoints—in part as a specific government policy in response to political and demographic changes; in other part as a resource for shoring up political and minority interests. Multiculturalism is acknowledged as a bold but ambiguous social experiment in the "management" of race and ethnic relations in ways both innovative and integrative, yet fractious and controversial. The extent to which multiculturalism enhances the re-constitutionalizing of Canada along pluralist lines completes the analysis.

The first chapter in this section, Chapter 9, examines official multiculturalism as a compelling if imperfect strategy for engaging race and ethnic diversity. Interest will focus initially on conceptual issues related to policy, perspectives, problems, reactions, and prospects for accommodating diversity in Canada. Chapter 10 emphasizes the practice of multiculturalism with respect to putting diversity to work at institutional levels. Multicultural principles do not necessarily translate into practice because of barriers created by institutional structures and individual mindsets. Gaps in the accommodation of diversity at institutional levels, despite promises to do so at the level of policing, media, or education, say a lot about the disparities between rhetoric and reality. Failure to close the institutional gaps has proven detrimental to Canada's integrity in a diverse and changing world. The final chapter looks at the broader relationship of multiculturalism to citizenship and society building in Canada. The challenges of diversity may be complex and time consuming, but ultimately indispensable if Canada is to retain its status as one of the least imperfect countries in the world.

MULTICULTURALISM IN CANADA: "Engaging Diversity"

CASE STUDY 9–1	Cultural Defence or Culturally Offensive? Drawing the Multicultural Line

Many agree that multiculturalism has lived up to its billing as an instrument of planned social change—to the approval of many, the disapproval of some—without any radical transformation of Canada's institutional structure (Woodley 1997). But the very presence of cultural diversity poses a challenge to conventional ways of doing things in a multicultural society. How acceptable are cultural practices that bring minority women and men into conflict with the law? Should cultural factors be included for explaining or excusing people's behaviour in a multicultural society? Is the recourse to "**cultural defence**" to explain and justify criminal actions a genuine attempt to put multicultural principles into practice or, alternatively, a smokescreen to condone or rationalize cul-

turally offensive actions? These questions are not only of interest as theoretical debates about abstract principles. Both questions and responses reflect the everyday realities that Canadians confront, particularly as diverse cultures with divergent values and expectations clash with mainstream expectations, agendas, and institutions.

Consider the controversy that came to light in early 1998 when two Haitian-Canadian males, who had sexually assaulted a young adult Haitian-Canadian woman in July 1996, were sentenced to an 18-month sentence, to be served at home, in addition to 100 hours of community service and a 10:00 p.m. curfew for one year. Many were shocked—even outraged—by the leniency of the sentence for a crime that normally is punishable by jail. According to the judge, Monique Dubreuil, mitigating circumstances justified the leniency, including the age of the victim (she was an adult), the status of the rapists (one was at university, the other had a job), and lack of previous conviction for a similar crime. That the men "behaved like two young roosters in need of sexual pleasure without caring about the young woman" (*Toronto Star,* 28 January 1998:A-26) may have confirmed their guilt, ruled Dubreuil, but left open the questions of motive and personal responsibility. Of greater interest was the judge's willingness to invoke the disclaimer of "particular cultural context" (*Globe and Mail,* 29 January 1998:A-1), primarily because of the *lack of remorse shown by the Haitian men over their actions.* In the words of Dubreuil, "The absence of regret of the two accused seems to be related more to the cultural context, particularly with regard to relations with women, than a veritable problem of a sexual nature" (*Kitchener-Waterloo Record,* 28 January 1998:A-3).

Many were incensed by this ruling and its implications. It was argued that the decision (a) was racist and sexist, (b) sent out the message that Haitians were insensitive to violence and victims of violence, (c) insulted Haitian woman by suggesting their complicity in rape, (d) further deterred women from seeking justice in court, (e) advocated a set of cultural values that did not exist, and (f) perpetuated the mistaken idea that violence is condoned in black communities. A false impression was conveyed that ethnic communities are not people like everyone else, but subhumans with little respect for life or rights. Even the logic proved baffling: It was not an instance of arguing that "culture made me do it," as was the case when a New Zealand Maori male shoved a 12-cm crucifix up a woman's nose, but escaped sentencing on the grounds of "makutu" ("witchcraft"). Rather, the cultural defence was based on inferences from

people's actions and responses to their actions. The underlying subtext becomes astonishingly clear: Haitian culture dictates how men relate to women, and if men are not contrite for their actions, it must be "normal" for Haitian men to carry out gang rape.

It's not our intent to second-guess the ruling or its rationale. What is relevant for our purposes is the extent to which cultural defence arguments stand up to scrutiny in a multicultural society. The issue seems straightforward enough: If Canada takes pride in being a multicultural society that promotes diversity, then where do we draw the line in terms of what is acceptable and not acceptable. Should Canadian multiculturalism tolerate only those cultural practices that are consistent with mainstream values and institutions? Or should this multiculturalism embrace cultural diversity in all its forms, even if it violates laws, infringes on people's rights, or subverts core values? After all, the very bedrock of multiculturalism is predicated on the principle that culture is the key variable in influencing peoples' behaviour and explaining differences and similarities from one context to another. Yet references to culture are problematic insofar as reliance on a cultural defence argument tends to essentialize (treat something as a singular, fixed, and homogenous entity) what, in reality, is fluid, situational, provisional, variable, changing, inconsistent, and contradictory. Culture may provide a blueprint for behaviour, but this blueprint is provisional, contextual, socially constructed, and, more often than not, consulted after the fact to justify or excuse actions.

Coming to terms with cultural diversity can pose a paradox in the multicultural management of differences; that is, on too many occasions our tolerance of diversity reaches its limits at the very point where cultural differences begin to have a real consequence). Stanley Fish (1997) captures the essence of this paradox when distinguishing between

weaker and stronger versions of multiculturalism, namely, boutique, abstracted, and radical multiculturalisms: A "boutique" multiculturalism, Fish argues, is supportive of
diversity but only in its most superficial sense,
since a deeper commitment to the principles
of universalism and liberal pluralism prevails.
Acceptance of pluralism and tolerance of differences, including those associated with a
cultural defence strategy, are conceded but
only as long as these differences are consistent with mainstream values and institutions.
Put bluntly, differences are not taken seriously inasmuch as they constitute a matter
of lifestyle choice that must mesh with the
commonality that universalizes humanity.
That is, the principle of diversity is vigorously endorsed yet abstracted in that it cannot
seriously embrace any particular difference
when that difference suppresses the differences of others. Any difference that is intolerant of other differences or rights is
indefensible because any intolerance is in-
tolerable in a liberal democracy. Multicultural
diversity is supported as long as everyone
"agrees to disagree"; support is withdrawn
from groups who prefer to "disagree to disagree." Finally, a "radical" multiculturalism
goes to the wall with a particular instance of
diversity, even if this difference involves the
suppression of other cultural distinctiveness
or individual rights. This "radical" multiculturalism would be inclined to accept the cultural defence arguments of the judge in
sentencing the Haitian men as a necessary

and logical—if regrettable—cost of living in
a genuinely multicultural society.

The dilemma should be obvious: How
does an immigrant society such as Canada
engage diversity when "the other" becomes
part of society yet wishes to retain its "otherness." The conundrum is aptly phrased by
Bernard Lewis in the *American Scholar*
(1997:21) when he writes:

> How do we deal with the unbeliever who
> persists in his unbelief; the alien who ac-
> cepts citizenship but does not fully share
> our identity and loyalties as we perceive
> them; the barbarian who wants to retain
> his barbarous customs, or at least cus-
> toms that we regard as barbarous.

How much diversity can be tolerated in a multiculturalism society? Too little diversity
makes a mockery of multiculturalism; too
much diversity is an existential nightmare that
may preclude the possibility of living together
with our sometimes uncomfortable differences. Where, then, should the line be drawn
between acceptable and unacceptable without undermining the very social order that
made the expression of diversity possible in
the first place? Working through differences
that are minor or abstracted may be one thing;
living together with differences that are substantive yet contrary to the "norm" is quite
another challenge (see Fish 1997). It remains
to be seen if multiculturalism can provide a
blueprint for rising to that challenge.

INTRODUCTION: MULTICULTURAL DISCOURSES

People overseas marvel at two aspects of Canada. First, some ask, How can Canada maintain
its independence and integrity despite proximity to the world's most powerful economic and
military machine? That Canadians have retained their distinctiveness and autonomy under the
shadow of this colossus, yet have managed to secure an enviable standard of living, is a tes-

timonial to the resiliency and tenacity of its people. Second, others ask, How can Canada remain united and prosperous when confronted by such daunting levels of diversity? For example, English-speaking Canadians seem to be perpetually embroiled with the Québécois over language issues; aboriginal assertiveness has ushered in a sea of challenges to the status quo; and Canada annually accepts thousands of immigrants and refugees with radically different cultures, any one of which is capable of subverting the status quo. The potentially fragmenting perils of diversity, notwithstanding, Canada remains one of the world's oldest federal systems, a country that is routinely acknowledged by the United Nations as having the world's best standard of living, and a society that many believe is strategically positioned to take advantage of twenty-first century demands. Responses to each of these questions and observations are diverse and complex, but surely "multiculturalism" is central in contributing to Canada's enviable reputation as one of the world's least imperfect countries.

Canada represents one of several democratic societies that has taken advantage of diversity as a basis for bolstering national identity and society building. Since 1971 multiculturalism has served as a formal means for defining government policy and programs at federal and provincial levels. Originating in part to ensure social harmony among competing ethnicities but without losing control of the overall agenda, multiculturalism has been perpetuated for a variety of political and economic considerations related to state functions, private interests, and electoral survival. Multiculturalism is associated with redefining the relational status of minority women and men in the same way that the principles of assimilation or segregation once offered competing frameworks for "managing" race and ethnic relations. A combination of demographic and political upheavals in recent years has helped to redefine the government's multicultural agenda. The cumulative effect of these changes has also had the effect of channelling Canada into directions scarcely conceivable even a generation ago.

This chapter will deal with multiculturalism in terms of policy, perspectives, problems, and prospects. The chapter focuses on official multiculturalism as a strategic device for addressing the challenge of living together with our differences in ways that are workable, necessary, and fair. It will also look at public responses to official multiculturalism, then analyze and assess the role of official multiculturalism in addressing the needs of a changing and diverse society. Comparison of Canada's "consensus" multiculturalism with the "critical" multiculturalisms of the United States will provide a useful counterpoint in contrasting alternative approaches for engaging diversity. Several themes prevail.

1. References to multiculturalism are shown to reflect different levels of meaning, including fact, ideology, policy, practice, and critique (see Kallen 1982; Fleras 1998). Failure to separate these analytically different but mutually connected levels of multicultural discourse will generate confusion and backlash.

2. Multiculturalism is explored primarily from the vantage point of official government policy. What is official multiculturalism? How did it originate as a policy, and why does it continue to exist? What is its impact on unequal relations? What are its implications for Canadian society? An ongoing struggle to balance national unity with diversity without provoking vested interests is a recurrent policy theme, but should never be used to underestimate the potentially "subversive" properties inherent in multiculturalism.

3. Not all multiculturalisms are the same. A comparison of multiculturalism with other forms of "isms" yields valuable insights into how Canadian official multiculturalism is but one of several ways for dealing with diversity as different yet equal.

4. Multiculturalism is exposed to scrutiny to determine whether it accomplishes what it sets out to do. Multiculturalism is hardly immune to criticism; nevertheless, a reassessment of this criticism provides an opportunity to debunk many of the myths that hobble its potential.

5. Multiculturalism must be seen in relation to the challenges of society building. Multiculturalism is neither the root of all evil nor the source of all solutions to Canada's problems, but a largely imperfect social experiment that for better or worse has transformed Canada into what it is today.

DEFINING MULTICULTURALISM

Pluralistic societies confront a paradox in grappling with the question of how to make society safe "for" diversity yet safe "from" diversity (see Schlesinger Jr 1992). A social and political framework must be established that can engage differences as different yet equal, but without eroding national unity and social coherence in the process. White settler dominions such as Australia and Canada have endorsed multicultural principles as a framework for "accommodating" immigrant minorities (Pearson 1996; Vasta and Castles 1996). Yet staunch support for multiculturalism has not congealed into any consensus over definition, attributes, or applications (Editorial 1997). Todd Gitlin (1995:228) describes the disarray when dismissing the state of multiculturalism:

> The word is baggy, a melange of fact and value, current precisely because it is vague enough to serve so many interests. Partisans may use the term to defend the recognition of difference, or to resist policies or ideas imposed by conquerors, or to defend cosmopolitanism—the interests and pleasures that each may take in the profusion of humanity. The purists of identity politics use it to defend endless fission, a heap of monocultures. On the other side, multiculturalism and its demonic twin, "political correctness," serve conservatives as names for a potpourri of things they detest—including an irritating insistence on the rights of minorities.

Contradictions compound the definitional process: On the one hand, multiculturalism may encourage the very thing ("ethnicity") that it sets out to control or discourage; on the other, it ends up controlling ("diversity") that which it purports to encourage. A deconstructed multiculturalism exposes a social formation both "westocentric and masculinist" (Hesse 1997); yet the interrogating of multiculturalism as discourse and practice has proven effective in challenging both conventions and complacency (Goldberg 1994). Multiculturalism simultaneously evokes a preference for consensus, but does so alongside a platform of criticism and reform; of hegemony yet resistance; of conformity yet diversity; of control yet emancipation; of exclusion yet participation; of compliance yet creativity (see Vasta 1996). In short, multiculturalism can mean whatever meaning is assigned to it—from a hegemonic tool of control to an oppositional ideology of resistance (see Pearson 1995). Such flexibility can be helpful at times; it may also foster needless disappointments as interactants grope about for common ground.

The centrality of multiculturalism to contemporary discourses has yielded such an array of meanings that many despair of any clarity or consensus. Both championed and maligned, idealized as well as demonized, the term has absorbed a broad range of often conflicting social articulations that resist integration (Caws 1994). References to multiculturalism without a qualifier have proven misleading in that its use as a stand-alone concept can be stretched to mean everything yet nothing. As a "thing" or "attribute" or "relationship" or "process" or "condition," multicultural references span the spectrum from a focus on cultural identity and social equality at individual or group levels to an emphasis on national interests or society building—at times concurrently, at other times in opposition. Of note in expanding its scope are the multiple ways in which differences may be constructed and coded under multiculturalism, with the main codifications reflecting a continuum of multicultural styles from the conservative and liberal to the postmodern and critical (McLaren 1994). Analytically distinct yet interconnected layers of meaning must also be taken into account in defining multiculturalism, including its existence at the level of (a) fact (what is); (b) ideology (what should be); (c) policy (what is proposed); (d) process (what really happens); (e) critical discourse (what is being contested); and (f) social movement (collective resistance) (Fleras and Elliott 1991). Failure to separate these diverse interpretive levels will invariably generate chaos or confusion, particularly when responding to questions such as, Is Canada a multicultural society?

Multiculturalism continues to elude any simple and straightforward definition. Such an admission may strike the reader as unusual, even paradoxical, given the profile of multiculturalism in Canada (and more recently the United States). Part of the problem is related to the definitional process itself: Should a definition emphasize what a thing or process looks like (structure), what it should do (function), or what it really does (process)? Many like to define multiculturalism around its promotional qualities; that is, multiculturalism is equated with promoting ethnic diversity and traditional cultures, while fostering a commitment to acceptance and mutual coexistence. Popular versions of multiculturalism tend to dwell on the celebrating of differences as differences, as valuable in their own right or in challenging for cultural space. Other definitions focus on multiculturalism as a "tool" for promoting an inclusive society by "accommodating" diversity in a proactive manner (Fleras 1994). Still others prefer a political dimension: Multiculturalism consists of an official doctrine, along with a corresponding set of policies and practices, for advancing the related goals of cultural differences, social equality, societal integration, and national unity (Wilson 1995). The best definitions intuitively focus on the relationship of multiculturalism to social inequality. Multiculturalism is inseparable from issues related to unequal power relations, and its role in supporting or challenging these inequities cannot be ignored. The better definitions also include a dynamic and contested component. Too static an interpretation of multiculturalism such as that conveyed by "stew" or "quilt" or "smorgasbord" cannot capture what is formative and evolving. References to multiculturalism as a "mosaic" are also unhelpful if they reinforce a view of society as a series of compartmentalized cultures separated by grouting (Gates Jr 1994). The dynamism and clamour attending contemporary multiculturalism is aptly captured by Amyn B. Sajoo (1994:17), who writes:

> Ours is more like an orchestral symphony, complex and energetic in its flow. If the result sometimes strains harmony, blame it on tough rehearsals by an ambitious if relatively young orchestra.

Multiculturalism in general can be defined as *a process of engaging diversity as different yet equal.* With multiculturalism, a framework is established for the full and equal participation of minority women and men through removal of discriminatory institutional barriers (both cultural and structural). Cultural space is created that confirms a minority right to be different yet the same ("equal"), depending on the circumstances. Under multiculturalism, a social and political climate is fostered in which diversity initiatives can be introduced without inciting a backlash or social turmoil. Inasmuch as multiculturalism engages diversity by challenging society to move over and make space, the remapping of Canada along pluralist lines promises to be a brave but contentious endeavour.

LEVELS OF MEANING OF MULTICULTURALISM

How would you respond to the question, Is Canada a multicultural society?

(a) Yes _____

(b) No _____

(c) It Depends _____

Any response will depend on how multiculturalism is defined. Such open-endedness implies the possibility of different levels of meaning associated with multiculturalism. It also confirms how multiculturalism has evolved from an emphasis on tolerating differences to the promotion of cultural rights, from the removal of prejudicial barriers to the restructuring of society and its institutions along more inclusive lines (see also Kurthen 1997). Multiculturalism can be interpreted at the level of (a) **empirical fact** of what is, (b) an **ideology** with a corresponding galaxy of ideas and ideals, (c) explicit government **policy** and programs, (d) a set of **practices** for promoting political and minority interests, and (e) a **critical discourse** that invites challenge and resistance (see Table 9.1). Failure to separate these different levels of meaning will invariably foster misunderstanding, especially when responding to the question, Is Canada a multicultural society? Responses will vary according to the level of meaning that is employed. Table 9.1 provides a brief overview.

TABLE 9.1	Levels of Meaning of Multiculturalism			
As Fact	**As Ideology**	**As Policy**	**As Practice**	**As Critical Discourse**
Descriptive statement of what is	Prescriptive statement of what ought to be	Explicit government initiatives to foster social equality, cultural diversity, and national interests	Putting it into practice: (a) political; (b) commercial; and (c) minority women and men	Challenge and resist distribution of cultural power

Multiculturalism As Fact

As fact, multiculturalism makes an empirical statement about "what is." It may be stating the obvious, but the obvious is sometimes overlooked for precisely that reason: Most countries are ethnically diverse, composed of people from a variety of different backgrounds who speak, think, worship, and act differently. Nearly all countries comprise different race and ethnic groups whose identities are stoutly defended and demanding of recognition or resources. Many of these groups wish to remain culturally distinct, yet are equally anxious to enjoy the benefits of full societal involvement.

Employed in the descriptive sense of the term, few would dispute the notion of Canada as a multicultural society. The existence of aboriginal, Charter, and multicultural minorities attests to this empirical fact (Elliott 1983). Adding to this variety is the realization that Canadians come from 170 different countries and speak over 100 different languages. Recent immigration patterns suggest that Canada will continue to be ethnically diverse in terms of population composition. (See Chapter 8, "Immigration and Multicultural Minorities.")

Multiculturalism As Ideology

Unlike its descriptive counterpart, multiculturalism as an ideology refers to a prescriptive ("normative") statement of "what ought to be." It prescribes a preferred course of thought or action with respect to how a society should be organized. This prescriptive state of affairs is modelled after liberal virtues of freedom, tolerance, and respect for individual differences. Multiculturalism is a value, in other words, and living in a multiculturalism allows for a more varied and richer experience than in a monocultural society (Poole 1996).

Several assumptions underlie a multicultural ideology. First and foremost is the belief that minority cultures constitute living and lived-in realities that impart meaning and security to adherents at times of stress or social change. Ethnocultural affiliation does not imply an element of mental inferiority, stubbornness, or lack of patriotism. Rather, these differences can be woven into a workable national fabric with a common set of overarching values ("unity within diversity"). Universalizing the right to a particular identity acknowledges that people are more than individuals, but social beings whose well-being depends on a shared identity within the cultural framework of an ethnic community.

Second, multiculturalism does not downgrade diversity as contrary to the goals of national unity or social progress. Cultural differences are not disparaged as incompatible with national goals, but endorsed as integral components of a national mosaic, a reflection of the Canadian ideal, and a source of enrichment and strength. Toward that end, multiculturalism points to a utopian state of affairs whereby the integration of minority differences creates a unique but unified whole as people become aware of each other's differences. More importantly, multiculturalism endorses the ideal that these differences can coexist and prosper. As Robert Hughes writes in his otherwise scathing indictment of multiculturalism (*The Culture of Complaint* 1994):

> [The premise of multiculturalism is] that people with different roots can co-exist, that they can learn to read the image banks of others, and they can and should look across the frontiers of race, gender, language, and age without prejudice or illusion.... It proposes—modestly enough—that some of the most interesting things in history and culture happen at the interface between cultures.

Third, a multicultural ideal builds upon the principles of cultural relativism. Multiculturalism fosters an open-minded philosophy around the principles of tolerance and mutual respect. This doctrine holds that all cultural practices are relative to a particular time and place. No cultural lifestyle is regarded as superior to another. If anything, cultural relativism reinforces the equality of diversity when examined in a specific historical and environmental context. That is not to say that everything *is* equally good; nor is anyone espousing the philosophy that "anything goes." Rather, to preclude prejudgment, diversity must be treated *as if* it were an equally valid expression of the human experience. Secure in the knowledge of *thoughtful relativism*, a commitment to multiculturalism reflects the premise that those confident in their cultural background will concede a similar tolerance to others (Berry et al. 1977).

Attainment of multicultural ideals is contingent on the following goals: (a) enhancing individual self-esteem through strong cultural identification; (b) eliminating prejudice and racism through sensitivity to others; (c) fostering improved intercultural exchanges through increased empathy and understanding; and (d) fostering conditions for distinct yet mutually related coexistence among different ethnic communities or identities. There is no guarantee of satisfactorily solving that perennial conundrum of "us" versus "them." But multicultural ideals are aimed at brokering such a relationship by emphasizing our commonality and shared values, not only our differences. Or as Trudeau explained back in 1971, if national unity is to mean anything in the deeply personal sense, it must be anchored on confidence in one's own identity, for it is out of this that respect for others grows (in Roy 1995). This notion—that if the state respects people for who they are, they, in turn, will be loyal to the state—was put to the test when the so-called "ethnic vote" in the October 1995 referendum temporarily de-railed the separatist aspirations of the Québécois (see also Cardozo and Musto 1997).

Multiculturalism may be ideological in a radically different sense. Ideology may be used to describe a set of ideas and ideals that have the intent or effect of securing the status quo. Cultural patterns of the dominant sector are bolstered as natural or normal, while sub-dominant patterns are dismissed as irrelevant or inferior. In setting out to do the ideological work of reinforcing patterns of power or inequality, multiculturalism is hegemonic in intent or outcome. Hegemony can be defined as the process by which people's attitudes are being manipulated without their knowledge but with their consent or involvement. Multiculturalism serves as a hegemonic tool of social control in different ways, from the commodification of culture for commercial purposes to the co-optation of ethnic leaders into a reality that remains monocultural in values, priorities, and practice.

Multiculturalism As Policy

Policy considerations are central to any official multiculturalism. By capitalizing on a mix of idealism and self-interests, governments throughout the world have embarked on official strategies for controlling immigration, managing ethnic relations, accommodating differ-ences, and integrating ethnocultural minorities into the mainstream. Multiculturalism rep-resents but one of the policy options open to central authorities for "coping" with diversity. Other policy frameworks, such as assimilation and integration, have been tried but proven inadequate in balancing societal needs with minority demands. Multiculturalism policies embrace the reality of ethnic diversities and validate their legitimacy at cultural, political, eco-nomic, and social levels. As a political principle, government must be seen to protect this di-versity, at the very least by preventing discrimination, or maximally by positively promoting and sustaining these differences (Poole 1996). Two policy levels can be discerned: One, multiculturalism consists of specific government initiatives to transform multicultural ideals into official programs and practices that acknowledge diversity as different yet equal. A new symbolic order is constructed under multicultural policies, along with a corresponding mythology, that helps to paper over any inconsistencies at odds with present realities (Breton 1984; Stasiulis 1988; Helly 1993). Two, multiculturalism can also be interpreted as a broader policy framework that justifies the design and implementation of diversity-driven programs without fear of inciting public concern over the possibility of creeping socialism or cultural apartheid. This framework may not be openly articulated; nevertheless, it supplies the "un-derlying agenda" that justifies specific decision making.

To say that Canada is officially multicultural is stating the obvious. Yet the irony is im-probable: From its inception in 1971, when it barely garnered a paragraph in Canada's na-tional paper, official multiculturalism has evolved to the point where it constitutes a formidable component of Canada's national identity, having profoundly altered how Canadians think about themselves and their relationship to the world (Fleras and Elliott 1991). Nearly thirty years of official multiculturalism have been instrumental in orchestrating a national consensus around majority acceptance of minority participation. Multiculturalism originated around the quest for integrative society-building functions; it continues to persist for precisely the same reason: the "containment" of ethnicity by modifying the rules of engagement and entitlement in a modern democratic society. Only the means for "managing" diversity have evolved in response to demographic upheavals and political developments, with cultural solutions giving way to structural reforms and, more recently, the promotion of shared citizenship (Annual Report 1997). An initial focus on "celebrating differences" as a means of eradicating prejudice and securing acceptance was superseded by an emphasis on "accommodating diversity" through institutional adjustment and removal of discriminatory barriers. The ground has again shifted in recent years to concerns about citizenship and belonging. For the sake of simplicity these shifts can be partitioned into three stages: **folkloric, equity,** and **civic multiculturalism,** keeping in mind that overlap between these stages is the rule rather than exception. First, a brief look at cultural politics in the premulticulturalism era.

Sowing the Multiculturalism Seeds

Pre-World War II government in Canada did not seriously address the issue of ethnic diversity. Central policy structures overlooked ethnic heterogeneity as inimical to broader interests. The Canada of this era was predominantly French and English, and the intent was to keep it that way. To be sure, religious and cultural differences were tolerated as private matters, but deemed divisive or dangerous when foisted on the public. Governments instead relied on time-honoured strategies that embraced the virtues of assimilation as essential for national unity and prosperity. Expressions of assimilation reflected a commitment either to Anglo-Canadian conformity or to a melting pot (or "fusion") in the American sense of the term (Hudson 1987). Anything that departed from the standards of God, King, and Empire was contemptuously dismissed as incompatible with national identity or loyalty to the Dominion.

But national consensus and commitment to Anglo-American ideals began to crumble with the intake of immigrants from Europe and later from Third World countries (Knowles 1992). If only to assist in the integration of immigrants and to foster community harmony, successive governments sought to modify the existing concept of Canada in line with new demographic realities. Passage of the first Citizenship Act in 1947 announced Canada's willingness to sever its colonialist identification with the United Kingdom. Changes of such magnitude forced a rethinking of Canada's character and the place of the "other ethnics" in the evolving configuration of Canadian society. A commitment to recognize diversity, the need for equality, and duty to protect the disadvantaged arose in response to these shifts. Pressure to create a new symbolic order was further heightened by the forces of Québécois nationalism in the aftermath of the Quiet Revolution (Breton 1989). The multicultural nod to ethnic minorities was envisaged as a potential counterbalance to neutralize (or depoliticize) an excessively bicultural focus of Canada (Webber 1994). Official bilingualism emerged as part of a new national unity strategy based on a new vision of Canada, not as a bicultural partnership between founding peoples, but as a multicultural mosaic of equality-seeking individuals (McRoberts 1997).

In brief, multiculturalism as Canadian policy originated as a pragmatic response by vested interests for achieving political goals in an electorally astute manner (Peter 1978). Of particular note in promoting a political agenda was mounting pressure on the state to "accommodate" and "manage" the vast scale of postwar immigration by expanding the rights of social citizenship (Pearson 1995; Wilson 1995). Multiculturalism was endorsed as a device for facilitating the absorption of new Canadians on the then unprecedented assumption that unity could be forged from elements of diversity. By making a virtue of necessity, in other words, multiculturalism would parlay a potential weakness into strength without necessarily revoking a commitment to social cohesion, national identity, domestic peace, economic advantage, and global status (Kurthen 1997).

Folkloric Multiculturalism ("Celebrating Differences") (1971–80)

Multiculturalism arose in the aftermath of the publication of the Report of the Royal Commission on Bilingualism and Biculturalism in 1969. Various ethnic minority groups, especially the Ukrainians and the Germans, had lobbied vigorously, arguing that their language and culture were as vital as Quebec's to Canadian society building (Wilson 1993). A compromise solution was eventually struck to take "into account the contribution made by the other ethnic groups to the cultural enrichment of Canada" (see Jaworsky 1979). A policy of multiculturalism within a bilingual framework was articulated by the Liberal government when Prime Minister Pierre Elliott Trudeau rose in Parliament and declared on 8 October 1971:

> There cannot be one cultural policy for Canadians of British or French origins, another for the originals, and yet a third for all others. For although there are two official languages, there is no official culture. Nor does any cultural group take precedence over another.... We are free to be ourselves. But this cannot be left to chance.... It is the policy of this government to eliminate any such danger and to safeguard this freedom.

This all-party agreement sought to assist those ethnic minorities who were relatively new to Canada. The objective was to integrate new Canadians into the mainstream through cultural adjustments on both sides. In the government's own words, multiculturalism would "strengthen the solidarity of the Canadian people by enabling all Canadians to participate fully and without discrimination in defining and building the nation's future." Four major principles prevailed in this commitment to resculpt a new Canada based on the equality of individuals and freedom from the tyranny of culture (McLeod 1983; McRoberts 1997):

- *Equality of status:* Canada does not have an official culture; all cultures are equal to each other.
- *Canadian identity:* Diversity lies at the heart of Canadian identity.
- *Personal choice:* The ability to choose lifestyles and cultural traits is a positive factor in society.
- *Protection of individual rights:* To be free of discrimination that precludes equality and participation.

To put these principles into practice, the government proposed initiatives (a) to assist those cultural groups that demonstrated the desire and effort to continue to develop, a capacity to grow and contribute to Canada, as well as a clear need for assistance; (b) to assist the members of all cultural groups to overcome cultural barriers to full participation in Canadian society; (c) to promote creative encounters and interchange among all Canadian cultural groups in the interests of national unity; and (d) to assist immigrants to acquire at least one of Canada's official languages to ensure full participation in Canadian society. It seems apparent, then, that multiculturalism did not focus exclusively on cultural preservation—at least not beyond an initial period when powerful ethnic lobbyists prevailed—but on fostering involvement and institutional participation as well as individual mobility and freedom of choice through elimination of "cultural jealousies" and "discriminatory attitudes" (McRoberts 1997; Cardozo and Musto 1997).

Funds were set aside for specific initiatives in securing language and culture, cultural sharing, official language learning, and removal of cultural barriers to equality. Government funding in these areas was positively received because of the political legitimacy conferred by federal support of a wide variety of ethnic concerns and activities. Agencies were also established. A multicultural directorate within the Department of Secretary of State was instituted in 1972 for the promotion of multicultural ideals, social integration, and racial harmony (Report, *Equality Now,* 1984). Efforts were directed at consolidating human rights, strengthening Canadian identity, preventing discrimination, fostering citizenship involvement, reinforcing national unity, and promoting cultural diversity. To assist federal authorities, the Canadian Consultative Council on Multiculturalism was established in 1973. The Council was later restructured and renamed the Canadian Ethnocultural Council in 1983 in the hopes of improving its advisory, research, and monitoring capacities. Later developments included the creation of a Ministry of Multiculturalism to monitor government departments. A federal Department of Multiculturalism and Citizenship was established in 1991 with passage of the **1988 Multiculturalism Act**, but subsequently scrapped in 1993. Federal multiculturalism has been downgraded to one of many programs or portfolios (including Parks and Amateur Sport) within the superministry of Canadian Heritage.

Official multiculturalism was not restricted to federal levels. Most Canadian provinces have formally endorsed the principles of multiculturalism as a guideline for government–minority relations. Saskatchewan was the first province to become officially multicultural when it established its Multicultural Council and Multicultural Directorate in 1974. The Government of Ontario followed soon, with its commitment to acknowledge all citizens, regardless of racial or religious background, as equal before the law with full political rights and equal access to government services. Quebec is also committed to a version of multiculturalism known as "interculturalism," the objective of which is the integration of allophones into French language and culture as revealed by this passage:

> ...*Désireux que toutes communautés culturelles et les nations autochtones du Québec puissent continuer de s'épanouir et contribuer pleinement a l'édification et au progrès d'une société regnent paix et harmonie.* Translation: All cultural communities and aboriginal nations in Quebec should be able to continue to flourish and fully contribute to the building and progress of a society in which peace and harmony reign (Robert Bourassa et al. 1986).

Quebec has rejected any federal multiculturalism that glosses over Quebec's collective rights as a full-fledged nation or at minimum, a distinct society. Federal multiculturalism is denounced as yet another centralizing intrusion into Quebec's internal affairs, a calculated plot to transform a founding people into another folkloric ethnic minority rather than an equal partner within a linguistically and culturally bifurcated Canadian state. Proposed instead of the federal mosaic is a "tree" version of multiculturalism in which minority branches are grafted onto a Québécois trunk (see Webber 1994). Under interculturalism, French is the official language and culture, with diversity tolerated and accepted only to this point (Talbani 1993). The main objectives of interculturalism can be identified as follows: (a) to ensure the reality of cultural communities; (b) to sensitize Québécois to the value of ethnic diversity; (c) to promote integration of minorities into Quebec society; and (d) the removal of discriminatory barriers and promotion of equal opportunity for all (Jantzen 1992). This focus is on affirming the cultural plurality and equal participation—without compromising the non-negotiable primacy of French language and culture, sovereignty of the National Assembly, a secular state, and equality between sexes (Hudson 1987; Helly 1993; Webber 1994).

Aboriginal peoples are likewise skeptical of multiculturalism as a solution to their problems. Like the Québécois, they make no claims to be part of a pluralistic society but a distinct people with shared history and a common homeland (see also Carter 1995). The levelling provisions within multiculturalism are perceived as a threat to cultural survival (Kallen 1987). Worse, still, multiculturalism is criticized as downsizing aboriginal status to that of a minority/ethnic group, thereby foreclosing the fiduciary relationship between First Nations and central authorities (Sanders 1987). Also dismissed as inadequate were federal attempts to promote aboriginal cultural preservation outside a general framework of self-determination and aboriginality. That being the case, aboriginal peoples, like the Québécois, prefer to negotiate from within a bicultural framework that recognizes their collective right to special status and distinct entitlements.

Equity Multiculturalism: Institutional Accommodation (1981–90)

Federal multiculturalism underwent a discernible shift in focus by the early 1980s. Initially, multiculturalism came to mean the introduction of government programs to protect the distinct ethnic identities that immigrants brought with them; it was also used to indicate increased government involvement in dealing with social problems that immigrant communities confronted (Poole 1996). Multiculturalism was directed almost exclusively at the European ethnic sector. It sought to enhance social status through symbolic affirmation of their language and culture as well as to improve participation in society through removal of cultural barriers and prejudicial attitudes on both sides of the ledger.

But the discourse on multiculturalism shifted to embrace the more equity-focused concerns of non-European immigrants. Pre-1970s immigrants shared with their hosts a broad commitment to Eurocentric values and priorities, thus facilitating assimilation into the mainstream; by contrast, the prejudice and discrimination associated with non-European visibility and differences precluded integration without government intervention (Sajoo 1994). For new immigrants, the need for dismantling racial barriers to opportunity or inclusion was more important than the celebration of their cultural differences (McRoberts 1997). The earlier emphasis on ethnicity and culture was subsequently replaced by a commitment to equity, social justice, and institutional accommodation through removal of discriminatory barriers at structural levels. Funding disbursements corresponded with this reversal in mandate. Rather than simply doling out money to ethnocultural organizations or events as had been the case, authorities have refocused multicultural spending on pragmatic goals. For the 1993–94 fiscal year, grants from federal multiculturalism totalled $25.5 million, with $13.3 million earmarked for community support and participation (assist in the settlement of new Canadians), another $6.5 million for public education and antiracism, and $5.5 million to promote the principle of heritage cultures and languages (Thompson 1994).

Subsequent developments further advanced the profile of multiculturalism. The Charter of Rights and Freedoms, which came into effect in 1985, constitutionally entrenched multiculturalism as a distinguishing characteristic of Canadian life. Its emergence as a tool of interpretation at the highest levels of national decision making reinforced a fundamental multicultural right in Canadian society: the right to be different (culture) as well as the right to be the same (equality). Its prominence was further advanced when Canada became the first country to formally endow multiculturalism with legal authority. The Multiculturalism Act in 1988 sought to promote cultures, reduce discrimination, and accelerate institutional accommodation through the "preservation and enhancement of Canadian multiculturalism." The act obligated federal institutions to engage diversity in a manner consistent with Canada's multicultural character, thus compelling state institutions to relate to Canadians increasingly on ethnic grounds rather than on a geographical or functional basis (Pearson 1996).

Passage of the Multiculturalism Act did not occur without acrimony or incident (Parel 1992). The Multiculturalism Act may well have sought to more effectively and positively manage Canada's growing diversity. But it may have had the effect of reconstituting and legitimating ethnic inequality since state initiatives such as law are socially constructed to appear as if they were a detached and objective expression of societal values that transcend the interest of any particular group. In reality, however, the state must accommodate a multiplicity of interests while fulfilling two often contradictory functions of capitalism: accumulation and legitimation (Jakubowicz et al. 1994). In other words, the Act was in no position to deliver what it set out to promise, except perhaps in the most superficial sense. Still, the significance of the Act cannot be underestimated. The Act rationalized government objectives by reaffirming within a statutory framework what existed previously as *de facto* policy. It also imbued multiculturalism with the cloak of legal authority and the weight of Canadian law, thus making it less vulnerable to political party politics and electoral whims (Report, *Multiculturalism,* 1987). It has also endowed multiculturalism with the legitimacy to coexist in harmony with (and equal to) the principle of bilingualism in Canada.

Civic Multiculturalism: Belonging Through Inclusion (1991–)

Multiculturalism continues to attract adherents for celebrating differences. Its commitment to engaging diversity is no less important and is manifest in the mainstreaming of key institutions to ensure minority access, representation, and equitable treatment. Equally evident is a trend toward twinning multiculturalism with citizenship, a relationship that was consummated during the short-lived era of the Department of Multiculturalism and Citizenship. Even the current arrangement aligns multiculturalism with the citizenship and Canadian identity portfolio within the superministry of Canada Heritage. This downgrading to program is not insignificant. The government may remain officially committed to multiculturalism, but its support is increasingly muted and is not beyond the scope of axing certain multicultural programs (see also Poole 1996).

Civic multiculturalism is oriented toward society building by emphasizing the ideal of a commonly shared citizenship (see also Chapter 11 for a closer examination of citizenship). It hopes to foster a sense of belonging and a shared sense of Canadian identity as one way of enhancing national unity without forsaking those differences that give practical effect to the idea of unity in diversity. Emphasis is on what we have in common as rights-bearing and equality-seeking individuals rather than on what separates or divides us. Policy objectives under this civic multiculturalism include a commitment to social justice, an emergent Canadian identity, and increased civic participation (Cardozo 1997). Objectives focus on inclusion and integration, with points of emphasis that vary from integrating diverse cultures into a uniquely Canadian identity to removing discriminatory barriers that preclude the incorporation of all Canadians into a civic culture. In contrast to the past, when multiculturalism was ostensibly aimed at racial and ethnic minorities, the scope of civic multiculturalism is directed toward society at large. The objective, according to the minister of multiculturalism, is to "break down the ghettoization of multiculturalism." This notion of "diversity" within "unity" is nicely captured in this passage from the noted British ethnicist, Bhikkhu Parekh:

> Multiculturalism doesn't simply mean numerical plurality of different cultures, but rather a community which is creating, guaranteeing, encouraging spaces within which different communities are able to grow at their own pace. At the same time it means creating a public space in which these new communities are able to interact, enrich the existing culture, and create a new consensual culture in which they recognize reflections of their own identity (cited in Giroux 1994:336).

But as noted elsewhere, it may prove difficult to implement an inclusive and civic-oriented multiculturalism when economic realities appear to be eroding those very programs and initiatives to meet the civic needs of ethnic minorities (Rivzi 1994). It remains to be seen whether a social justice policy can be comfortably located within the framework of an economic agenda that attempts to improve Canada's competitive advantage. Table 9.2 compares and contrasts the different stages in the evolution of Canada's multiculturalism policies.

TABLE 9.2	Multiculturalism Policies		
	Folkloric Multiculturalism (1970s)	**Institutional Multiculturalism (1980s)**	**Civic Multiculturalism (1990s)**
Focus	Celebrating differences	Managing diversity	Society building
Reference point	Culture	Structure	Community
Mandate	Ethnicity	Race relations	Citizenship
Magnitude	Individual adjustment	Accommodation	Participation
Problem source	Prejudice	Systemic discrimination	Exclusion
Problem solution	Cultural sensitivity	Employment equity	Inclusion
Key metaphor	Mosaic	Level playing field	Belonging

Multiculturalism As Practice

A raft of platitudes about celebrating and sharing cannot disguise the pragmatic components of multiculturalism. Multiculturalism as practice refers to its use by both political and ethnic sectors to promote respective goals and ambitions. Politicians and bureaucrats look upon multiculturalism as a resource with economic or political potential to be exploited at national or international levels for practical gain. For minority women and men, multiculturalism provides a political platform for articulating their concerns and drawing attention to grievances around gaps between multicultural ideals and institutional practices. This focus on practising multiculturalism will reinforce its status as a renewable resource in the ongoing reconstruction of Canadian society. It will also demonstrate how putting multiculturalism into practice does not always coincide with the policy ideals.

Political Gain/Commercial Advantage

If politics is the art of conflict resolution (Van Loon and Whittington 1981), then multiculturalism is indeed political because of its inseparability from "managing" conflicting interests. The politics behind the origins of Canada's multiculturalism are widely known: Multiculturalism originated from the customary interplay of good intentions and political opportunism (Gwyn 1994). It hoped to formulate a new founding myth of Canada as the land of opportunity and equality for all Canadians, thus uniting all Canadians at a time of political turmoil, but without any fundamental redistribution of power (Helly 1993). It also sought to shore up electoral strength in urban Ontario, to counterbalance Western resentment over perceived favouritism toward the Québécois, to preempt the encroachment of American cultural imperialism, and to thwart political unrest from changes to immigration (see Burnet and Palmer 1988). The governing apparatus of the Canadian state also relied on multiculturalism to fulfill a variety of legitimating functions involving national unity, economic prosperity, and electoral survival.

In the final analysis, multiculturalism is first and foremost a political program to achieve political goals in a politically astute manner (Peter 1978). At its crassest level, multicultural politics are animated by a belief in ethnic support as relevant for (re)election. The vast majority of Canada's multicultural minorities are concentrated in major urban centres such as Toronto, Montreal, and Vancouver, a trend likely to be amplified by future immigration patterns. The growing heterogeneity of Canada's population has prompted all political parties to pursue the multicultural vote through promises of increased representation, funding, and affirmative action at federal levels. At another level is the preoccupation with the commercial potential of multiculturalism. Prime Minister Brian Mulroney outlined this challenge in his "Multiculturalism Means Business" speech at a Toronto conference in 1986 when he stated:

> We, as a nation, need to grasp the opportunity afforded to us by our multicultural identity to cement our prosperity with trade and investment links the world over and with a renewed entrepreneurial spirit at home.... But our multicultural nature gives us an edge in selling to that world.... Canadians who have cultural links to other parts of the globe, who have business contacts elsewhere are of the utmost importance to our trade and investment strategy (Report, Secretary of State, 1987).

By enhancing Canada's sales image and competitive edge in a global economy, particularly by cultivating and tapping into the lucrative Asian market (Hage 1997), multiculturalism is touted as having the potential to harness lucrative trade contracts, establish international linkages and mutually profitable points of contact, and penetrate hitherto difficult-to-access export markets. Even success in local and regional markets is increasingly correlated with serving the needs of a multicultural population (Stinson 1994). But this commercial commitment is not without costs: The growing popularity of diversity as a lifestyle statement has resulted in the commercial appropriation of multicultural differences, a process where differences often are taken out of context and repackaged to meet consumer stereotypes. Under multiculturalism, cultures are commodified by freezing them in time or romanticizing as exotic, in effect compartmentalizing minorities into ethnic ghettoes while diverting attention away from real issues that have a destablizing effect on individual lives such as racism, unemployment, recession, free trade, and cutbacks to social services (Philip 1995). Multiculturalism is currently promoted as a desirable Canadian export with marketable value in the same way staple products were in the past (Moodley 1984; Crane 1995). According to Katharyne Mitchell, in her 1993 article on "Multiculturalism: the United Colors of Capitalism," multiculturalism has been actively deployed by Canada to attract members of the transnational elite and wealthy global citizens. Emphasis is on Canada as a welcoming country of many different cultures—"hey, look at us, we're multicultural"—rather than a single, exclusive national culture as is the case in Britain. A second tactic in attracting international capital is to emphasize the role of multiculturalism in reinforcing Canada's much-vaunted racial harmony, thus allaying fears of racial friction. The reworking of multiculturalism as an ideology of racial harmony and cooperative coexistence, Mitchell (1993) says, provides a degree of reassurance for nervous investors and fidgety capital. It also ensures the integration of Canada into the international networks of an ongoing expansion of global capitalism. As the globalization of capitalist market economies continues to expand, multiculturalism may well provide the mindset for confronting the challenges of a shifting and increasingly borderless twenty-first century society (see Gwyn 1997).

Multiculturalism and Multicultural Minorities

Multicultural minorities are inclined to see multiculturalism as a resource for attaining practical goals (Burnet 1981). Needs are basic: Many want to become established, to expand economic opportunities for themselves and their children, to eliminate discrimination and exploitation, and to retain access to their cultural heritage without loss of citizenship rights. Multiculturalism is employed as a tool for meeting these needs by opening up economic, social, and cultural channels. Many are increasingly reliant on multicultural mechanisms to combat discrimination in areas of employment, education, housing, and criminal justice (Report, *Equality Now*, 1984). As far as multicultural minorities are concerned, the driving principle behind multiculturalism is equality not nationalism. There is no desire for separate homelands or an autonomous government, but a desire to be Canadians, to be accepted as part of the national fabric (Cardozo and Musto 1997:92). The modest demands for protection of language, culture, and identity cannot be construed as an excuse for autonomy.

The resource value of multiculturalism is evident in other ways. Multicultural minorities are often unable to influence central policy structures because of geographical dispersal, cultural heterogeneity, and negligible negotiatory powers. With multiculturalism, an otherwise powerless sector now possesses the leverage to prod, embarrass, and provoke central policy structures by holding them accountable for failure to practise what they preach. Issues over power sharing, resource distribution, and meaningful decision making take precedent over food courts, folk dancing, and ethnic festivals. A new moral authority has evolved that portrays minorities as legitimate contenders in the competition for power and resources. Minority groups are now empowered with yet another resource in staking out their claims and articulating their demands alongside those of the first and second force. Appeals to multiculturalism are thus calculated to extract public and global sympathy, in the same way aboriginal peoples in Canada have relied on the United Nations as a bargaining chip against the federal government.

Multiculturalism As Critical Discourse

Multicultural principles and practices continue to animate the cultural politics in Canada and the United States, albeit in fundamentally different ways. References to Canada's official multiculturalism embrace a commitment to **consensus** by way of "conformity" and "accommodation." Attainment of these multicultural goals is varied, spanning the spectrum from promoting proactive measures to fostering tolerance toward diversity, reducing prejudice, removing discriminatory barriers, eliminating cultural ethnocentrism, enhancing equitable access to services, expanding institutional engagement, and improving intergroup encounters.

By contrast, the thrust of popular multiculturalisms in the United States is **critical** in contesting the organization and control of cultural space. Yet many are baffled by the emergence of any multiculturalism in a society whose ideological moorings were anchored on a melting pot mentality. The recency of the transformation is staggering: A Nexis database of major newspapers as recently as 1988 yielded no references to multiculturalism; by 1994, 1,500 entries had appeared (Glazer 1997). Expansion of multiculturalism has been applauded for reasserting people's control over lives, detested as political correctness gone mad, deplored for "fetishising" diversity at the expense of national vision and collective goals, and dismissed as a humanizing ideal that is somewhat prone to excessive zeal and "political correctness" (see Higham 1993). But multicultural discourses have challenged the venerable *e pluribus unum* (one out of many) principle that individuals are endlessly variable yet fundamentally alike. Advocated instead is the distinctly "un-American" axiom that personal patterns of engagement and entitlement should reflect disadvantage or birthright rather than merit, identity rather than conformity, and diversity rather than universality (McLaren 1994).

In the broadest sense, American multiculturalism is the contemporary expression of liberal antiracism (D'Souza 1995). It offers a critical investigation of prevailing political relations on the premise that cultural institutions are fundamentally racist in privileging westocentric values at the expense of minority struggles and aspirations (Early 1993). In seeking respect and equality for all cultures, multiculturalism can be pictured as a social movement based on the denial of Western cultural superiority and celebration of the other. Of course, not all multicultural discourses in the United States are cut from a critical cloth. Under a "happy face" multiculturalism, a universalist centre is promulgated that ostensibly celebrates diversity while simultaneously scaling it back for the purpose of control or containment (Eisenstein 1996; Hesse 1997). These liberal pluralisms may pay lip service to multiculturalism, but any commitment to diversity is devoid of critical content, historical context, or patterns of power (Giroux 1994). In contrast with these "consensus" multiculturalisms is the surge of "subversive" multiculturalisms in interrogating the culture of whiteness that historically defined public perception of what was necessary, normal, and inevitable (D'Souza 1995; Eller 1997). A critical multiculturalism transcends the simple construction of identities or celebration of tolerance. Embraced instead is a discourse of resistance that challenges the authority and legitimacy of white supremacy by contesting the racism, sexism, and patriarchy embedded in American society (Giroux 1994). Differences do not merely exist under critical multiculturalism; they exist as part of the struggle to create a new public culture. Inasmuch as multicultural interests are openly contesting the power to shape the production and reproduction of knowledge in institutions from education to media, critical multiculturalism promises to melt the assimilationist pot.

Multiculturalism as critical discourse pivots around four themes: postmodernism, cultural relativism, identity politics, and collective rights. The link between critical multiculturalism and postmodernism is inescapable (Goldberg 1994). In forsaking a reality that is coherent, objective, and amenable to rational analysis by dispassionate language, postmodernism espouses a mind-dependent world that has no centre or authority, only different viewpoints where everything is relative and true because nothing is absolutely knowable. Gerald Early (1993:223) captures the postmodernity at the heart of critical multiculturalism by emphasizing the "crisis of representation" that underpins intellectual reality:

> Postmodernism's goal is to expose the bourgeois intellectual order as inherently political and interested, as all political orders are, in maintaining the set of social and political relations that give it both authority and prestige. In short, what postmodernism...wishes to accomplish is undermining bourgeois's intellectual assumptions about a search for universal truth and the ideal of objectivity by arguing that...[these] were illusions to mask its own quest for power by hiding the epistemological roots of its own politicization.

Acceptance of a postmodernist reality as perspectival and provisional as well as socially constructed and culturally constrained has the effect of fragmenting society into a multiplicity of pluralisms (Adam and Allan 1995). It also has the effect of challenging the patterns of power that traditionally bolstered societal definitions of truth, rules of normalcy, and standards of legitimacy, many of which were at odds with the lived experiences of minority women and men (Harris 1995). In the final analysis, challenging the "dominant silencing of diversity" (Eisenstein 1996) fosters a framework by which new identities are (re)formulated, new communities are constructed, knowledge and power are contested, and Eurocentric universalisms are exposed for what they are: self-serving discourses in defence of dominant ideology.

Central to critical multiculturalism is the relativist assumption that nothing is neutral or impartial because everything/everyone is located in time and space. In the absence of absolute standards of right or wrong, criteria for criticizing a culture must be framed from within the culture, since cultures are not entitled to impose values on others (D'Souza 1996). The verdict of essentialism is mixed, as might be expected in any critical discourse. To one side is the essentialist stance that each group has its own culture; to the other is an antiessentialist rejection of all experiences or classifications that are defined as singular, fixed, or homogenous in favour of those that endorse multiplicity, fluidity, situationality, and hybridity; the concrete and particular rather than abstract and universal; and the contingent and provisional rather than rigid and doctrinaire (Eisenstein 1996). Identity politics and the politics of difference are part of this tug of loyalties to politicize, recover, preserve, or promote the differences of a threatened collectivity—often involving minority demands for separate yet equal recognition of cultural differences within academic or cultural institutions (Turner 1994). Society can only become equitable and inclusive if the perspectives of those historically marginalized by the dominant group's colonialist discourse are taken into account (Schneiderman 1996). Equally important to the "postmulticulturalism" turn is the notion of collective rights. Just as earlier social movements had challenged the ideas and structures that once justified oppression, the new identity politics concede that moves to eliminate group differences in favour of individual rights are equally oppressive—in consequence if not necessarily in intent (Eller 1997). The following Case Study compares the critical multicultural discourses in the United States with the consensus model in Canada and emphasizes their differences through a set of contrasts.

CASE STUDY 9–2	"Duelling Discourses": Canadian Versus American Multiculturalisms

Many have said that Canadians and Americans use the same words but speak a different language. Nowhere is this antimony more evident than in references to multiculturalism. Canada may claim to be a multicultural mosaic, but its multiculturalism is geared toward integrating ethnic Canadians into the mainstream. The *e pluribus unum* of the United States seems conducive to conjuring up the melting pot, but an "insurgent" multiculturalism has precipitated cultural wars involving identity politics and ethnic identities that threaten to undermine any coherent national vision (Simpson 1998). The magnitude of these differences suggests a new "postmulticulturalism" turn in contrast with the modernist multicultural project in Canada.

Canadian multiculturalism differs from its American counterpart at several points of discourse. (Canadian multiculturalism is featured first in each set of contrasts.) One multiculturalism is directed at transforming the mainstream without straining the social fabric; the other multiculturalisms are concerned with empowering minorities by eroding the monocultural firmament of society. One is officially political, yet seeks to depoliticize diversity for society-building purposes; the other falls outside the policy domain, but politicizes differences as a catalyst for minority empowerment and entitlement. One is rooted in the modernist quest for unity, certainty, and universality; the other in embracing a postmodernist zeal for differences, provisionality, and fragmentation. Of particular note is how the one transforms cultural differences into a discourse about social inequality, while the other reformulates social inequalities into a discursive framework of cultural differences and public culture. One is based on outward-looking public goals; the other on the inward-looking needs of victims for self-esteem, recognition, compensation, and role models, all of which are difficult to measure and impossible to challenge (Higham 1993). There is nothing inherently right or wrong in conceding the multiplicity of multicultural discourses. Difficulties arise when varying discourses are employed indiscriminately or interchangeably, with predictably distorting effects on expectations and communication.

Multiculturalism in Canada is primarily a political program for pursuit of national interests. In shifting from colonialism to pluralism as a basis for a new moral order, official multiculturalism in Canada is a form of state legitimacy rather than a vehicle of broader emancipation (see also Goodman 1997). It is more concerned with drawing people into the idea of a nation rather than in protecting social and cultural rights (see also Vasta 1993). This hegemonic discourse in defence of dominant ideology endorses those policies and initiatives that subordinate minority needs to the "greater good" of society. Multicultural principles and practices are inseparable from a neoassimilationist commitment to consensus and commonality as keys to social harmony. The potential disruptiveness of diversity is dispelled by homogenizing differences around a singular commonality so that everyone is similarly different, not differently similar, under a "monocultural" multiculturalism (Eisenstein 1996). By contrast, the postmodernist discourses that animate America's critical multiculturalism subvert as they resist. Critical multiculturalism transcends the constraints of official policy initiatives; it is not compromised by the demands of political engineering or electoral pandering. Discourses in the service of resistance are advocated instead, which challenge Eurocentricity by relativizing the white capitalist patriarchy with its exclusionary designs on the "other" (Giroux 1994; Eisenstein 1996). In contrast with liberal multiculturalism's emphasis on individual diversity, a critical multiculturalism addresses the issue of group differences and how power relations function to secure inequities and structure identities. Unlike consensus multiculturalism, which connotes a pluralism that is devoid of historical context and specificities of power relations, a critical multiculturalism signifies a site of struggle around the reformation of historical memory, national identity, self-

and social representation, and the politics of difference (Giroux 1994:336).

In other words, multiculturalism in Canada is essentially a society-affirming exercise that seeks to depoliticize differences through institutional accommodation. It is grounded in the liberal pluralist credo that what we have in common as rights-bearing, equality-seeking individuals is more important than what divides us through placement in an exclusive ethnic heritage. Compare this with American multiculturalism's group differences and identity claims, which are politicized by challenging the prevailing distribution of cultural power for moving over and making cultural space. A "playful" inversion is called for in juxtaposing these duelling discourses: Rather than making *society* safe from diversity, safe for diversity as is the case in a multicultural Canada, the underlying logic of critical multiculturalism is to make *diversity* safe from society as well as safe for society.

ATTITUDES TOWARD MULTICULTURALISM

Timing has played politics with multiculturalism. Multiculturalism may have originated in an era of optimism and accommodation, but is under scrutiny at a time of discontent. Multiculturalism was carried along by a wave of reform, but is now being buffeted by the undertow of retrenchment (Cardozo and Musto 1997). What started out as a good idea with noble intentions (to assist newcomers into Canada) has evolved into a flashpoint for tension between multiculturalism advocates (Levitt 1997) and those who recoil in horror at the very prospect of foisting yet more government on an unsuspecting public (Field 1994). Not surprisingly, public perception of multiculturalism in Canada is varied. Some Canadians are vigorously supportive; others are in total rejection or denial; still others are indifferent; and yet others are uninformed (see Musto 1997). The majority appear to be caught somewhere in between, depending on their reading of multiculturalism and its legitimacy in advancing a new vision of Canada (see also Goot 1993). Variables such as age, income, level of education, and place of residence are critical in gauging support, with higher levels of approval among younger, more affluent, better educated, and urban individuals. To the extent that most Canadians are unsure of what Canada's official multiculturalism is trying to do, and why, and what it can realistically accomplish in a capitalist democracy, the scenario described above by Goot may become the rule rather than the exception.

There is some disagreement on the extent to which Canadians accept official multiculturalism. Opinion polls are known to provide different answers, depending on the kinds of questions asked (Poole 1996). Nevertheless, national surveys on multiculturalism suggest a solid base of support (Angus Reid 1991; Berry 1993). Three recent studies have confirmed this: The first, conducted by Environics Research Group 1995 (and reported in Musto 1997), indicates that 66 percent of Canadians recognize the existence of federal multiculturalism policy. Of these, 62 percent approve of federal multiculturalism, although support appears to have declined slightly between 1989 and 1995 because of economic uncertainty. Another study by Eikos Research Associates (also 1995 and cited in Musto 1997) indicates that almost one-half of Canadians (48 percent) lack familiarity with federal multiculturalism policy. In response to whether people would support or oppose the following elements in a federal multiculturalism program, the vast majority endorsed the idea of multiculturalism when (a) assisting new Canadians to settle into Canada, (b) removing discriminatory barriers, and (c) promoting tolerance. A multiculturalism policy that helped people integrate into society without having to give up their ethnic identity was also heavily supported by 74 percent. Just barely one-half (55 percent) thought that multiculturalism should help ethnic minorities to preserve their culture. A third study, in 1997, also by the Environics Research Group (and cited in the Metropolis Project [1997]) suggests swings in public attitudes toward multiculturalism. Multiculturalism policy awareness had increased from 41 percent in 1976 to 69 percent in 1997, while approval for official multiculturalism had climbed to 62 percent in 1997, reversing a drop from 63 percent in 1989 to 50 percent in 1995. It is interesting to note that 41 percent of the respondents thought that tolerance and respect for others were key multicultural goals. Far fewer felt that multiculturalism ought to encourage cultural retention (26 percent) or assist in adaptation (18 percent).

What can we infer from these national surveys? First, support is not the same as enthusiasm. Canadians appear to embrace multiculturalism as a reality to be tolerated rather than an ideal to be emulated. The *idea* of multicultural tolerance may be widely supported, in that a mix of cultures makes Canada a more interesting place, but there is little dedication to its implementation. Approval persists only as long as costs are low and demands reasonable (Fleras 1998). Second, support is conditional; that is, people are prepared to accept different levels of multiculturalism. Multiculturalism is acceptable if it means that everyone has a right to his or her culture in Canada. Support vanishes when multiculturalism is seen to endorse a mishmash of different but equal cultures, with no centre and in a constant state of tension because of inner contradictions. Multiculturalism is OK if it's about learning of other cultures or eliminating discriminatory barriers to improve minority access and participation. It is not OK if endorsement of multiculturalism is thought to erode Canada's sense of national identity, challenges authority or core values, encourages separation or division, or fixates on demonizing the mainstream. Third, support or rejection tends to be selective. Most Canadians support some aspect of multiculturalism; for example, a tolerance toward diversity and acceptance of pluralism are embraced as the definitive attributes of Canada (Gwyn 1996). Yet those aspects of policy that encourage minorities to challenge cherished symbols of Canadian identity are rejected. In other words, resentment is directed not at multicultural diversity *per se,* but at those aspects involving policy, immigration, or the equity agenda.

Criticism of Multiculturalism

Official multiculturalism is unevenly supported across Canada. Residents of Ontario and Western Canada appear receptive, but the Québécois (Bourassa 1975; Ryan 1975) and First Nations (Sanders 1987) have demonstrated less enthusiasm. Many observers of Canada's political scene have criticized the government's initiatives in this area (Peter 1978; Kallen 1982; Burnet 1984; Bibby 1990; Thobani 1995; Das Gupta 1994; Bissoondath 1994; Falding 1995). Multiculturalism is accused of fostering ethnic separatism while discouraging the integration of ethnic Canadians into an increasingly fractured society. Robert Fulford (1997) does not mince words in rubbishing multiculturalism when he writes:

> Pluralism, the side-by-side existence of many forms of human association, is an essential quality of modern life. Official multiculturalism, the automatic classification of citizens according to race and ancestry, was a bad idea in the beginning, and in time will probably be seen as one of the gigantic mistakes of recent public policy in Canada.

Scholarly opinion has been equally dismissive of multiculturalism. Multiculturalism is portrayed as a colossal hoax perpetuated by vested interests to ensure minority co-optation through ideological indoctrination ("false consciousness") (Duncan and Cronin 1997/98). The fact that multiculturalism has become little more than a mantra for politicians and industry leaders to trot out for dignitaries, public relations, or reelection may reflect its unthreatening status for those in positions of power and privilege. Critics on the left have pounced on multiculturalism as ineffective except to provide symbolic redress to minorities; those on the right repudiate it as a costly drain of resources. Those in the middle concede the existence of multiculturalism to be a form of ideological indoctrination but whose egalitarian impulses promote a more compassionate society. Multiculturalism may sound good in theory, but is extremely difficult to implement because of the difficulties in integrating differences without undermining the integrity of the whole. This challenge of fostering integration without capitulating to assimilation remains a basic paradox of multiculturalism.

Others have argued that the government is willing to lavish funds on folk festivals and ethnic performing arts in an elaborate game of "pretend pluralism" (Kay 1999), but is reluctant to support minority demands for collective rights or socioeconomic enhancement (Kallen 1987). Minorities are ghettoized instead into certain occupational structures and residential arrangements, thereby preserving the prevailing distribution of power and wealth (Porter 1965; Moodley 1984). Public awareness of cultural diversity may be bolstered under multiculturalism, critics contend, but cultural solutions cannot possibly solve the structural problems of discrimination and systemic racism (Bolaria and Li 1988). The charge that multiculturalism is the last refuge of the racist raises questions of whether multiculturalism represents an authentic policy alternative or an interim measure for easing minorities into the mainstream, a kind of "assimilation by slow motion." Finally, criticism of multiculturalism is directed at its often unintended consequences for society at large. According to Kenneth McRoberts (1997), Trudeau's multiculturalism is undermining national unity, despite its avowed promotion as part of a national unity strategy, in part by alienating francophone Quebeckers, whose vision of Canada as a partnership is at odds with official multiculturalism. Gina Mallet (1997:D-2) captures a sense of this "good gone bad" when she writes:

> Although the drive to honour diversity through official multiculturalism was originally undertaken in order to promote tolerance, it is accomplishing the opposite. By setting Canadians against one another and emphasizing our differences rather than the many things we have in common, diversity has, in fact, gone too far.

Of Canada's critics, few have been as vocal in their condemnation of multiculturalism as author Neil Bissoondath (1994). He likens multiculturalism to a shibboleth that has been shamelessly manipulated by politicians and ethnic opportunists for ulterior purposes. An obsessive preoccupation with accommodating diversity, he argues, may embolden minorities by demanding that Canada adopt their customs and languages, rather than the other way around, in effect fanning the flames of hatred and tribalism at the expense of Canadian unity, identity, and culture. Not only has multiculturalism become impervious to criticism—to criticize is to be accused of racism—it also comes across as condescending paternalism in a country where the prevailing mindset endorses British and French as real Canadians, while regarding others as not-quite-Canadians. Multiculturalism tends to impede what it was created for, that is, the full and equal acceptance of immigrants into society. Diversity is endorsed, but migrants are then forced to conform to the superficially exotic image that Canadians have imposed on them, thus reinforcing a perception of them versus us. Multiculturalism also fosters sentiments that exclude minorities from full and equal participation, trivializes minority contributions, stigmatizes minorities as foreigners or outsiders, and patronizes minorities as inferior or incapable of accomplishment without outside assistance. Finally, multiculturalism encourages a reckless cultural relativism (Bibby 1990) that culminates in a Canada of marginalized and hyphenated Canadians with divided loyalties and fractured values.

Rethinking Criticism: "A Pox on Both Houses"

In its role as the self-appointed catalyst for social engineering, multiculturalism has attracted its share of criticism. Multiculturalism has become the scapegoat for a thicket of thorny problems, in particular, Canada's inability to resolve national divisions involving the British, French, and aboriginal peoples (Kymlicka 1999). National shortcomings for some reason tend to polarize and be magnified around minority relations. But much of this criticism tends to be misguided in that it glosses over the multidimensional nature of multiculturalism (Kymlicka 1998). As far as we are concerned, those who stoutly defend multiculturalism at all costs are as ideological as those who disparage multiculturalism as lacking any redeeming value whatsoever. Multiculturalism is neither all good nor all bad; rather, it is both good and bad, depending on the context and frame of reference. Multiculturalism can be liberating yet marginalizing, unifying yet divisive, inclusive yet exclusive (Vasta 1993). On the one hand, multiculturalism provides minorities with a platform for participating in society without the imposition of heavy-handed government tactics. On the other, minorities are lured into the dominant culture, since measures to improve access or participation often have assimilationist consequences. Even efforts at resistance are perceived as self-defeating exercises that have the effect of absorbing minorities into the very system they are rejecting (Pearson 1996).

Canada's official multiculturalism is double-edged in impact and implications (Fleras 1994). To one side, the existence of counterhegemonic multicultural discourses cannot be discounted, thus reflecting the ability of the powerless and dispossessed to convert the very tools for controlling them into levers of resistance and change (Pearson 1996). Minority women and men are not passive actors in the political arena, but have dissembled official multiculturalism into sites of struggle for access to symbolic and material resources (Pearson 1995). To the other, an emphasis on official multiculturalism has proven a politically workable strategy for deradicalizing ("depoliticizing") ethnicity, in part by legitimizing state-approved differences as integral to society; in other part by transforming institutions into public spaces where minorities can participate without ethnic entanglements. Far from being a threat to the social order, in other words, Canada's official multiculturalism constitutes a discourse in defence of ideology by circumscribing the permissible range of acceptable behaviour (Thobani 1995). No voice shall predominate in creating a community of communities under multiculturalism, the saying goes, except the voice that says no voices shall predominate (James 1997). In defining which differences count, what counts as difference, containment by multiculturalism could hardly be more artfully articulated.

Official multiculturalism can be interpreted as double-edged where strengths are linked with weakness, benefits with costs (see also Dorais et al. 1994). In the same way that ethnicity can empower or divide, depending on a particular frame of reference, so too can multiculturalism enhance yet detract. Positive and negative effects coexist uneasily, with one prevailing over another because of circumstances, but its opposite ready to reappear under different conditions. To the extent that multiculturalism prevents the forced assimilation of minorities into the mainstream, this policy is to be congratulated; insofar as multiculturalism as a bureaucratic set of rules and categories prevents individuals from breaking out of their ethnic shells to participate fully and equally in society, multiculturalism leaves much to be desired (Keohane 1997). Even operationalizing the terms "costs" and "benefits" can be difficult, in many ways reflecting observer bias and competing visions of society. Take the symbolic value of multiculturalism: Some are dismissive of government policies as "symbolic" or superficial. Others recognize that conferral of symbolic legitimacy is of formidable value in bolstering the status and legitimacy of minorities (Breton 1984; Webber 1994). This symbolism of respect, equality, tolerance, and accommodation appears to have fostered a strong ethnic commitment to Canada, a situation that proved serendipitous when the "ethnic vote" proved pivotal in the 1995 Quebec referendum (Cardozo and Musto 1997). Table 9.3 illustrates the hydra-headed character of multiculturalism by indicating how cost and benefit are not mutually exclusive but complementary yet oppositional.

TABLE 9.3 Costs and Benefits of Multiculturalism	
Costs	**Benefits**
Divisive: undermines Canadian unity and identity through endorsement of diversity ("balkanization")	**Unifying:** promotes unity and coherence by depoliticizing diversity (society building)
Regressive: ghettoizes minorities and keeps them in their place	**Progressive:** provides platform for articulation of interests and stepping stone for success
Symbolic: without substance, full of fury, signifying nothing except preservation of the status quo	**Substantive:** symbols can move mountains by legitimizing diversity as part of the national agenda
Fraud: instrument of control that deludes, conceals, evades, and distorts; that is, it promises a lot, but delivers little	**Catalyst:** instrument of opportunity through creation of a social climate for diversity to flourish

Criticism of multiculturalism is often misplaced in that its strengths and weaknesses are misunderstood. Canada's multiculturalism operates at two levels. First, it acknowledges the right of each individual to identify with the cultural tradition of choice, as long as this ethnic affiliation does not interfere with the rights of others, violate the laws of the land, or infringe on core values or institutions. Everyone has the right to be treated the same irrespective of ethnicity; everybody also has the right to be treated differently because of ethnicity without incurring a penalty in the process (Breton 1998). Cultural differences are thus transformed into a discourse about social inequalities in need of government intervention (McLaren 1994; Hesse 1997). Second, official multiculturalism is concerned with society-building functions. Multiculturalism does not set out to celebrate ethnic differences *per se* or promote cultural diversity. Nor does it condone the creation of segregated ethnic communities with parallel power bases and special collective rights. The objective of an official multiculturalism is to create a cohesive society in which differences are incorporated as legitimate and integral without undermining either interconnectedness or distinctiveness. Diversity is endorsed, to be sure, but only to the extent that all differences are equivalent in status, subject to similar treatment, and comply with the state's self-proclaimed claim to define the limits of permissible differences (see Johnson 1994). Reducing all differences to the same level by sanitizing their salience may sully multiculturalism's reputation as a progressive force. But this very depoliticization of ethnicity is precisely the reason behind its political popularity.

DEBUNKING MULTICULTURAL MYTHS: SEPARATING FACT FROM FICTION

Politically speaking, Canadian society can be envisaged as socially constructed around a series of national compromises, from federalism to regional equalization payments. In such a system of checks and balances, multiculturalism is aptly suited as a mediator for working the area between competing ethnicities. A compromise in its own right, multiculturalism provides a "solution" for reconciling ambiguities that are inherent in a diverse and changing society, including a host of contradictions in navigating the shoals between particularism (differences must be respected) and universalism (nobody should be treated differently without just cause). A capacity for speaking the language of "compromise" has enabled multiculturalism to secure the priority of the whole without destroying the constituent elements in the process. A commitment to multiculturalism furnishes a symbolic rationale for reconciling what otherwise would lapse into dismemberment and chaos. It also steers a path between the conflicting demands of stifling state conformity on the one hand and divisive ethnic tribalism on the other.

The objectives, scope, and limitations of multiculturalism must be clearly articulated if its full potential as a workable concept is to be realized. Yet Canadians remain curiously misinformed about what multiculturalism is, what it does or is supposed to do, why, and how it goes about doing its job. In a 1995 Eikos Research Associate Survey cited by Louis Musto (1997), only 18 percent of Canadians were extremely (2 percent) or quite (16 percent) familiar with multicultural policy, while 48 percent were unfamiliar. Yet a 1996 Environics Research Group survey (cited in Musto 1997) indicated that multiculturalism was perceived as an important symbol of Canadian unity and identity by 71 percent of all respondents, ahead of the CBC, bilingualism, and hockey, but behind Canada's health-care system and Charter of Rights. One way of explaining these anomalies in public perception of multiculturalism is to separate fact from fiction:

Fiction: Multiculturalism is ineffective/not working.

Fact: Who says so, why, on what basis, and compared to what? Multiculturalism possesses neither the power nor resources to make sweeping changes. As policy or program, it cannot single-handedly eliminate discrimination or racism. Nor can it automatically improve minority opportunities and life chances. Its strength resides in fostering a social climate responsive to diversity as legitimate and integral to society building.

Fiction: Multiculturalism divides/ghettoizes minorities.

Fact: Multiculturalism is not about isolating minorities in ethnic enclaves. To the contrary, the whole point of multiculturalism is to engage diversity through sharing, interaction, and participation (Kymlicka 1999). Rather than retention of foreign cultures, multicultural policies encourage ethnic groups to achieve greater social cohesion and mutual respect by promoting intergroup relations and fostering an inclusive society (Cardozo and Musto 1997).

Fiction: Multiculturalism is for "ethnics."

Fact: An official multiculturalism is not about targeting ethnic minorities. Emphasis is directed at transforming the ethnic mainstream—both attitudes and institutions—by modifying public perception of and response to diversity through modification of rules, rewards, structures, mindsets, and symbols. In the final analysis, multiculturalism is an exercise in society building by which all citizens are incorporated as legitimate and distinctive contributors to a united and inclusive society.

Fiction: Multiculturalism tolerates anything because of "political correctness."

Fact: Multiculturalism does not endorse a mindless relativism in which "anything goes" in the name of tolerance. Multiculturalism is clear about what is permissible in Canada. It rejects any customs that violate Canadian laws, interfere with the rights of others, offend the moral sensibilities of most Canadians, or disturb central institutions or core values. Multiculturalism emphasizes a kind of symbolic ethnic identity; that is, the right of individuals to identify with select aspects of their tradition, as long as these preferences are in accord with Canadian laws.

Fiction: Multiculturalism encourages diversity at the expense of unity.

Fact: Multiculturalism does not encourage diversity *per se*. More accurately, it seeks to depoliticize this diversity by channelling potentially troublesome conflicts into relatively harmless avenues pertaining to identity or culture. Differences are further depoliticized by treating all difference as the same, by circumscribing the outer limit of acceptable differences, and by scrubbing public places of an ethnic presence. Nor is there any truth that multiculturalism fragments Canada by making it less cohesive or too differences oriented. The loyalty of ethnic Quebeckers to Canada in the 1995 Quebec referendum is proof of that.

Fiction: Multiculturalism is all about politics.

Fact: True, but it is also much more. Multiculturalism may have originated as a calculated government ploy for balancing power in Canada, but people should never underestimate the power of ideas or the creativity of people in taking advantage of policies that may not have had their interests at heart (Philip 1995). Besides, diversity needs to be actively "managed" if conflicts are to be avoided and benefits gained. Neither the market nor voluntary compliance has made much headway in accommodating diversity. Government intervention is required instead, and certain political strings are inevitable in forging a social climate conducive to inclusiveness.

Fiction: Multiculturalism is an expensive luxury during times of fiscal restraint.

Fact: Multiculturalism is not expensive. Federal spending on multiculturalism stands at around $20 to $25 million, or less than $1 per person per year, most of which is directed at antiracism, settlement and integration, and cultural sharing. Compare this with the $700 million expended for official bilingualism. To put it in another perspective: Multiculturalism in 1992–93 received less than 1 percent of the government (both federal and provincial) spending allocated for arts and culture.

Fiction: Multiculturalism is experiencing a backlash.

Fact: Criticism of multiculturalism is real and valid. But criticism in its own right does not signal a backlash any more than silence is proof of tacit acceptance. Disgruntlement may stem from discontent that is growing among the already disenchanted rather than a new legion of the malcontent. A small but vocal minority may be the source behind this anti-multiculturalism, emboldened, as it were, by a social and political climate conducive to criticism without public censure. Moreover, it is difficult to determine what people dislike about multiculturalism. Many may agree with the principles of multiculturalism, but are irked by its status as formal government policy, a tax-funded set of programs and practices, or linkage with employment equity and immigration—with multiculturalism swept up in the criticism because of guilt by association.

To Sum Up One of the nice things about living in Canada is our general willingness to agree to disagree without resorting to threats or fear of reprisals. Multiculturalism is famed for its promise to accommodate diversity by acknowledging disagreements as long as people play by the rules. A willingness to agree to disagree is simple enough when the differences are superficial and choices are easy. Shall we order Szechuan tonight? How about a falafel? Anyone care for perogies? Things get more complex when fundamentally different and mutually opposed values come into contact. Even more complications occur when one set of values prefers to disagree with our commitment to agree to disagree. The Salman Rushdie case (in which a Muslim writer is under a death sentence by members of his own religion because some of his writings are considered blasphemous) is a primary example of the paradoxes that can surface when groups threaten to disagree to agree. The resolve for compromise and adjustment stiffens visibly when cultural differences are perceived as contrary to fundamental Canadian values such as gender equality and secular pluralism. Consider the controversies created by the Sikh turban in the halls of Canadian legions and among the RCMP. The wearing of the hijab, a head covering (or scarf) worn by some Muslim women, has also provoked debate for violating school dress codes in a predominantly secular school environment. The limits to multiculturalism are stretched even further with customs such as female genital mutilation that are totally at odds with core Canadian values. Do we impose Eurocentric values in outright condemnation, or do we capitulate to social chaos because of our failure to agree on what is disagreeable even when human rights abuses are involved? Such dilemmas raise the issue of what is tolerable in a multicultural society. Where, then, do we draw the line between what is acceptable and what is not? Are there limits to tolerance within Canada's multiculturalism commitments?

MULTICULTURALISM: IS THERE ANOTHER CANADIAN WAY?

Canada's commitment to multiculturalism has contributed to its image as an open, secular, and largely tolerant society. Some measure of proof is gleaned from Canada's lofty status (as deemed by various United Nations panels) as a socially progressive society with an enviable standard of living. Multiculturalism has proven a beacon of tolerance in a largely intolerant world. A social framework has evolved for balancing diversity with unity, even if that balancing act is not to everyone's liking. How do we gage the success of multiculturalism? In contrast with the alternatives that it has replaced, including racism and exclusion, multiculturalism starts to look a lot better than critics give it credit (Keohane 1997). Compared to a utopia of perfect harmony, Canada's multiculturalism falls short of the mark; compared with the grisliness of reality elsewhere, it stands as a paragon of virtue. The fact that Canada has avoided much of the ethnic strife that currently convulses many countries speaks well of its stature in proactively working through differences.

The worldwide reputation for tolerance that Canada enjoys is largely deserved (Kurthen 1997). The majority of Canadians, especially the younger and the well educated, are relatively open to diversity and proud of our multicultural heritage, despite undercurrents of fear and hostility toward certain newcomers. Even whole-hearted support, however, is no excuse for glossing over its imperfections. However potent a mechanism for engaging diversity, the principle and practice of official multiculturalism remain riddled with inconsistencies. Everyone agrees that there are enough loopholes in federal multiculturalism to dishearten even the most optimistic. Few would deny its vulnerability to manipulation by politicians and minority leaders. Fewer still would dismiss its potential to deter, divide, diminish, or digress. But criticism is one thing; proposals for alternatives to multiculturalism are quite another.

Critics may be relentless in their attacks on multiculturalism as regressive or irrelevant. But most critiques rarely offer constructive criticism. Many are fond of pulling down multiculturalism, but are less skilled at proposing positive alternatives that are workable and fair (see Loney 1998). Our stand is unequivocal: Multiculturalism is hardly an option in a modern Canada with deep diversities and competing citizenships. There are no alternatives to multiculturalism (see also Sajoo 1994). Neither assimilation nor segregation stands much chance of survival in a postglobalizing era. A much-touted return to traditional values as a glue for cementing Canadians into a unified and coherent whole sounds good in theory (Bibby 1990; Bissoondath 1993; 1994). In reality, such wishful thinking also may camouflage a hidden agenda for a return of the so-called "good old days," when minorities knew their place in society and acted accordingly.

A sense of perspective is overdue. Multiculturalism is not the cause of Canada's problems, any more than it can be the cure-all. There is no risk of Canada unravelling because of multiculturalism: The politics of "distinct society" and the "nations within" will see to that first. Nor should we get worked up over the absence of a common culture, as if multiculturalism destroyed what was not there in the first place. Perhaps Canada's core value is the absence of any common culture—in the same way that Canada's identity is rooted in the constant search for "who we are." Except for a basic decency, a respect for rule of law, and a commitment to individual equality, the only thing that Canadians appear to have in common, culturally speaking, is our differences (see Sajoo 1994). Diversity, not uniformity, is Canada's strength. To expect otherwise is unrealistic in a society organized around overlapping citizenships of the First Nations, the Québécois, and multicultural minorities (Kaplan 1993; Kymlicka 1995). Disagreement and conflict are inevitable in such a context. Just as shared ethnicity does not entail a unanimity of vision, as Bissoondath (1994) reminds us, albeit in a different sense, so too can a multicultural society survive on a "multiplicity of voices and visions, or the interplay of conflicting views," provided that, within limits, we agree to disagree.

Multiculturalism, in short, remains the policy of necessity if not of choice for a changing and diverse Canada. As policy or practice, it symbolizes an innovative if imperfect social experiment for engaging diversity within the framework of postcolonial society building. Multiculturalism has excelled in catapulting Canada from its colonialist past to its much-ballyhooed status as a trailblazer in engaging diversity. The Canada of today no longer consists of a British (or French) mainstream with ethnically related tributaries (Burnet and Palmer 1988). In many parts of urban Canada, minorities are the mainstream, and this revolutionary shift holds out the promise and the perils of reshaping our institutions, priorities, and mindsets. Under the circumstances, it is not a question of whether Canada can afford multiculturalism. More to the point, Canada cannot afford not to embrace multiculturalism in its constant search for political unity, social coherence, economic prosperity, and cultural enrichment. The final words belong to Michael Adams, president of Environics Research Group, in acknowledging that what once was seen as a multiculturalism-inspired weakness (lack of strong distinct identity) may in fact prove to be multiculturalism-driven strength in the twenty-first century: "Ours is a population that is resigned to—and may even take some pride in—the relatively weak attachments that bind us to each other. It is my feeling that we will continue on much as we have...forever pragmatic, forever flexible, forever Canadian."

CHAPTER HIGHLIGHTS

- This chapter has focused on the concept of Canadian multiculturalism. Multiculturalism is properly examined as a process for engaging diversity as different yet equal within the context of Canadian society building.

- With traditional styles of race relations management (including assimilation and integration) on the decline, multiculturalism has emerged as the key option in the pluralistic package for addressing the challenges of diversity.

- Official multiculturalism is defined as a policy and a practice concerned with creating a society that engages diversity as a legitimate and integral component without destroying either the unity or integrity of the system or distinctiveness of the constituent parts in the process.

- Is Canada a multicultural society? Responses to this question indicate the need to examine multiculturalism at different levels of interpretation, that is, as a sociological fact, an ideological system of beliefs and values, a set of policies involving government–minority relations, a renewable resource in serving political and minority interests, and a critical discourse that challenges as it resists.

- Canadian multiculturalism has historically been concerned with improving minority equality and participation in society, initially through elimination of ethnocentric biases ("folkloric"), then through removal of discriminatory barriers and institutional accommodation ("equity"), and currently through enhancing a sense of belonging to Canada ("civic").

- Official multiculturalism is not intended to celebrate differences or promote diversity. Diversity is endorsed to the extent that it allows individuals to identify with the cultural tradition of their choice, provided this affiliation does not violate human rights or laws of the land. The focus is on depoliticizing diversity by channelling it into harmless outlets, thus short-circuiting their potential for disruption. This reinforces the notion of multiculturalism as essentially a technique for society building rather than ethnic promotion.

- Multiculturalism originated and continues to exist for a variety of social, economic, and cultural reasons, most of which uphold the legitimacy of the state in managing diversity. This perspective confirms the adage that multiculturalism is essentially a political program to achieve political goals in a politically acceptable manner.

- The subsequent depoliticization of diversity under official multiculturalism has had the effect of isolating Canada's "consensus" multiculturalism from the "insurgent" discourses that animate "critical" multiculturalisms in the United States. Insofar as critical multiculturalisms invoke challenges whereas consensus multiculturalism invites accommodation, the two "isms" suggest a variety of ways for engaging diversity.

- At once an asset as well as a hindrance, multiculturalism has been regarded as a source of social tension, in addition to an innovative means for minority conflict management. Just as multiculturalism cannot be blamed for all social problems in Canada, so too should it be exempt from lavish and undeserved praise as the solution to its ills. Its influence exists somewhere in between: Rather than a magical formula for success, it is but one component—however imperfect—for managing diversity in a complex yet unequal context.

- Multiculturalism is often associated with several misconceptions that are ripe for plucking, including (a) fact: multiculturalism is not expensive (only $1 per year per Canadian in federal expenditures); (b) fact: multiculturalism is not divisive (ideally, it seeks to promote unity through preservation, participation, and integration); (c) fact: multiculturalism does not detract from national identity (Canada's collective self-image is dependent on accepting diversity); and (d) fact: multiculturalism is not a failure (compared to what?).

- Multiculturalism is usually criticized as being divisive, regressive, a symbol without substance, and an instrument of containment. Multiculturalism can also be shown to be unifying, progressive, a symbol with substance, and a social catalyst. The degree of criticism or praise may vary with a person's vision of Canadian society and the role of multiculturalism in fostering this vision.

- While official multiculturalism is riddled with inconsistencies and contradictions, critics have been unable to propose a viable alternative for engaging diversity in ways that are workable, necessary, and fair.

- The balancing act implicit in a country of compromises follows from this. Multicultural initiatives must simultaneously preserve a precarious balance of power between the imperatives of the state and majorities on the one hand, with the rights of minorities on the other, and citizenship rights of individuals on yet another. Confronted by such challenges and conflicts, liberal-democratic governments have stumbled in resolving these issues to everyone's satisfaction.

- Official multiculturalism is not simply a set of programs for splashing a dash of colour or pageantry into Canada's anglocentric agenda. For minorities, multiculturalism provides a platform that enables a transformation of the national agenda in terms of who gets what and why (entitlement).

- Multiculturalism is not a coherent set of policies or programs that are fixed in perpetuity. Multiculturalism undergoes renewal and reform through adaptation to political, social, and demographic changes. The open-ended and resilient nature of multiculturalism provides it with the flexibility to shift agendas (for example, from focus on ethnicity to equity to citizenship) as the context dictates.

- What are the limits of multicultural tolerance? Which ethnocultural differences can be absorbed within a multicultural society without undermining incontestable values and beliefs? The dilemma is self-evident: Too many differences can create anarchic conditions which inhibit the effective functioning of a social system, while too many restrictions make a mockery of multicultural principles. Nevertheless, the question arises, Where do we draw the line?

KEY TERMS

civic multiculturalism
consensus multiculturalism
critical multiculturalism
cultural defence
depoliticizing diversity
equity multiculturalism
folkloric multiculturalism
multiculturalism
Multiculturalism Act, 1988
multiculturalism as critical discourse
multiculturalism as empirical fact
multiculturalism as ideology
multiculturalism as policy
multiculturalism as practice
multiculturalism as society building

REVIEW QUESTIONS

1. Indicate how multiculturalism differs from other techniques for managing race and eth-
    nic relations.
2. Compare and contrast the different phases in the development of Canada's multicul-
    turalism policy in terms of objectives, assumptions, means, and outcomes.
3. How would you respond to the assertion that Canada is a multicultural society? Be sure
    to focus on the different levels of meaning associated with multiculturalism.
4. Demonstrate some of the benefits and costs associated with multiculturalism. Defend
    whether or not you regard multiculturalism as a society-affirming process or a society-
    destroying phenomenon.
5. Compare and contrast the multiculturalisms in Canada and the United States in terms of
    what each is trying to do, why, and how. State which you prefer as a basis for engaging
    diversity and justify your answer.
6. Multiculturalism is viewed differently by diverse sectors of Canadian society. Discuss
    the validity of this statement by examining public reaction to multiculturalism as gov-
    ernment policy.
7. Multiculturalism is about knowing limits and drawing lines as a basis for living together
    with our differences. Explain, and provide an example to illustrate your answer.

PUTTING MULTICULTURALISM TO WORK

CASE STUDY 10-1	Challenging Ivory Tower Racism

It is taken as axiomatic that racism is a pervasive feature of Canadian institutions (Henry et al. 1995; Satzewich 1998). The magnitude and scope of this racism, as well as its intensity and intent, are expressed in different ways. Educational institutions are no exceptions to this rule. Both primary and secondary schools have been criticized as sites of racism and discrimination, in effect sullying Canada's reputation as a pacesetter for progressive social change (Mukherjee 1993). Considerable energy has gone into the design and implementation of appropriate antiracist policies. Since 1992, for example, school boards in Ontario have parlayed multicultural and ethnocultural equity programs into everyday practice—in theory if not always in reality (Ministry of Education and Training 1993). By contrast, postsecondary initiatives for engaging diversity through antiracist measures have been inconsistent at best, nonexistent at worst, and motivated by a preference for crisis management or public relations rather than a commitment to social justice.

A seeming indifference to campus racism beyond the symbolic or token cannot be taken lightly. The demographic revolution of the past twenty years has had a profound effect on postsecondary schooling. The composition of the student body has been irrevocably altered; course content is increasingly contested; faculty of colour are growing in numbers and assertiveness; orthodox pedagogical styles are being challenged; and a business-as-usual mindset can no longer abide by conventional rules, roles, and responsibilities (Price 1993; Schuman and Olufs 1995; Henry et al. 1995). Rather than being above the fray, as popularly depicted, colleges and universities are no less susceptible than other institutions to the challenges of diversity (Exum 1980; McCaskill 1995; Modood and Acland 1998).

The Problem: Ivory White

Survey studies provide some insight into the magnitude and scope of campus racism (Ramcharan et al. 1991). The results of these studies have been published elsewhere (Fleras 1995), but the following points appear consistent across Canadian universities and community colleges:

- The number of *reported* race-related incidents on postsecondary campuses is not especially high, averaging around 20 to 120 per year at those Canadian universities and community colleges that keep such records.

- Most of the incidents that come to the attention of authorities do not involve physical retaliation, but consist of verbal slurs (from innuendos to stereotypes) and ethnic jokes. Racist graffiti is common but has yet to be analyzed for frequency.

- Students by virtue of their numbers are predominantly involved in most racial encounters, with most incidents occurring in residences, pubs, cafeterias, and classrooms.

Some tentative conclusions can be drawn from these surveys. First, the numbers themselves may say more about the survey instrument than anything about campus racism. The recording of an incident as racist or racial is not necessarily proof of racism; it may reflect interpersonal conflict that entails a racial dimension because people of different backgrounds are involved. Rather than any absolute increase *per se,* increases

in reported incidents may convey a greater willingness to report racial violations than was the case in the past. Second, there may be a strong tendency to underreport racial incidents, partly from fear of reprisals or from being branded a malcontent. Minority women and men may be deterred from coming forward with legitimate concerns because of worries that a complaint could be dismissed as frivolous if not upheld (McGill 1994). Complainants take the risk of being stereotyped as hypersensitive and overreactive, thus diminishing the force of their claims. Visa minority students rarely report racial incidents for fear of losing their visa status or compromising academic standing (Ramcharan 1991). Many individuals are unsure of where or when to report an incident, in some cases preferring the security of confiding in friends only. Third, racism "hurts" even if its magnitude and scope cannot be statistically assessed. Numbers cannot possibly convey a victim's humiliation or sense of betrayal that may intensify feelings of isolation or exclusion (OFS 1991). Unless victimized themselves, few can appreciate either the pain inflicted by racist graffiti or the paralyzing fear imposed by hate groups and racist literature. Even a seemingly harmless prank or thoughtless remark can create psychological distress every bit as emotionally devastating and socially debilitating as open bigotry (Stern 1992).

Yet there is more to campus racism than polite slurs or open hatred. The true nature of ivory tower racism is neither sporadic nor random; nor is it restricted to the deranged actions of a few social misfits. Campus racism is not so much about what happens but more about what doesn't happen. Racism is properly located in the system and institutionalized, with deep roots in organizational structures and dynamics that disempower and exclude. It may be created and is secured by official policies and practices, however inadvertently, then incorporated into structures and operations as normal or necessary, and sustained through ideologies that rationalize inequities as aberrations from an otherwise fair and open system of competition (Chesler and Crowfoot 1989). Postsecondary institutions are organized around tacit assumptions, mission statements, culture and subcultural values, power relations, organizational structure, operating principles, reward systems, and intended outcomes that tend to privilege some at the expense of others (McIntyre 1993; Schuman and Olufs 1995). As noted by Robert Blauner (1972:277), the university is racist because people of colour continue to be systematically excluded from full and equal participation and power—as students, professors, administrators, and, particularly, in the historic definition of the character of the institution and its curriculum:

> ...[F]or the liberal professor...racism connotes conscious acts, where there is an intent to hurt or degrade or disadvantage others because of their color or ethnicity.... He does not consider the all-white or predominantly white character of an occupation or institution in itself to be racism...acts of omission, indifference, and failure to change the status quo.

Contrary to popular belief, policies and programs that appear neutral on the surface may rest on structures and patterns that distribute rewards unequally (Schuman and Olufs 1995). Take, for example, a reliance on an exclusively westocentric curriculum as a tacitly assumed point of departure for class content and conduct. This exclusiveness may appear to be natural and normal, yet may be interpreted as systemically racist, regardless of motive or intent, in that alternative perspectives never appear. Such a monocultural agenda not only excludes or invalidates minority experiences; such exclusionary reference points also have a detrimental effect on those who fail to play by the rules of the game.

Solutions: Toward Institutional Inclusion

Perceptions of racism in the ivory towers have elicited responses ranging from denial to bandwagon. Few, however, would deny the existence of campus racism even if its intensity, scope, and tone are subject to dispute. Postsecondary institutions have conceded the ineffectiveness of *ad hoc* responses to racist incidents. Impromptu solutions may magnify tensions rather than dampen hostilities. Indecisiveness is equally detrimental when an administration is accused of foot dragging in censuring racist actions (Stern 1992). Failure to act quickly with zero tolerance can escalate a crisis by fostering an impression that antiracism has a lower priority than pandering to contented alumni. Administrative promises may be dismissed as misguided or cosmetic devices for calming "troublesome constituents" through conflict management or damage control. To avoid chaos or institutional paralysis yet convey a sense of justice being seen to be done, two types of responses have been articulated.

Many universities have *reacted* to the reality of racism by instituting policies and offices expressly for diversity issues (Fleras 1996). Universities these days are more responsive to the diverse needs of minority students (Ford 1998). Efforts to create a more welcoming environment, such as special prayer rooms for Muslim students, are intended to foster social harmony. Harassment codes and antidiscrimination guidelines have been implemented in conformity with provincial human rights codes. Reactive response plans consist of rehearsed contingency measures about what to do in an emergency and who should do it. Formal mechanisms are instituted in the hopes of opening the lines of communication for grievance resolution and conflict mediation. Resource persons are appointed to provide advisory and consultative services for students in need. Recruitment of committees from a cross section of the campus may assist in planning policy and procedures for worst-case scenarios. Disciplinary codes are implemented as a last resort for punishing offenders or to deter would-be offenders.

Proactive measures concentrate on prevention and problem solving. Universities and community colleges across the country have conducted research and drawn up plans to identify and solve problems (Gray 1993). Formal positions have been instituted, for example, a race relations office and human rights committees. In conjunction with these support committees are formalized mission statements and reports that denounce campus racism. Recommendations from these reports tend to follow a common script by focusing on issues related to policy, offices, committees, admissions, hiring and rewards, equity measures, and complaint procedures (Queen's 1991; University of Western Ontario 1993; McGill 1994; O'Neill and Yelaja 1994). Among the more common proposals are the following:

1. Facilitate the participation of members from underrepresented groups at institutional levels of decision making. Foster equity in terms of recruitment and minority hiring within acceptable time frames. Establish clearly articulated guidelines about appointment, promotion, and tenure. Review all procedures, policies, and practices to ensure freedom from systemic bias. Indicate that those in positions of authority are answerable for failure to accommodate institutionally.

2. Encourage the entry of aboriginal and minority students through more flexible admission requirements and the removal of hidden barriers.

3. Include non-Eurocentric perspectives and minority concerns across the entire post-secondary spectrum, from governing bodies to classrooms, curricula, resource centres and libraries, ethics, and research. Accommodate minority religious observance within the demands of class or exam scheduling. Establish "minority-friendly" student and support services.

4. Investigate complaints. Reduce incidents of discrimination and racism on campus by dealing firmly with violations through consultation or counselling. Recommend corrective action.

5. Foster an inclusive university climate for work and study free of both discrimination and racial harassment. Introduce race relations awareness education for all university members. Provide skills-training programs that assist in addressing racial problems.

6. Design workshops to assist departments in promoting an inclusive environment. Publicize an awareness of complaint procedures and disciplinary channels that are universally accessible, free of reprisals from peers or authority, and complainant friendly without infringing on the principles of due process.

Universities and community colleges appear to be moving in the right direction. Policy and mission statements are increasingly commonplace—nearly twenty documents were in place by late 1993 (Gray 1993)—with a broad array of chairs, committees, advisors, and offices for advising, consulting, monitoring, recommending, and initiating disciplinary action. Admittedly, the effectiveness of these offices and policies is open to conjecture (Henry et al. 1995). Solutions lean toward moderate reforms such as additional courses or sensitivity training, all of which provide insights but do not disrupt institutional structures, curricular content, academic freedom, standards of merit, and hierarchies that shore up entrenched interests. There are additional risks in dealing with racism that is individualized and overt: The establishment of offices and officers may help individual victims, but may do so at the risk of individualizing racism rather than focusing on the systemic but asymmetrical power relations within the ivory towers (Carniol 1991; Hick and Santos 1992). In other words, despite a spate of administrative concessions and reforms, the question remains as baffling as ever: How willing are universities to go the inclusiveness route, given its potential to provoke or disrupt?

Prospects: From Ivory Towers to Institutions of Colour?

Institutions of higher learning are expected to comport themselves in an exemplary fashion. They are looked upon as bastions of enlightenment; yet they are saddled with the messy responsibility of spearheading progressive social change. Their mission and objectives related to teaching and research must somehow strike a balance between empowering the dispossessed while enhancing excellence in understanding (Proceedings 1993; Schuman and Olufs 1995). The challenge is common to all postsecondary institutions: how to appear progressive and liberal minded without subverting the foundational core of the system (McIntyre 1993). How

can diversity be accommodated without undermining the interconnectedness of the constituent parts? Who will participate in redefining the role and responsibilities of postsecondary education; what values will predominate; and whose interests will they serve (Banks 1992)? Responding to this challenge will entail both political will and financial muscle, at a time of fiscal restraint and minority assertiveness. It will demand personal courage to brush off charges of "political correctness" for speaking out against racism and sexism (Richer and Weir 1995). Compromise and commitment will be sorely tested in balancing the apparent clash between quality and equality, of freedom with inclusiveness. In the final analysis, debates about the inclusiveness of higher education are really about power and control—who has it, who wants it, and who is going to do something about it (Schuman and Olufs 1995). Despite costs and disruptions to "the way things are done around here," the benefits from this struggle will be worthwhile in advancing postsecondary institutions, in ways both inclusive and equitable yet thoroughly postmodern in outlook.

INTRODUCTION: ENGAGING DIVERSITY

Multiculturalism in Canada has evolved as a central discourse around issues related to the construction of a national identity, definition of citizenship, and reformation of historical memory (Kymlicka 1998). Inception of official multiculturalism has brought about a shift in political attitudes toward the place of minority women and men in Canada. Historically, Canadian society tended to ostracize or demean minorities. Prejudice and discrimination reinforced a dismissive belief in diversity as inimical to society building. Ethnic minorities were expected to fit into the existing institutional framework as the price of admission into Canada. With the inception of multiculturalism, however, response to diversity has been stood on its head. Diversity is currently promoted as an integral and legitimate component of Canada's social fabric, with untapped potential for improving national wealth and international standing. Multicultural differences are no longer dismissed as a bothersome anomaly, of no redeeming value outside a personal or private context. Social trends instead point to an engagement with diversity as indispensable in the ongoing reconstruction of Canadian society.

Preliminary efforts at putting multiculturalism to work have proven uneven. Demographic pressures have altered the way institutions conduct their business by confirming the inappropriateness of established ways of "doing things" in a changing and diverse world. Public and private institutions are seeking to enhance organizational effectiveness by taking into account that all Canadians—not simply the more affluent and privileged—have something to contribute. This commitment to inclusiveness is especially pressing in service-oriented institutions, including the media, schooling and education, and policing, since their mandate as agencies of socialization and social control subjects them to greater accountability and criticism. Both socialization and control strike at the very core of social existence; they also influence whether or not we perceive ourselves in harmony with or alienated from our communities. Media and schools furnish the "blueprint" for acceptable behaviour; the police, in turn, control the limits of acceptable behaviour by disciplining those who break the rules. Each of these institutions has little option but to establish the necessary linkages for "bridging the gap" by engaging diversity positively and proactively. To the extent that they are successful in "putting multiculturalism to work," the feasibility of multicultural principles will take root in society.

This chapter makes it clear that the principles of institutional inclusion are here to stay, whether people approve or not. Institutions can no longer afford the luxury of remaining aloof from the demographic and cultural revolutions taking place in Canada. Conventional ways of doing things—from working with others to delivery of a service or a product—are less acceptable than in the past. The combination of minority pressure and government edicts has compelled many institutions to redefine themselves in ways both inclusive and equitable. Barriers continue to plague the transformation process, since those in positions of power dislike the prospect of relinquishing privilege. Institutional subcultures and organizational procedures may not lend themselves to inclusive change, as demonstrated in the next Case Study on **multicultural policing.** Yet the benefits of inclusiveness by way of engagement cannot be dismissed. The extent and pace to which Canadian institutions can "move over and make space" will largely determine the direction and pace of society building.

The theme of putting multiculturalism to work at institutional levels is analyzed in this chapter. The chapter examines how major institutions, such as the media, education, and police, are responding to the challenges of engaging diversity in ways that balance inclusiveness with the realities of organizational dynamics. The chapter explores programs and policies aimed at fostering institutional diversity both internally (in terms of organizational procedures and workforce) and externally (with respect to service delivery and community relations). Each institution is analyzed in terms of the problems that must be confronted in coping with the challenges of a multicultural society; what has been accomplished to date in accommodating diversity at organizational levels; and what should be done to improve patterns of inclusiveness. Also discussed are the challenges, the dilemmas, and contradictions associated with the multicultural "management" of diversity. The police, formal education, and media are employed as illustrative examples to accentuate the contested nature of putting multiculturalism to work. First, however, we need to explore the concept of institutional inclusiveness to determine the magnitude of the challenge before us.

INSTITUTIONAL INCLUSIVENESS: PRINCIPLES AND PRACTICE

It is one thing to encourage the diversification of Canada through immigration. It is another thing to promote a multiculturalism policy that endorses the reality of diversity as a legitimate component in Canadian society building. It may be something altogether different to transform these principles and put them into institutional practice in a way that makes an appreciable difference. The danger signals are everywhere for those impervious to the demands of diversity. Consider only the damage to personal careers and institutional reputation. Better still, imagine the potential for social strife unless minority women and men are convinced they have a stake in Canadian society. Aboriginal violence in Ontario and British Columbia and protracted police–minority youth tensions are just two of the indicators of a system in trouble. The option is clear: Unless we move over and make institutional space for *all* Canadians, our much-vaunted multicultural mosaic will shatter into fragments too numerous to retile.

Defining Institutional Inclusiveness

What is meant by the term "inclusive institution"? **Institutional inclusiveness** can be defined as a process by which institutions proactively and positively engage diversity, both internally and externally. Inclusiveness is about acceptance and promotion of differences as necessary, normal, and beneficial. As Joan Wallach Scott points out in her article "Campaign Against Political Correctness," the concept of inclusiveness entails a process of responding appropriately to an institution's diversity mix, keeping in mind that diversity is not a state of separate being in which people are slotted into a preexisting category. Rather, diversity is properly thought of as a hierarchical relation of power and inequality undergoing constant evaluation and adjustment in response to social changes. In other words, diversity is not a thing but a relationship that derives its meaning from context and consequences, and failure to understand the often unequal nature of this relation glosses over the dynamic of living together with our differences.

An inclusive institution is anchored around three conceptual levels (Cox Jr 1993). First, attention must be directed at employees who are expected to act in a nondiscriminatory manner in discharging their obligations to colleagues or customers. Of particular note is the need to modify personal attitudes toward differences, from perceptions as inferior or irrelevant to acceptance as normal, necessary, and beneficial. Second, groups and subcultures within institutions are singled out as potential problem areas. These informal groupings that exist within all organizations not only exercise control over members' behaviour; they also have the ability to facilitate or subvert the implementation of management diversity initiatives. Third, emphasis is devoted to organizational structures and corporate cultures. Institutions have a tendency over time to become ends in themselves and to satisfy only their own criteria for excellence. Resistance to reforms and accommodation are not situational but structurally embedded, and this makes it important to dislodge structural and cultural barriers. The interplay of these three levels is intended to minimize disadvantage for minority employees and service receivers; they are also expected to maximize potential advantages for all stakeholders.

Why Institutional Inclusiveness?

There are good reasons why institutions should become inclusive of diversity, especially at a time when both the workforce and the community at large are increasingly diverse and demanding. For service organizations, a commitment to diversity can reap institutional dividends by easing workplace tensions, generating creative synergies, facilitating community access, and improving the quality of service delivery. For private companies, the accommodation of diversity may be good for business. Methods of wealth creation have changed from mass-produced goods and one-size-fits-all service to a growing reliance on meeting the multicultural needs of ethnically driven niche markets, both domestically and internationally. Diversity connections can provide a platform for internationalizing domestic businesses and improving competitive advantage in global markets, as Bill Cope and Mary Kalantzis point out in their 1996 book *Productive Diversity. A New Australian Approach to Work and Management.* In an era of global markets and local needs, institutions increasingly rely on the language skills, cultural knowledge, life experience, and international connections that people of diversity bring to the workplace. The languages and cultural heritages of multicultural minority communities have the potential to assist in priming partnerships that are required for institutions to internationalize. An inclusive institution is able to capitalize on an expanded pool of talent, foster more cooperative working relations, promote a positive corporate image, and secure open lines of communication with diverse communities.

Components of an Inclusive Institution

Five components would appear uppermost in specifying the attributes of an inclusive institutions: *workforce representation, organizational rules and operations, workplace climate, service delivery,* and *community relations.* First, an institution's workforce should be representative, that is, relatively proportional to the composition of the regional labour force, taking into account both social and cultural factors as extenuating circumstances. Canada's Employment Equity Program is based on the hiring of workers of colour in federally regulated workplaces in numbers consistent with Canada's labour diversity patterns (Beeby 1998). Such a numerical accommodation applies to entry-level jobs; it also extends across the board to include all levels of management. Second, institutional rules and operations cannot hinder the recruitment, selection, training, promotion, and retention of minority personnel. This commitment to root out systemic bias demands a careful scrutiny of company policy and procedures. Third, the institution must foster a working climate conducive to minority health and productivity. At minimum, such a climate cannot tolerate harassment of any form; at best, diversity is actively promoted as normal, even beneficial, to effective functioning. Fourth, an inclusive institution ensures that delivery of its services is community based and culturally sensitive. This multicultural commitment to culturally sensitive services entails a willingness on the part of the organization to engage in genuine dialogue and negotiation in partnership with the community at large. Outcomes must be based on bilateral decision making rather than unilaterally imposed. Fifth and finally, institutions do not operate in a social or political vacuum. They cannot hope to remain outside community control and public accountability if open and productive lines of communication are to be secured.

In short, institutional inclusiveness is all about compromise. These compromises go beyond the realm of celebrating diversity or promoting minorities *per se.* Rather, they deal with creating institutions that are receptive to diversity as legitimate and integral without abdicating their traditional role of service delivery. Inclusiveness is necessary but in conjunction with institutional coherence and bottom line profitability. A dual focus is required to foster an institutional setting both representative of and accessible to minorities, as well as equitable in treatment and culturally sensitive. The adjustment process must occur at the level of institutional structure as well as within individual mindsets. It must also concentrate on the relationships within (the workplace environment) in addition to relationships without (clients). Fostering an inclusive workplace climate requires careful calibration of rules, procedures, and outlooks. After all, underemphasizing the relevance of differences when needed is as discriminatory as overemphasizing them when uncalled for. The end result may prove an elusive and enigmatic balancing act, but critical in securing cooperative work relations.

Barriers to Inclusiveness

Numerous barriers exist that interfere with the inclusion process. Stumbling blocks include *people, hierarchy, bureaucracy, corporate culture,* and *occupational subcultures.* People as institutional actors are a prime obstruction. People in general tend to be egocentric; that is, they have a tendency to interpret the behaviour of others on the basis of what they would have thought or done under similar circumstances. But such rationale will prove problematic. Appeals to inclusion may fall on deaf ears when people do not understand what is going on and why. Resistance to inclusiveness is sharpened when people's self-interest is threatened. That revelation should come as no surprise; unless convinced or compelled, few individuals are inclined to relinquish power or share privilege, especially with those once perceived as inferior or irrelevant.

The dimension of hierarchy will also inhibit inclusiveness initiatives. Those in higher echelons may be highly supportive of institutional change for a variety of reasons, ranging from genuine concern to economic expediency, with an eye toward public relations in between. Yet those in positions of power may be long-winded on platitudes but short-minded on practice or implementation. Middle and lower management may be less enthusiastic about changes, preferring to cling to traditional authority patterns instead, since this level of management is most likely to be affected by institutional adjustments. Those at the bottom of the employment pecking order may be least receptive to institutional change, even to the point of ignoring or sabotaging such directives. Bureaucratic structures can also inhibit institutional inclusion. Larger systems operate on bureaucratic principles of hierarchy and rational control. Such a controlling imperative is not conducive to adjustment and accommodation, especially if the reform process interferes with the "business as usual" syndrome. Institutional cultures are no less inimical to change. The operational philosophy encompassed by corporate cultures may recoil from adjustment when perceived as a threat to the bottom line or the "way we do things around here." Finally, occupational subcultures may derail the best of intentions in "inclusivizing" institutions. Subcultural values of front-line workers may differ from that of management because of differences in experiences or expectations. This slippage may prove disruptive to the inclusion process.

Engaging diversity at institutional levels is confronted by an array of personal and social barriers. Institutions are filled with people who are resolutely opposed to and resist change at all costs. The structural embeddedness of barriers makes it difficult to move over and make space. An official policy on inclusiveness will not necessarily translate into practice in any consistent fashion, with the result that decisions concerning promotion or recruitment may be clouded by prejudice, nepotism, patronage, and the "old boys' network" (Travis 1998). Advances in this field are further complicated by those who advocate change without much thought to the complexities involved. Implementing institutional changes is not like installing a new computer technology. Institutions are complex, often baffling landscapes of domination and control as well as resistance and sabotage. Conservatives confront progressives in a struggle for power and privilege. Conventional views remain firmly entrenched as vested interests balk at discarding the tried and true: Newer visions are compelling but lack the singularity of purpose or resources to scuttle traditional ways of "doing business."

The interplay of these juxtapositions can be disruptive as the **institution** is transformed into a "**contested site**" involving competing world views and opposing agendas.

Our position rests somewhere in between these extremes. We believe that institutional inclusion is necessary and overdue; but we also acknowledge the tenacity and logic of organizational inertia. The diversification of Canada's population demands a rethinking of orthodox ways of doing business or delivering service—if not for social justice, then for institutional effectiveness. We also believe that institutional inclusiveness is workable once the impediments to adjustment and change are isolated and challenged. Institutions and the people who inhabit them are not entirely rigid and unbending. Compromises and adjustments will materialize if there is a promise of payoff. The next sections will examine how three key institutions have addressed the notion of institutional inclusiveness, in the process revealing the perils and pitfalls—and successes and benefits—of putting multiculturalism to work in a multicultural society. First, however, a Case Study that demonstrates how intentions for inclusion can be thwarted by institutional barriers.

CASE STUDY 10–2	"Bending Granite": Resistance to Inclusive, Community-Based Policing

Interest in **community policing** has expanded to the point where it no longer symbolizes only a promising experiment in redesigning police–community relations (see last section of this chapter for additional detail) (Fleras 1998). The principles of community policing have catapulted to the forefront of contemporary Canadian policing, even if the rhetoric is known to outstrip reality. Its appeal may reflect an ability to evoke powerful emotional symbols that pluck at contemporary cultural concerns, including "democracy," "power to the people," and "small town morality" (Seagrave 1997). Its acceptance appears to be consistent with trends elsewhere in view of commitments to the principles of decentralization, human resources management, and customer satisfaction. This commitment to community policing has focused on transforming the police from a technically driven, bureaucrat-oriented, and professional crime-fighting force to a customer-inspired service that is community responsive, culturally sensitive, problem oriented, and "user-friendly."

Good intentions notwithstanding, initiatives in institutional inclusion are fraught with perils and pitfalls when principles clash with personal self-interest and organizational inertia (Fleras 1998). Not everyone is supportive of this shift in priorities from crime fighting and law enforcement to public service and peacekeeping in consultation with an increasingly multicultural community. For example, the Metro Toronto Police Association has voiced its opposition to community policing, despite (or in spite of) wholesale endorsement by senior management (Gillmor 1996). Resistance is to be expected: Community policing principles appear to be at loggerheads with conventional police work. Many perceive community policing as inconsistent with long-standing police practices, contrary to "real" police work, a threat to cherished values and images, an impediment to career enhancement, and erosion of police powers and relative autonomy. Its endorsement by senior administration simply reinforces rank and file perception of a management out of touch with reality and beholden to political rather than police interests (Gillmor 1996). The warning signs are all too clear: Implementation of community policing will invariably challenge vested interests; it will also encounter resistance from bureaucratic structures and occupational subcultural values (Chan 1997).

Occupational Subcultures

People who occupy a similar occupation may develop distinctive ways of perceiving and responding to their social environment (Chan 1996). They also are likely to endorse a common system of norms and values related to work. The police are no exception. They belong to a type of occupational subculture defined by the demands of the job and constraints of public expectations (Desroches 1998). A distinctive set of norms, values, and beliefs has evolved and has become entrenched through shared experiences, similar training, common interests, and continual interaction.

The grounds for this police occupational subculture are not difficult to uncover. Most police officers in Canada are male, white, able-bodied, French or English speaking, and of working class origin. This homogeneity in gender, social class, ability, and ethnicity is reinforced by similar socialization pressures related to common training and peer group influence. The resultant solidarity is reinforced by patterns of isolation from the ethnic community ("us versus them"), by police perception of the public as ignorant and unsupportive of law enforcement activities, and by the nature of police work, which encourages a degree of caution or defensiveness. Suspicion toward those outside the profession compounds the pressures of isolation, mutual distrust, and alienation. Police solidarity and estrangement from the community are further reinforced by the requirements of the job, including shift work and mutual support in times of crisis and danger.

The values and priorities underlying this occupational subculture are inconsistent with those of community policing (Seagrave 1997). The police openly resist those as-

pects of community service at odds with the reassuring confines of traditional policing subculture. Many police officers do not want to be seen as "facilitators" or "resource personnel" or "peacekeepers." The preferred image is that of law enforcement agents who define success by the number of arrests and citations. Many resent a "social welfare" tag preferring, instead, a "take charge" identity that reinforces their self-perception as professional crime fighters (Oettmeier and Brown 1988). With its focus on service, however, community policing does not coincide with popular perceptions of police as "crime busters." Those who identify with community policing principles may experience isolation and alienation even from colleagues as allegiances are perceived to shift from the brotherhood to the neighbourhood (Asbury 1989). Wilson and Kelling (1989:52) speak of the anguish:

> In every department we visited, some of the incident-oriented officers spoke disparagingly of the problem-oriented officers as "social workers," and some of the latter responded by calling the former "ghetto blasters." If a community-service officer seems to get too close to the community, he or she may be accused of "going native."

The gap between policing and multicultural communities could not be more striking (see Eck and Rosenbaum 1994). Community policing culture endorses the virtues of trust, familiarity, cooperation, and respect. The community is perceived as a "resource" with unlimited potential for dealing with local issues. Opposing this is the occupational subculture of the police with its detachment from multicultural communities. The community is dismissed as disinterested in social control work, indifferent and passive (waiting to be policed), incompetent to carry out even simple tasks, disorganized to act in unison, and misinformed about the pressures and demands placed upon the police. In short, the community is perceived as irrelevant to the point of an impediment for effective policing except in the most passive way of providing information (Gillmor 1996). This clash of visions makes it is difficult to imagine a situation more conducive to misunderstanding and distrust.

Bureaucratic Blocks

No less inhibiting of institutional inclusiveness is the pervasiveness of police bureaucracy. The police as an institution are organized around bureaucratic principles whose paramilitaristic overtones rarely coincide with community-based initiatives. Police organizations are governed by a central command and control structure, with a ranked hierarchy, complex division of labour, impersonal enforcement of formal rules, carefully stipulated procedures, and the provision of a rationally based service. These bureaucracies exist to control a large number of persons (both internally and externally) without displaying favouritism or making any concessions to specific contexts. This control function is attained through a combination of rational control procedures, standardization, conformity through rule following, and accountability to the organizational chain of command. The police may not deliberately set out to control, but the nature of their mandate as "functionaries" has the effect of controlling those who fall outside the rule of law. Such a commitment to control would appear consistent with a traditional **professional crime-fighting model,** but inconsistent with ethnic community demands or positive changes in police–community relations (Clairmont 1988).

The principles of bureaucracy and community policing appear diametrically opposed. The partnership ethos inherent in community policing clashes with the principles of bureaucracy and bureaucratic control. Community policing emphasizes collaboration, creativity, joint problem solving, answerability to clients, and co-responsibility for crime control and order maintenance

(Normandeau and Leighton 1990). Bureaucracies by contrast are destined to be remote, isolated, and case oriented; they are also bound by rules, organizational procedures, and hierarchy. A bureaucratic mindset is programmed for routinizing interaction with others to ensure standardization. By contrast, community policing is geared toward flexibility, creativity, lateral thinking, and spontaneity to creatively solve recurrent problems. In other words, a fundamental reorientation is called for that entails a debureaucratization of role, status, functions, reward structures, operational styles, training programs, and objectives. But fundamental questions remain: How can creative problem-solving techniques flourish under organizational conditions that expect obedience and compliance while discouraging questioning, self-motivation, and innovation (Tomovich and Loree 1989)? Can innovative—even risk-taking—solutions be reconciled with a managerial mindset based on "not rocking the boat" or "shut up, and do as you're told"?

From the Thin Blue Line to Inclusive Circles

Even the brightest proposals for change will not take hold without an adequate analysis of barriers and constraints. The introduction of new ideas is likely to encounter resistance from entrenched interests or established values, especially when a conservative bureaucracy renown for its reluctance is asked to move over and make space with the formerly discredited. The introduction of community policing principles represents such a threat. Achievement of these goals is likely to meet with resistance and resentment unless management finds a way to (a) break down the barriers to social change; (b) educate all police officials about the benefits and advantages; (c) address manageable problems before embarking on widespread reforms; (d) convey the inevitability and necessity of community policing as good policing; (e) provide clear indications of changes in training, reward structures, and career enhancement; (f) indicate willingness to experiment with new ideas and structures in the shift from "force" to "service"; (g) reveal how administrative styles and management techniques will address "coalface" concerns; and (h) clear up misunderstanding and misconception regarding the goals, content, and scope of community policing (Brown 1989). Community policing will not make its mark until police are convinced of its credibility to police and the policing of the "real" world. Nor will it make much of an impact until the goals of community policing are shown to be attainable, realistic, and rewarding, especially for those officers who stand to benefit or lose from its introduction. As along as individual officers believe they have nothing to gain from community policing and that rewards lie with "kick-ass policing," the prospect of attitudinal change is remote. In the final analysis, the success and failure of community policing as institutional will depend on its capacity to convince front-line officers of its vision of an "inclusive blue line."

MINORITIES AND THE MEDIA

Canada is universally proclaimed as a multicultural society whose diversity commitments at institutional levels are globally admired. But these accolades gloss over discrepancies between reality and rhetoric (Fleras 1997). Criticism by academics (Bibby 1990) and authors (Bissoondath 1994) has proliferated with charges of multiculturalism as irrelevant, wasteful, divisive, counterproductive, expedient, naive, decorative, and misplaced (Fleras and Elliott 1991). Failure by major institutions to incorporate diversity into the organizational "mainstream" has made them particularly susceptible to criticism. Few institutions, however, with the possible exception of schools and police agencies, have attracted as much criticism and concern as the media.

The media have been singled out as visibly negligent in responding positively to Canada's evolving diversity (Siddiqui 1997). Passage of the Multiculturalism Act in 1988 has obligated all government agencies, such as the CBC, to improve access, equity, and the representation of minorities, both within the organization (in terms of hiring, promotion, and training) and outside (through delivery of culturally sensitive services to a diverse public). But media treatment of minorities in Canada remains mixed at best, deplorable at worst (Kunz and Fleras 1998). Criticism applies across the board, from employment opportunities for minorities in the media, on the one hand, to media portrayals of minorities, on the other. The media have been reproached for biased and inaccurate coverage of aboriginal peoples and racial minorities, many of whom continue to be insulted, stereotyped, and caricaturized, when not actually ignored as irrelevant or infantilized as inferior. The cumulative impact of this dismissive treatment is unmistakably clear: Failure to improve the representation and the presentation of minority women and men will squander the benefits of Canada's multicultural potential.

Why should the media be under such scrutiny? To say the media are powerful and pervasive is merely stating the obvious. This potency lies in the media's ability to articulate what is important and acceptable in society as natural and normal. This function is referred to as "reality construction" (see Harris 1993). Reality construction is doubly articulated: The media construct the images around which reality is created, then confer legitimacy on the constructed image through selective exposure. To one side, media values and priorities impose an ideological context for framing our experiences of social reality. The media are ideological insofar as they reflect a constructed view of the world; they also are ideological in advancing the ideas and ideals of the dominant sector in ways that have the intent or effect of reinforcing prevailing discourses (Abel 1997). Alternative or minority perspectives are dismissed as irrelevant or inferior. To the other, the media themselves are socially constructed by powerful forces in stabilizing the status quo by "manufacturing consent" (Herman and Chomsky 1988). The owners of the media as well as their commercial sponsors are pivotal players in this reality construction process. As a result, ruling class interests are better served by the media than minority needs. Minority concerns are compromised by a pervasive Eurocentrism, a process whereby cultural differences are slotted into a single perspective that elevates westocentric traditions (related to values, institutions, realities, and accomplishments) as the standard by which others are judged and found wanting (Shohat and Stam 1994).

The consequences of being ignored or trivialized by the media should not be underestimated. The media serve as a window on the world in terms of what is or should be as well; they also provide a mirror that reflects cultural values and priorities. The media constitute a primary source of information about the world we live in. Distortions in this information can only undermine people's ability to act upon this knowledge in a productive and progressive manner. The media may not directly determine behaviour; rather, they are likely to create a cultural climate in which certain persons or objects are "normalized" as acceptable and desirable. These images become a cultural point of reference for defining what is right or wrong, good or bad. To be sure, the media do not necessarily set out to control; nevertheless, their control of images has a controlling effect on those who are subjected to unflattering portrayals. The consequences of mismanaging media images reflect poorly on Canada. If the media represent a mirror that reflects an image of society, Canadians still have a long way to go in achieving a multicultural "looking glass self."

Portraying Minority Images: "Safe, Exotic, and Somewhere Else"

The world we inhabit is pervaded and transformed by images. The control of knowledge and its dissemination through media images is fundamental to the exercise of power in society. Media images are critical for conveying shared cultural beliefs and underlying assumptions in organizing our way around society. These images not only assist in the identification and construction of ourselves as social beings. They also serve as "windows" that provide insight into social patterns and cultural values of society. The proliferation of media images makes it impossible to distinguish fantasy from reality, as Angus and Jhally (1989) explain, especially since the "real" is so thoroughly "media-ted" through media images that any separation of the two (except for analytical purposes) is futile. For minority women and men, the circulation of images is both a strength and a weakness:

> Visual images in that sense are congealed social relations, formalizing in themselves either relations of domination or those of resistance. The politics of images is the same as any politics; it is about being the subjects not the objects of the world that we live in (Bannerji 1986:20).

With images as powerful as they are, the onus is on minority women and men to reclaim control over representations about who they are and what they want to be. Several questions strike at the heart of media portrayals of minority images: How do the media portray an image of aboriginal peoples and minority women and men? How do the media reflect and represent minorities in Canada? Are prevailing media images the result of conscious or unconscious decisions? What, if anything, can be done to improve this level of representation (Jakubowicz et al. 1994)? Four themes appear to characterize media (mis)treatment of minority women and men, reflecting recurrent images in news casting, TV programming, advertising, and filmmaking.

Minorities As Invisible

Numerous studies have confirmed what many regard as obvious. Canada's multicultural diversity is poorly reflected in the advertising, programming, and news casting sectors of the popular media (Fleras 1994). Visible minorities are reduced to an invisible status through underrepresentation in programming, staffing, and decision making. Even substantial presentation in the media may be misleading if minority women and men are slotted into a relatively small number of programs such as TV Ontario's *Polka Dot Door* or reduced to victim/ assailant in reality-based programming. Nor is there much sign of improvement: In 1989, Robert MacGregor acknowledged the invisibility of visible minority women in Canada's national news magazine (*Maclean's*) when measured by the quantity and quality of their appearances over a thirty-year span. A follow-up study indicates that women of colour continue to be "couched in compromise" by virtue of mixed messages (Kunz and Fleras 1998). Or consider the plight of African-Americans on television. Shows whose casts are all black are common enough, but most TV sitcoms continue to be segregated; there is not a single drama built around black actors (in the belief that there is no sizable demographic audience for this kind of material), and black theme programs border on the demeaning or stereotypical (Gray 1995). A recent report for the Screen Actors Guild conducted by George Gerbner of Temple University has reconfirmed that, with the exception of blacks, minorities such as Hispanics, Asians, and Native Americans are underrepresented compared to their numbers in real life (*Toronto Star,* 23 December 1998).

It would be inaccurate to say that the news media ignore minorities. Rather, a "shallows and rapids" treatment is a more accurate appraisal. That is, under normal circumstances, minorities are ignored or rendered irrelevant by the mainstream press ("shallows"). Otherwise, coverage is guided by the context of crisis or calamity, involving natural catastrophes, civil wars, and colourful insurgents ("rapids"). When the crisis subsides, the media interest subsides until the next big thing. Conflicts and calamities occur in minority communities, of course, but the absence of balanced coverage results in distorted perceptions of needs, concerns, and aspirations. This distortion may not be deliberately engineered. Rather, the misrepresentation reflects media preoccupation with readership and advertising revenues. The flamboyant and sensational are highlighted to satisfy audience needs and sell copy, without much regard for the effects of sensationalism on the lives of those sensationalized. The media may shun responsibility for their discriminatory impact, arguing they are reporting only what is news. Nevertheless, such an exclusive focus has the effect of portraying minorities as "subhuman" and less than worthy of our sympathy or assistance.

No less disturbing than media "whitewashing" is the absence of diversity in creative positions in the industry. Despite some improvement, minorities are largely excluded from roles as producers, directors, editors, and screenwriters. Fewer still are destined to attain the upper levels of management where key decision making occurs. One consequence of such exclusion is that minority realities are inevitably refracted through the prism of a white-controlled media. For women of colour, the situation is even more perilous. They are doubly jeopardized by "pale male" ideologies that devalue contributions, distort experiences, limit options, and undermine self-confidence and identity as Canadians. In this type of situation, one might conclude, what is not included by the media is just as significant as what is.

Minorities As Stereotypes

Minorities have long complained of **stereotyping** by the mainstream **media**. Historically, people of colour were portrayed in a manner that did not offend prevailing prejudices. Liberties taken with minority depictions in consumer advertising were especially flagrant. In an industry geared toward image and appeal, the rule of homogeneity and conservatism prevailed. Advertisers wanted their products sanitized and bleached of colour for fear of lost revenue. People of colour were rarely depicted in the advertising of beauty care and personal hygiene products, so entrenched was the image of "whiteness" as the preferred standard of beauty (Bledsloe 1989). Elsewhere, images of racial minorities were steeped in unfounded generalizations that emphasized the comical or grotesque. This stereotyping fell into a pattern. People from the Middle East continued to be portrayed as sleazy fanatics or tyrannical patriarchs where terrorism and religion (for example, "Islamic guerrillas" in the film *The Seige*) are inextricably linked. Asians have been typecast either as sly and cunning or as mathematical whizzes. Blacks in prime time shows remain stuck as superheros/athletes or sex-obsessed buffoons and surrounded by a host of secondary characters, such as hipsters, outlaws, and working class blokes (Cuff 1996).

Consider how the media have historically portrayed Canada's aboriginal peoples as the "other," a people removed in time and remote in space. This image of aboriginal peoples as the "other" has filtered through Eurocentric lenses and has ranged in scope, from their eulogization as "noble savage" and "primitive romantic" to their debasement as "villain" or "victim" or "comical simpleton," with the stigma of "problem people" or "menacing subversives" sandwiched in between (also Blythe 1994; Wall 1997). Images of tribalism continue to resonate with a spicy mixture of meanings, from backwardness to spiritual mysticism to ecological custodians (Jakubowicz et al. 1994). Most portrayals embraced a mythical image of an imaginary warrior who occupied the Plains between 1825 and 1880 (Frances 1992). The standard for the generic North American Indian could be packaged with ingredients from a so-called "Indian Identity Kit" (Berton 1975), which consisted of the following items, few of which even were indigenous to aboriginal peoples prior to European settlement: wig with hair parted in the middle into hanging plaits; feathered war bonnet; headband (a white invention to keep the actor's wig from slipping off); buckskin leggings; moccasins; painted skin tepee; and armed with a tomahawk and bows and arrows. This one-size-fits-all (seen one, seen them all) image applied to all First Peoples, regardless of whether they were Cree or Salish or Ojibwa or Blackfoot. These images could be further broken down into a series of recurrent stereotypes, in effect reinforcing a "seen one Indian, seen them all" mentality. Collectively, these images reinforce the notion of aboriginal peoples as a people from a different time and place, whose histories began with the arrival of the white man, and whose reality only makes sense in terms of interaction with whites. Collective resistance to their colonization is rarely depicted, although individual acts of protest may be valorized, in effect depoliticizing aboriginal concerns and contributions to Canada. The net effect ensured an image of aboriginal peoples as "safe, exotic, and somewhere else," as Philip Hayward writes with respect to music industry co-optation of Australian aboriginal artists.

Negative portraits inflict a degree of symbolic and psychological violence on aboriginal lives. Their sense of self-worth plunges through images that secure their status as a devalued "other." To be sure, the media have begun to invert conventional stereotypes between whites and First Peoples, with much greater emphasis on the courage or durability of the indigenous people of the land versus the rapacious greed of white settler colonization (think *Dances With Wolves*). Nevertheless, there is a long way to go, as Maurice Switzer, a member of the Elders' Council of the Mississaugas of Rice Lake First Nations, at Alderville, Ontario, writes in *Windspeaker* (1997:21–22):

> The country's large newspapers, TV and radio news shows often contain misinformation, sweeping generalizations and galling stereotypes about natives and native affairs. Their stories are usually presented by journalists with little background knowledge or understanding of aboriginals and their communities.... As well very few so-called mainstream media consider aboriginal affairs to be a subject worthy of regular attention.

Why stereotyping? Stereotyping simplifies the media process. Media movers and shakers prefer to tap into a pool of aboriginal stereotypes as a kind of convenient shorthand. Reliance on these simplistic and reductionist images creates readily identifiable frames (tropes) that impose a thematic coherence that audiences can relate to because of a shared culture code (Taylor 1993). Over time, these stereotypes solidify into definitive statements about "reality," and, while not "real" in the conventional sense, stereotypes are real in their social consequences.

The social dimension of stereotyping should not be overlooked. Rather than an error in perception, stereotyping constitutes a system of social control through the internalization of negative images. Stereotypes are employed to keep aboriginal peoples in their place and out of sight, thus sanitizing the colonization of First Peoples by assuaging white guilt (Churchill 1994). With stereotypes, it becomes progressively easier to disregard their humanity and status as a distinct people. The racially coded discourses that comprise stereotyping not only tap into public fears, but also feed public demands for tougher measures of social control. Such stereotyping may also contribute to white identities (Davis 1996). Imaginary Indians are filtered through the prism of European prejudice and preconceptions, in the process projecting Euro-Canadian onto the "other." To the extent that whites have long resorted to certain images of the "other" as a basis for collectively defining who they are in relation to the world around them, these images really do say more about the "creators" rather than the "created."

Minorities As Problem People

Minority women and men are frequently singled out by the media as a "social problem," that is, as "having problems" or "creating problems" in need of political attention or scarce national resources. As **problem people,** they are taken to task by the media for making demands that may imperil Canada's unity or national prosperity. Consider the case of Canada's aboriginal peoples when they are depicted as (a) a threat to Canada's territorial integrity (the Lubicon blockade in 1988 or the Oka Mohawk confrontations in the summer of 1990) or to national interests (the Innu protest of the NATO presence in Labrador); (b) a risk to Canada's social order (the violence between factions at the Akwesasne Reserve or occupation at Gustafsen Lake, British Columbia); (c) an economic liability (the costs associated with massive land claims settlement or recent proposals to constitutionally entrench inherent self-governing rights); and (d) a problem for the criminal justice system (ranging from the

Donald Marshall case to police shootings of aboriginal people, including the killing of Dudley George at Ipperwash, Ontario) or an unfair player (cigarette smuggling or rum running across borders). Aboriginal activism will be framed as a departure from established norms. Protestors are frequently framed as dangerous or irrational: The subsequent demonization marginalizes the legitimacy of dissent, trivializes minority issues, and distracts from the issues at hand. As a result, many news stories involving assertive minorities are framed as a narrative involving a conflict of interest between the forces of destruction to one side and the forces of order, reason, and stability on the other (Abel 1997). Compounding this negativity are reports of an excessive reliance on welfare, a predilection for alcohol and substance abuse, a pervasive laziness and lack of ambition, and an inclination to mismanagement of what little they have. The combined impact of this negative reporting paints a villainous picture of Canada's First Peoples. Time and again they come across as "troublesome constituents" whose demands for self-determination and the right to inherent self-government are inimical to Canada's liberal-democratic tradition. Success stories are rarely reported, and those that make it simply confirm the exception to the rule.

Nonaboriginal minorities are also problematized by the media. People of colour, both foreign- and native-born, are targets of negative reporting that dwells on costs, threats, and inconveniencies. Media reporting of refugees usually refers to illegal entries and the associated costs of processing and integration into Canada. Immigrants are routinely cast as potential troublemakers who steal jobs from Canadians, cheat on the welfare system, take advantage of educational opportunities without making a corresponding commitment to Canada, engage in illegal activities such as drugs or smuggling, and imperil Canada's unity and identity by refusing to discard their culture. This negativity may be coded in different ways, from content to positioning and layout of the story, length of article and size of type, content of headlines and kickers (phrases immediately after the headline), use of newspeak or inflammatory language, and use of quotes, statistics, and racial origins. The cumulative effect of this largely one-sided portrayal racializes the notion of "them" as a problem "other."

Minorities As Adornment

The media tend to portray minority women and men as mere adornments to society at large. This decorative aspect is achieved by casting minorities in roles that are meant only to amuse or embellish. Minorities are associated with the exotic and sensual, portrayed as congenial hosts for faraway destinations, enlisted as superstar boosters for athletics and sporting goods, or ghettoized in certain marketing segments related to "rap" or "hip-hop." Most minority roles on television consist of bit parts, usually restricted to sitcoms or dramas, both of which stereotype minority women and men as superfluous to society. Blacks on television are locked into roles as entertainers or athletes. Rarely is there any emphasis on intellectual or professional prowess, much less recourse to positive role models to which youth can aspire outside of athletics or entertainment (Cuff 1996). Such a restriction may prove inherently satisfying to mainstream audiences who historically have enjoyed laughing at blacks when cast as comics or buffoons. The depoliticizing of blacks as "emasculated" cartoons ("playing 'em for laughs") has the effect of reassuring nervous audiences that the world turns as it should (see Farli 1995).

Media relations with minority women are no less demeaning (Jiwani 1992; hooks 1992; Creedon 1993; Graydon 1995). Both women and men of colour are vulnerable to misrepresentation as peripheral, stereotypes, problem peoples, and the other. Women also are subject to additional media mistreatment because of gender: The intersection of gender and race relegates aboriginal women, women of colour, and immigrant women to the status of decorative props. Minority women are generally reduced to commodities; this objectification equates women with objects for control or consumption. They are sexualized in a way that equates existence with "snaring" and supporting a man to the exclusion of anything else. This sexualization is thought to infantilize women by casting them as silly or childlike, obsessed with appearances, and devoid of intelligence. They also are racialized in a manner that draws inordinate attention to their status as "other," together with the demeaning implications associated with being "otherized." Their bodies are gratuitously paraded to sell everything from esoteric fashions and sensuous perfumes to a host of exotic vacation destinations in between (see Graydon 1995). Minority women are cast in roles of domestication, a process that tends to reduce their lives and life chances to a singular process. Finally, women of colour are portrayed as dangerous or evil, with the potential to destroy everything good about society or civilization (Jiwani 1992). The end result? Gender is superimposed on and intersects with race to perpetuate patterns of inequality in ways that are mutually reinforcing yet contradictory (Stamm 1993). These complex articulations tend to trivialize the realities and contributions of minority women to the level of adornments in an environment where style prevails over substance. The interplay of gender and race comes through nicely in the following critical look at Disney animation.

INSIGHT 10–1 — Disney: Wholesome of Hegemonic?

What image comes to mind when we say "wholesome film"? Many would respond with "Disney." Disney's animated films, from *Sleeping Beauty* to *Beauty and the Beast,* are endorsed as models of wholesome entertainment that extol family values while reinforcing cultural values at the core of American greatness. But what Disney says or sets out to do is not necessarily what it accomplishes. Beneath this glossy exterior of playful animation lurks a more disturbing discourse that, at best, reveals cultural naiveté or political insensitivity and, at worst, borders on sexism and racism, albeit in a subtle and disguised manner that may have an unintended but real effect on its audience (Giroux 1995). This distortion is compounded by the nature of the medium: The need to frame all stories around the theme of conflict such as good versus evil puts an onus on dividing the world into "good guys" and "bad guys."

The women in Disney's animated world are almost completely defined by their relationships to males. Their lives are geared toward securing and supporting a man even if any sense of self and identity dissipates in the process of catering to patriarchal whims. Love with a man conquers all, and marriage with "Mr Right" will ensure both live happily ever after. In the *Beauty and the Beast,* for example, Belle, the heroine of the film, is portrayed as a feisty and independent woman who inhabits some remote French provincial village. To her credit, Belle rejects the advances of a male chauvinist pig named Gaston; however, she capitulates to the gruff charms of Beast who holds her captive in the hopes of eroding her resistance. Belle not only falls in love with the Beast; she also civilizes him by transforming this narcissistic tyrant into a sensitive, new-age guy.

Some argue that Belle is a Disney feminist because she rejects a vain macho male.

Others are not so sure. They see Belle as simply another woman whose life is valued primarily for who she is rather than what she does. The fact that she is forcibly kept and controlled speaks volumes about coercive love and male privilege. Or take the acclaimed animation movie *Mulan,* where a Japanese woman must become disguised as a man to achieve acceptance and goals. Other Disney animations, such as the *Lion King,* are even more openly sexist. All rulers in this animal kingdom are males, in effect reinforcing the message that patriarchal entitlement and high social standing confer independence and leadership. The animated version of *Pocahontas* drew a chorus of boos not only for taking liberties with history, but also for its portrayal of the heroine as cute and curvaceous. Of course, Disney would have endured similar criticism for stereotyping First Peoples and strong-willed women had it chosen to portray Pocahontas as "unattractive."

The magical world of Disney is not impervious to charges of racism. Disney has of course long relied on denigrating images of aboriginal people and people of colour as a basis for characterization and plot development. *The Jungle Book* lampooned South Indians, while frontier land stories such as *Davy Crockett* revelled in racist representations of aboriginal peoples as "injuns" or "redskins." Recent releases have also come under fire, including the *Lion King* for its racist stereotypes in promulgating the popular perception of Africa as nothing more than an animal kingdom. Even the portrayal of the evil lion as black in contrast with the light-coloured good lion reinforces colour-coded stereotypes while condoning the virtues of imperial rule in the face of indigenous rabble (Coren 1994). The 1989 release of *Aladdin* drew particular concern. From the opening song, "Arabian Nights," with its depiction of Arabian culture with racist overtones and popular stereotypes, to its portrayal of supporting charac-

ters as violent or cruel, the film manipulated an audience already primed by the media portrayal of the Gulf War. Racism is also evident in racially coded language and accents. The bad Arabs speak in thick foreign accents, while Jasmine and Aladdin speak in standardized English. In *Lion King,* all members of the royal family speak in received British pronunciation, while Banzai and Shenzi styles resemble the nuances of inner-city gangs (Giroux 1995).

What do children learn from these racist depictions? Racism in Disney films is rarely conveyed by what is said, but by what is not. Overtly negative representations are combined with the absence of complex characterization to create an impact that is racist in consequence if not always in intent. Through images and codes, children are taught that cultural differences outside the imprint of white middle class culture are inferior, deviant, irrelevant, or threatening. Children of colour also learn to dislike who they are because of these depictions. A spokesperson for an American Islamic association said this about the film *Aladdin* (quoted in Giroux 1995:40):

> All of the bad guys have beards and large, bulbous noses, sinister eyes and heavy accents, and they're wielding swords constantly. Aladdin doesn't have a big nose; he has a small nose. He doesn't have a beard or a turban. He doesn't have an accent. What makes him nice is they've given him this American character.... I have a daughter who says she's *ashamed to call herself an Arab, and it's because of things like this* (emphasis added).

In short, Disney films are widely perceived as models of wholesome family entertainment. Such a perception is true only to the extent that Disney endorses narrowly defined social arrangements consistent with Western values. The reality is that Disney films embrace a racist and sexist subtext that may be difficult for young audiences to decode. No one is accusing Disney of blatant misogyny or open racism. But in the manipulation of consensus in defence of a racialized and patriarchal status quo, Disney discourses are hegemonic in consequence if not in intent. Presumably nobody intends to deliberately put down minority women or men. Rather, the largely unintended consequences of seeing the world through Eurocentric and androcentric filters creates this dissonance. Perhaps the animated character induces people to take liberties: People tend to assume that with animation (=cartoons?) they can relax by letting down their guard. Parents may think these full-length cartoons are essentially harmless; but the subliminality of racist and sexist images may have an extremely adverse effect on children. Until people realize that there is no cultural free space or time out in a media-ted world—that if you aren't putting things in your head, then someone else is—the dangers of being "hegemonized" are all too real.

To Sum Up   Visible minorities are rendered invisible through underrepresentation in programming, staffing, and decision making. Conversely, they are visibly overrepresented in areas that count for less, including tourism, sports, international relief, and entertainment. Media portrayals tend to depict minorities as the *other*. While whites are portrayed as the norm and the standard by which others are judged and found wanting, minority women and men are given short thrift as humans removed in time and space and outside the pale of civilization. Minorities complain of being treated as "foreigners" or "outsiders," whose lives seem to revolve about their "defining" status of race or religion, to the virtual exclusion of other attributes. They serve as a foil with which to praise or condemn contemporary values in society. Images of "them" as "those people" are filtered through the prism of European prejudice and preconceptions, in the process projecting mainstream fears or yearnings on to the other. Such demeaning images serve as lightening rods to absorb public hostility over unpopular changes in society. Ethnocentrism and white superiority may not be openly articulated by media "whitewashing," but are assumed and normalized as the standard that disparages the other. Portrayal of minorities as the other typically entails a cultural Catch-22: They are criticized for being too different yet may be chided for not being different enough; they are taken to task for aspiring to be the same yet denounced when differenced (Stamm 1993).

Accounting For the Problem

Neglect of minorities in the media may occur for a variety of reasons. These may span the spectrum from hard-boiled business decisions that reflect market forces to a lack of cultural awareness to deep-seated prejudice among media personnel. Certain working assumptions about racial minorities may also inhibit progressive action. Does **media** mistreatment of minorities imply the presence of personal prejudice or overt **discrimination**? Is it a case of unwittingly cramming minority realities into Eurocentric categories as a basis for description or evaluation (Shohat and Stam 1994)? Or does it reflect a preference to act out of self-interest and the dictates of the marketplace, especially during economic recessions and periods of corporate restructuring (Jhally and Lewis 1992)? Key personnel may be unsure of how to integrate Canadians of colour into the media without attracting the whiff of paternalism or tokenism. Advertising personnel may fear making mistakes that could attract negative product publicity or incite a consumer boycott. Minorities themselves may be reluctant to enter media professions because of the low status associated with such employment. Answers to these questions are critical but elusive. Nevertheless, studies in this area suggest that media–minority relations are tainted by discrimination and racism—at times deliberate, at other times inadvertent.

How do the media discriminate systemically? At the core of media actions is an unswerving Eurocentrism—a set of beliefs about the superiority of westocentric values and practices that is so pervasive as to escape detection. Yet the unspoken nature of these tacit assumptions is powerful in privileging the West at the expense of the rest (Shohat and Stam 1994). Consider the news media: News media may be defined as **discourses in defence of dominant ideology** (ideology = a set of ideas and ideals that establish and sustain relations of power) (Herman and Chomsky 1988). The news media are ideological in that they privilege (or normalize) certain points of view as normal and acceptable; other views are discredited as a threat or violation of the norm. News media are also ideological in that they themselves are loaded with ideological assumptions that influence how news stories are "**framed.**" The framing of news stories is critical for signposting a preferred way of reading the event (see Guerrero 1997). References to "tunagate," "zippergate," and "whitewatergate" provide handy reference points for quickly framing issues. Incidents that are framed to fit conflict formats or given a racial or gender "spin" intend to generate interest or intensify an angle (for example, "gender wars"). But this "framing" experience is not neutral; it reflects the interests of those who own or control the media. For example, a dominant discourse shared by many Canadians is a commitment to the ideal of unity within diversity. Such a perspective ensures that protest actions that disrupt this unity are framed accordingly.

The use of language can reflect a systemic bias in how media issues are framed. For example, reference to the expression "Oka Crisis" is part of our vocabulary. It is a convenient media shorthand that has the effect, if not the intent, of localizing aboriginal concerns into one irrational flashpoint, while ignoring a history of aboriginal grievances across Canada. Or consider the language employed by a Toronto columnist who described the funeral of Georgina Leimonis (accidentally shot in a robbery at a neighbourhood restaurant called Just Desserts) as a ritual of innocence: "Four young women in white, each holding a single white rose, led a gleaming white coffin to the altar. A wedding dress and a veil; a corpse as pale as the moon...." Compare this with her assailant—a bearded brown man with a facial mole and a dangling earring (see also Irshad Manji, "Nation's Newsroom a Pale Reflection of our Diverse Society," *Toronto Star,* 9 August 1994). There is no malevolent intent here to verbally bash minorities. Rather, a clear dichotomy of good versus evil is inadvertently conveyed by media framing of issues into a conflict framework. The combined impact of these images tends to demonize minorities by racializing crime while criminalizing minority groups.

Multiculturalizing the Media

The media in Canada are under scrutiny to make appropriate adjustments. Multicultural minorities and aboriginal peoples have asked some tough questions of the media regarding their commitment to accommodate Canada's ethnic diversity. Proposed changes include the incorporation of minority perspectives into the media process, multicultural programming, balanced and impartial news casting, and sensitivity training for journalists and decision makers (Abel 1997). Alternative arrangements include the creation of separate minority networks for enhancing minority input into the media process and outcomes (see also Spoonley and Hirsch 1990). Responsible coverage of minority interests and concerns is predicated on the need to stop (a) selective and sensationalistic accounts, (b) images and words that demean and malign, (c) portrayals that are biased and unbalanced while lacking any sense of context, and (d) stereotyping that inflames hatred and fear (Rees 1986). But a conflict of interest is inevitable: The commercial media do not see themselves as reform agencies to promote progressive change or to accommodate, even if they may have a social responsibility to do so. They are a business whose *raison d'être* is simple: To make money by connecting audience to advertisers through ratings. Institutional practices that once worked to generate revenues (for example, stereotyping) will be retained; those that don't will be discarded. Such a bottom-line mentality will invariably be at odds with minority demands for balanced and contexted coverage, given media preference for morselization over context, conflict over cooperation, and personalities over issues (see Atkinson 1994).

Institutional Responses

To some extent, many changes are already in progress. The government Task Force on Broadcasting Policy, co-chaired by Gerald Caplan and Florian Sauvagneau in 1986, singled out the need to include aboriginal peoples and racial minorities (Raboy 1988). The 1988 Broadcasting Act has come out in favour of "cultural expression" by expanding air time for ethnic and racial minorities. Reforms include sensitivity training for program and production staff, language guidelines to reduce race–role stereotypes, and monitoring of on-air representation of racial minorities. Rules are in place to deter abusive representations of individuals on the basis of race or ethnicity as well as age, gender, religion, or disability. Taken together, the programming of multicultural minorities in a positive manner is an enlightened and overdue commitment.

In Southern Ontario, CFMT, the multicultural channel, delivers a much-needed service. Serving 18 cultural groups and 15 languages, CFMT is unique in the world, not only in producing 23 hours of original programming per week, but also because 60 percent of the programming is non-French or non-English (Quill 1996). Vision TV also hosts about 30 programs largely about different religious faiths and practices. Inroads are also evident in the private sector, where multicultural issues since 1984 have been addressed by Toronto's CITY-TV station through two large blocks of non-English, non-French programming produced by CHIN on Saturdays and Sundays. Toronto is served by six ethnic radio stations, two closed-circuit audio services, an ethnic television station, three ethnic specialty services, and another six channels accessible with special receiving equipment (Lawton 1998). On-air programming such as the racially acclaimed series *North of Sixty* and the *Rez* are also pushing the frontier of acceptance, but have been dropped. In the field of advertising, racial minorities are appearing more frequently across a broader range of products and services. Companies that utilize diversity are now perceived as sophisticated and cosmopolitan compared with their all-white counterparts, who come across as staid and outdated. Demographics may be pushing the changes: When people of colour comprise over 30 percent of the populations in Vancouver and Toronto, the media have little choice but to acknowledge that diversity is "cool."

Media executives concede the importance of improving the quantity and quality of minority representations. The combination of a growing ethnic market and an increased competition for consumer loyalty and dollars has sounded the death knell for monomarketing. But moves to convey a positive image of minorities have tended to misfire. Media efforts to improve minority representation are as likely to be greeted with hoots of derision or an air of skepticism as they are with calls for support and encouragement. Positive portrayals and inclusive programming may be dismissed as window-dressing, condescending, tokenistic, or "politically correct." Media find themselves in a no-win situation: Portrayal of minorities in high status and stable relations (such as the *Cosby Show*) are rebuked for creating unrealistic and unattainable expectations that can only foster resentment; depictions of minorities as poor or depraved are seen as perpetuating stereotypes. Benetton ads that prominently display minorities in a variety of controversial situations are praised by some as progressive; by others as exploitative and insulting. Such an apparent dichotomy puts the media in a double bind, that is, in a lose–lose situation, where they are damned if they do and damned if they don't. Bewildered and taken aback by criticism for either action or inaction, the media have treaded cautiously for fear of detonating yet another cultural landmine that could backfire on corporate profits and personal careers.

The Third Media

The expansion of the "third media" (minority presses and broadcast programs) is a prime example of minority empowerment. One of the more successful stories in the third media is located in Northern Canada, where aboriginal communities have wrested control over the local media in large part by appropriating satellite technology to meet social and cultural needs (Meadows 1995). Historically, the CBC has had a commitment to include all Canadians as part of its society-building process. This commitment to Canada as a community has encountered difficulties in areas that are isolated and sparsely populated. Without access to media, it becomes difficult for these Canadians to establish a sense of national identity within the framework of Canada. Such is the situation for the indigenous peoples who occupy the barren lands near the Arctic Circle (see Quassar 1998). The fact that many Inuit communities are now serviced by a media that reflects their interests and priorities rather than those of the south is encouraging enough in its own right, as the following Insider Report demonstrates.

Insider Report
Indigenous Media

The CBC began operating a northern television service for some communities as far back as 1958 (radio broadcasting arrived in the north in the 1930s). But the objectives of this northern service were derived from a southern perspective (Quassar 1998). They tended to reflect political interests related to establishing Canadian sovereignty during the Cold War. Economic interests pertaining to industrial expansion were also important, but the service proved to be a commercially unfeasible proposition because of distance and isolation. This situation changed by the early 1970s with the availability of satellite technology. Passage of the Telsat Act in 1969 made Canada the first country to establish a domestic satellite transmission policy (Roth 1995). The launch of Canada's domestic satellite in 1973, Anik-B, ensured all but the most remote Inuit communities eventually were connected by satellite services in terms of radio, telephone, and TV. For example, the 4,000 members of the community of Iqaliut on the southern tip of Baffin Island can subscribe to twenty channels from mainland Canada and the United States (Bergman 1996). The availability of popular entertainment was attractive; but indigenous communities remained dependent on the CBC funding for survival. TV programming also posed a problem in reconciling traditional values with the modern images conveyed by broadcasting. Many feared the introduction of television would result in a loss of time-honoured pursuits and social interactions as well as accelerate a growing generation gap. That made it even more imperative for the Inuit to gain control over television messages and images.

In 1981, the Inuit Broadcasting Corporation came into being as one way of dealing with the paradox. The IBC promised a balance of CBC programming and Inuit language programming that reflected the realities and concerns of the local communities. The northern broadcasting policy promised a significant measure of Inuit participation in programming and regulation, with funds to create a limited amount of Inuit-produced programs over issues that dealt with language, culture, and society (Raboy 1990). IBC currently produces five hours of original programming per week that is nonviolent, family oriented, and respectful of Inuit traditions. Surveys indicate that 90 percent of the Inuit watch one to three hours of IBC programming, including *Takuginai* (*Look Here*), a kind of Inuit Sesame Street, and *Kippinguijautit* (*Things to Pass Time By*), which showcases Inuit talent and storytelling (Bergman 1996). Funds were also set aside to redub CBC programming into Inuit. The introduction of this new northern service proved that

modern technology, when locally owned, community based, and culturally sensitive, could be used to preserve indigenous language and culture.

The CRTC established Canada's current Aboriginal Broadcasting Policy in 1990 (Meadows 1995). A consortium of government and private interests, later called TVNorthern Canada, had argued for programming that reflected northern rather than southern interests. First Nations people wanted diversity in programming; but their expectations differed from southern audiences. Communication was endorsed as a powerful tool to ensure cultural survival, with the result that programming had to mirror the social, cultural, and linguistic realities of the Far North. Aboriginal programming was defined as any program about some aspect of native life directed toward an aboriginal audience or a program involving one of the indigenous languages. Limitations were also imposed on the kind and the amount of advertising on aboriginal radio and television.

Additional developments under the Aboriginal Broadcasting Policy have further decolonized the North. The inception in January 1992 of TVNorthern Canada, a trans-Arctic aboriginal TV network, was the culmination of a twenty-year struggle to gain access to northern airwaves while reducing dependency on the CBC (Meadows 1995). Primarily an aboriginal network with an audience base of 100,000, TVNorthern Canada proposed to produce 100 hours per week of programming for 94 communities in 13 different indigenous languages. Its rationale was straightforward: If aboriginal society was to survive, it was imperative to foster a sharing of ideas and experiences between dispersed communities from the Arctic Inuit to the Cree-Ojibwa of Northern Ontario.

This exercise in local self-determination not only enhanced Inuit pride and identity by reflecting Inuit values and survival skills. It also empowered Inuit communities through control over the electronic media by filtering southern realities through Inuit sensibilities while countering nonindigenous constructions that continue to dominate mainstream media. Primary attention is directed at indigenous youth with programming directed at skills enhancement, language and culture preservation, and entertainment through music videos (including aboriginal artists), talk-back shows hosted by young people, and magazine-style programs. Finally, indigenous broadcasting has served to politicize Northern peoples by aligning and drawing Inuit awareness to human rights issues as viable alternatives in other parts of the world. Knowledge that the concerns and challenges confronting the Inuit are similar to those of other indigenous peoples has united otherwise disparate Inuit communities into a more globally aware and progressive society.

The emancipatory potential of local media has altered our perception of traditional mass media (Meadows 1995). Commodity-driven mass media tend to obliterate identity in an avalanche of American-style programming, yet local productions may assist in locating or consolidating a collective affiliation. But even these efforts will fail unless indigenous peoples can gain local ownership over programming and a sense of community commitment and involvement. That appears to be the case with TVNorthern Canada and the IBC. Local programming has elicited high levels of interest in TV and radio programs; the popularity of shows related to language learning, skills acquisition, and northern exposure to regional organizations also indicates a bright future. To be sure, cutbacks in funding have led to uncertainty because of increased reliance on the government with its potential to compromise the integrity of indigenous cultures. For example, the federal government cut the IBC budget by 36 percent between 1990 and 1995 ($2.6 million to $1.6 million), even though 65 percent of its operating budget is dependent on federal spending (Bergman 1996). Nevertheless, evidence suggests that there will be no turning back, even with cutbacks, as Canada's indigenous people reestablish their rightful place in Canadian society.

To Sum Up   The media play an influential role in defining what is socially desirable or normal. This is accomplished in large part by defining a specific cultural framework that provides a reference point for acceptance or validity. As a primary channel of communication, the media have the potential to articulate a powerful statement about the legitimacy of diversity in our society. But they are likely to send out mixed messages about a commitment to accommodate diversity. That would suggest the media will continue as a contested site, with advocates of the economic, political, and social status quo in competition for the forces of change for control of the agenda. At the core of this redefinition process is power. Until the issue of power is resolved—in terms of who owns it, who has access to it, and whose values will dominate—media–public relations will remain riddled with ambiguity and fraught with frustration.

MULTICULTURAL SCHOOLING AND EDUCATION

The educational system has for the most part reflected a fundamental commitment to mono-culturalism. Historically, education was inseparable from the amalgamation of diversity into the mainstream. This conformist ideology sought to absorb immigrant children directly into Canadian society by stripping them of language and culture (Alladin 1996; Allingham 1992; McAndrew 1992; Moodley 1993). All aspects of schooling, from teachers and text-books to policy and curriculum, were aligned with the principles of angloconformity. Anything that veered outside this anglocentric framework was ignored as irrelevant or dangerous and punished accordingly. (See Case Study on residential schools in Chapter 6.) Special curricula and references to other languages or cultures were rejected as inconsistent with the long-term interests of Canadian society building. The conclusion was inescapable: Schooling, had evolved into a site for the reproduction of social inequality in that it denied equal opportunity and fostered outcomes at odds with minority students (Dei 1996).

The explicit assimilationist model that once prevailed within educational circles is no longer officially endorsed, even if assimilation remains an unspoken but powerful ethos at all schooling levels. The site encompassed by schooling and education has turned into a contested space, involving the struggles of those who endorse the status quo versus those who have historically been excluded and are seeking to multiculturalize the agenda (Giroux 1994). In theory, the impetus for **multicultural education** constitutes a departure from conventional ways of doing things. Its introduction has not only challenged how schools should relate to diversity, but also raised questions about the form, function, and processes of formal education in a changing and diverse society. By fostering a learning environment that acknowledges the culture of its students (Henry et al. 1995), multicultural education initiatives wrap themselves around the rhetoric of "cross-cultural communication," "racial awareness and sensitivity," and "healthy identity formation." In its more demanding versions, multicultural education emphasizes cultural diversity as a basis for challenging and relativizing the basic principles associated with dominant and subdominant cultures in the hopes of establishing a more dynamic schooling culture (Turner 1994). The most radical forms are expressed in an antiracism education that not only challenges those relationships of power that racialize the school social order, but also invoke direct actions for dismantling the structural roots of educational inequality (Giroux 1994). The extent to which multicultural education seeks to institutionally accommodate diversity is eminently worthwhile. That multicultural education may not accomplish what it sets out to do is indicative of the entrenched interests that seek to blunt, deflect, absorb, or crush any move toward inclusiveness.

Monocultural Education: Socialization As Social Control

Both the media and education are secondary agents of socialization whose social functions are often at odds with formal mandates. The following functions of education prevail in society: (a) socialization, or transmission of culture; (b) self-actualization and individual self-development; (c) preparation for the workplace, consumerism, and citizenship; (d) improvement in Canada's competitive edge; and (e) reproduction of the social order. Education plays both a conservative and a progressive role in society, depending on the level of schooling under examination. For example, elementary school education discharges a conservative function whereby cultural assumptions are tacitly inculcated along with the three R's. Child-centred curricula, with their focus on self-esteem and personal creativity, are moving beyond those limitations. Postsecondary education, by contrast, endorses creative and informed debate as a basis for progressive change—at least in theory if not in practice. But a tacit commitment to assimilation remains a central objective. Alok Mukherjee (1992:73) writes:

> Traditionally, the school has been a conservative institution. Its function, on the one hand, is to legitimize the dominant social, political, economic, and cultural ideas of society and, on the other, to perpetuate existing relations. The ownership, organization, and activities of the school reflect this dual role.

From daily routines to decision making at the top, education is organized to facilitate cultural indoctrination and social control of minority students. These reproductive functions can be accomplished in a direct manner by the selection of textbooks that reflect mainstream experiences and values. The streaming of minority students into lower level programs restricts access to higher education and useful employment. Indirect and largely unobtrusive measures are also employed. The school system screens out certain information by projecting certain views of the world as necessary and normal, others as inappropriate. Issues are framed in a way that gives prominence to some, but ignores others. Diminished teacher expectation may be a problem. The widely accepted practice of grading students may have the effect of reinforcing competitive individualism to the exclusion of traditional cultural values. Through schooling, in other words, the reproduction of the ideological and social order is realized without much public awareness or open debate. In linking power with culture, the school ends up perpetuating the prevailing distributions of power and resources (Apple 1987). This "hidden curriculum" is nicely described by Alok Mukherjee (1992):

> Schools...help control meaning. They preserve and distribute what is perceived to be "legitimate knowledge"—the knowledge that "we all must have." Thus schools confer cultural legitimacy on the knowledge of specific groups (Apple and Franklin 1979, cited in Mukherjee 1992:76).

The assimilationist dynamic imposes constraints on expanding a multicultural agenda. A commitment to diversity and change may be fundamentally compromised in a context where monoculturalism prevails. Rarely do schools seriously contemplate the magnitude of commitment that must occur for changes to "kick in" at the level of curriculum, language, and culture programs for children, placement and assessment, employment and promotion, teacher training, and relations with the community (McAndrew 1992). Ad hoc adjustments are more common than radical restructuring. Nor does there appear to be any wholesale move to reject the assimilationist ethos of the school system (Cummins and Danesi 1990). Discriminatory structures are not easily dismantled in the light of entrenched interests and ideologies, many of which are unlikely to tolerate significant changes without considerable resistance. Changes when they do occur may be relegated to the cosmetic realm, and away from the key domains of decision making, agenda setting, and power sharing. These impediments should warn against any excessive expectations regarding the potential of multicultural education. Still, the fact that pluralist initiatives have materialized at numerous schools suggests that multicultural education is here to stay in principle and in practice.

Multicultural Education: Enriching, Enlightening, and Empowering

Multicultural education encompasses a variety of policies, programs, and practices for engaging diversity within the school setting. It can encompass the study of many cultures or an understanding of the world from diverse perspectives; alternatively, it may convey how power and politics are inextricably connected with unequal group relations (see Schuman and Olufs 1995). Different styles of multicultural education can be observed, ranging in scope and comprehension from "moderate" to "radical" approaches. Three of the more common moderate approaches are *enrichment, enlightenment,* and *empowerment.* An *antiracism approach* is constitutive of a fundamentally different style.

An **enrichment multicultural education** is aimed at all students. Students are exposed to a variety of different cultures to enhance a knowledge of and appreciation for cultural diversity. The curriculum is enriched with various multicultural add-ons. Special days are set aside for multicultural awareness; projects are assigned that reflect multicultural themes; and specific cultures are singled out for intensive classroom study. Additional perspectives include a focus on healthy identity formation, cultural preservation, intercultural sensitivity, stereotyping awareness, and cross-cultural communication. A desirable side effect of the enrichment process is greater tolerance, enhanced sensitivity, and more harmonious intercultural relations. A less beneficial consequence is a failure to initiate sweeping institutional changes, much less challenge the racism within and outside the school.

The enrichment model is widely acceptable because of its nonthreatening nature. Yet this very innocuousness has brought it into disrepute with critics. Enrichment styles have been criticized as too static and restrictive in scope. The style tends to focus on the exotic components of a culture that everyone can relate to, rather than to more substantive issues such as values and beliefs, and when taught by poorly trained teachers may inadvertently trivialize or stereotype (Henry et al. 1995). Diverse cultures are studied at the level of material culture, stripped of their historical context, and discussed from an outsider's point of view (Mukherjee 1992). There is also a danger of over-romanticizing minorities by focusing on a timeless past or, alternatively, of crippling them as social problems when dwelling on the present. Even sensitive presentations must grapple with dilemmas as varied as the following: (a) how to discuss elements of other cultures that are fundamentally opposed to Canada's democratic principles; (b) is it possible to emphasize the positive features of minorities to the exclusion of problems that many confront; (c) can cultural differences be presented without reinforcing stereotypes or an "us-versus-them" mentality; and (d) exactly how does one convey the idea that everyone is basically different in the same kind of way, or everyone is fundamentally the same in radically different ways (see McAndrew 1992). Henry Giroux (1994:327) puts its smartly in acknowledging the dilemma of "particularist" approaches: "A viable multicultural pedagogy and politics must also affirm cultural differences while simultaneously refusing to essentialize and grant immunity to those groups that speak from subordinate positions of power." That these questions have yet to be answered to everyone's satisfaction casts a pallor on the effectiveness of this approach.

A second approach that is compatible with the first is an **enlightenment model of multicultural education.** This approach is similar to the enrichment model insofar as both seek to modify people's attitudes by changing how they think about diversity. Enlightenment models are less concerned with celebrating differences as a basis for attitudinal change. The focus is on enlightening students about race relations in society and their impact on education and schooling. Enlightenment models go beyond description of specific cultures, focusing, instead, on a broader, analytical approach toward diversity not as a "thing" but as a relationship, both hierarchical and unequal. Attention is directed at how minority–majority relations are created and maintained; it also is aimed at what would be required to challenge and transform these predominantly unequal relationships. Stronger versions may expose students to Anglo-European complicity in crimes of racism, dispossession, and imperialism and the corresponding concentrations of power in white hands. Specific group victimization may be included, for example, genocide against First Peoples, while emphasizing the achievements of indigenous and immigrant peoples as a corrective to their marginalization in history, society, and culture (see Dinesh 1996). Applied to education, the enlightenment objective is to analyze those arrangements that have the intent or the effect of compromising minority success in schools, including (a) school policies and politics; (b) the school culture and "hidden" curriculum; (c) languages—official, heritage, and other; (d) community participation; (e) assessment, testing procedures, and program tracking; (f) instructional materials; (g) the formal curriculum; (h) the ethnic composition of the teaching staff; and (i) teacher attitudes, values, and competency.

Both the enrichment and enlightenment styles of multicultural education concentrate on the needs of nonminority pupils. In contrast is a third model, called **empowerment multicultural education,** which is directed essentially at the needs of the minority student. The minority-focus empowerment model is predicated on the belief that monocultural school systems are failing minority pupils. Minority students do not see themselves at the centre of culture and history in a westocentric curriculum that rarely acknowledges minority achievements and contributions to society. What minority students require is a school context that capitalizes on their strengths and learning styles as a basis for achievement. These empowerment models—largely exemplified in black focus schools—have proven controversial, since not everyone necessarily shares in the assumption that separate but equal is the appropriate multicultural path to take (Dei 1996; also Smith and Smith 1996).

An example of empowerment education can be seen in the struggle by aboriginal peoples to gain control of aboriginal education. Since the early 1970s, aboriginal peoples have sought to implement a variety of reforms involving the need to (a) decentralize the educational structure, (b) transfer funding control to local authorities, (c) devolve power from the centre to the community, and (d) empower parents to assume increased responsibility for their children's education. Aboriginal grievances and concerns over education are understandable. Historically, the government's educational policies have embraced an explicit commitment to assimilate aboriginal children through segregation and indoctrination. Federally directed native education sought to disrupt the cultural patterns of aboriginal children, then expose them to the values and priorities of the West, often in schools off the reserve and away from community, friends, and relatives. The abusive consequences of residential schools have been widely documented. Other consequences are less direct but no less real in denying aboriginal experiences, as the Métis scholar Paul Chartrand (1992:8–9) says: "It is easy to assert power over others if they are made to feel they have no identity, they have no past, or at least no past that matters." Only a relatively separate education system controlled by aboriginal people for aboriginal people is viewed as a corrective to these historically imposed disadvantages.

The aims of aboriginal-controlled education are twofold. First, it seeks to impart those skills that aboriginal children will need to succeed in the outside world. Second, it hopes to immerse children in an environment that is unmistakeably aboriginal in content, style, and outcome. The key is to produce children who possess a strong sense of who they are and where they came from, without forsaking the skills to compete in the dominant sector. With its emphasis on empowerment through behavioural changes and institutional restructuring, aboriginal-focus education may well have more in common with antiracism styles of education. To put this into perspective, see Table 10.1, which provides a succinct comparison and contrast of the focuses of enrichment, enlightenment, and empowerment models of multicultural education.

TABLE 10.1	Styles of Multicultural Education		
	Enrichment	**Enlightenment**	**Empowerment**
Focus	Celebrate	Analyze	Empower
Objective	Challenge prejudice	Remove discrimination	Achieve success
Goal	Diversity	Eliminate disparity	Self-esteem
Outcome	Lifestyle ("heritage")	Life chances	Biculturalism
Means	Cultures	Race relations	Cultural renewal
Style	Experience	Understand	Immersion
Target	Student	Institution	Minority students
Scope	Individual	Interpersonal	Collectivity

Antiracism Education

Multicultural education revolves around a philosophy for celebrating differences. It consists of activities and curricula that promote an awareness of diversity in terms of its intrinsic value to minorities and/or society at large (Ministry of Education and Training 1993). The aim of multicultural education is largely attitudinal, that is, to enhance sensitivity by improving knowledge about cultural differences (enrichment) and race relations (enlightenment). But there is no proof that enriched or enlightened attitudes will lead to behavioural changes. By contrast, *antiracism education* is concerned with the identification and removal of discriminatory barriers at interpersonal and institutional levels. It begins with the assumption that minority underachievement is not necessarily caused by cultural differences. Nor will cross-cultural understanding contribute to any fundamental change in uprooting the structural roots of inequality (Kivel 1996). Even analyzing inequality may lose its salience to inform and transform if such enlightenment endorses a view that contradictions in race and ethnicity can be harmonized within a prevailing structure of power relations (Giroux 1994). Improving minority status is contingent on removing the behavioural and structural components of racial inequality, along with the power and privileges that sustain racism through institutional policies, practices, and procedures (Ministry of Education and Training 1993). Sweeping changes in the curriculum are called for—not simply a tinkering with multicultural concessions.

Antiracism education is constructed around the commitment to antiracism. Both are dedicated to actively challenge and transform those discriminatory aspects of education through direct action. **Antiracist education** can be defined as a proactive and process-oriented approach that seeks to balance a value on difference with a sharing of power (Dei 1996). It involves at least four elements: (a) critical insight into the interlocking differences that are brought into the classroom; (b) a critical discourse that focuses on race and racism as issues of power and inequality rather than matters of cultural difference; (c) an interrogation of existing school practices to uncover the structural roots of monoculturalisms and inequality; and (d) challenge and rupturing of the status quo (rather than insertion into existing system) by fostering engagement through political and social activism (Dei 1996). Put bluntly, the goal of antiracist education is to delegitimize the supremacy and colonialism at the heart of contemporary society by interrogating the system of power relations that continue to racialize the social order and bestow privilege to whiteness.

Antiracism education differs sharply from multicultural education. While multicultural education is merely intolerant of racism in its practice, antiracism seeks to actively eradicate

racism through awareness, challenge, and confrontation (Kivel 1996). Antiracism education shifts attention away from subdominant cultures and any inclination to emphasize their
deficits to one that examines how racism in its different forms is historically created, sym-
bolically expressed, and institutionally embedded at various levels in society (Giroux 1994).
It goes beyond acknowledging differences (enrichment) and analyzing stereotypes (enlightenment) to that of understanding, engaging, and transforming the structural roots of
racism and racial discrimination. The pedagogy becomes political, Giroux points out, when
it addresses how the production of knowledge, social identities, and social relations may
challenge the racist assumptions and practices that inform the schooling and education.
Under an antiracism education, both students and teachers are offered the opportunity to
see how culture is organized, who is authorized to speak about different forms of culture,
which cultures are worthy of valorization, and which cultures are seen as unworthy of public esteem. They also come to understand how power operates in the interests of dominant
social relations and how such relations can be challenged and transformed (Giroux 1994).

Different styles of antiracism education can be discerned. Antiracism at individual levels
concentrates on behaviour modification through education and training (Stern 1992).
Institutional antiracism strategies are aimed at dismantling the structural basis of school
racism. These systemic biases are most apt to occur at the level of mission statement, culture
and subculture, power and decision making, structures (including rules, roles, and relationships), and distribution of financial and human assets. At one level antiracist education is
concerned with shifting minority presence into the centre of the curriculum. Emphasis is on
providing a platform for minority stories to be told in their own voices, while repudiating
the white-centredness of school knowledge as the only legitimate form of culture (Allingham
1992; Mukherjee 1992; McCaskill 1995). An inclusive or multicentric emphasis seeks to incorporate all students and the values they bring to school as a basis for improving successful
learning outcomes while bolstering a truly multicultural curriculum (Dei 1996). A minor-
ity-centred or minority-focused school provides an alternative learning environment that
caters to students for whom mainstream schools are inappropriate even with incorporation of
"other centred knowledge to achieve a multicentric, inclusive school" (Dei 1996:106). For example, an Africentric or African-focused school arrangement seeks to improve academic
and social achievement by emphasizing the centrality of black experiences in social history
and cultural development for those minority students who are alienated and disengaged from
a Eurocentric educational system. Table 10.2 provides a summary comparison of multicultural
and antiracism education in terms of focus, objectives, concerns, scope, and outcomes.

**TABLE 10.2   Multicultural and Antiracism Education:
Comparisons and Contrasts**

	Multicultural Education	Antiracism Education
Focus	Culture	Structure
Objective	Sensitivity	Removal of discriminatory barriers
Concerns	Ethnocentrism	Systemic racism
Scope	Student	Institutions
Style	Accommodative	Challenge/Resist
Outcome	Understanding	Equality

POLICING MULTICULTURAL MINORITIES

The criminal justice system should be no less responsive to the demands of inclusion than other institutions. For this reason, the slow and erratic nature of the response has proven cause for concern. This indictment is especially evident at the level of policing and law enforcement, where miscalculations are not always measured by inconvenience but in deadly consequences. The police have been accused of underpolicing (slow response rates) and overpolicing (excessive and oppressive coverage), thus reinforcing allegations of racial prejudice and discriminatory treatment of minorities (Holdaway 1996). The consequences of this breakdown in interaction have had the effect of racializing crime in Canada while simultaneously criminalizing minorities (Henry et al. 1995).

Both political and community pressure has drawn attention to anomalies in police–minority relations at odds with Canada's multicultural ethos. An increasingly fractious policing environment is evolving, given the combination of changing demographics, new legislation, diverse ethnocultural communities, minority activism, and public demands for accountability. Concern over the so-called crisis in police–minority relations has gained prominence in recent years, in the process eroding minority confidence in aspects of Canadian policing. Police initiatives to stem this crisis in credibility by restoring legitimacy to policing functions should be acknowledged. Authorities at various levels have cast for ways to ease the tension, calm troublesome constituents, patch up the crisis, and improve police–minority dialogue without impairing police effectiveness in the process. Initiatives in community-based, multiculturally sensitive policing have proven pivotal in easing the crisis. The fact that each step forward appears to be undermined by another step backward is indicative of the challenges and complexities of institutional accommodation (Fleras et al. 1989).

Crisis in Policing

Police–minority relations are undergoing a profound reassessment that borders on crisis and chaos. The sensibilities of many Americans and Canadians were deeply offended by the Rodney King-inspired riots that killed 50 people in Los Angeles in early May 1992. The fact that a similar, smaller-scale riot was reenacted in Toronto with considerable property damage to the Yonge Street strip laid to rest the fabled superiority of Canada's race relations. Shock, outrage, and sadness greeted news of the destruction in what many had congratulated as a model city in multicultural engagement. Elsewhere across Canada the police came in for biting criticism. In Montreal, a coroner's inquest castigated the police for the callous and racist indifference to human life following a display of sheer incompetence in the bungled shooting of an unarmed black male. Criticism has also uncovered a reliance on strip searches to humiliate the loud and uncooperative or to punish those likely to slip through the system (Editorial, 7 November 1998). This breakdown in police–minority relations has had the effect of eroding the legitimacy of the police in certain multicultural communities (Baker 1994).

Perceptions of a crisis in police–minority relations stem from incidents involving young urban male African-Canadians (also Holdaway 1996). In the greater Toronto Census Metropolitan Area, a total of eight young blacks were shot by the police between 1988 and 1992, compared with ten whites, even though African-Canadians comprise only a small percentage of the total population of the metropolitan area. Of the ten people shot in Montreal between 1988 and 1993, five were black and three were Hispanic. Minority parents and community leaders did not see these shooting incidents as isolated cases, but as reflecting a pattern of police harassment, brutality, and oppression, in the same way Marc Lepine's shooting of 14 women in Montreal in 1989 has been interpreted as a logical extension of male violence toward women. Many believe that blacks are harassed more often because of double standards; they are also charged, arrested, convicted, and jailed at a rate far beyond their proportion in the community. Police, in turn, are accused of being excessively preoccupied with the belief that minorities are predisposed to crime ("overpolicing") yet underoccupied in their attention to ethnic communities when needed ("underpolicing") (Henry et al. 1995). This situation appears to be typical elsewhere (Chan 1996; Holdaway 1996). In Britain, only a quarter of those racially attacked in the previous year had reported the incident to the police; only half of reported cases were satisfied with police response, with the predominant feeling being that police were disinterested in the complaint or sympathetic to the perpetrators (Modood and Berthoud 1997). Confidence in the police service has plummeted accordingly: The police continue to be perceived as representatives of white power establishment in communities of colour (Kivel 1996).

The police would dispute this assessment of their relationship with targeted minority communities. The spate of shootings involving minority males is perceived as isolated and coincidental, reflecting the growing menace of guns and drugs. Racially motivated actions may exist, they concede, but excesses can be attributed to a small number of "rogue" officers rather than to any institutionalized racism. The apprehension of minority youths is not a case of discriminatory policing, according to the police, but a response to street culture crimes that invite police attention. And, as far as police officers are concerned, minority communities have only themselves to blame if misguided allegations of police brutality deter community members from seeking police protection.

Who is right? Or wrong? Is there a failure to communicate because of contrasting perceptions of the problem and proposed solutions? The police believe that excessive coverage of minority males reflects the realities of irresponsible behaviour by disaffected youths. By contrast, African-Canadians often see police as racist and trigger-happy, concerned only with protecting their turf against intruders. The fact that neither side can understand the other—much less engage in cooperative actions—intensifies the potential for crisis and confrontation. The result is a strained mutual avoidance: Minority youth stake out their patch by withdrawing legitimacy from the "machine." The police, in turn, encircle the wagons even more securely against what they perceive as unwarranted attacks by stroppy youths, community activists, an unsympathetic press, opportunistic politicians, and the forces of political correctness.

CASE STUDY 10-3	Black and White and "Red" In Between

If nothing else, the OJ Simpson trial and subsequent acquittal exposed a cultural rift that separates whites from blacks. Whites tend to accept the criminal justice system as a pillar of civilized society. The reasoning is simple: Not only does the criminal justice system reflect and reinforce mainstream values; but white experiences with the law have proven generally satisfactory, even if occasional miscarriages have tarnished the image of impartial policing. By contrast, black experiences with the law are largely distressful, at least judging by perceptions of double standards within the criminal justice system. For example, police in Ontario are twice as likely to stop black males between the ages of 18 and 24 than their white counterparts (43.2 percent versus 23.8 percent), according to the 1995 study of systemic racism in Ontario's criminal justice system. Blacks are also more likely to be jailed overnight or denied bail. Not surprisingly, so-called "uppity" blacks who challenge and resist the "white man's law" may be widely valorized by other blacks. Those successful enough to beat the system are often accorded hero status.

That urban police and certain sectors of the minority community do not mix well is an established fact (Ungerleider 1993). To some extent, conflict is inevitable; after all, the police are perceived as the most visible embodiment of a white establishment that criminalizes people on the basis of colour, in effect racializing "them" as the undeserving "other" (Ungerleider and McGregor 1995; Holdaway 1996). Police attitudes are condemned by the powerless as controlling and obstructive to service delivery which minorities would define as "safe" (Ramsden 1995). The high rate of incidents involving violence and death would attest to this: The seven minority males shot and killed by the Metro Toronto Police since 1991 represent nearly one-quarter of the 29 people killed in Toronto, but African-Canadians comprise only 7.5 percent of the population in the Metro region (Tyler 1996). Crimes by the poor are more likely to attract police attention, in contrast with white-collar crime, which is not nearly as visible or as easily detected. Such selective enforcement would suggest that minorities are not more criminal but more likely to be criminalized because of their visibility in the public domain.

Race, Lies, and Stereotypes

Police–minority encounters tend to augment stereotypes and prejudices on both sides of the interactional divide. The police employ styles of communication both verbal and nonverbal that inadvertently, perhaps, reinforce negative stereotypes about themselves

as aggressive defenders of white privilege. Conversely, oppositional interactional styles of black male youth may confirm police perceptions of youth as surly, defiant, uncooperative, disrespectful, deceptive, deviant, and deserving of increased surveillance. With such mutually derogatory views, who can be surprised that police–minority relations have deteriorated to almost crisis proportions, as confirmed by the scarcely concealed contempt that each side has for the other, in some cases culminating in fatal impacts.

At the core of this interactional breakdown are stereotypes, none of which flatter the other side. Black youth see police as racist for enforcing the law in a discriminatory and insensitive fashion. Police are accused of double standards, since blacks perceive themselves as harassed, charged, arrested, and convicted more often than whites—when not actually shot at and killed. The police tend to reject these accusations as unwarranted. As far as they are concerned, their job is to enforce the law evenly and without prejudice. Higher crime rates can only reflect greater criminal activity among blacks, in turn justifying special police attention. Blacks dismiss this allegation by suggesting that higher rates result from police preconceptions and preoccupations with highly visible street activities that inflate charge and arrest rates.

Not unexpectedly, the police are seen by some sectors as the "enemy," as a Toronto race relations consultant once reminded us, whose status is that of an "occupying army" and not to be trusted (see also Modood and Berthoud 1997). By mandate and by action, police are perceived as agents of coercive control in contexts both unequal and dominating. They are also seen as overzealous in policing black youth, taunting and baiting them as part of a "cops and robbers" game. Police actions are viewed as part of a broader institutional pattern of racism and discrimination. Many blacks reject the excuse that police excesses are isolated or random, preferring instead to see police misconduct as institutionalized in perpetuating white privilege and power. In other words, the police are likened to just another gang in the city, black youths argue, with uniforms, patches, weapons, and an internal code of ethics. Only the legal right to wield force in staking out their "turf" distinguishes police from the "hood."

Police stereotypes are equally one-sided. The police tend to see blacks as problem people whose frequent brushes with the law must be quashed before chaos rules. Blacks are rarely viewed as normal and adjusted; most are labelled as criminals, drug pushers, pimps, welfare cheats, or malcontents, even if evidence suggests a small proportion of youth are blowing things out of proportion, in effect demonizing an entire community for the actions of a few (Henry 1994). Black teens are seen as criminally inclined with a predisposition toward guns, gangs, and drugs, along with a taste for violence imported to some extent from the violent street cultures of the Caribbean. Rarely is much consideration given over to perceptions of black youth as alienated and underprivileged, without much stake in a system where few seem to care if they live or die. Black activists are also denounced as self-serving malcontents whose loose rhetoric and self-serving grandstanding only serve to inflame public resentment toward the police.

Subcultures in Collision

Many of the stereotypes that each has of the other are subculturally driven. Minority youths may identify with "nonwhites" and define themselves in opposition to a white society and everything that it symbolizes (Henry 1994). For male black youth subculture, toughness and assertiveness are core values. Animosity toward police may be part of defining a young male identity (Neugebaur-Visano 1996), what Elijah Anderson (1994) calls an oppositional culture that reflects the code of the street with its craving for respect, power, bravado, and deference. Few are willing to back down from a challenge, especially when group dignity and personal honour are at stake. This assertiveness is given a menacing edge because of the growing presence of guns and drugs. Complicating the relationship is a fatalistic perception that life is cheap, even disposable. In other words, the very masculinities that offer deference and respect will feed directly into actions that bring minority youth into conflict with the law (Gillborn 1998).

Police occupational subcultures are also concerned with the virtues of toughness, assertiveness, and control. Subcultural values are organized around a perception of police as the "thin blue line" between the civilized "us" and the hordes of "them." Core values within the occupational subculture include the following: deference to police authority and control, respect for the badge, a dislike of uncertainty or disorder, an endorsement of even extreme police tactics, a limited tolerance for deviance, a relatively rigid definition of right versus wrong, and a suspicion of those who criticize police authority (Ungerleider 1995). To no one's surprise, those segments of the community that defy police authority or resist arrest for any offence are deeply resented and fiercely resisted. To hit an officer is a breach of trust in the sanctity of the uniform, Simon Holdaway (1996) writes, and any "dis" of the sacred invites a retaliation of physical force. The need to appear in control at all times is especially pivotal to an occupational self-image (James and Warren 1995). Police are employed by the state to exercise control through law and order, and enforcement can occur only when taking charge. Conflict, when it occurs, is likely in situations that are difficult to control because of resistance to arrests, hostile audiences, uncooperative victims, abusive offenders, and intoxicated patrons (Ungerleider 1995).

To what extent is "normal policing" different from policing of minorities? According to Holdaway (1996), police do not activate a separate compartment of their mind labelled "race" or "black" when they encounter minority youth, but assimilate general ideas about routine policing into interaction with "others." The distinction between "normal policing" and policing of minorities may be overstated, in other words, in that the variable "race" may be irrelevant in racializing outcomes, depending on the social and cultural context. Thus any abuse of police power is often triggered by interactions that influence the manner in which everybody is policed—black or white. Those situations that (a) challenge police conception of normalcy and order, (b) invoke disrespect for police advice or refusal to defer to their status as legitimate authority, or (c) involve those who are typecast as deviant, dangerous, complaining, and discredited may be more likely to elicit a physical retaliation (James and Warren 1995). The potential for confrontation is only too real when such a controlling authority confronts an increasingly uncontrollable force.

Black and White and Red In Between

It is quite obvious that both police and minority youths display stereotypical perceptions of each other. However inaccurate, these misconceptions do not make them less real in terms of their consequences. Perception *is* reality where interaction and communication are involved. The cumulative impact of these stereotypes is particularly hard on both sectors. The combination of low police morale, high suicide rates, and increased attrition rates may reflect the costs of incorrectly reading the situation. Failure of police to go beyond stereotypes may take a toll by further marginalizing minority youth lives and life chances. The criminalization of minority street behaviour amplifies the labelling of youth as potential troublemakers, while the racialization of crime has the effect of perpetuating the criminal injustice cycle. Still, the onus of responsibility for identifying and eliminating barriers to improved service would appear to lie with the service provider rather than those who have little choice but to be processed by the system (also Ramsden 1995).

A democratic society expects its law enforcement agents to be answerable for their actions. Some degree of accountability to the community is also anticipated. Police initiatives to improve lines of communication with the community have been moderately successful. But attempts to initiate positive reform in preventative policing are undermined by entrenched subcultural values among police that revel in a "kick-ass" style of policing. The police as an institution appear reluctant to engage community involvement, preferring, for the most part, to remain a "closed shop" (Henry et al. 1995). The interplay of defensiveness, suspicion, and hostility is likely to isolate police from the community they serve and protect. This estrangement is reinforced by bureaucratic structures that endorse conservatism, distance from the community, hierarchy, division of labour, and a paramilitary chain of command. Any potential for positive police–minority relations is diminished by the realities of incident-driven policing, with its focus on charges and arrests. Interactional patterns are further hampered by ineffective race-awareness training. What little most officers receive has been conducted by poorly trained, sometimes unmotivated, officials. Much of the education has been geared toward cultural sensitivity, but such a focus may have the effect of reinforcing stereotyping while doing little to improve police–minority relations (Ungerleider 1992). Educating police officers about different cultures may have the opposite effect of reinforcing a view of "them" as really different and deserving of differential treatment (Holdaway 1996). Few police services have the resources—or the courage—to conduct antiracist training for uprooting the racist and discriminatory aspects of police behaviour (see Kivel 1996).

In short, police in Canada have come under pressure from different quarters. Urban police work under stressful conditions: Split-second decisions have to be made over matters of life and death in environments that rarely appreciate the pressure cooker of contemporary policing. Compounding the pressures of police work is the need to appear efficient and in control at all times (James and Warren 1995). They are accused of losing the fight against crime because of outdated workplace styles. Allegations of harassment, brutality, double standards, intimidation, abuse, corruption, and racism have fuelled the fires of criticism toward police. Additional questions arise over police effectiveness and efficiency in a society that is increasingly diverse, ever changing, and more uncertain. Loss of public confidence raises certain questions over breakdowns in police–minority relations: Is police misconduct an isolated act, or is it pervasive and structurally rooted? Is policing marred by a few "bad apples," or is it rotten to the core? What is it about policing that creates "bad" officers? Does the "badness" reside in (a) the recruitment and selection process; (b) the nature of police work; (c) the organizational framework; (d) negative work experiences; or (e) the type of personality supposedly attracted to policing? The concept of multicultural policing is seen as one way of deflecting this potential crisis in police legitimacy while restoring public confidence in policing a multicultural society (Fleras et al. 1989).

Bridging the Gap: Toward Multicultural Policing

Police throughout Canada have attempted to bridge this multicultural gap, if only to open lines of communication and to prevent any further deterioration in their relationship within a multicultural public (see also McNeill 1994). Recruitment of minority police officers is widely heralded as a first step in restoring community confidence in law enforcement. Specific initiatives have been designed and implemented to secure a proportion of visible minority officers commensurate with their numbers in the local population. Proactive recruitment strategies have included the following: (a) comprehensive advertising campaigns through the ethnic media; (b) career day and recruitment sessions at secondary and post-secondary schools; and (c) direct appeals to visible minority organizations within the community. Visible minority police officers are also encouraged to actively recruit within the community by virtue of their ethnic links. This reliance on sustained personal encounters and in-depth follow-ups (involving home visits and consultation) is perceived necessary to diffuse community misperceptions about the police. However, there is no assurance that minority police officers are anxious to serve in minority communities in light of conflicts of interests and competing loyalties (see McNeill 1994; Kivel 1996). Additional attempts to "multiculturalize" the police have incorporated the following organizational adjustments: looser weight and height restrictions, which traditionally discriminated against minority applicants; appearance regulations have also been modified in light of recent decisions by the RCMP to allow turbans as a head covering, by the Peel Regional Police to permit kirpans (Sikh ceremonial sword), and by the Calgary police (and RCMP) to accept braided hair among First Nations officers. These modifications, however modest or symbolic, do signify a growing willingness to make adjustments that are inclusive of Canada's diversity.

Of those initiatives at the forefront of multicultural policing, few have had the profile or potential as community policing (Fleras 1998). Broadly speaking, community policing is about redefining the nature of police work by reworking its relationship to the communities they serve and protect. More specifically, community policing can be seen as a reaction to limitations in conventional policing styles that had the intent and effect of distancing police from ethnic community involvement (Bayley 1994). Professional crime-fighting models promoted a view of police as a highly trained and mechanized force for crime control and law enforcement. Police work could be described as incident driven and complaint-reactive, and its effectiveness was measured by random car patrols, rapid response rates, and high conviction and clearance rates. Structurally, police were organized into a paramilitaristic model of bureaucracy involving a top down chain of command and control. Rewards and promotions were allocated on the basis of the big catch or unswerving loyalty to the force.

By contrast, community policing is about transforming the police from "force" to a "service." It can be defined as a strategy that police have adopted to deter crime by successfully engaging the public as partners in crime prevention (see Moir and Moir 1993). Community policing is about establishing a closer and more meaningful partnership with the local community as part of a coherent strategy to prevent crime through proactive efforts in problem solving. The community is defined as an active participant in crime prevention rather than a passive bystander. The police, in turn, are expected to shed their "crime-buster" image in exchange for proactive styles that embody a willingness to cooperate with increasingly diverse communities through the establishment of liaisons and communications (see Shusta et al. 1995). Four principles undergird the concept of community-based multicultural policing.

1. *Partnership perspective:* A partnership status entails adjustments in police perception of the community. A partnership is committed to the ideal of police working with the community to prevent crime. A working partnership rejects the view of the police as experts with exclusive credentials for crime control. In its place is an image of police as "facilitators" and "resource personnel" who cooperate by working alongside citizens.

2. *Prevention/Proactive:* Arguably, all policing is concerned with crime prevention. Whereas conventional policing endorsed law enforcement as the main deterrent to criminal offending, community policing endorses prevention through community partnership as the preferred alternative. Proactive approaches attempt to deal with problems before they arise rather than after the fact ("an ounce of prevention = a pound of cure"). Prevention strategies revolve around proactive mechanisms designed by the community in consultation with the police.

3. *Problem solving:* Problem solving cuts to the core of community policing. Many have criticized the futility of continuous responses to recurrent incidents in the same area by a small number of repeat offenders. What is required is a style that diagnoses the underlying causes rather than just responding to symptoms (Saville and Rossmo 1995). A problem-solving strategy seeks to (a) isolate and identify the underlying causes of recurrent problems, (b) evaluate alternative solutions, (c) respond by applying one or more solutions, (d) monitor the impact, and (e) redesign solutions if feedback is negative.

4. *Power sharing:* A commitment to power sharing with the community is essential to community policing. Without a sharing of power, community policing is simply tokenism or a publicity stunt to offload responsibilities for burdensome tasks. Police are

under pressure to share power by loosening up organizational structures, transferring authority and resources to communities, and implementing mutually agreed-upon goals. The ability to identify, prioritize, and apply creative solutions to problems by way of meaningful input into the design and delivery of programs is also predicated to some degree on a sharing of power.

To Sum Up A commitment to diversifying policing cannot be taken lightly. With Canada in the midst of a demographic revolution, it is only a matter of time before mandatory measures are imposed to improve effective multicultural policing for all sectors of Canadian society. Policing from top to bottom must become better acquainted with the multicultural community in terms of its varied needs, entitlements, demands, and expectations. A commitment to diversity also compels the police to view cultural differences as a resource of potential value in preventing crime. The principles of community policing appear to offer the best multicultural option for doing what is workable, necessary, and fair. But until there is a collective mindset shift toward acceptance of multicultural communities as partners in preempting crime before it starts, the vision of Canada as different yet equal will continue to stumble.

CHAPTER HIGHLIGHTS

- The concept of putting multiculturalism to work is concerned primarily with "engaging diversity" through institutional accommodation. But endorsement of multicultural principles is one thing; efforts to operationalize the multicultural engagement with diversity at institutional levels may be quite another challenge.

- The media, education, and police services are but three of the institutions that are called upon to respond to social, demographic, and political pressures in a society that is changing, diverse, complex, and uncertain.

- Institutional change is evident not only at the level of organization and delivery, but also in terms of initial assumptions and goals. Without diminishing the impact of the changes that have taken place, the gap between expectations and reality remains a cause for concern.

- The concept of institutional accommodation is concerned with improving an organization's representation, workplace climate, operational procedures and rules, and service delivery in a multicultural society.

- The most common barriers to institutional accommodation are people, hierarchy, bureaucracy, corporate culture, and occupational subculture.

- Canada's media industry has been remiss in responding to the challenges of diversity and institutional accommodation. Such an omission creates problems, since the media possess the cultural capacity to define what is acceptable and good in society.

- Media mistreatment of minorities falls into one of four categories, regardless of medium (print versus electronic) or outlet (advertising, news, TV programming): invisible, stereotypes, social problems, or ornaments.

- Recent initiatives to put multiculturalism to work are to be applauded. But accommodation is slow and gradual, in part because of resistance created by the commercial logic of the media.

- There are three approaches to education and diversity: assimilation, multiculturalism, and antiracism. Educational agendas have historically revolved around the principles of assimilation, creating a challenge to the development of an institution that is receptive to diversity under the multicultural umbrella.

- Three types of multicultural education are shown to exist. Enrichment multicultural education is concerned primarily with celebrating differences. Enlightenment education is focused on informed and critical understanding of Canadian race, ethnic, and aboriginal relations. Empowerment education is geared toward the empowering of racial minorities and aboriginal peoples by taking steps to overcome the monoculturalism of conventional schooling.

- Antiracist education differs from multicultural education. Antiracist education is concerned with isolating and challenging expressions of racism (both personal and institutional) through direct action.

- Police–minority relations are currently experiencing a crisis. The sources of the problem are varied but invariably include problems of perception, communication, lifestyle differences, and authority patterns in society. That gap in power suggests that police are in a difficult position when asked to solve problems that lie beyond their jurisdiction.

- Multicultural policing by way of community policing represents an effort to close the institutional gap between the police and multicultural communities. Initiatives in this area tend to ignore the social context in which police–minority relations are constructed and maintained.

- Community-based and culturally sensitive policing are riding a popular wave at present. The principles are widely accepted, but much more difficult to implement because of bureaucracy and occupational subcultures.

KEY TERMS

antiracist education
community-based policing
empowerment multicultural education
enlightenment multicultural education
enrichment multicultural education
framing the news
institutional accommodation
institutional inclusiveness
institutions as contested sites
media as systemic discrimination
media stereotyping
minorities as problem people
multicultural education
multicultural policing
news as discourse in ideology
professional crime-fighting model

REVIEW QUESTIONS

1. Compare and contrast the different models of multicultural education in terms of assumptions, objectives, and intended effects.

2. Compare and contrast antiracist education with multicultural education with respect to focus, objectives, concerns, scope, and outcomes.

3. How are multicultural minorities and aboriginal peoples portrayed by the media? Why? How does this present a problem in Canada's multicultural society?

4. Indicate what, if anything, can be done to improve media images of multicultural minorities and aboriginal peoples. Keep in mind both the commercial and organizational context in which changes must occur.

5. What are the basic problems underlying police–minority relations in Canadian metropolitan regions? What steps have been taken to alleviate these problem areas?

6. What is community policing, and how does it hope to improve minority–police relations? What problems may interfere with its implementation?

7. What do we mean by institutional inclusiveness? What are the components that comprise an inclusive institution? What barriers exist that may preclude the institutional inclusion of diversity?

RECONSTITUTIONALIZING CANADA

CASE STUDY 11-1	Political Correctness: The Politics of Inclusion

Political correctness is one of those curious turns of phrase that somehow manage to stop any conversation in its tracks. The concept itself is difficult to define, much less to defend, because of its lack of tangible referents. Moreover, since the early 1990s, the term has been in a linguistic free fall, with the result that it can refer to anyone or anything that departs from long-held custom (Hurst 1998). Nobody has ever defined herself as politically correct, although many take a perverse delight in sticking it to others. In conjuring up images of a humourless, pinched personality that unthinkingly hops aboard intellectual fashions or trendy causes and foists them on others, being labelled politically correct is worse than being called a racist (Hurst 1998). To make matters worse, politically correct is neither an identifiable ideology (such as Marxism) nor a coherent social movement (such as feminism), even if the terms have the effect of positioning the accuser as much as the accused. For leftists, political correctness serves as a reminder to speak and act correctly with respect to minority rights and values (for example, refusing to question immigration on racial terms). For conservatives, political correctness relays images of being forced to speak and act in ways that infringe on their rights and values (for example, the right to question unlimited immigration from certain sources). In the final analysis, political correctness is a notoriously hazy term that can be used across a range of often contradictory political positions. It can also mean whatever a person wants it to mean, for as James Raskin concludes: "As a description of political ideas, 'political correctness' expresses, literally nothing. It is an empty vessel of a signifier into which meaning is poured on a purely expedient and ad hominem basis."

Mindful of the disarray and the slippery terrain, any working definition of political correctness is likely to meet resistance. We prefer to define **political correctness** as a *term of derision* by the neoconservative right and liberal left for slandering those who promote a more inclusive society. Political correctness is situated within the context of a right wing backlash against active steps to improve "institutional inclusiveness" when these steps are seen as imperiling free expression because of a misguided attempt at social engineering (Abramowicz 1991). The politically correct have been caricaturized for their bullying tactics in making people afraid to say what they think for fear of being censured or criticized (see Brennan 1991). Those labelled as politically correct are denounced as "stooges" in defence of this proposed social/moral order; they also are castigated for their aggressiveness and rigidity in suppressing debate to silence opposition or terminate debate. In turn, those who hurl charges of political correctness are accused of hiding behind a smokescreen that camouflages reactionary agendas. At the core of this debate over political correctness are reaction and resistance to the principles of inclusion in a multicultural society. Political correctness symbolizes the site of a struggle between those who want to defend tradition and those who want a new kind of society. It also raises the challenge of whether intellectual freedom and multiculturalism are mutually exclusive. Or do social and cultural policies based on sensitivity to others lead to censorship in speech or action?

Such a contested struggle says a lot about the challenges of **reconstructing Canada** along pluralistic lines.

Genesis

The concept "political correctness" originated among socialist and middle class social movements during the 1960s (Kohl 1991; Weir 1995). Once employed in a mildly deprecating sense among leftists for occasional lapses into rigidity or dogma, the term evolved into a kind of in-joke within radical circles for chiding ideologues who either memorized an ideological lexicon or approved of the party line even in the face of contradictory evidence. The term was expanded to single out commitment from hypocrisy. Among cohorts, it provided a gently reproving way of admonishing those who mistakenly associated progressive political engagement with puritanical language codes, flamboyant posturing, and correct poses (Raskin 1992). The label was occasionally reserved for those "designer" radicals who sported all the right "buttons" or slogans, but rarely put principles into practice when confronting militarism or repression. The reproach also drew attention to inconsistencies in the lives of do-gooders, the same activists who protested against foreign injustice in some remote corner of the world, but who thought nothing of abusing their partners or ripping off the system. In short, to be rebuked as politically correct within leftist circles was not a case of being too radical, but rather of too much insincerity; that is, a level of engagement consisting of "frozen politics of empty gestures" with a surplus of "preachy self-righteousness, but a deficit of analysis and courage" (Raskin 1992:31).

From Irony to Putdown

The gist of political correctness as "cosmetic commitment," "doctrinaire rigidity," or "fabricated authenticity" has lingered into the present. Political correctness is perceived as a commitment to diversity and change, but one that is lacking conviction or is so abstracted as to preclude action. Not surprisingly, the politically correct are accused of failing to "walk the talk." Alternatively, it reflects a blind commitment to inclusiveness that is "rigidified" to the point of dogma. Or political correctness is applied to those who are afraid to criticize minority actions or government accommodation for fear of being criticized as "racist" (or sexist or homophobic). In all cases, there is no mistaking the more strident, even sneering, tone associated with the putdown against those who want to reform the world by modifying how we act or talk. The term is applied in a disparaging way to slander individuals who are seen to endorse a political position without critical reflection or any sustained commitment. By contrast, those who disagree with the politically correct dogma portray themselves as courageous and critical in reaction to such mealy-mouthed timidity and cowardice, as expressed in this self-serving phrase: "...this may not be politically correct, but..." (see Trillin 1993).

The revival of political correctness as a term of derision can be properly understood within the context of a conservative backlash against the forces of diversity and change. Stripped of its irony and applied to smear any progressive change, the concept has been co-opted by neoconservatives who wrap themselves around the flag of free speech to discredit any move toward inclusion of the historically disadvantaged (Richer and Weir 1995). Conservative elements have appropriated this expression as a semantic club with which to bash the credibility of these "zealots," in the same way the phrase "knee-jerk liberalism" once denounced everyone who hopped aboard every chic-leftist issue because of peer pressure (Raskin 1992). What we have, in other words, is a case of "theft" and "inversion"

(Brennan 1991). The conservative right has turned the tables on its enemies in an effort to discredit activism or stifle intellectual dissent without appearing reactionary in the process. The conservative right already has a prior record of appropriating the language of the left (consider the expression "reverse discrimination") to justify retention of traditional values. What sets it apart is its accusation of a left wing conspiracy, both sweeping and coercive, to suppress debate and enforce a politically motivated rewriting of history, society, and culture.

The New Silencers? Who Is Silencing Whom?

That political correctness is often associated with censorship of free speech is a curiosity in its own right. The politically correct are portrayed as the new "silencers," at the sinister edge of a new wave of repression and intolerance with respect to the free marketplace of ideas. But it might be argued that the opponents of political correctness are equally guilty of free speech infringement in their zeal to defend privilege and the status quo. The reactionary platform is no less anxious to restrain serious social analysis by relying on disparaging labels to silence and deter (Raskin 1992). Strangely enough, the politically correct credo—that you can change the world by changing how you talk about it—has been turned back upon the movement itself. This is evidenced by a host of unflattering references, such as the Thought Police, the new Puritanism, the Silencers, the new McCarthyism, the Kindly Inquisitors, the New Conformists, the Intimidators, and the Multiculturalists.

Speech codes are linked with political correctness as a social weapon in the cultural wars between tradition and inclusiveness. Political correctness is defined by the new *Concise Oxford English Dictionary* as "the avoidance of forms of expressions that exclude, marginalize, or insult racial or cultural minorities." It is speaking with regard for the rights and views of minorities, on the somewhat contested assumption that how we talk can influence how we act in advancing an antiracist society (Neuman 1998). The power to define is the power to rule. For example, people who are seen as politically correct may prefer the term "individual with disabilities" rather than "disabled person." The distinction, they believe, is important. The former expression focuses on the individual first, the disability second. The latter reverses the order and puts the disability first, in effect (if not in intent) reinforcing "ablism," that is, discrimination in favour of the able bodied. Those who think the distinction is irrelevant may not appreciate the role of language in the social construction of reality (but see Berger and Luckmann 1967). But use of one expression rather than another says a lot about the speaker and his or her politics—whether the speaker is aware of it or not.

This suggests a new spin on the debate. The struggle is not about political correctness and something else. More accurately, it is between competing versions of political correctness, with each seeking to impose their vision of society (Fish 1994). Of course, both adherents and opponents of political correctness are equally committed to very different political agendas. Both sides are political and neither has a lock on truth or justice. One tends to stress a more egalitarian and social vision of justice; the other is more inclined toward a libertarian and individual ideology. Thus the debate is not over who is in favour of free speech, but on the limits of free expression and how it is to be balanced against other values. Nor is the clash about ends— everyone agrees on equality and justice. The means are central to the debate, and the politically correct are accused of using the same repressive measures that created the problem in the first place (see also *The Economist* 1993). However, the antipolitically correct faction is no less political or politicized.

Instead of criticizing the reality of racism and sexism in society, conservative right factions prefer to offload their fears of inclusiveness on the messengers of change by referring to them as rigid, dogmatic, lacking in humour, and superficial. They also ignore how the consequences of free speech in an unequal society may have the effect of handicapping the historically disadvantaged.

Implications: Thought Control or Social Awareness?

Reference to political correctness can be interpreted in different ways. It symbolizes a struggle over competing visions of society, namely, an inclusive multiculturalism or the status quo. On the one hand are efforts to shore up the prevailing distribution of power and privilege; on the other are moves to challenge the status quo in favour of the historically disadvantaged (McIntyre 1993). To one side are the proponents of formal equality; to the other are advocates of substantive equality and an equality of outcomes. Either way, there are several misconceptions associated with political correctness in need of clarification. Just as it is problematic to see racism in everything spoken or done, so is it a problem to treat the impact of speech and actions as secondary to people's primary freedoms to express themselves. The forces of political correctness are not anti-free speech or against academic freedom, except in cases where free speech serves as a cover for hate speech (Fish 1994). There is no such thing as absolute free expression; restrictions exist by definition. Under political correctness, the concept of free expression is subjected to further negotiation and restriction, in the belief that the world can be changed by changing how you speak about it. In the final analysis, restricting the right of free expression for the powerful may secure the rights and freedoms of those who historically have been excluded from full participation. Herein lies the dilemma: Free speech debate is not between a good and an evil, but rather between two mutually exclusive yet equally valid goods. On the one hand are those who endorse the sanctity of free speech and view any effort at curbing it as nothing short of a civil liberty violation.

On the other are those who concede the primacy of free speech, but not in the absolute sense. The possibility that both positions are "right" poses a prickly challenge in living together with our differences.

INTRODUCTION: NEW GAME, NEW RULES, NEW STAKES

That we live in a period of convulsive social change is surely beyond dispute. Everything is changing so quickly that nothing is certain or predictable except a pervasive sense of unpredictability or uncertainty. The combination of feminist and civil rights movements has rocked the very foundations of society, in the process loosening the moorings that formerly secured a scripted Canadian society. What once were endorsed as universal truths and self-evident virtues are no longer accepted as morally valid. The rules of the established order, in addition to the structures and values around hierarchy and control, are openly challenged and resisted. The impact of this postcolonizing tumult is unshakeable: Canadian society is increasingly a "contested site," that is, a kind of battleground involving a struggle between opposing groups in constant competition over power, status, and resources. To be sure, compared to societies that are plagued by human and natural misery, as an editorial in the *Globe and Mail* (1 July 1996) observed, Canada's relentless inspection of itself reflects the indulgence of a country that by any measure is a solution in search of a problem. True, the challenge of Canadian **society building** may pale in comparison with India and its 16 official languages and five major religions, or an Indonesia of 200 million people across 17,000 islands and representing 300 ethnic groups and 500 languages/dialects (Gee 1998). Still, it is not overly dramatic to suggest that Canada is at a crossroads with regard to its future as a diverse society.

Recent events confirm that society building in Canada involves a series of interrelated but competing national projects. First and foremost is the still unfinished business of constructing a cohesive and overarching society by cobbling Canadians into a moral community of citizens rather than an aggregation of self-seeking individuals. Of equal importance as a national project is the sorting out of jurisdictions and entitlements as they pertain to various subnational units. Aboriginal issues pertaining to land rights and jurisdictions will dominate the agenda at the turn of the millennium. Both government and aboriginal initiatives are seeking a complete restructuring of their collective status and relationship, from one of a colonized dependency to that of a "nation within," with inherent rights to self-government. All eyes are focused on how far developments in "reconstitutionalizing" aboriginal peoples–government relations can be explored before public apathy or a political backlash interrupts this restructuring process. A parallel situation exists at the level of Charter member groups, where English- and French-speaking relations are bordering on collapse. A deepening polarization is increasingly evident as each side engages in acts of brinkmanship to see who blinks first. With the spectre of separation clearly before us, it remains to be seen whether a workable Canadian society can reconcile the "two solitudes" before splitting apart at the seams. At an equally critical juncture is the evolving prominence of Canada's "multicultural minorities."

The interplay of political, demographic, and social changes has initiated a fundamental shift in the bargaining power of this once ignored sector. With the emergence of multiculturalism as a platform and pivot point, racial and ethnic minorities are poised to become major societal players, with the capacity to catapult Canada into as yet uncharted realms.

Few of these developments in society building have occurred without conflict or controversy. That much can be expected in a society where the politicization of diversity has profoundly challenged the very notion of what Canada is for (as described in the Case Study above). Canada is currently in the midst of a social revolution so profound in its impact and implications that it threatens to obliterate conventional definitions of acceptability. What once were vices are now embraced as virtues; strengths, in turn, lapse into weaknesses as the politics of difference scuttle traditional assumptions about right and wrong. The lurching about from one diversity crisis to another has left many Canadians in a quandary over where to go next as both aboriginal peoples and the Québécois challenge the legitimacy of Canada as an exclusive sovereignty. These crises in Canadian identity have evoked different responses. For some, the prospect of a three-nation state within a framework of multiculturalism may provide Canada with the flexibility it requires to withstand the stresses of uncertainty and change. Others disagree, however, and continue to embrace attitudes inconsistent with wholesale renewal or reform. In trying to turn back the clock, they want to fortify Canada against the realities and pressures of the world at large. Still others fall somewhere in between. They are mentally predisposed for change but dismayed by the prospect of the magnitude of dealing with tomorrow's problems by way of yesterday's solutions. There is mounting dismay that many of the initiatives that seemed so promising in the 1970s and 1980s—from multiculturalism to employment equity—have been overtaken by a pessimism that nothing works and nobody cares (see also Kitaro 1997). With minority assertiveness unlikely to diminish in the near future, Canada's society-building skills will be sorely tested in seeking to balance the often competing demands of unity within diversity in a freewheeling global market economy.

Where, then, do we go from here? The title of this chapter, "Reconstitutionalizing Canada," may cast some illumination. Constitutionalisms are central to any reconstitutionalizing process. Constitutionalism refers to those first principles that govern how the different relations in a society are governed (Tully 1995). These first principles may be officially articulated or implicit. For example, the Constitution Act of 1982 officially endorsed the principle of equal opportunity without denying the principle of equal outcomes ("special measures") for the historically disadvantaged. At the same time, the act unofficially endorsed the principle of liberal-pluralism in confirming that what we have in common is more important than what separates or divides (Fleras 1998). The concept of constitutionalism can be applied in different ways. A macro-perspective portrays Canada as a socially constructed and contested site, that is, a diverse and complex yet unequal political arrangement undergoing constant change and adjustment in response to internal pressures and external forces. Group dynamics are being reshaped by the interplay of three major forces, each with competing agendas, unique histories, distinct legal statuses, and different entitlements. Society building in this "adventure called Canada," as Governor General Vincent Massey once deftly put it, is complicated by factors as disparate as geography, history, regionalism, proximity to the United States, the presence of deep diversities, and the temperament of its population. Over time, Ottawa has responded to the challenge of diversity with a package of compromises that continue to elicit admiration—or invoke wrath—at both national and international levels. That these initiatives consolidate Canada's reputation as a pacesetter for engaging diversity is accurate enough. Whether they go far enough in securing Canada's survival remains to be seen.

It would be folly to underestimate the magnitude of the problems confronting Canada. Formidable barriers impede the reconstruction of Canada along more pluralistic lines, as the following questions clearly testify: How will central authorities respond to the increasingly assertive demands of the three major ethnicities without compromising Canada's survival? Are constitutional structures capable of addressing these competing demands without unravelling the social fabric or territorial integrity? Are deep diversities "meltable" into a workable and cohesive unit? Can an inclusive citizenship be formulated that acknowledges both commonalities and differences as a basis for innovative patterns of belonging? In this concluding chapter we set out to explore the possibilities for Canada at a critical juncture in its society-building process. Mindful of shifting tides and competing principles for engaging diversity, this chapter will explore emergent trends in the reconstruction of Canada along aboriginal, Charter group, and multicultural lines. Current debates over citizenship are shown to encapsulate many of the challenges and paradoxes associated with reconstitutionalizing an evolving Canada. A reassessment of Canada's so-called weaknesses as postmodernist strengths will provide a basis for peering into the immediate future. In other words, the chapter makes the following clear: It is imperative to know where we have been, where we are at present, and what the future holds in store if Canada hopes to consolidate its lofty status as a twenty-first-century template for living together with our differences.

DECONSTRUCTING CANADA: KEY THEMES, EVOLVING ISSUES, EMERGENT TRENDS

> We must always remember that Canada is a white man's country.
>
> Prime Minister Mackenzie King, 1948

> In my view, there isn't any one Canadian identity. Canada has no national culture.
>
> Sheila Finestone, Minister of Multiculturalism, 1995

These two quotes, separated by nearly fifty years, give a glimpse into Canada's evolution into possibly the world's first **postmodernist society** (Gwyn 1994). Postmodernism is employed as a rejection of structure, coherence, authority, hierarchy and centredness of any sort; to aspire to these goals is futile and by their nature repressive. In its place is a sense of impermanence and mutability in a radically skeptical world where everything is relative and nothing is absolute (Gwyn 1996). Postmodernist philosophies reject the priority of uniformity and order, best exemplified in the Enlightenment's obsession with universal progress through reason and science. Postmodernists acknowledge the lived experiences of Canadians as fragmented and eclectic, with no obvious centre or continuity, except perhaps in an endorsement of "ephemeralness" as real and unavoidable. Under postmodernism, society is no longer organized around conventional rules of engagement or entitlement. Advocated instead is a new game with a new set of rules whose stakes have the effect of inverting the conventional traditions of right as wrongs, vices as virtues, weaknesses as strengths, and absolutes as uncertainties. The periphery is moving into the centre as a result of these upheavals, while the centre is under pressure to move over and make space. This pluralist ("postmodernist") critique of conventions and values has catapulted debate over diversity to the point where it commands public attention and political concern (Webber 1994).

Liberal democratic societies such as Canada have reacted to diversity by framing policy responses along a continuum that has a bipolar vision of exclusion at one end, assimilation at the other, with varying degrees of incorporation in between (Castles 1997). Three additional responses ply the area in between (see Raz 1994). First is the promotion of tolerance. Minorities are allowed to conduct themselves as they please without penalty, as long as this diversity does not interfere with the culture and public space of the dominant sector. Second is the promotion of nondiscrimination. A nondiscriminatory commitment upholds the principle that minorities have a right to be free from discrimination on grounds unrelated to merit. They also possess an inalienable right to equal opportunity as a natural extension of the individual rights. Third is the promotion of multiculturalism. Multiculturalism can consist of situations where different cultures coexist in territorially separate units (for example, the Inuit in Canada). More commonly, however, it will refer to situations where individuals must share the same space without forsaking either differences or equality. That being the case, individuals of different cultural backgrounds are accorded full and equal participation in society, in effect reinforcing this commitment to equality through accommodation of differences (Raz 1994).

Contemporary debate over the status of diversity in society is highly politicized. The politicization of diversity signals a shift from earlier eras when government policies routinely endorsed the superiority of majority values and institutions. But a profound cultural and demographic shift has uprooted Canada from its anglocentric moorings, with a corresponding reassessment (deconstruction) of race, ethnic, and aboriginal dynamics. Aboriginal peoples and minority groups are no longer willing to bide their time on the sidelines; they are actively and openly competing for scarce resources. In this sense, minority women and men are cresting the wave of what Michael Adams (1997) calls a sea change in Canada's social values—from an authoritarian pyramid to a more egalitarian model of societal functioning anchored in pragmatism, flexibility, and egalitarianism. Whereas the minority poor and different were socially indoctrinated to stay in their place, nobody knows their place anymore in a postmodernist world, and many are unwilling to stay below the deck, metaphorically speaking, of a sinking Titanic. Transformations of such magnitude make it doubly imperative to delve into what is going on, and why. The following emergent trends and evolving issues appear foremost as key themes in the reconstitutionalizing of Canada.

From Assimilation to Diversity

Historically, government–minority relations were structured around the policy framework of assimilation and absorption into the mainstream. Loyalty to the Empire defined anglo-Canadian identity, and minorities were expected to tow the line. At times, government efforts to stamp out diversity bordered on the explicit and ruthless; at other times, assimilationist philosophies were consistently applied (if not always explicitly articulated) to achieve national goals; at still other times, the principles of assimilation were tacitly assumed, implicit within or derived from the consequences of government actions. Canada's immigration policy operated on the assumption that the further immigrants departed from the norm of British whiteness, the less desirable—or likely—they were to assimilate. The end result was predictable regardless of technique: the creation of a white anglo-Canadian society that upheld the virtues of God, Empire, and the Dominion. Differences, when tolerated, were relegated into the realm of the private or personal or restricted to the folkloric dimension. This assimilationist orientation was consistent with evolutionary philosophies and racial doctrines that extolled the virtues of Western progress, but denigrated the lowly status of non-Western populations as irrelevant to society building.

Explicit assimilationist agendas began to erode in the face of national and international pressures. Aboriginal organizations attacked the racist assumptions and objectives underlying government policies. In discarding the colonialist mentality of the past, aboriginal leaders displayed a marked preference for arrangements that reflected aboriginal models of self-determination by way of inherent self-government rights over land, identity, and political voice, as a basis for reengaging constructively. Elsewhere, Quebec's demands for quasi-independence drifted into open confrontation with federal authorities. In rejecting the relevance or legitimacy of official bilingualism and federal multiculturalism, Quebec's nationalistic aspirations pounced on issues from sovereignty association to distinct society to secure a French-speaking homeland within the framework of a renewed Canadian federalism (Talbani 1993). Adjustments in the relational status of the multicultural minorities are no less pivotal in the diversification of Canada. Much of this shift can be attributed to a major overhaul in Canada's immigration policies that had the effect of exercising demographic pressure for political institutions to move over and make space. Further adjustments in redefining the national agenda stemmed from the introduction of multiculturalism as government policy in 1971. Promotion of multiculturalism acknowledged the inevitability of diversity as a basis for national identity and society-building unity. It also confirmed how English Canada had been eclipsed by the vision of society as multicultural, with a single-language society, shared institutions and values, and a single citizenship.

From Exclusion to Inclusiveness

Racial, ethnic, and aboriginal groups have long been perceived as fringe players in the unfolding of Canadian society. By policy and practice, Canada perceived itself as a Dominion of white settlers; non-European minorities were routinely defined as a social problem or dismissed as a problem people with annoying and sometimes costly deficiencies. Government efforts were directed at excluding these differences that interfered with the smooth functioning of mainstream institutions, customs, and values. Specific sectors suffered exclusion in different ways. The First Peoples were deemed expendable—on occasion even as obstructionist—for society-building purposes. It took a crisis at Oka to startle policy makers from their complacency and indifference, to belatedly recognize aboriginal peoples as major stakeholders in any reconstruction of Canada. Multicultural minorities were routinely exploited and vilified, then excluded when deemed expendable, particularly if they were of non-European origin. Since the late 1960s, with the "new multiculturalism" (with its postfolkloric focus on equality, accommodation, and race relations), however, diversity has been recognized as a legitimate and integral component of Canada's identity and society building. Multicultural minorities are entitled to make demands on the Canadian state, demands that acknowledge their right to equal as well as equivalent treatment, that is, the same rights as all Canadian citizens as well as equity rights for remedying the effects of past discrimination. Multiculturalism entails support for both conceptions of equality: the right to integrate as equals into the public sphere yet acceptance of differences in both the public and private spheres (Modood 1997).

From Equality to Equity

At one time Canada espoused a racist system that routinely denied political equality and civil rights to racial, aboriginal, and ethnic minorities. Inequality was endorsed as normal and natural in the sorting-out process that determined who got what. There was no need to justify inequality; it simply existed because of accidents of birth or the wrath of God. By the 1960s another shift was apparent. The concept of formal equality was extended to include all individuals regardless of race or ethnicity. Discrimination would no longer be allowed in a system where everyone was equal before the law and initiatives were introduced to remove discriminatory barriers, cultural jealousies, and attitudinal prejudices. But notions of equality underwent a shift in emphasis when it became clear that inequality was deeply entrenched and beyond legislative reform. Formal equality, with its emphasis on equal (as in similar) treatment before the law, was insufficient for people who experienced discrimination on the basis of skin colour. Nor was a straightforward equality of opportunity an answer to the removal of discriminatory barriers; after all, applying formal equality to unequal situations will have the effect (however unintended) of freezing the status quo, further precluding the disadvantaged from competing equally because of staggered starting blocks. Proposed instead was a substantive equity, that is, one that took differences into account by recognizing minority women and men as having different needs and experiences. Under the new equity, in other words, equality of outcomes was more important than equal opportunities; race-specific initiatives than colourblind commitments; structural barriers than cultural impediments; and the collective rights of peoples than formal rights of individuals. Rather than slotting gender, race, and ethnicity into separate categories for entitlement or redress, they are approached as inseparable dimensions of identity and ascription that not only inform relationships between people, but also create interlocking hierarchies of subdomination (Hamilton 1996).

Equity initiatives reflect a change of thinking in framing the causes of inequality. It was widely assumed that cultural differences interfered with minority adaptation into Canada. Minority values and customs, though quaint, were irrelevant or regressive and had to be discarded or compartmentalized for acceptance and incorporation. But by the early 1980s a paradigm shift was in progress, prompted in part by a rapid increase of visible minorities through more liberal immigration policies. Cultural and attitudinal solutions could not solve what essentially was a structural problem. Impediments to advancement were not derived entirely from prejudice and culture, but from institutional constraints, both systemically and chronically embedded, as varied as segmented labour fields, racial division of labour, dual labour markets, and systemic structures of discrimination. These structures combined with relations of power to constrain minority opportunities and life chances. The onus, in other words, lay on the removal of these structural barriers to ensure a level playing field by way of equitable access, treatment, and outcomes.

From Laissez-Faire to Social Engineering

Central authorities have institutionalized diversity as a normal and necessary component of Canada's identity, unity, and prosperity both domestically and abroad. Through policy and practice, the government has adopted an active role in shifting diversity from the side stream to the mainstream, in effect leaving institutions with little choice but to move over and make space. Such was hardly the case in the past when the government played a passive role in the management of Canada's race, ethnic, and aboriginal agenda. Its role was restricted to that of disinterested neutrality—to eliminate the most blatant abuses in the system and ensuring that everyone played (more or less) by the rules. With the diversity agenda firmly in tow, the state has become critically involved in designing more inclusive institutional structures. These initiatives accept the idea that, left to its own, diversity provokes partition. A degree of "management" is required to put diversity to work for both national and ethnic interests. Federal multicultural initiatives are in place to ensure an equality of outcome through participation and involvement, but also to preserve ethnicity and support intercultural sharing. Passage of the Employment Equity Act in 1986/1996 has also confirmed government commitment to engineering social change. The government is now entitled to enact special measures for hiring and promotion to overcome historically imposed disadvantages for certain minorities. Moreover, rather than putting the burden of accommodation exclusively on minority women and men, institutions are under pressure to become more inclusive through a closer examination of rules and procedures that relate to minority representation, access, and equitable treatment.

From Individual Rights to Collective Rights

Passage of the Constitution Act in 1982 and the Charter of Rights and Freedom in 1985 has elevated public awareness of individual rights. Citizens are now better informed, more demanding, and increasingly articulate about their rights as individuals. With several exceptions, however, Canada has not been receptive to the notion of collective rights. Canadian society was steeped in a kind of liberalism that elevated the individual as the vehicle of our productivity and progress (Gwyn 1994). Society was envisaged as a collection of individuals in need of only limited state protection to exercise their rights and obligations from the excesses of the market or government. Anything that enhanced the group at the expense of the individual was viewed as retrograde.

The growing commitment to balancing individual rights with the collective rights of certain minority groups is discernible. Aboriginal peoples and minority groups are concerned that an exclusive focus on individual rights is a luxury that only those in positions of dominance can afford in sorting out who gets what. Collective rather than individual rights are more likely to procure and safeguard advantages for the disadvantaged on the grounds that strength lies in numbers. Collective rights are not opposed to individual rights; nor are they incompatible (Fleras and Spoonley 1999). Under collective rights, the community exercises some degree of control over individuals rights to preserve group solidarity, identity, and survival in the face of internal or external pressure. These collective rights apply only to nations or peoples, such as the Québécois or the First Nations, both of whom possess the mandate and the resources to establish the basis for putting collective rights into practice. Multicultural minorities as a rule are not entitled to collective rights, although initiatives such as employment equity would suggest an exception to this rule.

From Citizenship ("One Size Fits All") to Belonging ("Living Together With Differences")

Passage of Canada's first Citizenship Act in 1947 announced that Canada would no longer serve as another British outpost. Citizenship conferred statutory rights and equal obligations to all citizens without distinction or favouritism, on the assumption that citizenship is a universal category that transcends particular backgrounds and does not exclude others because of who they are or what they do. Core values undergird a universal citizenship: Individual citizens may be entitled to many beliefs and identities, but only one civic identity in public affairs with a mutual set of rights and obligations. But the abstract rationality of nineteenth-century citizenship may be incompatible with Canada's contemporary needs for addressing diversity. The dominance of a unified civic citizenship has been challenged by previously excluded and marginalized groups. The fragmented and decentred natures of these "identity" movements have combined to weaken the universalizing tendencies of a citizenship-based politics. Practitioners of identity endorse affiliation with race, aboriginality, or ethnicity as a basis for belonging to society (Kauffman 1990). For example, an individual may identify first as a Six Nations person, then as an aboriginal person without necessarily forsaking identification with Canada as a Canadian citizen. For citizenship to mean anything in an increasingly diverse and demanding society, it must expand from its universal focus to incorporate the identity demands of the different diversities *without denying differences in the process.* Such a challenge is formidable, especially when the members in question desire a different way of belonging than that envisioned by central authorities (Kaplan 1993).

CITIZENSHIP AS BELONGING: BEING CANADIANS

Shifts in Canadian society building are increasingly crystallized around debates over citizenship and belonging. What do we mean by citizenship? Why in a pluralistic society is there a relationship between citizenship and national identity? How is this relationship expressed? In what way does citizenship within a multicultural framework contribute to the goals of societal unity without ignoring those of minority equality and cultural retention? Can Canada incorporate radically different ways of belonging without shearing the social fabric of society in the process? Attempts to answer these questions induce a rethinking of citizenship as a tool for remaking Canadian society. Citizenship in the past entailed a social contract involving a mutually related set of rights and duties between individuals and the state—a kind of one size fits all. Contemporary citizenship is predicated on the principle that people can belong together in different ways without sacrificing a commitment to the whole or to its parts. Not everyone will agree with our notion of citizenship as (a) overlapping and situational, (b) inclusive of differences yet united in purpose, and (c) responsive to both individual and collective group rights. Many Canadians are baffled by a citizenship in which individuals can identify with the whole yet affiliate with subnational units without fear of contradiction. But a multidimensional view of citizenship not only provides the basis for reconstructing a distinct Canadian identity. It also confirms Canada's cutting-edge status in creating a new way of thinking about society. To the extent that we can accept this mindset shift will say a lot in answering these questions: What is Canada? What kind of country do we want to be? What does it mean to be a Canadian and belong to a country that is politically segmented, socially fragmented, regionally diverse, and increasingly multiethnic (Kaplan 1993)?

Conceptualizing Citizenship

Until 1947 and passage of the Citizenship Act, there was no such thing as a Canadian citizen apart from a Commonwealth context. All persons in Canada were defined as British subjects, with an obligation to conduct themselves in a manner that upheld the language, culture, and identity of England. The Citizenship Act established the framework for creating a new kind of belonging, consistent with being Canadian rather than anglocentric realities. The need to construct an indigenous citizenship became even more urgent with the diversification of Canadian society. Hundreds and thousands of emigrants from war-torn Europe had arrived in the hopes of rebuilding shattered lives. The rights of previously disenfranchised minorities—African-, Japanese-, and Chinese-Canadians—were restored in the rush to put democratic principles into practice. Even aboriginal peoples shook off a once dormant status in exchange for political activism to reclaim their rights. For central authorities, the challenge was unmistakable: This diversity had to be "managed" in a way that accommodated differences but did not impede the construction of a united, identifiable, and prosperous Canada. The challenge lay in cultivating a sense of community among a largely unconnected peoples, with a common sense of purpose and identity as a unifying principle. It is within this context that citizenship evolved as part of a society-building project to achieve the much-vaunted goal of unity within diversity.

Defining citizenship is not as simple as it might appear on the surface. As with multiculturalism, the concept of *citizenship* can be interpreted from different vantage points, depending on context or intent. Broadly speaking, **citizenship** may be defined as a social contract involving rules of entitlement and engagement: engagement, as in the mutually reciprocal set of duties, rights, and obligations that define a relationship between society (the state) and individuals; entitlement, in defining the patterns of who gets what and why. A social contract spells out what both parties are entitled to under an arrangement and what each must concede as part of the transaction. Citizens look to the state for protection of basic rights pertaining to security, opportunity, and survival. The state, in turn, expects citizens to abide by the laws of the country, even when this entails sacrifices and restrictions. Tim Schouls (1997:732) writes:

> The rights of citizenship empower individuals to claim the political entitlements made available to them by those rights, while the responsibilities of citizenship bind individuals to a reciprocal commitment to honour the terms of the rights each citizen exercises...citizenship is a universal entitlement, the position of all citizens is elevated to that of full and equal membership within the state.

Fostering a sense of community, identity, and purpose—a kind of national *esprit de corps*—is of paramount state concern especially when diversity is involved. Citizenship is thus directed at the integration of previously excluded minorities, in the hope of fostering a shared loyalty and society-building commitment to the whole of which they are part. Failure to achieve the goal of a uniform citizenry was generally perceived as a recipe for self-destruction. Not surprisingly, the rationale behind citizenship in Canada (and elsewhere) predictably lay in stamping out differences as inimical to national interests.

The emergence of assertive minority sectors has proven to be challenging to orthodox ways of defining citizenship as a social contract. Strategies that may have worked in the past have proven inadequate to address the highly politicized and collective claims of cultural minorities and ethnic nationalism. Canada, as most modern state-nations, must address the challenges of diversity within the framework of full and equal citizenship. How do societies long accustomed to the virtues of homogeneity create a common citizenship when confronted by the divisiveness of diversity? Some would argue that recognition and acceptance of differences are key to national unity. Efforts to deny differences or to exclude minorities because of language or cultural differences have not worked in the past, and there is no reason to believe that denying differences will be more effective at present. Entitlements under a "universal" citizenship often fail certain marginalized and dispossessed groups because they privilege individual rights over group differences, thus ranking all individuals as similar for political purposes (Schouls 1997). But this abstracted impartiality has proven detrimental in contexts where equal standards are applied to unequal contexts. As Iris Marion Young (1990:124) concedes, in acknowledging that unequals require unequal treatment:

> In a society where some groups are privileged and others are oppressed, insisting that as citizens persons should leave behind their particular affiliations and experiences to adopt a general point of view serves only to reinforce that privilege; for the perspectives and interests of the privileged will tend to dominate this unified public, marginalizing or silencing those of other groups.

Proposed instead under an expansive citizenship is an official recognition—no matter how symbolic—of minority differences coupled with institutional support (funding, language rights protection, political representation, and so on). As far as this position is concerned, equality and the full rights of citizenship can only be fulfilled when a people's differences are recognized and accommodated by way of rights or policies to overcome impediments and advance interests (Kymlicka 1995; Schouls 1997). Disenfranchised groups are entitled to special rights and collective entitlements commensurate with their distinct identities, unique circumstances, and evolving aspirations. The meshing of these differences into an integrated whole provides a rationale for exploring new styles of citizenship, even if minority cultures dissent from the cultural practices of the majority.

Others disagree with this view on two grounds. First, on principle: Citizenship differentiated into "this" and "that" cannot possibly fulfill its basic function of creating shared loyalty, common identity, and patriotic commitment. What is required instead is a type of citizenship in which every person is treated equally before the law. A differentiated citizenship, with its special and collective rights, cannot fit the bill when it induces the demise of a common culture and unifying symbols for bonding citizens into a single framework. Second, in practice: Specifying certain minorities for special citizenship entitlements raises questions about who is entitled to the largest concessions and why. Should special entitlements be aimed at those who have suffered the most and have more to lose without recognition of their rights? Can special citizenship rights be applied to groups that are dispersed or partially assimilated? Or must this concession be restricted to groups that are compact, self-conscious, territorially intact, institutionally complete, and culturally viable? Does such a preferred citizenship make sense only when extended to aboriginal peoples or the Québécois, both of whom joined Canada on the condition that they retain some degree of self-determination over land, language, and identity? Of some note are time concerns: Are special citizenship rights to last only as long as groups experience marginality, then removed when no longer required? Or do these rights exist in perpetuity to ensure equity? That these and related questions have not been adequately answered (at least to everyone's satisfaction) suggests a need to rethink citizenship not as a social contract but as a basis for belonging in a postcolonizing society.

The Kaleidoscope of Citizenship

Canadian society is anchored around the theme of unity within diversity. But this multicultural mantra is not without problems: Too much unity can culturally exclude minorities; too much diversity can dismember unity. The challenge is clear-cut: How does one create a common identity or citizenship in a country where people have the right to be different and belong to separate cultural communities? How are unity and identity fostered when citizens have shown a preference to belong through primary membership in a group (Kymlicka 1995; Editorial, *New Community,* 1997)? One way out of the impasse is through promotion of *universal citizenship.* An alternative route is by engaging diversity through a commitment to *differentiated citizenship.* A third way incorporates both universal and differentiated citizenship to create an *inclusive citizenship.*

Universal Citizenship

Few ideals are as widely admired by Canadians as the principles of *universal citizenship*. One of Canada's foremost sociologists, John Porter, endorsed a version of citizenship that treated everybody alike, with formal legal rights and equality before the law at the core of this universalism. A **universal citizenship** is rooted in the notion of a social contract between the individual and the state involving a mutual and obligatory exchange of rights and duties. In privileging the priority of individual rights, a universal citizenship rejects any type of entitlement rooted in collective or group rights. Promotion of group differences on racial or ethnic grounds—even in the spirit of inclusiveness and progress—can only deter and distract from universal citizenship's main goals (see Gwyn 1997).

A universal citizenship is anchored in the liberal-pluralistic principle that what we have in common as rights-bearing and equality-seeking individuals is more important than what divides us as members of specific identities or groups. Claims for preferential treatment derived from membership in a particular racial or ethnic group are rejected. The problems of inequality and cultural exclusion must be addressed—not by affirmative action plans for aggrieved groups, but through removal of discriminatory barriers that inhibit full institutional participation. To be sure, a universal citizenship does not deny the free and private expression of individual (and even group) cultural identity. Endorsement of these cultural differences, however, should not detract from the citizenship rights of individuals.

Differentiated Citizenship

For liberal thinkers, equality and progress stem from the renunciation of differences and conferral of universal citizenship. For cultural pluralists the opposite is true. Engaging differences as well as the recognition of group-based special needs are central to social equality and national unity. Overcoming a history of cultural exclusion requires a more "expansive" definition of citizenship, one that acknowledges special citizenship rights for meeting the distinct needs of the historically disadvantaged (Kymlicka 1992). As Iris Marion Young (1990) has argued, a universal conception of citizenship is unfair when applied to unequal contexts. Its universality runs the risk of needless conformity while freezing a racialized status quo. The unfairness arises from treating all citizens—regardless of race, class, or gender—as individuals in the abstract rather than as disadvantaged members of real groups. People who identify with minority groups *are* different: Collectively, they have different needs, aspirations, status, and experience; thus solutions must have a collective dimension to address group-based concerns. What is required in such pluralistic contexts is a *differentiated citizenship* that is sufficiently flexible to engage historically excluded groups. Three types of **differentiated citizenship** can be discerned (equity, self-determining, and multicultural), with profound implications for living together with our differences (Kymlicka 1992).

Equity   It is widely acknowledged that racial minorities are underrepresented in many parts of Canadian society. Different solutions for improving institutional representation have been proposed as ways of overcoming historical marginality. Citizenship in this case is "differentiated" because eliminating these inequities begins with recognition of minority needs above and beyond those of universal citizenship. As Kymlicka (1992) notes, equity citizenship rights are usually focused around improving institutional access and representation, especially in the political domain, because of historical exclusion from decision-making circles. The conferral of equity citizenship rights is not meant to repudiate the principle of universal citizenship as a basis for equality. It merely confirms its insufficiency in contexts where inequalities are chronic, embedded, and systemic. Nor is there any sense of permanence about these initiatives. Rather, equity and affirmative action measures stay in effect until citizens are no longer differentiated because of exclusion or inequity.

Self-determining   Another type of citizenship is endorsed by aboriginal peoples and the Québécois. In this view, the inherent rights of peoplehood coupled with the principle of self-determination are simply unworkable under a universal citizenship. The rationale is straightforward: Unlike other racial and ethnic minorities, aboriginal peoples and the Québécois are each historically a community, possess some degree of institutional self-sufficiency, occupy a territory or a homeland, share a distinct language and culture, and are encapsulated by the boundaries of a larger political community. As peoples or nations, their demands as citizens go beyond universal or equity citizenship; they include claims upon the state for control over land, culture/language, and identity; the right to self-government and jurisdiction over matters of direct relevance; and a transfer of power from central authorities (devolution) rather than mere political representation or institutional accommodation.

The collective and constitutional right to survive as a group is central to this notion of self-determining citizenship. Canada is envisaged as a federation of equal communities, each having the self-determining rights to flourish as "peoples" within a broader framework of citizenship. As far as they are concerned, both aboriginal people and the Québécois have entered into agreement with Canada—and have even transferred powers to this effect—but not at the expense of their self-determination rights over internal matters. Failure of Canada to meet the terms of this agreement entitles the "signatories" to withdraw from the arrangement. Not surprisingly, the concept of self-determining citizenship is perceived as threatening to many Canadians since it (a) treats some as more equal than others, (b) elevates special group rights over individual rights, and (c) undermines the legitimacy of the political community at large.

Multicultural   In between equity and self-determining citizenship is one that focuses on multicultural rights. Immigrant-based groups are anxious to secure some degree of official support for protection of their ethnocultural heritage. Multiculturalism has emerged as a tool for that advancement. A multicultural citizenship officially confirms the validity of diversity and provides institutional support (for example, funding) for its survival. Ethnicity is acknowledged as legitimate and valuable, and a long-term commitment to cultural support is part of the package for full and equal participation in society. In other words, a multicultural citizenship is concerned with preserving cultural particularities without, however, hampering access and equality in political or economic fields. Rather than proposing new structures, multicultural citizenship connotes instead a willingness to work within the system to attain a degree of integration and acceptance. It accepts and takes for granted the authority of the larger community, provided that some degree of accommodation is allowed for cultural differences to flourish.

Inclusive Citizenship

Should the rights of citizenship be vested in individuals or collectivities (see McRoberts 1996)? Is it possible to reconcile the individualistic notion of universalistic citizenship with the pluralistic notion of differentiated citizenship without creating severe social stresses (Sigurdson 1996)? The conferral of universal citizenship with its endorsement of formal individual rights is one thing; a differentiated citizenship with a focus on collective group rights and special treatment for minorities is quite another. An *inclusive citizenship* may provide the middle ground that can balance the competing rights and identities at the heart of contemporary citizenships. Each citizen is entitled to an "inclusive" citizenship of several strands. Each strand of citizenship is comprised of a different set of entitlements about who gets what and why. One of these strands emphasizes universal citizenship rights, with rights to individual equality and similar treatment. Another focuses on citizenship rights that acknowledge differences as a legitimate and integral component of belonging to Canada. Entitlements are justified in part on (a) the magnitude of need (formal equality versus special rights), (b) the status of group members (racial, ethnic, or indigenous), (c) the relationship to society at large (collective versus individual), and (d) the nature of the claims against the state (inherent versus conferred).

The concept of **inclusive citizenship** entails the notion of a shared identity. An inclusive citizenship works on the assumption that an equal and cohesive society cannot be constructed around differences alone. Also required is recognition of shared identity (Modood 1997). Attachment to specific ethnic communities is promoted, but this affiliation must be complemented by equally meaningful membership that brings all citizens together, regardless of ethnicity. A shared identity under an inclusive citizenship is based on two principles: First, all Canadians must come around to a sense of "peoplehood," with a pride in "things Canadian," such as respect for cultural differences. To do this, Canadians must concede the insufficiency of surface diversity (such as ethnic dances and foods). Instead, there must be a willingness to work through differences that are substantial and deep. Liberal democratic societies are poorly equipped to respond to demands for recognition of otherness when these "deep diversities" take the form of autonomous territories or separate power bases (Taylor 1992; 1993). Second, Canadians must recognize and accept different ways that each group expresses its citizenship as a belonging to Canada. This distinction is important. Tolerance of differences is less important for an inclusive citizenship than respect for a variety of approaches to diversity and different ways of belonging. Aboriginal peoples may identify primarily with their aboriginality without necessarily repudiating an equally powerful affiliation with Canada through membership in First Nations communities. National unity is thus derived from a shared commitment to value diversity as well as to value it in a different way.

Belonging Together With Our Differences

A half-century ago, the British sociologist TH Marshall argued that citizenship had evolved from the eighteenth-century focus on legal rights and a nineteenth-century emphasis on political rights to a twentieth-century commitment to social rights. The twenty-first century may prove to be the era of cultural citizenship rights. Citizenship will invariably revolve around cultural rights and the right of cultures to define who they are and how they will belong. The cultural politics of citizenship will make one thing very clear: Citizenship is neither uniform nor homogeneous but diverse and evolving and subject to challenge and contestation. Unity in a pluralistic society thrives in a citizenship environment that upholds the principle of agreeing to disagree. For example, aboriginal and Québécois approaches to citizenship may not concur with ours. Minority prescriptions for "managing" diversity may vary from the mainstream. But the survival of a multicultural society is dependent on creating different ways of relating as citizens of Canada. This is no time for the modernist notion of a unitary Canadian citizenship, with a dash of multicultural colour thrown in for good measure. What we need instead is a postmodernist Canada—a country that is moving ahead not in the conventional way of stamping out differences under a universal citizenship, but one that engages diversity as a basis for belonging together with our differences. The challenge is clearly before us, Ruth Lister (1997:66) concludes:

> [R]ejecting the "false universalism" of traditional citizenship theory does not mean abandoning citizenship as a universalist goal. Instead, we can aspire to a universalism that stands in creative tension to diversity and difference and that challenges the divisions and exclusionary inequalities which can stem from diversity.

The viability of an inclusive citizenship, both universal and differentiated yet within a shared identity, is subject to debate. People are alike in different kinds of ways; they also are different in similar ways. We will have to learn to respect both of these dimensions as part of our efforts at belonging together by being apart.

"THIS ADVENTURE CALLED CANADA"

Canada sits among a handful of modern countries including Australia and New Zealand that are in the vanguard of constructing a coherent yet pluralistic society (Vasta and Castles 1996; Pearson 1996). Its status as a global trailblazer in engaging diversity stems from the "atypical" way Canada has gone about solving its largely atypical problems (see Saul 1998). In shifting from a predominantly monocultural system to one consistent with multicultural principles and egalitarian practices, the canvas of Canada as a bilingual, three-nation state within a multiculturalism framework is being contested and challenged. This transformation is manifest at different levels. The ongoing postcolonization of Canada's aboriginal peoples has evolved to the point where the reality of inherent aboriginal self-government rights is falling into place. The proposed restructuring of Quebec–Ottawa relations within a renewed federalism has proven elusive, to be sure, and may not be resolved without a serious rethinking of what Canada is for. But the two interdependent solitudes have such a vested interest in avoiding disruptive political rupture that this mutual dependency may well yield the pragmatism, flexibility, and compromise to shore up an awkwardly coherent Canada. In the final analysis, the problem may be unsolvable, because of history and structure, and Canadians may have to tolerate a relatively high threshold of ambiguity in coping with the discordancies of society. No less relevant is the prominence of Canada's multicultural agenda, where a commitment to cultural identity, social equality, and civic citizenship has accelerated official multiculturalism to the forefront of strategies for engaging diversity, albeit not without criticism and backlash. Few Canadians have been untouched by these diversity initiatives. Nevertheless, the politics of working through differences has put Canada in the enviable position of, arguably, being the world's least imperfect society.

The challenges confronting liberal democracies such as Canada should not be underestimated. Minority demands for greater representation and inclusion in societies have brought into question a host of thorny questions about (a) the legitimacy of minority identity claims, (b) the affiliated notions of minority rights, and (c) the very assumptions that historically have undergirded state-nations. All societies, including Western liberal-democratic systems, exist as exercises of the collective imagination, in part because of people's desire to belong to something they can call their own (Anderson 1991). The onus is on creating a society that comprises a moral community of communities to be nurtured rather than a treasure trove for individuals to plunder. Equally important in this society-building process is a fostering of political union with a sense of shared core values, a common vision, a sense of belonging and commitment, a workable citizenship, and a singularity of collective purpose.

On balance, Canada appears to have been relatively successful in balancing these awkward demands with minority rights, even if the juggling act tends to be wobbly at times. Such an achievement is not to be sneered at. "Canada is not a real country," Lucien Bouchard reminded English-speaking Canadians, but a mishmash of immigrants. In the final analysis, Canada *is* an idea and a set of ideals ("ideology") rather than a nation with a history or a people, and it this fundamental ambiguity that underscores the contradictions in Canadian society building. So, too, does Jody Berland, writing in *Border/Lines,* point to Canada as an excuse waiting to happen: There is no real political, economic, or cultural reason to justify Canadian society, nationality, or identity. Canadians have little in common, not even a language, no shared ancestors or genetic pool, no origin myths, and few common rituals except a commitment to public institutions such as universal health care. Even Canada's economy is patterned on a natural north/south flow, rather than an east/west pull. In short, Canada is not so much a mosaic as a complex matrix of defining lines and "decomposable subelements" that expand or contract in response to the vagaries of multiple identities and competing sovereignties under a single polity.

External pressures complicate the society-building challenge of forging unity from diversity. The world we occupy is engulfed by two mutually exclusive yet extremely powerful forces (Nelson and Fleras 1998). On the one hand are the universalizing (and homogenizing) forces of a freewheeling global market economy. Transnational movements of goods and services, as well as jobs and investments, are conducted with little regard for societal boundaries. Advances in information technology tend to render national borders increasingly porous and difficult to monitor and control. On the other hand, the fragmenting forces of insurgent ethnicities are poised to dismember and destroy. Radical ethnicities and ethnic nationalisms are largely indifferent to the legitimacy of the nation-state, but often willing to jettison this arrangement for parochial interests (Ignatieff 1993). This interplay of centrifugal and centripetal forces promises to reconfigure the political landscape of societies large and small. These apparently dichotomous forces are also positioned to contest the concept of absolute state sovereignty in exchange for *de facto* sovereignties that are divided, overlapping, and interlocking.

Two scenarios loom large in light of these opposing forces. The first suggests that a decentralizing Canada may collapse because it lacks any coherent centre. The demise of Canada could stem from a failure to mend social fissures both old and new (Simpson 1993). Critics of multiculturalism (Bissoondath 1994), for example, are skeptical of Canada's prospects. Any policy that encourages diversity, they argue, fosters conditions for ethnic divisiveness because of real or imagined grievances. Others disagree with such a gloomy scenario. By virtue of its very decentredness, Canada stands on the cusp of becoming the world's first postmodernist society (Gwyn 1994; 1996). In a world that is rapidly changing and increasingly uncertain and diverse, Gwyn asserts, the lightness of being that constitutes Canada may provide a prototype for the ideal twenty-first-century society. Weaknesses conceal strengths or become strengths as priorities change in response to changing circumstances. The fact that Canada represents a political union born out of economic necessity rather than a national spirit created out of violent struggle may work in its favour (Simpson 1993; Eisler 1994). Canada's unity and identity question may perplex and provoke, even infuriate those who live it on a daily basis. But the paradox of Canada lies in its ability to take those differences that divide and transform them into a basis for a coherent yet distinct society (LaSalva 1996). This tension-to-be-negotiated-rather-than-a-problem-to-be-solved may have also contributed to Canada's reputation as open and tolerant, with a willingness to negotiate compromises to achieve workable arrangements (Saul 1998).

We, too, believe that Canada will survive and prosper despite any conclusive proof of this assertion. Societies that are wired for dealing with diversity will have an enormous competitive edge on coping with a freewheeling global marketplace. Canada's advantages stem from precedent and practice in engaging diversity—from the dynamics of French–English duality to the society-building challenges of immigration. Its fortuitousness may originate from yet another unexpected source. Canadians are frequently accused of lacking shared values or national character; our nationalism is muted, lamented, while our sense of peoplehood is fractured along regional and ethnic lines, without any root in history and homeland. This dispassionate, self-effacing nature should not be interpreted as an indifference to Canada, as Richard Gwyn notes (1994). Recent surveys indicate that a staggering 94 percent of Canadians agree that Canada is the best place in the world to live (the highest ranking among all industrialized societies). The United Nations has also placed a similar stamp of approval for five consecutive years, suggesting that Canadian perspectives are not out of line with international perceptions. Other surveys point out that Canadians are among (a) the happiest people in the world, (b) the proudest and most confident in their uniqueness, and (c) those inhabitants of a country that is admired most.

Put bluntly, in a world of diversity, uncertainty, and change, Canada's atypicalness may be its strength. Canadians may possess the kind of temperament best suited for the indeterminancies of the twenty-first century, namely, a dedication to pragmatism, a commitment to civility and tolerance, and a willingness to compromise as a way of constructively engaging the "others." Our multiple and nested identities will allow us to shift or reposition without necessarily experiencing contradiction or dissonance. Our historical experience of muddling through problems rather than having solutions unilaterally imposed by decree paves the way for negotiated settlements between seemingly incompatible aspirations as a preferred way of working through differences. The endless debates over power, resources, and jurisdictions after 130 years of accommodation have evolved into a kind of glue for binding Canadians as well as a lightning rod for defining who we are (Editorial, *Globe and Mail,* 1 July 1996). In a world where rules and conventions are being turned inside out, our threshold for uncertainty and tolerance for ambiguity may stand us in good stead. In a world where a passionate attachment to homeland or culture may maim or destroy, our redemption may reside in an inability to specify precisely what it means to be a Canadian, preferring instead to renegotiate the meaning in terms of rights, principles, obligations, and rules of engagement (MacQueen 1994).

It is in this sense that Canada represents the world's first postmodern society. Instead of a definitive centre that categorically defines identity and unity, Canada is constructed around the principle that when it comes to diversity, nothing is absolute and everything is subject to negotiation and compromise. As the Royal Commission on Aboriginal Affairs (1996) proclaims, such inclusiveness qualifies Canada as a social experiment in proving that dissimilar peoples can share land, power, and resources while respecting and sustaining their differences, including the right to be treated equally irrespective of ethnicity and the right to be treated differentially because of ethnicity. To the extent that Canadians are willing to work through differences, without capitulating to mindless relativism, Canada may yet achieve the goal of being the world's least imperfect society. And what many defined as Canada's weakness—its lack of unity and distinct identity—may prove a tower of strength in a world where certainty and authority may clash with the pervasive humanity-wide consciousness of a free-wheeling global market economy (Erickson 1997). The decentralization within Canada, long thought a bane of our existence, may hold up well in a world where calls for self-determination threaten to fragment and dismember countries. Once reviled in the past, diversity is reconstituted as a potential resource. Through the management of its race, ethnic, and aboriginal agenda, Canada has transformed former weaknesses into contemporary strengths in a way that may consolidate its unity and integrity while securing a competitive edge in a global economy. Perhaps this penchant for snatching virtue from vice will further promote the progressive— if somewhat contested—ways of living together with our differences.

CHAPTER HIGHLIGHTS

- Not everyone is hopping aboard the diversity bandwagon. Resistance and reaction are symbolized by debates over political correctness. Political correctness entails a struggle between those who want progressive change by altering how people think or talk versus those who regard demands for inclusiveness and power sharing as a threat to core cultural values, individual freedom, and national prosperity.

- With the First Nations, the Charter groups, and multicultural minorities vying for power and scarce resources, it is not far-fetched to describe Canada as the contested site of a struggle between opposing forces and competing agendas.

- The interplay and impact of rapid change, growing diversity, and increased uncertainty have contributed to this notion of Canada "at the crossroads" with respect to building a modern and progressive society.

- The reconstruction of Canada along pluralist lines will entail imaginative ways of "reconstitutionalizing" minority concerns while balancing the competing demands of Canada's three major forces.

- Key themes and evolving trends can be discerned in this reconstruction process. Foremost in terms of managing race, ethnic, and aboriginal relations is the shift from a monocultural, assimilationist framework to the accommodation of diversity not only as an important national resource, but also as a basis for government policy and institutional change.

- Other shifts are also noticeable, particularly with respect to changing definitions of equality (from formal to substantive), increased government involvement in managing inequality, a growing focus on the structural determinants of equality, a commitment to accommodate differences and colour-conscious programs, and recognition of the importance of balancing individual with collective rights.

- Many of these contemporary changes are reflected in and reinforced by debates over citizenship as a basis for redefining minority–state relations. This chapter makes it clear that conventional ways of thinking about citizenship ("universal citizenship") will need to expand into more inclusive styles if Canada hopes to survive.

- Talk is one thing when it comes to reconceptualizing citizenship; action is another. It remains to be seen whether the deep diversities envisioned by a more inclusive citizenship can be incorporated into the society-building process without irreparable damage to Canadian distinct society status.

- Canada is increasingly drawn into a set of largely untested rules because of demographic, political, ideological, and social changes. As a result, what once were virtues are increasingly regarded as vices, while former weaknesses are now interpreted as potential strengths.

- The challenges associated with society building should not be underestimated. Conflicting demands and opposing agendas complicate the process of "reconstitutionalizing" a three-nation society, bilingual and multicultural in both policy and practice.

- Canadians possess a relatively high threshold for ambiguity and change because of historical precedents. Such flexibility may enable Canada to emerge as the world's first postmodern society in the progressive management of race, ethnic, and aboriginal relations.

KEY TERMS

citizenship
differentiated citizenship
inclusive citizenship
political correctness
postmodern society
reconstructing Canada
society building
universal citizenship

REVIEW QUESTIONS

1. What are the challenges that await the reconstruction of Canada along pluralist lines?
2. How can Canada be transformed into an inclusive society that is both safe for diversity and safe from diversity?
3. Briefly outline the key themes and emergent trends in the management of Canada's race, ethnic, and aboriginal relations.
4. Discuss the demographic, political, ideological, and social changes that have altered the contours of Canada's social landscape.
5. Compare and contrast the different types of citizenship that are brought to bear in managing diversity.
6. What are the issues that surround the political correctness debate?
7. Evidence suggests that Canada may be advantageously positioned to redefine itself as the world's first postmodern society. Comment on what constitutes a postmodern Canada.

References

Abbate, Gay 1998 "Hate Crimes Increase in Toronto." *The Globe and Mail.* February 26.

Abel, Sue 1997 *Shaping the News. Waitangi Day on Television.* Auckland: Auckland University Press.

Abella, Irving 1989 *A Coat of Many Colours: Two Centuries of Jewish Life in Canada.* Toronto: Lester and Orpen Dennys.

Abella, Irving 1995 "Anti-Semitism is Declining." *Kitchener-Waterloo Record.* May 18.

Abella, Irving and Harold Troper 1991 *None is Too Many: Canada and the Jews in Europe 1933– 1948.* 3rd Edition. Toronto: Lester and Orpen Dennys.

Abramowicz, Lenny 1991 "Why Isn't It Wrong to be Correct?" *The Globe and Mail.* December 30.

Abu-Laban, Yasmeen and Daiva K. Stasiulis 1992 "Ethnic Pluralism Under Seige: Popular and Partisan Opposition to Multiculturalism." *Canadian Public Policy* XVIII(4):365–386.

Adam, Barbara and Stuart Allan 1995 *Theorizing Culture: An Interdisciplinary Critique After Postmodernism.* New York: New York University Press.

Adam, Heribert 1989 "Contemporary State Policies toward Subordinate Ethnics." In *Multiculturalism and Intergroup Relations.* James Frideres (ed.). pp. 19–34. New York: Greenwood Press.

Adam, Heribert 1992 "Ethnicity, Nationalism and the State." In *Beyond Multicultural Education. International Perspectives.* Kogila A. Moodley (ed.). pp. 14–22. Calgary: Detsilig Enterprises Ltd.

Adams, Michael 1997 *Sex in the Snow. Canadian Social Values at the End of the Millennium.* Toronto: Penguin.

Adelman, Howard, Allan Borowski, Meyer Burnstein, and Lois Foster (eds.) 1994 *Immigration and Refugee Policy. Australia and Canada Compared. Volume 2.* Toronto: University of Toronto Press.

Adorno, T.S. et al. 1950 *The Authoritarian Personality.* New York: Harper and Row.

Agòcs, Carol and Monica Boyd 1993 "The Vertical Mosaic Revisited." In *Social Inequality.* 2nd Edition. Jim Curtis (ed.). Scarborough: Prentice Hall.

Aguirre, Jr. Adalberto and Jonathan Turner 1995 *American Ethnicity: The Dynamics and Consequences of Discrimination.* New York: McGraw Hill.

Ahenakew, David 1985 "Aboriginal Title and Aborginal Rights: The Impossible and Unnecessary Task of Identification and Definition." *The Quest for Justice: Aboriginal Peoples and Aboriginal Title.* Menno Boldt and J. Anthony Long (eds.). pp. 24–30. Toronto: University of Toronto Press.

Alba, Richard and Victor Nee 1997 "Rethinking Assimilation Theory for a New Era of Immigration." *International Migration Review* XXXI(4):826–874.

Alberta Report 1994 "Last Rites for White Writers' Rights." April 25.

Alexander, Lincoln 1998 "Mandela and the Fight Against Racism." *The Toronto Star.* September 25.

Alfred, Gerald Robert 1995 *Heeding the Voices of Our Ancestors: Kahnawake Mohawk Politics and the Rise of Native Nationalism in Canada.* Toronto: Oxford University Press.

Alladin, Ibrahim 1996 "Racism in Schools: Race, Ethnicity, and Schooling in Canada." In *Racism in Canadian Schools.* I. Alladin (ed.). pp. 4–21. Toronto: Harcourt Brace.

Allan, Robert 1993 *His Majesty's Indian Allies. British Indian Policy in the Defence of Canada 1774–1815.* Toronto: Dundurn Press.

Alland, Alexander Jr 1996 "Review: The Eternal Triangle: Race, Class, and IQ." *Current Anthropology* 37 (Supplement):151–152.

Allen, Paula Gunn 1986 *The Sacred Hoop: Recovering the Feminine in American Indian Traditions.* Boston: Beacon Press.

Allingham, Nora Dewar 1992 "Anti-Racist Education and the Curriculum—A Priviledged Perspective." In *Racism and Education: Different Perspectives and Experiences.* Canadian Teachers Federation (ed.). pp. 15–29. Ottawa.

Allport, Gordon 1954 *The Nature of Prejudice.* New York: Doubleday and Company.

Amagoalik, John 1998 "The Rebirth of Nunavut." *Aboriginal Voices* (December):27–29.

Anderssen, Erin 1997 "Immigration Overhaul Urged." *The Globe and Mail.* December 3.

Anderssen, Erin 1997 "Lost Generations: Not Indian Enough by Law." *The Globe and Mail.* November 17.

Anderssen, Erin 1998 "Nunavut to be a Welfare Case." *The Globe and Mail.* June 5.

Anderssen, Erin 1998 "Canada's Squalid Secret: Life on Native Reserves." *The Globe and Mail.* October 12.

Angus, Ian 1995 "Multiculturalism as a Social Ideal." Paper presented to the Learned Society Meetings (CSAA) at Montreal. June.

Angus, Ian and Jut Jhally 1989 *Cultural Politics in Contemporary America.* New York: Routledge.

Angus, Murray 1990 "And the Last Shall be First." *Native Policy in an Era of Cutbacks.* Ottawa: Aboriginal Rights Coalition.

Angus Reid Group Inc. 1991 Multiculturalism and Canadians: Attitude Study, 1991. National Survey Report Submitted to the Department of Multiculturalism and Citizenship.

Annual Report 1992 *Annual Report of the Commissioner of Official Languages.* Ottawa: Minister of Supply and Services.

Annual Report 1993 *The Operation of the Canadian Multiculturalism Act.* Annual Report 1991/1992.

Annual Report 1994 *Canada Multiculturalism,* Minister of Supply and Services, Ottawa: Minister of Supply and Services.

Annual Report 1994/95 Annual Report of the Aboriginal and Torres Strait Islander Commission. Canberra Act: Government Press.

Annual Report 1997 "The Operation of Canada's Multiculturalism Act." Canadian Heritage. Ottawa: Minister of Public Works and Government Services.

Anthias, Floya 1998 "Evaluating 'Diaspora': Beyond Ethnicity?" *Sociology* 32(3):552–580.

Apple, Michael 1993 "Series Editor's Introduction." *Race, Identity and Representation in Education.* C. McCarthy and W. Crichlow (eds.). pp. vii–ix. New York: Routledge.

Appleby, Timothy 1998 "Top Court in U.S. Links Race to Crime." *The Globe and Mail.* May 16.

Armstrong, Pat 1996 *Wasting Away.* Toronto: Oxford University Press.

Arthurs, Harry 1993 Keynote Address. *National Symposium for University Presidents on Institutional Strategies for Race and Ethnic Relations at Canadian Universities.* Report of a symposium held at Queen's University at Kingston. February 2–4, 1992.

Asbury, Kathryn 1989 "Innovative Policing. Foot Patrol in 31 Division, Metropolitan Toronto." *Canadian Police College Journal* 13(3):165–181.

Asbury, Kathryn E. 1992 "Building Police-Community Partnerships With Culturally, Racially, and Linguistically Diverse Populations in Metropolitan Toronto." Published by the Council of Race Relations and Policing. Toronto.

Asch, Michael 1984 *Home and Native Land: Aboriginal Rights and Canadian Constitution.* Toronto: Methuen.

Asch, Michael 1989 "To Negotiate Into Confederation: Canadian Aboriginal Views on Their Political Rights." In *We are Here. Politics of Aboriginal Land Tenure.* Edwin N. Wilmsen (ed.). Berkeley: University of California.

Asch, Michael 1993 "Aboriginal Self-Government and Canadian Constitutional Identity: Building Reconciliation." In *Ethnicity and Aboriginality. Case Studies in Ethnonationalism.* Michael D. Levin (ed.). pp. 29–52. Toronto: University of Toronto Press.

Asch, Michael 1997 *Aboriginal and Treaty Rights in Canada. Essays on Law, Equality, and Respect for Differences.* Vancouver: UBC Press.

Asch, Michael and Norman Zlotkin 1997 "Affirming Aboriginal Title; A New Basis for Comprehensive Claims Negotiations." In *Aboriginal and Treaty Rights in Canada.* M. Asch (ed.). pp. 208–230: Vancouver: UBC Press.

Assembly of First Nations 1992 "To the Source." *The First Nations Circle on the Constitution.* Commissioners Report. Ottawa.

Atkinson, Joe 1994 "The State, the Media, and Thin Democracy." In *Leap Into the Dark. The Changing Role For the State in New Zealand Since 1984.* Andrew Sharp (ed.). pp. 146–177. Auckland: Auckland University Press.

Aubin, Benoit 1997 "How Quebec's Language Law May Save Us All." *The Globe and Mail.* October 4.

Auger, Michael C. 1997 "Two Visions, Two Results." *The Globe and Mail.* December 9.

Avery, Donald H. 1995 *Reluctant Hosts: Canada's Response to Immigrant Workers 1896–1994.* Toronto: McClelland and Stewart.

Awatere, Donna 1984 *Maori Sovereignty.* Auckland: Broadsheets.

Badets, Jane and Tina W.L. Chui 1994 *Canada's Changing Immigration Population.* Catalogue No. 96–311E. Published by Statistics Canada and Prentice Hall Canada Inc.

Baker, Donald (ed.) 1994 *Reading Racism and the Criminal Justice System.* Toronto: Canadian Scholars Press.

Baker, Judith (ed.) 1994 *Group Rights.* Toronto: University of Toronto Press.

Balthazar, Louis 1993 "The Faces of Quebec Nationalism." In *Quebec. State and Society.* 2nd Edition. Alain G. Gagnon (ed.). pp. 2–17. Scarborough: Nelson.

Balthazar, Louis 1996 "Identity and Nationalism in Quebec." In *Clash of Identities.* James Littleton (ed.). Scarborough: Prentice Hall.

Banks, James A. 1992 "A Curriculum for Empowerment, Action, and Change." *Beyond Multicultural Education. International Perspectives.* Kogila Moodley (ed.). pp.154–170. Calgary: Detsilig Enterprise Ltd.

Banks, Marcus 1996 *Ethnicity. Anthropological Constructions.* New York: Routledge.

Bannerji, Himani "Popular Images of South Asian Women." *Parallelogramme* 11(4):17–20.

Bannerji, Himani, Linda Carter, Kari Dehli, Susan Heald, and Kate McKenna 1991 "Introduction." In *Unsettling Relations. The University as a Site of Feminist Struggles.* H. Bannerji et al. (eds.). Toronto: Women's Press.

Banton, Michael 1967 *Race Relations.* London: Tavistock Publications.

Banton, Michael 1979 *The Idea of Race.* London: Tavistock Publications.

Banton, Michael 1987 *Racial Theories.* London: Cambridge University Press.

Banton, Michael 1997 *Ethnic and Racial Consciousness* 2nd Edition. London: Longman.

Barkun, Michael 1994 *Religion and the Racist Right. The Origins of the Christian Identity Movement.* Chapel Hill, NC: University of North Carolina Press.

Barnsley, Paul 1999 "Cree Chief Slams Gathering Strength." *Windspeaker* 16(9)(January):1.

Barnsley, Paul 1999 "AFN Poll Provides Ammunition for Minister." *Windspeaker* January.

Barrett, Stanley R. 1987 *Is God a Racist? The Right Wing in Canada.* Toronto: University of Toronto Press.

Barth, Frederick 1969 *Ethnic Groups and Boundaries.* Boston: Little, Brown.

Basch, Linda, Nina Glick Schiller, and Cristina Szanton Blanc 1994 *Nations Unbound. Transnational Projects, Postcolonial Predicaments, and Deterritorialized Nation-States.* Reading, GB: Gordon and Breach.

Bates, Stephen 1997 "One in Three Britons Admit to Racism." *Guardian Weekly.* December 28.

Bauer, William 1994 "How the System Works." *The Globe and Mail.* November 12.

Baureiss, Gunter 1985 "Discrimination and Response: The Chinese in Canada." In *Ethnicity and Ethnic Relations in Canada.* Rita M. Bienvenue and Jay E. Goldstein (eds.). pp. 241–262. Toronto: Butterworths.

Bayley, David "International Differences in Community Policing." In *The Challenge of Community Policing.* D. P. Rosenbaum (ed.). pp. 278–284. Thousand Oaks, CA: Sage.

Beddgood, Janet 1997 "Pakeha Ethnicity?" *SITES.* Spring 35:81–100.

Bedford, David 1994 "Marxism and the Aboriginal Question: The Tragedy of Progress." *The Canadian Journal of Native Studies* XIV(1):101–117.

Beeby, Dean 1998 "Military Sets Sights on Visible Minorities." *The Globe and Mail.* July 21.

Behrens, Gerd 1994 "Love, Hate, and Nationalism." *Time Magazine.* March 21.

Belich, James 1996 *Making Peoples. A History of New Zealanders From Polynesian Settlement to the End of the Nineteenth Century.* Auckland: The Penguin Press.

Bell, Avril 1996 "We're Just New Zealanders." In *Nga Patai: Racism and Ethnic Relations in Aotearoa/ New Zealand.* P. Spoonley et al. (eds.). pp. 144–158. Palmerston North, NZ: Dunmore Publishing.

Bell, Catherine 1997 "Metis Constitutional Rights in Section 35(1)." *Alberta Law Review* 36(1): 180–204.

Bell-Fialkoff, Andrew 1993 "Ethnic Conflict." *The World and I* July:465–477.

Bercuson, David and Barry Cooper 1997 "Some Teen Fatalities Matter Less." *The Globe and Mail.* December 6.

Berg, A. and P. Spoonley 1997 "Refashioning Racism: Immigration, Multiculturalism and an Election Year." *New Zealand Geographer* 53(2):46–51.

Berger, Brigitte 1993 "Multiculturalism and the Modern University." *Partisan Review.* pp. 516–530.

Berger, Peter and Thomas Luckmann 1967 *The Social Construction of Reality.* New York: Anchor.

Berger, Thomas R. 1991 *A Long and Terrible Shadow.* Vancouver: Douglas and McIntyre.

Berkely, Bill 1996/97 "The 'New' South Africa: Violence Works." *World Policy Journal* XIII(4):73–80.

Berry, John W., Rudolph Kalin, and Donald M. Taylor 1977 *Multiculturalism and Ethnic Attitudes in Canada.* Ottawa: Ministry of Supply and Services in Canada.

Berry, John and Rudolph Kalin 1993 "Multiculturalism and Ethnic Attitudes in Canada: An Overview of the 1991 National Survey." Paper Presented to the Canadian Psychological Association, Annual Meetings. Montreal. May.

Berton, Pierre 1975 *Hollywood's Canada: The Americanization of our National Image.* Toronto: McClelland and Stewart.

Bibby, Reginald W. 1990 *Mosaic Madness. The Potential and Poverty of Canadian Life.* Toronto: Stoddart.

Biddiss, Michael D. (ed.) 1979 *Images of Race.* New York: Holmes and Meier Publishers.

Bienvenue, Rita M. 1985 "Colonial Status: The Case of Canadian Indians." In *Ethnicity and Ethnic Relations in Canada.* Rita M. Bienvenue and Jay E. Goldstein (eds.). pp. 199–216. Toronto: Butterworths.

Billingsley, B. and L. Musynzski. 1985 *No Discrimination Here...* Toronto: Urban Alliance.

Bissoondath, Neil 1993 "A Question of Belonging: Multiculturalism and Citizenship." In *Belonging. The Meaning and Future of Canadian Citizenship.* William Kaplan (ed.). pp. 367–387. Kingston/Montreal: McGill-Queen's University Press.

Bissoondath, Neil 1994 *Selling Illusions. The Cult of Multiculturalism.* Toronto: Stoddart.

Black, Jerome H. and David Hagan 1993 "Quebec Immigration Politics and Policy: Historical and Contemporary Perspectives." *Quebec. State and Society.* 2nd Edition. Alain-G. Gagnon (ed.) pp. 280–303. Scarborough: Nelson.

Blauner, Rob 1972 *Racial Oppression in America.* New York: Harper and Row.

Blauner, Rob 1994 "Talking Past Each Other: Black and White Languages." *Race and Ethnic Conflicts.* Fred L. Pincus and Howard J. Ehrlich (eds.). pp. 18–28. Boulder, CO: Westview Press.

Bledsloe, Geraldine 1989 "The Media: Minorities Still Fighting for Their Fair Share." *Rythym and Business Magazine.* March/April:14–18.

Blumer, Herbert 1965 "Industrialisation and Race Relations." In *Industrialisation and Race Relations: A Symposium.* Guy Hunter (ed.). London: Oxford University Press.

Blumer, Herbert 1969 *Symbolic Interactionism: Perspectives and Methods.* Englewood Cliffs, NJ: Prentice Hall.

Blumer, Herbert and Troy Duster 1980 "Theories of Race and Social Action." In *Sociological Theories: Race and Colonialism.* UNESCO (ed.). pp. 211–238. Paris.

Blythe, Martin 1994 *Naming The Other. Images of the Maori in New Zealand Film and Televsion.* Metuchen, NJ: Scarecrow Press.

Boismenu, Gerald 1996 "Perspectives on Quebec-Canadian Relations in the 1990s: Is the Reconciliation of Ethnicity, Nationality, and Citizenship Possible? *Canadian Review of Studies in Nationalism* XXIII(1-2):99–109.

Bolaria, B. Singh and Peter S. Li 1988 *Racial Oppression in Canada.* 2nd Edition. Toronto: Garamond Press.

Boldt, Edward D. 1985 "Maintaining Ethnic Boundaries: The Case of the Hutterites." In *Ethnicity and Ethnic Relations in Canada.* Rita M. Bienvenue and Jay E. Goldstein (eds.). p. 87–104. Toronto: Butterworths.

Boldt, Edward D. 1989 "The Hutterites: Contemporary Developments and Future Prospects." *Multi-culturalism and Intergroup Relations.* James Frideres (ed.). pp. 57–72. New York: Greenwood Press.

Boldt, Menno 1993. *Surviving as Indians: The Challenge of Self-Government.* Toronto: University of Toronto Press.

Boldt, Menno and J. Anthony Long (eds.) 1985 *The Quest for Justice: Aboriginal Peoples and Aboriginal Rights.* Toronto: University of Toronto Press.

Bonacich, Edna 1972 "A Theory of Ethnic Antagonism: The Split Labour Market." *American Sociological Review* 37:547–559.

Bones, Jah 1986 "Language and Rastafaria." In *The Language of Black Experience*. David Sutcliffe and Ansel Wong (eds.). pp. 37–51. Oxford: Basil Blackwell.

Bonilla-Silva, Eduardo 1996 "Rethinking Racism: Toward a Structural Interpretation." *American Sociological Review* 62:465–480.

Booth, William 1998 "New Wave of Immigrants Tests a Dream." *Guardian Weekly*. April 17.

Borrows, John and Leonard Rotman 1997 "The Sui Generis Nature of Aboriginal Rights: Does it Make a Difference?" *Alberta Law Review* 36:9–45.

Bottomley, Gill, Marie de Leveranche, and Jeannie Martin 1991 *Gender/Class/Culture/Ethnicity*. Sydney: Allen and Unwin.

Bourassa, Robert 1975 "Objections to Multiculturalism." Letter to *Le Devoir*. November, 17, 1971. Reprinted in Palmer 1975.

Bourhis, R.Y., H. Giles, J.P. Leyens, and H. Tajfel 1979 "Psycholinguistic Distinctiveness: Language Divergence in Belgium." In *Language and Social Pyschology*. H. Giles and R.N. St. Clair (eds.). pp. 158–185. Oxford: Basil Blackwell.

Bradley, Harriet 1996 *Fractured Identities: Changing Patterns of Inequality*. Oxford, UK: Polity Press.

Bragg, Rebecca 1998 "Why Ph.D.s Are Working As Security Guards." *The Toronto Star*. May 24.

Brennan, T. 1991 "PC and the Decline of the American Empire." *Social Policy*. Summer:16–29.

Breton, Raymond 1964 "Institutional Completeness of Ethnic Communities and the Personal Relations of Immigrants." *American Journal of Sociology* 70:103–205.

Breton, Raymond 1984 "The Production and Allocation of Symbolic Resources: An Analysis of the Linguistic and Ethnocultural Fields in Canada." *Canadian Review of Sociology and Anthropology*. 21(2):123–140.

Breton, Raymond 1988 "The Evolution of the Canadian Multicultural Society." *Canadian Mosaic, Essays on Multiculturalism*. A.J. Fry and Ch. Forceville (eds.). pp. 25–47. Amsterdam: Free University Press.

Breton, Raymond 1989 "Canadian Ethnicity in the Year 2000." In *Multiculturalism and Intergroup Relations*. James Frideres (ed.). pp. 149–152. New York: Greenwood Press.

Breton, Raymond 1991 "The Political Dimensions of Ethnic Community Organization." In *Ethnicity, Structural Inequality, and the State in Canada and the Federal Republic of Germany*. Robin Ostow (ed.). New York: Peter Lang.

Breton, Raymond 1998 "Ethnicity and Race in Social Organizations: Recent Developments in Canadian Society." In *The Vertical Mosaic Revisited*. R Helmes-Hayes and J. Curtis (eds.). pp. 60–115. Toronto: University of Toronto Press.

Breton, Raymond, Wsevolod W. Isajiw, Warren E. Kalbach, and Jeffrey G. Reitz 1990 *Ethnic Identity and Equality: Varieties of Experience in a Canadian City*. Toronto: University of Toronto Press.

Briggs, Vernon M. Jr. and Stephen Moore 1994 *Still an Open Door? U.S. Immigration Policy and the American Economy*. Washington: The American University Press.

Bristow, Peggy (coordinator), Dionne Brand, Linda Carty, Afua A. Cooper, Sylvia Hamilton, and Adrienne Shadd 1993 *We're Rooted Here and They Can't Pull Us Up: Essays in African Canadian Women's History*. Toronto: University of Toronto Press.

Brock Kathy L. 1991 "The Politics of Aboriginal Self-Government: A Paradox." *Canadian Public Administration* 34(2):272–285.

Brown, David 1989 "Ethnic Revival: Perspectives on State and Society." *TWQ* 11(4):1–17.

Brown, Rosemary and Cleta Brown 1995 "Comments. Reflections on Racism." In *Perspectives on Racism and the Human Services Sector*. C. James (ed.). pp. 47–50. Toronto: University of Toronto Press.

Browne, Malcolm W. 1994 "What is Intelligence, and Who Has It?" *New York Times Book Review*. October 16.

Brunt, Stephen 1994 "It's all There in Black and White." *The Globe and Mail*. November 12.

Bryden, Joan 1997 "Aboriginals Request Protection." *The Globe and Mail*. February 18.

Brym, Robert J., William Shaffir, and Morton Weinfeld (eds.) 1993 *The Jews in Canada*. Toronto: Oxford University Press.

Brym, Robert J. 1991 "Ethnic Group Stratification and Cohesion in Canada: An Overview." In *Ethnicity, Structural Inequality, and the State in Canada and the Federal Republic of Germany*. Robin Ostow (ed.). pp. 49–78. New York: Peter Lang.

Buckley, Helen 1992 *From Wooden Ploughs to Welfare: Why Indian Policy Failed in the Prairie Provinces*. McMillian Collier: Toronto.

Buckley, Stephen 1996 "Wife Abuse is the Norm in Africa." *Kitchener-Waterloo Record*. May 4.

Buckner, H. Taylor 1993 "Minorities on Minorities. How Canada's Ethnic Minorities View Selected Canadian Minority Groups." *Working Paper. Centre for Community and Ethnic Studies*. Concordia University.

Bull, Sam 1994 "Federal Government Pursues Assimilation Policies Through Devolution Process." *Solidarité*. Newsletter by Aboriginal Rights Coalition. Vol. 4, No. 2.

Bullivant, Brian 1981 "Multiculturalism: Pluralist Orthodoxy or Ethnic Hegemony." *Canadian Ethnic Studies* XIII (2):1–22.

Burger, Julian 1987 *Report From the Frontier. The State of the World's Indigenous Peoples*. New Jersey: Zed Books.

Burgess, Michael 1996 "Ethnicity, Nationalism, and Identity in Canada-Quebec Relations: The Case of Quebec's Distinct Society." *Journal of Commonwealth and Comparative Politics* 34(2):46–64.

Burnet, Jean 1981 "The Social and Historical Context of Ethnic Relations." In *A Canadian Social Pyschology of Ethnic Relations*. Robert C. Gardiner and Rudolph Kalin (eds.). pp. 17–36. Agincourt, ON: Methuen.

Burnet, Jean 1984 "Myths and Multiculturalism." *Multiculturalism in Canada*. Ronald J. Samuda, John W. Berry and Michael Laferriere (eds.). pp. 18–29. Toronto: Allyn and Bacon Inc.

Burnet, Jean 1986 "Looking Into My Sister's Eyes." Toronto: Multicultural History Society of Ontario.

Burnet, Jean 1989 "Taking Into Account the Other Ethnic Groups and the Royal Commission on Bilingualism and Biculturalism." In *Multiculturalism and Intergroup Relations*. James Frideres (ed.). pp. 9–18. New York: Greenwood Press.

Burnet, Jean and Howard Palmer 1988 "Coming Canadians." *An Introduction to the History of Canada's People*. Toronto: McClelland and Stewart in conjunction with the Multicultural Directorate within the Secretary of State.

Burrell, G., and G. Morgan 1979 *Organizational Theory and Sociological Paradigms*. London: Heinemann.

Campbell, Murray 1997 "Canada Talks the Talk." *The Globe and Mail*. February 22.

Campbell, Murray 1998 "Mediation Suggested in N.B. Forest Dispute." *The Globe and Mail*. April 27.

Canadian Heritage 1997 Programs Headlines: Multiculturalism. Respect, Equality, Diversity. Ottawa.

Canadian Press 1997 "Canadian Aboriginals cited in UN Report." *Kitchener-Waterloo Record*. April 13.

Canadian Press 1999 "Aboriginal Population Expected to Increase Rapidly." *Kitchener-Waterloo Record.* January 14.

Cannon, Margaret 1995 *Invisible Empire. Racism in Canada.* Toronto: Random House.

Cardozo, Andrew 1994 "On Guard for Multiculturalism." *Canadian Forum.* April 14–18.

Carodozo, Andrew 1996 "Harris Tearing Apart System." *The Toronto Star.* September 21.

Cardozo, Andrew 1997 "Immigration Critics Can't Make a Case." *The Toronto Star.* September 8.

Cardozo, Andrew and Louis Musto (eds.) 1997 *Battle Over Multiculturalism: Does it Help or Hinder Canadian Unity.* Ottawa: Pearson-Shoyama Institute.

Carniol, Ben 1991 "The Way We Respond Can Become an Issue." Paper presented at the Remedies for Racism and Sexism Conference. University of Western Ontario, London.

Carter, Stephen L. 1995 "Let Us Pray." *New Yorker.* January:60–62.

Carty, Linda 1991 "Black Women in Academia: A Statement from the Periphery." In *Unsettling Relations: The University as a Site of Feminist Struggles.* Himani Bannerji et al. (eds.). pp. 13–44. Toronto: Women's Press.

Carty, Linda 1993 "African Canadian Women and the State." *We're Rooted Here and They Can't Pull Us Up: Essays in African Canadian Women's History.* Peggy Bristow et al. (eds.). Toronto: University of Toronto Press.

Cashmore, E. Ellis (ed.). 1984 *Dictionary of Race and Ethnic Relations.* London: Routledge and Kegan Paul.

Cassidy, Frank 1991 "First Nations Can No Longer Be Rebuffed." *Policy Options.* May:3–5.

Cassidy, Frank 1994 "British Columbia and Aboriginal Peoples: The Prospects for the Treaty Process." *Policy Options.* March:10–13.

Castells, Manuel (1997) *The Power of Identity.* Oxford: Blackwell.

Castles, S., B. Cope, M. Kalantzis, and M. Morrissey 1988 "The Bicentenary and the Failure of Australian Nationalism." *Race and Class* XXIX(3):53–68.

Castles, Stephen and Mark J. Miller 1998 *The Age of Migration.* 2nd Edition. London: Macmillan.

Castonguay, Claude 1994 "Why More Quebec Voices Aren't Arguing for Federalism." *The Globe and Mail.* July 25.

Caulfield Timothy and Gerald Robertson 1996 "Eugenics Policies in Alberta: From the Systematic to the Systemic" *Alberta Law Review* xxxv(1):59–81.

CAUT "CAUT Calls on Ontario Gov't to Withdraw Framework." *CAUT Bulletin ACPPU.* p.1. June 1994.

Caws, Peter 1994 "Identities. Cultural, Transcultural, and Multicultural." In *Multiculturalism. A Critical Reader.* D. T. Goldberg (ed.). pp. 371–387. Oxford: Blackwell.

Chagnon, Napolean 1998 *The Yanomamo.* 5th Edition. New York: Holt Rinehart and Winston.

Chambers, Gretta 1996 "Distinct Clause Needs Study, Not Merely Semantic Jigging." *The Globe and Mail.* April 22.

Chan, Janet 1996 "Police Racism. Experiences and Reforms." In *The Teeth Are Smiling. The Persistance of Racism in a Multicultural Australia.* E. Vasta and S. Castles (eds). pp. 160–172. Sydney: Allen & Unwin.

Chan, Janet 1997 *Changing Police Culture. Policing in a Multicultural Society.* Cambridge, UK: Cambridge University Press.

Chartrand, L.A.H. Paul 1993 "Aboriginal Self-Government: The Two Sides of Legitimacy." *How Ottawa Spends. A More Democratic Canada...?* Susan D. Phillips (ed.). pp. 231–256. Ottawa: Carleton University Press.

Chartrand Paul 1992 "Aboriginal Peoples, Racism, and Education in Canada: A Few Comments. In *Racism and Education: Different Perspectives and Experiences.* Ontario Teachers Federation (ed.). Ottawa. pp. 7–14.

Chartrand, Paul 1996 "Self-determination Without A Discrete Territorial Base?" In *Self-determination: International Perspectives.* D. Clark and R. Williamson (eds.). pp. 211–234. London: Macmillan.

Cheney, Peter 1998 "The Money Pit: An Indian Band Story." *The Globe and Mail.* October 24.

Chesler, Mark A. and James Crowfoot 1989 *Racism in Higher Education 1: An Organizational Analysis.* PCMA (Program in Conflict Management Alternatives). Working Paper No. 21. November.

Cheyne, Christine, Mike O'Brien, and Michael Belgrave 1997 *Social Policy in Aotearoa/New Zealand.* Auckland: Oxford University Press.

Clark, Bruce 1990 *Native Liberty, Crown Sovereignty: The Existing Aboriginal Right of Self-Government in Canada.* Kingston: McGill-Queen's University Press.

Clement, Wallace 1998 "Power, Ethnicity, and Class: Reflections Thirty Years After the Vertical Mosaic." In *The Vertical Mosaic Revisited.* R. Helmes-Hayes and J. Curtis (eds.). pp. 34–59. Toronto: University of Toronto Press.

Clift, Dominique 1989 *The Secret Kingdom. Interpretations of the Canadian Character.* Toronto: McClelland and Stewart.

Coates, Ken 1998 "International Perspectives on the New Zealand Government's Relationship with the Maori." In *Living Relationships. Kokiri Ngatahi: The Treaty of Waitangi in the New Millennium.* K. Coates and P. McHugh (eds.). pp. 18–65. Wellington: Victoria University Press.

Cockerill, Jodi and Richard Gibbins 1997. "Reluctant Citizens? First Nations and in the Federal Canadian State." In *First Nations in Canada.* J.R. Ponting (ed.). pp.383–403. Toronto: McGraw Hill Ryerson.

Codrescu, Andrei 1995 "Faux Chicken & Phony Furniture." *Utne Reader* May–June:47–48. Originally published in *The Nation.* December 12, 1884.

Cohen, Abner 1969 *Custom and Politics in Urban Africa.* Berkeley: University of California Press.

Cohen, Rob 1998 *Global Diasporas. An Introduction.* Basinstoke: UCL Press.

Cohen, Robin 1997 "Introduction." In *The Politics of Migration.* R. Cohen and Z. Laylor-Henry (eds.). pp. 1–14. Cheltanham, England: Edward Edgar Publishers.

Comeau, Pauline and Aldo Santin 1990 *The First Canadians. A Profile of Canada's Native Peoples Today.* Toronto: James Lorimer and Sons.

Commissioner of Official Languages 1995 *Annual Report 1994.* Ottawa: Minister of Supply and Services Canada.

Conlogue, Ray 1997 "Arret! You Are Entering a French-Speaking Area." *The Globe and Mail.* March 22.

Connor, W. 1972 "Nation-Building or Nation-Destroying." *World Politics* 24(3).

Connor, Walker 1973 "The Politics of Ethnonationalism." *Journal of International Affairs* 27(1):1–21.

Cook, Peter 1995 "In South Africa." *The Globe and Mail.* February 8.

Coren, Giles 1994 "Disney's Heart of Darkness." *The London Sunday Times.* July 20.

Cornell, Stephen 1988 *The Return of the Native: American Indian Political Resurgence.* New York: Oxford.

Cose, Ellis 1994 "Color-Coded 'Truths.'" *Newsweek.* October 24.

Cose, Ellis 1997 Color-Blind. *Seeing Beyond Race in a Race-Obsessed World.* NY: HarperCollins.

Coser, Lewis A. 1956 *The Functions of Social Conflict.* New York: Free Press.

Coser, Lewis A. 1967 *Continuities in the Study of Social Conflict.* New York: Free Press.

Cox, Jr. Taylor 1993 *Cultural Diversity in Organizations: Theory, Research, and Practice.* San Francisco: Berrett-Koehler Pub.

Cox, Oliver C. 1948 *Caste, Class, and Race: A Study of Social Dynamics.* New York: Doubleday.

Coyne, Andrew 1998 "One, Three, Many Nations" *Time.* January 19.

Coyne, Andrew 1998 "Lots to Like in Review of Immigration." *Kitchener-Waterloo Record.* January 15.

Crane, David 1995 "Canada Should Capitalize on its Multicultural Society." *The Toronto Star.* January 14.

Creedon, Pamela J. (ed.) 1993 *Women in Mass Communication.* 2nd Edition. Newbury Park: Sage.

Cryderman, Brian, Chris O'Toole, and Augie Fleras (eds.) 1998 *Policing, Race, and Ethnicity. A Guidebook for the Policing Services.* 3rd Edition. Toronto: Butterworth.

Cummins, Jim 1991 "Heritage Languages in Canadian Schools: Fact and Fiction." *Lectures and Papers in Ethnicity.* No. 6. November. University of Toronto Press.

Cummins, Jim 1994 "Heritage Language Learning and Teaching." In *Ethnicity and Culture in Canada. The Research Landscape* by J.W. Berry and J.A. Laponce (eds.). pp. 435–456. Toronto: University of Toronto Press.

Cummins, Jim and Marcel Danesi 1990 *Heritage Languages: The Development and Denial of Canada's Linguistic Resources.* Toronto: Garamond Press.

Curtis, James, Edward Grab and Neil Guppy (eds.) 1993 *Social Inequality in Canada.* Scarborough: Prentice Hall.

Curtis, Michael 1997 "Review Essay. Antisemitism: Different Perspectives." *Sociological Forum* 12(2):321–327.

D'Souza, Dinesh 1995 *The End of Racism. Principles for a Multicultural Society.* New York: Free Press.

Dahrendorf, R. 1959 *Class and Class Conflict in Industrial Society.* London: Routledge and Kegan Paul.

Dalhousie University 1989 *Breaking Barriers: Report of the Task Force on Access for Blacks and Native Peoples.* September.

Daost-Blais, Denise 1983 "Corpus and Status Language Planning in Quebec: A Look at Linguistic Education." In *Progress in Language Planning.* Juan Cobarrubias and Joshua K. Fishman (eds.). pp. 207–234. New York: Moulton Publishers.

Darder, Antonia 1990 *Culture and Power in the Classroom: A Critical Foundation for Bicultural Education.* Critical Studies in Education and Culture Series. Henry A. Giroux and Paulo Freire (eds.). New York: Bergin and Garvey.

Darroch, Gordon A. 1979 "Another Look at Ethnicity, Stratification, and Social Mobility in Canada." *Canadian Journal of Sociology* 4:1–25.

Darroch, Gordon A. and Wilfrid G. Marston 1984 "Patterns of Urban Ethnicity: Toward a Revised Ecological Model." In *Urbanism and Urbanization. Views, Aspects, and Dimensions.* Noel Iverson (ed.). pp.127–162. Leiden: E. J. Brill.

Das Gupta, Tania 1994 "Multiculturalism Policy: A Terrain of Struggle for Immigrant Women." *Canadian Women's Studies.* 14(2):72–76.

Davidson, Basil 1994 "Government by Massacre." *The Times Higher Education Supplement.* October 7.

Davis, Kingsley and Wilbert E. Moore 1945 "Some Principles of Stratification." *American Sociological Review* 5:242–249.

Davis, Peter 1996 *In Darkest Hollywood. Exploring The Jungles of Cinema's South Africa.* Athens: Ohio University Press.

de Toro, Fernando "Ontario's Zero-Tolerance Policy or the End of Academic Freedom: Between the Reign of Intellectual Terrorism and University Cleansing." *CAUT Bulletin ACPPU.* p.15. June 1994.

Dei, George 1996 "Black/African-Canadian Students' Perspectives on School Racism." In *Racism in Canadian Schools.* I. Alladin (ed.). pp. 42–61. Toronto: Harcourt Brace.

Dei, George J. Sefa 1993 "The Challenges of Anti-Racist Education in Canada." *Canadian Ethnic Studies* XXV(2):36–49.

Dei, George J. Sefa 1996 *Anti-Racism Education. Theory and Practice* Halifax: Fernwood.

Delacourt, Susan 1995 "Finally, To Be a Somebody." *Globe and Mail.* May 20.

Delgamuukw v British Columbia 1998 "Delgamuukw v British Columbia *AILR* 3(1):35–48.

Deloria Jr., Vine and Clifford Lytle 1984 *The Nations Within. The Past and Future of American Indian Sovereignty.* New York: Pantheon.

Denis, Claude 1996 "Aboriginal Rights In/And Canadian Society. A Syewen Case Study." *International Journal of Canadian Studies* 14(Fall):13–34.

Denis, Claude 1997 *We Are Not You: First Nations and Canadian Modernity.* Peterborough: Broadview Press.

Denis, Wilfrid B. 1990 "The Politics of Language." In *Race and Ethnic Relations in Canada.* Peter Li (ed.). pp. 148–185. Toronto: Oxford University Press.

Denley, Randall 1998 "Its Time to Talk About the Results of Our Policy." *Kitchener-Waterloo Record.* January 15.

Desroches, Frederick J. 1998 "The Occupational Subculture of the Police." In *Police, Race, and Ethnicity. A Guide for Law Enforcement Officers.* B. Cryderman et al. (eds.). pp. 121–132. Markham: Butterworths.

DeVoretz, Don 1988 "Bad Economics: Irrational Racism." Speech to a conference on Policing in Multicultural/Multiracial Ontario.

Diamond, Jack 1997 "Provinces Are Archaic. More Power to the Cities." *The Globe and Mail.* May 26.

DIAND 1997 "Historic Indian Treaties." *Information.* April.

Dickason, Olive Patricia 1992 *Canada's First Nations: A History of Founding Peoples from Earliest Times.* Toronto: McClelland and Stewart.

Dickman, Howard 1993 *The Imperiled Academy.* Transaction Publishers.

Doan, Ashley 1997 "Dominant Group Ethnic Identity in the United States: The Role of 'Hidden' Ethnicity in Intergroup Relations." *Sociological Quarterly* 38(3):375–397.

Donnelly, Patrick 1998 "Scapegoating the Indian Residential School." *Alberta Report* January 26.

Dorais, Louis-Jacques, Lois Foster, and David Stockley 1994 "Multiculturalism and Integration." In *Immigration and Refugee Policy: Australia and Canada Compared.* Howard Adelman et al. (eds.). pp. 372–404. Toronto: University of Toronto Press.

Dore, Lyette 1993 "Official Languages and Multiculturalism: Choices for the Future." Notes for a conference speech, "Linguistic Rights in Canada: Collisions or Collusions?" Canadian Centre for Linguistic Rights. University of Ottawa. November 5.

Dosman, Edgar 1972 *Indians: The Urban Dilemma.* Toronto: McClelland and Stewart.

Drakich, Janice, Marilyn Taylor, and Jennifer Bankier 1995 "Academic Freedom is the Inclusive University." *Beyond Political Correctness.* S. Richer and L. Weir (eds.). pp. 118–135. Toronto: University of Toronto Press.

Driedger, Leo (ed.). 1987 *Ethnic Canada: Identities and Inequalities.* Toronto: Copp Clark Pitman.

Driedger, Leo 1989 *The Ethnic Factor: Identity in Diversity.* Toronto: McGraw Hill Ryerson.

Drohan, Madelaine 1997 "Canada-Quebec Relations seen as Model in Spain." *The Globe and Mail.* December 5.

Drost, Herman, Brian Lee Crowley and Richard Schwindt 1995 *Marketing Solutions for Native Poverty* Toronto: CD Howe Institute.

Du Plessis, Rosemary and Lynn Alice 1998 *Feminist Thought in Aotearoa/New Zealand.* Auckland: Oxford University Press.

Duncan, Phil and Grant Cronin 1997/98 "Behind the Rise of Maori Sovereignty." *Revolution.* pp: 15–21.

Dyck, Noel (ed.) 1985 *Indigenous People and the Nation-State. Fourth World Politics in Canada, Australia, and Norway.* St John's, NF: Memorial University.

Dyck, Noel 1997 "Tutelage, Resistance and Co-optation in Canadian Indian Administration." *Canadian Review of Sociology and Anthropology* 34(3):333–348.

Dyer, Gwynne 1998 "How the 'New' Francophones will Save Canada." *The Globe and Mail.* March 28.

Easteal, Patricia 1996 *Shattered Dreams. Marital Violence Against Overseas-Born Women in Australia.* Canberra: Australia National University Press.

Easton, Adam 1998 "Women at Risk From Whitening Products." *New Zealand Herald.* July 25.

Eaton, Jonathan 1997 "Female Firefighters Seek Fair Equality." *The Toronto Star.* June 9.

Eck, John E. and Dennis P. Rosenbaum 1994 "The New Police Order. Effectiveness, Equity, and Efficiency in Community Policing." In *The Challenge of Community Policing.* D.P. Rosenbaum (ed.). pp. 3–26. Thousand Oaks, CA: Sage.

Eckholm, Erik 1994 "The Native and Not-So Native American Way." *New York Times Magazine.* February 27:45–52.

Editorial 1996 "Canada, The Unfinished Country." *The Globe and Mail.* July 1.

Editorial 1997 "Money and Ethics, Two Years Later." *The Globe and Mail.* December 1.

Editorial 1997 "Introduction." *New Community* 23(2):i–iv.

Editorial 1998 "Some Social Unions are Better Than Others." *The Globe and Mail.* December 4.

Editorial 1998 "Broaden Debate on Immigration Changes." *The Toronto Star.* March 2.

Editorial 1998 "Self-Government Alone is Not Enough." *The Globe and Mail.* January 22.

Edwards, Harry 1971 *The Sociology of Sport.* Homewood, IL: Addison-Wesley.

Edwards, John 1985 *Language, Society and Identity.* London: Basil Blackwell.

Edwards John and Lori Doucette 1987 "Ethnic Salience, Identity and Symbolic Ethnicity." *Canadian Ethnic Studies* XIX(1):52–62.

Eisenstein, Zillah 1996 *Hatreds. Racialized and Sexualized Conflicts in the Twenty-first Century.* New York: Routledge.

Eisler, Dale 1996 "Prairie Time Bomb." *Maclean's.* November 11.

Eller, Jack David 1997 "Anti-anti-multiculturalism. *American Anthropologist* 99(2):249–260.

Elliott, Jean Leonard (ed.) 1983 *Two Nations, Many Cultures. Ethnic Groups in Canada.* Scarborough: Prentice-Hall.

Elliott, Jean Leonard and Augie Fleras 1990 "Immigration and the Canadian Mosaic." In *Race and Ethnic Relations in Canada.* Peter S. Li (ed.). Toronto: Oxford University Press.

Elliott, Jean Leonard and Augie Fleras 1991 *Unequal Relations.* Scarborough: Prentice-Hall.

Erickson, Arthur 1997 "Our Lack of National Identity is Our Strength." *The Globe and Mail.* June 10.

Essed, Philomena 1991 *Understanding Everyday Racism. An Interdisciplinary Study.* Newbury Park, CA: Sage.

Exum, William H. "Plus ça change...? Racism in Higher Education." Paper presented at the Annual Meetings of the American Psychological Association. September 2–6, 1980. Toronto: OISE.

Eyoh, Dickson 1995 "From the Belly to the Ballot: Ethnicity and Politics of Africa." *Queen's Quarterly* 102(1):39–52.

Eysenck, H.J. 1971 *Race, Intelligence, and Education.* London: Temple, Smith.

Faces 1996 "No Labor of Love" Compiled by *Faces* staff. Spring.

Falding, Harold 1995 "Multiculturalism—A Great Shibboleth." *Policy Options.* March:42–47.

Farber, Bernie 1997 From Marches to Modems: A Study of Organized Hate in Metropolitan Toronto.

Farley, John 1995 "Old Loyalties and Identities Don't Fade Away." *The Globe and Mail.* December 27.

Farli, Paul 1995 "TV 'Ghetto' Has Last Laugh on Blacks." *Guardian Weekly.* January 29.

Fay, Brian 1996 *Contemporary Philosophy of Social Science.* London: Blackwell.

Feagin, Joe R. and Clairece Booher Feagin 1993/1998 *Racial and Ethnic Relations.* 4th/6th Edition. Englewood Cliffs, NJ: Prentice Hall.

Fellegi, Ivan P 1996 "Chief Statistician: Why the Census is Counting Visible Minorities?" *The Globe and Mail.* April 26.

Field, Dick 1994 "Multiculturalism Undermines Values Held by Canadians." *The Toronto Star.* December 23.

Financial Post 1998 "Don't Let BC Land Claims Hurt Economic Interests." February 4.

Fish, Stanley 1993 "Reverse Racism. How the Pot Got to Call the Kettle Black." *The Atlantic Monthly.* November:128–136.

Fish, Stanley 1994 *There's No Such Thing as Free Speech and It's a Good Thing, Too.* New York: Oxford University Press.

Fish, Stanley 1997 "Boutique Multiculturalism, Or Why Liberals Are Incapable of Thinking About Hate Speech." *Critical Inquiry* (Winter):378–394.

Fisher, Claude S. et al. 1998 *Inequality by Design. Cracking the Bell Curve Myth.* Princeton University Press.

Fishman, Joshua 1989 *Language and Ethnicity in Minority Sociolinguistic Matters.* Clevedon, England: Multilingual Matters.

Fiske, John 1994 *Media Matters.* Minneapolis: University of Minnesota Press.

Flanagan, Tom 1997 "Killing With Kindness." *The Globe and Mail.* September 11.

Flanagan, Tom 1998 "To Call Leaders to Account." *The Globe and Mail.* May 11.

Fleras, Augie 1987 "Redefining the Politics over Aboriginal Language Renewal. Maori Language Schools as Agents of Social Change." *Canadian Journal of Native Studies* 7(1):1–40.

Fleras, Augie 1989 "Inverting the Bureaucratic Pyramid: Debureaucratizing the Maori Affairs Bureaucracy." *Human Organization* 48(3):214–225.

Fleras, Augie 1990 "Race Relations as Collective Definition: Aboriginal-Government Relations in Canada." *Symbolic Interaction* 13(1):19–34.

Fleras, Augie 1990 "Towards a Multicultural Reconstruction of Canadian Society." *American Review of Canadian Studies* XIX(3):307–320.

Fleras, Augie 1991 "Aboriginal Electoral Districts for Canada: Lessons from New Zealand." In *Aboriginal Peoples and Aboriginal Reform in Canada.* Rob Milen (ed.). pp. 67–104. Toronto: Dundurn Press.

Fleras, Augie 1991 "Tuku Rangatatiratanga: Devolution in Iwi-Government Relations." In *Nga Take. Ethnic Relations and Racism New Zealand.* Paul Spoonley, Cluny McPherson, and David Pearson (eds.). pp. 171–193. Palmerston North, NZ: Dunmore Press.

Fleras, Augie 1992 "Managing Aboriginality: Canadian Perspectives: International Lessons." Paper presented to the Australian and New Zealand Association for Canadian Studies. Victoria University in Wellington, NZ. December 6.

Fleras, Augie 1993 "From Culture to Equality: Multiculturalism as Ideology and Policy." *Social Inequality in Canada.* 2nd Edition. James Curtis, Edward Grab, and Neil Guppy (eds.). pp. 330–352. Scarborough: Prentice- Hall.

Fleras, Augie 1993 "Heritage Languages in Canada. A Post-Multicultural Outlook." Paper presented to the Conference on Linguistic Rights in Canada: Collisions or Collusions? University of Ottawa. November 5–7.

Fleras, Augie 1994 "Walking Away From the Camera." In *Ethnicity and Culture in Canada. The Research Landscape.* J.W. Berry and Jean Laponce (eds.). pp. 340–384. Toronto: University of Toronto Press.

Fleras, Augie 1994 "Doing What is Workable, Necessary, and Fair. Multiculturalism in Canada." *Contemporary Political Issues.* Mark Charlton and Paul Barker (eds.). pp. 25–40. Scarborough: Nelson.

Fleras, Augie 1995 "Please Adjust Your Set: Media and Minorities in a Post-Multicultural Society." *Communications in Canadian Society.* 4th Edition. Benjamin Singer (ed.). pp. 281–307.

Fleras, Augie 1996 "The Politics of Jurisdiction." In *Visions of the Heart.* David Long and Olive Dickason (eds.). Toronto: Harcourt Brace. pp. 111–143.

Fleras, Augie 1996 "Behind the Ivy Walls: Racism and Antiracism in Academe." In *Racism in Canadian Schools.* I. Alladin (ed.). pp. 62–91. Toronto: Harcourt Brace.

Fleras, Augie 1998 "From Force to Service: Community Policing in Canada." In *Police, Race, and Ethnicity: A Guide for Law Enforcement Officers.* Brian K. Cryderman et al. (eds.). 3rd Edition. pp. 94–134. Toronto: Butterworths.

Fleras, Augie 1998 "Working Through Differences: The Politics of Posts and Isms in New Zealand." *New Zealand Sociology* 13(1):62–96.

Fleras, Augie 1999 "Politics of Jurisdiction: Pathway Or Predicament? In *Visions of the Heart.* David Long and Olive Dickason (eds). Toronto: Harcourt Brace.

Fleras Augie and Frederick J. Desroches 1989 "Bridging the Gap: Towards a Multicultural Policing in Canada." *Canadian Police College Journal* 13(3):153–164.

Fleras Augie and Jean Leonard Elliott 1992 *The Nations Within: Aboriginal-State Relations in Canada, the United States, and New Zealand.* Toronto: Oxford.

Fleras, Augie and Jean Leonard Elliott 1992 *Multiculturalism in Canada: The Challenge of Diversity.* Scarborough: Nelson.

Fleras, Augie and Paul Spoonley 1999 *Recalling Aotearoa. Cultural Politics and Ethnic Relations in New Zealand.* Auckland: Oxford University Press.

Fleras Augie and Vic Krahn 1992 "From Community Development to Inherent Self-Government: Restructuring Aboriginal-State Relations in Canada." Paper presented at the Annual Meetings of Learned Societies. Charlottetown, PE. June.

Flynn, Karen 1998 "I Prayed That the Killer Was Not Black." *The Toronto Star.* August 18.

Fontaine, Phil 1997 "Colonialist Approach to Aboriginal Issues." *The Globe and Mail.* December 31.

Fontaine, Phil 1998 "Cooperation, Not Confrontation." *Time.* January 19.

Fontaine, Phil 1998 "The Double Standard About First Nations is Starting to Get Tedious." *The Globe and Mail.* March 11.

Ford, Christine Tausig 1998 "Meeting the Needs." *University Affairs.* p. 2. December.

Ford Clyde W. 1994 *We Can All Get Along.* NY: Dell Publishing.

Foreman Jr., Christopher H. 1998 "Black America." *Brookings Review* 16(2):8–11.

Foster, Cecil 1997 "Whatever Happened to Equity?" *The Toronto Star*. February 17.

Foster, Cecil 1999 "Key to Immigration Success." *The Toronto Star*. January 18.

Foster, Lorne 1998 *Turnstile Immigration. Multiculturalism, Social Order, & Social Justice in Canada*. Toronto: Thompson Educational Publishing Inc.

Fournier, Pierre 1994 . *A Meech Lake Post-mortem: Is Quebec Sovereignty Inevitable?* Montreal: McGill-Queen's Press.

Francis, Daniel 1997 *National Dreams: Myths, Memory, and History*. Arsenal Pulp Press.

Francis Diane 1996 "Challenging Quebec's Language Law." *Maclean's*. March 25. p. 13.

Francis, Francis 1999 "Immigration: A Costly Nightmare." *National Post*. April 3.

Frankenburg, Ruth 1993 *White Women, Race Matters. The Social Construction of Whiteness*. Minneapolis, MN: University of Minnesota Press.

Frankenberg, Ruth (ed.) 1997 *Displacing Whiteness. Essays in Social and Cultural Criticism* Durham, NC: Duke University Press.

Fraser, Graham 1997 "What an African-Canadian Is." *The Globe and Mail*. August 30.

Fraser, John 1988 "Refugee Riddles, Dark Mirrors, and the National Honour." *Saturday Night*. pp. 7–8. March.

Freeden, Michael 1998 "Is Nationalism A Distinct Ideology?" *Political Studies* xvi:748–765.

Freitas, Leslie de 1996 "Outsider." *New Internationalist*. p. 21. March.

Frideres, James (ed.) 1989 *Multiculturalism and Intergroup Relations*. New York: Greenwood Press.

Frideres, James 1991 "From the Bottom Up: Institutional Structures and the Indian People." In *Social Issues and Contradictions in Canadian Society*. B. Singh Bolaria (ed.). Toronto: Harcourt Brace and Jovanovich.

Frideres, James 1998 *Aboriginal Peoples in Canada. Contemporary Conflicts*. 5th Edition. Scarborough: Prentice Hall.

Fry, A.J. and C. Forceville (eds.) 1988 *Canadian Mosaic: Essays on Multiculturalism*. Amsterdam: Free University.

Fukuyama, Frances 1994 "The War of All Against All." *New York Times Book Review*.

Fulford, Robert 1997 "Do Canadians Want Ethnic Heritage Freeze-Dried?" *The Globe and Mail*. February 19.

Furnivall, J.S. 1948 *Colonial Policy and Practice*. London: Cambridge University Press.

Gaertner, Samuel L. and John F. Dovidio 1986 "The Aversive Form of Racism." In *Prejudice, Discrimination, and Racism*. John F. Dovidio and Samuel L. Gaertner (eds.). pp. 61–90. New York: Academic Press.

Gagnon, Lysianne 1996 "Sorry to Be Boring, But Quebec Loves Its Constitutional Contradictions." *The Globe and Mail*. July 6.

Galt, Virginia 1998 "Language Proposals Fire Debate." *The Globe and Mail*. January 20.

Gans, Herbert J. 1979 "Symbolic Ethnicity: The Future of Ethnic Groups and Culture in America." *Ethnic and Racial Studies*. 2:1–20.

Garcia, J.L.A. 1996 "The Heart of Racism." *Journal of Social Philosophy* 27(1):5–45.

Gardner, Dan 1996 "Statscan's Task is Not Black-and-White." *The Globe and Mail*. September 17.

Gates Jr. Henry Louis 1994 "Goodbye, Columbus? Notes on the Culture of Criticism." In *Multi-culturalism: A Critical Reader*. D.T. Goldberg (ed.). pp. 203–217. Cambridge, MA: Basil Blackwell.

Gates Jr., Henry Louis 1998 "The Two Nations of Black America." *Brookings Review* 16(2):4–7.

Gee, Marcus 1998 "Is this the End for Suharto?" *The Globe and Mail.* January 14.

George, Daniel 1997 "Letter." *The Globe and Mail.* August 12.

Gherson, Giles 1994 "Playing Gatekeeper to a World That is Forever Pleading for Admission. *The Globe and Mail.* July 12.

Gibbins, Richard and J. Rick Ponting 1986 "Faces and Interfaces of Indian Self-Government." *Journal of Native Studies* VI:43–62.

Gibson, Gordon 1997 "The Land-Claims Ruling is a Breathtaking Mistake." *The Globe and Mail.* December 16.

Gibson, Gordon 1998 "Nisga'a Treaty: The Good, the Bad, and the Alternative." *The Globe and Mail.* October 13.

Gibson, Gordon 1998 "The Racial Question Must be Debated." *The Globe and Mail.* January 6.

Gillborn, David 1998 "Race and Ethnicity in Compulsory Education." In *Race and Higher Education.* T. Modood and T. Acland (eds.). pp. 11–23. Policy Studies Institute: University of Westminister.

Gillies, James 1997 "Thinking the Unthinkable and the Republic of Canada." *The Globe and Mail.* June 28.

Gillespie, Marie 1996 *Television, Ethnicity, and Cultural Change.* London: Routledge.

Gillmor, Don 1996 "The Punishment Station." *Toronto Life.* January:46–55.

Ginzberg, Effie 1986 "Power Without Responsibility: The Press We Don't Deserve." *Currents* (Spring):1–5.

Giroux, Henry E. 1994 "Insurgent Multiculturalism and the Promise of Pedagogy." In *Multiculturalism: A Critical Reader.* D.T. Goldberg (ed.). pp. 325–343. Cambridge MA: Basil Blackwell.

Giroux, Henry E. 1995 "Foreword." In *Culture and Difference. Critical Perspectives in the Bicultural Experience in the United States.* Antonia Darder (ed.). pp. ix–xi. Westport CT: Bergin and Garvey.

Gitlin, Todd 1995 "Prime Time Ideology: The Hegemonic Process in Television Entertainment." In *Television: The Cultural View.* 5th Edition. H. Newcombe (ed). New York: Oxford University Press.

Glazer, Nathan 1997 *We Are All Multiculturalists Now.* Cambridge, MA: Cambridge University Press.

Glazer, Nathaniel and Daniel P. Moynihan 1970 *Beyond the Melting Pot.* Cambridge, MA: MIT Press.

Glazer, Nathaniel and Daniel P. Moynihan 1975 *Ethnicity. Theory and Experience.* Cambridge: Harvard University Press.

Goar, Carol 1995 "Unequal Shares of the American Dream." *The Toronto Star.* May 14.

Goldberg, David Theo 1993 *Philosophy and the Politics of Meaning.* Oxford: Basil Blackwell.

Goldberg, David Theo 1994 "Introduction: Multicultural Conditions." In *Multiculturalism: A Critical Reader.* D.T. Goldberg (ed.). pp. 1–44. Cambridge MA: Basil Blackwell.

Goldbloom, Victor 1994 "Ottawa Urged to Support Bilingualism?" *The Globe and Mail.* April 13.

Gonick, Cy 1987 *The Great Economic Debate: Failed Economics and a Future For Canada.* Toronto: James Lorimer.

Goodman, James 1997 "Nationalism, Multiculturalism, and Transnational Migrant Politics: Australian and East Timorese." *Asian and Pacific Migration Journal* 6(3–4):457–472.

Goot, Murray 1993 "Multiculturalists, Monoculturalists and the Many in Between: Attitudes to Cultural Diversity and Their Correlates." *Australia and New Zealand Journal of Sociology* 29(2):226–254.

Gordon, Milton M. 1964 *Assimilation in American Life.* New York: Oxford University Press.

Gordon, Sean 1999 "Canada Blamed by U.N." *Montreal Gazette.* April 10.

Gosnell, Joseph 1997 "Let's Get On With Land Claims Settlements." *Vancouver Sun.* December 19.

Gosnell, Joseph, President, Nisga'a Tribal Council 1999 "Nisga'a Rights." Letters to *The Globe and Mail.* January 20.

Goudar, Ruth 1989 "Adjusting the Dream." *Saskatchewan Multicultural Magazine* 8(3):5–8.

Gould, Terry 1995 "Line of Fire." *Saturday Night.* February:35–41.

Government of Canada 1969 "White Paper." *Statement of the Government of Canada on Indian Policy.* Department of Indian Affairs and Northern Development.

Government of Canada 1994. "Federal Government Begins Discussions on Aboriginal Self-Government." News Release 1-9354.

Graham, Doug 1997 *Trick Or Treaty?* Wellington: GP Publications.

Granastein, J.L. 1994 "Universities Strangled by 'PC' Politicians." *Canadian Speeches: Issues of the Day.* July:2–8.

Grand Council of Cree 1995 *Sovereign Injustice. Forcible Inclusion of the James Bay Cree* and *Cree Territory into a Sovereign Quebec.* October. Nemaska Quebec.

Gray, Herman 1995 *Watching Race. Television and the Struggle for Blackness.* Minneapolis: University of Minnesota Press.

Gray, John 1994 "The Vanishing." *The Globe and Mail.* December 10.

Gray, John 1997 "AFN Rivals Embody Competing Visions." *The Globe and Mail.* July 28.

Gray, John 1998 "Mining Companies Reluctant to Invest After Ruling." *The Globe and Mail.* June 9.

Gray, Kathy 1993 "Racism Policies." *Memorandum to Canadian Universities Employment Equity Network.* September 10.

Grayson, J. Paul 1996 "'White Racism in Toronto." *Institute for Social Research.* Vol.11(1). Winter.

Green, Paul 1994 "Introduction." In *Studies in New Zealand Social Problems.* P. Green (ed). pp. 1–24 Palmerston North, NZ: Dunmore.

Greenspon, Edward 1998 "Sovereignty Outlook Weakening." *The Globe and Mail.* April 2.

Griffin, Richard 1996 "Canada was the Testing Site for Baseball's Racial Experiment." *Kitchener-Waterloo Record.* June 1.

Gross, Michael L 1996 "Restructuring Ethnic Paradigms: From Premodern to Postmodern Perspectives." *Canadian Review of Studies in Nationalism* xxiii(1-2):51–65.

Guibernau, Monsterrat 1996 Nationalisms. The Nation-State and Nationalism in the Twentieth Century. London: Polity Press.

Gutman, Amy (ed.) 1992 *Multiculturalism and the Politics of Recognition.* Princeton University Press.

Gwyn, Richard 1994 "The First Borderless State." *The Toronto Star.* November 26.

Gwyn, Richard 1997 "We Wave Our Flag and Waive Our Citizenship." *The Toronto Star.* February 2.

Gwyn Richard 1998 "The National Unity Problem is Not Meant to be Solved." *The Toronto Star.* June 10.

Gwyn, Richard 1998 "Home and Away." *The Toronto Star.* January 11.

Gwyn, Richard 1998 "Neverendum is the goal for Quebeckers." *The Toronto Star.* October 30.

Ha, Tu Thanh 1997 "Language Police Target Even Slight Differences." *The Globe and Mail.* August 26.

Hacker, Andrew 1993 "'Diversity' and Its Dangers." *New York Times Review of Books.* pp. 21–25. October 7.

Hage, Chasson 1997 "Multicultural Zoology. The Pro Asia Manual for the Display of Ethnics." *Poetica* 3(2):23–36.

Hall, Anthony J. 1986 "The N'ungosuk Project. A Study in Aboriginal Language Renewal." Unpublished paper.

Hall, Stuart 1996 "New Ethnicities." In *Stuart Hall in Critical Studies.* D. Marley and K.H. Chen (eds.). London: Routledge.

Hall, Tony 1986 "Self-Government or Self-Delusion? Brian Mulroncy and Aboriginal Rights." *Journal of Native Studies* VI:77 89.

Hall, Tony 1993 "The Politics of Aboriginality." *Canadian Dimension.* January-February:6–8.

Hamilton, Roberta 1996 *Gendering the Vertical Mosaic. Feminist Perspectives on Canadian Society.* Toronto: Copp Clark.

Hannaford Ivan 1996 *Race: The History of an Idea in the West.* Baltimore: John Hopkins University Press.

Harries, L. 1983 "The Nationalisation of Swahili." In *Language Planning and Language Change.* Chris Kennedy (ed.). pp. 118–131. London: George Allen and Unwin.

Harris, Debbie Wise 1993 "Colonizing Mohawk Women: Representation of Women in the Mainstream Media." *RFD/DRF* 20 (1/2) 15–20.

Harris, Fred 1995 *Multiculturalism From the Margins.* Westport, CT: Bergin and Garvey.

Harris, Paul 1997 *Black Rage Confronts the Law.* New York: New York University Press.

Harvey, Jim 1992 "Multicultural Education: An Undetheorised Romanticism." *Multicultural Teaching* xi(3):5–7.

Haslett Cuff, John "1996 Television." *The Globe and Mail.* April 18.

Hassan, Marwan 1995 "Articulation and Coercion: The Language Crisis in Canada." *Border/Lines* 36:28–35.

Havel, Vaclav 1994 "Needed: A New Spirit for a New World." *The Globe and Mail.* February 28.

Hawkes, David C. (ed.) 1989 *Aboriginal Peoples and Government Responsibility: Exploring Federal and Provincial Roles.* Ottawa: Carleton University Press.

Hawkes, David C. and Marina Devine 1991 "Meech Lake and Elijah Harper: Native-State Relations in the 1990s." In *How Ottawa Spends.* pp. 33–63. Ottawa: University of Carleton Press.

Hawkins, Freda 1975 "Recent Immigration Policy." In *Immigration and the Rise of Multiculturalism.* Howard Palmer (ed.). pp. 71–75. Toronto: Copp Clark Publishing.

Hawkins, Freda 1982 "Multiculturalism in Two Countries: The Canadian and Australian Experience." *Journal of Canadian Studies* (17):64–80.

Hawkins, Freda 1988 "Canadian Multiculturalism: The Policy Explained." *Canadian Mosaic. Essays on Multiculturalism.* A.J. Fry and Ch. Forceville (eds.). pp. 9–24. Amsterdam: Free University Press.

Hawkins, Freda 1991 *Critical Years in Immigration: Canada and Australia Compared.* 2nd Edition. Montreal/Kingston: McGill-Queen's University Press.

Hayes, Rose D. 1975 "Female Genital Mutilation, Fertility Control, Women's Role, and the Patrilineage in Modern Sudan." *American Ethnologist* 2(4):617–633.

Hayes-Bautista, David E. 1992 "Academe Can Take the Lead in Binding Together the Residents of a Multicultural Society." *The Chronicle of Higher Education.* October 28.

Hechter, Michael 1975 *Internal Colonialism: The Celtic Fringe in British National Development.* Berkeley: University of California Press.

Hedge, Mike 1997 "Aborigines Look Back in Horror At Stolen Lives." *New Zealand Herald.* May 31.

Hedican, Edward J. 1995 *Applied Anthropology in Canada. Understanding Aboriginal Issues.* Toronto: University of Toronto Press.

Helmes-Hayes, Rich and Jim Curtis (eds.) (1998) *The Vertical Mosaic Revisited.* Toronto: University of Toronto Press.

Helly, Denise 1993 "The Political Regulation of Cultural Plurality: Foundations and Principles." *Canadian Ethnic Studies* XXV(2):15–31.

Henare, Denise 1995 "The Ka Awatea Report: Reflections on its Process and Vision." In *Justice and Identity: Antipodean Practices.* M. Wilson and A. Yeatman (eds). pp. 44–61. Wellington: Bridget Williams Books.

Henderson, James [Sakej] Youngblood 1993 "Governing the Implicate Order: Self-Government and the Linguistic Development of Aboriginal Communities." Paper presented to the conference on Linguistic Rights in Canada: Collisions or Collusions? University of Ottawa. November 5–7.

Henderson [Sakej], James 1997 "Interpreting Sui Generis." *Alberta Law Review* 36:46–96.

Henry, Frances 1968 "The West Indian Domestic Scheme in Canada." *Social and Economic Studies* 17(1)83–91.

Henry, Frances 1994 *The Caribbean Diaspora in Canada.* Toronto: University of Toronto Press.

Henry, Frances and E. Ginzberg 1984 *Who Gets the Work: A Test of Racial Discrimination in Employment Toronto.* Urban Alliance on Race Relations and the Social Planning Council of Toronto.

Henry, Frances and Effie Ginzberg 1993 "Racial Discrimination in Employment." In *Social Inequality in Canada.* James Curtis et al. (ed.). pp. 353–360. Scarborough: Prentice-Hall.

Henry, Frances and Carol Tator 1985 "Racism in Canada: Social Myths and Strategies for Change." *Ethnicity and Ethnic Relations in Canada.* 2nd Edition. Rita M. Bienvenue and Jay E. Goldstein (eds.). pp. 321–335. Toronto: Butterworths.

Henry, Frances and Carol Tator 1993 "The Show Boat Controversy." *The Toronto Star.* May 28.

Henry, Frances and Carol Tator 1994 "The Ideology of Racism—'Democratic Racism.'" *Canadian Ethnic Studies* xxvi(2):1–16.

Henry, Frances, Carol Tator, Winston Mattis and Tim Rees 1995 *The Colour of Democracy.* Toronto: Harcourt Brace.

Henton, Darcy 1998 "Territorial Government." *The Toronto Star.* March 5.

Herberg, Edward 1989 *Ethnic Groups in Canada: Adaptation and Transition.* Scarborough: Nelson.

Herman, Ed and Noam Chomsky 1988 *Manufacturing Consent. The Political Economy of the Mass Media.* New York: Pantheon Books.

Hesse, B. 1997 "It's Your World: Discrepant Multiculturalisms." *Social Identities* 3(3):375–394.

Hewitt, Roger 1986 *White Talk, Black Talk.* New York: Cambridge University Press.

Hick Stephen and Ron Santos 1992 *Anti-Racism Student Organizing in Canadian Universities.* Sponsored by the Race Advisory Committee, School of Social Work, Carleton University, Ottawa.

Higham, John 1993 "Multiculturalism and Universalism: A History and Critique." *American Quarterly* 45(3):195–219.

Hill, Jennifer Leigh 1992 "Accessibility: Students with Disabilities in Universities in Canada." *The Canadian Journal of Higher Education* XXII(1):48–67.

Hinton, M., E. Johnson and D. Rigney 1997 *Indigenous Peoples and the Law.* Sydney: Cavendish Publishing.

Hochschild, Jennifer L 1998 "American Racial and Ethnic Politics in the 21st Century." *Brookings Review* 16(2):43–46.

Hockey News 1997 "Hurtful Slurs Now Thorny NHL Issue." December 12.

Holdaway, Simon 1996 *The Racialisation of British Policing.* NY: St Martin's Press.

Honderich, John 1996 "Referendum: One Year Later." *The Toronto Star.* October 26.

hooks, bell 1984 *Feminist Theory: From Margin to Centre.* Boston: South End Press.

hooks, bell 1992 *Black Looks.* Toronto: Between the Lines.

hooks, bell 1994 *Outlaw Culture: Resisting Representations.* New York: Routledge.

hooks, bell 1995 *Killing Rage.* Boston: South End Press.

Horn, Michael 1997 *Becoming Canadian: Memoirs of an Invisible Immigrant:* Toronto: University of Toronto Press.

Horsburgh, Susan 1998 "Hard Landing." *Time.* March 2.

Hou, Feng and T.R. Balakrishnan 1996 "The Integration of Visible Minorities in Contemporary Canadian Society." *Canadian Journal of Sociology* 21(3):307–327.

Howard, Ross 1998 "Immigration Proposal Faces B.C. Furor if Chinese Barred." *The Globe and Mail.* January 8.

Hudson, Michael R. 1987 "Multiculturalism, Government Policy and Constitutional Enshrinement— A Comparative Study." In *Multiculturalism and the Charter: A Legal Perspective.* Canadian Human Rights Foundation (ed.). pp. 59–122. Toronto: Carswell.

Hughes, Robert 1992 "The Fraying of America." *Time.* pp. 40–46. February 3.

Hummel, Ralph 1987 *The Bureaucratic Experience.* New York: St. Martin's Press.

Hurst, Lynda 1998 "Tug of Words Marks the '90s." *The Toronto Star.* February 21.

Hurtado, Aida 1996 *The Color of Privilege: Three Blasphemies on Race and Feminism.* University of Michigan Press.

Hylton, John H. (ed.) 1994 A*boriginal Self-Government in Canada. Current Trends and Issues.* Saskatoon: Purich Publishing.

Ignatieff, Michael 1994 *Blood and Belonging: Journeys into the New Nationalism.* Viking.

Ignatieff, Michael 1995 "Nationalism and the Narcissism of Minor Differences." *Queen's Quarterly* 102(1):1–25.

Ip, Manying 1990 *Home Away From Home: Life Stories of Chinese Women in New Zealand.* Auckland: New Women's Press.

Ip, Manying 1998 "Gender, Racism, and the Politics of Chinese Immigration." In R. Du Plessis and L. Alice. *Feminist Thought in Aotearoa/New Zealand.* Auckland: Oxford University Press.

Irwin, Colin 1989 "Lords of the Arctic: Wards of the State." *Northern Perspectives* 17(1). Ottawa: Canadian Arctic Resources Committee.

Isajiw, Wsevolod W. 1977 "Olga in Wonderland: Ethnicity in Technological Society." *Canadian Ethnic Studies* IX(1):77–85.

Isajiw, Wsevolod W. 1982 "Occupational and Economic Development." *A Heritage in Transition: Essays in the History of Ukrainians in Canada.* M. Lupul (ed.). pp. 59–84. Toronto: McClelland and Stewart.

Isajiw, Wsevolod W. 1990 "Ethnic-Identity Retention." *Ethnic Identity and Equality.* R. Breton et al. (eds.). pp. 34–91. Toronto: University of Toronto Press.

Isajiw, Wsevolod W. 1997 *Multiculturalism in North America and Europe. Comparative Perspectives on Interethnic Relations and social incorporation.* Toronto: Canadian Scholars Press.

Isbister John 1996 The Immigration Debate: Remaking America. West Hartford, CT: Kumarian Press.

Jackson, Peter 1998 "Constructions of 'Whiteness' in the Geographical Imagination." *Area* 30(2):99–106.

Jain, Harish C. and Rick D. Hackett 1989 "Measuring Effectiveness of Employment Equity Programs in Canada: Public Policy and a Survey." *Canadian Public Policy* XV(2):189–204.

Jain, Harish C. 1988 "Affirmative Action/Employment Equity Programs and Visible Minorities in Canada." *Currents*:3–7.

Jakobsh, Frank 1994 "Racist Foundations." *Kitchener-Waterloo Record.* September 3.

Jakubowicz, Andrew et al. 1994 *Racism, Ethnicity, and the Media.* St Leonards, NSW: Allen & Unwin.

James, Carl 1994 "The Paradoxes of Power and Privilege: Race, Gender, an Occupational Position." *Canadian Women Studies* 14(2):47–51.

James, Carl 1995 *Seeing Ourselves: Exploring Race, Ethnicity, and Culture.* Toronto: Thompson Publishing.

James, Carl and Adrienne Shadd (eds.) *Talking About Differences. Encounters in Culture, Language, and Identity.* Toronto: Between the Lines.

James, Jacqueline B. 1997 "What Are the Social Issues Involved in Focusing on Difference in the Study of Gender?" *Journal of Social Issues* 53(2):213–232.

James, Royson 1998 "Black Passengers Targeted in Airport Searches?" *The Toronto Star.* November 11.

James, Steve and Earl Warren 1995 "Police Culture." In *Cultures of Crime and Violence. The Australian Experience.* J. Bessant et al. (eds.). pp. 3–13. Bandoora Vic: La Trobe University Press.

Jantzen, Lorna 1992 "Multiculturalism in Quebec." Proceedings of the 1992 Waterloo-Laurier Multidisciplinary Graduate Student's Conference. W.T. Kinastowski and P.J. Misiaszek. Department of Political Science. University of Waterloo and Wilfrid Laurier University.

Jaret, Charles 1995 *Contemporary Racial and Ethnic Relations.* Scarborough, ON: Harper Collins.

Jawani, Yasmin "In the Outskirts of Empire. Women of Colour in Popular Film and Television." *Aquellarre* (Fall):13–17.

Jaworsky, John 1979 *A Case Study of Canadian Federal Government's Multicultural Policies.* Unpublished MA thesis. Political Science. Ottawa: Carleton.

Jencks, Christopher and Meredith Phillips 1998 "The Black-White Test Score Gap." *Brookings Review* 16(2):24–27.

Jenkins, Richard 1994 "Rethinking Ethnicity: Identity, Categorization, and Power. *Ethnic and Race Relations* 17(2):197–223.

Jensen, Arthur R. 1969 "How Much Can We Boost IQ and Scholastic Achievement?" *Harvard Educational Review* 39:1–123.

Jenson, Jane 1996 "Quebec: Which Minority?" *Dissent* (Summer):43–48.

Jhally, Sut and Justin Lewis 1992 *Enlightened Racism. The Cosby Show, Audiences, and the Myth of the American Dream.* Boulder, CO: Westview Press.

Jhappan, C. Radha 1990 "Indian Symbolic Politics: The Double-Edged Sword of Publicity." *Canadian Ethnic Studies* XXII(3):19–39.

Jhappan, Radha 1995 "The Federal-Provincial Power Grid and Aboriginal Self-Government." In *New Trends in Canadian Federalism.* F. Rocher and M. Smith (eds.). pp. 155–186. Broadview Press.

Jimenez, M. 1999 "Immigration Rules Costing Canada Billions." *The National Post.* February 18.

Johnson, Daniel 1995 "Daniel Johnson Urges Flexible Federalism." By John Gray. *The Globe and Mail.* January 19.

Johnson, James 1998 "In Brief." *Brookings Review* 16(2):3.

Johnson, P.M.G. 1994 "Examining A State Relationship. 'Legitimation' and Te Kohanga Reo." *Te Pua* 3(2):22–34.

Jordan, Deidre F. 1987 "Aboriginal Identity: The Management of a Minority Group by the Mainstream Society." *Canadian Journal of Native Studies.*

Joy, Richard 1971 *Languages in Conflict.* Toronto: McClelland and Stewart.

Jull, Peter 1998 "Nunavut or None of it? *Arena* (August/September):36–37.

Jull, Peter and Donna Craig 1997 "Reflections on Regional Agreements: Yesterday, Today, and Tomorrow." *Australian Indigenous Law Reporter* 2(4): 475–493.

Juteau, Danielle 1994 "Changing Forms of Nation-ness in the Canadian Context: The Quebec Case." University of Saskatchewan. Sorokin Lectures, No. 25.

Kallen, Evelyn 1982 "Multiculturalism: Ideology, Policy, and Reality." *Journal of Canadian Studies* (17):51–63.

Kallen, Evelyn 1987 "Multiculturalism, Minorities, and Motherhood: A Social Scientific Critique of Section 27." *Multiculturalism and the Charter: A Legal Perspective.* Canadian Human Rights Foundation (ed.). pp. 123–138. Toronto: Carswell.

Kallen, Evelyn 1989 *Label Me Human. Minority Rights of Stigmatized Canadians.* Toronto: University of Toronto Press.

Kallen, Evelyn 1995 *Ethnicity and Human Rights in Canada.* 2nd Edition. Toronto: Oxford University Press.

Kanter, Rosabeth 1977 *Men and Women of the Corporation.* New York: Vintage.

Kaplan William (ed.) 1993 *Belonging: The Meaning and Sense of Citizenship in Canada.* Montreal /Kingston: McGill-Queen's University Press.

Katz, Irwin, Joyce Wackenhut, and R. Glen Hass 1986 "Racial Ambivalence, Value Duality, and Behavior." In *Prejudice, Discrimination, and Racism.* John F. Dovidio and Samuel L. Gaertner (eds.). pp. 35–60. New York: Academic Press.

Kauffman, L.A. 1990 "Citizenship. Democracy in a Postmodern World." *Social Policy (*Fall):7–11.

Kaufman, Cynthia 1998 "The Making and Unmaking of Whiteness." *Socialist Review.* pp. 192–202.

Kazarian Shahe S. 1997 "The Armenian Psyche: Genocide and Acculturation." *Mentalities* 12(1-2):74–90.

Keating, Michael 1993 "Two Faces Under One Flag." *The Times Higher Education Supplement.* September 24. p.19.

Kelsey, Jane 1986 "Decolonization in the 'First World'—Indigenous Minorities Struggle for Justice and Self- Determination." *The Windsor Yearbook of Access to Justice* 5:102–141.

Kennedy, Chris (ed.) 1983 *Language Planning and Language Education.* London: George Allen and Unwin.

Keohane, Kieran 1997 *Symptoms of Canada: An Essay on Canadian Identity.* Toronto: University of Toronto Press.

Kessler-Harris, Alice 1992 "Multiculturalism Can Strengthen, Not Undermine a Common Culture." *The Chronicle of Higher Education.* October 21.

Kevles, Daniel J. 1995 *In the Name of Eugenics: Genetics and the Use of Human Heredity.* New York: Alfred A Knopf Inc.

Khayatt, Didi 1994 "The Boundaries of Identity at the Intersections of Race, Class, and Gender." *Canadian Women Studies* 14(2):6–13.

Kilgour, David 1988 *Uneasy Patriots: Western Canadians in Confederation.* Edmonton: Lone Pine.

King, Deborah 1988 "Multiple Jeopardy, Multiple Consciousness: The Context of Black Feminist Ideology." *Signs* 14(2):42–49.

King III, Martin Luther 1994 "Forward." In *We Can All Get Along.* Clyde W. King (ed.). pp. ix – x. New York: Dell Publishing.

Kinloch, Graham C. 1977 *Sociological Theory: Its Development and Major Paradigms.* Toronto: McGraw Hill.

Kinsella, Warren 1994 *Web of Hate: The Far-Right Network in Canada.* Toronto: Harper Collins.

Kirschbaum, Erik 1998 "German Racist Attacks on Rise." *The Globe and Mail.* May 7.

Kitaro, Harry 1997 *Race Relations.* Englewood Cliffs, NJ: Prentice-Hall.

Kleinman, S. 1978 "Female Premarital Sexual Careers." In *Shaping Identity in Canadian Society.* Jack Haas and William Shaffir (eds.). pp. 101–115. Scarborough, ON: Prentice-Hall.

Knight, David B. 1985 "Territory and People or People and Territory? Thoughts on Postcolonial Self- Determination." *International Political Science Review* 6:248–272.

Knowles, Louis L. and Kenneth Prewitt 1969 *Institutional Racism in America.* Englewood Cliffs, NJ: Prentice-Hall.

Knowles, Sidney 1998 "Letters to the Editor." *Society.* January/February.

Knowles, Valerie 1992 *Strangers at Our Gates. Canadian Immigration and Immigration Policy.* pp. 1540–1990. Toronto: Dundurn.

Knox, Paul 1997 "Doors Slamming on Refugees, UN Agency Says." *The Globe and Mail.* December 8.

Knox, Paul 1998 "Top UN Official Assails Canada's Refugee Policy." *The Globe and Mail.* November 10.

Kohl, Herbert 1991 "The Politically Correct Playground. Multiculturalism and the Schools." *Social Policy.* Summer:33–40.

Kohl, Howard 1994 "Service with a Sneer." *New York Times.* November 6.

Kostash, Myrna 1988 "Domination and Exclusion: Notes of a Resident Alien." In *Ethnicity in a Technological Age.* Ian H. Angus (ed.). pp. 57–66. Edmonton: Canadian Institute of Ukrainian Studies, University of Alberta.

Kralt, John and Ravi Pendakur 1991 "Ethnicity Immigration & Language Transfer." *Policy & Research. Multiculturalism Sector.* Multiculturalism and Citizenship, Ottawa.

Kramarae, Cheris 1984 "Introduction: Toward an Understanding of Language and Power." In *Language and Power.* Cheris Kramarae et al. (eds.). pp. 9–22. Beverley Hills: Sage Publications.

Kromkowski, John A. 1995 "To the Reader." *Race and Ethnic Relations. Annual Editions.* Sluice Dock, CT: Dushkin Publishing.

Krotkin, Joel 1992 *Tribes. How Race, Religions and Identity Determine Success in the New Global Economy.* New York: Random House. (As reviewed in the *New York Times Magazine.* March 8, 1993.)

Krotz, Larry 1990 *Indian Country: Inside Another Canada.* Toronto: McClelland and Stewart.

Kulchyski, Peter (ed.) 1994 *Unjust Relations. Aboriginal Rights in Canadian Courts.* Toronto: Oxford University Press.

Kunz, Jean Lock and Fleras, Augie 1998 "Women of Colour in Mainstream Advertising: Distorted Mirror or Looking Glass?" *Atlantis* 22(2):27–38.

Kurthen, Hermann 1997 "The Canadian Experience with Multiculturalism and Employment Equity. Lessons for Europe." *New Community* 23(2): 249–270.

Kymlicka, Will 1995 "Misunderstanding Nationalism." *Dissent* (Winter):131–137.

Kymlicka, Will 1998 *Finding our way. Rethinking Ethnocultural Relations in Canada.* Toronto: Oxford University Press.

Kymlicka, Will 1999 "Cracks in the Mosaic?" Interview in *University Affairs.* February:8–9.

Laczko, Leslie 1997 "Feelings of Fraternity in Canada. An Empirical Exploration of Regional Differences." *Asian and Pacific Migration Journal* 6(3-4):343–361.

Lahgi, Brian 1997 "Ottawa to Renegotiate Two Land Claims." *The Toronto Star.* December 23.

Laghi, Brian 1999 "Alarm Raised Over Missing Would-be Refugees." *The Globe and Mail.* January 16.

LaPiere, R. 1934 "Attitudes Versus Action." *Social Forces* 13:230–237.

Larner, Wendy 1996 "Gender and Ethnicity: Theorising 'Difference' in Aotearoa/New Zealand." In *Nga Patai.* P. Spoonley et al. (eds.). pp. 159–174. Palmerston North, NZ: Dunmore Publishing.

LaRoque, Emma 1975 *Defeathering the Indian.* Agincourt, ON: Book Society of Canada.

LaRoque, Emma 1990 "Preface, or Here are Our Voices—Who Will Hear?" *Writing the Circle: Native Women of Western Canada.* Jeanne Perreault and Sylvia Vance (eds.). pp. xv–xxx. Edmonton: NeWest.

Latouche, Daniel 1993 "Quebec, See Under Canada: Quebec Nationalism in the New Global Age." *Quebec. State and Society.* 2nd Edition. Alain-G. Gagnon (ed.). pp. 40–63. Scarborough: Nelson.

Latouche, Daniel 1995 "To Be or Not to Be a Province." *The Globe and Mail.* February 17.

Laurin, Camille 1978 "Charte de la Langue Française/French Language Charter." *Canadian Review of Sociology and Anthropology* 15(2).

Lawton, Valerie 1998 "CRTC to Study Ethnic Broadcasting." *The Toronto Star.* December 23.

Laxer, James 1993 "Buying Into Decline." *Canadian Forum.* April:5–7.

Laxer, James 1994 "Canada Can't Survive as a Union of 10 Equal Provinces." *The Toronto Star.* August 7.

Leah, Ronnie 1989 "Race, Class, Gender: Bonds and Barriers." *Socialist Studies/Etudes Socialistes.* 5:174–205.

Lee, Edward 1997 "Canada's Chinese Still Stereotyped." *The Toronto Star.* December 15.

Légaré, André 1997 "The Government of Nunavut (1999): A Prospective Analysis." In Ponting 1997:404–432.

Lehr, John C. 1987 "Government Perceptions of Ukrainian Immigrants to Western Canada 1896–1902." *Canadian Ethnic Studies* XIX(2):1–13.

Lemarchand, Rene 1993 *Ethnocide as Discourse and Practice.* New York: Cambridge University Press.

Leo, John 1988 "An Apology to Japanese Americans." *Time Magazine.* May 2.

Lerner, Gerda 1997 *Why History Matters. Life and Thought.* NY: Oxford University Press.

Levin, Michael, D. (ed.) 1993 *Ethnicity and Aboriginality: Case Studies in Ethnonationalism.* Toronto: University of Toronto Press.

Levin, Michael D. 1995 "Understanding Ethnicity." *Queen's Quarterly* 102(1):71–89.

Levine, Alissa 1999 "Female Genital Operations: Canadian Realities, Concerns, and Policy Recommendations." In *Ethnicity, Politics, and Public Policy.* H. Troper and M. Weinfeld (eds.). pp. 26–53.

Levitt, Howard 1994 "Employment Equity Act Ill-Conceived." *The Toronto Star.* July 18.

Lewis, Oscar 1964 "The Culture of Poverty." In *The Explosive Forces in Latin America.* J. Tepaske and S. Fisher (eds.). pp. 149–173. Columbus, OH: University Press.

Lewycky, Laverne 1993 "Multiculturalism in the 1990s and into the 21st Century: Beyond Ideology and Utopia." In *Deconstructing A Nation. Immigration, Multiculturalism and Racism in 90s Canada.* Vic Satzewich (ed.). pp. 359–402. Halifax: Fernwood Press.

Li, Peter S. 1988 *Ethnic Inequality in a Class Society.* Toronto: Wall and Thompson.

Li, Peter S. 1988 *The Chinese in Canada.* Toronto: Oxford University Press.

Li, Peter S. (ed.) 1990 *Race and Ethnic Relations in Canada.* Toronto: Oxford.

Li, Peter S. 1994 "A World Apart: The Multicultural World of Visible Minorities and the Art World of Canadians." *Canadian Review of Sociology and Anthropology* 32(4):367–398.

Li, Peter S.1994 "Unneighbourly Houses or Unwelcome Chinese: The Social Construction of Race in the Battle Over 'Monster Homes' in Vancouver, Canada." *International Journal of Comparative Race & Ethnic Relations* 1(1):14–33.

Li, Peter S.1995 "Racial Supremacism Under Social Democracy." *Canadian Ethnic Studies* xxvii(1):1–17.

Linden, W. 1994 *Swiss Democracy.* New York: St Martin's Press.

Lipset, Seymour Martin and Earl Raab 1995 *Jews and the New American Scene.* Harvard University Press.

Lister, Ruth 1997 *Citizenship: Feminist Perspectives.* London: Macmillan.

Little Bear, L., Menno Boldt and J. Anthony Long 1984 *Pathways to Self-Determination: Canadian Indians and the Canadian State.* Toronto: University of Toronto Press.

Littleton, J. 1996 *Clash of Identities.* Scarborough: Prentice-Hall.

Loney, Martin 1998 *The Pursuit of Division. Race, Gender, and Preferential Hiring in Canada.* Montreal/Kingston: McGill-Queen's University Press.

Long, David and Olive Dickason (eds.) 1996 *Visions of the Heart.* Toronto: Harcourt Brace.

Loury, Glen 1997 "The Conservative Line on Race." *The Atlantic Monthly.* November:144–148.

Loury, Glen C. 1998 "An American Tragedy." *Brookings Review* 16(2):38–42.

Lupul, M.R. 1988 "Ukrainians: The Fifth Cultural Wheel in Canada." In *Ethnicity in a Technological Age.* Ian H. Angus (ed.). pp. 177–192. Edmonton: Canadian Institute of Ukrainian Studies, University of Alberta.

Lupul Manoly R. 1994 "Multiculturalism, Ethnic Studies, and the Present Economic Crisis in Alberta. *Shevchenko Lecture.* University of Alberta. March 24.

Lyons, Noel 1997 "Feds Criticized." (Cited in) *Windspeaker.* November.

Maaka, Roger and Augie Fleras 1998 "Rethinking Claims-Making As Maori Affairs Policy." *He Pukenga Korero* 3(2):43–51.

Macionis, John, and Linda Gerber 1999 *Sociology.* 3rd Canadian Edition. Scarborough: Prentice Hall Allyn and Bacon.

Mackie Marlene 1985 "Stereotypes, Prejudice, and Discrimination." In *Ethnicity and Ethnic Relations in Canada.* 2nd Edition. Rita M. Bienvenue and Jay E. Goldstein (eds.). pp. 119–159. Toronto: Butterworths.

Macklem, Patrick 1993 "Ethnonationalism, Aboriginal Identities, and the Law." In *Ethnicity and Aboriginality: Case Studies in Ethnonationalism.* Michael D. Levin (ed.). pp. 9–28. Toronto: University of Toronto Press.

MacQueen, Ken 1994 "I am a Canadian. Don't Let Me Screw Up." *Kitchener-Waterloo Record.* April 23.

Madely, Steve 1994 "Immigration and Crime." *Ottawa Sun.* July 20.

Malek, Kenan 1996 "Universalism and Difference: Race and Postmodernists." *Race & Class* 37(3):1–20.

Mallet, Gina 1997 "Has Diversity Gone Too Far?" *The Globe and Mail.* March 15.

Marable, Manning 1998 "Ethnic Nationalism. Black Fundamentalism." *Dissent.* Spring.

Marcus, Alan Rudolph 1995 *Relocating Eden. The Image and Politics of Inuit Exile in the Canadian Arctic.* Hanover, NH: The University Press of New England.

Marger, Martin N. 1994 *Race and Ethnic Relations. American and Global Perspectives.* 2nd Edition. Belmont, CA: Wadsworth.

Marger, Martin N. and Phillip J. Obermiller 1987 "Emergent Ethnicity Among Internal Migrants: The Case of the Maritimers in Toronto." *Ethnic Groups* 7:1–17.

Marin, Peter 1995 "Secularism's Blind Faith." *Harpers.* September:20–22.

Martin, James G. and Clyde W. Franklin 1973 *Minority Group Relations.* Columbus, OH: Charles E. Merrill Publishing Company.

Martin, Jerry 1993 "The Postmodern Argument Considered." *Partisan Review.* pp. 638–646.

Matas, Robert 1994 "Putting a Price on Immigration." *The Globe and Mail.* February 11.

Matas, Robert 1997 "Abuse Reported by Early 1900s." *The Globe and Mail.* December 11.

Matas, Robert 1998 "Nisga'a People Make History With B.C. Pact." *The Globe and Mail.* July 16.

Matas, Robert, Erin Anderssen, and Sean Fine 1997 "Natives Win on Land Rights." *The Globe and Mail.* December 12.

Matthews, David Ralph and Jason Lian 1999 "Does the Vertical Mosaic Still Exist?" *Canadian Review of Sociology and Anthropology.* 36(2).

Mawani, Nurjehan 1997 "Is Refugee Determination Fair." (Letter) *The Globe and Mail.* December 13.

McAndrew, Marie 1992 "Combatting Racism and Ethnocentrism in Educational Materials: Problems and Actions Taken in Quebec." In *Racism and Education. Different Perspectives and Experiences.* Ontario Teachers Federation (ed.). pp. 49–60. Ottawa.

McBride, Stephen and John Shields 1993 *Dismantling a Nation: Canada and the New World Order.* Halifax: Fernwood.

McCall, George J. and J.L. Simmons 1978 *Identities and Interactions. An Examination of Human Associations in Everyday Life.* Revised. New York: Free Press.

McCarthy, Cameron and Warren Crichlow (eds.) 1993 *Race, Identity, and Representation in Education.* New York: Routledge.

McCaskill, Tim 1995 "Anti-Racist Education and Practice in the Public School System." *Beyond Political Correctness.* S. Richer and L. Weir (eds.). pp. 253–272. Toronto: University of Toronto Press.

McConohay, John B. 1986 "Modern Racism, Ambivalence, and the Modern Racism Scale." In *Prejudice, Discrimination, and Racism.* John F. Dovidio and Samuel L Gaertner (eds.). pp. 91–126. New York: Academic Press.

McCormack, Thelma 1991 "Political Correct?" *The Canadian Forum.*

McCormack, Thelma 1998 "Multiculturalism, Racism and Hate Speech." *Newsletter. Institute for Social Research.* York University.

McFarlane, Scott 1995 "The Haunt of Race." *Fuse* 18(3):18–31.

McGarry John and Brendan O'Leary 1994 "The Political Regulation of National and Ethnic Conflict." *Parliamentary Affairs.* pp. 94–115.

McGill 1994 *Anti-Racism and Race Relations.* Prepared by Monique Shebbeare. McGill's Equity Office. July.

McGregor, Robert M. 1989 "The Distorted Mirror: Images of Visible Minority Women in Canadian Print Advertising." *Atlantis* 15(1).

McGregor, Roy 1989 *The Fearless Vision of Billy Diamond.* Markham, ON: Viking.

McHugh, Paul 1998 "Aboriginal Identity and Relations—Models of State Practice and Law in North America and Australasia." In *Living Relationships. Kokiri Ngatahi. The Treaty of Waitangi in the New Millennium.* K. Coates and P. McHugh (eds.). pp. 72–113. Wellington: University of Victoria Press.

McIntosh, Peggy "White Privilege and Male Privilege: A Personal Account of Coming to See Correspondences Through Work in Women Studies." *Working Paper No. 189.* Wellesly College, Centre for Research on Women, MA.

McIntyre, Sheila 1993 "Backlash Against Equality: The 'Tyranny' of the 'Politically Correct.'" *McGill Law Journal/Revue de Droit de McGill* 38(1):3–63.

McKague, Ormand (ed.) 1991 *Racism in Canada.* Saskatoon: Fifth House Publishing.

McKee, Craig 1996 *Treaty Talks in British Columbia.* Vancouver: UBC Press.

McKenna, Ian 1994 "Canada's Hate Propaganda Laws—A Critique." *British Journal of Canadian Studies.* pp. 15–42.

McKenzie, Robert 1996 "Polls Show Quebecers Not Racist, PQ Says." *The Toronto Star.* October 29.

McLaren, Peter 1994 "White Terror and Oppositional Agency. Towards A Critical Multiculturalism." In *Multiculturalism. A Critical Reader.* D.T. Goldberg (ed.). pp. 45–74. Oxford: Blackwell.

McLemore, S. Dale 1994 *Racial and Ethnic Relations in America.* 4th Edition. Toronto: Allyn and Bacon.

McLeod, Keith A. (ed.) 1983 *Multiculturalism, Bilingualism, and Canadian Institutions.* Toronto: University of Toronto Guidance Centre.

McMillan, Alan D. 1988 *Native Peoples and Cultures of Canada.* Vancouver/Toronto: Douglas and McIntyre.

McNeill, Michelle 1994 "Policing in a Multicultural Society." National Police Research Unit. Sydney.

McNeill, William H. 1986 *Poly-Ethnicity and National Unity in World History.* Toronto: Butterworths.

McRae, K.D. 1974 *Consociational Democracy: Political Accommodation in Segmented Societies.* Toronto: McClelland and Stewart.

McRoberts, Kenneth 1989 *Quebec Social Change and Political Crisis.* 3rd Edition. Toronto: McClelland and Stewart.

McRoberts, Kenneth 1993 "English-Canadian Perceptions of Quebec." *Quebec. State and Society.* Alain-G. Gagnon (ed.). pp. 116–129. Scarborough: Nelson.

McRoberts, Kenneth 1995 "Living With Dualism and Multiculturalism." In *New Trends in Canadian Federalism.* F. Rocher and M. Smith (eds.). pp. 109–132. Broadview Press.

McRoberts, Kenneth 1996 "Introduction (Citizenship and Rights)." *International Journal of Canadian Studies* 14(Fall):5–12.

McRoberts, Kenneth 1997 *Misconceiving Canada. The Struggle for National Unity.* Toronto: Oxford University Press.

McRoberts, Kenneth 1998 "Are Canadians a People? Are Quebeckers?" *The Globe and Mail.* March 19.

Mead, Walter Russell 1993 "This Land is My Land." *New York Times Book Review.* November 7.

Meadows, Michael 1995 "Northern Exposure. Indigenous Television Developments in Northern Canada." *Media International Australia* 78(November):109–118.

Medjuck, Sheva 1988 "From Self-Sacrificing Jewish Mother to Self-Centered Jewish Princess: Is This How Far We've Come." *Atlantis: A Women's Studies Journal* 14(1):90–97.

Mercredi, Ovide and Mary Ellen Turpel 1993 *In the Rapids: Navigating the Future of First Nations.* Toronto: Penguin Books.

Metge, Joan 1976 *The Maoris of New Zealand: Rautahi.* London: Routledge and Kegan Paul.

Mickleburgh Rod 1998 "Natives Underscore Landmark Judgement." *The Globe and Mail.* December 12.

Mickleburgh Rod 1998 "British Columbians Want Vote on Nisga'a Treaty, Surveys Say." *The Globe and Mail.* November 12.

Miles, Robert 1982 *Racism and Migrant Labour.* London: Routledge and Kegan Paul.

Miles, Robert 1993 *Racism after Race Relations.* New York: Routledge.

Miles, Robert and Ann Phizacklea 1984 *White Man's Country: Racism in British Politics.* London: Pluto Press.

Miliband, Ralph 1973 *The State in Capitalist Society.* London: Quartet Books.

Miller, J.R. 1996 *Singwaulk's Vision, A History of Native Residential Schools in Canada.* University of Toronto Press.

Miller, J.R. 1989 *Skyscrapers Hide the Heavens: A History of Indian-White Relations in Canada.* Toronto: University of Toronto Press.

Millman, Joel 1997 *The Other Americans: How Immigrants Renew Our Country, Our Economy, and Our Values.* NY: Penguin.

Milroy, S.T. 1997 "Maori Issues." *New Zealand Law Review.* Part 2:247–273.

Miner, Michael 1986 *Police Intercultural Training Manual.* Published by the Canadian Association of Chiefs of Police with the support of the Multicultural Directorate of the Secretary of State. Ottawa.

Ministry of Municipal Affairs 1988 *Employment Equity.* Toronto.

Ministry of Education and Training 1993 *Antiracism and Ethnocultural Equity in School Boards. Guidelines for Policy Developent and Implementation.* Toronto.

Minogue, Kenneth 1998 *The Treaty of Waitangi: Morality Or Reality?* Wellington: The Business Roundtable.

Mirza, Heidi Safia 1998 "Race, Gender, and IQ: The Social Consequence of a Pseudo-Scientific Discourse." *Race, Ethnicity, and Education* 1(1):109–124.

Mirza, Heidi Safia 1998 "Black Women in Education: A Collective Movement for Social Change." In *Race and Higher Education.* T. Modood and T. Acland (eds.). pp. 39–50. Policy Studies Institute. New Westminster.

Mitchell, Alana 1994 "Study Debunks Immigration Myths." *The Globe and Mail.* July 13.

Mitchell, Alana 1995 "Members of Minorities Hold More Degrees." *The Globe and Mail.* June 14.

Mitchell, Alana 1998 "Sensitivity Required in Using Race Data." *The Globe and Mail.* February 17.

Modood, Tariq and Tony Acland (eds.) (1997) "Introduction." In *Race and Higher Education.* T. Modood and T. Acland (eds.). pp. 1–10. Policy Studies Institute: University of Westminster.

Modood, Tariq and Richard Berthoud (eds.) 1997 *Ethnic Minorities in Britain. Diversity and Disadvantage.* London: Policy Studies Institute.

Moir, Peter and Matthew Moir "Community-based Policing and the Role of Community Consultation." In *Policing Australia.* P. Moir and H. Eijkman (eds.). pp. 211–235. Melbourne: Macmillan.

Molloy, Tom 1998 "Inside the Nisga'a Treaty." *The Globe and Mail.* July 28.

Montgomery, Moses and W.G. MacDonald 1991 "Human Rights and Race Relations Policy in Canadian Universities and Colleges. *International Education Magazine.* pp. 8–16, 22.

Monti, Lorne 1997 "Mercredi's Legacy." *New Federation* (October/November):12–14.

Moodley, Kogila 1984 "Canadian Multiculturalism as Ideology." *Ethnic and Race Studies* 6(3):320–332.

Moodley, Kogila (ed.) 1992 *Beyond Multicultural Education. International Perspectives.* Calgary: Detsilig Enterprises.

Moore, Charles W. 1997 "Christmas isn't Supposed to be Multicultural." *The Globe and Mail.* December 23.

Morris, Barry and Gillian Cowlishaw (eds.) 1997 *Race Matters. Indigenous Australians and 'Our' Society.* Canberra: Aboriginal Studies Press.

Morrissey, Rick 1996 "Colour Barrier Splits Players." *The Globe and Mail.* September 4.

Morse, Bradford, W. (ed.) 1985 *Aboriginal Peoples and the Law.* Ottawa: Carleton University Press.

Mukherjee, Alok 1992 "Educational Equity for Racial Minorities and the School: The Role of Community Action." In *Racism and Education: Different Perspectives and Experiences.* Ontario Federation of Students (ed.). pp. 73–81. Ottawa.

Mukherjee, Alok 1993 "Educational Equity for Racial Minorities and the School: The Role of Community Action." In *Human Rights. Issues and Trends.* Abdul Q. Lodhi and Russell A. McNeilly (eds.). pp.135–144. Toronto: Canadian Schools Press.

Mulgrew, Ian 1996 "B.C. Unfinished Business." *BCB* (September):36–45.

Murray, Charles and Richard J. Herrnstein 1994 *The Bell Curve: Intelligence and Class Structure in American Life.* New York: The Free Press.

Myrdahl, Gunnar 1944 *The American Dilemma. The Negro Problem and the Problems of Democracy.* New York: Harper.

Nadeau, Richard, N. Nevitte, E. Gidengil, and A. Blais 1998 "Why Public Support is Low for Increased Aboriginal Spending." *The Globe and Mail.* February 23.

Nadkarni, M.V. 1983 "Cultural Pluralism as a National Resource: Strategies for Language Education." In *Language Planning and Language Education.* Chris Kennedy (ed.). pp. 151–159. London: George Allen and Unwin.

Nagel, Joane 1994 "Constructing Ethnicity: Creating and Recreating Ethnic Identity and Culture." *Social Problems* 41(1):152–170.

Nagel, Joane and Susan Olzak 1982 "Ethnic Mobilization in the New and Old States: An Extension of the Competition Model." *Social Problems* 30(2):127–142.

Nagle, Patrick 1994 "Manitoba Takes First Steps to Axe Indian Act." *The Toronto Star.* April 24.

Nelson, Adie and Augie Fleras 1998 *Social Problems in Canada: Conditions and Consequences.* 2nd Edition. Scarborough: Prentice-Hall.

Neufeld-Rocheleau, Melody and Judith Friesen 1987 "Isolation: A Reality for Immigrant Women in Canada." *Saskatchewan Multicultural Magazine* 6(2):12–13L.

Nevitte, Neil and Allan Kornberg 1985 *Minorities and the Canadian State.* Oakville, ON: Mosaic Press.

Newsweek 1995 "Holes in the Glass Ceiling Theory." March 27.

Ng, Roxana 1989 "Sexism, Racism, Nationalism." In *Race, Class, Gender: Bonds and Barriers.* Jesse Vorst (ed.). Toronto and Winnipeg: Between the Lines and the Society for Socialist Studies.

Ng, Roxana 1994 "Sexism and Racism in the University: Analyzing a Personal Experience." *Canadian Women Studies* 14(2):41–46.

Nielson, Kai 1996 "Against Partition." *Dalhousie Review.* pp: 216–222.

Nielson, Kai 1996–97 "Cultural Nationalism, Neither Ethnic Nor Civic." *The Philosophical Forum* xxviii (1–2).

Nipp, Dora 1996 "Chinese Canadians Have Long History of Fighting Injustice." Letter to *The Toronto Star.* November 16.

Normandeau, Andre and Barry Leighton 1990 "A Vision of the Future of Policing in Canada: Police Challenge 2000." A Background Document for the Policy and Security Branch, Ministry Secretariat. Solicitor General of Canada. Ottawa: Minister of Supply and Services.

O'Bryan, K.G., J. Reitz, and O. Kuplowska 1976 *The Non-Official Languages Study.* Ottawa: Minister of Supply and Services.

O'Neill Brian J. and Shankar A. Yelaja 1994 "Multiculturalism and Postsecondary Education." In *Ethnicity and Culture in Canada. The Research Landscape.* J.W. Berry and J.A. Laponce (eds.). pp. 483–506. Toronto: University of Toronto Press.

Oettmeier, Timothy E. and Lee P. Brown 1988 "Role Expectations and the Concept of Neighborhood-Oriented Community Policing in the Houston Police Department." Prepared for the International Association of Police Chiefs. Washington.

Oliver, Melvin and Thomas M. Shapiro 1995 *Black Wealth/White Wealth: A New Perspective on Racial Inequality.* London: Routledge.

Omi, Michael 1989 "In Living Color: Race and American Culture." *Cultural Politics in Contemporary America*. Ian Angus and Sut Jhally (eds.). pp. 111–122. New York: Routledge.

Omi, Michael and Howard Winant 1993 "On the Theoretical Concept of Race." *Race, Identity and Representation in Education*. C. McCarthy and W. Crichlow (eds.). pp. 3–10. New York: Routledge.

Ongley, Patrick 1996 "Immigration, Employment, and Ethnic Relations." In *Nga Patai: Racism and Ethnic Relations in Aotearoa/New Zealand*. P. Spoonley et al. (eds.). pp. 13–34. Palmerston North, NZ: Dunmore Publishing.

Oommen, T.K. 1994 "Race, Ethnicity and Class: An Analysis of Interrelations." *International Journal of Social Sciences*. February:83–94.

Pal, Leslie 1993 *Interests of State. The Politics of Language, Multiculturalism,and Feminism in Canada*. Montreal/Kingston: McGill-Queen's.

Palmer, Alison 1998 "Colonial and Modern Genocide: Explanations and Categories." *Ethnic and Racial Studies* 21(1): 89–101.

Palmer, Douglas L. 1996 "Determinants of Canadian Attitudes Toward Immigratioin: More Than Just Racism?" *Canadian Journal of Behavioural Science* 28(3):180–192.

Palmer, Howard (ed.) 1975 *Immigration and the Rise of Multiculturalism*. Toronto: Copp Clark Publishing.

Parekh, Bhikkhu 1997 "Foreword." In *Ethnic Minorities in Britain*. T. Modood and R. Berthoud (eds.). London: Policy Studies Institute.

Parel, A.J. 1992 "Multiculturalism and Citizenship." In *George Grant and the Future of Canada*. Yusuf K. Umar (ed.). pp.139–150. University of Calgary Press.

Parenti, Michael 1992 *Make Believe Media:Tthe Politics of Film and TV*. New York: St Martin's Press.

Parillo, Vincent N. 1990 *Strangers to These Shores: Race and Ethnic Relations in Canada*. New York: MacMillan.

Parizeau, Jacques 1996 "The Objective is Sovereignty, Not Partnership." *The Globe and Mail*. December 19.

Passaris, Constantine 1998 "The Role of Immigration in Canada's Demographic Outlook." *International Migration* 36(1):93–106.

Patience, Allan 1998 "Warming to a Global Society." *AQ* (September/October):6–11.

Patterson, Lorraine, James E. Cameron, and Richard N. Lalonde 1996 "The Intersection of Race and Gender: Examining the Politics of Identity in Women's Studies." *Canadian Journal of Behavioural Science* 28(3):229–239.

Patterson, Orlando 1998 "Affirmative Action." *Brookings Review* 16(2):17–23.

Pearlstein, Steven 1998 "Court Sets Rules for Quebec Secession." *Guardian Weekly*. August 30. p. 16.

Pearson, David 1990 *A Dream Deferred. The Origins of Ethnic Conflict in New Zealand*. Wellington: Allen and Unwin.

Pearson, David 1995 "Multi-Culturalisms and Modernisms. Some Comparative Thoughts." *Sites* 30:9–30.

Pearson, David 1996 "Crossing Ethnic Thresholds: Multiculturalisms in Comparative Perspective." In *Nga Patai*. P. Spoonley et al. (eds.). pp. 247–266. Palmerston North, NZ: Dunmore.

Pedraza, Silvia 1994 "The Sociology of Immigration, Race, and Ethnicity in America." *Social Problems* 41(1):1–6.

Pendakur, Krishna and Ravi Pendakur 1995 "Earning Differentials Among Ethnic Groups in Canada." Social Research Group. Hull. Department of Canadian Heritage. Ref SRA-34.

Penner, Keith 1983 *Indian Self-Government in Canada*. Report of the Special Committee chaired by Keith Penner. Ottawa: Queen's Printer for Canada.

Perry, Michael 1997 "The Cries of a Stolen People." Christchurch Press. May 26.

Persons, George 1998 *Race and Ethnicity in Comparative Perspectives*. Rutgers: Transaction Publishers.

Peter, K. 1978 "Multi-cultural Politics, Money, and the Conduct of Canadian Ethnic Studies." *Canadian Ethnic Studies Association Bulletin* 5:2–3.

Petrone, Penny (ed.) 1990 *Native Literature in Canada: From the Oral Tradition to the Present*. Toronto: Oxford University Press.

Pettigrew, Thomas F. 1994 "New Patterns of Prejudice: The Different Worlds of 1984 and 1964." *Race and Ethnic Conflict*. Fred L. Pincus and Howard J. Ehrlich (eds.). pp. 53–59. Boulder, CO: Westview Press.

Pettman, Jan 1987 "Combatting Racism within the Community." In *Prejudice in the Public Arena: Racism*. Andrew Markus and Rahda Rasmussen (eds.). Monash University, Victoria University: Centre for Migrant and Intercultural Studies.

Philip, M. Nourbese 1992 *Frontiers. Essays and Writings on Racism and Culture*. Stratford, ON: Mercury Press.

Philip, M. Nourbese 1995 "Signifying Nothing." *Border/Lines* 36:4–27.

Philip, M. Nourbese 1996 "How White is Your White?" *Border/Lines* 37:19–24.

Philp, Margaret 1998 "Walking Wounded." *The Globe and Mail*. October 12.

Picard, Andre 1994 "Quebec Drops Old Sign-Law Changes." *The Globe and Mail*. April 13.

Pilger, John 1998 "Freedom Next Time." *The Guardian Weekend*. April 11. p. 14–19.

Pincus, Fred L. and Howard J. Ehrlich (eds.) 1994 *Race and Ethnic Conflict. Contending Views on Prejudice, Discrimination, and Ethnoviolence*. Boulder, CO: Westview Press.

Platiel, Rudy 1995 "UN Praises Quebec Cree Band for Setting Fine Example." *The Globe and Mail*. June 20.

Platiel, Rudy 1996 "Key Proposals Likely to be Lost in Debate." *The Globe and Mail*. November 20.

Plaut, Rabbi W. Gunther 1989 "Unwanted Intruders or People in Flight." *Perception* 13(2):45–46.

Poata-Smith, Evan S. Te Ahu 1996 "He Pokeka Uenuku I Tu Ai: the Evolution of Contemporary Maori Protest." *Nga Patai*. P. Spoonley et al. (eds.). pp. 97–116. Palmerston North, NZ: Dunmore Publishing.

Ponting, J. Rick 1986 *Arduous Journey: Canadian Indians and Decolonization*. Toronto: McClelland and Stewart.

Ponting, J. Rick 1997 *First Nations in Canada: Perspectives on Opportunity, Empowerment, and Self- determination*. Toronto: McGraw Hill Ryerson.

Ponting, J. Rick and Roger Gibbins 1980 *Out of Irrelevance: A Socio-Political Introduction to Indian Affairs in Canada*. Toronto: Butterworths.

Poole, Ross 1996 "National Identity, Multiculturalism, and Aboriginal Rights: An Australian Perspective." *Canadian Journal of Philosophy Supplement* 22:407– 423.

Porter, John 1965 *The Vertical Mosaic*. Toronto: University of Toronto Press.

Posner, Michael 1997 "A Battlefield Primer on Multiculturalism." A Review. *The Globe and Mail*. July 12.

Price, Christopher 1993 "Schools of Thought." *New Statesman and Society*. August 20.

Price, Richard 1991 Legacy. Indian Treaty Relationships. Edmonton: School of Native Studies. University of Alberta.

Priest, Lisa 1989 *Conspiracy of Silence*. Toronto: McClelland and Stewart.

Prince, Michael J. 1987 "How Ottawa Decides Social Policy: Recent Changes in Philosophy, Structure and Process." In *The Canadian Welfare State: Evolution and Transition*. Jacqueline S. Ismael (ed.). Edmonton: University of Alberta.

Proceedings 1992 *Challenges of Measuring an Ethnic World: Science, Politics, and Reality.* Joint Canadian-United States Conference on the Measurement of Ethnicity. Cosponsored by Statistics Canada and the U.S. Bureau of the Census. Washington: U.S. Government Printer.

Proceedings 1993 *National Symposium for University Presidents on Institutional Strategies for Race and Ethnic Relations at Canadian Universities.* Report of a symposium held at Queen's University at Kingston February 2–4, 1992.

Puddington, Arch 1995 "What to do About Affirmative Action." *Commentary.* June 22–28.

Purich, Donald 1986 *Our Land: Native Peoples in Canada.* Toronto: James Lorimer.

Purvis, Andrew 1999 "Whose Home and Native Land?" *Time Magazine,* pp. 16–26. February 15.

Qaadri, M. Shafiq 1997 "Pakistan's Expatriates Savor Best of Both Worlds." *The Toronto Star.* August 13.

Quassar, Paul 1998 "Technology Links the Arctic to the World." *Aboriginal Voices.* December. pp. 32–33.

Queen's University 1991 "Towards Diversity and Equity at Queen's: A Strategy for Change." Final Report of the Principal's Advisory Committee on Race Relations. *Queen's Gazette Supplement.* April 8.

Quill, Greg 1996 "CFMT. The World in Miniature." *The Toronto Star.* May 19.

Raboy, Marc "Two Steps Forward, Three Steps Back. Canadian Broadcasting Policy From Caplan-Sauvagneau to Bill C -36." *Canadian Journal of Communications* 14(1):70–75.

Ramcharan, Subhas 1982 *Racism: Nonwhites in Canada.* Toronto: Butterworths.

Ramcharan, Subhas, James Chacko and Roxanne Baker 1991 *An Attitudinal Study of Visible Minority Students at the University of Windsor.* Windsor, ON.

Ramsden, Irihapeti 1996 "Cultural Safety: Implementing the Concept." *NZ College of Midwives Journal* October:6–9.

Raskin, James 1992 "The Fallacies of 'Political Correctness.'" *Z Magazine* (January):31–36.

Raz, Joseph, 1994 "Multiculturalism: A Liberal Paradox." *Dissent* (Winter):67–80.

Raza, Racheel 1994 "Silent Shame." *The Toronto Star.* August 5.

Razack, Sherene 1994 "What is to be Gained by Looking White People in the Eye? Culture, Race, and Gender in Cases of Sexual Violence. *Sign* (Summer):894–922.

Regional Municipality of Waterloo 1986 *Equal Employment Opportunity. Phase 1.*

Reitz, Jeffrey and Raymond Breton 1994 *The Illusion of Difference: Realities of Ethnicity in Canada and the United States.* Toronto: C.D. Howe Institute.

Reitz, Jeffrey G. and Sherrilyn M. Sklar 1997 "Culture, Race, and the Economic Assimilation of Immigrants." *Sociological Forum* 12(2):223–247.

Rensberger, Boyce 1994 "The Case for One Race." *The Toronto Star.* December 24.

Report 1984 *Equality Now! Report of the Special Committee on Visible Minorities in Canadian Society.* Bob Daudlin, MP Chairperson. Ottawa: Queen's Printer.

Report 1987 *Multiculturalism... Being Canadian.* Report of the Secretary of State of Canada (Multiculturalism). Ottawa: Minister of Supply and Services.

Report 1987 *Multiculturalism: Building the Canadian Mosaic.* Report of the Standing Committee on Multiculturalism. Gus Mitges, MP, Chairperson. Ottawa: Queen's Printer.

Report 1988 *Multiculturalism in Canada.* Draft prepared by the Policy Analysis and Research Division, Multiculturalism, Secretary of State. Ottawa.

Report of the Royal Commission on Aboriginal Affairs. "Looking Forward, Looking Backward." Volume 1. Ottawa: Minister of Supply and Services.

Report 1988 *Towards a National Agenda for a Multicultural Australia.* Goals and Principles Report of the Advisory Council on Multicultural Affairs. Canberra: Australian Government Publishing Service.

Report 1991 *Towards Managing Diversity: A Study of Systemic Discrimination at DIAND.* Report by the Deputies Council for Change. Ottawa: Minister of Supply and Services.

Resnick, Philip 1990 *The Masks of Proteus: Canadian Reflections on the State.* Montreal and Kingston: McGill-University Press.

Rex, John 1983 *Race Relations in Sociological Theory.* London: Routledge and Kegan Paul.

Rhea, Joseph Tilden 1997 *Race Pride and the American Identity.* Cambridge, MA: Harvard University Press.

Richardson, Benjamin, Donna Craig, and Ben Boer 1994 "Indigenous Peoples and Environmental Management: A Review of Canadian Regional Agreements and Their Potential Application to Australia. Part 1." Proceedings from conference. pp. 320–356.

Richardson, Laurel 1988 *The Dynamics of Sex and Gender. A Sociological Perspective.* 3rd Edition. New York: Harper and Row.

Richer, Stephen and Lorna Weir (eds.) 1995 *Beyond Political Correctness: Toward the Inclusive University.* Toronto: University of Toronto Press.

Richmond, Anthony H. 1988 *Immigration and Ethnic Conflict.* Basingstoke, England: MacMillan.

Rieff, David 1993 "Multiculturalism and the Global Information Society." *Deconstructing a Nation: Immigration, Multiculturalism, and Racism in the 90s Canada.* Vic Satzewich (ed.). pp. 351–357. Halifax: Fernwood.

Rimmer, Alan 1998 "PQ Win Means Return to the Referendum Debate." *Echo.* December 3–9. p. 4.

Rioux, Marcel 1973 "The Development of Ideologies in Quebec." In *Communities and Cultures in French Canada.* Gerald Gold and Marc-Adelard Tremblay (eds.). Toronto: Holt Rinehart and Winston.

Rizvi, F. 1994 *The New Right and the Politics of Multiculturalism in Australia. Multiculturalism and the State.* Vol 1. London: Institute of Commonwealth Studies.

Roberts, David 1996. "Native Residential Schools Leave Often-Brutal Legacy." *The Globe and Mail.* October 22.

Roberts, David 1999 "Some Immigrant Groups Fare Badly, New Study Asserts." *The Globe and Mail.* February 1.

Roberts, Julia 1996 "Hate Crimes Common—Study." *The Toronto Star.* February 2.

Roberts, Lance W., and Rodney A. Clifton 1990 "Multiculturalism in Canada: A Sociological Perspective." In *Race and Ethnic Relations in Canada.* Peter S. Li (ed.). pp. 120–147. Toronto: Oxford University Press.

Robertson, Heather 1998 Review of *Stolen from Our Embrace: The Abduction of First Nations Children and the Restoration of Aboriginal Communities.* By S. Fournier and E. Crey. Douglas & McIntyre. In *Canadian Forum* (January/February):46–47.

Rocher, Francois and Miriam Smith 1995 *New Trends in Canadian Federalism.* Broadview Press.

Ross, J.A. 1979 "Language and the Mobilization of Ethnic Identity." In *Language and Ethnic Relations.* H. Giles and B. St.-Jacques (eds.). pp. 1–14. Oxford: Pergammon Press.

Ross, Jeffrey A. 1982 "Urban Development and the Politics of Ethnicity: A Conceptual Approach." *Ethnic and Racial Studies* 5(4):440–456.

Roth, Lorna 1995 "(De)Romancing the North." *Border/Lines* 36:36–43.

Rothchild, Donald and Alexander J. Groth 1995 "Pathological Dimensions of Domestic and International Ethnicity." *Political Science Quarterly* 110(1):69–79.

Rotman, Leonard Ian 1996 *Parallel Paths. Fiduciary Doctrine and the Crown-Native Relationship in Canada.* University of Toronto Press.

Roy, Patricia E. 1995 "The Fifth Force: Multiculturalism and the English Canadian Identity." *Annals of the American Academy, AAPSS* 538 (March):199–212.

Royal Commission 1992 *Framing the Issues: Discussion Paper No 1.* Royal Commission on Aboriginal Peoples. Ottawa.

Royal Commission 1993 *Overview of the Second Round.* Prepared for the Royal Commission on Aboriginal Peoples by Michael Cassidy Ginger Group Consultants. Ottawa, Minister of Supply and Services Canada.

Rubin, J. 1983 "Bilingual Education and Language Planning." In *Language Planning and Language Education.* Chris Kennedy (ed.). pp. 4–16. London: George Allen and Unwin.

Rushton, P. 1994 *Race, Evolution, and Behavior: A Life History Perspective.* NY Transaction.

Ryan, Claude 1975 "Biculturalism or Multiculturalism?" Speech 1972. Reprinted in *Immigration and the Rise of Multiculturalism.* Howard Palmer (ed.). Toronto: Copp Clark Publishing.

Ryan, Stephen 1997 *Nationalism and Ethnic Conflict.* New York: St. Martin's Press.

Ryan, William 1971 *Blaming the Victim.* New York: Vintage.

Saggers, Sherry and Dennis Gray 1998 *Dealing with Alcohol. Indigenous usage in Australia, New Zealand, and Canada.* Melbourne: Cambridge University Press.

Said, Edward W. 1997 Revised edition. *Covering Islam.* New York: Vintage Books.

Sajoo Amyn B. 1994 "New Dances With Diversity." *Policy Options.* December:14–19.

Salée, Daniel 1995 "Identities in Conflict: The Aboriginal Question and the Politics of Recognition in Quebec. *Racial and Ethnic Studies* 18(2):277–314.

Salée, D. and W. Coleman 1997 "The Challenges of the Quebec Question: Paradigm, Counter-Paradigm and the Nation-State." In *Understanding Canada.* W. Clement (ed.). Kingston/Montreal: McGill-Queen's Univeristy Press.

Samuel, T. John 1995 "Let's Make Multiculturalism Work." *The Toronto Star.* January 23.

Samuel, T. John 1997 "Why Canada Should Celebrate Its Impressive Array of Languages." *The Toronto Star.* December 12.

Samuel, T. John 1998 "Debunking Myths of Immigrant Crime." *The Globe and Mail.* June 17.

Samuel, LaSalva 1996 *The Moral Foundations of Canadian Federalism. Paradoxes, Achievements, and Tragedies of Nationhood.* Montreal/Kingston: McGill-Queen's University Press.

Samuels II, Raymond 1997 National Identity in Canada and the Cosmopolitan Community. Ottawa: The Angora Cosmopolitan.

Sapsted, David 1998 "White Men Can't Jump—or Run." *Dominion.* January 9.

Sarick, Lila 1997 "Federal Documents Spell Out Immigrant Targets for Staff." *The Globe and Mail.* September 16.

Satzewich, Vic 1991 "Social Stratification: Class and Racial Inequality." *Social Issues and Contradictions in Canadian Society.* B. Singh Bolaria (ed.). pp. 91–107. Toronto: Harcourt Brace.

Satzewich, Vic (ed.) 1992 *Deconstructing a Nation: Immigration, Multiculturalism, and Racism in the 90s Canada.* Fernwood Publishing and the Social Research Unit. Department of Sociology, University of Saskatchewan.

Satzewich, Vic (ed.) 1998 *Racism and Social Inequality in Canada. Concepts, Controversies, and Strategies of Resistance.* Toronto: Thompson Educational Publishing.

Schermerhorn, R.A. 1956 "Power as a Primary Concept in the Study of Minorities." *Social Forces* 35:53–56.

Schermerhorn, R.A. 1970 *Comparative Ethnic Relations: A Framework For Theory and Research*. New York: Random House.

Schlesinger, Arthur M. Jr. 1992 *The Disuniting of America. Reflections on a Multicultural Society*. New York: W.W. Norton.

Schmitt, David E. 1998 "Ethnic Structure, Conflict Processes and the Potential for Violence and Accommodation in Canada." *The Journal of Conflict Studies*.

Schnauer, Patricia 1997 "Government Discrimination Lives On." *The Independent Business Weekly* (NZ). November 11.

Schneiderman, David 1996 "Theories of Difference and the Interpretation of Aboriginal and Treaty Rights." *International Journal of Canadian Studies* 14(Fall):35–52.

Schouls, Tim 1997 "Aboriginal Peoples and Electoral Reform in Canada: Differentiated Representation versus Voter Equality." *Canadian Journal of Political Science* xxiv (4):729–749.

Schuler, Corinna 1999 "Mandela Opens Parliament for the Last Time As Country Faces a New Era." *The National Post*. February 5.

Schwartz, Bryan 1985 *First Principles: Constitutional Reform with Respect to Aboriginal Peoples of Canada 1982–1984*. Kingston: Institute of Intergovernmental Relations, Queen's University.

Scott, Craig 1996 "Indigenous Self-determination and the Decolonization of the International Imagination." *Human Rights Quarterly* 18:815–820.

Scott, James C. 1998 *Seeing Like a State*. Princeton: Yale University Agrarian Press.

Scrivener, Leslie 1997 "Canada's Refugee Apartheid." *The Toronto Star*. February 23.

Seagrave, K. 1997 *Policing in Canada*. Scarborough: Prentice Hall.

Sebahara, Pamphile 1998 "The Creation of Ethnic Division in Rwanda." *The Courier* 168:12–21.

Seccombe, Allan 1998 "Africa's Killing Fields." *Christchurch Press*. April 25.

See, Katherine O'Sullivan and William J. Wilson 1988 "Race and Ethnicity." In *Handbook of Sociology*. Neil J. Smelzer (ed.). pp. 223–242. Newbury Park, CA: Sage.

Seguin, Rheal 1994 "Native Self-Rule Talks Plunged into Disarray." *The Globe and Mail*. May 19.

Seguin, Rheal 1997 "PQ Still Can't Land Ethnic Vote." *The Globe and Mail*. March 11.

Seguin, Rheal 1998 "A 'Canadian People' Nonexistent, Lawyer Says." *The Globe and Mail*. March 6.

Seguin, Rheal 1998 "Quebec Offers Natives New Political Ideal." *The Globe and Mail*. April 3.

Sells, Michael A. 1997 *The Bridge Betrayed. Religion and Genocide in Bosnia*. Berkeley: University of California Press.

Senese, Guy B. 1991 *Self-Determination and the Social Education of Native Indians*. New York: Praeger.

Shaffir, William and Cyril Levitt 1987 *Riot at Christie Pits*. Toronto: Lester and Orpen Dennys.

Shallot, Jeff 1994 "Canada's Refugee Body has Freedom to Offend Friends." *The Globe and Mail*. August 19.

Sharp, Andrew 1990 *Justice and the Maori*. Auckland: Oxford.

Shipler, David 1997 *A Country of Strangers. Blacks and Whites in America*. New York: Alfred Knopf.

Shkilnyk Anastasia M. 1985 *A Poison Stronger Than Love*. New Haven, CT: Yale University Press.

Shkilnyk, Anastasia M. 1986 *Progress Report—Aboriginal Language Policy Developments*. Unpublished Report for the Assembly of First Nations.

Shohat Ella and Robert Stamm 1994 *Unthinking Eurocentrism. Multiculturalism and the Media*. New York: Routledge.

Shusta, R.M. et al. 1995 *Multicultural Law Enforcement. Strategies for Peacekeeping in a Diverse Society.* Englewood Cliffs, NJ: Prentice Hall.

Siddiqui, Haroon 1998 "Muslims Unfairly Labelled." By the Toronto Star Ombudsoffice. *The Toronto Star.* January 10.

Siddiqui, Haroon 1998 "Budget Cuts Fray Cultural Diversity." *The Toronto Star.* June 14.

Siddiqui, Haroon 1998 "Quebec's Three Emerging Solitudes." *The Toronto Star.* December 3.

Siddiqui, Haroon 1999 "A New Conundrum on Immigration." *The Toronto Star.*

Siegel, Fred 1991 "The Culture of Multiculturalism." *The New Republic.* February 18:34–39.

Sigurdson, Richard 1996 "First People, New Peoples, and Citizenship in Canada." *International Journal of Canadian Studies* 14(Fall):53–76.

Silman, Janet (ed.) 1987 *Enough is Enough. Aboriginal Women Speak Out.* Toronto: Women's Press.

Simmons, Dale 1994 "How the West Won." *Faces* (Saskatchewan Multicultural Magazine). Winter:12–14.

Simmons, Alan B. and Kieran Keohane 1992 "Canadian Immigration Policy: State Strategies and the Quest for Legitimacy." *Canadian Review of Sociology and Anthropology* 29 (4):421–452.

Simone, Rose 1994 "Immigration Act Criticized as Sexist." *Kitchener-Waterloo Record.* October 15.

Simpson, G.E. and J.M. Yinger 1972 *Racial and Cultural Minorities: An Analyis of Prejudice and Discrimination.* New York: Harper and Row.

Simpson, Jeffrey 1993 *Faultlines. Struggle for a Canadian Vision.* Toronto: Harper-Collins.

Simpson, Jeffrey 1997 "Canadians Still Lack Confidence in the Refugee Process." *The Globe and Mail.* December 5.

Simpson, Jeffrey 1997 "Canada's Policies Will Continue to be Generous to Immigrants." *The Globe and Mail.* October 29.

Simpson, Jeffrey 1998 "Aboriginal Conundrum." *The Globe and Mail.* October 15.

Simpson, Jeffrey 1998 "Winning Conditions." *The Globe and Mail.* October 6.

Simpson, Jeffrey 1998 "Canadian Melting Pot Remains Sturdy, but U.S. One is Cracking." *The Globe and Mail.* April 2.

Sivanandan, A 1997 "Introduction." *Race and Class* 39(ii):v–vi.

Slambrouck, Paul Van 1999 "It's Lonely at the Top of the Class." *National Post* (originally *Christian Science Monitor*). March 22.

Slattery, Brian 1997 "Recollection of Historical Practice." In *Justice for Natives. Search for a Common Ground.* Andrea P. Morrison (ed). pp. 76–82. Montreal/Kingston: McGill-Queen's Press.

Sleeper, Jim 1997 *Liberal Racism.* New York: The Free Press.

Sleeter, Christine E. 1991 *Empowerment Through Multicultural Education.* Albany: State University of New York Press.

Smaje Chris 1997 "Not Just a Social Construct: Theorising Race and Ethnicity." *Sociology* 31(2):307–327.

Smelser, Neil 1993 "Contested Boundaries and Shifting Solidarities." *ISA Bulletin.* pp. 58–59.

Smith, A.D. 1994 "The Problem of Nationalist Identity: Ancient, Medieval, or Modern." *Ethnic and Race Relations.*

Smith, Anthony D. 1996 "LSE Centennial Lecture. The Resurgence of Nationalism? Myth and Memory in the Renewal of Nations." *British Journal of Sociology* 47(4): 1–16.

Smith, Bobbi Jo 1992 "Curbing Racism on Campus." *Campus Scene.* pp. 12–15.

Smith, Dan 1997 *The Seventh Fire. The Struggle for Aboriginal Government.* Toronto: Key Porter Books.

Smith, Earl and Wilbert M. Leonard II 1997 "Twenty-Five Years of Stacking Research in Major League Baseball: An Attempt At Explaining This Re-Occurring Phenomenon." *Sociological Focus* 30(4):321–332.

Smith, Melvin H. 1995 *Our Home or Native Land?* Toronto: Stoddart.

Smith, Michael G. 1965 *The Plural Society in the British West Indies.* Berkely: University of California Press.

Smith, S. 1991 *Report: Commission of Inquiry on Canadian University Education.* Ottawa. Association of Universities and Colleges in Canada.

Smolicz, J.J. 1997 "Australia: From Migrant Country to Multicultural Nation." *JMR* 31(1):171–186.

Sniderman, David, David A. Northrup, Joseph Fletcher, Peter Russell, and Philip E. Tetlock 1993 "Psychological and Cultural Foundations of Prejudice: The Case of Anti-Semitism in Quebec." *Canadian Review of Sociology and Anthropology* 30(2):242–267.

Snyderman, Mark 1994 "How to Think About Race." *National Review* September 12:78–80.

Sociological Quarterly 1997 "Dominant Group Identity in the United States." 38(3):375–391.

Solomos, John and Les Back 1996 *Racism and Society.* London: Macmillan.

Sowell, Thomas 1989 *Preferential Policies: An International Perspective.* Morrow.

Spencer, Martin E. 1994 "Multiculturalism." *Sociological Focus* 9(4):550–566.

Spiers, Rosemary 1998 "Slowing Stream of Asian Immigrants a Sensitive Topic." *The Toronto Star.* January 22.

Spiers, Rosemary 1998 "Apology to Natives Should Have Come From Chretien." *The Toronto Star.* January 8.

Spoonley, Paul 1993 *Racism and Ethnicity in New Zealand.* Auckland: Oxford University Press.

Spoonley, Paul 1997 "Migration and Reconstruction of Citizenship in Twentieth Century Aotearoa." Asia-Pacific Migration Research Network, Department of Sociology, Massey University. Albany Auckland

Spoonley, Paul and Walter Hirsch 1990 *Between the Lines. Racism and the New Zealand Media.* Auckland: Heinemann Reed.

Spoonley, Paul, David Pearson and Cluny Macpherson (eds.) 1991 *Nga Take. Ethnic Relations and Racism in Aotearoa/New Zealand.* Palmerston North, NZ: Dunmore Press.

Stamm, Robert 1993 "From Stereotype to Discourse: Methodological Reflexions." *Cineaction.* No. 32.

Stasiulis, Daiva K. 1980 "The Political Structure of Ethnic Community Action. A Reformation." *Canadian Ethnic Studies* XII:19–44.

Stasiulis, Daiva K. 1988 "The Symbolic Mosaic Reaffirmed: Multiculturalism Policy." In *How Ottawa Spends 1988–89.* Katharine A. Graham (ed.). pp. 81–111. Ottawa: Carleton University Press.

Stasiulis, Daiva K. 1990 "Theorizing Connections: Gender, Race, Ethnicity, and Class." In *Race and Ethnic Relations in Canada.* Peter S. Li (ed.). pp. 269–305. Toronto: Oxford University Press.

Stasiulis Daiva K. 1991 "Symbolic Representation and the Numbers Game: Tory Policies on 'Race' and Visible Minorities." *How Ottawa Spends.* pp. 229–253. Ottawa: Carleton University.

Stasiulis, Daiva K. and Abigail Bakan 1997 *Not One of the Family: Foreign Domestic Workers in Canada.* Toronto: University of Toronto Press.

Statistics Canada 1998 "The Daily. 1996 Census: Ethnic Origins, Visible Minorities." February 17.

Stea, David and Ben Wisner (eds.) 1984 "The Fourth World: A Geography of Indigenous Struggles." *Antipodes: A Radical Journal of Geography* 16(2).

Stekete, Mike 1997 "Sorry: The Hardest Word." *The Australian.* May 24.

Stepan, Nancy 1982 *The Idea of Race in Science: Great Britain, 1800–1960.* London: Macmillan Press.

Stern, Kenneth S. "Battling Bigotry on Campus." *USA Today Magazine.* pp. 58–62. March 1992.

Sternberg, Robert J. and Elena Grigorenko 1997 *Intelligence, Heredity, and Environment,* New York: Cambridge University Press.

Steward, Jenny 1997 "Dismantling the State." *Quadrant* April:35–39.

Stewart, Edison 1994 "Being No. 1 Isn't Enough for Quebec." *The Toronto Star.* November 13.

Stewart, Edison 1998 "Language Watchdog Reports Progress." *The Toronto Star.* April 1.

Stinson, Marion 1994 "Real Estate Spoken Here." *The Globe and Mail.* October 26.

Stocking Jr., George 1968 *History of Anthropological Theory.* New York: Free Press.

Stoffman, Daniel 1994 "Marchi's Big Change is to Factor in National Interests." *The Toronto Star.* November 5.

Stoffman, Daniel 1997 "Making Room for Real Refugees." *International Journal* (Autumn):575–581.

Stoffman, Daniel 1998 "Toward a 'Moderate Level of Immigration.'" Letter to *The Globe and Mail.* January 29.

Stonequist, E.V. 1937 *The Marginal Man: A Study in Personal and Culture Conflict.* New York: Scribners.

Sudol, Stan 1994 "Economic Realities Demand a Reduction in Immigration Quotas." *The Toronto Star.* August 16.

Sudol, Stan 1998 "Stop Spending on Immigrants." *The Globe and Mail.* January 31.

Sugiman, Momoye (ed.) 1992 *Jin Guo: Voices of Chinese Canadian Women.* Women's Book Committee, Chinese Canadian National Council. Toronto: Women's Press.

Sunahara, Ann G. 1981 *The Politics of Racism.* Toronto: James Lorimer.

Sutcliffe, David 1986 "Introduction." In *The Language of Black Experience.* David Sutcliffe and Ansel Wong (eds.). pp. 1–14. London: George Allen and Unwin.

Swift, Richard 1996 "Spitting in the Soup." *New Internationalist* (March):20–21.

Switzer, Maurice 1998 "The Canadian Media Have Declared Open Season on Indians." *Aboriginal Voices.* December:8.

Synnott, Anthony and David Howes 1994 "Visible Minority: Concept and Reality." *Working Paper. Centre for Community and Ethnic Studies.* Concordia University.

Talbani, Abdulaziz 1993 "Intercultural Education and Minorities: Policy Initiatives in Quebec." *McGill Journal of Education* 28(3):407–421.

Tambiah, Stanley J. 1989 "Ethnic Conflict in the World Today." *Ethnology* 16(2):335–339.

Taylor, Charles 1992 "The Politics of Recognition." *Multiculturalism and the Politics of Recognition.* Amy Gutman (ed.). pp. 25–74. Princeton University Press.

Taylor, Charles 1993 "The Deep Challenge of Dualism." *Quebec. State and Society.* 2nd Edition. Alain-G. Gagnon (ed.). pp. 82–95. Scarborough: Nelson.

Taylor, Charles 1997 "Deep Diversity and the Future of Canada." *Canadian Forum* September:15–18.

Taylor, D.M. and H. Giles 1979 "At the Crossroads of Research and Language and Ethnic Relations." In *Language and Ethnic Relations.* H. Giles and B. St. Jacques (eds.). p. 231–241. Oxford: Pergammon Press.

Taylor, Donald M. 1998 "The Quest for Collective Identity: The Plight of Disadvantaged Ethnic Minorities." *Canadian Psychology* 38(3):175–190.

Taylor, John P. and Gary Paget 1989 "Federal/Provincial Responsibility and the Sechelt. In *Aboriginal Peoples and Government Responsibility*. David Hawkes (ed.). pp. 297–348. Ottawa: Carleton University Press.

Tebege, Ainamlem 1989 "Cultural Interaction of Canadians and Ethiopian Newcomers in Canada." Policy Analysis Directorate, Immigration Policy Branch. Ottawa: Employment and Immigration.

Tennant, Paul 1985 "Aboriginal Rights and the Penner Report on Indian Self-Government." *The Quest for Justice: Aboriginal Peoples and Aboriginal Rights*. pp. 321–332 In Menno Boldt and J. Anthony Long (eds.). Toronto: University of Toronto Press.

Tepper, Elliot L. 1988 *Changing Canada: The Institutional Response to Polyethnicity. The Review of Demography and Its Implications for Economic and Social Policy*. Ottawa: Carleton University.

The Economist 1993 "Three Other-Visioned Mice." April 17: 89–90.

Thernstrom, Abigail and Stephan Thernstrom 1998 "Black Progress." *Brookings Review* 16(2): 12–16.

Thobani, Sunera 1995 "Multiculturalism: The Politics of Containment." *Social Problems in Canada Reader*. Adie Nelson and Augie Fleras (eds.). pp. 213–216. Originally published in Aquelarre (1992). Scarborough: Prentice-Hall.

Thompson, Allan 1994 "MPs Attack Multiculturalism." *The Toronto Star*. February 8.

Thompson, Allan 1995 "Economist Debunks 'Head Tax.'" *The Toronto Star*. May 17.

Thompson, Allan 1997 "Refugee Overhaul in the Wind." *The Toronto Star*. December 17.

Thompson, Allan 1997 "Investor Immigrants Targeted to Pay More." *The Toronto Star*. March 22.

Thompson, Allan 1998 "New Course on Immigration." *The Toronto Star*. January 11.

Thompson, John Herd and Morton Weinfeld 1995 "Entry and Exit: Canadian Immigration Policy in Context." *Annals of the American Academy AAPSS*, 538, March:185–198.

Thompson, Richard 1998 "Ethnic Minorities and the Case for Collective Rights." *American Anthropologist* 99(4):786–798.

Thomson, Dale 1995 "Language, Identity, and the Nationalist Impulse: Quebec." *Annals of the American Academy AAPSS*, 538, March:69–81.

Thornicroft, R. 1983 "A Multicultural Research Survey Summary."

Thorsell, William 1995 "Who Are We." *Report on Business Magazine*. January:21–22.

Thorsell, William 1998 "The Hostages Have Left the Building." *The Globe and Mail*. January 2.

Tinker, George 1993 *Missionary Conquest. The Gospel and Native American Cultural Genocide*. Fortress Press, Minneapolis.

Tobias, John L. 1976 "Protection, Civilization, and Assimilation: An Outline History of Canada's Indian Policy." *Western Canadian Journal of Anthropology* 6(2):13–30.

Tomlinson, Asha 1998 "New World Youth Battle Age-old Biases." *The Toronto Star*. October 27.

Tomlinson, John 1998 "The International Underdevelopment of Aboriginal Communities." Nekeneke News/Internet. April 8.

Tomovich, V. A. and D. J. Loree 1989 "In Search of New Directions. Policing in the Niagara Region." *Canadian Police College Journal* 13(1):29–54.

Toronto Star 1994 "Immigrants Do Not Commit More Crime." *Editorial*. July 23.

Toronto Star 1995 "The Color of Learning." February 11.

Toronto Star 1998 "Minorities Hardly Exist in U.S. TV, Report Says." December 23.

Travis, Alan 1998 "Home Office Aims to Root Out Racism." *Guardian Weekly*. August 30.

Trillin, Calvin 1993 "Smoking Incorrectly." *The Globe and Mail.* April 8.

Troper, Harold and Morton Weinfeld 1989 *Old Wounds: Jews, Ukrainians and the Hunt for Nazi War Criminals in Canada.* Chapel Hill: University of North Carolina.

Troper, Harold and Morton Weinfeld 1999 *Ethnicity, Politics and Public Policy. Case Studies in Canadian Diversity.* Toronto: University of Toronto Press.

Tully, James 1995 *Strange Multiplicity. Constitutionalism in an Age of Diversity.* Cambridge, UK: Cambridge University Press.

Turner, Terence 1994 "Anthropology and Multiculturalism: What is Anthropology that Multi-culturalists Should Be Mindful of It?" In *Multiculturalism: A Critical Reader.* D.T. Goldberg (ed.). pp. 406–425. Cambridge, MA: Basil Blackwell.

Tyler, Tracey "Police Probe Shootings of Blacks, Families Say." *The Toronto Star.* September 28

Ucarer, Emek M. 1997 "Introduction: The Coming of an Era of Human Uprootedness: A Global Challenge." In *Immigration into Western Societies. Problems and Policies.* E.M. Ucarer and D.J. Puchala (eds). pp. 1–16. London: Cassells.

Underhill-Sem, Yvonne and Thomas F. Fitzgerald 1997 *Paddling a Multicultural Canoe in Bicultural Waters. Ethnic Identity and Aspirations of Second Generation Cook Islanders in New Zealand.* Macmillan-Brown Working Paper Series No 4. Christchurch: University of Canterbury.

Ungerleider, C.S. and F.H. Echols 1985 "Police Intercultural Education Project in Vancouver and Ottawa." *Currents* 3(2)18–21.

Ungerleider, Charles 1993 "Police-Minority Relations in Democratic Societies." *Currents* 8(1):3–5.

Ungerleider, Charles "Police, Race, and Community Conflict in Vancouver." *Canadian Ethnic Studies.* pp. 91–104.

Ungerleider, Charles and Josette McGregor 1995 "Training Police for Intercultural Sensitivity. A Critical Review and Discussion of the Research." *Canadian Public Adminstration* 36(1):77–89.

University of Guelph 1994 *Final Report of the President's Task Force on Anti-Racism and Race Relations.* Summer.

University of Toronto 1994 *First Report of the Race Relations and Anti-Racist Initiative Office.* April.

University of Western Ontario 1989 *Survey of Race Relations at the University of Western Ontario.* President's Advisory Committee on Race Relations.

University of Western Ontario 1993 "Report of the Race Relations Policy Review Committee." M.W. Westmacott, Chair. *Western News Supplement.* September 16.

University of Windsor 1993 "Fourth Annual Report. July 1, 1992–June 30th 1993." *Ombudsperson and Race Relations Officer.* September 8.

Unland, Karen 1997 "Study of Figures Reveals 43% More Blacks." *The Globe and Mail.* February 8.

Vallieres, Pierre 1971 *White Niggers of America.* Toronto: McClelland and Stewart.

Valpy, Michael 1994 "Mr Marchi's Flawed Doomsday Argument." *The Globe and Mail.* June 15.

van Dijk, Teun A. 1987 *Communicating Racism: Ethnic Prejudice in Thought and Talk.* Newbury Park: Sage Publications.

van den Berghe, Pierre 1967 *Race and Racism.* New York: John Wiley.

van den Berghe, Pierre 1970 *Race and Ethnicity.* New York: Basic Books.

van den Berghe, Pierre 1981 *The Ethnic Pheonomenon.* New York: Elsevier.

van den Berghe, Pierre 1985 "Race and Ethnicity: A Sociobiological Perspective." *Ethnicity and Ethnic Relations in Canada.* 2nd Edition. Rita M. Bienvenue and Jay E. Goldstein (eds.). pp. 19–30. Toronto: Butterworths.

van den Berghe, Pierre and Karl Peter 1988 "Hutterites and Kibbutzniks: A Tale of Nepotistic Communism." *Manitoba (NS)* 23(3):522–539.

Van Rijn, Nicolaas 1999 "Expert Immigrants Are Being Left Out in the Cold." *The Toronto Star.* February 21.

Vancouver Sun 1998 "Nisga'a Negotiators are on Right Road." *Opinion.* February 2.

Varadarajan, Tunku 1998 "Deal With Tribe Starts." *The Dominion.* August 25.

Vasil, Raj and D.H. Yoon 1996 *New Zealanders of Asian Origin.* Wellington: Institute of Policy Studies, Victoria University of Wellington.

Vasta, Ellie 1993 "Multiculturalism and Ethnic Identity: The Relationship Between Racism and Resistance." *Australia and New Zealand Journal of Sociology* 29(2):209–225.

Vasta, Ellie and Stephen Castles 1996 *The Teeth Are Smiling. The Persistance of Racism in A Multicultural Australia.* Sydney: Allen & Unwin.

Venne, Sharon 1998 "Analysis of Delgamuukw." Internet. March 3.

Vipond, Robert C. 1996 "Citizenship and the Charter of Rights and Freedoms: The Two Sides of Pierre Trudeau." *International Journal of Canadian Studies* 14(Fall):179–192.

Waldie, Paul 1998 "More Refugees Sheltered in Canada by New Rules." *The Globe and Mail.* November 14.

Walker, James W. St. G. 1985 *Racial Discrimination in Canada. The Black Experience.* The Canadian Historical Association Booklet No. 41.

Walker, James W. St. G. 1989 "Race Policy in Canada. A Retrospective." *Canada 2000: Race Relations and Public Policy.* O.P. Dwivedi et al. (eds.). pp. 1–19. Guelph: University of Guelph. Department of Political Science.

Walker, James W. St. G. 1997 *"Race." Rights and the Law in the Supreme Court of Canada.* Waterloo: Wilfrid Laurier Press.

Walkom, Thomas 1997 "Hong Kong Exodus Worries B.C." *The Toronto Star.* September 29.

Walkom, Thomas 1998 "The Big Power Shift." *The Toronto Star.* December 5.

Wall, Melanie 1997 "Stereotypical Constructions of the Maori 'Race' in the Media." *New Zealand Geographer* 53(2):40–45.

Walser, Michael 1992 "Comment." *Multiculturalism and the Politics of Recognition.* Amy Gutman (ed.). pp. 99–104. Princeton University Press.

Wardhaugh, Ronald 1983 *Language and Nationhood: The Canadian Experience.* Vancouver: New Star Books.

Waterloo 1994 "Discrimination and Harassment. A Student's Perspective." *An Educational Package for Students.* Lisa DuCharme. Office of Ethical Behaviour and Human Rights.

Watson, J.K.P. 1983 "Cultural Pluralism, Nation-Building and Educational Policies in Penninsular Malaysia." In *Language Planning and Language Education.* Chris Kennedy, (ed.). pp. 132–150. London: Routledge and Kegan Paul.

Watson, Paul 1995 "Reality Bites New South Africa." *The Toronto Star.* January 1.

Watson, Paul 1998 "Australia's Lost People." Three Parts. *The Toronto Star.* March 7–9.

Watson, Warren 1993 "Cultural Diversity's Impact on Interaction Process and Performance." *Academy of Management Journal* 16(3). As reviewed in *The Economist,* August 7, 1993.

Watts, Franklin 1975 "Introduction." In *The White Mans Burdensome Business.* Murray L. Wax and Robert W. Buchanan (eds.). pp. 1–5. New York: A New York Times Book/New Viewpoints.

Weaver, Sally M. 1981 *Making Canadian Indian Policy: The Hidden Agenda, 1968–1970.* Toronto: University of Toronto Press.

Weaver, Sally M. 1984 "Struggles of the Nation-State to Define Aboriginal Ethnicity: Canada and Australia." *Minorities & Mother Country Imagery.* pp. 182–210. In G. Gold (ed.). Institute of Social and Economic Research Number 13. St. John, NF: Memorial University Press.

Weaver, Sally M. 1991 "A New Paradigm in Canadian Indian Policy for the 1990s." *Canadian Ethnic Studies* XXII(3):8–18.

Weaver, Sally M. 1993 "First Nations Women and Government Policy 1970–1992: Discrimination and Conflict." *Changing Patterns: Women in Canada.* 2nd Edition. Sandra Burt et al. (eds.). Toronto: McClelland and Stewart.

Weaver, Sally M. 1993 "Self-Determination, National Pressure Groups, and Australian Aborigines. The National Aboriginal Conference 1983–1985." In *Ethnicity and Aboriginality. Case Studies in Ethnonationalism.* Michael D. Levin (ed.). pp. 53–74. Toronto: University of Toronto Press.

Weaver, Sally M. 1997 "An Assessment of Federal Self-Government Policy." In *Justice for Natives. Search for a Common Ground.* A.P. Morrison (ed). pp. 111–117. Montreal/Kingston: McGill-Queen's Press.

Webber, Jeremy 1994 *Reimaging Canada. Language, Culture, Community, and the Canadian Constitution.* Montreal and Kingston: McGill-Queen's University Press.

Weber, Max 1947 *The Theory of Social and Economic Organization.* New York: Oxford University Press.

Weigel, Russell H. and Paul W. Howes 1985 "Conceptions of Racial Prejudice: Symbolic Racism Reconsidered." *Journal of Social Issues* 41(3):117–138.

Weimann, Gabriel and Conrad Winn 1986 *Hatred on Trial: The Zundel Affair, the Media, and Public Opinion in Canada.* Oakville, ON: Mosaic Press.

Weinfeld, Morton 1985 "Myth and Reality in the Canadian Mosaic: 'Affective Ethnicity.'" *Ethnicity and Ethnic Relations in Canada.* 2nd Edition. Rita M. Bienvenue and Jay E. Goldstein (eds.). pp. 65–86. Toronto: Butterworths.

Weinfeld, Morton et al. 1981 *The Canadian Jewish Mosaic.* Toronto: John Wiley.

Weir, Lorna 1995 "PC Then and Now: Resignifying Political Correctness." *Beyond Political Correctness.* S. Richer and L. Weir (eds.). pp. 51–87. Toronto: University of Toronto Press.

Wells, Paul 1998 "Separatism Skewered on its Logic." *Kitchener-Waterloo Record.* January 21.

West, Shearer 1997 *The Victorians and Race.* Aldershot, UK: Scolar Press.

Wetherell, M. and J. Potter 1993 *Mapping the Language of Racism. Discourse and the Legitimation of Exploitation.* New York: Columbia University Press.

Whitaker, Reg 1991 *Double Standard: The Secret Story of Canadian Immigration.* Toronto: Lester and Orpen Dennys.

Whitaker, Reginald A. 1993 "From the Quebec Cauldron to the Canadian Cauldron." *Quebec. State and Society.* 2nd Edition. Alain-G. Gagnon (ed.). pp. 18–39. Scarborough: Nelson.

Whitaker, Reginald A. 1996 "Sovereign Diversions: A Nationalism Between Liberalism and Ethnicity." In Littleton. pp. 73–87.

White, Jack E. 1998 "It's Still White Supremacy." *Time Magazine.* July 27.

White, Patrick 1997 "Linguistic Vigilantes to Boost Quebecois." *Otago Daily Times.* March 19.

White, Rob 1997 *Crime and Social Control: An Introduction.* Melbourne: Oxford University Press.

Wieseltier, Leon 1989 "Scar Tissue." *The New Republic.* June 5:18–22.

Williams, Allison M. 1997 "Canada Urban Aboriginals: A Focus on Aboriginal Women in Toronto." *Canadian Journal of Native Studies* xvii(1): 75–101.

Wilson, Clint III, and Felix Gutierrez 1995 *Race, Multiculturalism, and the Media. From Mass to Class Communication*. Thousand Oaks, CA: Sage.

Wilson, James Q. and George L. Kelling 1989 "Making Neighborhoods Safe." *The Atlantic Monthly* February:46–52.

Wilson, Margaret 1995 "Constitutional Recognition of the Treaty of Waitangi. Myth Or Reality?" In *Justice and Identity: Antipodean Practices*. M. Wilson and A. Yeatman (eds.). pp 171–192. Wellington: Bridget Williams Books.

Wilson, V. Seymour 1993 "The Tapestry Vision of Canadian Multiculturalism." *Canadian Journal of Political Science* XXIV(4).

Wilson, V. Seymour 1995 "Canada's Evolving Multicultural Policy." In *Canada's Century. Governance in a Maturing Society*. C.E.S. Franks et al. (eds.). Montreal/Kingston: McGill-Queen's University Press.

Wilson, William J. 1978 *The Declining Significance of Race*. Chicago: The University of Chicago Press.

Winant, Howard 1997 "Behind Blue Eyes. Whiteness and Contemporary U.S. Racial Policy." *New Left Review* 225:73–88.

Winant, Howard 1998 "Racism Today: Continuity and Change in the Post-Civil Rights Era." *Ethnic and Racial Studies* 21(4):89–97.

Witte, Rob 1996 *Racist Violence and the State: A Comparative Analysis of Britain, France, and the Netherlands*. Essex, England: Addison Wesley Longman Ltd.

Wong, Jan 1998 "Why Should I? This is My Home." *The Globe and Mail*. November 26.

Wooldridge, Adrian 1994 "Left with an Aptitude Problem." *Times Higher Education Supplement*. December 2.

Wotherspoon, Terry (ed.) 1987 *The Political Economy of Canadian Schooling*. Toronto: Methuen.

Wotherspoon, Terry and Vic Satzewich 1993 *First Nations. Race, Class, and Gender Relations*. Scarborough: Nelson.

Woycenko, O. 1982 "Community Organizations." In *A Heritage in Transition: Essays in the History of Ukrainians in Canada*. M. Lupul (ed.). pp. 173–194. Toronto: McClelland and Stewart.

Yalden, Maxwell 1993 "Language, Human Rights, and the New World Order." Speech to a Conference on "Multilingualism in an Interdependent World." Sponsored by the OISIE and the Goethe Institute, Toronto, September 9. Reprinted in the *Canadian Speeches of the Day*. October 1993.

Yinger, J. Milton 1994 E*thnicity. Source of Strength. Source of Conflict?* Albany, NY: SUNY Press.

York, Geoffrey 1989 *The Dispossessed: Life and Death in Native Canada*. Toronto: Lester and Orpen Dennys.

York Geoffrey 1994 "Self-Rule Discussions Yield Little." *The Globe and Mail*. March 29.

York, Geoffrey 1997 "Russians Admire Canadian Constitution." *The Globe and Mail*. October 8.

Young, Iris 1990 *Justice and the Politics of Difference*. Princeton University Press.

Yuval-Davis, Nira 1997 "*Gender & Nation*, London: Sage.

Zerbisias, Antonia 1994 "Media Accused of Inflaming Conflicts of Language and Race." *The Toronto Star*. May 30.

Zhou, Min 1997 "Segmented Assimilation: Issues, Controversies, and Recent Research on the New Second Generation. *International Migration Review* XXXI(4):975–1008.

Glossary

Aboriginal peoples Includes the New Zealand Maori, Australian Aborigines, the Saami of Scandinavia, and Native Americans in the United States. Aboriginal peoples represent the original ("indigenous") occupants of a particular country or territory, never having relinquished these rights of self-determination over jurisdictions pertaining to land, identity, and political voice. Canada's aboriginal peoples regard themselves as (a) fundamentally autonomous political communities, each of which is sovereign in its own right yet sharing in the sovereignty of Canada as a whole; (b) entitled to special considerations because of their original occupancy; (c) in possession of a special relationship with the state with a corresponding set of entitlements and engagements; and (d) a relatively independent "nation within" the framework of Canadian federalism. Also indigenous peoples.

Aboriginality The concept of aboriginality can be defined as a political statement that establishes a unique and irrevocable relationship between aboriginal peoples and the state in a manner that sharply curtails state jurisdictions while bolstering aboriginal models of self-determination. Appeals to aboriginality not only challenge the legitimacy of the sovereign state as the paramount authority in determining who controls what and why. These appeals provide the catalyst for advancing innovative patterns of belonging that embody the postsovereign notion of a nation with multiple yet overlapping jurisdictions.

Affirmative action Affirmative action in the United States consists of policies and programs that since the late 1960s have sought to improve minority status in the workplace through preferential treatment and special programs. These programs tend to rely on quotas and deadlines as a way of complying with federal laws in contrast with Canadian initiatives, which focus on goals and timetables. See also employment equity.

Antiracism A commitment to identify, isolate, and challenge racism in all its forms through direct action at individual and institutional levels.

Apartheid Apartheid represented the official race relations policy in South Africa. Derived from the Dutch word meaning "separate," apartheid involved a racialized system of laws and procedures that segregated whites from nonwhites. Central to the notion of apartheid was creation of semi-autonomous, black homelands whose primary purpose was to provide cheap and disposable labour for white-owned industry. Also included under apartheid was a powerful belief in the virtues of racial purity and white supremacy. Apartheid was officially abolished in 1993.

Assimilation The concept of assimilation is derived literally from the process whereby nutrients are absorbed by a living organism. Sociologically speaking, assimilation also consists of a complex and dynamic process in which minorities begin to lose their distinctiveness through absorption into the ongoing activities and objectives of the dominant society. As policy, assimilation can refer to specific and formal government directives for the transformation and incorporation of minority populations. It can also encompass an overarching political framework for introducing, promoting, and justifying program initiatives by which minorities internalize dominant culture values with a corresponding diminishment of their own. The assimilation processes may (a) entail forced or voluntary compliance with laws and institutions, (b) proceed at varying rates of change or scope, (c) involve explicit or implicit policy guidelines, and (d) consist of outward compliance rather than wholesale conversion. The impact of assimilation can also vary depending on whether the process of change occurs at the level of culture, social structure, individual, or group. Also known as anglo-conformity.

Bilingualism Bilingualism entails the coexistence of two languages, each of which can be expressed at territorial, institutional, or individual levels. Canada is officially bilingual at institutional levels: Both French and English are legally and constitutionally entrenched as official and equal languages. Official bilingualism is applied primarily to federal institutions; that is, people have the right to work in either language or to receive services in French or English. Parliament and federally funded organizations (from Air Canada to Parks Canada) are bilingual for public service purposes. Official language minorities are also entitled to certain guarantees to official language services in areas where numbers warrant. Of the ten provinces only New Brunswick is officially bilingual. Approximately 16 percent of all Canadians regard themselves as bilingual speakers.

Capitalism Capitalism can be defined as an economic (and social) system dedicated to the rational pursuit of profit. It is also characterized by (a) the presence of exchange (involving money) and market relations (including class relationships), (b) the organization of production and distribution of goods at prices determined by the "laws" of supply and demand, and (c) the use of modern technology and machinery for bolstering the production process.

Charter groups The French and English comprise the second major force in Canadian society. The 1867 British North America Act acknowledged and enshrined the rights of the French and English settlers/colonizers as the foundational members of Canadian society, with the right to establish agendas and define priorities. Much of the current political crisis revolves about competing visions of Canada as "compact," "contract," or "three-nations."

Charter of Rights and Freedoms Canada passed the Charter of Rights and Freedoms in 1982. The Charter constitutionally entrenched the right of individuals to be free from discrimination on irrelevant grounds; it guaranteed individuals freedom from unnecessary state intrusion. The concept of collective rights was also endorsed as a reasonable limitation on individual rights when taking into account the common good.

Citizenship The reciprocal rights and duties that exist between a person and the state in which "they" live. Citizenship has historically revolved around the concept of treating everyone the same through conferral of similar rights and obligations. The concept of "one-size-fits-all" citizenship is currently contested by the notions of differentiated and inclusive citizenships, each of which recognizes that different kinds of belonging to society can exist without necessarily undermining a commitment to the whole.

Civic nationalism This term is usually employed to indicate state initiatives in society building. Civic nationalism is concerned with creating a society that entails a community of individuals in whom resides ultimate authority ("sovereignty to the people"). Under civic nationalism all people are citizens who (a) possess equal rights, (b) are conferred citizenship on the basis of common loyalty to shared values and institutions, and (c) coexist with their differences in a spirit of live and let live. See ethnic nationalism.

Class An aggregate of persons who occupy a similar status or strata in society because of similarities in power, wealth, or status. Those of a Marxist persuasion prefer to see class as the division of society in terms of people's relationship to the means of production and private property. Those who own productive private property are the ruling class; those who must sell their labour power to survive are called the working class. Those of a Weberian bent tend to see class as a complex interplay of factors such as wealth, power, and prestige, not all of which coincide, in effect leading to different class systems, including a division of society into the ever popular categories of upper, middle, and lower class.

Collective definition A distinct if somewhat underutilized approach to the study of race and ethnic relations. Collective definition endorses a view of race and ethnic relations as dynamic and contested, involving competing sectors within both the dominant and subdominant groups, each of which defines the situation differently and acts accordingly. The intersection of these competing actors encourages a dynamic view of society that ranges from cooperation or co-optation to open confrontation and conflict. See dualism.

Colonialism Colonialism refers to a specific era of European expansion into overseas territories from the sixteenth to the mid-twentieth century. It entailed the process whereby a European power took control and exploited an indigenous sector by appropriating land and resources, extracting wealth, and capitalizing on cheap labour. Racial doctrines that reinforced patterns of superiority were often invoked to justify, explain, and promote the blatant exploitation of indigenous minorities. White settlement often accompanied the colonialist enterprise; that in turn led to the displacement of indigenous populations as barriers to progress.

Compact Refers to an interpretation of Canadian federalism as a special union between the French and English rather than a contract of federal and provincial subunits. According to the compact vision, the Québécois are not an ethnic minority or even a province, but a distinct people with a common homeland, culture, language, and identity whose status is equivalent to that of the English as a founding (Charter) group. See Charter groups.

Conflict theory One of several sociological perspectives that can be applied to a study of race and ethnic relations. Conflict theory takes as its starting point the idea that con-frontation and change are critical components of society. Race and ethnic relations are interpreted as competitively different groups that compete for scarce resources in contexts that favour some groups, not others. See also internal colonialism.

Contested site Conventional ways of thinking and doing are increasingly challenged because of demographic, social, and political changes. The concept of contested site captures this notion of society as a kind of battleground in which opposing groups with conflicting visions struggle to impose their agendas and priorities at the expense of others. The outcome is open to debate and rarely resolved. For example, the contemporary university can be interpreted as a contested site involving those who wish (a) to retain its ivory tower status, (b) to move it closer to a business enterprise, and (c) to engage higher education in progressive social change.

Cultural relativism Cultural relativism consists of a belief that cultures are relative to the society in which they exist. It also entails the notion that cultural practices are relative to the social context from which meaning and significance are derived. Likewise, cultural relativism can mean that each culture (or cultural practice) should be assessed on its own terms rather than by some arbitrarily selected external criteria. It is widely (but incorrectly) thought that in the absence of absolute standards cultural relativism embraces all cultural practices as good and valid ("anything goes"), even when in violation of basic standards of human decency. But cultural relativism is not a blanket endorsement of all cultural practices. Proponents of a thoughtful cultural relativism argue instead that cultural practices can be defined *as if* equally good and valid for purposes of understanding without necessarily condoning or prejudging them.

Culture Social scientists normally employ the concept of culture in a more comprehensive sense than nonacademics. The concept of culture can be defined as a complex and socially constructed system of rules, meaning, knowledge, artifacts, and symbols that (a) guide human behaviour, (b) account for pattern regularities of thought and action, (c) provide a standard for right or wrong, good or bad, and (d) contribute to human social and physical survival. More specifically, culture can refer to the integrated lifestyle of a particular group of people who differ from others in terms of beliefs, values, world views, and attitudes.

Discourse A conceptual framework with its own internal logic and underlying assumptions that may be readily recognizable to the audience. A discourse involves a distinct way of speaking about some aspect of reality. It also suggests that the item under discussion is not a natural attribute of reality but socially constructed and defined. For example, approaching race and ethnic relations as relationships of inequality is one kind of discourse; the analysis of race and ethnic relations within the framework of the assimilation cycle or theories of prejudice is another discursive framework. Also paradigm.

Discrimination Discrimination represents a denial of equal treatment to some group or member of a group because of race, ethnicity, gender, or disability. Often viewed as the behavioural counterpart of prejudice (attitudes), discrimination consists of actions that have the effect (whether deliberate or not) of denying or excluding because of a person's inclusion in socially devalued category. Diverse types of discrimination can be discerned, ranging from the personal, intentional, and direct to the impersonal, inadvertent, and systemic. See also racism.

Distinct society The concept of distinct society is usually applied to describe the political aspirations of the Québécois. The Québécois assert that they constitute a "distinct society," that is, a historical people with a unique language, culture, and identity whose homeland of last resort is Quebec. The notion of distinct society does not necessarily mean outright separation from Canada, but some kind of association that acknowledges Quebec's distinctiveness and its right to self-determination over internal matters. See nations within.

Dominant group The collectivity of persons in society with both power and authority to preserve and promote the prevailing distribution of privilege in society. The dominant sector represents that part of society with the capacity to define itself and its culture as the standard or norm by which others are judged and evaluated. Competition over the good things in life is likely to nudge the dominant sector into conflict with those who are excluded for one reason or another.

Dual labour market The observation that the labour market is not uniform or homogeneous but divided along major racial lines. Patterns of employment involving racially different groups in urban areas can entail qualitative differences that reflect advantage and relative disadvantage. The primary market (usually associated with the privileged sectors of the labour force) provides high wages and career opportunities, in contrast with the reduced opportunities and rewards of the secondary labour market.

Dualism A term at the core of collective definition perspective. The concept of dualism suggests a series of binary division ("factions") within society. One faction within the dominant sector is anxious to incorporate minorities into the mainstream; another prefers to maintain a degree of separation between the competing groups. Within the subdominant sector are those who endorse closer ties with the dominant sectors; others want to remain separate. The interplay of these dualisms imparts the dynamic quality to pluralist societies.

Egalitarian The term "egalitarian" does not mean that everyone is or should be the same. It connotes instead the idea that everyone has relatively equal and unimpeded access to the basic necessities of life as defined by society. Egalitarian may also imply a more equitable distribution of scarce resources.

Employment equity Employment equity is a concept that can be interpreted as a principle, a policy, and a set of practices. As a principle, employment equity embraces the notion of institutional accommodation by improving the hiring and treatment of minorities. As law, employment equity refers to official policies such as the Employment Equity Act of 1986, which enshrined equity principles as formal government initiative. The policy is aimed at providing equitable employment opportunities for all Canadians through removal of discriminatory barriers and implementation of proactive measures to accommodate differences. As practice, employment equity consists of formal programs and procedures by which companies draw up plans to hire and promote targeted minorities (women, people of colour, individuals with disabilities, and aboriginal people) in compliance with federal or provincial laws. Unlike affirmative action in the United States, companies only have to establish goals and timetables rather than quotas and deadlines. They are also expected to exhibit reasonable progress toward attainment of these particular goals, although penalties for not doing so remain unclear. Also affirmative action.

Entitlement The conferral of certain rights and privileges ("who gets what") to a particular group or category of groups by virtue of their collective and relational status in society. Canada's First Nations, for example, are entitled to additional consideration from the federal government because of their status as the original occupants and politically autonomous communities whose rights to indigenous models of self-determination over jurisdictions related to land, identity, and political voice have never been extinguished.

Equality of outcome A pattern of distribution by which the good things in life (wealth, power, and privilege) are allocated on the basis of people's needs rather than on market skills or ability to generate revenue. Compare this egalitarian pattern of allocation with the concept of equal opportunity and its connotation of individual competition and abstract merit as a basis for sorting out who gets what.

Equity The belief that each individual is entitled to an equitable share of scarce resources. Attainment of equity may entail treating people differently and the recognition of collective rights.

Essentialism The belief in unchanging human characteristics that are uniform and stable within a certain category and impervious to social context or historical modification.

Ethnic The largely ascriptive identity of a group of individuals who see themselves as belonging to a certain cultural affiliation because of their identification with a common language, ancestry, homeland, and historical and cultural symbols.

Ethnic boundaries The "membrane" that keeps an ethnic group in and unwanted influences out. It consists of socially constructed divisions that are constructed, negotiated, and adjusted between groups to ensure a sense of "peoplehood" among the different members. Certain beliefs and practices that people have in common are employed as symbols to demarcate one group from another and from society at large. Boundaries between groups can also be maintained through certain practices such as prohibition of mixed marriages, rules regarding exit and entry, and establishment of ethnic institutions for catering to member needs.

Ethnic groups Ethnic groups consist of a kinship-based community of individuals with a shared awareness of a common identity and cultural symbols. Key characteristics include (a) a common ancestry, (b) awareness of a historical past, (c) identification with select cultural elements as symbolic of their peoplehood, (d) a set of related experiences, interests, history, origins, and descent, (e) the potential to interact with others up to and including the point of a community, and (f) a self-awareness of themselves as a "people." The viability and persistence of an ethnic group as a community depend to some degree on the level of boundary maintenance, cultural strength, institutional completeness, and shared interests.

Ethnic nationalism Those who share an ascriptive ethnic identity are mobilized into an action group ("social movement") for attainment of certain goals related to land, recognition, honour, or revenge. Ethnic nationalism entails a community of "like-minded" people whose attachments reflect ethnic ascription and defence of the homeland rather than loyalty to society at large or universalistic principles of equality or human rights. On occasion associated with "ethnic cleansing" or doctrines of "racial purity." See civic nationalism and nationalism.

Ethnic stratification A hierarchical ranking of racial and ethnic minorities in ascending/descending order on the basis of the criteria of income, education, or social class. Canadians of British or northwestern European background have historically ranked near the top of the hierarchy. Groups such as aboriginal First Nations and certain visible minorities occupy the bottom of the stratificatory system, with others in between.

Ethnic surge This concept is employed to refer to the explosion of ethnicity in recent years. The ethnic surge is reflected in the growing assertiveness of minorities who have utilized cultural or racial symbols as strategic resources in the competition over scarce resources. Ethnic minorities throughout the world have shifted from a marginal status at the edges of society to a position as a force to be reckoned with in competition with the nation-state as the basis of a morally legitimate political community.

Ethnicity A principle by which people are defined, differentiated, organized, and rewarded on the basis of commonly shared physical or cultural characteristics. Ethnicity can consist of a consciously shared system of beliefs, values, loyalties, and practices of relevance to group members who regard themselves as different and apart. The salient feature of ethnicity is its shared awareness of differences as a basis for engagement or entitlement ("peoplehood"). Other characteristics and traits that symbolize and reinforce this shared system—including religion, language, and homeland—can vary in importance or strength depending on the nature of the situation.

Ethnicity and culture The two are not synonymous despite some overlap. Culture refers to an integrated whole that lives naturally and is organized around tacitly accepted beliefs and practices of a community. Ethnicity, by contrast, represents a self-conscious expression of culture that not only is subject to manipulation and open articulation, but also depends on open competition with other cultures for its existence.

Ethnocentrism A tendency to see reality from a person's cultural perspective. It also includes a belief in the superiority of one's culture or cultural inventory as necessary and normal when compared with other practices or values, with a corresponding inclination to dismiss or denigrate others as inferior or irrelevant. Incorrectly applied, ethnocentrism can interfere with our capacity to understand or empathize with others because of a tendency to interpret the world from our cultural point of view. Refusal to see the world outside our "filter" can also breed intolerance and bigotry toward others because of their differences.

Eugenics A science and a social movement that attained considerable popularity during the first part of the twentieth century, eugenics is concerned with improving the quality of the human species through selective reproduction. Eugenics involves a move to encourage the creation of large families among the socially superior, while discouraging breeding within so-called inferior stock (that is, the poor or minorities). Eugenic-type organizations remain in existence today, often underwriting those persons or agencies that embrace racism or racist codes.

Eurocentrism A belief in the moral superiority of European thoughts and practices as the norm or standard by which others are judged and interpreted. European values and institutions are viewed as the apex of human development, while European achievements are rarely linked with developments in other parts of the world.

Everyday racism Racism that is expressed and reinforced in the minutiae of daily life and interaction. Everyday racism can be interpreted as an interplay of actions involving the individual (beliefs), the system (organizational rules and priorities), and culture (social values).

Genocide An orchestrated effort by members of a society to eradicate members from a devalued group. Genocide can be open, deliberate, and violent; it can also be systemic and nonviolent in process.

Group This concept has been widely and indiscriminately employed to encompass a broad range of meanings. It can be applied to include anything from statistical categories of persons who may be unrelated to each other except for some single unifying characteristics to a relatively cohesive social community with a distinctive cultural pattern, social norms, and common identity.

Hegemony That constellation of everyday practices by which the prevailing distribution of power and resources in society is secured and maintained without people's awareness of their involvement. It entails beliefs and practices so ingrained and deeply embedded as to be outside the realm of normal discourse and immune to challenges. For example, the participation of boys in organized team sports reinforces certain values that are conducive to perpetuating "masculinity" as a cherished ideal. Compare hegemony with the different types of "isms" that constitute intellectual explanations of the world.

Heritage languages Heritage languages are those non-French, non-English, and non-aboriginal languages associated with multicultural minorities. Canadian governments tend to be supportive of heritage languages, in part from principle, in other part from economic expediency. This support, however, remains constrained within the framework of two official languages as a public system of communication. Also called world languages to reflect their growing importance in global affairs.

Identity politics Also known as politics of recognition. The term is used in two ways. First, it acknowledges the desire of groups to have their identities recognized and accorded respect *on their own terms,* rather than on the conditions espoused by central authorities. Acknowledgement of differences provides the basis for rewards and recognition. Second, it concedes that certain issues involving aggrieved minorities are claimed as the exclusive jurisdiction of those who are directly victimized. For example, only a person of colour can identify and talk about the experience of racism. Both variants impart a key dynamic to contemporary politics.

Ideology Defined in its broadest sense, ideology refers to a complex of ideas that attempt to explain, justify, legitimate, and perpetuate a specific set of circumstances. Ideology can be employed in the Marxian sense as a complex of ideas underlying particular material ("class") interests that distort and falsify an account of the real world. Thus racism is construed as an ideology established by the ruling class to justify and extend the exploitation of the working class.

Immigrant Refers to any person born outside Canada ("foreign-born"), but who is seeking or has received permanent resident status. Immigrants include those who are seeking family reunification or improvement in economic status. Refugees are seen as a special category of immigrants (fleeing because of persecution fears), while visa students would not normally be included, since their status is temporary. With the exception of the First Nations, all Canadians are immigrants or descendants of immigrants. About 16 percent of Canada's population is foreign-born (that is, immigrant), a figure that has remained relatively constant since the early 1950s.

Institutional inclusiveness The idea that mainstream institutions must move over and make space for the historically disadvantaged. Both the Employment Equity Act of 1986 and the Multiculturalism Act of 1988 specify the need to hire and promote minorities through removal of discriminatory barriers and introduction of proactive measures to improve minority representation, treatment, and equity. Also institutional accommodation, managing diversity.

Institutionalized racism Institutionalized racism involves an explicit set of discriminatory policies, priorities, and practices that openly deny and exclude minorities from full participation within the organization.

Integration Integration involves a set of policy ideals that oppose the principles of segregation or separation. As policy or practice, integration is concerned with incorporating minorities into the mainstream so that they can participate as equals. In theory, integration differs from assimilation as a technique for the management of race and ethnic relations. Assimilation involves a one-way process of minority compliance or conformity with majority beliefs and practices; by contrast, integration allows the adaptation and acceptance of the minority without sacrifice of their cultural identity. In practice, however, the difference between assimilation and integration in terms of impact is more nominal than real.

Internal colonialism Internal colonialism is a concept applied to settler control and domination of indigenous ("aboriginal") groups. A colonized indigenous minority is forced to live in society not of its own making, but one where (a) political and social involvement is curtailed; (b) the cultural basis of society is undermined; and (c) bureaucratic structures are constructed to regulate movements or aspirations.

Ku Klux Klan The Ku Klux Klan originated in the United States after the Civil War in reaction to the conferral of legal and political rights to blacks. The organization sought to uphold white supremacy and the purity of the white Anglo-Saxons. Terrorist threats and violent actions accompanied the Klan's efforts to unilaterally keep minorities in their place. Targets have included not only blacks but also Jews, Catholics, communists, and Mormons. The KKK remains a formidable presence in Canada and Britain as well as the United States; its underground status makes it difficult to assess the strength and scope.

Mainstreaming A process whereby minorities are incorporated into institutions as legitimate and integral contributors. The term is employed in opposition to "sidestreaming," a process that relegated minorities to the margins of society. Also institutional inclusiveness.

Melting pot A metaphor that is used to describe the preferred ideal in American race and ethnic relations. The concept of a melting pot suggests the fusion of minority differences to create a new and improved national culture. The ideal, however, does not match the reality for many racial minorities who by choice or circumstances remain unmeltable. See mosaic.

Merit/Meritocracy The act of rewarding a person on the basis of credentials or achievement. Three features make a judgment meritocratic: the measurement of achievement against a commonly accepted scale is applied to all candidates; every candidate is measuredly impersonally, that is, on the basis of performance rather than identity; and a reliance on examiners who are selected on the basis of their excellence and impartiality.

Minority group The concept of minority group does not refer to numbers or statistical proportions. Sociologically, the concept of minority group refers to any group (whether based on race, ethnicity, or gender) that is disadvantaged, underprivileged, excluded, discriminated, or exploited. More accurately, it refers to a socially defined category of individuals who are perceived as different and treated accordingly by the majority and whose disproportionate share of resources stems from a lack of power, discriminatory barriers, and denial of opportunity. The one thing all minorities have in common is their lack of access to wealth, power, and privilege. Also subdominant.

Mosaic A metaphor to describe the ideal arrangement involving various racial and ethnic groups in societies such as Canada. The proposed image is that of a patterned entity comprising disparate and distinct elements arranged into a cohesive whole. Proponents admire the positive images associated with the mosaic; detractors denounce it as a gross distortion that neither fits reality nor escapes the conceptual trap of cultural coexistence both fixed in time and separated by inequality.

Multicultural minorities One of the three major forces in Canada, multicultural minorities comprise those Canadians who are immigrants or descendants of immigrants. Multicultural minorities have the same citizenship rights as Canadians at large, in addition to special rights because of inclusion under Canada's official multiculturalism. Both visible minorities and European ethnics are known to possess a distinct set of problems and have proposed a set of solutions consistent with this problem definition. Their goals are less political than those of the First Nations or the Québécois and tend to focus on institutional accommodation, removal of discriminatory barriers, and establishment of cultural space. Also known by racial or ethnic minorities, or as "others."

Multicultural thinking What does it mean to think like a multicultural person? One characteristic would reflect a pattern of thought that is nonjudgmental yet informed and critical, flexible yet multidimensional and complex. Multicultural thinking revels in diversity not as a threat or as irrelevant, but as something to be enjoyed for its own sake and as a way of learning about ourselves and the world at large. In contrast, ethnocentric or stereotyped thinking is judgmental, morally evaluative, rigid and unbending, static, uncritical, and dismissive of alternatives.

Multiculturalism Multiculturalism can be defined as a technique for engaging diversity as different yet equal. The different levels of multiculturalism range from a fact or an ideology to a policy or practice. We prefer to define multiculturalism as a doctrine and a corresponding set of practices that officially acknowledge and promote a society in which diversity is defined as legitimate or integral without necessarily undermining the interconnectedness of the parts that hold it together.

Nation A nation consists of a moral community of people who share a common home-

land, language, identity, set of grievances, and cultural and historical symbols. Essentially a kinship or descent group, it can also be seen as an imagined but fundamentally autonomous political and social community based on symbols of identification and a sense of belonging. Both Quebec and the First Nations prefer to see themselves as "nations" within Canadian federalism.

Nationalism Nationalism entails the notion of a world divided naturally into identifiable and distinct populations, each with the right to self-determination over territory, institutions, and values. Nationalism evolved into a formidable political force in Europe during the nineteenth century and provided the basis for the creation of nation-states in the twentieth century. Paradoxically, nationalism now competes with the civic notions of a nation-state, to the detriment of stability and conventional world order.

Nations within A term normally employed to describe aboriginal ambitions for self-determination in Canada. The "nations within" concept acknowledges the relative autonomy of the First Nations, but does not advocate outright secession as an independent state with control over external affairs. See self-government.

Notwithstanding clause Canada possesses a written constitution with provisions that apply equally to all provinces. It also retains clauses that allow provinces to override these provisions if detrimental to provincial well-being. The notwithstanding clause in Section 33 of the Constitution allows provinces the right to opt out of the Charter agreements for up to five years without a court challenge, provided the province is explicit about the suspension of civil liberties to pursue collective goals.

Official language minorities The Official Languages Acts of Canada (1969/1988) offer protection to Canada's official languages. French-speaking Canadians who live outside Quebec and English-speaking Canadians who reside in Quebec have certain rights that not only allow them access to services in their language, but enable them to exercise control over institutions such as education.

Official Languages Act The Official Languages Act of 1969 officially declared Canada a bilingual society (see bilingualism). The act was updated in 1988 to consolidate changes since 1969 as well as to strengthen the rights of official language minorities.

People of colour Those Canadians who are nonaboriginal, nonwhite, and non-Caucasian in origin, and are defined as such by the government or have agreed to be defined in such a way for employment or census purposes. People of colour share one attribute in common: Most generally lack access to power, wealth, and privilege as compared with the dominant sector.

Plural society First popularized by Furnivall in his study of Dutch overseas colonies, the concept focuses on societies where settler domination of subordinate groups leads to social, political, and cultural separation. Only the marketplace allows these groups to come together for the purposes of exchange involving goods, services, and labour. Without a common or unifying consensus, plural societies are held together by the threat of force or heavy-handed ideological indoctrination.

Pluralism Pluralism can be defined as a society that entails the coexistence of culturally different groups. This cultural coexistence is achieved through the creation of an overarching set of values or institutions. A commitment to multiculturalism represents one variant of a pluralist society.

Politically correct A putdown for criticizing those who want to change society. A term of derision employed by the conservative "right" to criticize as rigid or undemocratic those who wish to enhance inclusiveness to society by transforming how people talk and think. Political correctness can also be employed to symbolize the struggle between the traditional order and a new more inclusive society.

Politicization The process by which issues are taken out of the personal or private domain and situated instead within the public domain in the competition for scarce resources.

Postmodernism A term that does not lend itself to a quick-fix definition. We prefer to see postmodernism as a discourse that rejects the modernist claim for a unified and organized way of thinking about the world from a fixed and objective point of view. Postmodernism shares much in common with the principles of a radical cultural relativism. That alone makes postmodernism suitable for addressing the challenges of diversity and change, in addition to the uncertainties that accompany such transformations.

Power Power refers to the capacity of dominant groups (or at least the elites within the dominant sector) to enforce a degree of compliance ("obedience") in accordance with needs and aspirations. A key concept in the study of race and ethnic relations, power can be acquired and applied in different ways, ranging from the exercise of physical coercion to the construction of ideologies that sustain the prevailing patterns of power and privilege. Power should not be thought of as a thing, but inherent to relationships. The relational nature of power shifts from context to context, suggesting that minorities can wield power in certain situations.

Prejudice Prejudice can be defined as a set of biased and generalized prejudgments about out-groups that are derived from inaccurate and incomplete information. It represents a dislike of others based on faulty and inflexible generalizations, involving an irrational and unfounded set of assumptions that influence our ability to treat minority groups in an impartial or equitable manner. Prejudice is "framed" as a social construction rather than a purely psychological phenomenon; it originates when the dominant sector invokes negative ideas to justify and entrench its power and privilege over the subordinate sector.

Refugees A refugee is defined by the United Nations as people who flee their country because of a well-grounded fear of persecution. Currently, there are about 25 million refugees in the world, with Canada accepting around 20,000 to 40,000 each year. Canada distinguishes between sponsored (hand-selected by private agencies or the government) refugees and refugee claimants who arrive unannounced and request asylum. The grounds for admittance have expanded in recent years; for example, Canada now extends refugee status to include gender-based persecution.

Race Race is currently defined as an arbitrary and socially constructed classification of persons into categories on the basis of real or imagined physical characteristics such as skin colour. Under race, the world is divided into a fixed number of immutable groups of individuals (2 to 160) who are differentiated on the basis of inherited biological (and sometimes sociological) traits. Race is generally regarded as having no empirical validity or scientific merit. It exists instead as a social construction that is manipulated to define and reinforce the unequal relations between dominant and subordinate groups.

Race and ethnic relations Race and ethnic relations consist of those recurrent and unequal patterns of interaction that evolve between groups who are defined as biologically or culturally different. Race and ethnic relations are inseparable from relationships of inequality, and this puts the onus on sociologists to determine how these inequities are constructed, maintained, challenged, and transformed within contexts of control and exploitation.

Race types Race types invoke the social construction of categories of persons who share one or more physical properties, according to some system of classification. Each racial type is usually assigned a set of social, moral, and psychological characteristics as well.

Racial typologies The concept of racial typologies includes a process whereby racial groups are evaluated and hierarchically arranged in ascending and descending orders of superiority or inferiority. Racism

becomes inevitable when this kind of typologizing is employed to justify patterns of privilege and power.

Racialization The idea that race relations do not exist (since no such thing as race) but focuses on why certain relations between groups become defined by reference to race. Racialization refers to patterns of interaction that reflect perceptions of biological differences to account for differences and similarities. It also entails the idea that certain ideas or activities become linked with race (racialized). Minorities may also be racialized in that they are invested with negative biologically determined attributes that are seen as creating problems, posing a threat to society, and providing unwanted competition for scarce resources.

Racism Racism not only refers to a relatively complex and organized set of ideas and ideals ("ideology") that assert natural superiority of one group over another in terms of entitlements and privileges. It also consists of the power to put these beliefs into practice in a way that denies or excludes those who belong to a devalued category. The components of racism are often summarized in this popular equation: racism = prejudice + discrimination + power. It is important to discern different types of racism, from the personal and direct to the impersonal, institutional, and systemic. Racism also exists at diverse levels, including the individual, the institutional, the cultural, and the everyday.

Racism as biology/racism as culture/racism as power It is useful to make a distinction between variants of racism. Employed in the narrow sense of hatred, racism involves the belief that biology is the primary determinant of group attitudes and the entitlements they deserve. Racism can be employed to indicate a dislike of others because of their cultural attributes or practices. The term is also employed in the broader sense of power and privilege that one group has over another.

Scapegoating A situation in which a particular group is singled out and unjustly blamed for the misfortunes, failures, and shortcomings of another.

Segregation The process and practice of separating groups on the basis of race or culture. This separation can occur voluntarily or involuntarily and can be formal or informal.

Self-determination A claim to assume control over jurisdictions (or domains) of immediate concern to a particular group of people.

Self-government A term that is usually employed in the context of aboriginal demands for inherent self-determination rights. The First Nations argue that they continue to possess their Creator-given right to take control of their destinies at political, economic, social, and cultural levels. Self-government is the political expression of this demand for control over internal jurisdictions. The types of self-government will vary from those that resemble provincial governments to those that operate along community-based municipal governments to those that confer aboriginal control over the delivery of social services within cities. Demands for self-government are invariably tied with restoration of aboriginal lands, not simply out of justice but to provide a viable resource base for renewal and healing.

Society building The challenge that confronts contemporary societies as they attempt to create a political and moral community through the accommodation of diversity.

Sovereignty Another term that can mean whatever the context allows or the author wants to convey. It generally refers to the attainment of autonomy without having to put up with outside interference. Applied to the distinct society aspirations of Quebec, the concept can apply to a variety of political arrangements, ranging from more flexible federalist arrangements to outright secession with only minimal ties to Canada. Applied to aboriginal peoples, many are looking for a relationship with Canada that recognizes their sovereignty as fundamentally autonomous political communities while sharing in the sovereignty of the whole.

State A political, legal, and administrative unit that exercises political sovereignty over a specific territory, monopolizes the legitimate use of authority, and is ruled by a government that alleges to speak for the inhabitants.

Stereotype A stereotype is a shorthand way of classifying social reality into convenient categories on the basis of common properties. As a generalization, it provides an oversimplification or exaggerated version of the world based on preconceived and unwarranted notions that extend to all members of the devalued group; for example, Germans are "industrious"; blacks are natural "athletes." Stereotypes become harmful when individuals are judged and evaluated according to the norms of their group rather than on personal merit. They can also be damaging if employed to deny equality of opportunity or participation.

Stratification Every society can be divided into layers or hierarchies that can be ranked according to certain criteria in ascending or descending order. This suggests that inequality is not random or fleeting, but is patterned and predictable and tends to cluster around certain devalued categories related to race or ethnicity.

Subdominant Also called subordinate, subdominant groups stand in an unequal relation to dominant groups, although this inequality may be contested and transformed.

Substantive equity Substantive equity is based on the idea that differences sometimes have to be taken into account for achieving genuine rather than formal equivalence. This colour-conscious approach to equality appears to be at variance with colourblind notions where everyone is treated the same ("mathematical equality"). Also equality of outcome.

Symbolic ethnicity Symbolic ethnicity (also situational ethnicity) constitutes a process in which an individual retains a cognitive or emotional affiliation with a cultural past. Involvement in the daily and organizational life of that particular ethnic group is kept to a minimum without necessarily abdicating any sense of belonging or attachment. This type of ethnicity is popular in Canada, reflecting a type of continuity with the past that is voluntary and without the costs and sanctions of primary group participation. Canada's multiculturalism is based on endorsement of symbolic ethnic affiliation. It remains to be seen if Canada can accommodate the "deep" ethnicities at the core of contemporary society-building processes.

Systemic discrimination Systemic discrimination is based on the principle that inequality can be built into the institutional system in a way that hinders minorities without much awareness of this bias. It can be defined as any action that has the effect (rather than intent) of denying or excluding persons because of their membership in devalued groups. An action is systemically discriminatory if it indirectly impacts on some group because of inappropriate standards or tacit assumptions within the workplace.

Three major diversities For analytical purposes, Canada can be divided into three major racial and ethnic groups. Each of these groups (the original, the Charter, and the others) differs from the others because of legal status, major problems, proposed solutions, and anticipated outcomes. Also three major forces, three major ethnicities.

Three-nation state A term that reflects the emergent reality of Canada as a society of three founding nations: the French, the English, and the First Nations. Each of these possesses the privilege of contributing to the national agenda as it relates to Canada's national interests.

Vertical mosaic A twist on the notion of Canada as a multicultural "mosaic," the term originated with publication of the book *The Vertical Mosaic,* by John Porter, the eminent Canadian sociologist. According to Porter, Canada's multicultural mosaic is organized and aligned along a system of stratification that has disadvantages for certain racial or ethnic minorities. Any policy or program that involves the promotion of diversity, Porter contends, would only serve to entrench and perpetuate the hierarchical notions of racial or ethnic inequality. See stratification.

Visible minorities Also people of colour. The term "visible minority" is used to designate nonwhite, non-Caucasian racial minorities in Canada with distinctive physical characteristics pertaining largely to skin colour. The government recognizes about ten geographic areas that "produce" visible minority immigrants or refugees. Not everyone is happy with this expression; after all, the concept is arbitrary, subjective, reductionist, simplistic, and unrealistic (Synnott and Howes 1994). However unacceptable, the term represents an improvement over other pejorative connotations; it also has the bonus of acknowledging the common problems encountered by members of this category because of their visibility.

Index